Third Edition

PRACTICAL BUSINESS LAW

John Jude Moran, J.D., M.B.A.
Associate Professor, Department of Business and Economics
Wagner College

Prentice Hall, Englewood Cliffs, New Jersey 07632

Library of Congress Cataloging-in-Publication Data

Moran, John Jude.
    Practical business law / John Jude Moran.—3rd ed.
      p. cm.
    Includes index.
    ISBN 0-13-138660-3
    1. Commercial law—United States.   I. Title.
KF889.M67   1995
346.73'07—dc20
[347.3067]   94-25594
                                      CIP

To my mother and
grandmother

Acquisitions Editor: Don Hull
Cover Designer: Tom Nery
Buyer: Paul Smolenski

© 1995 by Prentice-Hall, Inc.

A Division of Simon & Schuster

Englewood Cliffs, New Jersey 07632

Printed in the United States of America

10 9 8 7 6 5 4 3 2 1

ISBN   0-13-138660-3

Prentice-Hall International (UK) Limited, *London*
Prentice-Hall of Australia Pty. Limited, *Sydney*
Prentice-Hall Canada Inc., *Toronto*
Prentice-Hall Hispanoamericana, S.A., *Mexico*
Prentice-Hall of India Private Limited, *New Delhi*
Prentice-Hall of Japan, Inc., *Tokyo*
Simon & Schuster Asia Pte. Ltd., *Singapore*
Editora Prentice-Hall do Brasil, Ltda., *Rio de Janeiro*

Contents

Part 2 Contemporary Topics

Part 3 Contract Law

Preface

Successful teaching begets successful learning. To accomplish this, this text presents principles of law in a simple step-building approach, illustrates those principles with stimulating examples, and aids the student in remembering the many principles of law by employing a variety of memory devices.

Practical Business Law is a simple approach to the law with a foundation of legal principles explained in laymen's language. The principles are illustrated through the use of practical cases and examples. This provides the student with a book he or she can truly understand and appreciate. At the same time, the text affords the professor the opportunity to discuss the principles more fully by introducing his or her own examples and instances of practical experience.

The purpose of an example is to explain a principle of law by utilizing factual circumstances. Examples, if vivid and interesting, can help the student remember particular points of law. To capture the student's interest, each chapter contains tailor-made examples using a different set of characters and scenarios based on history, mythology, astrology, art, science, film, literature, and athletics. Some of these examples are humorous. The usual examples concerning transactions between *A* and *B* or *XYZ* corporation are monotonous and do not lend themselves to easy memorization.

The ultimate task in learning is to apply the principles of law to factual situations. This can be accomplished through the use of cases and chapter review questions to stimulate class discussions. Cases are included in each chapter that focus on the important principles of law to be learned. These cases and the review questions at the end of each chapter are extracted from actual cases to enhance class discussions while providing the student with a pragmatic view of the reasoning behind court decisions.

Memory techniques are further exemplified in the text by employing mnemonics. Mnemonics are catch phrases or codes wherein each letter represents a point of law. The elements of a contract might prove difficult to remember; however, the task is simplified by the student's remembering PALACE (Promise, Agreement, Legal capacity, Act, Consideration, Executed in proper form).

This book contains forty chapters divided into six categories—introduction to law, contemporary topics, contract law, commercial law, property law, and business law.

The third edition has three innovative additions. First, more than 150 new cases have been included in the text. These cases are current from 1990 through 1993.

Second, a current topics section has been added to the book. Its purpose is to address those topics of business law that are timely. Discussion of these topics is timely because even though they are business related they have a profound effect on our personal lives. The chapters included in this section are Environmental Law, International Law, and Employment Law.

Third, a special topic section on business ethics has been included at the end of each of the six parts of the book.

In addition, the chapter on products liability has been expanded with the introduction of additional case material, and a chapter on Consumer Law has been added to the Commercial Law section.

Finally, I wish to express my sincerest appreciation to the individuals who made the publication of this book possible: Don Hull, my editor at Prentice Hall, whom I found to be the finest editor I have worked with; my mom, Rita, for typing the original manuscript and instructor's manual and for her neverending love and support; and my grandmother, Rita, for her prayers and devotion.

J.J. Moran, J.D.

1

The History of Law

Introduction

The Origin of Law

Roman Law

Revival of Roman Law

Common Law

Law of the Merchant

INTRODUCTION

There are two basic systems of law in the free world. One system is based on a code; the other system is based on case law. The code system was founded on Roman law, conceived during the Roman Republic and the Roman Empire. Roman law was codified in the sixth century by Justinian I and was called the Justinian Code. After the fall of the Roman Empire, Roman law lay dormant for over 600 years until it was revived in the twelfth century in Italian universities. Students studied the Justinian Code, and the popularity of Roman law soon spread throughout the European continent. After the French Revolution Napoleon codified Roman law into the Napoleonic Code, which has become known as the French Civil Code. This code has served as the model and the foundation for the law of many countries throughout the world, including those in continental Europe, Central and South America, and South Africa. The province of Quebec and the state of Louisiana also have legal systems based on the Napoleonic Code.

The case law system has evolved out of the English common law, which had its birth in the Middle Ages. English common law relies on the written opinions of judges and the principle of precedent, the latter being commonly known by its Latin name, *stare decisis*. For example, if a case has been decided one way in the past, English common law dictates that all similar cases thereafter should be decided in the same way for purposes of uniformity unless such a decision would be clearly against the weight of the evidence or in violation of one's conscience. Common law came into its own in the seventeenth, eighteenth, and nineteenth centuries. The widespread use of the printing press played a large part in its development because judges' opinions could be reproduced in volume for reference and study.

The importance of case law can best be appreciated through its role in interpreting the endless stream of statutes, some of them vague, that come from the legislatures.

The laws of the United States, Great Britain, and most of Canada are based on the case law method. The origins of the legal systems of these countries can be traced back to the common law of England. The development of both the code system and the case law system is interrelated with religion, philosophy, history, politics, and sociology. The discussion that follows is a brief description of the historical origins of the two systems of law that prevail today.

THE ORIGIN OF LAW

When people lived in caves, the parents, as heads of the family, had the primary responsibility for ensuring that family customs were passed on to their children, who in turn passed them on to their children, and so on.

Conformity was often imposed upon the young through severe physical tests or even torture. It was believed that torture ensured conformity. As families grew, tribes developed. The customs of the family then became the customs of the tribe. When tribes fought with one another, the victors imposed their customs upon the conquered, who usually became enslaved or melded into the victorious tribe. Property rights were an outgrowth of this consequence. Children were taught that what was given to them, what they found or hunted, and what they conquered in battle was theirs. The right of personal property ownership extended to tools, hunting and fishing equipment, food, and slaves. If one member of the tribe stole from another, the punishment imposed might include exile or death. The right to own real property was the most highly regarded of all rights. With ownership of land came power. Greater territorial rights meant a greater hunting and fishing area and perhaps the choice of a safer location for shelter. Tribal battles were fought over land and personal property. Many battles began because of a violation of territorial rights. As societies became more developed, central governments were established and laws were enacted to govern people.

Laws are only as successful as the willingness of people to abide by them. There is a need for uniformity of laws among people. Alexander the Great conquered the world, but his empire fell apart because he had no uniform laws with which to govern. The Roman Empire endured for such a long time because, after their conquests, the Romans governed the conquered people with an established set of laws and regulations.

ROMAN LAW

The Romans worshipped many gods and believed that the will of the gods controlled human conduct. The Romans' early system of government was controlled by individual clans independent of one another. They were self-governing, implementing their clan customs. The elders held executive, legislative, and judicial power. The clans grew and eventually formed the city of Rome. Roman law developed from the customs of the clans. The priests were considered the custodians of the law because they were usually very powerful and among the most highly educated. People sought them out for advice and asked them to settle disputes.

Property had great importance to the Roman family because power to govern usually went with it. It was out of property law that contract law developed. The law of contracts gave people the right to trade their property with one another. The making of a contract was considered sacred; it required a ritual performed by a priest before whom promises were made. A promise was binding as long as the proper formalities were carried out. Contracts were used for the following purposes: transfer of property; making of loans; employment; sale of goods; and formation of syndicates, joint ventures, agencies, and partnerships. A monetary system was created as a substitute for bartering, and contracts for buying and selling became prevalent with the use of coin money. The banking system was predicated on the lending of money in return for the payment of interest. Loans were based on a pledge of collateral as security or on the general credit of the borrower; if payment could not be made, the borrower would be taken as a slave until the loan was repaid. Usury laws were established to set a maximum rate of interest that could be charged on a loan. As commerce grew, partnerships originated, involving two or more individuals who decided to administer their businesses jointly by sharing in the profits and by assuming liability for the partnership's debts. Joint ventures were also established for a single common goal, usually a trading voyage. The joint venture was dissolved upon the completion of the voyage. Syndicates, consisting of many members and managed by boards of directors, similar to our corporations, were formed to develop and finance various businesses and projects. Guilds and unions of craftsmen were also formed.

The law of wills was created to determine the disposition of a person's real and personal property upon death. The father, as patriarch, had a duty to support and protect his family. On his death, his property passed down his bloodline. This meant that children could inherit only from their fathers.

Tort law grew in response to the right of the people to be secure in their persons and in their property. Tort laws concerning fraud, duress, and negligence developed, with restitution being the remedy for the redress of a private offense, along with the imposition of a penalty to deter future wrongdoing. People were also responsible for the acts of agents or servants in their employ. Personal injuries including mutilations were also torts, but the remedy at that time was retribution: "an eye for an eye."

REVIVAL OF ROMAN LAW

The revival of Roman law began in the twelfth century in the Italian universities, where students began to study the Roman Civil Code. This practice spread throughout continental Europe over the centuries that followed. In 1795, after the French Revolution, the French drafted a constitution creating a conservative republic held by five directors. The constitution also provided for separation of church and state, abolition of slavery, implementation of the metric system, and scientific codification of French law.

Napoleon Bonaparte established a coup d'état under the guise of parliamentary and democratic reform and set up a consulate with himself as the first consul. This form of government and the term *consul* were derived from the Roman Republic. Napoleon also created the Bank of France, but his greatest achievement came in 1804 when the first of five codes, known originally as the Code Napoleon, was finally completed. The codes were based on the Roman Civil Code. The first one was the Civil Code, containing 2,281 articles. Four more codes were drafted in 1807, 1808, and 1811. These four codes were the Code of Commerce, the Penal Code, the Administrative Code, and the Acts of the Chambers of Deputies. These five codes of law and procedure captured the revolutionary ideals of liberty and equality. The five codes of Napoleon, as modified and supplemented by other laws, case decisions, and treatises, became known as the French Civil Code. This code has been adopted around the free world, except in countries where English common law has been adopted.

COMMON LAW

In England, the common law originated during the Middle Ages in the kings' courts. Laws were made by the judges, whose decisions depended on their common sense. This was a vast improvement over the previous methods, such as trial by ordeal and trial by battle. Nevertheless, harsh decisions resulted either from the judges' temperaments or from their adherence to a strict construction of the law. The necessity to curtail this problem led to the birth of the King's Court of Chancery, which dealt with matters equitably, on the basis of fairness. The chancellors, now using principles of equity, would hear cases when a common law remedy was not satisfactory. At times, chancellors would advocate strict construction of the law, and the differentiation between the law of equity and the common law would be slim; however, equity would soon prevail. Our present system of law permits courts to administer both legal and equitable remedies.

The common law provided the parties with the right to a jury trial. The basic remedy under the common law was money damages, as opposed to the many possible equitable remedies. Modern case law encompasses both common law and the law of equity. In our legal system statutory or code law is promulgated by the legislature. Statutory law preempts case law where it is applicable; in all areas not preempted, case law has precedence.

The common law differed from the Roman law in that common law was centered around the decisions of judges, whereas Roman law was centered around a code promulgated by the legislature. The Roman Civil Code covered all areas of the law. The judge needed only look to the code for the resolution. In the Anglo-American system founded on common law, the jury must interpret the facts and the judge must apply the appropriate law. The common law (or case law) system is centered on the judge and the jury. Under this system the law changes with society's norms because judges have the discretion to fashion their decisions to each case's particular set of facts. In a code system, on the other hand, change can come about only through legislative amendments to the code.

LAW OF THE MERCHANT

The age of commerce reigned supreme from 1350 to 1650, starting with the birth of the Hanseatic League. This was a compact formed by various cities for the purpose of trading with one another without the imposition of tariffs. The league adopted a federal constitution, and an assembly met once a year to discuss issues of foreign policy and internal management and to legislate regulations. Cities that did not observe the regulations were expelled from membership in the league. As nations gained internal strength, the cities no longer had use for the league.

The law of the merchant had its birth in the league and continued to grow thereafter. The law of the merchant developed along with the growth of commerce. There was a need for a uniform set of laws for national and international commerce. Promissory notes were invented to allow travelers to thwart pirates and robbers. Bills of exchange were also used; these became promissory notes upon endorsement. The merchants' law of trade and commerce was recognized as early as 1600 by Lord Coke, the chief justice of England. He permitted the law to be used as evidence of a custom. In 1750 the law of the merchant was adapted into the English common law and enforced by the courts; in the late 1800s it was codified and thus given statutory authority. In the same century the French codified it into their Civil Code. The law of the merchant was finally codified by the United States into what is now called the Uniform Commercial Code (UCC). The law of the merchant provided the foundation for the development of the following areas of the law:

Contracts for the sale of goods, known simply as Sales

Commercial Paper, also known as Negotiable Instruments

Agency

Partnerships, including Joint Ventures

Insurance

Trademarks

2

The American Legal System

HISTORY OF THE AMERICAN LEGAL SYSTEM

In 1607 Jamestown became the first permanent English settlement in America. It was funded by a group of merchants known as the London Company. The first local council was assembled in 1608, with John Smith as its president. The House of Burgesses was the first representative assembly in America. It was convened in 1619, just eleven years after that first council was called together. The House of Burgesses was composed of two representatives from each settlement.

In 1620 a group of Pilgrims landed at Plymouth Rock in Massachusetts. They were funded by the Plymouth Rock Company, a group of stockholders. Upon arriving in America, forty-one Pilgrims signed the Mayflower Compact, the first constitution in America, thereby forming a "civil Body politick . . . to enacte, constitute, and frame such juste and equall laws, ordinances, acts, constitutions, and offices, from time to time, as shall be thought most meete and convenient for the generall good of the Colonie unto which we promise all due submission and obedience." The right to vote was based on the ownership of property; citizenship was restricted to the religious orthodox; trial by jury was guaranteed for criminal matters, trespass, and nonpayment of debts; and estates of decedents had to be administered one month after death.

Though there were local interpretations, the English common law became the basis for law in America where the English colonized and conquered. It soon spread throughout America as the nation expanded. The practice of law was recognized as a profession in 1701. A lawyer's oath was formulated and required upon admission to the bar.

UNITED STATES CONSTITUTION

The United States Constitution was adopted on September 17, 1787, and ratified thereafter by the original thirteen states. There are seven articles in the Constitution. The first article speaks to the legislative powers of the Congress, which consists of a Senate and a House of Representatives. The Senate is representative of the states, with each state having two senators. The House is representative of the people, with the number of representatives apportioned among the states according to population. Congress can exercise its legislative power to create laws through the origination of a bill and its passage in both the House and the Senate. The bill is then presented to the president for confirmation. The president can sign the bill—in which case it becomes law   or veto it and return it to the House with presidential objections. After reconsidering the bill the House and the Senate can override the president's veto by a two-thirds majority vote.

Congress has the power to collect taxes and duties, pay the debts of the United States, provide for the common defense and general welfare of the people, borrow money, regulate interstate and foreign commerce, establish uniform bankruptcy laws throughout the United States, coin money, establish courts inferior to the Supreme Court, declare war, and make all laws necessary and proper for executing its congressional powers. Congress's two most effective ways of regulating individuals and businesses are the taxing power and the power to regulate interstate and foreign commerce.

The taxing power has a strong effect on the activity of businesses and individuals who are subject to the particular taxes enacted. The main thrust of the tax must be to raise money, not to regulate. This must be accomplished through a method that is uniform throughout the states. A determination must be made as to the purpose of the tax. The provisions of the tax must be examined, and a projection of the effect of the tax must be made. The fact that the main purpose of the tax must be to raise revenue does not, in practice, curtail Congress's power to regulate because raising revenue is relatively easy to justify. Even if the main purpose of a tax is regulatory, the tax may still be upheld if it is necessary and proper. For a tax to be necessary and proper, collecting or enforcing the tax must be its primary purpose, and it must not be in violation of any of the constitutional protections afforded by the Bill of Rights.

Congress has the power to regulate anything that directly or indirectly has a substantial effect on commerce. Congress has exclusive power concerning foreign commerce. In regard to interstate commerce, Congress's power is concurrent with the states' except where there is a conflict between Congress and a state legislature. In such cases Congress can preempt the state legislature. Interstate commerce extends to all commercial matters that affect more than one state, including crime, labor disputes, wage and price controls, and racial discrimination. Even intrastate activities that have an effect on interstate commerce are within the purview of regulation under the commerce clause. The only criteria that must be satisfied are that a rational basis exists for finding that commerce is affected by goods, services, or people's conduct and that the means selected by Congress to regulate are reasonable, appropriate, and not in violation of any fundamental rights protected by the Bill of Rights. The spending power is another important power that must be considered. Under its spending power Congress can create federally funded programs, such as social security and welfare, that have a profound effect on the lives of individuals.

The second article of the Constitution describes the executive branch of government, which is invested in a president and a vice president for a four-year term. The power of the president includes the authority to act as commander-in-chief of the armed forces; to make treaties; and to appoint ambassadors, judges of the Supreme Court, cabinet members, and other executive officials with the advice and consent of the Senate. The president takes an oath of office to execute faithfully all laws of the United States.

The third article of the Constitution creates the judicial branch of the government. The power of judicial review is given to one Supreme Court and to other inferior courts created by Congress. The power to exercise judicial review encompasses cases where a legal remedy is sought as well as cases where an equitable remedy is requested. The jurisdiction of the Supreme Court and the other inferior courts is restricted to cases arising under the Constitution and the federal statutes, controversies in which the United States is a party, and disputes between two or more states or between citizens of two different states.

The fourth article of the Constitution delineates the full faith and credit laws: Each state shall give full faith and credit to the laws of every other state. The privileges and immunities clause prohibits arbitrary discrimination against citizens of other states. The individual states are guaranteed a republican form of government and protection against both invasion from without and domestic violence from within.

The fifth article provides the method for making amendments. A two-thirds vote of both the House and the Senate is required to propose an amendment to the Constitution. The amendment must be ratified by three-fourths of the state legislatures.

The sixth article declares that the Constitution shall be the supreme law of the land and that the courts in every state shall be bound by it. The officers in each of the three branches of government must take an oath binding them to support the Constitution.

The seventh article conditioned the establishment of this Constitution on the ratification of the conventions of nine states.

BILL OF RIGHTS

On December 15, 1791, the fifth article of the Constitution was invoked, and the first ten amendments were adopted and immediately ratified. These amendments were in response to the widespread feeling in several state conventions that the Constitution did not adequately safeguard individual liberties. These ten amendments are known as the Bill of Rights because they define individuals' rights with respect to liberty and because they are analogous to the Bill of Rights adopted by England in 1689, which proclaimed political liberties for all Englishmen.

Many of our individual rights and freedoms are protected by the First Amendment: freedom of religion, freedom of speech, and freedom of the press; the right of the people to assemble in a peaceful manner; and the right of the people to petition the government for redress of grievances. The establishment clause of the First Amendment prohibits the government from establishing a national religion, thus ensuring freedom of religion. The Second Amendment protects the rights of the people to keep and bear arms in order to secure and maintain a free state. There have been many attempts, some successful and some not, to restrict this amendment through the regulation of arms by gun control laws. The Third Amendment protects the rights of homeowners to be secure in their homes by providing that soldiers shall not be allowed to take shelter in a home without the owner's permission.

The Fourth, Fifth, and Sixth Amendments have a profound impact on criminal proceedings. The Fourth Amendment protects people, their homes, and their effects against unreasonable search and seizure by the state or federal government. The Fifth Amendment guarantees the protection of life, liberty, and property by means of the due process clause; the right to an indictment by a grand jury for a capital offense; the right to be tried only once for a crime, thus prohibiting double jeopardy; and the right to just compensation for property condemned for public use. The Fifth Amendment also guarantees the right to remain silent inherent in the privilege against self-incrimination. This is used most often in criminal investigations and is known as "taking the Fifth." The Sixth Amendment ensures the right to a speedy and public trial by an impartial jury of one's peers in the state where the crime was committed; the right to counsel in the preparation of a defense; the right, if indigent, to be provided with counsel without charge; and the right to be confronted by opposing witnesses.

The Seventh Amendment ensures the right to trial by jury in civil cases. The use of cruel and inhuman punishment is prohibited by the Eighth Amendment. The Ninth Amendment states that the rights set forth in the Constitution do not restrict or discredit other rights held by the people. The reserve clause of the Tenth Amendment states that all powers not delegated to the United States by the Constitution are reserved to the states or to the people.

Initially, the Bill of Rights guaranteed protection of individual freedoms solely in relation to the federal government. It was not until 1868 that the Bill of Rights was applied to the states through the due process clause of the Fourteenth Amendment. The Fourteenth Amendment also established the equal protection clause, which prohibits invidious discrimination against a class of people because of their religion, race, sex, or national origin. There have been only sixteen additional amendments to the Constitution since the Bill of Rights was ratified in 1791.

FEDERAL COURT SYSTEM

The power of the federal courts to hear and decide legal issues is limited to causes of action involving $50,000 or more, based on violations of the Constitution or federal statutes, and to cases where there is diversity of citizenship. Diversity arises when plaintiff and defendant are citizens of different states. In cases involving multiple parties, diversity arises when there are no plaintiffs and defendants from the same state. These cases may be started in either federal or state court. A federal court will apply the law of the state that has the controlling interest in the lawsuit. If a plaintiff chooses to proceed in state court, the defendant may make a motion to move the case to federal court. The purpose of hearing diversity cases in federal court is to provide the out-of-state party with an impartial forum. This is designed to overcome potential bias of a state court in favor of the party who is domiciled there. Domicile is the state in which a person has his or her principal place of residence, votes, and pays taxes. The domicile of a corporation is the state in which it was incorporated and in which it has its principal place of business.

A plaintiff who brings a cause of action based upon a violation of a constitutional right must prove that the violation directly inflicts an injury on the interest the plaintiff is seeking to protect. This interest must be within the zone of interests that the Constitution or a federal statute is seeking to protect. In other words, the plaintiff must have a personal stake in the outcome of the case. This gives the plaintiff sufficient standing to sue in federal court.

The federal court system is composed of the following trial courts: Court of Claims, bankruptcy courts, Tax Court, and district courts; and the following appellate courts: circuit courts and the Supreme Court. (See Figure 2-1.)

The *United States Supreme Court* is the highest court of the United States and is the only court directly created by the Constitution. Nine justices with lifetime terms sit on the Court. They hear appeals from the following: the highest court of each of the fifty states, the eleven circuit courts of appeals, and the Court of Claims. The Supreme Court reviews cases brought by right of appeal or writ of certiorari. Right of appeal is an appeal taken by a losing party from a decision made by any of the previously men-

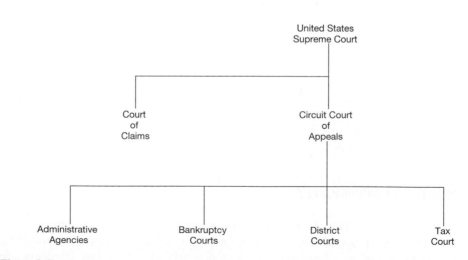

Figure 2-1

tioned courts. Although a person has a right to bring an appeal, the Supreme Court may affirm the lower court's decision without an opinion or summarily dismiss the appeal without a hearing. The Supreme Court will hear a case on a writ of certiorari when the dispute is timely and of great importance and where conflicting decisions have been made regarding the case. When the Supreme Court hears a case, a majority of votes is required for a decision. An opinion is usually written by one of the justices in the majority; those agreeing for different reasons may write concurring opinions, and those disagreeing may write dissenting opinions espousing their beliefs.

The *circuit court of appeals* is the first appellate court to which federal appeals are taken. The country is divided into ten circuits, with a court being located in the major city in each circuit. The eleventh circuit is the District of Columbia, which requires its own circuit because of the large number of appeals involving the federal government. Appeals are heard from the bankruptcy courts, the Tax Court, and the district courts, and from administrative agencies such as the Interstate Commerce Commission, Federal Trade Commission, and Federal Communications Commission.

The *Court of Claims* is a court of original jurisdiction with the authority to hear all claims made against the United States government except tort claims, which are heard by the district courts.

Bankruptcy courts are located in all areas where there are district courts. They have original jurisdiction in all matters involving bankruptcy.

The *Tax Court* is located in Washington, D.C. It hears all matters regarding the Internal Revenue Code.

District courts are located in geographical districts throughout the United States. Each state has at least one district court, with some states, such as New York, California, and Texas, having as many as four. District courts are trial courts that have unlimited general jurisdiction over all diversity cases and federal matters except special matters that are covered by the trial courts with limited jurisdiction.

Administrative agencies are not courts; rather, each agency holds hearings regarding issues under its jurisdiction. The rulings made as a result of these hearings are appealable to the circuit courts of appeals. However, because of the technical nature of the subject matter, the decisions made by the agencies will generally not be overturned unless they are clearly arbitrary and capricious. Some of the better-known agencies are the Environmental Protection Agency (EPA), Federal Communications Commission (FCC), Federal Trade Commission (FTC), Interstate Commerce Commission (ICC), Internal Revenue Service (IRS), and Securities and Exchange Commission (SEC).

REVIEW QUESTIONS

1. What are the three branches of government established by the Constitution?
2. How does the United States Constitution, as adopted, safeguard our individual liberties?

3. What is the Bill of Rights?
4. When and how was the Bill of Rights applied to the states?
5. In what situations will the federal courts hear and decide cases?
6. Describe the structure of the federal court system.
7. What is the significance of the Fourteenth Amendment?

3

Court Practice and Procedure

INTRODUCTION

To begin a journey through the legal system, an individual must have a legal cause of action. A cause of action gives a person the legal right to sue another for damages suffered. It is one's ticket of admission to the American legal system. A person initiating a lawsuit based on his or her legal right to sue is known as the plaintiff. The person against whom the suit is brought is called the defendant. Damages are awarded for the harm suffered by the plaintiff. The defendant is the person who allegedly caused the harm or is allegedly accountable for it. The person is held to be "allegedly" responsible until the outcome of the case is decided, under the theory that a person is innocent until proven guilty. The determination of actual liability is the reason the suit is brought: to see whether or not the defendant is responsible. Once a lawsuit is initiated, there are many rules of practice and procedure that the plantiff must follow to establish and prove a case. These include jurisdictional and evidentiary guidelines.

JURISDICTION

Jurisdiction is the authority the court must possess to hear and decide particular legal issues and to bind the parties involved to the court's decisions. The rules of jurisdiction vary from state to state; the following discussion is predicated on the rules that are most representative.

Subject matter jurisdiction is the authority the court must possess to hear and decide particular legal issues. The requirement of subject matter jurisdiction may not be waived by either the court or the parties to the action. Personal jurisdiction is the court's authority over the parties involved in the lawsuit. The plaintiff must follow a procedure to obtain jurisdiction over the defendant's person, property, or both in a civil case. Once jurisdiction is obtained, the court having subject matter jurisdiction may hear the case and render a decision that will bind both the plaintiff and the defendant.

Subject Matter Jurisdiction

The structure of a typical state court system is outlined in Figure 3-1. This structure is representative of that in most states, if not more complex, because some states do not have intermediate courts of appeals. There are two types of courts: trial and appellate courts. A lawsuit must begin in a trial court. The purpose of a trial is to resolve questions of fact. In most states the supreme court is the highest court of the state, but in New York the highest court is referred to as the Court of Appeals.

Appellate courts handle appeals from the trial courts. When a party is not pleased with a decision—that is, he or she feels that the law has been incorrectly applied—a *motion for an appeal* may be made, and a notice of appeal must be served on the

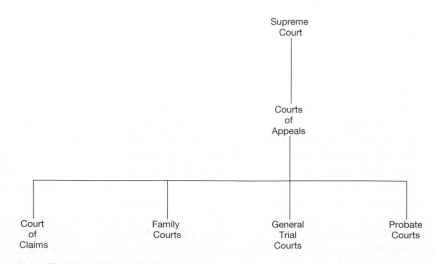

Figure 3-1   The Court System of a Typical State

opposing party and filed with the trial court. The county courts and the courts below that level are the trial courts where most cases are tried and decisions determined.

An appeal is a review by a higher court as to the appropriateness of a lower court's application of law to the facts of the case. An appellate court may not review questions of fact unless they are against the weight of the evidence. A *question of fact* is an actual event that is disputed by the parties and that must be resolved in order for the principle of law to be applied. Where a jury trial is requested, the jury will determine questions of fact; otherwise the judge will make the resolution. *Questions of law* are the application of principles of law to an agreed-upon or resolved factual determination and are reserved to the judge.

The Court System of a Typical State

The *state supreme court* is the highest court in all states except New York, where the highest court is known as the Court of Appeals. The supreme court decides appeals from the intermediate appellate courts, or from trial courts in states that do not have intermediate courts. The supreme court's decisions bind all of the courts in the state as well as its citizens unless preempted by the United States Supreme Court.

Appellate courts are intermediaries that act as a buffer between the trial courts and the supreme court. They are the first courts of appellate review. They hear appeals from all of the trial courts: county courts, family courts, probate courts, and courts of claims. In states heavily congested with court cases, the appellate courts relieve the supreme court of the burden of deciding all appeals. They act as a filter that allows only the most important cases to flow to the supreme court.

The *general trial courts* are located in each county of the state. They are known as county courts, district courts, circuit courts, superior courts, courts of common pleas, and—in New York—as supreme courts. They are courts of unlimited general jurisdiction. This means that they may hear any legal matters, with the following general exceptions: federal suits (federal courts), family altercation suits (family court), monetary suits against the state (court of claims), and matters relating to decedents' estates (probate court). Furthermore, the general trial courts' jurisdiction may be monetarily limited: for example, to suits involving $10,000 or more. If this is the case, there is another trial court of unlimited general jurisdiction to hear matters involving less than $10,000. This court is usually known as the civil court or municipal court. Appeals from the general trial courts are made to the appellate court having jurisdiction over that particular county.

Courts of claims have exclusive jurisdiction concerning monetary suits against the state. Appeals are made to the appellate court in the appropriate district.

Family courts hear matrimonial actions and family altercation proceedings such as those concerning support, neglect, juvenile delinquency, and paternity. A family courts is located in each county, and appeals are made to the appropriate appellate court.

A probate court, located in each county, administers decedents' estates. Appeals are made to the appellate court in the appropriate district.

Civil courts are generally located in all major cities. There is usually a monetary ceiling, such as $10,000. Cases requesting damages in excess of the monetary ceiling would be heard in the county courts. There may be separate parts for landlord-tenant altercations and for traffic violations. Appeals are made either to the county court or to the appellate court in the appropriate district.

Criminal courts are located in major cities. Appeals are made to the appellate courts.

Municipal courts and justice of the peace courts are generally located in smaller cities and towns and have a much lower monetary limitation. They usually have both civil and criminal jurisdiction and may be seen as a combination of the civil and criminal courts on a smaller scale. Appeals are made to the county court in the appropriate county.

There are also small claims courts, which have monetary ceilings ranging from $1,000 to $5,000. These courts provide individuals with the opportunity to resolve small cases without retaining lawyers. Small claims courts open the legal system to individuals who would otherwise be prevented from commencing lawsuits because of the high legal costs involved. Many small claims courts have evening sessions to accommodate working people. Formal procedural and evidentiary rules are relaxed, with the judge acting more like a mediator.

Effect of Jurisdiction

Obtaining personal jurisdiction over a defendant allows the plaintiff to commence an action against the defendant in a court of law. Jurisdiction and a cause of action against the defendant give the plaintiff the right to sue that particular defendant. Jurisdiction is important to the plaintiff: If the plaintiff can obtain jurisdiction in his or her state over an out-of-state defendant, he or she may have the convenience of suing in a familiar court with a familiar attorney.

Jurisdiction, together with a cause of action, gives a person the right to sue another for a legal remedy. It is important to note that securing jurisdiction does not mean that the person has a cause of action. Even if there is a cause of action, it does not guarantee that the case is won. The plaintiff must still prove the facts set forth in the cause of action that he or she is alleging has caused the injury.

PLEADINGS

Pleadings are the written declarations of the plaintiff and the defendant. They consist of the plaintiff's complaint, which is served upon the defendant, and the defendant's answer to the complaint. In a civil case, the plaintiff is the party who is commencing the lawsuit on the basis of a cause of action with the hope of being granted a remedy. A cause of action gives the plaintiff a legal right to sue. The defendant is the party against whom the action is brought and from whom the plaintiff is seeking a remedy. To commence a lawsuit, the plaintiff must serve the defendant a summons and a complaint. The *summons* gives the defendant constitutional notice of the commencement of the action. The *complaint* explains why the plaintiff is suing the defendant and describes the relief requested. It sets forth the factual allegations upon which the plaintiff is claiming the relief requested and the reasons why the defendant should be responsible for this relief. If the complaint is not served with the summons, it may be served later on the defendant's demand.

The defendant's response to the plaintiff's complaint is called an *answer.* An answer must admit or deny the plaintiff's allegations. A general denial indicates that all the plaintiff's allegations are believed to be untrue. A special denial is used when the defendant denies particular allegations and admits the rest. All allegations that are not denied are deemed admitted.

The defendant may also raise an affirmative defense or a counterclaim in his or her answer. An affirmative defense is raised in situations where the defendant admits that the plaintiff's allegations are true but argues that his or her own actions are justified under the circumstances. Many of these affirmative defenses, such as bankruptcy discharge, nonpayment, release, and incapacity, are described in Chapter 17, "Contractual Defenses."

A *counterclaim* is a cause of action the defendant has against the plaintiff. The counterclaim need not arise out of the plaintiff's claim; it may pertain to a totally different matter. If a counterclaim is raised by the defendant, the plaintiff must respond to it. This response is known as a *reply.* It is similar to a defendant's answer in that the plaintiff must deny all of the allegations set forth in the counterclaim; otherwise the allegations will be deemed admitted.

To summarize, an answer is a defendant's response to a plaintiff's complaint; a reply is a plaintiff's response to a defendant's counterclaim, if one is raised in the defendant's answer. After serving the answer, the defendant may implead a third person who is, or may be, liable to him or her for all or part of the plaintiff's claim. The defendant must serve a separate complaint upon the third party in order to bring that person into the action. It is then up to the court's discretion to admit the third party into the lawsuit.

Pleadings are liberally construed, and immaterial defects are ignored. A pleading should be sufficiently particular to apprise the other party of the material elements giving rise to the cause of action or defense. Parties may amend pleadings to correct errors or to add causes of action. Generally this may be done once without the court's permission. After that, the court's permission is necessary and will be granted as justice requires.

DISCOVERY

Discovery is the next step before trial. *Discovery* allows each party to examine the other's witnesses, property, documents, and records prior to trial to get a clear picture of the evidence that will support the factual allegations and denials set forth in the complaint and the answer, respectively. It prevents surprise and helps to even out discrepancies in the parties' resources. Full disclosure of all material and necessary evidence is required except for the following: privileged information, the attorney's trial strategy, and evidence prepared for litigation. However, the latter must be disclosed to the other party upon his or her request in cases where the evidence is material and necessary, cannot be duplicated, and would cause undue hardship to the party if he or she would have to proceed without it. An example of this would be opinion evidence or evidence of tests regarding personal property that has subsequently been destroyed. The evidence requested must have a significant relationship to an issue in the case. Substantial or irrelevant requests that are intended to burden or harass the other party need not be acknowledged. The main types of discovery devices are **DIE.**

> **D**epositions (oral and written)
> **I**nspections
> **E**xaminations (physical and mental)

A deposition can be either oral or written. An oral deposition is often referred to as an examination before trial (EBT). The *deposition* gives each party the opportunity to ask questions of the opposing party, and that party's witnesses, before trial. This is the most popular discovery device. A written transcript of the testimony is usually made with the aid of a legal stenographer. Testimony of individuals who will not be able to appear at trial may be preserved by deposition, and the written transcript of the deposition may be introduced at trial. A written deposition is called an *interrogatory*. It consists of questions submitted to the opposing party in writing, to which the opposing party must respond if the questions are reasonable.

Inspections of certain premises, personal property, documents, and records under the control of the opposing party may be requested through discovery upon sufficient notice where they relate to the issues in the lawsuit.

Examination of the physical or mental condition of an opposing party may be had, by court order, when that party's condition is at issue in the action. The need for the information must be great; it must outweigh the right to privacy of the party to be examined.

PRETRIAL CONFERENCE

A *pretrial hearing* is often held between the judge and the attorneys of the opposing parties after discovery. The judge may encourage the parties to settle out of court if the circumstances warrant. If not, the triable issues of fact are discussed, and the agenda of the trial is planned.

TRIAL

The trial may be by judge or by jury. The right to a trial by jury is guaranteed under the Seventh Amendment to the United States Constitution and under the constitutions of the individual states, but one party must exercise the right to a jury trial by requesting it.

At the outset of the trial, opening statements are made by the attorneys of both parties. In the opening statement the plaintiff's attorney presents to the jury the allegations of fact set forth in the complaint and the relief requested. The jury, at this point, has not had the opportunity to learn of the complaint. The plaintiff's attorney then tells the jury how he or she will prove the allegations through the production of real evidence and the testimony of witnesses. The opening statement by the defendant's attorney will usually be in the form of a rebuttal to the statements made by the plaintiff's attorney. The attorney for the defendant will deny the factual allegations made by the plaintiff and will tell the jury how he or she intends to disprove them.

The plaintiff has the burden of proving the cause of action set forth in the complaint. The plaintiff's attorney begins the trial by calling witnesses to testify to the truth of the allegations listed in the plaintiff's complaint. After direct examination of each witness by the plaintiff's attorney, the attorney for the defendant is given the opportunity to cross-examine that witness. The defendant's attorney will attempt to discredit the plaintiff's witness by trying to show prior inconsistent statements, bias, unjustifiable hostility toward the defendant, or a reputation for untruthfulness. The attorneys have the option to reexamine witnesses. The attorney who called the witness may elect to reexamine that witness on redirect examination in order to clear up any inconsistencies brought out in that witness's testimony on cross-examination. The same procedure described for examination of the plaintiff's witnesses applies to the defendant's witnesses as well.

The plaintiff and the defendant may present further evidence, in rebuttal, to negate each other's positions. After the attorneys for both sides have rested their cases, they make their closing statements to the jury. The closing statement consists of an attorney's plea to the jury to return a verdict for his or her client, including the reason why the attorney believes they should. The plaintiff's attorney will usually explain how the evidence presented proves the factual allegations recorded in the complaint. The defendant's attorney will argue that the evidence presented on the defendant's behalf disproves the allegations set forth in the complaint.

After the closing statements, the judge will instruct the jury with regard to the particular law that applies to the case. The jurors, triers of fact, must make a decision based upon the factual evidence presented. Then the jury will apply the law, as the judge instructed them, to their factual determination and pronounce a verdict for either the plaintiff or the defendant. If the verdict is for the plaintiff, the jury may be requested to resolve the issue of the amount of money damages to be awarded.

EVIDENCE

Evidence is the medium for proving disputed facts. Each party presents evidence on his or her own behalf. Evidence may be in the form of testimony, writings, or documents. The court may also take judicial notice of matters of common knowledge without requiring the parties to prove their existence. Example of facts of which courts will take judicial notice include the metric system, the calendar, the law of gravity, and the population of a state. Real evidence, which is the actual production of the object that is in issue or related to the issues, may also be introduced.

To be admissible, evidence must be material, relevant, and competent. Evidence is material and relevant when it is probative of (tends to prove) a fact in issue. Evidence is competent when the person testifying is capable of understanding the oath and able to perceive, remember, and recall the facts. A competent witness can testify to the facts but may not interpret or draw conclusions from them unless (1) the evidence is related to the senses and involves speed, color, emotion, taste, sound, or smell or (2) the person testifying is an expert witness. Expert witnesses may be qualified by proof of their skill, knowledge, or experience. They may give opinions based on the evidence presented but not based on hearsay evidence.

Hearsay is an out-of-court statement offered as proof of the truth of the matter asserted. Generally, when a person is testifying as to what another person said, that is considered hearsay evidence. Hearsay is not admissible as evidence in a court of law to prove the issue in dispute, but it may be admitted to show a person's state of mind at a particular time related to the issue.

The burden of proof rests with the plaintiff in a civil case and with the state in a criminal case. In a civil trial the plaintiff must prove his or her case by a preponderance of the evidence, which means over 50 percent. The plaintiff has the burden of producing evidence that will prove his or her cause of action. If the evidence presented by the plaintiff is not sufficient, the judge will direct the verdict for the defendant because the plaintiff has not met the burden of proof. If the evidence presented by the plaintiff is sufficient to prove the cause of action, then the defendant must rebut this evidence or justify his or her actions by presenting a valid defense. If the defendant succeeds he or she will win the case; if not, the judgment will be entered for the plaintiff.

In a criminal trial, the state must prove its case beyond a reasonable doubt, which is a much more difficult requirement than that demanded in a civil case. The burden of going forward with proof rests on the state, and the outcome depends on whether the state can meet that burden and, if so, whether the defendant can rebut the state's evidence or present a justifiable defense to acquit himself or herself of the alleged crime.

ARBITRATION

Arbitration is an alternative to the use of the court system. It is a means for the expeditious and inexpensive settlement of a dispute pursuant to a written arbitration agreement. The agreement will provide for the selection of an arbitrator, a mediator who is free to examine the facts and grant a judgment based on a factual determination. An arbitrator has a duty to be unbiased. The arbitrator makes the award in writing, and this then is served upon the losing party. Upon confirmation of the award, a judgment is entered in the court records. It is binding on both parties and generally not appealable unless the arbitrator acted in an arbitrary or capricious manner or had an interest in the outcome.

Many states now require mandatory arbitration of all civil cases below $10,000 because the courts have become so inundated with lawsuits that they are unable to handle their caseloads. Many states have instituted arbitration panels consisting of local attorneys who sit once a month and hear all cases within their jurisdictions. Arbitration is an extremely fast, efficient, and inexpensive means for disposing of minor civil cases. It appears to be the trend of the future.

JUDGMENTS

A *judgment* from a court action or an award from an arbitrated case is the final determination of the rights of the parties. After the court enters a judgment in favor of one of the parties, that party may attempt to collect it from the other. The person who is awarded the judgment is known as the judgment creditor; the person against whom it is directed is the judgment debtor. The enforcement of a judgment is another matter. Most people erroneously believe that once the judgment is pronounced in their favor, the opponent will expeditiously pay the award granted. Although most people abide by the judgment rendered by the court, many do not.

There are various methods of collecting judgments. When a judgment concerns the title to real or personal property, the judgment creditor may enforce it by having the county sheriff seize the property, pursuant to an execution order, and transfer it to the creditor. Money judgments may be derived from any property legally transferable or assignable by the judgment debtor, with certain exceptions designated by statute for subsistence. Property may be seized by the county sheriff pursuant to an execution order and sold at public auction, and the proceeds of the sale may be applied to the judgment. The judgment creditor may also obtain a lien against property owned by the judgment debtor. A judgment lien against property means that the property cannot be sold until the amount of the lien is satisfied by payment. An income execution order may also be issued against the judgment debtor, but the amount garnished may not exceed 10 percent of the salary or wages earned. In spite of these methods of collection, a judgment is often worthless. The judgment debtor may be judgment proof. He or she may have filed voluntary bankruptcy, or other creditors may have forced the judgment debtor into involuntary bankruptcy. The judgment debtor may be unemployed and may have no other assets from which to collect the judgment; perhaps the judgment debtor has disappeared and cannot be located. Judgments usually can be enforced for as long as ten to twenty years, but individuals rarely pursue the matter for that length of time.

APPEAL

The party against whom the judgment is made has the right to *appeal* the case to a higher court, which is referred to as an appellate court. An appeal may be made only in regard to the law applied in the trial, not in regard to the facts. No evidence will be heard by the appellate court. A notice of appeal must be filed with the clerk of the trial court within the prescribed time limits after the judgment is entered in the court records. The person making the appeal is the appellant; the person against whom the appeal is made is known as the appellee. The appellant's attorney must file the record of the trial with the appellate court, together with a brief presenting the appellant's argument. The appellee must also submit a brief refuting the appellant's argument. The appellant may, at his or her option, file a reply to the appellee's brief. Both parties, through their attorneys, may supplement their briefs by presenting oral arguments before the court.

The appellate court then makes its determination and either affirms the decision of the trial court for the appellee or reverses it in favor of the appellant. If this appellate court is an intermediary appellate court, a party may appeal its decision to the state supreme court by submitting a petition within the allotted time frame. The trial record, along with the intermediary appellate court's opinion, will be filed with the state supreme court for review. New briefs must be filed and new arguments presented.

The decision of the state supreme court will be final unless a federal issue is involved, in which case an appeal to the United States Supreme Court would be possible. The state supreme court will either affirm the decision of the lower court for the appellee or reverse it with instructions to enter a judgment for the appellant. There are times when the appellate court's instructions call for a new trial to be granted by the trial court. This means that the entire trial process must be started over. Only a very small percentage of the cases appealed from the trial court's decisions are changed by the appellate courts. In fact, many cases do not even go to trial but rather are settled out of court because of the time and expense involved.

The cost of commencing an appeal presents financial obstacles for many individuals who feel that questions of law have been unjustly resolved. Many appeals are thus lost or abandoned, with the victorious party being the one willing to spend the most and tie up the case the longest. This is clearly evident where the amount in dispute is relatively small and the individual's opponent is a large corporation such as an insurance company.

NEED FOR LAWYERS

By reading this book you will acquire a certain amount of knowledge concerning the law. It is important to understand the danger inherent in trying to be your own lawyer. There is an old saying, "A person who acts as his own lawyer has a fool for a client."

REVIEW QUESTIONS

1. Define jurisdiction, summons, complaint, answer, counterclaim, reply, discovery, deposition, pretrial hearing, appeal, arbitration, judgment, evidence, and hearsay.
2. What is the structure of a typical state court system?

3. What is the jurisdiction or function of each court in the state court system?
4. What is the difference between a trial court and an appellate court?
5. What is the difference between a question of fact and a question of law?
6. What are the documents that constitute the pleadings?
7. What is the difference between the burden of proof in a civil case and in a criminal case?
8. Who are the plaintiff and the defendant?
9. Describe the various stages of a trial.
10. What is the function of the jury? The judge?

4

Criminal Law
and Procedure

INTRODUCTION

Criminal law is an entire and separate branch of law unto itself. It is concerned with identifying criminal conduct and providing the appropriate penalties to punish criminals and to deter them from committing future offenses. All of the other areas of law, including those discussed in this book, come under the heading of civil law.

BUSINESS CRIMES

The impact of criminal law on business is evidenced by the amount of money and property lost through theft by employees and customers as well as by outright criminals.

    When most people think about crimes against business, they think of shoplifting. But shoplifting by customers pales in comparison with employee theft. Employees are insiders who have greater access to merchandise, cash, and supplies than customers do. The trust and confidence placed in them by their employers often make it easy for them to steal. Their co-workers often look the other way. Estimates have been placed at upward of $1,000 per employee for direct, tangible loss of money and property.

24

Computer crimes also plague businesses. By using computers some individuals have embezzled funds through unauthorized electronic transfers. Others have erased or dismantled programs, causing disruption of operations and loss of important records

The use of bribes or kickbacks is rampant in negotiations for business deals. Buyers of large quantities of merchandise are often tempted to make deals in return for something "under the table."

Businesses are also faced with acts of burglary, robbery, arson, and vandalism. In response, businesses spend large sums of money on crime detection and security protection in the form of cameras, televisions, alarms, guards, watchdogs, fencing, and lights.

RICO

RICO is the Racketeer Influenced and Corrupt Organizations Act. The original purpose of the act was to prevent organized crime from using legitimate business as a cover to launder money from illegal activities. The concept of RICO has been expanded to include anyone who uses a business enterprise to perpetrate criminal activities, the most prevalent of which is fraud, which accounts for three out of every four causes. For RICO to be enforced, a pattern of criminal activity—that is, two or more occurrences over a ten-year period—must be established. RICO is the main weapon against white-collar crime. A crime under RICO is punishable by a fine of up to $25,000, twenty years' imprisonment, or a combination of fine and imprisonment.

Crimes Against Business

The crimes that have the most profound effects on businesses are **BAFFLE.**

Burglary
Arson
Fraud or embezzlement
Forgery
Larceny
Extortion, bribery, and blackmail

Computer Crime

Computer crime has become a serious problem transcending the antiquated penal codes of many states. The crime of larceny was intended to apply to the theft of tangible property, which would include computers, yet funds transferred by computer are intangible. Financial, educational, and employment records as well as stock, insurance, and bank accounts can be altered; bills paid by checks issued without authorization; and credit reports falsified through unauthorized computer access. It is difficult to catch the culprit, but even more frustrating to prosecute.

OBJECTIVES OF CRIMINAL PROCEDURE

The main objective of criminal procedure is to realize fast and accurate investigation of crimes while protecting the individual freedom of citizens. Criminal procedure differs from civil procedure, discussed in Chapter 3. When a crime has been committed or is about to be committed, an arrest may be made, the accused and his or her property may be searched, and any incriminating evidence found may be seized.

CONSTITUTIONAL RIGHTS AT TIME OF ARREST

The test to determine whether a lawful arrest was made and whether the search and seizure were proper is found in the Fourth Amendment to the Constitution. The Fourth Amendment protects people, their homes, and their effects against unreasonable searches and seizures by the state or federal government. Search and seizure must be carried out pursuant to a warrant based on probable cause, the reasonable belief that a person committed a crime or that a certain person or item incident to a crime may be found at a particular place. A search warrant issued on probable cause must be supported by an oath and affirmation describing the place to be searched or the person or property to be seized. A deliberate falsification of any of this information by the maker of the warrant is grounds for suppression of the evidence seized or for release of the person. A search may be made without a warrant only under special circumstances.

The Fifth and Sixth Amendments also have an important impact on the rights of the accused when he or she is arrested. These rights have resulted in the Miranda warning. In 1966 the United States Supreme Court, in *Miranda* v. *State of Arizona,* 384 U.S. 436, promulgated these rights when it held,

> At the outset, if a person in custody is to be subjected to interrogation, he must first be informed in clear and unequivocal terms that he has a right to remain silent. . . . The warning of the right to remain silent must be accompanied by the explanation that anything said can and will be used against the individual in court. This warning is needed in order to make him aware not only of the privilege, but also of the consequences of foregoing it. . . .
>
> . . . an individual held for interrogation must be clearly informed that he has the right to consult with a lawyer and to have the lawyer with him during interrogation under the system for protecting the privilege we delineate today. . . . it is necessary to warn him not only that he has the right to consult with an attorney, but also if he is indigent, a lawyer will be appointed to represent him.

Because these warnings were not given to Miranda, the Supreme Court reversed the decision of the Arizona Supreme Court and awarded judgment for Miranda.

PROCEDURE AFTER ARREST

After arrest the accused is taken to the police station to be booked, that is, charged with a specific crime. The police will then question the accused for the purpose of obtaining more information about the crime or a voluntary confession. Often a suspect will be requested to stand in a lineup so the identity of the perpetrator of the crime can be verified. The accused will then be brought before a judge, who will advise the accused of his or her rights and set bail. Then formal proceedings begin.

In felony cases, about half the states provide for indictment by grand jury. The other states allow the prosecutor to use his or her discretion in a proceeding on the basis of either a grand jury indictment or information similar to a plaintiff's complaint in a civil case. The court grants a preliminary hearing where the prosecutor has brought forward the proceedings on information without a grand jury indictment.

After the indictment or information is filed, the accused is arraigned. Arraignment takes place when the accused is brought into court for the purpose of being informed of the charges against him or her. The accused is again advised of his or her constitutional rights, and the indictment or information is recited. The accused is then afforded an opportunity to respond to the charge. It is here that plea bargaining takes place. Often, the accused will plead guilty to a lesser crime. This avoids the need for a time-consuming and expensive trial and helps clear the congested trial calendar. If the accused does not plead guilty to a charge, then a trial will begin. The Sixth Amendment guarantees the accused a trial by jury in a case involving a serious offense such as a felony.

TRIAL

The trial begins with a reading of the indictment or the information by the clerk of the court. The accused's plea is also given. The prosecution and defense counsel make their opening statements. Because the burden of proof is on the prosecution, it will proceed with the introduction of real evidence and the testimony of witnesses to prove beyond a reasonable doubt the allegations set forth in the indictment or information. This burden of proof is much greater than that required in a civil trial. The defense counsel may cross-examine each witness introduced by the prosecution. The right to confront or cross-examine opposing witnesses can be found in the Sixth Amendment. After the prosecution concludes, the defense counsel may introduce real evidence and the testimony of witnesses to disprove the prosecution's evidence and thus try to create a reasonable doubt in the minds of the jurors. The prosecution will cross-examine the witnesses introduced by the defense in an attempt to discredit or minimize their impact on the outcome of the trial.

After the defense rests its case, the judge will charge the jury with principles of law pertinent to the issues raised by the evidence. The jury is instructed to deliberate and arrive at a verdict based on the judge's charges. If the accused is found guilty, a judgment convicting him or her will not be entered until a sentence is imposed.

SENTENCING

Sentencing is administered through a separate hearing in which additional arguments and evidence are presented so the appropriate punishment can be determined. During the time lapse between the jury's verdict and the sentencing, the judge may authorize either that bail be continued or that the defendant be taken into custody. After a sentence is imposed, the judge will inform the defendant of his or her right to appeal the conviction or the sentence.

REVIEW QUESTIONS

1. What is criminal law?
2. What are the various business crimes?
3. What constitutional rights does a person have when arrested?
4. A prosecutor may proceed against a person accused of a crime on the basis of an indictment or information. What is the difference between the two?
5. What is the procedure after a person is arrested?
6. What is the burden of proof in a criminal trial?
7. What was the significance of the United States Supreme Court's decision in *Miranda* v. *State of Arizona?*

5

Torts

INTRODUCTION

Torts are private civil wrongs committed by people against people, their privacy, or their property. Torts are distinguished from crimes, which are public wrongs committed against the state. However, many crimes are also torts, in which victims have the legal right to sue for money damages to redress the wrongs committed.

EXAMPLE | Robert Suskind is walking crosstown to his east-side apartment after seeing a Broadway show. He is mugged by Wilfred Malone, who slashes Suskind's arm with a switchblade and steals his wallet. Malone is apprehended two days later. Is Malone's action a crime or a tort? Both! The state may criminally prosecute Malone for robbery. The crimes of larceny and criminal assault are included in robbery. Suskind may sue Malone for civil assault and battery to recover for the injuries he sustained. He may also sue Malone for conversion of his wallet to regain the lost money and credit cards.

There are two types of torts: intentional and unintentional. Intentional torts include assault, battery, conversion, defamation, fraud, false imprisonment, invasion of privacy, interference with business relations, malicious prosecution, nuisance, strict liability, and trespass. Unintentional torts include negligence, product liability, and misrepresentation.

INTENTIONAL TORTS

Assault and Battery

An *assault* is the apprehension of a harmful or offensive contact. It is distinguished from the contact itself, which is a battery. An assault is an attempt, with force, to injure another. There must be some act denoting apparent present ability and the intention to assault, and the person against whom the attempt is directed must be aware of this act.

A *battery* is an intentional, unpermitted contact made by one person with another. The contact may be made with any part of the body or anything connected with it, such as a hat, necklace, or pocketbook. Battery includes contacts that do actual physical harm as well as less serious ones that are nonetheless offensive and insulting, such as kissing or pinching a stranger in public. The relationship of the parties and the circumstances under which the act is committed will necessarily affect the unpermitted character of the contact.

The difference between assault and battery is the difference between physical contact and the apprehension of it; the first is a battery and the second is an assault. It is an assault when a person swings a fist to strike another and a battery when the fist hits the victim's nose.

Infants are liable for their torts; however, an infant under age four is generally thought to be incapable of formulating the necessary intent to commit a tort.

EXAMPLE | The Bobsey Twins are strolling along a cobblestone street in a dense fog after a splendid evening at the theater. Meanwhile Simon LeGree is lurking in an alley waiting to devour them. Approaching from the opposite direction is Steve Townsend out for an evening stroll. He looks up to the sky, and through the mist he sees a full moon. Suddenly he cringes and falls limp to the ground. The Bobsey Twins rush to his aid, the figure slowly rises, and the Wolf Man appears. The Bobsey Twins shriek and then faint, receiving severe head injuries when they hit the cobblestone. The Wolf Man approaches Simon Legree, who does not clearly see the Wolf Man because of the fog. The Wolf Man grabs LeGree and flips him twenty feet. Have the Bobsey Twins and Simon LeGree any recourse against the Wolf Man? Yes! The Bobsey Twins may sue the Wolf Man in tort for assault. There was no battery because the Wolf Man never touched them. Simon LeGree may sue the Wolf Man in tort for battery. There was no assault because Simon never saw the Wolf Man.

Conversion

Conversion is the unlawful taking of personal property from the possession of another, the converting of another's property for one's own use. Conversion may be made by mistake, but if it is done intentionally it amounts to criminal theft, which is considered under the headings of larceny, embezzlement, and robbery.

EXAMPLE | Jack the Ripper and Bluebeard are out at a muggers' convention. After checking their coats they proceed to enjoy an informative and educational series of lectures on new devices and tactics as well as retirement plans and tax shelters. On the way out Bluebeard mistakenly takes Jack's coat, which contains his favorite pushbutton switchblade. Is Bluebeard liable for the mistake? Yes! Jack the Ripper may sue him in tort for conversion, which is the wrongful taking of property. If Bluebeard's action was intentional, he would have committed a theft, the crime of larceny.

Defamation

Defamation is a false statement that is communicated to at least one other person orally or in a permanent form such as writing and that causes harm to a third person's reputation. Libel is written defamation, whereas slander is oral defamation. Libel is actionable without proof of special damages because a writing remains in existence and could be distributed widely; oral defamation is usually temporary and limited to the range of a person's voice, except when the oral statement is recorded and broadcast continually on television, radio, or soundtrack.

The requirement for libel is a false statement published and read by someone other than the one about whom it is written. The true intention of the writer is that which is apparent from the natural and ordinary interpretation of the written words and—when an individual is concerned—the interpretation placed upon those words by people acquainted with the plaintiff and the circumstances. General damages are automatically awarded for harm to reputation in the community or in business and for personal embarrassment and mental anguish. Special damages may be awarded if the victim can prove he or she suffered an actual pecuniary loss from the harm to his or her reputation.

EXAMPLE | The *Fort Night Quarterly* published an article claiming that Dracula, a reputable funeral director by day, was a vampire by night. As a result his business died off. Has Dracula any recourse against the paper? Yes! He may sue them for libel by claiming that the statement was false and proving that it led to a decline in his business.

Piersall v. Sportsvision of Chicago
595 N.E. 2d 103 (Ill. App. 1 Dist. 1992)

Jimmy Piersall, a former major league all-star, was hired by Jerry Reinsdorf, owner of the Chicago White Sox, to be a commentator for *Sports Vision*, a cable TV program. Piersall was also a radio announcer for WMAQ. During the early 1980s Piersall made the following statements:

1. Wives of baseball players are "horny broads who say yes very easily."
2. "The writers for the *Sun Times* were a bunch of alcoholics."
3. In response to a recent player trade, "There is no one in the White Sox organization smart enough to hold a gun to anyone's head."

After the first game of the 1983 season, Piersall was discharged. Reinsdorf made the following statements about Piersall and former White Sox announcer Harry Caray:

> I don't mind criticism, but they both told a lot of lies. They wanted us to lose. They thought they were bigger than the club and did not want the attraction shifting to the field. (*Chicago Sun Times,* September 19, 1983)

> and

> The public could not know the truth about them; they are both liars. They both said things on the air they knew were not true. (*Chicago Tribune,* September 19, 1983)

Piersall sued Reinsdorf for libel. The issue is whether Reinsdorf's statements were made with actual malice.

The court held, "Nothing in the record, even with the benefit of reasonable inferences, supports a finding of knowing falsity on Reinsdorf's part. Therefore, Piersall has not established a genuine issue of material fact as to whether Reinsdorf acted with actual malice." The court continued, "[T]he general statement that someone is a liar, not being put in context of specific facts, is merely opinion." Judgment for Sportsvision.

Slander requires a defamatory statement heard by someone other than the person against whom it is directed. Special damages must be proved except in four situations where general damages are recoverable without proof. These situations include derogating some characteristic important to a person in that person's trade or business, such as honesty or integrity; accusing a person of committing a crime of moral turpitude; denouncing someone by stating that he or she has contracted a loathsome disease; and imputing that a woman is unchaste.

EXAMPLE | Prince Yussupoff was running against Rasputin for political office in Siberia. Knowing of Rasputin's immense popularity with the women voters, the prince called Rasputin a debaucher and a mad monk. Rasputin was able to prove that these statements were false. Is Prince Yussupoff guilty of slander? Yes.

Truth is an absolute defense when the statement made is fully true, but the truth must be proved. There is a special rule pertaining to defamatory statements made by the media concerning public figures. Even if the statement cannot be proved to be true, the media will not be liable unless malicious intent can be substantiated. Malice is the making of a false statement with the intent to injure another.

In the previous example, assume that Prince Yussupoff's allegations concerning Rasputin are the truest words ever spoken but that he has no way of proving them. What result? The result will be the same: Rasputin will recover general damages. Although truth is an absolute defense, the burden of proof is on the person who made the statement.

Tyson v. L'Eggs Products, Inc.
351 S.E. 2d 834 (N.C. App. 1987)

L'Eggs Products, Inc. released an article to the press stating that tendinitis was not a work-related condition. Tyson and Bennett, employees, wrote a letter to the *Richmond County Daily Journal* accusing their employer of misstating the conclusion of the medical study. Later they appeared on local television to further their cause. The management of L'Eggs responded in a company newsletter that the allegations of Tyson and Bennett were "a bunch of hogwash." A defamation suit against L'Eggs followed.

The issue is whether the statement was defamatory. The court concluded that the opinion of the management of L'Eggs was written with hostility, but that Tyson and Bennett expressed their own feelings with strong accusations and therefore could not be thin-skinned. The statements of both parties were within the realm of proper debate and were not defamatory. Judgment for L'Eggs.

Fraud and Misrepresentation

Fraud involves the intentional misrepresentation of a material fact that induces another person to act in reliance on that fact to his or her detriment. When the false statement of a material fact is made unintentionally, then the tort of *misrepresentation* not fraud applies. Fraud and misrepresentation are contractual defenses as well as torts. A lawsuit involving them may be based on tort law or contract law. A further discussion of fraud and misrepresentation appears in Chapter 17, Contractual Defenses.

EXAMPLE | Dr. Jekyll placed an ad in the *Transylvania Times* offering to pay $25 to a person who would volunteer for an experiment with no risk. Mr. Hyde, who was down and out, figured he could use the money, so he accepted the offer. Dr. Jekyll falsely informed Mr. Hyde that the experiment was to be a behavioral study with no risk of permanent effects.

Mr. Hyde drank a potion prepared by Dr. Jekyll and turned into a monster. Later he returned to his normal self, but the change came upon Mr. Hyde again, and it seems to occur whenever he becomes nervous and excited. Mr. Hyde sued Dr. Jekyll for fraud. What result? Mr. Hyde will recover damages for his permanent injuries. He justifiably relied on Dr. Jekyll's representations to his detriment.

Atkins v. Kirkpatrick
823 S.W. 2d 547 (Tenn. App. 1991)

The Atkinses bought land through a realtor, Mrs. Kirkpatrick. The realtor advised the Atkinses that it was a buildable lot but suggested they contact the health department. The health department approved the lot so long as it had not been disturbed by landfill. The land turned out to have been disturbed. The Atkinses sued the realtor, claiming fraud and misrepresentation.

The issue is whether the realtor had the responsibility for determining whether the lot was buildable and whether the Atkinses relied on the realtor's opinion to their detriment.

The court held, "In the case before us, there is absolutely no evidence that . . . Kirkpatrick possessed knowledge of the defective condition of the property. Plaintiffs never inquired whether the lot had been 'disturbed.' There was no proof that plaintiffs relied upon the statements made by any of the defendants. To the contrary, plaintiffs made their own independent investigation." Judgment for Kirkpatrick.

False Imprisonment

False imprisonment and *false arrest* are the confinement of a person to an area against his or her will, with no opportunity to escape. The restraint may be accomplished by means of physical barriers or threats of force. Most states have enacted new laws that allow merchants to detain customers when there is reasonable suspicion that shoplifting has occurred and where the confinement is reasonable. Confinement that is not reasonable and not consented to will result in false imprisonment; the same may be said for false arrest. General damages are normally awarded for the embarrassment and mental distress suffered.

EXAMPLE | Christopher Daniels works as a security guard in Hutton's Department Store. One day he notices a customer take off her jacket, lay it aside, and put on one from the racks. He follows her at a distance but loses her in the crowd. He figures he will catch her as she leaves the store. Mistakenly he apprehends Gloria Henn, who is wearing a similar jacket that she purchased a few weeks before. Daniels asks Gloria Henn to accompany him to the manager's office, where both he and the manager intimidate her as they attempt to elicit a confession. Gloria, in tears, asks if she may call her husband. They refuse permission until the police arrive. Later Gloria's husband appears, producing the receipt for her jacket. The store manager and the detective apologize, but Gloria sues them for false imprisonment. What result? In most states a merchant has the legal right to detain a customer when there is a reasonable suspicion that the person has engaged in shoplifting and the confinement is reasonable. Here, the intimidation used to secure a confession, coupled with the refusal to permit Gloria the opportunity to extricate herself by calling her husband, who could produce the receipt, amounts to unreasonable confinement. Gloria may be awarded general damages for the embarrassment and mental distress she has suffered.

Invasion of Privacy

Personal privacy is protected against invasions causing economic loss or mental suffering. There are four distinct invasions: intruding on a person's physical solitude, publishing private matters violating ordinary decencies, putting a person in a false position in the public eye by connecting him or her with views he or she does not hold, and appropriating some element of a person's personality for commercial use such as photographs.

EXAMPLE | Statler Beer is introducing a new beer called Sparkling Lite. To market the product, Statler is featuring an unauthorized poster of the Reverend Luther Winthrop advocating the purchase of Sparkling Lite. The Reverend Winthrop is a well-known fundamentalist minister who openly decries the consumption of alcohol. Has Reverend Winthrop any recourse? Yes! He may sue Statler Beer, asserting that he did not consent to the poster and that it puts him in a false position in the public eye by connecting him with a view that he does not hold and a product that he does not deem appropriate.

Publication of private matters that are newsworthy is privileged as long as it does not violate ordinary decencies. A false report by the media of a matter of public interest is protected by the First Amendment right of free press, in the absence of proof that it was published with malice.

Morgan v. Hustler Magazine, Inc.
653 F. Supp. 711 (N.D. Ohio 1987)

In January 1973 Donda Morgan posed for a professional fashion photographer in connection with her career as a fashion model. *Hustler Magazine, Inc.* published one of these pictures on the front cover of its December 1975 issue. Donda brought this action on the basis of libel and invasion of privacy. Donda alleged that this was done without her consent and that her prominent display on the front cover implied that she supported the views of *Hustler Magazine*, which she did not. Donda argued further that this event had placed her in a false light in the public eye and that her personal esteem, her character, and her peace of mind had been destroyed.

Hustler argued that Donda had executed a release covering the photograph in question, which had been given to the photographer. The words "or distorted in character or form" had been deleted by Donda from the provisions of the release.

Because this action was brought approximately ten years after the publication, *Hustler* argued that the lawsuit was biased by the one-year statute of limitation for libel. Donda argued that she had not become aware of the publication until 1984 and that the one-year time limitation should have run from this date.

The issues are whether the libel action is timely and whether the release prohibits the invasion of privacy claim.

The court held, "It has been held that a cause of action for libel when there is a publication in a national magazine accrues on the date of publication. This is known as the single publication rule." As to the invasion of privacy claim, "It is the view of this Court that the release signed by the plaintiff Donda R. Morgan was clear and unambiguous. . . . In addition, the plaintiff Donda R. Morgan excised certain language from the printed form of the release to distortions. If she had wanted to or had intended to exclude the use of her pictures from a magazine such as *Hustler,* she could have included this language in the release." Judgment for *Hustler.*

Interference with Business Relations

A person who intentionally interferes in a business relationship through the use of fraudulent inducement or other unethical means that result in an unfavorable contract, or in the loss or breach of a favorable contract, is liable for damages. The victim must prove damages, such as the specific loss of a customer, except where the nature of the falsehood is likely to bring about a general decline in business.

EXAMPLE Figaro was producing an opera at the Met starring Madame Butterfly as the Last of the Red-Hot Mamas. On opening night, November 17, a capacity crowd was in attendance, with some people paying as much as $100 a seat. As the curtain rose and Madame Butterfly began singing her opening aria, the piano player stopped the music and jumped on top of the piano. When the spotlight diverted the piano player's attention, who did he turn out to be? None other than the Phantom of the Opera! The audience shrieked and evacuated the theatre. Later many of them sued for a return of their money. As a result the show failed, costing Figaro over $700,000. Has Figaro any recourse? Yes! Figaro can sue the Phantom of the Opera for damages resulting from interference with advantageous business relations. Figaro lost his patrons and the show because of the Phantom's intentional acts.

Nuisance

A *nuisance* is the unreasonable, negligent, or unlawful use of property. People may not use their property in such a way as to deprive others in turn of the reasonable use and enjoyment of their property. Zoning laws have been developed as a result of nuisances. Zoning segregates designated areas for certain purposes; it protects the reasonable use and enjoyment of property.

EXAMPLE | Dr. Frankenstein and Dr. Dracula are interns at the South Bronx Morgue and Psychiatric Center. Dr. Dracula does much of the embalming at the morgue, while Dr. Frankenstein handles the lobotomies at the psychiatric center. They live in Coney Island. Every Saturday night they have an all-night monster mash with their friends. The noise is very disturbing to their neighbors. Do the neighbors have any recourse? Yes! They can sue Dr. Frankenstein and Dr. Dracula in tort for nuisance because the interns are impairing the neighbors' right to the use and enjoyment of their homes. The neighbors may ask the court to grant an injunction prohibiting the interns from playing loud music and carrying on past a certain hour.

The *attractive nuisance doctrine* was formulated to protect children from hazardous conditions. An attractive nuisance is anything that attracts unsupervised children and could prove dangerous to their safety, such as an unfenced swimming pool. The attractive nuisance doctrine is invoked when the owner knows or should know that children might be trespassing and when the condition caused by the owner imposes a danger to children who, because of immaturity, do not appreciate the danger involved. Owners are held liable under this doctrine for any injury to children caused by the attractive nuisance. The risk of injuring children far outweighs the presence of the attractive nuisance.

EXAMPLE | Nevada Smith owns an estate in Reno, Nevada. He constructs an above-ground swimming pool but neglects to enclose it with a fence. One day Dennis the Menace, a neighbor's five-year-old child, wanders onto the unfenced deck area and falls into the pool. Unable to swim, Dennis drowns. His parents sue Nevada Smith for the wrongful death of their son. What result? The parents will win because the unfenced swimming pool created an attractive nuisance that led to the boy's death.

Strict Liability

Strict liability in tort imposes a responsibility on a person who increases the risk of harm to others in the community by lawfully bringing something onto his or her land that is or could be dangerous, such as wild animals, explosive devices, and the like. If other individuals are harmed as a result, the person who brought about the danger will be absolutely liable even though he or she was not negligent in any manner. One party must bear the loss. The party who brought about the danger is the logical choice even where he or she acted without fault by taking every possible precaution. There is no liability for merely increasing the risk of harm to others; liability occurs only when damage results.

EXAMPLE | Rita Mullins is the owner of Babette, Muffin, and Scruffy, three poodles who are colored grey, black, and champagne. Phil Fogarty lives next door to Rita. On one sunny afternoon in July, he is preparing a barbecue for his family and friends. He lays out twelve porterhouse steaks on a picnic table. He goes inside to look for the grill and charcoal. In the meantime, Babette, Muffin, and Scruffy have wandered into his yard to sniff around. By the time Phil returns, the dogs have devoured three of the steaks and licked the rest a few times. Phil sues Rita for the value of the twelve steaks. Will he be able to collect? Yes! Rita is absolutely liable for the damages done by the dogs under the theory of strict liability.

There is no liability for anything that exists naturally on the surface of the land unless a person interferes with it and this action results in injury to the property or the person of another. There is liability if anything that is brought onto the land, or under the land, escapes and causes damage. This is true regardless of that precautions are taken except if the event causing the damage occurred through an act of God.

EXAMPLE | In the example concerning Nevada Smith's pool, assume that after twelve years the walls of the pool give way, spilling 15,000 gallons of water. In a neighboring yard the Adams family is holding an outdoor reception for their daughter's wedding. Most of the water comes pouring into their yard, overturning the elaborate buffet and soaking tablecloths, guests' feet, and the wedding gown and veil and ruining the entire occasion. Have the Adams family, their daughter, and their guests any recourse? Yes! They may sue Nevada Smith for damages under the theory of strict liability in tort. Nevada Smith is absolutely liable even though he was not negligent. He must assume direct responsibility for the damage caused by the collapse of the pool's walls regardless of the precautions he took.

Trespass

Trespass is the unlawful entry onto the land of another. An owner owes no duty to a trespasser except to refrain from willful conduct in disregard of human safety, such as the setting of bear traps or a spring gun.

EXAMPLE | Two youngsters, Pat and Mike, climbed a twelve-foot-high fence on the perimeter of a junkyard. Once inside they began to jump on all of the wrecked vehicles. Pat landed on the windshield of a 1966 Plymouth and fell through, suffering a broken leg. Mike ran to the office to telephone for help. When he opened the door, he was confronted with a full-size Doberman pinscher. There was no posted warning, and the dog could not bark because its vocal cords had been removed. Mike ran as fast as he could, but he was caught from behind. Pat and Mike sued the junkyard dealer for their injuries. Have they any recourse? Both Pat and Mike were trespassing. The owner owes them no duty except to refrain from willfully causing them harm. Pat has no recourse because the junkyard owner is not responsible for the safety and condition of the vehicles. The presence of the watchdog is permissible. But, where no warnings are posted and the dog's bark cannot be heard, willful intent to cause harm may be inferred. Mike will be able to collect for the injuries he sustained from the silent Doberman.

Wrongful Death

When a person commits a tort that results in the death of another, an executor or personal representative of the decedent may bring a wrongful death action on behalf of the estate. The lawsuit may be brought for any wrongful act or any neglect that causes death. Some states allow the victim's beneficiaries, usually consisting of the immediate family, to bring a wrongful death action against the defendant. Recovery may include damages for the decedent's pain and suffering, loss of earnings, medical expenses, and, most important, the survivors' loss of the decedent's support and services. There is no compensation given to the family for grief, mental suffering, or loss of the loved one.

The actual amount awarded for future loss of support and services is measured according to guidelines that take into account the decedent's life expectancy, current and projected income, health, and past contributions to the family. The jury is generally given wide latitude in making an award rather than being restricted to compliance with a definite formula. Juries have awarded high verdicts to parents, even in cases involving minors where the parents would actually have received no pecuniary benefit had the child lived because children generally cost more to rear than they contribute.

EXAMPLE | David Sands was a lifeguard at Malibu Beach. On a hot afternoon he was preoccupied in a social conversation with a bikini-clad beauty and failed to observe Walter Roberts drowning. By the time he responded, Roberts had died. Roberts's estate sued Sands for Roberts's wrongful death. Is this a good cause of action? Yes! Wrongful death may result from neglect. Sands had a duty to observe and act, and because he failed to do so, he is responsible. Suppose Walter Roberts's drowning was caused by a friend who playfully held him under water without intending to drown him. Could a wrongful death action be brought against the friend? Certainly! The fact that Roberts's death was accidental does not affect the cause of action. What matters is that Roberts is deceased.

UNINTENTIONAL TORTS

Negligence

Negligence is the failure to perceive a risk that results in an injury that was foreseeable. Negligence is caused by conduct that falls below the standard established by law for the protection of others against risks of harm. The negligent party must have had a duty to perceive the risk of harm, which he or she fails to meet. The key to negligence is that the defendant failed to act as a reasonable person would in light of the risk. The plaintiff has the burden of proving this. The elements that give rise to negligence are contained in **NOCIL** (pronounced "nozzle").

Negligent act
Owed a duty
Cause was proximate
Injury was foreseeable
Loss or damage resulted

There must be a negligent act caused by the defendant, who owed a duty to exercise reasonable care. The negligent act must be the proximate cause of a foreseeable injury that results in loss or damage to the injured party.

Negligence is an act performed in a careless manner, or an omission to act, that proximately causes injury to another. Liability for the negligence does not arise until it is established that the person who was careless owed a duty toward the person bringing suit. A duty to exercise reasonable care arises whenever there is a danger of one person's causing injury to another. The injury to the plaintiff must have been proximately caused by the negligent act of the defendant. Proximate cause means that the negligent act must have been reasonably connected to the plaintiff's injury. The injury to the plaintiff must have been foreseeable. A foreseeable injury is that which would reasonably be anticipated as a consequence of the defendant's negligence. In most states the defendant is responsible for damages resulting only from foreseeable injuries.

The plaintiff must sustain a definable loss or damage and prove that this loss or damage resulted from the injury caused by the defendant's negligence. The plaintiff's loss is recompensed with money damages.

Palsgraf v. Long Island Railroad Company
248 N.Y. 339, 162 N.E. 99 (1928)

Palsgraf sued the Long Island Railroad for injuries sustained as a result of the alleged negligence of its employees.

Mrs. Palsgraf was standing on a platform waiting for a train. A man carrying a package was running to catch a train that was already moving. As the man jumped aboard, two guards attempted to assist him for fear he might fall. One guard grabbed his arm while the other pushed from behind. The package in the man's arms was dislodged in the process. It fell on the tracks and exploded because it contained fireworks. The explosion caused a set of scales several feet away on the platform to overturn and fall upon Mrs. Palsgraf.

> The Long Island Railroad contended that they owed no duty of care to Mrs. Palsgraf because the injuries she received were not the result of any foreseeable harm.
>
> The court agreed with the railroad's contention and established the doctrine of foreseeability, which states, "Negligence is not actionable unless it involves the invasion of a legally protected interest, the violation of a right." In this case the railroad did not violate Mrs. Palsgraf's rights because the risk of harm to her was not foreseeable. "One who jostles one's neighbor in a crowd does not invade the rights of others standing at the outer fringe when the unintended contact casts a bomb upon the ground. The wrongdoer as to them is the man who carries the bomb, not the one who explodes it without suspicion of danger." Judgment for Long Island Railroad.

The doctrine of foreseeability may also be applied to situations where one party's negligence has injured a person and caused others to attempt to rescue. Under the doctrine of "danger invites rescue," the negligent party is responsible for injury to the rescuers, where they act reasonably and where it is foreseeable that people might go to the rescue of the injured person.

EXAMPLE | The Gargoyles, a French family-owned corporation, are building a trestle bridge across Niagara Falls. They employ Sweeney Todd, known to be good with a saw, as their chief carpenter and general contractor. One day Sweeney, who is rushing to finish work so he can leave for his home on Fleet Street, omits three of the four nails securing one of the tracks. Two months later the bridge opens and the first train rolls across. Jack the Ripper and his cousin Mack the Knife are among the last to board the train. They have a big date in Toronto with Apple Annie and her sister Orange Blossom. They are forced to stand between the cars because the train is overcrowded. Casey Jones, the train's engineer, misjudges the correct speed needed to round a curve smoothly and sends Jack flying out the door. The train stops 100 feet down the tracks. Mack bolts off the train to look for his cousin. When he steps on the track that is not properly secured, it gives way and he joins his cousin in the falls. Their estates sue the Gargoyles for wrongful death. The Gargoyles acknowledge their responsibility for Jack only. What result? Mack's estate may also recover under the doctrine that danger invites rescue because it was foreseeable that Mack might go to the rescue of his cousin.

Contributory Negligence

People must exercise reasonable care in looking out for themselves. To recover damages for a defendant's negligent conduct, a plaintiff must not have been negligent in any way that might have contributed to the resulting injury. Some states have enacted comparative negligence statutes that apportion the fault between the plaintiff and the defendant according to their degrees of negligence when a plaintiff is contributorily negligent. If the plaintiff is 25 percent negligent, that person may recover only 75 percent of the damages for the injury received. The purpose of comparative negligence statutes is to protect those who were slightly negligent from being barred from recovery. If the plaintiff's own negligence was the proximate cause of the injury, many states will bar any form of recovery. Contributory negligence consists of the plaintiff's failure to discover or appreciate a risk that would be apparent to a reasonable person. Even when this is the case, the plaintiff may still recover if the defendant had the last clear chance to avoid injury to the plaintiff.

EXAMPLE | Lucrezia Borgia owns a diner in the Bensonhurst section of Brooklyn. One day she is applying, around the perimeter of the room, a new poison that she developed to kill ants and roaches. She leaves the bottle on one of the tables in the far corner of the diner, near where she is working. The bottle is properly labeled with the word *poison* and with the skull and crossbones. Albert DeSalvo, aka the Boston Strangler, is sitting at the next booth waiting for his pepper steak. When it arrives he reaches back to the table behind him and grabs the poison, thinking it is Worcestershire sauce. Albert applies it generously to the pepper steak. When he takes a bite, it has a very spicy taste. He likes it. Suddenly he falls over. DeSalvo is rushed to the emergency room of a nearby hospital. Dr. Crippin, whose motto is "We either cure or kill," pumps DeSalvo's stomach and saves his life. Assume that Lucrezia is assessed 90 percent of the fault and DeSalvo is considered to be 10 percent contributorily negligent. What result? Under comparative negligence statutes Albert would be able to recover 90 percent of his damages. Under a contributory negligence statute, he may be barred from any recovery unless it is determined that Lucrezia had the last clear chance to avoid Albert's injury.

Assumption of Risk

Assumption of risk is intentional exposure by the plaintiff to a danger or risk of which the plaintiff is aware, such as riding in a car with a drunken driver. The court determines the reasonableness of the injured party's conduct by balancing the risk against the value of the action taken. The risk of being in an accident while riding with a drunken driver will be compared with the value or importance of getting a ride home.

Assumption of risk is a matter of knowledge of the danger and intelligent acquiescence to that danger. A plaintiff must know and appreciate the risk involved. The choice to incur the risk must be made voluntarily. The effect of an assumption of risk is to relieve the defendant of all legal duty toward the plaintiff. This happens in situations where the plaintiff voluntarily enters into a relationship with the defendant knowing that the defendant will not protect him or her against the risk. One example of such a case would be a person being hit by a baseball while watching a game at the ballpark.

However, assumption of risk does not apply where the plaintiff acted in a reasonable manner during an emergency. Under these circumstances the defendant is not relieved from his or her legal duty to the plaintiff.

EXAMPLE | Papillon is a free-lance travel writer on a guided tour of the caves of Devil's Island. The entrance to one cave is blocked by huge signs reading "Do Not Enter—Haven of the Bats." Papillon figures a few snapshots would enhance his story. He sneaks into the cave and snaps a few pictures. When the flash goes off, he is attacked by the bats and sustains severe injuries. Does he have any recourse against the proprietors of Devil's Island? No! Once he disregarded their conspicuous warnings, Papillon assumed the risk of injury.

REVIEW QUESTIONS

1. Define torts, assault, battery, conversion, defamation, fraud, false imprisonment, invasion of privacy, interference with business relations, nuisance, attractive nuisance doctrine, strict liability, trespass, wrongful death, and misrepresentation.

2. What are the elements of negligence?

3. William Buckley is a well-known lecturer, a columnist syndicated in 350 newspapers, and the author of over twenty books. Liberty Lobby is an incorporated not-for-profit lobbying organization that publishes a weekly paper, *The Spotlight.* Willis A. Carto, the founder of Liberty Lobby, contended that in Buckley's new book the sentence "*The Spotlight's* distinctive feature is racial and religious bigotry" defamed it. Buckley claimed that his opinion about *The Spotlight* was constitutionally protected by the First Amendment. What result? *Carto* v. *Buckley,* 649 F. Supp. 502 (S.D.N.Y. 1986).

4. Byron Brown, a senior counselor at a drug rehabilitation facility, engaged in sexual intercourse with Kimberly Bunce, a patient. This happened several times with her consent. Thereafter Bunce sued Brown in civil court for sexual assault, battery, and malpractice. Brown argued that consent is a defense. What result? *Bunce* v. *Parkside Lodge of Columbus,* 596 N.E. 2d 1106 (Ohio App. 10 Dist. 1991).

5. After renting the videotape *Who Framed Roger Rabbit* from Pathmark for his four- and seven-year-old children, the Reverend Alan Thomas was astonished to discover a pornographic passage added onto the tape. He sued Pathmark for negligent infliction of emotional distress. Pathmark countered that it had no duty to inspect the tape. What result? *Thomas* v. *Supermarkets General Corp.,* 586 N.Y.S. 2d 454 (Sup. 1992).

6. Sidney Rosenberg applied to Equitable Life Assurance for a policy. He was 51 years old and had had a heart attack seven years before. Equitable required a stress test and arranged for him to see Dr. Arora. A month later Rosenberg died of a heart attack. The stress test was found to be the proximate cause. Rosenberg's estate brought suit against Equitable for wrongful death. What result? *Rosenberg* v. *Equitable Life Assurance Society,* 584 N.Y.S. 2d 765 (Ct. App. 1992).

7. In September 1983 the owner of the Chicago White Sox, Jerry Reinsdorf, called baseball announcer Jimmy Piersall a liar in response to earlier statements that Piersall made on the air. In November 1983 Piersall's employer WMAQ fired him. Piersall sued Reinsdorf for tortious interference with Piersall's broadcasting contract with WMAQ. WMAQ contended that Reinsdorf's statements had nothing to do with Piersall's termination. What result? *Piersall* v. *Sportsvision of Chicago,* 595 N.E. 2d 103 (Ill. App. 1 Dist. 1992).

8. While visiting his brother at Meyers's Joy Ranch, Cory Grote was kicked by a colt he was releasing from a corral while helping his brother, an employee, with Meyers's permission. The colt was known to the ranchers to have uncontrollable behavior. Cory sued the ranch for the head injuries he suffered. Meyers countered that Cory had assumed the risk because he volunteered. What result? *Grote* v. *Meyers Land and Cattle Co.,* 485 N.W. 2d 748 (Neb. 1992).

9. Richard Bloom worked as an associate dentist in Allan Dampf's office. While the plaintiff took a vacation, Dr. Bloom made a photostatic copy of the plaintiff's computer-generated "recall list," which contained all of his patients' names, addresses, telephone numbers, dates of last appointments, and dates due for next checkups. This list was kept in Dr. Dampf's home for security reasons. After he was fired, Dr. Bloom opened his own office and began soliciting the plaintiff's patients. What result? *Allan Dampf, P.C.* v. *Bloom,* 512 N.Y.S. 2d 116 (A.D. 2 Dept. 1987).

10. Lenzer was employed as a physician assistant by ARC under the supervision of Drs. Baucom and Harman. She was in the process of satisfying the requirement for state certification. However, Drs. Baucom and Harman withdrew supervision from Lenzer, causing her to lose the certification she needed to maintain her position with ARC. The physicians' reason was that Lenzer counseled patients about child abuse. This was outside the scope of a physician assistant's duties. There was no dispute over Lenzer's competence, and actually her counseling had been tolerated for a long time. Lenzer claims that her counseling is protected by the First Amendment's free speech clause. Lenzer is suing for Drs. Baucom and Harman's interference with her contract with ARC. What result? *Lenzer* v. *Flaherty,* 418 S.E.2d 276 (N.C.App. 1992).

Special Topic: Business Ethics

INTRODUCTION

Ethics is a very important topic in our society. This is because many individuals, politicians, and businesses lacks ethics. Business ethics may be defined as acting in an honest manner while conducting business. This means that conduct that involves deceit, coercion, suppression of material facts, or any other action resulting in aggrandizement while causing injury to another falls short of an ethical standard of behavior.

SOCIAL RESPONSIBILITY

Do businesses have a social responsibility toward society and the environment? Should they just barely meet standards, or should they exceed them? Should businesses lobby against more stringent pollution, plant safety, and health standards, or should they take the initiative to promote them? Should corporate management be held criminally responsible for grossly negligent acts that result in accidents causing the death of others (for example, Union Carbide's plant accident at Bhopal, India)? How far do we extend ethical behavior and social responsibility? These questions must be resolved, but by whom? If we allow businesses to regulate themselves, the answer is clear: Maximize profit—minimize cost. Businesses will be quick to point out that they contribute to the arts and fund grant programs for charity, research, and education, but these contributions are tax-deductible. Installing pollution safety devices or dumping toxic wastes in designated sites is expensive and not always tax-deductible.

There are now laws protecting the environment, consumers, and workers, but many of these laws are not enforced. Ethical behavior should be applauded, but how can we mandate it? Adoption and strict enforcement of laws, increased consumer and government awareness, and education in business ethics for young people who will enter the business world are sorely needed.

IS IT FAIR OR FOUL?

Atkins v. Glen Falls City School District
75 A.D. 2d 239, 429 N.Y.S. 2d 467 (3rd Dept. 1980) rev'd
53 N.Y. 2d 325, 441 N.Y.S. 2d 644, 424 N.E. 2d 531 (1981)

A spectator named Atkins was observing a high school baseball game while standing outside the third base line. A batter lined a drive foul that struck Atkins, causing him severe injuries. In denying an award to Atkins, the New York Court of Appeals reasoned that "an owner of a baseball field is not an insurer of the safety of its spectators" and that "many spectators prefer to sit where their view of the game is unobstructed by fences or protective netting." The court added that a spectator seated in an area not protected by screening will not be permitted to recover for injuries sustained if there exists one empty seat in the protected area. The rationale is that if a spectator were so concerned about his or her safety, he or she would purchase a seat in the protected area.

A strong dissent was voiced by Chief Judge Cooke. He reasoned that if there were no vacant seats in the protected areas, the spectator would have to assume the risk of being hit or not attend the game. He also exclaimed that there was an arbitrary distinction between the screened areas down the first and third base lines. Clearly the degree of danger was not significantly different, and "limiting the area to be protected to that area behind home plate does nothing more than to artificially limit the liability of . . . park owners." Judgment for Glen Falls.

Davidoff v. Metropolitan Baseball Club, Inc.
459 N.Y.S. 2d, 475 N.Y.S. 2d 367 (1984)

Jennifer had been struck by a foul ball; the incident caused her to lose the sight in one eye. She had been seated in a box seat behind first base. Only a three-foot fence separated her seat from the ballfield. The court stipulated that as long as protective seating behind home plate, the area of greatest danger, is provided, the proprietor of the stadium has satisfied its duty to exercise reasonable care and cannot be held liable for negligence.

Both *Atkins* and *Davidoff* rejected the implied premise that the owner of the ballpark could be thought of as an "insurer of spectators."

The nature of baseball is such that a risk of injury exists no matter where one is seated. However, in *Atkins* the court determined that the risk of getting struck with a foul ball is considerably greater behind home plate than outside the first and third base lines.

In *Atkins* the court rejected the notion that "every spectator injured by a foul ball no matter where he is seated or standing in the ballpark, would have an absolute right to go to the jury on every claim of negligence, regardless of the owner's efforts to provide reasonable protection." Judgment for the Mets.

Clapman v. City of New York
63 N.Y. 2d 669, 479 N.Y.S. 2d 515, 468 N.E. 2d 697 (1984)

In July 1977 David Clapman and his wife were occupying box seats behind the home team dugout at Yankee Stadium. A foul ball struck David Clapman, causing him to sustain injuries. Clapman argued that the protective screening should have been extended to the area in which he was seated and that a vendor blocked his view of the oncoming foul ball.

The New York Court of Appeals responded to the first argument by stating that a proprietor's duty of reasonable care toward spectators is satisfied by the provision of adequate screening behind home plate, the area where foul balls present their greatest danger. With regard to Clapman's obstructed view, the court decided that the Yankees had no duty to ensure that roaming vendors would not block a spectator's view. Judgment for the Yankees.

Clark v. Goshen Sunday Morning Softball League
493 N.Y.S. 2d 262, 129 Misc. 2d 401 (1985),
aff'd 505 N.Y.S. 2d 655, 122 A.D. 2d 769 (1986)

Alexsis Delgado overthrew his receiver in a warm-up catch prior to a game, and the ball struck a spectator, Morvin Clark. Alexsis Delgado and his receiver were warming up twenty feet apart, parallel to the third base line. An errant throw sailed over the head of the receiver, striking Morvin Clark, who was leaning over the perimeter fence and looking in the opposite direction from the oncoming ball. Clark alleged that Delgado and the softball league were negligent in failing to take precautionany measures to avoid such an accident.

Adequate screening was provided behind the backstop where Clark and his friends could have conversed. Clark did not avail himself of this opportunity. Delgado was where he should have been: adjacent to the playing field, warming up. It has long been the rule in New York that spectators assume the risk of being hit and injured by a baseball. Considering the circumstances there was no duty on the part of Delgado or the league to warn Clark of the inherent dangers of baseball. Judgement for Goshen.

Neinstein v. Los Angeles Dodgers, Inc.
229 Cal. Rptr. 612, 185 CA 3d 176 (Second Dist. Ct. App.)

While attending a ballgame at Dodger Stadium, Shirley Neinstein was struck by a foul ball, sustaining injuries. In denying recovery for her personal injuries, the court cited Atkins. In the Atkins case the court detailed the widely recognized principle that an owner of a baseball field is not an insurer of the safety of its spectators.

The court went on to hold,

> In the instant case, plaintiff impliedly consented to take her own chances that she would not be injured. She voluntarily elected to sit in a seat which was clearly unprotected by any form of screening. Rather than request a seat in a section where injury was unlikely to occur, plaintiff chose to accept a highly sought after seat, close to the sphere of action, where the likelihood of foul balls entering the stands remained a possibility. She was sufficiently warned of the risk by common knowledge of the nature of the sport and by the warning provided on the back of her ticket. The Dodgers were under no duty to do anything further to protect her from that hazard.

Judgment for the Dodgers.

Falkner v. John E Fetzer, Inc.
317 N.W. 2d 337, 113 Mich. App. 500 (1981)

Kathy Falkner was struck by a baseball during a Detroit Tigers game at Tiger Stadium. She alleged that the defendant had failed to provide protective screening where she was seated, failed to inform her of the availability of seats with protective screening, failed to offer her a choice between protective and unprotective seating, failed to provide a sufficient number of seats in the most hazardous areas, and failed to post signs to warn her of the hazards of foul balls.

The trial court returned a directed verdict on the first four counts for the defendant. On the fifth count the jury found the defendant neligent and awarded the plaintiff $258,850.

On appeal, the Michigan Appellate Court overturned the jury verdict, stating, "It is a generally accepted proposition that there is no duty to warn of the risk of being hit by batted balls when attending a baseball game, because the risk is obvious."

The court continued that although the plaintiff argued that the magnitude of the risk involved was much greater than commonly believed, the plaintiff presented no evidence to establish proximate cause. The plaintiff did not prove that had she been given proper warning, she would have acted in a manner that would have prevented the injury. Judgment for Fetzer.

Friedman v. Houston Sports Assoc.
731 S.W. 2d 572 (Tex. App. 1 Dist. 1987)

Eleven-year-old Karen Friedman was struck by a baseball near her right eye in the Houston Astrodome. Karen had left her seat and proceeded to stand behind the first base dugout when a line-drive foul ball clocked her. Friedman argued that recovery should be allowed in accordance with the comparative negligence statute.

The appellants misconstrued the purpose of comparative negligence. Comparative negligence does not create a duty; it simply allows partial recovery for a plaintiff who is no more than 50 percent at fault. The appellants in this case still had the burden to prove that the appellee owed them a duty to warn.

The court held, "We find that a stadium owner has no duty to warn spectators of the danger of foul balls. The stadium owner's duty is to provide 'adequately screened seats' for all those desiring them." Judgment for Houston.

Uzbavines v. Metropolitan Baseball Club
454 NYS 2d 238 (1982)

On July 5, 1978, the New York Mets were playing the Philadelphia Phillies in a night game at Shea Stadium. Marie Uzbavines was in attedance with her husband and two children in box seats forty feet behind home plate. In the third inning Jerry Martin of the Phillies lined a foul straight back. The ball went through the screening and struck Marie Uzbavines in her right cheekbone, causing her severe injuries. The screening behind home plate is made of the same anchor-type mesh wire used in fences. However, the location where the ball passed through the screening had previously been damaged. The repair was made with thin chicken wire. When the ball struck it, the chicken wire could not withstand the force and thus allowed the ball to pass through.

The duty owed by the Mets was to exercise reasonable and ordinary care to protect spectators from injuries that were foreseeable. It was certainly foreseeable that a baseball coming into contact with and passing through screening repaired with thin wire, which could not withstand the force of the fouled baseball, might cause injury to a spectator.

The court held, "[D]efendant was at all times under a duty to maintain and control the protective screening for the safety of plaintiff who has purchased a ticket seating her behind the safety screen, thereby causing her to rely on its protection; and the injury from a foul ball was an accident that would not have occurred in the absence of defendant's negligence." Judgement for Uzbavines.

REVIEW QUESTIONS

1. Is being hit by a baseball an assumption of risk? Who should decide?
2. Discuss whether each of the above cases was decided in an ethical manner.
3. Should the doctrine of assumption of risk be modified or eliminated?

6

Environmental Law

INTRODUCTION

Our environment sustains our physical life. Clean air and clean water are precious gifts that we must cherish and safeguard. Pollutants in the air and water eventually wind up in our bodies. Our bodies can withstand the infiltration of only so many contaminants before they will become diseased and die.

People generate a tremendous amount of waste. The environment will suffer wherever the waste is dumped. What people often fail to understand is that when we harm the environment—the air, water, and soil—we harm ourselves. When industry, landfills, and automobiles pollute, we in turn breathe the polluted air, drink the contaminated water, and eat the food from the putrified soil. We contract cancer, parasites, and breathing difficulties. We damage our lungs, intestines, and livers. We pay the consequences for our pollution.

Our environment is at a critical stage. It is in serious need of protection from corporate executives who forget that they are breathing the same air and drinking the same water they are polluting. The consequence of continuously maximizing profit while minimizing cost is that we all suffer.

Often people blame business or government, and those entities are at fault. But individuals still want to drive automobiles, use aerosol cans, and enjoy air conditioning. Are they sending a message to business and government to protect the environment? No! Are people willing to recycle and possibly to pay more for recycled goods? Many are not. Then what can they expect? When individuals decide to change their outlook and sacrifice some of their conveniences and luxuries, then businesses and government will be forced to follow.

NATIONAL ENVIRONMENTAL POLICY ACT

The National Environmental Policy Act (NEPA) was enacted by Congress in 1969, to encourage harmony between humans and the environment. There is often conflict between people and the environment. The goal of a national environmental policy must be realistic. Pollution and waste will not disappear; they must be minimized. Recycling, mass transportation, alternative fuel sources (e.g.,) electric or natural gas-driven vehicles, less packaging, biodegradable products, and composting are some of the solutions. The emphasis must be on balancing the need to pollute with the health and welfare of the people. The Council on Environmental Quality was formed to establish a national policy to improve the quality of the environment. The main goal of the NEPA was to create a national environmental policy to restore and maintain the quality of the environment. This act also created the Environmental Protection Agency to enforce the environmental laws enacted by Congress, to monitor businesses, and to curtail their deleterious effects on the environment.

AIR POLLUTION

The Clean Air Act of 1970 established national air quality standards. Areas that do not meet the standards are required to implement pollution control devices such as those used on factories and automobiles. Areas that meet the air quality standards are advised to maintain their status. The three pollutants that cause the most problems in the atmosphere are hydrocarbons, carbon monoxide, and sulfur dioxide.

Clean Air

Air pollution is caused primarily by factory and auto emissions. Because most Americans live in metropolitan areas, these areas have the greatest concentration of industry and automobiles, which, in turn, produce air pollution. State and local governments have the primary responsibility for controlling air pollution. Air pollution damages crops, livestock, and land as well as human health.

The Clean Air Act established strict measures for improving air quality. The EPA sets emission standards to be followed by cities and states. The laws are adequate, but their enforcement is not. The EPA has for many years maintained lists of hazardous waste sites that it has designated for cleanup. The problem is that the sites have not been cleaned up. Strict adherence to the laws is needed if the dilemma is to be solved.

Hazardous Air Pollutants

The Clean Air Act contains a list of more than 190 cancer-causing pollutants. The EPA must identify major sources of these pollutants—that is, facilities emitting more than ten tons per year of any chemical on the list or twenty-five tons per year of any combination of chemicals on the list. The EPA then sets standards for emission. The purpose is to require the maximum reduction in pollutants while taking into account the financial cost of achieving it, as well as any other health, environmental, or energy impact that would result. Specifically, the Clean Air Act requires reduction of toxic pollutants through implementation of changes in the manufacturing process; substitution of other, less toxic materials; system enclosure; or capture of toxic emissions from stacks. The strategy was to reduce cancer attributable to hazardous air pollutants by 75 percent per year. Supposedly the air is cleaner today than in 1970, when the Clean Air Act Amendments went into effect, but the incidence of cancer is still on the rise.

State of Idaho v. Bunker Hill Co.
635 F. Supp. 665 (D. Idaho 1986)

Gulf Resources and Chemical Corporation purchased Bunker Hill Company in 1968. In 1982 the State of Idaho brought an action against Bunker Hill and its parent, Gulf, claiming that Bunker Hill violated the Comprehensive Environmental Response, Compensation, and Liability Act (CERCLA) by exceeding the limitations authorized for the releasing of hazardous wastes.

CERCLA Section 107(f) provides, "There shall be no recovery . . . where such damages and the release of a hazardous substance from which such damages resulted have occurred wholly before" (December 11, 1980).

The first issue is whether liability attaches where the releases occur before December 1980 but where the damage occurs afterward. The court held, "To the extent the release occurred prior to the enactment, but the resultant damages occurred postenactment, Section 107(f) does not bar recovery."

The second issue is whether Gulf is liable and, if so, whether it can be held liable for damages caused by releases of hazardous waste by Bunker Hill that occurred before its acquisition of Bunker Hill in 1968. The court held "that Gulf was an owner or operator for purposes of CERCLA liability." However, the court determined, "While the acts of the Bunker Hill Co. prior to 1968 may be in question, Gulf cannot be held liable for such acts." The reason is that Gulf was not an owner or an operator before 1968. Liability attaches only during the period of ownership or operation. Judgment for the state of Idaho against Bunker Hill Company, but not against its parent, Gulf.

Auto Emissions

Auto emissions are the main culprit in air pollution. In Staten Island, New York, known as the home of the world's largest dump, a study found that auto emissions resulted in 85 percent of the air pollution, with the dump and the New Jersey chemical refineries being responsible only for the remaining 15 percent. Clearly, the catalytic converter was not the answer. Although it has been helpful to some extent, the auto companies used it to circumvent the real problem, redesigning the engines for better propulsion and for alternative fuel use. Hydrogen, electricity, natural gas, methanol, and ethanol, while not pollution free, emit less toxicity than petroleum-based gasoline. The auto companies stubbornly resist any effort for movement and change.

Even if auto emissions could be reduced significantly, the reduction would be more than offset by the increase in the total number of drivers as well as the total number of miles driven per driver. Total number of drivers does not tell the whole story, either. As the number of drivers increases, so does the amount of congestion. It takes each of those drivers longer to drive each mile, and thus the amount of emissions per mile increases. Bumper-to-bumper traffic on the major highways tells the real story.

An example illustrates this situation. Sam travels fifty miles to work on the Long Island Expressway (LIE). It used to take him one and one-half hours; now it takes him two hours. The amount of emissions has increased 25 percent because he is covering the same distance but taking more time to do it. If the number of drivers using the LIE increases from 200,000 to 250,000, then the number of driver hours spent on the road increases from 300,000 to 500,000. The result is 66 2/3 percent more emissions.

Indoor Pollution

Air pollution is not restricted to the outdoors. Indoor air pollution has become a major problem in both the home and the office. If you check your bathroom and kitchen cabinets, you will likely find an array of household cleaners, air fresheners, and pesticides that contain many ingredients with names not easily pronounced. Many of these chemicals are toxic. When they are used in the confinement of the bathroom or kitchen, the toxicity becomes concentrated. This can have harmful effects on the lungs, liver and kidneys. Ventilating the room or working with nontoxic products is preferred.

Office buildings that do not permit the free flow of outside air into the interior cause people to have headaches, nausea, and fatigue. This is commonly referred to as the "sick building syndrome." In tall office buildings, air ducts, where present, are often placed at street level and take in motor exhaust, dirt, and sewer gases. This costs businesses a great deal of money in sick time or poor job performance by affected workers.

SOLID WASTE DISPOSAL

Most solid waste is disposed of on land in dumps and landfills. This can present a danger to people's health and to the environment. Open dumping pollutes the air, the land,

and possibly the water through underground seepage. Recycling solid waste is an alternative to dumping and a potential source of energy. However, separating out the usable solid waste is cumbersome and expensive.

The Solid Waste Disposal Act was created in 1976 to address the mounting quantity of solid waste from products generated by industry to service the nation's increased standard of living. Careful planning is required to avoid air and water pollution, which in turn poses substantial risks to human health. Through the EPA the federal government will lend its expertise to the states to ensure that land disposal facilities are capable of long-term containment of hazardous wastes. Millions of tons of material that could be recycled take up landfill space each year. Motor oil is an example of a substance extremely harmful to the environment that can be reused instead. Solid waste may also be utilized to produce energy. These are examples of ways in which careful planning can reduce land disposal of waste.

WATER POLLUTION

The Federal Water Pollution Control Act (Clean Water Act), as amended in 1972, established the national goal of eliminating the discharge of pollutants into the nation's waterways by 1985. The problem of water pollution is not decreasing, nor is there any real chance of eliminating it. New York City used to boast of having the cleanest, best-tasting water in the country because of its upstate reservoir system. Now, because of increased pollution, encroachment by developers, and the building of waste treatment facilities, New York City's water system is less than adequate. The federal government may soon mandate that New York City build a $6 billion filtration system. The city is trying to buy all land adjacent to the reservoirs to convince the government that the filtration system is not necessary. Development and toxic dumping by factories are the main contributions to the pollution of our water systems. The oceans are being used as dumping grounds; the result is high levels of mercury and lead in the popular varieties of fish that we eat.

Pollution of many of our important inland waterways is causing fish to die and depriving us of clean water to drink. Certain bays in large cities are so polluted that swimming will not be possible for at least a decade. Our oceans are now beginning to feel the ill-fated effects of our waste. Many species of fish and shellfish contain contaminants from toxic waste.

The major pollutants of water are sewage, metals, toxic chemicals, fertilizers, sediment caused by unnatural erosion from development, bacteria from human and animal waste, and agricultural byproducts. The latter include sediment, pesticides, and bacteria, as well as nitrogen and phosphorus, that promote algae growth.

The 1972 amendments to the Federal Water Pollution Act set forth an agenda:

- Eliminate the discharge of pollutants into navigable waters by 1985.
- Sustain the fish, shellfish, and wildlife that live near or in water.
- Prohibit the discharge of toxic pollutants into water.
- Develop a national policy for alternative waste disposal.

Clean Water

The Clean Water Act applies a technology-based approach wherein the EPA sets standards of allowable discharge based on the pollution control devices existing at the time. These standards are suppose to be reviewed every five years; that review has not been accomplished so far.

Safe Drinking Water

The Public Health Service Act, also known as the Safe Drinking Water Act, was instituted to ensure a constant supply of safe drinking water. A maximum level is established for each contaminant. Quality control procedures are mandated, with follow-up testing to ensure that the contaminants do not exceed the limitations.

Bradley Mining Co. v. U.S. EPA
972 F. 2d 1356 (D.C. Cir. 1992)

Bradley Mining owns the Sulfur Bank Mine, which is adjacent to an inlet of Clear Lake in California. Mining of sulfur and mercury took place between the 1850s and the 1950s. The mine is now inactive. The EPA placed the mine on the National Priorities List of sites containing hazardous substances because mercury was found in Clear Lake. Bradley contended that EPA's decision was arbitrary and capricious because the agency had miscalculated the risk of contamination of usable ground water by the mercury.

Placement on the National Priorities List is based on an EPA formula that reflects risk to human health. It is arrived at as follows:

> The potential for a release into the ground water is rated based, among other factors, on how close the site is to an aquifer, the permeability of the soil, and the existence of barriers that would contain the hazardous substances—i.e., through an examination of the factors that might inhibit migration. The factors relevant to potential releases into surface water are the terrain near the site, the distance of the surface water from the site, annual rainfall, and containment.

Ratings for toxicity and persistence, quantity of a release, and the potential targets are then added to the scores, reflecting the risk of harm to human health in a potential or actual release.

The issue is whether the ground water must be contaminated or have the potential to be contaminated.

The court decided the latter. It held,

> The EPA saw no observable release in the ground water. It therefore calculated a ground water score based on the risk of release. . . . As the

area has significant precipitation, and the soil is permeable, the Agency
concluded that the possibility that substances would be released into the
ground water was high. It found wells that served 1,245 year-round residential homes within three miles of the site.

Judgment for the EPA.

Ocean Dumping

The Marine Protection, Research, and Sanctuaries Act of 1972, more commonly referred to as the Ocean Dumping Act, requires a permit for all ocean dumping. Its purpose is to limit the dumping of sewage, solid waste, medical waste, high-level radioactive waste, and chemicals into the ocean to cases where it poses an unacceptable risk of
harm on the land and no other solution is feasible.

   In the mid-1980s illegal dumping of toxic chemicals and medical waste was rampant off the New York-New Jersey coast. One year all the beaches of the New Jersey
shore were closed. Millions of visitors had nowhere to swim. Shore merchants lost millions of dollars as a result. A little dumping caused a lot of harm.

Oil Pollution

The Oil Pollution Act of 1990 was enacted to shift the cost of oil spills from the government to the parties at fault. Exceptions exist for spills caused by an act of God or an
act of war. The problem with this law is that it limits liability to $10 million—a sum
clearly inadequate when damage is severe.

RENEWABLE RESOURCES

The Forest and Rangeland Renewable Resources Planning Act of 1974 was enacted to
preserve the renewable resources of the forest and the range. According to its terms the
Secretary of Agriculture must assess impact of the wood mills on the forest and must
require that the wood mills use up-to-date technology to minimize waste.

COASTAL MANAGEMENT

The Coastal Zone Management Act of 1972 was instituted to preserve the habitats
of fish, wildlife, and other organisms living in ecologically fragile areas. The demands placed upon coastal areas have been heavy: residential development, recreation, industry, commerce, and waste disposal. The effect has been loss of living
marine resources, wildlife, and nutrient-rich areas and permanent damage to the
ecosystem.

ENDANGERED SPECIES

The Endangered Species Act of 1973 was designed to prevent the extinction of wildlife, fish, and plants whose populations have been depleted by the nation's unrestricted economic growth and development. The Secretary of Commerce must prevent the destruction of the habitat of an endangered species, using scientific and commercial data as primary sources of evidence.

Seattle Audubon Society v. John L. Evans (U.S. Forest Service) and Washington Contract Loggers Association
771 F. Supp. 1081 (W. Dist. Wash. 1991)

The Seattle Audubon Society sued for a permanent injunction to prevent the U.S. Forest Service from selling logging rights to the Washington Contract Loggers Association. The purpose of the suit was to preserve the old-growth forest, which is the habitat of the northern spotted owl. The loggers contended that the Pacific Northwest mills had a timber supply shortage. Job losses would result. They parlayed the dispute in the media into a jobs-versus-owls conflict, with the phrase "Shoot an owl, save a job" as their slogan.

The Audubon Society countered that the loggers had deforested much of the public and private land without replanting trees. They were subsidized by federal taxpayers as timber was sold to loggers at below-market prices. The government built and maintained logging roads that comprised seven times the mileage of the interstate highway system.

The issue is whether the habitat of the northern spotted owl should be protected from loggers.

The court ruled, "Job losses in the wood products industry will continue regardless of whether the northern spotted owl is protected . . . 30,000 jobs will be lost to worker-productivity increases alone."

The court continued,

> The problem here has not been a shortcoming in the laws, but simply a refusal of administrative agencies to comply with them. . . . This invokes a public interest of the highest order: the interest in having government officials act in accordance with law. . . . The loss of an additional 66,000 acres of spotted owl habitat. . . . would risk pushing the species beyond a threshold from which it could not recover.

Judgment for Seattle Audubon Society.

CONCLUSION

The solution to our environmental problems lies in convincing government as well as business leaders that without clean air and water, life will end. This reality seems self-evident, yet difficult for many leaders to comprehend.

REVIEW QUESTIONS

1. What is the National Environmental Policy Act?
2. What is the function of the EPA?
3. List and describe the main federal Acts designed to battle pollution.
4. Stop-N-Go, Inc. contracted to sell sixteen of its stores to The Pantry. The contract warranted that the stores complied with state environmental regulations. Five of the Kentucky stores had retail gasoline pumps. Stop-N-Go did not have a permit to dispose of waste at any of its stores. Petroleum products leaked from the underground storage tanks and contaminated the soil and ground water.

   Kentucky law states: "Solid waste means any garbage, refuse, sludge, and other discarded material, including solid, liquid, semi-solid, or contained gaseous material resulting from industrial, commercial, mining (excluding coal mining wastes, coal mining by-products, refuse and overburden), agricultural, operations, and from community activities. . . ."

   The issue is whether petroleum qualifies as waste. What result? *Pantry, Inc. v. Stop-N-Go Foods, Inc.,* 796 F. Supp. 1171 (S.D. Ind. 1992).
5. Magnolia Petroleum Company was granted an easement by L.A. Collier to dump oil waste and saltwater in Cottonwood Creek, which flowed through Collier's property. Magnolia Petroleum assigned this easement to Mobil Oil Corporation. Mobil was sued for polluting Cottonwood Creek by Branch, who bought Collier's property. Was the assignment of the easement valid? *Branch v. Mobil Oil Corp.,* 772 F. Supp. 570 (W.D. Oh. 1991).
6. The Department of Environmental Resources (DER) required Richard Winn to remedy a hazardous condition at the Strasbourg Landfill at a cost to him of over one million dollars. Winn complied under threat of criminal prosecution. Later it was determined that he was not responsible. He sued the DER for the moneys he had expended, claiming that the state was unjustly enriched. The DER retorted that the landfill was not owned by the state. What result? *Dept. of Environmental Resources v. Winn,* 597 A. 2d 281 (Pa. Cmwlth. 1991).
7. Ferebee became afflicted with pulmonary fibrosis as a result of exposing his skin to the herbicide paraquat over a long period. Chevron, the manufacturer, argued that the EPA had found that paraquat did not have any adverse effects on the environment and the product was so labeled. What result? *Ferebee v. Chevron Chemical Co.,* 736 F. 2d 1529 (D.C. Cir. 1984).

8. Papas was injured through exposure to pesticides manufactured by Upjohn. He claimed that the pesticides were not adequately labeled. Upjohn argued that the pesticides were labeled in accordance with the EPA's determination that the labeling was adequate protection against risk of injury. What result? *Papas* v. *Upjohn Co.,* 926 F. 2d 1019 (11th Cir. 1991).

9. Mobil Oil deposited oil waste, salt water, and other dangerous substances in Cottonwood Creek, which runs through the Branches' property. Mobil argued that it had a right to deposit these substances in Cottonwood Creek because of an easement and release granted to it by L.A. Collier, prior owner of the Branches' property. The Branches' contended that this contract was against public policy because it encouraged pollution. What result? *Branch* v. *Mobil Oil Corp.,* 722 F. Supp. 570 (W.D. Okl. 1991).

10. John Alter purchased Dual 8E, a herbicide manufactured by CIBA-GEIGY, based on the representations of its agent, Ron Wulfkuble. The six-page label contained the following information:

Conditions of Sale and Warranty
CIBA-GEIGY warrants that this product conforms to the chemical description on the label and is reasonably fit for the purposes referred to in the Directions for Use subject to the inherent risks referred to above. CIBA-GEIGY makes no other express or implied warranty of fitness or merchantability or any other express or implied warranty. In no case shall CIBA-GEIGY or the Seller be liable for consequential, special, or indirect damages resulting from the use or handling of the product.

Directions for Use
FAILURE TO FOLLOW ALL PRECAUTIONS ON THIS LABEL MAY RESULT IN POOR WEED CONTROL, CROP INJURY, OR ILLEGAL RESIDUES.

Precaution: Injury may occur following the use of Dual 8E under abnormally high soil moisture conditions during early development of the crop.

While Alter was applying Dual 8E, it rained. Two months later the corn crop was ruined. What result? *CIBA-GEIGY Corp.* v. *Alter,* 834 S.W. 2d 136 (Ark. 1992).

7

International Law

INTRODUCTION

International laws are not as clear and definite as the domestic laws of the United States because there are so many countries involved in the international arena. Each country has its own laws and customs as well as its own particular biases. However, the free flow of international commerce could not be guaranteed without some agreement on ways to resolve conflicts. Treaties perform this function: They are contracts between countries. The United States Constitution gives the president the power to negotiate treaties with the advice and consent of the Senate. The United Nations and the European Community are outgrowths of treaties.

GATT

GATT is the General Agreement on Tariffs and Trade. Tariffs are protectionist in nature and inhibit free trade. The term GATT refers to both the document drafted in 1947 and the organization created to implement it. The purpose of GATT is to reduce tariffs and other trade barriers, which might otherwise lead to trade wars, and to promote free trade. To accomplish these ends, participants hold rounds every so often to resolve disputes. The Uruguay Round was the latest. More than 100 countries, representing 80 percent of world trade, participated.

One of the guiding principles of the agreement is the Most Favored Nation Rule, found in Article I of GATT: "Any advantage, favor, privilege, or immunity granted by any other contracting party to any product originating in or destined for any other country shall be accorded immediately and unconditionally to the like product originating in or destined for the territories of all other contracting parties." The purpose of this rule is to prevent a nation from favoring one country over another by granting concessions on tariffs to the favored country. The Most Favored Nation Rule states that if a rate reduction is granted to one country, it applies to all countries.

EXAMPLE | South Korea charges a 15 percent import tariff on beer. German beer is not sold in South Korea because of the high tariff. South Korea wants to encourage Germany to export beer to South Korea, so it lowers the tariff for Germany to 5 percent. Then, under the Most Favored Nation Rule, beer imported into South Korea from every other country will be subject to only a 5 percent tariff.

GATT also seeks to prohibit countries from favoring their own domestic goods ("Buy American") over imported ones. In particular the use of import quotas, such as the one the United States imposes on cars made in Japan, is not condoned because it discriminates against Japan. Although Japan is doing the same thing to the United States, the point is to try to eliminate protectionism in both countries.

Unfair trade practices such as dumping and subsidies are also violations of GATT. Dumping is a form of price discrimination whereby producers from one country sell a particular product for a price substantially less than that charged in the producers' home market. The idea is to build recognition, market share, and perhaps—in the case of semiconductors—dependence, with the idea that prices will be raised and the lost profit will be recouped later.

EXAMPLE | Japanese companies dump semiconductors in the United States for $10 each, when the price charged in Japan is the equivalent of $20 and U.S. companies routinely charge $15. The result is that U.S. manufacturers buy the Japanese semiconductors, thereby establishing Japanese recognition, market share and dependence. After this the price of the Japanese semiconductors rises. Meanwhile, Japanese firms have agreed to buy only from domestic suppliers. Although U.S. semiconductors were $5 cheaper, their manufacturers could not realize any market share. This is in violation of GATT's Antidumping Code.

National governments use subsidies to build up industries to compete more effectively with those from other nations. The negative side of subsidies is that they often create unfair advantage, sustain unproductive industries, and destroy comparative advantage.

EXAMPLE | *Domestic subsidy.* The United States pays farmers to grow wheat and corn even though the market is saturated and the grains will never be used. The purpose is to keep these farmers in business.

Export subsidy. To gain entry into the European VCR market, Thailand subsidizes its producers even though the cost per VCR is 20 percent higher than for competing brands. With credit guarantees and favorable tax treatment, Thai producers are able to undersell their foreign competitors. This hurts international trade because other VCR makers are now operating at a distinct disadvantage in the export market.

When a dispute arises it may be submitted to a dispute resolution panel. This panel is made up of experts who hold hearings and make recommendations to the GATT Council of Representatives on ways to resolve the dispute. If the recommendations are adopted but subsequently ignored by the offending party, the victimized country may petition GATT for permission to seek retaliatory measures.

NAFTA

The North American Free Trade Association is the United States, Canada, and Mexico's answer to the European Community. Its purpose is to eliminate tariffs between the member countries, thereby facilitating free trade, and to establish common barriers to those outside. NAFTA will be home to 360 million people with a $6 trillion–plus gross national product (GNP). Mexico's cheap labor market will be opened up much more than it already is to U.S. and Canadian companies.

Two major fears surroundings NAFTA have to do with labor and the environment. Labor unions fear that many workers will lose jobs. Environmentalists fear that heavily polluting companies will relocate on the Mexican border to circumvent U.S. pollution regulations. The result may be cleaner air in the Midwest and much more polluted air across the southern border. A major benefit will be an increase in the Mexican standard of living, which might mimimize the financial reason that many Mexicans emigrate illegally to the United States.

DOCTRINE OF SOVEREIGN IMMUNITY

The doctrine of sovereign immunity is based on the theory that a nation cannot be sued for its actions in the courts of another country. This doctrine was considered absolute until after World War II. Socialist countries, in which all companies were state owned, would qualify for immunity in all business transactions. Because of this, the doctrine was restricted to the governmental activities of the nation, not the commercial activities.

EXAMPLE | A Russian state-owned manufacturer sold defective bobsleds to the Jamaican Olympic bobsled team. The Jamaican bobsled team could sue the Russian government because this is a commercial transaction to which the doctrine of sovereign immunity no longer applies.

Foxworth v. Permanent Mission of Uganda
796 F. Supp. 761 (S.D. N.Y. 1992)

Mrs. Foxworth was severely injured by an automobile owned by the Mission of Uganda to the United Nations. A default judgment was awarded to Mrs. Foxworth against Uganda for $250,000. When she sought to have Uganda's Chemical Bank account attached, Uganda claimed diplomatic immunity under the United Nations charter: "Representatives of the Members of the United Nations and officials of the Organization shall similarly enjoy such privileges and immunities as are necessary for the indepedent exercise of their functions in connection with the Organization." Uganda argued that the $250,000 judgment exceeded the amount in its bank account and that it would be forced the cease operations if the judgment were enforced.

The issue is whether diplomatic immunity applies when the tort of negligence has been commutted.

The court ruled,

> [A]ttachment of defendant's bank account is in violation of the United Nations Charter and Vienna Convention because it would force defendant to cease operations. Moreover, defendant should not conclude that because I have granted its motion that I condone either its cavalier attitude toward the serious injuries it has inflicted on an 80-year-old woman or its selective disregard for the laws of the United States and the jurisdiction of this nation's courts.

The $250,000 judgment remains outstanding, but it is unenforceable. This means that it may be paid at the discretion of the government of Uganda when and if that government has sufficient funds. Judgment for Uganda.

ACT OF STATE DOCTRINE

The act of state doctrine requires a court to refuse to decide a case where it has jurisdiction and where the matter clearly violates international law when it is in the best interests of the government's foreign policy to do so. A domestic court should not interfere where the matter has significant foreign policy implications. The reasoning is that an adverse decision could precipitate the severing of relations, trade embargoes, or outright war. These matters are best left to the executive and legislative branches.

EXAMPLE | In Iran, Habib Oil contracted to sell 100,000 barrels of oil to Hasseim Oil for $18 per barrel. Subsequently the price of oil jumped to $21 per barrel. Habib refused to deliver the oil to Hasseim, instead, selling it to Exxon for $21 per barrel. Hasseim attempted to block the sale in the Iranian courts, but was unsuccessful because of Habib's close political ties. Hasseim brought suit in the U.S. District Court, claiming breach of contract. Although it had jurisdiction, the U.S. District Court declined to hear the matter, invoking the Act of State Doctrine because of the foreign policy implications.

NATIONALIZATION

The term *nationalization* is synonymous with expropriation, that is, the taking of private property for public use with just compensation. The reason for the taking must be legitimate, not politically motivated. *Just compensation* means that the payment must be fair, prompt, and freely transferable.

EXAMPLE | Mustafa Ali, a citizen of Morocco, owned a villa in Barcelona. The Spanish government took possession of Mustafa's villa because it was located on the site of a venue for the Olympics. The fair market value of the villa was $157,000. Spain was obligated to pay Mustafa that amount in cash promptly and permit him to remove the entire amount from Spain or allow him to convert it into the currency of his choice. There could be no blocking of the currency transfer.

If a government fails to cooperate, the aggrieved individual may sue the government in the courts of that country. The problem lies in the fact that the courts may be politically connected to the government and unsympathetic to the individual, especially where a friendly government has been deposed and a hostile one has taken over. The first thing such a government may do is to nationalize all property belonging to foreigners. Then the foreigner's best choice is to sue in a country where the hostile government owns assets, preferably the foreigner's home country. The plaintiff will have a friendly forum and, if victorious, the opportunity to attach the assets of the hostile government and apply it to the debt owed.

EXAMPLE | Françoise Chevalier, a French citizen built, a factory in Port-au-Prince, Haiti, to manufacture Barbie-like Fifi dolls. With the overthrow of the Haitian government, Françoise's factory was expropriated for the new regime's use. The factory was worth $6 million. Françoise learned of bank accounts and real estate held by the Haitian government in the United States. She sued in the U.S. District Court to recover the amount owed. Although the U.S. court has proper jurisdiction and could subject the Haitian assets to attachment to satisfy Françoise's claims, it might defer to the State Department's judgment to preserve the national interests and forgo hearing the case because of the doctrine of sovereign immunity and the Act of State doctrine. This would leave Françoise with no recourse.

CHOICE OF LAW

Freedom to contract carries over to international law. If contracting parties have incorporated a provision that the laws of a particular nation shall govern their contract, then the courts will uphold that. Absent that, the court will apply either the law of the nation that has the closest relationship with the conflict or the law of the nation upon which the outcome will have the greatest effect. With contracts, questions of validity will be governed by the law of the nation where the contract was made; questions of performance will be determined in accordance with the law where performance was to be rendered. Torts will be decided where the wrong occurred, and real property issues will be governed by the nation where the property is located.

CHOICE OF FORUM

Choice of forum is the selection by the parties of the state or country in which any lawsuit shall be brought.

EXAMPLE | Annemarie Carter, owner of Idaho Potatoes, Inc. contracts to ship 500 tons of potatoes to the Bulgarian Food Commissary. The contract provides that Idaho law shall govern and that the U.S. District Court in Boise, Idaho, shall have exclusive jurisdiction. The Food Commissary believes that the condition of the potatoes upon arrival is unsatisfactory. Under the contract it must sue Annemarie in Idaho, with Idaho law governing. What if the Food Commissary brings suit in Bulgaria? Then it is up to the discretion of the Bulgarian courts either to enforce the provision by dismissing the case or to ignore the provision and hear the case. If the Bulgarian courts hear the case and resolve it against Annemarie, there is no guarantee that U.S. courts will enforce the Bulgarian judgment against Annemarie, given the circumstances under which the judgment was obtained.

ARBITRATION

Another choice open to contracting parties is to agree to arbitrate any disputes. This is the preferred method of dispute resolution because it is expeditious, inexpensive, and private. Throughout the world there are many arbitration organizations that can provide arbitrators. An arbitration provision can be overruled by a court that is unwilling to relinquish jurisdiction. In most cases, though, arbitation is the preferred way to resolve conflicts.

CISG

CISG, which stands for Contracts for the International Sale of Goods, is a treaty that incorporates common law, civil law, and socialist law. CISG is like an international version of the Uniform Commercial Code (UCC). It has been adopted by the United States as well as thirty-three other nations. CISG preempts the UCC when a party from another nation is involved, but questions regarding the validity of the contract and product liability are still governed by local law.

DOCUMENTARY TRANSFERS

In order for a buyer to obtain title to goods shipped, certain documents must accompany the transfer. A draft is an order to pay drawn by the seller and presented to the buyer along with the goods. A sight draft requires immediate payment before the goods are released. A time draft allows the buyer to take title to the goods, with payment to follow in thirty, sixty or ninety days. The draft is accompanied by a collection letter providing payment instructions. The documents are transferred by the seller's bank to the buyer's bank, which then demands payment from the buyer.

EXAMPLE | Big Foot, a shoe store for people with big feet, orders 2,000 pairs of assorted styles and sizes from Scapezzi, an Italian shoe manufacturer. The cost is $50,000. Scapezzi issues a sixty day time draft with the following supporting documents: collection letter, commercial invoice, U.S. customs form, certificate of origin form, certificate of insurance, and bill of lading. The documents pass from the Bank of Milan to the Bank of New York, which then demands payment from Big Foot within sixty days.

LETTERS OF CREDIT

Without some form of guaranteed payment, sellers might be afraid to ship goods internationally. How do they know if buyers will pay for the goods. Letters of credit provide this guarantee. An international bank acting on behalf of the buyer guarantees payment for the goods upon receipt of conforming goods and required documentation. Because the seller will not likely have a relationship with the foreign bank, the seller will involve its own bank as an intermediary. That bank can be involved in two ways: as an advising bank or as a confirming bank. An advising bank merely notifies the seller upon receipt of the letter of credit but does not become liable on the letter of credit, as does a confirming bank. For a confirmed letter of credit, the seller is charged a higher fee because of the risk the bank is undertaking. If the confirmed letter of credit is not paid, the seller may proceed against its own domestic bank rather than having to sue the foreign bank, which issued the letter of credit.

A bank adheres to the strict compliance rule when making payment on a letter of credit. The documents are matched against the terms of the letter of credit. If the documents are incomplete, payment will not be made. Before a bank will issue a letter of credit, it will require cash or some other form of collateral.

EXAMPLE | Scapezzi, from the previous example, requests that Big Foot supply it with a $50,000 letter of credit issued by a recognized international bank. Big Foot uses its current inventory as collateral for the Bank of New York, which issues the letter of credit in Scapezzi's favor to the Bank of Milan. Upon receipt of conforming goods and the appropriate documents, the Bank of New York will pay the $50,000 to the Bank of Milan, which will then credit Scapezzi's account sixty days henceforth in accordance with the terms of the contract.

A standby letter of credit is a special instrument used to guarantee performance. Unlike letters of credit, which require payment to be made, standby letters of credit are a form of insurance, with payment made only upon default. If all goes well the standby letter of credit will remain dormant.

EXAMPLE | Trade Winds Shipbuilding, a Brazilian company, is manufacturing three oil tankers for Royal Dutch Petroleum Shell, a Dutch company. Shell requires that Trade Winds issue a standby letter of credit to guarantee that the three oil tankers will be completed by July 1, 1997 and that they will be free of defects. If the tankers are delivered free of defects on or before July 1, 1997, the standby letter of credit will go unpaid. However, if a breach occurs, payment to rectify the damages will be made.

FORCE MAJEURE

Force majeure is a term used to describe an act of God (e.g., earthquake, volcano, or hurricane) or an act of Man (e.g., war, pollution, or embargos). It is wise to incorporate a force majeure clause in an international sales contract and to describe the circumstances under which the parties will be relieved from performing. These events are beyond the control of the parties.

EXAMPLE | Melbourne Wool Company, an Australian firm, is shipping wool to the Indonesian Textile Corporation. in Bali. The contract contains a *force majeure* clause, which states that the parties are relieved from performing if the goods are destroyed because of volcanos, fire, earthquake, or other acts of God or strike, war, or other acts of man. En route a tidal wave flips the ship, causing it to sink. Is the seller excused from performing? Yes! A tidal wave is a natural disaster. That is why it is best not only to list several types of *force majeure* but to include an encompassing clause as well.

SELLING GOODS OVERSEAS

Agents

Selecting the most advantageous method for selling goods overseas requires deliberation. A variety of strategies may be employed. Commercial agents may be hired to find buyers for the seller's services or goods. General principles of agency law serve as a guide, but local laws do vary. There should be a stipulation as to whether the agent will be able to contract on the seller's behalf or whether the agent will serve as an intermediary, passing information along. If the agent handles the negotiation, the transaction is more efficient, but the seller will be bound by the contract even though the terms may not be favorable.

EXAMPLE | Penguins Plus, Inc. is a manufacturer of marine animal paraphernalia in Iceland. It wishes to distribute its products throughout Canada. It hires Jacques Lefleur as its agent, giving him total authority to negotiate contracts. Jacques is given a price list by Penguins Plus and is told to remain within ten percent of the listed prices. In his exuberance Jacques authorizes delivery of 50,000 items by December 1, in time for the Christmas season at a 20 percent discount. This is beyond the capacity of Penguins Plus and is not in line with its philosophy of low volume and greater profit margins. Jacques has bound Penguins Plus to a contract of high volume and low markup.

Distributors

Unlike agents, distributors purchase goods from sellers and are responsible for resale. They bear the risk of loss if the goods are not sold. The distributors compensation is much larger than the agent's, and therefore the seller's profit margins are correspondingly lower. The distributor is responsible for maintaining inventory and promoting the product. If the seller wishes to terminate the arrangement, it must compensate the distributor for its investment in promoting the product. Servicing of products during the warranty period may also be handled by the distributor. This is subject to negotiation.

EXAMPLE | Flush Me, I'm Full, Inc. is a high-volume manufacturer of toilets and other waste disposal products. Its skills lie in design, and because of domestic demand it has not developed a sound marketing program. After attending an international trade convention and realizing the keen interest in its products, Flush Me, I'm Full decided to hire a distributor to sell its products throughout Europe. Profit margins for Europe were only half of those in the domestic market, but Flush Me, I'm Full decided this was the only way it could take advantage of overseas demand for its products.

Licensing

A license to sell, manufacture, or use a product may be given to an overseas company by the seller. Licenses involve intellectual property: trademarks, patents, and copyrights. Trademarks are unique symbols, words, or designs that represent particular products or services. A patent gives the inventor the exclusive right for a seventeen-year period to sell, make, or use the item for which the patent was granted. Copyrights are granted to authors for expressions of their ideas in writing, music, dance, and computer programs. The licensee can reproduce, manufacture, use, or sell the product or service in return for a fee. The licensee must make a substantial commitment. Upon termination of the license, the licensee must compensated for its investment. The trademark, patent, or copyright information must be returned. The licensing agreement must stipulate that there be no infringement either during the contract or upon its termination. The potential for abuse is high.

EXAMPLE | The Copycats, a Korean company, obtain a license to manufacture and sell Weetabix, an English cereal, in Korea for a 10 percent royalty payment. Subsequently the Copycats, through a subsidiary, replicate the cereal and sell it under the name Wheat-a-Treat, saving themselves the royalty payment. Wheatabix would have to discover the fraud, which might be difficult because the cereal is being sold by a subsidiary. Then the license would be revoked, and Weetabix would sue for loss of profits.

Franchising

Franchising is a form of licensing wherein the seller permits the franchisee to replicate the seller's establishment (e.g., Mc Donald's, Baskin-Robbins, Midas Muffler) and operate it in accordance with a set of established rules. The appearance, products, and services of all outlets of a particular franchise may be similar, regardless of the countries in which they are located. Employment of local workers, advertising, and adherence to the host country's customs help ingratiate a franchise with the local market. Chapter 40, "Corporate management," gives more information on franchises.

EXAMPLE | When Kentucky Fried Chicken (KFC) franchised its restaurants in Japan, it translated its service manuals into Japanese, sent American managers to train local workers in the KFC tradition, and adjusted menus to meet the customs and desires of the Japanese people.

Direct Investment

Direct investment is serious long-term commitment to a particular country. A direct investor may acquire a local company, create a branch or subsidiary, or enter into a joint venture. Acquisition is probably the preferred method because the company is already established within the country. The problem is that many countries restrict acquisitions, requiring some percentage of local ownership. In such cases joint venture, a form of partnership, is an alternative. Often the form of direct investment depends on the industry involved. Air transportation, broadcasting, and industries with national security impact may be totally restricted.

EXAMPLE | It Suits Us, a Singapore manufacturer of men's and women's suits, attempts to acquire a garment manufacturer in Sri Lanka. The country requires It Suits Us to allow the local firm to retain 40 percent ownership in the joint venture. This is an example of an acquisition turned joint venture.

If a company wishes to establish a presence overseas, it may do so through a branch or a subsidiary. A branch is an extension of the company. The company is in control, but the trade-off is that the company is subject to the jurisdiction of foreign courts. A subsidiary is a separate corporation, which may be wholly owned by the parent corporation. In most countries the liability of the parent corporation is limited to the value of the subsidiary.

EXAMPLE | Nuclear Technologies Corporation and Radioactive Waste, Inc. want to expand operations into India. Nuclear Technologies establishes a branch in Calcutta. Radioactive Waste sets up a subsidiary called Chemical Waste in Bombay. Major accidents occur at both plants. Nuclear Technologies is subject to a lawsuit because the company is operating in Calcutta through its branch office.

Chemical Waste, not Radioactive Waste, is subject to the lawsuit. Chemical Waste is a separate corporation; its shareholder, Radioactive Waste, is liable only for the amount of its investment in Chemical Waste.

REVIEW QUESTIONS

1. What is GATT?
2. What effect will NAFTA have on labor and the environment?
3. What is the difference between the doctrine of sovereign immunity and the Act of State Doctrine?
4. Was the court's decision in the Foxworth case ethical?
5. Explain the difference between choice of law and choice of forum.
6. What is CISG?
7. Discuss the importance of letters of credit.
8. What is *force majeure*?
9. Explain the different methods for selling goods overseas.
10. Shute was injured on a Carnival Cruise and brought suit in his home state. Carnival argued that a choice of forum provision required that the lawsuit be brought in Florida. What result? *Carnival Cruise Lines, Inc.* v. *Shute,* Ill. S. Ct. 1522 (1991).

8

Employment Law

Employment Discrimination
Affirmative Action
Sex Discrimination
Sexual Harassment
Age Discrimination

Discriminating against People with
 Disabilities
Labor Law
Review Questions

EMPLOYMENT DISCRIMINATION

Title VII of the Civil Rights Act of 1964 is the main authority governing employment discrimination. It is a federal law, which means that it is binding on all employers throughout the United States. An employer is a person or business employing at least fifteen individuals for twenty weeks of the year. The employer's business must have some connection with interstate commerce for Title VII to be applicable.

   The main thrust of Title VII is that it is an unlawful practice to discriminate in hiring, promotion, compensation or any other aspect of the employment relationship because of an individual's religion, race, sex, ethnic heritage, or participation in an investigation relating to any of the above.

   Violations of Title VII are brought before the Equal Employment Opportunity Commission (EEOC). Within ten days of receipt of a complaint, the EEOC notifies the employer and conducts an investigation, which entails questioning employees, obtaining physical evidence, or both. A determination must be made within four months. None of these proceedings are made public.

   If there is reasonable cause to believe the charge is true, the EEOC will attempt to persuade the offending employer to change its practices. The offender has thirty days to comply. If the employer refuses, the EEOC can initiate a civil lawsuit in federal district court. At the court's discretion, an attorney may be appointed for the complainant, with all fees waived. A determination by the court of intentional discrimination can result in reinstatement and back pay. These are compensatory damages, which are intended to return the party to status quo, the position he or she would have been in had the unlawful practice not been committed.

EXAMPLE | Marshall Jackson, who is black, has been a sales representative for Tucker Machinery Corporation for twenty years. His district is predominantly black. He has applied for promotion to sales manager. Although his credentials are superior to those of the other candidates, he is overlooked because management feels he will not command the respect of the sales force, which is overwhelmingly white. Is this employment discrimination? Yes! Tucker Machinery has violated Title VII because the sole reason Jackson was not selected was that he was black. Jackson will be entitled to the promotion together with the pay differential from the date when he should have been selected.

Under the Civil Rights Act of 1991, Congress expanded the means to deter employment discrimination by including punitive damages, which may be awarded to punish an offending employer who has acted with reckless disregard or malice. When awarded, punitive damages are usually quite high.

In addition to contesting whether discrimination actually occurred, an employer may argue that discrimination was a business necessity or was related to a bona fide occupational qualification. The 1991 Civil Rights Act also expanded the right of an employee to challenge a seniority system that was instituted to discriminate purposely.

Congress has found that there still exist barriers to the advancement of women and minorities in the workplace. These groups remain underrepresented in management and decision-making positions. In 1991, Congress established the Glass Ceiling Commission to address this problem. The commission must consider how prepared women and minorities are for advancement, the opportunities available, the policies businesses follow in making promotions, comparisons with businesses that have actively promoted women and minorities, and reasons for their success.

Keeping of records on employees gender, race, and ethnic heritage is required for the purpose of monitoring affirmative action programs and showing whether employers' selection procedures have an adverse impact on particular groups. (The officially recognized racial and ethnic groups are: Blacks, American Indians, Asians, Hispanics, and Whites.) The Equal Employment Opportunity Standard Form 100 is used for such monitoring. The employer must ensure that the information is not used improperly.

The "80 Percent Rule"

The employment selection rate on minorities must be within eighty percent of the selection rate for non-minorities; otherwise the selection procedure utilized is discriminatory.

EXAMPLE | In 1993, 1,000 people applied for a position with Zit, Inc., and 230 people were selected.

Group	Applied	Selected	Selection rate
Minorities	200	30	15%
Nonminorities	800	200	25%

Minorities selection rate 15% / Nonminorities selection rate 25% = 60%

This selection falls short of the 80 percent rule. Therefore, Zit's selection procedure has an adverse impact on minorities. Zit, Inc. must enact a plan to remedy this deficiency.

AFFIRMATIVE ACTION

Affirmative action attempts to achieve equal employment opportunity by actively selecting minorities and women where they have been underrepresented in the work force. Although affirmative action programs are considered temporary, many remain in force for a long time until equilibrium is achieved. To determine whether an affirmative action program is needed, one must consider a number of factors: the minority population of the area, in absolute numbers and as a percentage of the total population; the number of minority individuals employed and unemployed, together with their respective percentages; the skills of the minority labor pool; the amount of training the employer can reasonably offer; and the availability in the organization of other minorities or women who can be promoted or transferred. The same criteria determine the need for an affirmative action program for women. After affirmative action procedures are in place, the goals must be achieved on reasonable timetables; and the rate of success must be measured.

SEX DISCRIMINATION

In the past gender was considered a bona fide occupational qualification. Stereotypes ruled. Men were physicians, lawyers, construction workers, and policemen; women were nurses, flight attendants, secretaries, and teachers. This situation had the effect of discriminating against both men and women in certain job classifications. The effect on women, particularly with regard to better-paying positions, was noticeable. Section 703 of Title VII makes it unlawful to discriminate in employment because of gender. Because of this, prescribing limits for lifting or carrying weight or for working before or after childbirth are prohibited. Any provisions or benefits must be provided to both sexes.

EXAMPLE | Mitchell Freeman is a vice-president at Bulls and Bears, Inc., an investment banking firm. There is an opening for an assistant vice-president to work directly underneath Freeman. There are two in-house candidates: Tom Folino, a competent securities trader with five years of experience, and Mary Michaels, a senior bond trader with seven years of experience. Freeman selects Tom because they have common interests—they go to hockey games after work and have a few beers together. Mitchell and Tom are both single, whereas Mary is married with children. Freeman and she have nothing in common outside of work.

Does this qualify as sexual discrimination? Yes! Freeman's decision is not based on job performance but rather on personal interests that he shares with one candidate.

Equal Pay

The Equal Pay Act of 1963 is an amendment to the Fair Labor Standards Act, which regulates child labor, minimum wage, and overtime pay. The Equal Pay Act prohibits the payment of different wages to men and women performing the same job. This act covers all types of job categories, from clerical to executive. To be subject to the terms of the act, the jobs must be eqauivalent with regard to required skill, knowledge, or experience, and the conditions under which the work is performed must be similar. For example, a person working overseas is entitled to be paid more than one performing the same job domestically.

EXAMPLE | Keith Peterson and Jennifer Rivers were both hired after graduation for entry-level positions with an accounting firm. Their scholastic achievements were comparable. Keith was offered $32,000, and Jennifer was offered $30,000. Does this constitute sex discrimination? Yes! This is in violation of the Equal Pay Act because the jobs are exactly the same.

Comparable Worth

Comparable worth was an attempt to assign values to male-dominated and female-dominated occupations on the basis of worth. Where the values equated, equal pay would be required. The underlying theory is that most female-dominated jobs pay less than most male-dominated jobs. This argument has not found favor with the courts because assigning values is arbitrary and interferes with compensations based on supply and demand.

EXAMPLE | Gary Josephson is a construction worker. Jessica Tremont is a stenographer. He earns $36,000. She earns $22,000. Jessica argues that both jobs have comparable worth and that she should earn the same as Gary. Is she correct? No! Although her argument is based on comparable worth, the courts have decided not to enforce this doctrine.

SEXUAL HARASSMENT

There are two distinct situations of sexual harassment for which the company may be liable: quid pro quo and hostile work environment.

Quid pro quo means this for that. It involves situations where a superior is eliciting sexual favors from a subordinate in return for some form of work-related benefit.

EXAMPLE | Clarence Worthington, a hospital administrator, approaches one of the nurses' aides and informs her that he can arrange a schedule change from nights, weekends, and holidays to day work if she is willing to sleep with him. Is this quid pro quo? Yes! The hospital is liable for the sexual harassment of its employee because a benefit was denied to her unless she agreed to have sex.

In some instances, people use sex to gain advancement. "Sleeping one's way to the top" is the old expression.

EXAMPLE | Christine Wiley was an administrative assistant at Bay Ridge Publishing when she met Joe Flanagan, the president, at a company picnic. Joe immediately became infatuated with Christine, and they began an affair. During the next two years, she was promoted seven times and finally became vice-president of corporate affairs. Her skills were not particularly impressive. Every other vice-president had been in a managerial position at least fourteen years before attaining the position of vice-president. Is this sexual harassment? Yes! In the opposite sense, though. The employees who were passed over for promotion were sexually harassed because of the favoritism shown to Christine.

In some cases sexual harassment can be used as a threat against management: "Promote me or else I will file a claim against you."

EXAMPLE | It is obvious to everyone at Parker Management Company that Charlie Harris is very fond of Marie Copley, a marketing research assistant. He complements her every day and often brings her flowers. Marie is tired of doing research. She would prefer to earn commissions and work with people. This would be tantamount to a transfer and promotion. Marie approaches Charlie, who is vice-president of marketing, and asks him to grant her request. Charlie informs Marie that although he is fond of her, he cannot grant the request because she is not qualified. Marie tells Charlie that unless he grants her wish, she will file a complaint against him, alleging that he demanded sex for the promotion. What should Charlie do? This is blackmail. Charlie is in a delicate situation because his conduct, although not constituting sexual harassment, has laid the foundation for a false claim to be leveled against him. Charlie should seek the advice of upper management as well as legal counsel. From an ethical standpoint Marie's request should not be granted because it is false. Practically, Charlie or the company may grant it to avoid future public embarrassment and litigation. If Charlie adopts an ethical viewpoint and refuses Marie's request and the company is sued, Charlie must be prepared at best to be severely reprimanded or at worst to lose his job as a consequence of damage done to the company.

Hostile work environment encompasses touching, verbal communication, and distribution of material of a sexual nature that an individual has not consented to and finds offensive. The aggrieved individual may initiate a lawsuit against the offending party personally or may proceed against the company. Unpermitted touching gives rise to the torts of civil assault and battery. Sexual comments made with a particular individual in mind would constitute slander. Such comments written or drawn would be libel. If generic comments were made that degraded the gender, an individual could claim the tort of infliction of emotional distress.

EXAMPLE | George Miles works as an insurance underwriter. In the office he has openly stated his view that women are good only for sex and do not belong in the workplace because they are always complaining about PMS. Susan cringes when she hears these remarks and tries to hide from George's view lest she become a target. George continues to fondle Amanda's backside when she has repeatedly admonished him. He has photostated a caricature of Debbie, a co-worker, as a naked woman with large breasts. George speaks about the pornographic films that he has viewed and describes them in detail. He also has commented that he is due for a promotion after having sex with Margaret, the vice-president for operations. What recourse do these women have against George? Amanda may sue George for the tort of battery because it is unpermitted touching that she has found offensive and embarrassing. Margaret may sue for slander because George's remarks are untrue and damaging to her reputation. Debbie may sue for libel because the sexually offensive drawing has been distributed. Susan may sue for infliction of emotional distress because Georges comments, although not directed at her personally, are degradating to who she is—a woman.

Most instances of sexual harassment have involved men harassing women, but there are occasions where men have been harassed by women or other men and where women have been harassed by other women. That harassment equally unacceptable.

EXAMPLE | Phil Thomas is a construction worker who lives with his mother. After work every day he rushes home to tend to her needs. When he won't join them for a few beers, his co-workers taunt him continually, claiming that he's a Mama's boy, a wimp, tied to his mother's apron strings. This happens regularly throughout the day. The co-workers leave notes, photostat caricatures, and openly make remarks. Is this sexual harassment? Yes! Phil's co-workers are inflicting emotional distress upon him.

EXAMPLE | Steve Hart is a happily married man with three children. His superior, Linda Evert, finds him very attractive. She invites him to dinner, to a show, or to her apartment. Steve politely declines each time. Linda stresses to Steve that if he wants to get promoted he must have an intimate relationship with her. Is this sexual harassment? Yes! It is an unwelcome sexual advance.

Most victims of harassment seek recovery from their company. The rule of thumb is, Sue the deepest pocket.

AGE DISCRIMINATION

The Age Discrimination in Employment Act (ADEA) was enacted to discontinue mandatory retirement and to shift the requirement for employment from age to ability. There is an exception. Companies can force executives in high policy-making positions to retire.

EXAMPLE | Lawrence Wright is the chief financial officer for Code Blue Medical Supplies, Inc. Miriam Hodges is a quality control analyst. Both will be seventy in March. Code Blue has a policy of compulsory retirement at age seventy. Will Lawrence and Miriam both have to retire? Under ADEA, Miriam can continue to work as long as she is able to do the job. Lawrence will be forced to retire as CEO because he is a high policy-making executive. This does not prevent him from doing consulting work for the company, however.

DISCRIMINATING AGAINST PEOPLE WITH DISABILITIES

The Americans with Disabilities Act (ADA) requires employers with fifteen or more employees to refrain from discriminating against any individual who has an impairment that limits major life activities. This includes impairments to sight, speech, hearing, walking, learning, and so on. It also applies to people with cancer, heart disease, AIDS, and disfigurement. The ADA requires employers to make reasonable accommodations to enable people with disabilities to work. This includes making the work site accessible, modifying equipment, and changing work schedules. The disabled person must be qualified to do the job—that is, able to perform the essential function with reasonable accommodation. The ADA was not designed to force employers to hire disabled workers who were not qualified. The qualifications required, however, must be essential to the job. If another applicant is more qualified than a disabled applicant, the employer is not required to give the disabled individual preferential treatment.

EXAMPLE | Lisa Conroy applied for a paralegal position with the law firm of Moran, Holochwost, and Mullins. Lisa is a paraplegic who uses a wheelchair. The firm is located on the second floor of an office building with no elevator. The firm employs eighteen individuals. What must the law firm do? The firm must refuse to hire Lisa. Existing businesses are not required to install elevators. If the law firm occupied the first floor as well, it would be required to make a reasonable accommodation for Lisa on the first floor. If the firm were going to construct its own office building, an elevator would be required if the building had three stories or more.

    If the law firm were located on the first floor but there were two steps inside and the bathroom entrance were not wide enough for a wheelchair, what would the firm have to do? It would have to install a ramp and widen the bathroom entrance. These modifications are reasonable. To not make them would be to refuse to hire Lisa solely because of her disability.

EXAMPLE | Patricia Krakowski was fifty-two years old. She applied for a position as a high school history teacher with the Monroe Township Academy. Although her credentials were superior, she was passed over for a younger applicant. Patricia had had a cancerous kidney removed. The academy feared that she might be a candidate for dialysis. This situation could cause its health insurance costs to increase. Because the academy was operating within a tight budget, Patricia posed a potential risk that it did not want to take.

    Has Patricia been discriminated against? Yes! If not for her disability, Patricia would have been hired. The academy must give Patricia the position or reimburse her until she finds another suitable one.

Eyerman v. Mary Kay Cosmetics, Inc.
967 F. 2d 213 (6th Cir. 1992)

Dobi Eyerman, an independent contractor, was terminated from her position as a National Sales Director for Mary Kay Cosmetics because of alcoholism. She had a drunk driving conviction and an accident attributed to alcohol. She behaved poorly at a meeting because of her inebriated condition. Eyerman was informed that she could file for disability.

The law provides,

It shall be an unlawful discriminatory practice: For any employer, because of the race, color, religion, sex, national origin, handicap, age, or ancestry of any person, to discharge without just cause, to refuse to hire, or otherwise to discriminate against that person with respect to hire, tenure, terms, conditions, or privileges of employment, or any matter directly or indirectly related to employment. . . . Alcoholism is one of the handicaps protected by this provision.

The issue is whether the relationship between an employer and an independent contractor is covered by this statute.

The court ruled, "We decided that independent contractors would be covered by Title VII if, under an 'economic realities' test, they are susceptible to the types of discrimination Title VII meant to prohibit." Economic realities are determined by "the employer's ability to control the job performance and employment opportunities" of the independent contractor. The court continued, "[T]here is no indication in the record that Mary Kay Cosmetics controlled Eyerman's work in any significant way." Judgment for Mary Kay Cosmetics.

LABOR LAW

Norris-LaGuardia Act

The first major federal employment law was the 1932 Norris-LaGuardia Act. This act gave employees the right to freely associate, organize, and designate representatives for the purpose of collective bargaining without interference from the employer. However, the weakness of this act was that collective bargaining was not mandated. The employer could refuse to deal with the union.

The Norris-LaGuardia Act also stipulated that an employment contract could not contain a provision that the employee promised not to join a union; otherwise, the contract would be unenforceable. The act gave employees the freedom to engage in lawful strikes. A lawful strike may be undertaken if the workers are employed for an indefinite period or if their term of employment has ended. An employer can prevent a strike through the use of an injunction only where the employment contract is for a definite term or where the President of the United States has interceded because the strike would jeopardize national health or safety.

Wagner Act

The Wagner Act of 1935 (National Labor Relations Act) imposed a duty on employers to recognize collective bargaining. This meant that employers would be forced to sit down at the bargaining table with union leaders. The Wagner Act also created the National Labor Relations Board for the purpose of administering the act and investigating unfair labor practices engaged in by management.

The Wagner Act has been amended twice. The Taft-Hartley Act of 1947 (Labor Management Relations Act) restricted unions from engaging in unfair labor tactics against management.

The Landrum-Griffin Act of 1959 created a bill of rights for union members, many of whom were being treated improperly by the very unions created to protect them.

Occupational Safety and Health Act

The Occupational Safety and Health Act (OSHA) was enacted in 1970 to reduce safety and health hazards in the workplace, thereby preventing injury, loss of wages, lost production, and incurrence of medical and disability expenses. Employees must be provided with a safe environment free of toxic substances and damaging particulates. Provisions must be made for first aid, eye and face protection, and safety at excavation sites to prevent cave-ins. Employees must be accorded work environments with adequate lighting, heat, and ventilation, and tools and equipment that are in proper working order. The Department of Labor has the right to inspect the work environment to ensure adherence to the OSHA requirements. The Occupational Safety and Health Review Commission is the initial review body for violations of the act.

Workers' Compensation

The purpose of workers' compensation is to provide monetary relief to an injured employee in an expeditious manner even if he or she should be at fault. With total liability shifted to the employer, it was thought that employers would make working conditions as safe as possible to minimize the number of injuries requiring payouts.

Discharging of Employees

Discharging of employees must be done in good faith. It is well recognized that companies cannot guarantee employment for life. When a company wishes to lay off employees, it must do so without discriminating against any of them because of race, religion, gender, national origin, age, or disability.

A company may discharge an individual if his or her work is unsatisfactory, but the decision must be made in good faith.

Zep Manufacturing Co. v. Harthcock
824 S.W. 2d 654

Zep Mfg Company hired Harthcock as a chemist. The terms of the contract provided no definite term of employment:

> If the President of Zep, in his sole discretion, determines that Employee's performance of duties hereunder is unsatisfactory, Employee's employment hereunder may be terminated by written notice from the President of Zep or his designee, and Employee shall receive Employee's salary for the two(2) months (including the month in which notice is given as one full month) following the giving of such notice.

The issue is whether this contract can be terminated at will by the employer or only for cause.

The court held,

> [A] contract by which one agrees to employ another as long as the services are satisfactory, or which is otherwise expressed to be conditional on the satisfactory character of the services rendered, gives the employer the right to terminate the contract and to discharge the employee whenever the employer, acting in good faith, is actually and honestly dissatisfied with the work. There must be a bona fide dissatisfaction that must be founded on acts such as would induce action on the part of a reasonable person. The employer may not act arbitrarily or without reason in the matter. If the employer feigns dissatisfaction and dismisses the employee, the discharge is wrongful.

The court continued,

> Although an employment-at-will contract allows severance of the employment relationship at any time without cause, when an employment agreement is a satisfaction contract, there must be a bona fide dissatisfaction or cause for discharge. The employment agreement here contains terms that limit Zep's right to terminate Harthcock's employment. Although the determination of the quality of Harthcock's performance is within the Zep president's "sole discretion." Texas law implies that the determination to terminate Harthcock will be made in good faith. The limitation on Zep's right to terminate Harthcock if he satisfactorily performed his duties changed the normal employment-at-will relationship.

Judgment for Zep.

Whistle Blowing

Whistle-blowing occurs when an employee decides to go public with an allegation of wrongdoing on the employer's part. The employer often argues that the employee's only duty is to perform the task assigned and not to be concerned with consequences. The affected employee views this conflict as a choice between company and society. Choosing to protect the company means job security and being seen as a company person, someone on whom the company can depend. Opting for society means possibly sacrificing one's employment for the greater good of all people or a class thereof.

REVIEW QUESTIONS

1. What is affirmative action?
2. What is the significance of the Civil Rights Act of 1964?
3. What is the difference between quid pro quo and hostile environment with regard to sexual harassment?
4. Explain comparable worth and give examples to illustrate the concept.
5. What is the mandatory retirement age now?
6. What is the 80 percent rule?
7. Who qualifies under the ADA?
8. The NFL agreed to pay developmental squad players a fixed salary of $1,000 a week. The NFL Players Association (NFLPA) objected and insisted that these players be allowed to negotiate their salaries. The NFLPA is a labor organization and has exclusive bargaining rights for all NFL players. This extends to developmental squad players. The 1982 Collective Bargaining Agreement gave NFL players the right to negotiate the salary terms of their contracts. Is this in violation of the antitrust laws? *Brown* v. *Pro Football, Inc.* 782 F. Supp. 125 (D.D.C.1991).
9. William Clark had performed legal services for Nellie Ellis for many years. His firm prepared a petition for Mrs. Ellis when she was diagnosed with Alzheimer's. A temporary guardian was appointed for Mrs. Ellis. Mr. Clark refused to release Mrs. Ellis's records and filed a counterpetition claiming that Mrs. Ellis had retained him to fight the conservatorship. Was there a conflict of interest? *In re Ellis,* 822 S.W. 2d 602 (Tenn. App. 1991).
10. John Mack was an FBI agent in New York. Because he was associated with another FBI agent who dealt in drugs, Mack was suspected of drug use and asked to submit to a urinalysis. When the urinalysis revealed the presence of cocaine, the FBI fired him. Mack contended that by forcing him to give a urine sample, the FBI violated his common-law right to privacy, his Fourth Amendment right against unreasonable search and seizure, and his Fifth Amendment right against self-incrimination. What result? *Mack* v. *U.S., F.B.I.,* 653 F. Supp. 70 (S.D.N.Y. 1986).

Special Topic: Business Ethics

AIDS DISCRIMINATION

Employers' concerns are many with regard to AIDS, (Acquired Immune Deficiency Syndrome). Whenever an employee is asked whether he or she has the disease or whenever that information is related to other employees, an invasion of privacy may occur. If an assertion that an employee is suffering from the AIDS virus turns out to be unfounded, defamation may occur. If an employee is refused employment because he or she has the AIDS virus, employment discrimination may be charged. When a current employee who is capable of working is discharged because he or she has the AIDS virus, a violation of the Federal Rehabilitation Act or state law protecting the people with handicaps may result. Under the circumstances, how can an employer maintain harmony in the workplace? Employers must develop policies governing the treatment of current employees with AIDS— regarding fringe benefits policies including sick leave, dental and medical benefits, alternative work locations, and reassurance of support by the company. Job applicants who have AIDS must receive equal treatment. As long as a person with AIDS is capable of performing the work, he or she should be treated no differently than any other employee. Employers are encouraged to develop educational programs to ease fears of co-workers who worry about catching the virus. The key is successful planning. Companies that have no known current cases of AIDS should plan now because, according to the Center for Disease Control's projections, the number of AIDS cases is increasing dramatically each year.

Shuttleworth v. Broward City Office
No. 85-0624
Florida Commission on Human Relations (1985)

Mr. Shuttleworth, a public employee of Broward County, was discharged when it was discovered that he had contracted AIDS. Shuttleworth had been in the employ of the county for sixteen months when he was dismissed. His work performance had been satisfactory during this time. The county's defense centered around its unwillingness to assume the risk of a co-worker contracting AIDS from Shuttleworth in the workplace.

In determining whether the term *handicap* applies to people with AIDS, the Florida Commission on Human Relations determined that the term should be defined by common usage. "A person with a handicap does not enjoy, in some manner, the full and normal use of his sensory, mental or physical faculties." The Florida Commission on Human Relations decided, "Based upon the plain meaning of the term handicap and the medical evidence presented, an individual with acquired immune deficiency syndrome is within the coverage of the Human Rights Act of 1977 in that such individual does not enjoy . . . normal use of his sensory, mental or physical faculties."

The Florida Commission on Human Relations concluded that there was no reasonable basis to support Broward County's conclusion that Shuttleworth posed a substantial risk of future injury to his co-workers by continuing in the county's employ.

Subsequently Shuttleworth brought a discrimination claim in the Southern District Court of Florida, which was settled in December 1986. The terms of the settlement were payment of $196,000 to Shuttleworth and reinstatement as an employee of Broward County. This was the first case in which AIDS was determined to be a handicap under a state antidiscrimination statute. Judgment for Shuttleworth.

Cronan v. New England Telephone
No. 80332
Mass Sup. Ct. (Suffolk Cty 1986)

Paul Cronan was a repair technician for the New England Telephone Company. He had been in the company's employ since 1973. In May 1985 Cronan requested permission on two separate occasions to leave work for an hour and a half for a medical appointment. His supervisor, O'Brien, granted both requests. However, on the third occasion O'Brien demanded to know the details of Cronan's medical problems, assuring confidentiality, even though he had received a note from a physician stating that Cronan was under medical care. Cronan acquiesced to O'Brien's demands and revealed that he had ARC (AIDS related complex). Cronan explained to O'Brien the difference between AIDS and ARC, ARC being the less serious of the two.

O'Brien informed his superiors, who then placed Cronan on disability. According to Cronan the company officials assembled Cronan's co-workers in two group meetings, informing them of Cronan's condition. Cronan received intimidating phone calls from his co-workers, some of whom threatened to lynch him if he returned to work. In August 1985 Cronan attempted to contact his supervisor to inform him of his desire to return to work, but his calls were never answered. In September 1985 Cronan was hospitalized and, after undergoing extensive blood tests, was diagnosed as having AIDS. Subsequently Cronan filed a lawsuit in the Massachusetts Superior Court of Suffolk County, claiming breach of privacy, employment discrimination, and violation of civil rights.

Subsequently this case was settled out of court, with Cronan being allowed to return to work in October 1986. When they learned of Cronan's reinstatement, his co-workers requested that they receive their assignments outside to avoid close contact with Cronan in a confined setting. New England refused, and 75 percent of the workers walked off the job. The company quickly assembled three physicians, who convinced the workers that the AIDS virus could not be transmitted through casual contact with Cronan. Even after this, not all were convinced: Someone left on a bulletin board a note reading, "Gays and bisexuals should be shipped to an island and destroyed." Cronan responded, "It's bad enough I have a disease that'll probably kill me. Now I have to deal with insults." The reaction to Cronan's return and the subsequent education and return of his co-workers is proof that fear of AIDS is caused by false rumor and ignorance of the facts and that proper and timely education given before mass hysteria develops will help to maintain harmony in the workplace. Judgment for Cronan.

Dept. of Fair Employment and Housing v. Raytheon Co.
No. Frep 83-84 L 1-031p L-336 76 87-04
(Fair Employment and Housing Comm. of Cal. 1987)

John Chadbourne was hired by the Raytheon Company in 1980. Chadbourne worked as a quality control analyst in an office shared with five co-workers. His work required him to come into casual contact with many other employees throughout the plant.

In December 1983 Chadbourne was diagnosed as having AIDS by Doctor Hosea and subsequently released into his care. Patricia Heyble, the nurse in charge of medical services for the division of Raytheon for which Chadbourne worked, requested medical documentation concerning Chadbourne's condition. She received a letter from Dr. Hosea's associate stating that Chadbourne had AIDS. Ms. Heyble contacted Dr. Juels, a medical consultant for the Communicable Disease Control Center in Santa Barbara County. Dr. Juels toured the Raytheon plant and viewed Chadbourne's work environment. He concluded that Chadbourne's coworkers would not be at risk of contracting AIDS from him through contact in the workplace. Dr. Juels offered the training services of the Santa Barbara Department of Public Health to educate Raytheon's employees about AIDS.

After receiving a letter from Dr. Hosea in mid-January stating that Chadbourne was physically able to return to work, Raytheon postponed Chadbourne's reinstatement to gather more information. Ms. Heyble contacted Dr. Kenneth Kastro of the Center for Disease Control in Atlanta, who advised her of the center's position with regard to AIDS. AIDS is communicable only through the exchange of blood and body fluids not through casual contact in the workplace.

Even with the affirmation of Raytheon's Medical Director, Dr. Stephen Alphas, regarding permission for Chadbourne to return to work, Raytheon decided to stall his comeback attempt, postponing reinstatement in 1984 from February 6 to February 26, March 3, June 15, and then indefinitely. By August 1984 the effects of AIDS had overtaken Chadbourne, preventing him from working again. He died five months later. His estate filed a complaint with the Department of Fair Employment and Housing, which instituted an action on the estate's behalf with the Fair Employment and Housing Commission of the State of California for back pay, compensatory damages for pain and suffering, and punitive damages for malicious and deliberate harm.

Raytheon's first argument was that Section 503 of the Rehabilitation Act of 1973 preempted the physical handicap provisions of the Fair Employment and Housing Act. The Fair Employment and Housing Commission rejected this argument, stating that the former lacked either express or implicit congressional intent to preempt.

Raytheon's second argument was that AIDS did not constitute a physical handicap as defined in the Fair Employment and Housing Act. The commission disagreed, stating that the California Supreme Court mandated a broad interpretation of the term *physical handicap* when it defined the term as any physical condition that has a disabling effect, making it difficult to achieve. The California Supreme Court expanded the definition further by including physical conditions that will be disabling in the future but cause no present signs of disability. On the basis of this reasoning, the California Fair Employment and Housing

Commission decided,

> Under this standard there can be no doubt that AIDS does constitute a physical handicap. It is plainly a physical condition of the body. And while AIDS did not impair Chadbourne's physical ability to do his job until long after he was first excluded from it by respondent, there was not simply a possibility but a tragic certainty that the condition would at some time in the future seriously impair his physical ability and ultimately kill him. AIDS thus falls squarely within the physical handicap coverage of the Act.

In assessing Raytheon's liability the commission resolved,

> There is no dispute that respondent discriminated against Chadbourne because of. . . physical handicap within the meaning of the Act. . . . There is no question here that Chadbourne's AIDS was the sole reason that respondent denied him reinstatement to his job and we therefore determine that respondent discriminated against him under the Act.

Raytheon then attempted to justify the discrimination, claiming that reinstating Chadbourne would endanger the health and safety of his co-workers. The burden of proving this rested with Raytheon and could not be shifted to the Department of Fair Employment and Housing. The commission concluded, "The great weight of the evidence demonstrates that Chadbourne would not have endangered the health or safety of his co-workers any more than would an employee without AIDS." Judgment for Chadbourne.

School Board of Nassau County, Florida v. Arline
U.S. No. 85—1277 / (1987)

Gene Arline first contracted tuberculosis in 1957, when she was a teenager. After that the disease was in remission for twenty years until she suffered three relapses in 1977 and 1978. At this point she was an elementary school teacher in Nassau County, Florida, as she had been since 1966 and continued to be until 1979, when she was dismissed by the school board because of her recurring relapses of tuberculosis.

Arline argued that Section 504 of the Rehabilitation Act of 1973 prohibited discrimination against the handicapped. Arline contended that persons with contagious diseases fell within the definition of *handicapped.* The school board retorted that it would be unreasonable to believe the term *handicapped* could include persons with contagious diseases.

Section 504 of the Rehabilitation Act of 1973 states in part, "No otherwise qualified handicapped individual in the United States, as defined in section 706 (7) of this title, shall, solely by reason of his handicap, be excluded from participation in, be denied the benefits of, or be subject to discrimination under any program or activity receiving Federal financial assistance. . . ."

Congress expanded this definition in 1974 to include "Any person who (i) has a physical or mental impairment which substantially limits one or more of such person's major life activities, (ii) has a record of such an impairment, or (iii) is regarded as having such an impairment."

The issue is whether a person having a contagious disease may be considered handicapped under Section 504 of the Rehabilitation Act.

The court decided that a person suffering from a contagious disease is handicapped under Section 504 of the Rehabilitation Act of 1973. The court stated,

> The fact that some persons who have contagious diseases may pose a serious health threat to others under certain circumstances does not justify excluding from the coverage of the Act all persons with actual or perceived contagious diseases. Such exclusion would mean that those accused of being contagious would never have the opportunity to have their condition evaluated in light of medical evidence and a determination made as to whether they were otherwise qualified. Rather, they would be vulnerable to discrimination on the basis of mythology—precisely the type of injury Congress sought to prevent. We conclude that the fact that a person with a record of a physical impairment is also contagious does not suffice to remove that person from coverage under Section 504.

Judgment for Arline.

CONCLUSION

Employers should educate themselves concerning the legal and medical issues surrounding AIDS and develop company policies to deal with affected employees. Following are guidelines for a model policy.

A Model for a Company Policy on AIDS

1. Employees with AIDS will receive equal treatment with regard to the right to work, to seek promotions and raises, and to be protected from discrimination and harassment by managers and co-workers

2, An employee suspected of having AIDS will not be approached, and no statement will be made to co-workers regarding the suspected illness. This guards against an invasion of privacy suit as well as a defamation action should the suspicion prove to be false.

3. The resources staff will be well informed and trained in dealing with all aspects of the AIDS dilemma. Employees with AIDS will be encouraged to confide in the human resources staff. The staff will help those employees cope with unfriendly co-workers and protect them from harassment and discrimination through education and, if necessary, disciplinary action. The human resources staff will explore the possibility of flexible work hours or work at home via computer and modem. The future course of the AIDS virus will be discussed with affected employees, and available medical and disability will be explained. A counselor will be employed to help employees cope with the psychological trauma associated with the disease. Affected employees will be referred to community service programs that are geared to addressing their needs outside of the workplace.

4. Confidentiality will be extended to information received by the company from an employee with AIDS. This information will not be placed in the employee's personnel file but may be documented in the employee's medical file with consent. This procedure guards against invasion of privacy.

5. An educational program will be implemented and print materials provided on the causes of AIDS, living with AIDS, and working with someone who has AIDS. Seminars may be held with a physician and psychologist invited to discuss the physical and emotional consequences of AIDS and how to deal with them. The purpose of the program will be to create a comfortable atmosphere in which both employees and their co-workers can function productively.

6. The company will educate and counsel co-workers to dispel their fear of catching the AIDS virus from casual contact. An employee's refusal to work with an employee who has AIDS will not be given preferential treatment beyond that accorded a normal request for a transfer.

7. Employees who hold positions of leadership in the community will be encouraged to express their concern for AIDS awareness.

8. An employer's right to dismiss an employee with AIDS is based solely on an evaluation of the employee's work. If the quality of work has suffered because of excessive absences or a weakened physical condition, the employer may legally exclude the employee from the workplace by placing him or her on disability. Before doing so, the employer will meet with the employee and discuss the health benefits the company will provide.

REVIEW QUESTIONS

1. Should people with AIDS be considered handicapped?
2. Discuss whether each of the cases described in this section was resolved ethically?
3. Who should bear the cost of the medical bills of individuals with AIDS?

9

Contracts: An Introduction

Elements of a Contract	Significance of a Written Contract
Validity of a Contract	Types of Contracts
Contractual Rights and Duties	Proper Application of State Laws
Freedom to Contract	Uniform Commercial Code
Importance of Contracts	Review Questions
How Contracts Relate to Us	

ELEMENTS OF A CONTRACT

A *contract* is a legally enforceable agreement. For an agreement to be legally enforceable, the following elements must be present: a mutual agreement, executed in proper form, voluntarily made by two or more capable parties wherein each party promises to perform or not to perform a specific legal act for valuable consideration. Each element in this definition must be satisfied by each party for the contract to be valid. The validity of the contract is what gives it legal effect.

A useful aid in remembering the elements of a contract is **PALACE.**

> **P**urpose (lawful)
> **A**greement
> **L**egal capacity
> **A**ct (promise to perform)
> **C**onsideration
> **E**xecution in proper form

Each element will be treated in a separate chapter. A simple explanation of each term at this juncture will help you understand the correlation of the elements as you study each chapter.

Purpose (Lawful)

The purpose for which the contract was consummated and the acts undertaken to accomplish that purpose must be lawful. Lawful means that the purpose and the acts must not contravene any federal statute or any statute of the state that has subject matter jurisdiction over the contract. When both the means employed and the end result are consistent with the law, then the contract will be valid. If the agreement contemplates the performance of an illegal act or the achievement of an illegal purpose, the contract is invalid.

Agreement

An agreement is arrived at through an offer on one party's part that another party accepts voluntarily. An agreement in and of itself is not binding because it confers no legal obligation without the other five contractual elements. Often the terms *contract* and *agreement* are used interchangeably. Keep in mind that for the two terms to be synonymous, the other five elements giving rise to a legal obligation must be present.

Legal Capacity

For a contract to be valid and enforceable, the parties involved must have the legal capacity to enter into a contract. Because the parties are binding themselves to a legal obligation, each one must be competent to contract. The parties must be responsible for their actions to ensure that the performance of their promises will be completed in accordance with the terms of the contract. The fulfillment of the requirements of legal age and sanity create the presumption that a party is capable of entering into a contractual relationship.

Act (Promise to Perform)

A promise is a commitment to perform or not perform a specific act, in the present or in the future. The act must be one that is possible to perform, not something illusory. A party becomes legally obligated to perform an act when he or she makes a promise to perform. The performance of the act is the reason why each party entered into the contract.

Consideration

Consideration is something valuable given in exchange for something valuable received. The promise to perform a certain act or acts is the consideration given by each party. Generally, what is given need not be identical in value to what is received. It is sufficient that the performance of the act has some intrinsic value.

Execution in Proper Form

Certain contracts must be executed in writing in order to be valid. This requirement is known as the statute of frauds requirement; its main purpose is to prevent fraud. Whenever possible all contracts, except those of nominal value, should be reduced to writing. This practice evidences the existence of a contract, preventing ambiguity and protecting the parties involved.

VALIDITY OF A CONTRACT

A valid contract, which is created by the presence of the six elements, can be enforced in a court of law should a breach arise. If one or more of the contractual elements is lacking, then the contract is void. A void contract can be carried out by the parties, but it is not a legal contract and cannot be enforced in a court of law. A contract may also be voidable. A voidable contract is valid unless one party who has a special right to disaffirm the contract decides to do so, thus rendering the contract void. Generally, at the time a party possesses a contractual defense, the contract becomes voidable. When the party exercises his or her right to disaffirm the contract by presenting a defense, the contract becomes void. Chapter 17, "Contractual Defenses," covers this matter in detail.

Wade v. Brooks
413 S.E. 2d 33 (S.C.App.1992)

Hazel Wade and her children moved into a house with Nelson Edwards. The rent was $25 per month. Hazel made payments irregularly. She helped Nelson farm until he became disabled, at which time she took care of his personal needs. At age ninety, Nelson fathered Hazel's fourth child. After Nelson's death, Hazel requested the estate to reimburse her for the personal services she had rendered him.

The issue is whether the parties intended to form a contract or their living arrangement was for their mutual benefit.

The court held,

A contract is an obligation which arises from actual agreement of the parties manifested by words, oral or written, or by conduct. Without the actual agreement of the parties, there is no contract. . . . An implied contract, like an express contract, rests on an actual agreement of the parties to be bound to a particular undertaking. The parties must manifest their mutual assent to all essential terms of the contract in order for an enforceable obligation to exist. If one of the parties has not agreed, then a prerequisite to formation of contract is lacking.

In the absence of actual agreement by the parties, an obligation to pay for benefits may be implied by law if: (1) the plaintiff conferred a benefit on the defendant; (2) the benefit was not conferred gratuitously but with an expectation of compensation; (3) the circumstances were such that the defendant knew or ought to have known the plaintiff expected compensation; and (4) the defendant chose to accept the benefit with such knowledge. This obligation is variously described as rising in quasi-contract, quantum meruit, or restitution. In this case, there is no evidence Mr. Edwards knew Mrs. Wade expected money compensation for her services and accepted them on that basis.

Judgment for Brooks.

CONTRACTUAL RIGHTS AND DUTIES

A contract is a legal relationship comprising certain rights and duties. A duty arises to perform specifically what is promised. This duty is a legal one that, if breached, gives the aggrieved party a legal cause of action. A cause of action is a right to sue for a legal remedy. The remedy most often awarded is money damages; however, under certain circumstances, the court may grant the equitable remedies of specific performance or rescission. A more thorough discussion of remedies is provided in Chapter 16, "Remedies for Breach of Contract." In certain instances, the individual committing the breach may have had just cause for doing so. This just cause will be raised as a contractual defense that, if proven, will relieve the individual from liability for the breach of contract.

FREEDOM TO CONTRACT

The parties to a contract have the freedom to set up their own rights and duties concerning such things as payment and time and place of delivery. This freedom facilitates the smooth and efficient operation of business and individual transactions. However, this freedom to contract is not absolute. Contracts that involve price fixing or discrimination, or that are unconscionable, are invalid because they are unduly harsh or one-sided. Except for certain limitations such as the ones just mentioned, freedom to contract is protected by Article I, Section 10 of the United States Constitution and by the laws of the individual states. The states enact laws for the interpretation of contractual terms and for the enforcement of promises. These form the laws of contracts.

Freedom to contract is a well-established principle of contract law. The Constitution, in Article I, Section 10, prohibits any state from passing a law impairing the obligation of contracts. Although freedom to contract is a fundamental right in our country, it is not absolute. Contracts that unreasonably restrain trade are illegal and unenforceable.

IMPORTANCE OF CONTRACTS

The law of contracts is the foundation of business law. Our economy operates through contracts, as the following example illustrates.

EXAMPLE Many interrelated contracts enable the *Daily Planet* to publish its newspaper and enable people to buy it. Following are the contracts involving the *Daily Planet* organization, its employees, and the people who buy the newspaper.

The *Daily Planet* is published in Sun Valley, Idaho, with a daily circulation approaching 55,000. The *Daily Planet* has an individual contract, for a set salary, with each member of its editorial staff, including its editor-in-chief, Mars Hanley. The reporters also have contracts with the *Planet,* particularly Jupiter Jones, its star reporter. Jupiter's contract is negotiated by his agent, Sun Spots, Inc. Jupiter has an agency contract with Sun Spots to represent him in contractual matters. The terms are a 10 percent commission of any salary paid above the *Planet's* original offering. Haley's Comics has a contract with the Planet for the weekly inclusion of Pluto in the Sunday comic section. Venus, a syndicated columnist, is paid a royalty stipulated by contract for each beauty aid column that the *Planet* publishes. There is also a contract with Global Weather Forecasting Services allowing the *Planet* to reprint its forecast.

The advertising that appears in the paper is placed with the Asteroid Advertising Agency, which works on a commission basis. The local television commercials that are responsible for the *Daily Planet's* skyrocketing circulation are also devised by Asteroid Advertising in return for a fee. The paper on which the *Daily Planet* is printed is supplied by Universal Paper Corporation in Crater Lake, Oregon. The trees and the paper mills are located in the Petrified Forest in Arizona. This weekly delivery of pulp is crucial to the publication of the *Daily Planet.* Failure to deliver would result in a loss of profits.

The actual printing of the newspaper is handled by employees belonging to the Mercury Printer's Union. The union contracts with the *Planet* on behalf of all employees engaged in printing operations. The *Daily Planet* engages the law firm of Galaxy and Globe to represent it in contract negotiations with the union. The Solar System Underwriting Syndicate underwrites the insurance needs of the *Planet,* including fire insurance; insurance against liability, including personal injury and libel; and life and health insurance for employees.

Neptune Newsstands, Inc. provides a forum in which the newspapers are sold. Neptune contracts with the *Daily Planet* for delivery of a certain number of newspapers to each stand, on consignment, with a commission paid according to the number of papers sold. The unsold newspapers are returned.

The actual delivery of the newspapers from the *Daily Planet* to the Neptune newsstands is handled by the Star Delivery Corporation. The *Planet* gives them a delivery location sheet and pays a fixed fee per truck and driver on a weekly basis. This contract is renewable yearly, with the standard weekly fee being set at the beginning of the renewal period. If negotiations concerning the fee break down, the paper is not delivered. The contract between Star Delivery and the *Planet* provides for an arbitrator to be brought in to settle disputes, with the arbitrator's fee to be apportioned between both parties. The purpose of this arrangement is to avoid lengthy contract disputes and to resolve matters expediently. Finally, when a conflict is reconciled and the papers are delivered to the newsstands, individuals may purchase them. The purchase of a newspaper is a contract.

This scenario illustrates the law of contracts in only one instance. It is typical of situations involving contracts, yet it is unique, as you will understand when you read further in this book. The factual circumstances surrounding a contract will be the guiding principle. The parties to a contract may be individuals, corporations, partnerships, or governments. The *Daily Planet,* Sun Spots, Universal Paper, Neptune Newsstands, and Star Delivery are corporations. Galaxy and Globe, Asteroid Advertising Agency, and Solar System Underwriting Syndicate are partnerships. Individuals include Jupiter Jones, Venus, Haley, and Mars Hanley. The parties may act for themselves or through agents. Jupiter Jones hired Sun Spots as his agent. The *Daily Planet* used the law firm of Galaxy and Globe as its agent. Two or more parties may be involved in a particular contract. The *Daily Planet's* contract with the printers' union involves three parties: the *Daily Planet,* Mercury Printers' Union, and individual employees. Certain individuals, such as Mars Hanley, Jupiter Jones, and the printers; are employees. The others, such as Star Delivery, Neptune Newsstands, and Asteroid Advertising Agency, are independent contractors. Independent contractors are not employees but rather act independently in the means they employ to achieve the agreed-upon result, such as delivery of newspapers to newsstands each morning.

Most of the contracts referred to here have been expressed in writing for the purpose of avoiding ambiguity and protecting the parties involved by evidencing the existence of the transaction. The aforementioned contracts do not include every possible type of contract. They are merely a sample of the contracts having a direct effect on the *Daily Planet,* its employees, the independent contractors involved, and the individuals buying the newspaper. Contracts are interwoven throughout the *Planet's* operations. Without contracts the parties involved in this business would not be in agreement on how to operate. Although the *Daily Planet* is only one business out of thousands, its case illustrates the dependence of a business on contracts and the dependence of those connected with the business. Contracts truly provide the basis for business operations.

HOW CONTRACTS RELATE TO US

In the previous section we saw the importance of contracts to the people involved at all levels of a business. We must now turn our attention to the manner in which contracts relate to us, especially when we are adversely affected.

EXAMPLE | Tommy Moon walks to his local Neptune newsstand, flips the proprietor a quarter, and returns home with the morning edition of the *Daily Planet.* Did Tommy Moon make a contract with Neptune Newsstands? Yes! He made a contract to purchase the newspaper. Although there was no written or oral agreement to that effect, there is a contract implied in the actions of the parties. The factual circumstances give rise to the contractual obligation.

Let us check to see if all the contractual elements are present: There are lawful purpose, agreement, legal capacity, promise to perform a specific act, consideration, and execution in a proper form. There is an agreement to buy and sell a newspaper. Both Tommy Moon and the representative of the Neptune newsstand are presumed to have the requisite legal capacity to contract. There is the promise to exchange a newspaper for a quarter. This act is legal. The newspaper and the quarter furnish the required consideration. And because the contract does not have to be in writing, it is executed in proper form, implied from the actions of the parties. A valid contract has been made.

Although the contract is simple, all of the required elements must be present for it to be valid. The example illustrates the contractual significance of a transaction that we make every day in our lives. Why must we be aware of this? Because certain legally enforceable rights and duties have been created. Suppose Tommy Moon moves to a new house that is not within walking distance of a Neptune newsstand. Being an avid reader of the *Daily Planet,* Tommy Moon has bought a three-year subscription to the newspaper for $300. After six months the paper is no longer delivered. Tommy figures, "No big deal." Upon calling the *Planet* to register his complaint, he is advised that all subscriptions are handled exclusively by Saturn Subscription Services, as stated in the subscription contract. Saturn informs Tommy that the primary responsibility lies with the *Planet.*

Tommy Moon is now concerned about the existence of his contractual rights and the contractual duties of the *Daily Planet* and Saturn Subscription Services to deliver the newspaper. He checks to see if all the contractual elements are present. Then Tommy Moon wants to know what legal remedies are available to him and whether the defenses raised by the *Planet* and Saturn are viable. How can Tommy learn more about his contractual rights? He can begin by reading this book, with special attention to the chapters dealing with contracts.

The ensuing discussion points out other areas where contracts touch our lives and the lives of our families. Perhaps contract law, along with income tax law, are the two types of law that most directly affect you. Think of how many contracts you and your family enter into each month. Mortgage or rent payments are paid pursuant to the respective mortgage contract or lease. A mortgage note is a contract between the homeowner and the mortgage holder, generally a bank or the previous owner. A lease is a contract between landlord and tenant. Contracts are entered into with the following companies, which impose monthly service charges: electric, gas, telephone, fuel, credit card, and insurance (life, health, automobile, and homeowner coverage). Furthermore, when home repairs are made, contracts are entered into with electricians, carpenters, roofers, plumbers, and painters, to name a few. Daily or weekly purchases of food, gas, and newspapers are also contracts; so are school tuition payments. Contracts run the gamut from the simple to the highly complex. Often we do not realize that we are entering into simple contracts. We seem to do so unconsciously. However, our realization quickly develops when something goes wrong, such as when the milk purchased is sour, the plumber does not adequately fix the bathtub leak, or the landlord sues for nonpayment of the rent.

We realize that we have certain rights and defenses, and we intend to take full advantage of them. The chapters devoted to contracts will explain what these rights and defenses are and how businesses and individuals can make use of them. It is important to understand and appreciate contracts so that when we enter into contracts, we can view them from the proper perspective, whether they are simple or complex.

SIGNIFICANCE OF A WRITTEN CONTRACT

Generally there is no problem with the validity of an oral contract; the difficulty arises when one tries to prove its existence. Many valid contracts are dismissed by the courts because their terms cannot be proved. In an oral contract, if one party does not fulfill his or her obligation, the other party, without witnesses, will have an arduous task trying to prove the existence of the contract. The old saying "It's my word against yours" is very true and applicable to oral contracts. Even when witnesses are available, there are still problems. Over time witnesses tend to forget; their testimony is often conflicting and may even be perjured. For convenience, simple contracts, particularly those of nominal value, tend to be oral; but parties should make valuable and important contracts in writing to evidence their existence. All states have recognized this principle by adopting a statute of frauds requiring certain contracts to be in writing. The underlying main purpose of the statute is to prevent fraud by requiring evidence of a contract's existence. This protects the parties involved by preventing misunderstandings. A more detailed discussion of the statute of frauds is presented in Chapter 14, "Form and Interpretation."

A contract expressed in oral or written form is referred to as an *express contract*. Contracts may also be implied from the actions of the parties. These contracts are referred to as *implied contracts*. They come about when no words are spoken by the parties and no writing is made but when the actions of the parties dictate agreement to the terms of the contract. Implied contracts arise in situations involving simple transactions, such as the buying of food, gasoline, or newspapers. When a person boards a bus or a train and deposits a token or hands the driver or conductor a receipt for payment, there is an implied promise to transport the individual to any of the various scheduled stops.

TYPES OF CONTRACTS

There are basically four categories of contracts. Remember to **R.S.V.P.**

Real property contracts
Sales contracts
Variety of special contracts
Personal service contracts

Real property contracts are contracts for the sale of land.
Sales contracts cover the broad range of contracts for the sale of personal property. The Uniform Commercial Code (UCC) is the controlling authority in states that have adopted and incorporated it into state law.

A personal service contract is a contract in which one person promises to perform a service for an individual in return for that individual's promise to provide compensation for the services rendered. Personal service contracts include employment contracts, where an individual is employed on a salary basis, as well as contracts with professionals or independent contractors, where performance is on an hourly or per-case basis.

Special contracts are contracts that are so important and specialized that a separate body of law is devoted entirely to each of them. The following areas of law are based on contract law: bailments, insurance, agency, partnership, and commercial paper. Each of these legal subjects is addressed in a separate chapter of this book. Basic contract law is still applicable and often serves as both the foundation and the supplement for the law regarding these special contracts.

PROPER APPLICATION OF STATE LAWS

Each state has its own law of contracts. States enact laws to interpret and enforce contracts. When terms or phrases in a contract are ambiguous, a conflict may develop. The courts interpret the contract to determine the intentions of the parties. The language of the contract is construed according to its fair and reasonable meaning. A court makes this determination by considering the language within the context of the entire transaction. For the state to have jurisdiction, there must be some substantial connection between the state and the contract or the parties to the contract. The state must have sufficient interest to interpret the contract and legally enforce the rights and duties of the parties involved. The following rule determines the application of state law: When a contract is made between two parties of a state and the contract is to be performed in that state, the law of that state will govern.

An example of this principle is the *Daily Planet's* contract with Galaxy and Globe, a local law firm, to represent it in contract negotiations with the Mercury Printers' Union. When a contract will be performed in a state other than the one where the contracting parties are located, the presumption is that the law of the state where performance will take place will govern. The *Planet* has a separate contract with Star Delivery to deliver newspapers across the Idaho border into Montana. The presumption is that Montana law will govern this contract. The parties may override this presumption by stipulating in the contract that the law of the state where the contract is made, Idaho, will govern. A contract involving real estate is governed by the law of the state in which the property is located. Personal service contracts are generally governed by the state in which substantial performance is to take place; however, as stated before, the parties may stipulate otherwise.

UNIFORM COMMERCIAL CODE

The Uniform Commercial Code (UCC) was created for the purpose of establishing among individual states a uniform set of laws that would be compatible with the growth of commerce. A uniform set of laws was needed because of the numerous contracts between parties of different states and the need for a consistent way to resolve the conflicts arising out of those contracts. The UCC has been adopted in the District of Columbia and in all fifty states except Louisiana, which has adopted it only in part. The code has the following ten articles, with each article devoted to a different aspect of a commercial transaction.

Article 1: General Provisions
Article 2: Sales
Article 3: Commercial Paper
Article 4: Bank Deposits and Collections
Article 5: Letters of Credit
Article 6: Bulk Transfers
Article 7: Documents of Title
Article 8: Investment Securities
Article 9: Secured Transactions
Article 10: Effective Date and Repealer

This book will deal with all of the articles to some degree, devoting separate chapters to the more important topics, such as sales (contracts for the sale of goods), commercial paper, and secured transactions.

The purpose of the UCC is threefold. First, it simplifies the laws governing commercial transactions. Second, it allows for the growth of commercial practices through the incorporation of customs and terms used in particular trades. Third, it makes the law of commercial transactions uniform throughout the United States. Its main purpose is to make the law of contracts simple and clear, to make the law uniform throughout the states, and to make it flexible enough to give the parties freedom to determine their respective rights and duties. When each state adopted the UCC, it became part of that state's contract law. The UCC is controlling in respect to contracts for the sale of goods. Basic contract law supplements the code and fills in the gaps. However, the elements of a contract must still be present in all commercial transactions. The code has expanded contract law and made important modifications.

In a commercial transaction involving the sale of goods, the buyer, the seller, and the property contracted for are often in different states. The *Daily Planet's* contract with Universal Paper Corporation typifies this situation. The *Daily Planet* is located in Sun Valley, Idaho; Universal Paper Corporation is in Crater Lake, Oregon; and the paper to be delivered is from the Petrified Forest in Arizona. Because performance— delivery of newspapers—is to be made in Idaho, and because one of the parties is domiciled in Idaho, Idaho law would govern unless the contract stipulated otherwise. To avoid conflicts wherein each party would want the law of the state most favorable to itself to govern, the UCC has simplified the matter by making the law of contracts for the sale of goods uniform in all states.

However, when the UCC became a part of each state's contract law, it also became open to judicial interpretation by the individual courts in each state. In time, this situation may lead to varying interpretations of the provisions of the UCC. This means that it will be important to a party in conflict to have the case decided in the court giving it the most favorable interpretation of the code, whether that interpretation be a liberal or a strict construction.

REVIEW QUESTIONS

1. Define a contract.
2. What are the elements of a contract?
3. How does an agreement become legally enforceable?
4. What is the importance of contracts?
5. How do contracts relate to us?
6. What are the various types of contracts?
7. Universal Paper Corporation (Oregon) contracts to sell the land it owns in the Petrified Forest (Arizona) to the *Daily Planet* (Idaho). Which state's law governs?
8. The *Daily Planet* in Sun Valley, Idaho, buys the *Morning Star* newspaper, which is based in Jupiter, Florida. Meteor Mike signs a contract with the *Planet* to be editor-in-chief of the *Morning Star.* After six months, the *Planet* is suing Meteor Mike for nonperformance of his duties. Which state's law governs? Could the jurisdiction have been altered by contract?
9. What is the significance of the UCC?
10. In the example given in the text, Tommy Moon wants to know what his rights are in respect to the cancellation of his subscription. Can you advise him?

10

Agreement

INTRODUCTION

An *agreement* is a definite understanding between two or more parties wherein each party promises to perform or forbear from performing a specific act. An agreement is constituted by an offer on one party's part that another party accepts voluntarily. An *offer* communicates the offeror's intention to be bound by the terms of the offer, which must be set forth, and requests the offeree to accept those terms. When we speak of an offer, we mean an enforceable offer, where acceptance of the terms results in a contract. This presupposes the presence of the other contractual elements: lawful purpose, legal capacity, promise to perform a specific act, consideration, and execution in proper form.

The *offeror* is the person making the offer. This individual has the freedom to set the terms of the offer, a freedom largely unrestricted because the offeree is protected by the right to refuse the offer. The *offeror* may modify or revoke the offer at any point prior to acceptance. Upon acceptance, the offeror is bound to the terms of the offer. The *offeree* is the person to whom the offer is made. This person is under no obligation to accept the offer. The offeree may accept, make a counteroffer, reject, or allow the offer to lapse. An *acceptance* indicates the offeree's willingness to be bound by the terms of the offer. Acceptance of the offer binds the parties to each other by contract.

EXAMPLE | John Smith arrived in Plymouth, Massachusetts, on a boat from England. He was on a sightseeing tour with the Pilgrims when he first saw Plymouth Rock. Smith told the tour guide, Pocahontas, that he wanted to speak with the owner of Plymouth Rock. Pocahontas took Smith to Jamestown, Virginia, to speak with her father, Powhatan, who was the owner of Plymouth Rock.

The great Indian chief did not fancy John Smith. Pocahontas interceded on Smith's behalf and was able to convince her father to offer him Plymouth Rock. The wise old chief acquiesced to his favorite daughter's request, but he asked for $48 in trinkets, double the price for Manhattan Island, and made Smith promise not to marry Pocahontas. Smith gladly accepted. Is there an agreement between the parties? Yes! An agreement was made when Smith accepted Powhatan's offer. So Smith lost Pocahontas, but ended up with a piece of the rock!

CHARACTERISTICS OF AN OFFER

An offer has three essential characteristics:

> Definite terms
> Communication to offeree
> Validity for a reasonable time

Definite Terms

An offer generally must be clear and definite in its terms, especially in regard to quantity, price, time, place of delivery, identification of the parties, and description of the goods being offered. The mnemonic **STIPND** (pronounced "stipend") is useful for remembering those key terms.

> **S**ubject matter description
> **T**ime
> **I**dentification of the parties
> **P**rice
> **N**umber, quantity
> **D**elivery place

An offer must be clear and definite so that the offeree can recognize that the offeror wishes to make a valid contract based on acceptance of the terms indicated. Both parties should know the exact terms to which they are agreeing. Specifically, the offeree wishes to know what is required of him or her and what the offeror intends to do in return. It is rare that someone purchases something without asking what the price is, determining where and when the item can be delivered, and ascertaining that the needed quantity is available. These are basic facts you should agree upon before buying. If the offeror makes a mistake that is not reasonably evident in one of the material terms, then he or she is bound if the offeree accepts the offer before receiving notification of the error.

EXAMPLE | Powhatan's offer to John Smith must include the description of the property, the price he is asking, and the time and place he intends to deliver the deed. The quantity term is not significant except as it relates to the acreage of land sold, which is part of the legal description of the property. If Powhatan tells Smith that he intends to sell him the northern section of Plymouth Rock, but mistakenly includes part of the eastern section, and Smith accepts the offer as stated, is Powhatan bound by his mistake? Yes! There is an agreement as long as Smith is not aware of Powhatan's mistake.

The terms of an offer must be clear and definite in order for the court to interpret the rights and duties of the parties in case of a dispute. Terms that are ambiguous or indefinite cannot be enforced. The court does not have the power to create terms because to do so that would restrict the parties' freedom to bargain with each other. The UCC looks to the actions of the parties to determine what their course of performance or course of dealing has been. This approach helps to resolve ambiguities because the parties themselves know best what they meant by the phrases they used in the contract, and their actions are the best source for clarifying that meaning. The court will also ascertain the meaning attributed to a disputed term in the particular trade or business.

Certain contracts are permitted to be indefinite when particular terms cannot be defined in advance.

The UCC does not require contracts for the sale of goods to be definite in all respects. It liberalizes rules pertaining to the formation of a contract. A contract exists even where certain material terms have been left out, if the intentions of the parties to make a contract are clear and there is a reasonable basis for supplying the omitted term and granting an appropriate remedy should a breach occur. The gap-filler provisions of the code will supplement the contract, which thus will not fail because of indefiniteness. "Reasonable price" and "reasonable time" will be substituted where a contract does not provide for these terms. Place of delivery will be at the seller's place of business in a case where this term is not mentioned. The three other key terms—quantity, identification of the parties, and description of the goods—must be stipulated, or the contract will fail for indefiniteness.

EXAMPLE Ben Franklin in Lexington, Massachusetts obtains a newspaper concession. He is approached by Thomas Paine, the publisher of *Common Sense* who offers to deliver 150 copies to Franklin on a daily basis. Is this an enforceable offer? Yes! Paine's offer to Franklin is enforceable under the UCC even though certain terms have been omitted. The price must be a reasonable price for wholesale delivery of newspapers. The delivery time must be reasonable for Franklin to be able to sell the newspapers. If Franklin had wanted to receive the papers at his newsstand at 4 A.M. for sale to early morning commuters, he should have requested this term before the contract was made.

Rutgers, State University v. Martin Woodlands Gas Co.
974 F. 2d 659 (5th Cir. 1992)

Rutgers University entered into a five-year contract with Martin Woodlands Gas Company to purchase natural gas. The initial price for the first year was $3.30 per MMBtu.

The following are guidelines for negotiating price increases:

At the end of the initial year hereunder and annually thereafter the Price hereunder for the succeeding year shall have been agreed upon by BUYER and SELLER. It is agreed that said redetermined net burner-tip price shall not escalate more than ten percent for the second year hereunder. The price for the third year shall not increase more than fifteen percent of the second year Price; the percent of the fourth year Price not more than twenty percent over the third year Price; and the fifth year Price not more than twenty-five percent of the fourth year price. If less than the maximum allowed increase is hereafter agreed upon for a given year, the unused margin shall carry forward in computing the price cap for future years.

The price of gas declined substantially by the end of the first year. A reduction in gas prices was not anticipated by the parties when the contract was made. When a price adjustment could not be worked out for the second year, Rutgers sent the following letter to Martin Woodlands: "To demonstrate our good faith we will make gas purchases at the $3.30 price on a month to month basis while we continue discussing future pricing without prejudice to Rutgers' right to terminate our arrangement in the event we are unable to agree on price." Martin did not respond but continued to deliver gas well into the third year. At that point Rutgers gave written notice of its refusal to accept future deliveries.

Rutgers argued that the contract terminated at the end of the first year because the parties failed to agree on a price. Rutgers was seeking a price reduction, while Martin Woodlands contended that $3.30 per MMBtu was an established minimum.

The issue is whether the contract is ambiguous with regard to negotiation of a new price below the initial price of $3.30 per MMBtu.

The court stated,

We hold that the contract is not ambiguous and that it does not expressly or impliedly limit potential negotiated price changes to price increases. As appellants pointed out, no one expected dramatic decreases in gas prices when the contract was signed in 1985. Consequently, no floor was built into the contract, because the parties anticipated that increasing gas prices made that an unnecessary precaution. The parties failed to agree on a new price at the end of the first year of the contract. We find that the contract lapsed at that time.

Judgment for Rutgers.

Communication to Offeree

An offer must be communicated through the method selected by the offeror. An offer becomes effective when the offeree receives it. If the offeree learns of the offer through another source, the offer is not enforceable. An offer is not assignable because the offeree has no contractual rights to what is offered. Only upon acceptance, when a contract is made, are legal rights and duties created. At that time a contract may be assigned subject to certain restrictions. Assignments and applicable restrictions will be discussed in Chapter 15, "Rights of Third Parties."

EXAMPLE | At a public campground near West Point, Benedict Arnold overhears George Washington offer to sell West Point to a group of cadets in order to raise money for his revolutionary cause. Benedict Arnold, knowing that Sir Henry Clinton and his men have always wanted to occupy West Point, sends Major André, a trusted informant, to him. Clinton accepts the offer and notifies Washington of his intent to occupy West Point. Washington refuses by saying that Clinton's acceptance is not valid. Is Washington correct? Yes! Washington is correct because the offer can be accepted only by the cadets, the party to whom it was made.

Validity for a Reasonable Time

An offer is valid only for a "reasonable time" unless a definite time is stated. What is reasonable depends on what is being offered and on the terms of the offer. An offer for perishable goods would logically be open for a shorter period than an offer for durable goods; likewise, an offer for the sale of securities at a fixed price would be open for a shorter time then an offer for the sale of real estate.

The way the offer is made also affects the duration of its validity. An offer that arises during a conversation in person or on the phone must be accepted during the conversation or it lapses, unless a definite time for acceptance is stated.

EXAMPLE | In a Charlottesville pub, Thomas Jefferson and his neighbor James Monroe are having a few beers. During the conversation Jefferson offers to sell Monroe for $100,000, his home, Monticello, which Monroe has always admired. Nothing more is said during the conversation. The next day Monore visits Jefferson at Monticello and accepts the offer. Jefferson claims that Monore's acceptance was not timely made. Is he correct? Yes! Jefferson is correct because an offer that arises during a conversation must be accepted before the conversation ends or it lapses.

M.T. Bonk Co. v. Milton Bradley Co.
945 F. 2d 1404 (7th Cir. 1991)

Mark Bonk invented a game entitled "Play It Again, Juke Box." Each Player had to complete a phrase from a song after being given a few lyrics. Milton Bradley and Bonk began to negotiate a licensing agreement. Bonk was warned that a game could be removed from the review process at any time. Milton Bradley expressed concern over Bonk's right to use copyrighted song lyrics. Bonk replied that he was entitled under the Fair Use Doctrine. Subsequently Milton Bradley terminated all negotiations because it believed that Bonk's game was not protected by the Fair Use Doctrine. Meanwhile Bonk refused all other offers and stopped promoting and marketing the game.

The issue is whether there is an oral agreement between the parties.

The court ruled,

> In determining whether an oral contract exists, the trier of fact must determine whether there was a meeting of the minds between the parties with respect to the terms of an agreement and whether the parties intended to be bound to the oral agreement. In order for an oral contract to be binding and enforceable the contract terms must be definite and certain.

Judgment for Milton Bradley.

PRELIMINARY NEGOTIATIONS

Preliminary negotiations include all communications between parties that do not constitute an enforceable offer. Their purpose is to lead to an offer by providing buyers with information concerning products, services, or real estate. A buyer may be negotiating with several businesses at the same time to determine the most advantageous deal. If each negotiation were said to be an offer, the buyer might become involved in several contracts that he or she would be unable to perform. This would inhibit parties from negotiating. Preliminary negotiations may go through several stages, especially in complicated contracts. Each discussion may involve a different contractual provision or even an aspect of a provision.

The following is a list of statements that do not qualify as offers because they are generally considered to be preliminary negotiations: **ICE CAPS.**

Invitations
Circulars
Emotional statements

Catalogs
Advertisements
Price quotes
Social invitations

Invitations

A statement that leaves terms open for negotiation is not an enforceable offer but an invitation to negotiate. An invitation to negotiate is a communication requesting people to make offers. It cannot be accepted because its terms are not definite. A key to determining whether a statement is an offer or an invitation is the class of people to whom the offer is directed. A statement made to the general public must be construed as an invitation; otherwise an offeror would be reluctant to deal with the general public for fear of breaching the contract if the general public's needs could not be met. If the statement is restricted to a certain few, the odds are greater, though not conclusive, that the statement is an offer.

A reward, although open to the general public, is an offer because the requested performance can be made only by one or at most, by a few individuals. Acceptance of the reward requires some knowledge of the reward coupled with actual performance.

EXAMPLE | George Washington offers a reward for the arrest of Benedict Arnold. Nathan Hale, while picnicking with Betsy Ross atop Bunker Hill, sees Benedict Arnold, who fires a shot-mortally wounding Hale. Hale, noted for his bravery and patriotism, captures the traitor and while dying in Betsy Ross's arms proclaims, "I regret that I have but one life to lose for my country." But then he remembers the reward and makes a miraculous recovery. Has Hale accepted the offer for the reward? Yes, by capturing Benedict Arnold.

Circulars, Catalogs, Advertisements, and Price Quotes

Circulars, catalogs, advertisements, and price quotes are all forms of invitations intended to acquaint prospective purchasers with certain products, property, or services the seller provides. In disseminating these invitations, the seller hopes that prospective customers will discuss terms that will eventually lead to enforceable offers. These forms of invitations are not enforceable unless they are so clear and definite that no terms are left open for negotiation. However, laws have been enacted to protect consumers from false advertising by imposing criminal penalties on an advertiser who deliberately attempts to mislead the public.

When the recipient of an invitation or advertisement offers to buy something, the seller may accept or reject the offer depending on whether the particular size, color, and style requested are available. As you know, not all sellers do carry every color, size, and style of every product that is made. They are free to carry what they feel are the most popular items. To require them to do otherwise would restrict their freedom.

EXAMPLE | Abe Lincoln is spending a quiet day at home, leafing through a Sears catalog, when suddenly an advertisement catches his eye, "Sears Paints Great American Homes." Lincoln concludes that he is a great American and that Sears should paint his home. Abe hurries down to accept the offer. The store manager, John Wilkes Booth, informs Lincoln that although Scars acknowledges that he is a great American, it is the company's belief that his log cabin is not a great American home. Has Lincoln any recourse? No! The advertisement was an invitation for Lincoln to make a request. Its terms were not definite enough to constitute an offer. Lincoln splits and makes tracks for Washington.

Emotional Statements

If a reasonable person would believe tht an offer was made during an emotional statement in anger, excitement, or jest, such an offer would not be enforceable. Whether or not a statement was made in anger, excitement, or jest depends on the objective actions of the parties, not on their subjective states of mind. The key is what the person said and the context in which it was said, not what may have been in that person's mind at the time. The person seeking to enforce the agreement must reasonably believe that the other party seriously intended to enter into a contract. The surrounding circumstances are helpful in the determination of such intention.

Social Invitations

Social invitations, such as dates or invitations to parties or weddings, are not legally enforceable offers, although they can be accepted. As a matter of public policy, it has been decided that one should not be subject to a breach of contract suit for breaking a date or changing one's mind about going to a party. People can have agreements concerning social affairs, and breaking these agreements may have moral and social implications, but there no legal consequences.

EXAMPLE | Miles Standish has admired Priscilla for a long time and finally gets up enough courage to ask her for a date. She accepts and invites Miles to meet her family. Miles is too shy to meet her family, so he asks his friend John Alden to call for Priscilla in his stead. Alden, being a good friend, does as Miles requests. He meets the family but, after one look at Priscilla, decides to take her out himself. Has Miles any recourse against Priscilla or Alden for the broken date or his broken heart? No! Dates are not offers; they are social invitations that have no legal consequences.

SPECIAL OFFERS

Invitations requesting bids are called soliciting offers. At an auction the auctioneer is inviting the audience to bid on particular items. When someone from the audience bids, that person is making an offer. A higher bid has the effect of canceling all the lower ones. Acceptance rests with the auctioneer, who by pounding the gavel, creates a contract of sale to the highest bidder. Bidders who have second thoughts may retract their offers but must do so before the auctioneer has banged the gavel. The auctioneer may refuse the highest bidder and withdraw the item if a fair price has not been bid. However, if the auction is being held "without reserve," the auctioneer must accept the highest bid. The words *without reserve* must be specifically stated. These words signify that the owner is agreeing not to withdraw the property no matter how low the highest bid might be.

An auctioneer is an agent for the seller. Auctioneers are generally professional salespeople who act on behalf of the seller to get the highest possible bid for each item offered for sale. An auctioneer may represent an individual seller or many sellers in a general auction; he or she may conduct a sale of public property or an estate auction in which a deceased's personal effects are sold off in settlement of the estate.

EXAMPLE | James Madison has come to the conclusion that the federal deficit must be reduced. He decides that the government should auction off some of the national treasures. He appoints Ben Franklin, an auctioneer, to hold the auction at Independence Hall in South Philadelphia. When Franklin asks, "What am I offered for the Liberty Bell?" the highest bid is $50,000 by Patrick Henry. Madison believes that the Liberty Bell is worth at least $100,000 and instructs Franklin to refuse the offer. Patrick Henry shouts, "Give me the Liberty Bell or give me death." Has he any recourse? Unless the auction is held without reserve, Madison is not bound to accept the highest bid.

Sales of stocks, bonds, and commodities are transacted on a bid-asked basis. The seller will be trying to get the highest bid for their securities and commodities, just as the buyer will be trying to purchase at the lowest possible bid. The prices bid and asked generally have some relationship to the price of the previous sale. When a bid is accepted, a contract is made. Auction sales and sales of securities on the stock exchange floor are contracts, implied from the actions of the parties through recognized sign language.

Construction bids that a landowner requests from general contractors are not offers. The bids submitted by the general contractors are offers. The land-owner has the opportunity to accept or refuse the lowest bid. To arrive at their bids, general contractors will request bids from subcontractors in specialized fields such as electricity, masonry, plumbing, and carpentry. The bids submitted by subcontractors are offers. A general contractor's use of a subcontractor's bid does not constitute an acceptance of that bid even if the general contractor is subsequently awarded the contract. When the contract is awarded, the general contractor is free to accept or reject the subcontractor's bid. A subcontractor has the freedom to retract the bid at any point prior to the general contractor's acceptance.

OPTION CONTRACTS

An *option* gives the offeree the exclusive right for a specified period to accept or reject the stipulated offer. An option is a contract because the offeree must give some form of consideration in return. The offeree is paying for time and may use the time to attempt to negotiate a better deal, either with the offeror or with another party. The offeree may well be in a better position to make a decision three or even six months down the road. He or she may foresee an improvement in personal finances or an economic recovery that might make the option more valuable. Even if the offeree rejects the offer initially, he or she may later accept it as long as the option has not expired. The offeror is restricted from selling to another party for the duration of the option.

EXAMPLE | John Adams and his son John Quincy Adams own Valley Forge. They are approached by George Washington, who inquires if he may purchase the land for his men to use as a winter retreat. The Adams family offers to sell Valley Forge to Washington for $50,000. Washington wants to talk the price over with his men, so he asks the Adams family to hold the offer open for thirty days in return for payment of $50. They agree. Ten days, later Washington notifies the Adams Family that his men intend to move on to New York. The Adams family immediately sells the property to a group of Englishmen who are seeking to build their own nation in America. Fifteen days later a turn of events dictate that Washington and his men return to Valley Forge to spend the winter. Washinton calls on the Adams family to exercise his option. Is Washington better later then never? Yes! Washington may still accept the offer to buy Valley Forge because the option has not expired.

TERMINATION OF AN OFFER

An offer may be terminated by **ROLD DICE**.

> **R**evocation
> **O**peration of law
> **L**apse of time
> **D**estruction of subject matter
>
> **D**eath
> **I**ncompetency
> **C**ounteroffer
> **E**xpress rejection

Revocation

The offeror may cancel by revoking the offer for any reason at any time prior to the offeree's acceptance. The revocation must be communicated to the offeree and does not become effective until the offeree receives notice of it. The revocation is effective even if the offeree learns of it through another source. If the offeree accepts prior to receiving notice of revocation, a valid contract is made.

EXAMPLE | Ben Franklin offers to sell the first copy of his *Poor Richard's Almanac* to the Marquis de Lafayette, a French nobleman, if Lafayette accepts within ten days. One week later

Lafayette, while vacationing with Jefferson at Monticello, tells him of Franklin's offer. Jefferson informs Lafayette that Frankilin has decided to donate the first copy for display at Independence Hall in Philadelphia. Lafayette asserts that the ten days have not expired. Is Franklin bound by the ten-day limit? No! Franklin is not bound by the limit because Lafayette has given no consideration in return. Franklin can revoke at any time, and Lafayette's learning of the revocation from Jefferson fufills the requirement of proper notice.

The UCC provides that if the offeror makes an offer to the offeree and then sells to a third person in the ordinary course of business without notifying the offeree, who then accepts the original offer, the third person may retain the goods, and the offeree's remedy will be limited to loss of profits. This rule was enacted as protection for the buyer in the ordinary course of business who would otherwise be reluctant to enter into a contract for fear an offer might have been made to another. A buyer in the ordinary course of business is a person who buys in good faith and for valuable consideration without knowledge that someone else may have superior rights to the goods purchased. An offeror may reserve the right to sell to another without notice to the offeree, as long as this right is stipulated in the offer. Revocation of an offer to the general public may be made through the medium used to convey the offer. Individual notification is not necessary because it would be costly and practically impossible.

A promise by the offeror not to revoke for a stated period is not enforceable unless the offeree provides consideration in return, which would make it an option contract. There are certain situations where an offeror may not revoke an offer: **CAP**.

Changing position in reliance on the offer

Acceptance of the offer

Partial performance

Operation of Law

Enactment of a new law that makes the offer legal cancels the offer. If the offer was accepted before the change in law, the validity of the contract depends upon whether or not the law is retroactive.

EXAMPLE | The Green Mountain Boys, seniors at Fort Ticonderoga High School, often cross the Hudson to buy distilled spirits from the Saratoga Springs Emporium. A surprise party is planned for the men stationed at the fort by Ethan Allen, the captain of the Green Mountain Boys. Ethan Allen orders 50 cases of distilled spirits from the emporium. In the interim Peter Stuyvesant, governor of New York, raises the drinking age from eighteen to nineteen. When Allen attemps to pick up his order, Saratoga Springs refuses because he is only eighteen. Has Ethan any recourse? No! Ethan Allen has no recourse because the enactment of the new law has effectively canceled the offer.

Lapse of Time

An offer is enforceable for the length of time stated in the offer. When the time expires the offer is canceled. If the offeror fails to restrict the duration of the offer, it is enforceable for a reasonable time. What is reasonable depends upon what is being offered and the surrounding circumstances. An offer for securities or commodities at a fixed price on an exchange may be enforceable only for a matter of minutes or seconds because of the volatility of price fluctuations. Real estate offers and offers to render personal service are generally of longer duration because the prices do not fluctuate as rapidly. Once an offer lapses, a party wishing to accept may only make a new offer. In a situation where no time is fixed and the offeror receives the acceptance after what is believed to be a reasonable time, the offeror must notify the offeree immediately that the acceptance is not valid or run the risk that his or her silent conduct will operate as an acceptance. If it is important for the offeror to restrict the duration of the offer, it is always best to state the length of time that the offer is open. Otherwise, the other party may bring a lawsuit to determine whether acceptance was made within a reasonable time.

EXAMPLE | William Penn owned a large oat farm. In June Penn contacted the Quakers, a food-processing concern, and offered to sell them his oats. The Quakers finally accepted Penn's offer in September, long after the oats had been harvested. By this time Penn had made other arrangements. Penn refused to ship the oats to the Quakers, claiming that an unreasonable amount of time had passed. Do the Quakers have any recourse? No! Because contracts are generally made before harvest, Penn is right: A reasonable time to accept the offer has elapsed.

Destruction of Subject Matter

Destruction of the subject matter—land or personal property—will nullify the offer if the subject matter was unique or had been specifically designated for the purchaser in a sales contract. This is because it would be impossible to replace the destroyed subject matter. Each parcel of real estate is unique; so are certain goods that are handcrafted or are one of a kind. An offer for goods that can easily be replaced does not terminate unless the seller had separated certain goods from the rest and designated them for the purchaser or the contract specified that the goods would come from a particular crop or shipment and these goods subsequently were destroyed.

EXAMPLE | While strolling through South Philadelphia, George Washington came upon an upholsterer's shop with a star-spangled banner in the window. Washington approached the proprietor, Betsy Ross, and offered to buy the flag; he told her he would return the next day with the money. That night a fire consumed the shop and destroyed the flag. Did George's offer go up in smoke? Yes! The offer to purchase the star-spangled banner has been nullified by its destruction.

Death or Incompetency

Death or incompetency of either the offeror or the offeree terminates the offer unless there is a firm offer or part performance by the offeree that can be completed by the offeror's personal representative. An offer is personal, and if the offeror dies, the offer dies with that person. This is generally true whether or not the other party has been notified. An offer is enforceable only by the person to whom it is made; if the offeree dies, no one else has the power to accept it. A contract is not terminated by incompetency or death because certain legal obligations have been created that must be carried through. Otherwise physicians and hospitals would hesitate to make contracts with terminal patients for fear of not getting reimbursed. An exception to this rule would be personal service contracts. An individual's services are unique; in the absence of that person, there is no way to enforce the contract or provide a remedy. An offer carries no legal obligations. This is generally why offers do not survive the people who make them or the people to whom they are made.

EXAMPLE | The Marquis de Lafayette, a wealthy French entrepreneur, owned the Statue of Liberty. Patrick Henry, a true patriot and admirer of the Sons of Liberty organization, offered to buy the statue from Lafayette with the intention of donating it to the revolutionary group. Lafayette told Patrick Henry to bring the money and said that they would discuss the offer further. On the way up to Lafayette's home in Harlem Heights, Patrick Henry was mugged by a Tory. His last reported words echoed his offer: "Give me the Statue of Liberty or give me death." Lafayette's acceptance of the offer is precluded by Patrick Henry's death.

Counteroffer

A counteroffer is a reply to the original offer where at least one of the key terms has been altered. The addition or alteration of material terms impliedly amounts to a rejection of the original offer with the substitution of a new offer. Once a counteroffer is made, the offeree cannot have a subsequent change of heart and accept the original offer. It is important to distinguish between a counteroffer altering a material term and an inquiry asking if a material term may be changed. The latter is not a counteroffer.

An inquiry may be merely a suggestion or a request. An inquiry is worded so as not to amount to a rejection of the original offer and a proposal of a new offer. "Is this your highest offer?" and "Is it possible for you to make delivery at my place of business?" are inquiries, whereas, "In reply to your offer of $4,000, my price is $5,000" and "I accept your offer only if delivery is made at my place of business" are counteroffers.

An inquiry may also be expressed in the following way: "I am considering your offer, but I would like to inquire whether you are flexible in regard to the price." The words "I accept your offer to buy 100 Polaroid cameras for $5,000, and I hope you will sell me an additional 100 for $4,550" amount to a valid acceptance of the first 100 cameras. This contract is not affected by the buyer's subsequent offer to purchase an additional 100 cameras.

In contracts between merchants for the sale of goods, the UCC provides that additional terms contained in the acceptance become part of the contract unless they alter the material terms of the offer; acceptance is restricted to the terms set forth in the offer; or the offeror gives notice of objection within a reasonable time

---

Nuco Plastics v. Universal Plastics
601 N.E.2d 152 (Ohio App. 11 Dist. 1991)

Nuco entered into a contract with Universal Plastics to manufacture 500,000 "door guards" at 23.5 cents each. Universal Plastics made an offer to modify the contract by requesting a change in the composition of the door guards. Nuco accepted on condition that the price be raised to 40 cents each. Universal Plastics ordered 105,000 door guards at 40 cents each. Nuco billed Universal Plastics for 500,000 door guards, claiming that was the minimum purchase agreed upon to cover the costs of developing the models.

The issue is at what point did the terms of the contract become finalized.

Nuco's conditional acceptance amounted to a counteroffer because a material term, the price, was changed. Universal Plastics then conditionally accepted Nuco's offer by agreeing to the price adjustment but lowering the quantity. This amounted to a counteroffer by Universal Plastics because a material term, the quantity, was altered. Nuco then accepted Universal Plastic's counteroffer of 105,000 door guards at 40 cents each by accepting $42,000 as payment for these parts delivered. Judgment for Universal Plastics.

Express Rejection

The offeree may reject the offer by communicating his or her refusal to the offeror. The rejection becomes effective only upon receipt. If the offeree does not reply, the lapse of time will signify a rejection. Once the offeree communicates notice of rejection to the offeror, the offeree cannot later have a change of mind and accept the offer. When offers are solicited from the general public, an offer may not be rejected solely because of the offeree's race, religion, nationality, or sex. This rule applies to public service companies providing electricity, gas, telephone service, fuel, medical care, and insurance, and to hotels, restaurants, employers, landlords, and other vendors.

EXAMPLE | Chief Massasoit, the local Indian Chief, observes that a Dutch ship has pulled into Manhattan Bay and that a wealthy tycoon named Henry Hudson has stepped off the boat. The chief offers to take Hudson on a boat tour around the bay, but Hudson replies that he has already made the tour. What is the effect of Hudson's reply? It is a rejection of Chief Massasoit's offer. The chief tries a different angle. He offers to sell Hudson the island for $24. Hudson replies, "I will accept it if I can pay with traveler's checks." The chief laughs and walks away saying, "Not without a credit reference." Later Hudson returns with the cash, but the chief says that he has already sold the Island to Peter Minuit for $24 in trinkets. What is the status of Hudson's reply? Hudson's reply concerning the traveler's checks is a counteroffer changing a material term of the offer.

METHODS OF ACCEPTANCE

An offeree has the legal power to consummate a contract by accepting the offer in the manner requested. Acceptance of an offer must be made by the party to whom the offer was made. An offer cannot be assigned to a third party unless it is an option contract. There must be an unconditional acceptance of the material terms of the offer. Incidental additions do not operate as a rejection. An acceptance that adds or alters material terms is a counteroffer, and a contract will not result except in those situations allowed by the UCC. Where similar acceptances will be made repeatedly or at certain intervals, those acceptances already made are contracts; however, the rest can be rejected if notice is given to the offeror.

Acceptance must be communicated to the offeror in the manner requested in the offer. Acceptance of an offer by mail is effective when it is mailed, even if the mail is delayed or lost. This is a general rule that the offeror can change if he or she states in the offer that acceptance is effective upon upon receipt. This is illustrated in the following case. The best way to phrase an offer is to state that acceptance must be received by a specific date. In this way, the risk of the acceptance being lost is transferred from offeror to offeree. If after mailing a rejection the offeree changes his or her mind, an acceptance will be effective only if it is received before the rejection is received.

American Heritage Life Ins. Co. v. Koch
721 S.W. 2d 611 (Tex. App.–Tyler 1986)

In February 1984 Alfred Koch enrolled in a group insurance policy that provided $100,000 in accidental death benefits. In 1985 Koch received an application to increase his coverage to $150,000. On March 29, 1985, Koch mailed the signed application with a check to Kirk Van Orsdel, American Heritage's agent. Van Orsdel received the check and application on April 3, 1985. The application provided that the coverage would "become effective upon the first day of the month following the receipt of the premium payment."

On April 16, 1985, Koch died in an automobile accident. His widow argued that her husband's acceptance had become effective when it was mailed on March 29, 1985. This would mean that the increased coverage should have begun on April 1, 1985. American Heritage contended that acceptance had become effective when the payment was received, on April 3, 1985, with the policy becoming effective on May 1, 1985.

The issue is whether the coverage became effective prior to Koch's death.

The court held that

> The "mailbox rule" actually provides that when a party makes an offer through the mail, the contract is created when a written acceptance by the offeree, properly addressed and stamped, is deposited with the post office. This rule does not apply, however, if the offer contains a stipulation that the acceptance must be received before the contract is completed. The plain language of this offer requires that the acceptance be actually received before calculating when coverage began.

Judgment for American Heritage Life.

EXAMPLE   Clark in St. Joseph, Missouri, writes to his friend Lewis in Sacramento, inviting him to sail up the Missouri and Columbia rivers and explore the Oregon Territory. Clark mails his offer on April 3, stating that acceptance must be made within one week. Delivery by mail takes five days. Later Clark realizes that Lewis is no fun and decides to revoke his offer, mailing the notice on April 7. Lewis receives the offer on April 8 and does not send his acceptance until April 11. The next day Clark's notice of revocation arrives. Lewis's acceptance does not reach Clark until two weeks later because of a delay in the mail. Will Lewis join Clark in their search for the Oregon Territory? Yes! Lewis's acceptance on April 11 is well within the one-week time limit, which expires April 15. The fact that there was a delay in the delivery of the mail does not affect Lewis's acceptance. Clark's notice of revocation is not effective because it was received on the day after Lewis accepted.

If the offeree responds in a manner different from that stipulated, then acceptance is effective upon receipt. The offeror may change the general rule by providing that acceptance is effective only upon receipt. The parties may agree that the contract will be valid only when a written document is prepared that contains all the key terms, is drafted in a clear and definite manner, and is signed by both parties.

The UCC provides that acceptance in response to an offer for the sale of goods may be made in any reasonable manner unless the offeror specifies otherwise. Acceptances in contracts that are implied by the actions of the parties may be made by certain expressions of assent, such as the nodding of the head or the exchange of goods in return for money. There must be some affirmative movement on the offeree's part to signify acceptance.

EXAMPLE | Peter Minuit offers trinkets totaling $24 to Chief Massoit in exchange for Manhattan Island. The parties understand the nature of the transaction although neither speaks the other man's language. The Chief accepts the trinkets. Is this acceptance valid? Yes! The contract created through the offer by Minuit and the acceptance by Chief Massasoit is implied from the actions of the parties.

Acceptance may be made through performance or forbearance of an act such as the prompt shipment of goods in a sales contract. The offeror must be given notice of acceptance. Immediate performance or forbearance by the offeree will usually be sufficient to apprise the offeror of acceptance. If not, the offeror must be informed by other means within a reasonable time.

EXAMPLE | The Marquis de Lafayette, writing from his quarters in Southern Virginia, sent a letter to George Washington asking him to supply Baron von Steuben with food and blankets whenever the baron requested them and promising to be responsible for the debt if the baron could not make payment. During the onslaught of winter, the baron made the request, and Washington crossed the icy Potomac with the food and blankets. The baron failed to pay for the goods, and Washington then became involved with more pressing affairs and did not request payment from Lafayette for one year. Lafayette, unaware that delivery had been made, refused to pay when he was billed. Did Washington cross the Potomac for naught? Yes! Although acceptance was made by George's outright performance, prompt notification of performance should have sent to Lafayette because he had agreed to be liable for the baron's debt. Because notification was not given to Lafayette, he is not responsible for payment.

Silence will generally not constitute acceptance even if the offeree states that it will because one person cannot be forced to reply to an offer. If this were not true, some unscrupulous individuals could offer to buy other people's houses or personal effects, or even hire their services, by informing them that unless offers were expressly rejected, silence would constitute acceptance. Innocent people would be besieged by offers of this type and forced to go to great lengths to inform the offerors of their refusal. Merchandisers have followed this practice with such items as books sent through the mail, along with letters stating that acceptance would be implied if the merchandise were not returned within a certain time period, which was usually on the short side. Most states have adopted the Postal Reorganization Act of 1970, which provided that unordered merchandise need not be paid for or returned.

In certain situations silence will operate as an acceptance. These exceptions to the general rule are **SCRAP**.

Stipulation in the contract
Conduct of the offeree
Received benefit of services with knowledge
Actions of the parties
Prior dealings

Stipulation in the Contract

The parties have the freedom to stipulate in the contract that, for their convenience, silence will operate as an acceptance. This stipulation must be made freely by the parties. It often arises in contracts which are repetitive.

EXAMPLE | Aaron Burr writes to Alexander Hamilton requesting weekly deliveries of *The Federalist*. Hamilton offers to make prompt shipment to Burr each week unless otherwise notified. Burr agrees. Will Burr's continued silence operate as an acceptance of the weekly delivery of the newspaper? Yes! Each delivery of *The Federalist* is a contract made by offer and acceptance. The parties have stipulated that Burr's silence will constitute an acceptance; therefore Burr's continued silence signifies acceptance in these repetitive contracts.

Conduct of the Offeree

If the offeree's conduct leads the offeror into reasonably believing that silence will constitute an acceptance, and if delay through silence causes the subject matter to become unmarketable or if other damages are sustained, then acceptance through silence may be inferred. The offeree has a duty to speak and inform the offeror of his or her refusal.

EXAMPLE | Samuel Adams informed John Hancock that he would like to purchase fire insurance on property he owned on Bunker Hill near Boston. John Hancock accepted by issuing the policy. Every year on July 4 the policy was automatically renewed, and a bill was mailed to Samuel Adams two weeks later. One year on July 11 a fire totally destroys the property and John Hancock refuses to pay the face value of the policy on the grounds that silence does not constitute acceptance. Does Samuel Adams have any recourse? Yes! John Hancock's conduct has reasonably led Samuel Adams to believe that the insurance has been granted for another year. If John Hancock wishes to cancel the policy, he must inform Adams in advance, thereby giving him a reasonable time to find insurance elsewhere.

Received Benefit of Services with Knowledge

An offeree who receives the benefit of services performed with knowledge and who has reason to know they were offered in the expectation of profit has impliedly accepted the benefit, and he or she is responsible for the reasonable value of the services performed.

EXAMPLE | The Pilgrims boarded the Mayflower and were provided bed and board. When they reached Plymouth, their destination, the Mayflower Company demanded payment for the services provided. The Pilgrims asserted that the Mayflower's offer had not been accepted by them because of their silence. Upon initiating a suit does the Mayflower get more than the silent treatment? Yes! The Pilgrims derived a benefit from the services the Mayflower Company provided with the knowledge that the Company expected to be paid. The Pilgrims' silence will operate as an acceptance.

Actions of the Parties

Contracts implied by the actions of the parties may be accepted in silence although an affirmative act on the offeree's part is required. Depositing a token in a turnstile is such an action. So is the banging of the auctioneer's gavel.

Prior Dealings

When a transaction is based on prior dealings where the offeree has given the offeror reason to believe that silence will be the method of acceptance, silence will be effective in the present case as well.

EXAMPLE | John Rolfe and his wife Pocahantas ran a pub in Jamestown. Sir Walter Raleigh, an English captain, made frequent trips between Jamestown and England. On each trip Raleigh returned with several cases of Scotch whiskey, which Rolfe and Pocahantas gladly accepted. On his last voyage to England, Raleigh returned with the usual shipment for Rolfe and Pocahantas, but this time they refused to accept it. Raleigh, a tobacco man, had no use for the whiskey. Must he suffer the loss? No! Although silence is generally not effective as an acceptance, Raleigh acted upon their silence on the basis of prior dealings.

REVIEW QUESTIONS

1. Define the following terms: agreement, offer, acceptance, offeror, offeree, and option.
2. List and explain the ways an offer may be terminated.
3. In what situations may silence be effective as an acceptance?
4. Pharmaceutical Horizons developed an idea for a stick deodorant that would relieve muscular ache, similar to Ben-Gay. Sterling Drug signed an agreement with Horizons to evaluate the product's potential and to develop and market it if it appeared to be feasible. Sterling would pay 5 percent of the net sales as royalties. At any time before royalties accrued to Horizons, Sterling could terminate the contract. Sterling never manufactured the product, and Horizons sued for breach of contract. What result? *Pharmaceutical Horizons* v. *Sterling Drug*, 512 N.Y.S. 2d 30 (A.D. 1 Dept. 1987).
5. R. C. Foster was in the employ of Hickman Datsun as their used car manager until April 1983, when he was discharged. Foster claimed that Hickman Datsun breached their employment contract with him. Datsun retorted that the contract was for an indefinite period and therefore could be terminated by

either party at will. What result? *Hickman Datsun, Inc.* v. *Foster*, 351 S.E. 2d 678 (Ga. App. 1986).

6. Albert and Raymond Martin owned Martin's News Service, Inc., a retail store that sold lottery tickets, newspapers, cigarettes, and small variety items. When they began having difficulty working together, the brothers entered into a buy-out agreement that gave each one the first right to purchase the other's stock. On November 3, 1983, Albert notified Raymond that his half was for sale. Raymond began sending checks in August 1984 in accordance with the buyout agreement. Albert refuse to accept the checks and never cashed any of them. Raymond asserted that the agreement was a binding contract supported by adequate consideration in the form of reciprocal promises. Albert claimed that his brother had abrogated the agreement because he did not respond within a reasonable time to the offer. What result? *Martin* v. *Martin's News Service, Inc.*, 518 A.2d 951 (Conn. App. 1986).

7. Tuneup Masters had an option to extend their original lease for an additional five years. Jenkins, the landlord, required that notice of acceptance be "sent by certified United States Mail, return receipt requested." After the tenant had sent the notice of acceptance, it was lost in the mail. The landlord contended that the notice had not been mailed in the manner required by the lease. Did Tuneup Masters satisfy the landlord's mode of acceptance? *Jenkins* v. *Tuneup Masters*, 235 Cal. Rptr. 214 (Cal. App. 3 Dist. 1987).

8. U.S.D., a manufacturer, and Magid, a distributor, orally agreed that U.S.D. would sell Magid certain respirator products for resale. The parties did not discuss the duration of the proposed relationship or sales quotas. Was the contract valid? *Magid Mfg. Co., Inc.* v. *U.S.D. Corp.* ,654 F. Supp. 325 (N.D. Ill. 1987).

9. Harry S. Field Jr. owned property in Texas. His daughter and her husband, the Barretts, had resided in an adjacent dwelling since 1977 and had been paying Field $100 per month with the intent of buying the property. When the Barretts agreed to buy, Field applied the $100 rental payments to the purchase. The parties also agreed that the purchase price was to be the appraised value of the property and that the payments were to be $100 per month. Field contended that the Barretts had not agreed to any purchase price in regard to the property. Was the contract enforceable? What result? *Penwell* v. *Barrett*, 724 S.W. 2d 902 (Tex. App. San Antonio 1987).

10. Plaintiff works as a manager for W. C. Realty Company, a real estate management firm owned by the defendant. In consideration for receiving one-half of the defendant's interest in the property, plaintiff was to "supervise the refurbishing of the building." Plaintiff contends that his services constitute valid consideration, which makes the oral agreement enforceable. What result? *Azoulay* v. *Cassin*, 512 N.Y.S. 2d 900 (A.D. 2 Dept. 1987).

11

Consideration

INTRODUCTION

Consideration is something valuable given in exchange for something valuable received. Parties enter into a contract for a reason: They want to receive something they think is valuable. That something is the consideration given by the other party. In return they too must be willing to give something. What they give constitutes their consideration, given in exchange for what they receive. The consideration given by each party may take the form of performance, forbearance, or the promise to perform—or forbear from performing—a specific act.

Performance is valuable consideration because the act performed establishes the existence of a contract and the rights and duties of the parties to the contract.

EXAMPLE | A sower called a supplier for a 100-pound bag of mustard seed, the least of seeds from the tallest of plants. The supplier was informed that payment would be made upon delivery. Is the sower bound by the delivery? Performance by delivery of the mustard seeds will bind the sower to pay for them. The supplier's consideration is the delivery.

Forbearance constitutes a valuable consideration because one party is forfeiting a legal right or freedom to act, within prescribed limits. There must be no impairment of constitutional rights in return for a promise. Once the forbearance is undertaken, a contract is created. It does not matter whether the person making the promise in return for the forbearance receives a benefit.

Hammer v. Sidway
124 N.Y. 538, 27 N.E 256 (1891)

William E. Story II brought an action to recover money promised to him by his uncle.

At a family reception, Uncle Bill promised William II $5,000 if he would forbear from drinking, smoking, swearing, and gambling at cards or billiards until the age of twenty-one. The promise was witnessed by many family members. The nephew agreed and adhered to his part of the bargain. After reaching twenty-one he wrote to his uncle asking for the $5,000 stating that he had kept his part of the bargain. The uncle wrote back saying, "I have no doubt but you have, for which you shall have five thousand dollars, as I promised you. I had the money in the bank the day you was twenty-one years old that I intend for you and you shall have the money certain." He went on to describe how hard he had worked for the money and how he hoped William II would not squander it. He also said in the letter that he had purchased fifteen sheep when the nephew was born. After he put them out to pasture repeatedly, they multiplied to a number approaching 600. He promised the sheep to young Bill as well.

After an exchange of correspondence, it was agreed that the uncle should retain the sheep and the money in trust for his nephew. Two years later Uncle Bill died. The executor refused to deliver the money or the sheep because young Bill had given no valuable consideration in return for the uncle's promise.

The court held that the nephew had had a legal right to drink and smoke before twenty-one. Forbearance from this legal right was valuable consideration to support a promise of payment. The promise of the sheep was gratuitous. The matter would be resolved according to whether the gift was completed—that is, document of title or physical possession of the sheep was transferred to William II. Judgment for William II.

A promise to perform or forbear is valuable because people are bound by promises they make that have legal value. Most contracts involve performance or forbearance in the future but are made in advance. Because parties cannot be bound by a performance or forbearance that has not occurred, they are bound by their promises to perform or forbear. This enables the contract to become viable immediately, fixing the rights and duties of the parties in regard to future performance or forbearance.

Both parties must be bound by a legal duty. There must be a mutual obligation. Consideration satisfies this mutual obligation by creating in each party a legal right in return for giving the consideration and a duty in return for receiving it. This is why consideration is probably the most important element of a contract.

EXISTENCE OF CONSIDERATION

Consideration must exist for a contract to be valid. The requirement that consideration be valuable refers to legal value. This criterion was established to resolve conflicts concerning which agreements ought to be enforced. For a contract to be valid, each party must give something of legal value. Social agreements, gifts, and agreements backed by family seals are not elevated to contract status because considerations of this sort have no legal value. Years ago, in the case of a family seal, a person's good name was sufficient consideration to uphold a contract because people knew and trusted one another. The development of commerce has led people to contract with parties throughout the country whom they have never met. This form of progress diminished the significance of the family seal.

As a general rule the law will not look into the adequacy of consideration unless it is grossly one-sided. The reason is that people attach different values to different things, depending upon such variables as tastes, interests, desires, and needs. Personal values are subjective. Whether a person has benefited from a contract depends on subjective values, on how the person feels. The law acknowledges people's freedom to contract and it respects their judgment as to the legal value of the consideration they receive.

EXAMPLE | A man owned a vineyard. Early one morning he saw some men standing idly by; he offered to employ each one for the day in return for a silver piece. They agreed. Later in the day he came upon some other men standing idle. He asked them why they were idle, and they replied that no one had hired them. He instructed them to go to his vineyard to work and said that he would give them just compensation. At the end of the day, he gave each man a silver piece. The men who had begun work in the morning argued that they had received inadequate consideration because those who worked for only one hour had received as much as they themselves did. Are these men correct? No! The law is concerned with the existence of consideration, not its adequacy. The silver piece was valuable consideration, and these men exercised their freedom to contract by agreeing to accept it for a day's work. The fact that someone else worked less and received the same is of no significance because an employer may be as generous as he pleases with his or her own money.

Individuals making imprudent contracts with unfavorable results are not given recourse (unless one has entered into the contract as a result of fraud, duress, or an unconscionable act) because they have exercised their freedom to contract. Only in certain circumstances will people's freedom be restricted and their judgments overruled.

EXAMPLE | A man entered into two contracts: one to borrow a huge sum of money and one to lend a small sum of money. Both loans were to be repaid in two years; however, each conract contained a covenant giving the lender the right to demand payment at any time. Shortly thereafter, hard times fell upon all. The man was called by his lender to repay the debt immediately. When he pleaded with the lender to have patience, the lender forgave him the debt. The man then went to his borrower and demand full payment immediately. The borrower pleaded with him to have patience, but the man would not. What is the fate of the borrower? The convenant in the contract is unconscionable because it is unduly harsh and one-sided; it will be stricken from the contract. The borrower will be allowed the full term to repay the debt.

When money is exchanged the amount given must be equal to the amount received; otherwise the discrepancy constitutes a gift. Allowances are made for accrued interest and other compensating factors, such as advance payment in return for a reduction in interest. People and institutions do not lend money with the expectation of receiving less except when the loan is actually a gift in whole or part or when some other consideration, such as services or property, is given to supplement the reduced payment.

EXAMPLE | A man felt sorry for a poor widow he met. Desiring to share his wealth with her, he told her, "In consideration of the $11,000 which I will give you, you must pay me $1,000." She did as he stated. Is the consideration she gave valuable? No! Where money is concerned, the exchange must be equal; otherwise a gift will be presumed. Here, there is a contract for $1,000 loan and a gift of 10,000

Illusory contracts fail because of extreme inadequacy of consideration where one party is bound by a promise and the other party is not. Illusory promises are unreasonably disproportionate in allowing one party the privilege of acting at will. The power to cancel with notice, or for cause, is not illusory as long as the parties act in good faith.

A promise subject to a future condition, known as an aleatory promise, is valuable consideration and not illusory even though the contract may never materialize.

EXAMPLE | A man contracted with another to purchase the latter's house. The contract contained a clause conditioning the sale of the house upon the purchaser's obtaining a mortgage. This is a form of an aleatory promise. If the contract contained another clause giving the purchaser the right to cancel the contract at will, the purchaser's promise would be illusory.

PRIOR LEGAL OBLIGATION

A promise to pay more than the agreed-upon price for the performance of an existing contract, or a promise to accept less than the amount owed, has no valuable consideration unless something additional is given to serve as consideration. When a person promises to perform an act that he or she is legally obligated to perform, this does not constitute valuable consideration. A contract based on a promise of this sort is not valid and cannot be enforced. This rule concerning preexisting legal obligation applies to people's duty to observe the law; to individuals who have responsibilities through public service and public administrative positions, and to parties bound by contract.

EXAMPLE | A man hired a builder to construct a house for him by July 1 for 140 gold pieces. The man insisted that time was of the essence because he was selling his old house on July 15. The builder, aware of the situation, informed the man in June that the house could not be completed before the end of September unless an additional sum of ten gold pieces was paid. The man agreed to this but later refused to pay. Is he bound by his promise? No! The builder was under a prior legal obligation to build the home for 140 gold pieces. He gave no consideration for the additional ten gold pieces.

A party who requests more money or time to complete a contract is not giving any consideration in return for the other party's consent because the first party is already legally obligated to complete the contract under the original conditions. If the other party acquiesces, that promise is not enforceable. This situation often presents itself in a form of economic duress exerted by a contractor at a point where the owner has no alternative but to allow the contractor to proceed at a price greater than that agreed upon.

There are two exceptions to the rule that a preexisting legal obligation is not sufficient as consideration. First, where a significant change is made in contract, that change will be valuable consideration if it supports a return promise to pay more money or grant more time. The change may include additional work to be performed, alteration in the nature of the work, or performance in a shorter time.

EXAMPLE | Solomon was hire to build a temple. The contract provided that he was to have ten years in which to complete it. After four years he was told of a great celebration that was to occur in the seventh year. Solomon accepted, and, true to his word, the temple was completed in time for the celebration. For his efforts Solomon received only the original contract price. Has he any recourse? Yes! Although Solomon was under a prior legal obligation to build the temple, he gave valuable consideration by performing something that he was not legally obligated to do: finish the temple three years earlier.

Port Chester Elec. Const. Corp. v. HBE Corp.
782 F. Supp. 837 (S.D.N.Y. 1991)

Port Chester Electrical Construction Corporation entered into a subcontract with HBE Corporation for $1,222,000. The original contract work was delayed by significant alterations which amounted to $877,845. Port Chester was compensated for the original work and the alterations. Port Chester sued HBE for the additional costs it incurred in performing the original work because of delay caused by the change.

> The issue is whether Port Chester should be compensated for the additional cost.
>
> The court held, "In sum, Port Chester established that conduct for which it was not responsible and for which HBE was responsible, caused delay in the completion of its base subcontract work. It also established that these delays, which required it to be at the site two and a half years longer than expected, caused increased expense, principally from enhanced labor cost." Judgement for Port Chester.

The second exception to the rule involves unforeseen situations that arise and make performance more difficult. Unforeseen situations also provide sufficient consideration to support a promise to pay more or to grant additional time. The unforeseen event must not have been reasonably apparent to the parties at the time the contract was made. The parties must have been taken by surprise. Unforeseen circumstances generally do not include inclement weather, shortages, price changes, or strikes, because these problems are readily foreseeable by the parties.

EXAMPLE | A wealthy man entrusted a certain sum of money with each of his three employees for a period of seven years. He gave 500 gold pieces to the first, with 1,000 due upon his return; 200 gold gold pieces to the second, with 400 due; and 100 gold pieces to the third, with 200 due. After seven years the wealthy man settled his accounts. The first and second employees fulfilled their promises, but the third man did not. He had buried the money for fear of losing it. He asked the wealthy man to accept less than what he owed. The wealthy man accepted the small sum but then later decided to collect the rest. Once he has accepted the small sum, has he any recourse? Yes! The wealthy man's promise to accept less than what was owed to him is not binding because the third individual gave no consideration to support the promise. Suppose a banking crisis had developed that caused the third individual to bury the money out of fear of losing the principal. Would this qualify as an unforseen occurrence? No! Monetary problems in the banking environment are forseeable and do not excuse the third individual's performance.

American Demolition v. Haperville Hotel
413 S.E 2d 749 (Ga App. 1991)

In demolishing a building for Haperville Hotel, American Demolition encountered a problem of a more extensive foundation than they had anticipated.

The contract provided,

> The intent of the Contract Documents is to include all of the work for the Stipulated Contract Sum and within the Contract Time. . . . any work

> which is obviously necessary to complete the work within the limits established by the Drawings and Specifications, all shall be considered as part of the Contract and shall be executed by the Contractor in the same manner and with the same character of material as other portions of the Contract without extra compensation.

American Demolition did not complete the job. The issue is whether the unanticipated problem qualifies as an unforeseen occurrence that entitles American Demolition to receive additional compensation in order to complete the job.

The court held,

> In order to determine whether American can recover additional money for the unforseen performance costs involved we must look in the contract itself to see who bore the risk of unknown obstacles. The contract here contained no changed conditions clause, unequivocally limited the contract payment to a sum certain, and contained an inspection clause. It is clear from theses provisions that the contract imposed the risk of uncertainty of subsurface conditions on American Demolition. . . . Parties laboring under no disabilities may make contracts on their own terms, and in the absence of fraud or mistake of terms that are illegal or contrary to public policy, they must abide by the contract. The fact that it is unwise or disadvantageous to one party furnishes no reason for disregarding it. . . . Because the contract placed the risk of extra expense on it, American Demolition is not entitled to recover additional compensation just because the work required to be performed was more expensive than it had anticipated.

Judgment for Haperville Hotel.

A person who makes part payment and asks to be relieved from paying in full, after services have been performed, is not giving any consideration for the reduction in price. Even if the part payment is accepted, the balance may still be collected unless the party has been released from his or her legal obligation. Otherwise the reduction in price is valid only when some other form of consideration is given as a substitute for the remainder or when the amount is validly disputed and a settlement called an accord and satisfaction is made. Accord and satisfaction will be discussed later in this chapter.

Parties may release each other from their duties to perform by mutual agreement. One party may release the other party from the obligation to continue performance after that performance has been partially or substantially completed: A party's right to release another is part of the freedom to contract. The release must be in writing, supported by consideration, and signed by the releasing party. In the writing the releasing party must express the intent to discharge the other party from his or her legal obligation. No particular set of words is required to make a release effective, as long as the releasing party's intent is evident. Where the party's intent is clearly conveyed in the writing, the requirement of consideration is not always necessary. For example, the UCC requires delivery of a signed writing, but no consideration is necessary.

PAST CONSIDERATION

Each party must give valuable consideration, either in the present or in the future. Past consideration is legally insufficient to support a present promise because it is no longer valuable. A party wishing to reciprocate at a later date may do so; however, the promise to reciprocate is not enforceable because it is not supported by valuable consideration. The promise is merely gratuitous, or it is one made through a sense of moral obligation. An agreement to return what was given by another in the past, based upon a moral obligation, is admirable but not binding because the necessary legal consideration is not present. There are exceptions to this rule, which will be discussed later.

EXAMPLE | A man was riding along a road when he was attacked by a band of thieves who robbed him and left him for dead. Later two men came by, noticed the injured man, and kept on going. A third man who came by was moved by compassion. He aided the injured man by bringing him to an inn and seeing to it that the injured man was restored to health. Years later the two men met again. The recipient of the Good Samaritan's kindness offered to repay him. The Good Samaritan declined at first, but when man insisted he reluctantly accepted and gave the man his address. The man never repaid the money. Has the Good Samaritan any recourse? No! The man is not bound by his promise. The Good Samaritan's action was past consideration revived by a sense of moral obligation the man felt upon seeing the Good Samaritan again. This moral obligation is sufficient to support the man's promise if he chooses to repay the money, but it is not sufficient to bind him legally to do so.

LOVE AND AFFECTION

Love and affection are not sufficient consideration to enforce a return promise because they have no legal value. There is no legal value because there is no way to measure the value of love and affection.

Love and affection are an important reason why people give gifts. A gift is a transfer of title to property that passes when one party expresses a present intention to transfer property. To do this the donor delivers the property or some form of ownership to another, who then accepts it. Property may be transferred via a gift because of love and affection. However, a gift is not a contract, and a mere promise to give a gift is not enforceable because there is no consideration to support it.

The Story of the Texas Gentleman

There was a man living in Texas who was known throughout the state as the Texas Gentleman. Now, the Texas Gentleman was not an ordinary individual. He was an exceptionally tall man, standing six feet six inches tall, and he seemed even taller when he wore his ten-gallon hat. One Friday morning, on the spur of the moment, the Texas Gentleman decided to visit the Big Apple. He took the weekly special to JFK Airport and the express train to Grand Central Station. The Texas Gentleman stepped out at noon onto Forty-Second Street, where he was unknown to everyone. He wandered aimlessly for a while, but finally, by chance, he met a beautiful young woman who offered to show him the sights of Manhattan. They visited the Empire State Building, the Statue of Liberty, and Rockefeller Center. After their excursion they stopped on a street corner for a momentary rest. It was here that the Texas Gentleman exclaimed, "Darlin', for bein' so kind to me and showin' me all the gorgeous sights, I'd like to express my appreciation to you by buyin' you a few li'l trinkets in this here five-and-dime." The "five-and-dime" he referred to was Tiffany's. They went inside, and the young woman proceeded to select $5,000 worth of trinkets. The Texas Gentleman did not bat an eye. He opened his checkbook and began to write a check for the full amount. The cashier beckoned to the manager, who informed the stranger that his credit must be verified before the check could be accepted. At this time it was after 4 P.M. in New York, which meant it was after 3 P.M. in Texas, and the Texas banks were closed.

The manager anxiously explained his position because he did not wish to lose the sale. The Texas Gentleman interrupted the manager: "Sir, I understand your position. You don't know me, and here I'm gonna write out a check to you for $5,000. I tell you what we'll do. Give me that little box over there and we'll stuff these trinkets in it. I'll mark my name in big red letters on the box. Bright and early Monday morning, we'll be by, and by then you could have checked my credit balance." The manager was happy, the young woman was happy, everybody was happy. The young woman pranced away with the Texas Gentleman, holding tightly to his arm. Bright and early Monday morning, the Texas Gentleman came sauntering through the door wearing his ten-gallon hat, with the young woman at his side. The manager hastened to greet them. "Sir," he exclaimed, "we checked with your bank and you do have an account, but nowhere near $5,000!" With that the young woman began to scream and yell as she stormed out the door. The Texas Gentleman was unmoved by all of this. The manager began to apologize, but he was quickly interrupted by the Texas Gentleman who said, "Sir, never you mind, 'cause thanks to you I just had one helluva weekend."

Does the young woman have any recourse against the Texas Gentleman? No, because his promise to buy the trinkets was merely gratuitous. Consideration was lacking on her part, because love and affection are not deemed legally sufficient.

Even though a promise to give a gift is unenforceable, if a gift is given and title has passed, the party receiving it is not obligated to return the gift or any other form of consideration upon request.

In a social agreement, parties have no intention to make their promises legally binding. They intend to carry them through and usually they do. The moral and social obligations inherent in a social promise are often sufficient. Society has agreed, as a matter of public policy, that no legal right or duty arises from a social agreement. This permits social engagements to be more free and less restricted than business arrangements—a fundamental distinction between the two.

EXAMPLE | A man was invited to a wedding banquet in another town. He traveled at great expense to reach the reception, only to be refused admission. Is he entitled to his travel expenses or damages for the embarrassment he suffered? No! A social invitation is not binding on either party. Although social pressure is usually sufficient to enforce the invitation or engagement, it may be terminated at a whim without recourse.

EXCEPTIONS TO CONSIDERATION

Even though consideration is one of the requirements of a valid contract, there are some exceptions to this requirement: **MECCA**.

Moral obligation
Estoppel (promissory)
Commercial Code exceptions
Composition of creditors
Accord and satisfaction

Moral Obligation

Moral obligation, that sense of fairness and responsibility toward others, may cause a person to revive a past debt discharged by the statute of limitations or because of infancy. The moral obligation, by itself, is not legally binding. To be legally enforceable, the promise to repay must be in writing.

A statute of limitations is a time limit within which a lawsuit must be brought by an aggrieved party. The time limit varies depending upon the area of the law involved. A debt avoided through the defense of infancy may be ratified by the debtor when he or she reaches majority. The statute of limitations and the defense of infancy safeguard individuals from lawsuits resulting in possible judgments against them. This safeguard is a legal one that a debtor may waive in writing after the statute of limitations has run out, or—in the case of infancy—when he or she reaches majority.

The moral obligation to repay the debt always exists, but it is not legally enforceable until the new promise is made in writing. A writing is required in most states to evidence the intention of the debtor. The writing may be informal and may be explained by other evidence. When the new promise is made in writing, the past consideration supported by the moral obligation will revive the original debt. Part performance will also revive an old debt and create an implied promise to repay the balance. It is within the debtor's purview to dispense, in whole or part, with the legal protection afforded. The debtor, although under no legal obligation, may choose to repay part of the debt or may condition repayment on an event such as attainment of financial stability. This condition must be satisfied before the creditor has a right to repayment of the debt.

EXAMPLE | A creditor had two debtors: One owed him a great sum and the other owed a small sum. Both of the debtors were infants who had no money with which to repay the debts. The creditor forgave them both. Upon reaching majority the debtor who owed the greater sum promised orally to repay the forgiven debt, while the debtor who owed the lesser sum made his promise to repay in writing. Thereafter both of the debtors changed their minds. Has the creditor any recourse? The creditor has no recourse against the person who made the oral promise. An oral promise to repay a past debt that was forgiven is not enforceable. The creditor has recourse against the person who promised in writing to repay the debt. The writing coupled with the moral obligation revives the past debt.

Estoppel (Promissory)

When a person changes his or her position in reliance on a promise and that change in position is foreseeable, the person making the promise will be stopped from asserting that there is no consideration to enforce the contract. This is the doctrine of *promissory estoppel*. It is equitable in that enforcement of a promise may be upheld for reasons of fairness and justice even though the recipient of the promise gave no consideration in return. To invoke the doctrine of promissory estoppel, the person making the promise must reasonably expect it to motivate the other person to change his or her position by taking some substantial and justifiable action in reliance on the promise. The person taking the action must be going to suffer a detriment from his or her reliance on that promise if it is not carried out. This is the reason for enforcing the promise—to prevent the person relying on the promise from suffering a loss.

The doctrine of promissory estoppel extends to charitable, religious, and educational organizations that ask people to pledge money for particular causes. Such organizations rely upon these subscriptions to fill their needs. This reliance is justifiable. Although the charitable organization is giving no consideration in return, potential donors will be bound by their promises under the promissory estoppel exception.

Commercial Code Exceptions

The UCC has provided certain exceptions where the need for consideration may be dispensed with to allow for the smooth operation of contracts for the sale of goods.

Modifications   Modification of a contract for the sale of goods requires no new consideration if it is made in good faith. The good-faith requirement protects each party against any unconscionable modification of the contract attempted by the other party. The modification may be oral unless the contract is required to be in writing by the Statute of Frauds. Also, where a contract provides that all changes must be in writing, a party to the contract who is a consumer must be advised in the written contract that oral modifications are not binding. This rule protects the consumer against oral misrepresentations.

Modifications of contractual provisions occur too often for parties to be required to draft a new contract each time an alteration is made. The UCC has simplified the consideration requirement by providing that the original consideration given to create the contract will support any future modification made in good faith. This enables the parties to make adjustments, as needed, at any point during the contract. By making it compulsory for all alterations to be made in good faith, the UCC has developed a built-in safeguard for the freedom to contract.

Firm Offers   Firm offers are similar to option contracts except that no consideration is given to support them. A firm offer must be made in a signed writing and may be irrevocable for up to three months at the offeror's discretion.

Discharge of Debts   A claim for breach of contract for a debt that is due and certain may be discharged in whole or in part when a release is signed and delivered by the party against whom the breach was committed. Under the UCC the release is binding upon the party who made it even though there is no consideration to support it.

Composition of Creditors

A composition of creditors is a procedure where two or more creditors may agree to accept less than the amount the debtor owes to avoid the debtor's filing for bankruptcy. The percentage received under such an agreement is generally greater than that received under a bankruptcy settlement because of fees and expenses. Although the debtor is giving no valuable consideration for the creditor's agreement, the agreement is enforceable because of the debtor's forbearance from filing for bankruptcy.

EXAMPLE | A widow who had always given from her want, unlike others who gave only from their surplus, could not meet her creditor's demands. She informed them that she would have to declare bankruptcy. All of her creditors gathered together and mutually agreed to accept half of what was owed. The widow payed the creditors according to this agreement. Are the creditors bound by this agreement, or can they sue for the balance? The composition of creditors is bound by the agreement to accept less than the amount owed to them. The widow's consideration for this agreement is her forbearance from filing for bankruptcy.

Accord and Satisfaction

Accord and satisfaction occur when one party substitutes some other form of consideration for that which was originally promised and the other party accepts the substituted consideration as full satisfaction of the legal duty owed. When there is a valid dispute over the amount owed, the cashing of a check marked "paid in full" operates as an accord and satisfaction. The party sending the check is offering substituted performance in return for a release from claim, and the receiving party is accepting the accord as full satisfaction of the debt owed.

REVIEW QUESTIONS

1. Define consideration, promissory estoppel, and accord and satisfaction.

2. List and explain the exceptions to consideration.

3. The Atkinses bought a lot through a realtor, Mrs. Kirkpatrick. It turned out that the lot was not buildable. The Atkinses sued the realtor, claiming failure of consideration—that they did not get what they bargained for. What result? *Atkins* v. *Kirkpatrick*, 823 S.W. 2d 547 (Tenn. App. 1991).

4. John Kottis agreed to sell shares of stock in Hammersmith Farms to Benedetto Cerilli for $1,360,000. A deposit for $12,000 was given by Cerilli. When the closing did not take place, negotiations continued, but a dispute arose over possession of the deposit. Cerilli contended that he had agreed to let Kottis keep the deposit in return for canceling the deal. Does this constitute an accord and satisfaction? *Kottis* v. *Cerilli*, 612 A. 2d 661 (R.I. 1992).

5. Dennis Harris was police chief of Plano, Illinois, when Bud Johnson was elected mayor. Harris asked Johnson if Johnson wanted Harris to remain police chief; if not he would take advantage of some other opportunity offering similar pay. Johnson told Harris that he would appoint him if he stayed on, but Johnson later terminated Harris's employment. Harris was forced to take another position at a substantial reduction in pay. Harris sued Johnson for breach of promise, asked for the difference in pay as the measure of damages, and cited the promissory estoppel doctrine. What result? *Harris* v. *Johnson*, 578 N.E. 2d 1326 (Ill. App. 2 Dist. 1991)

6. In formulating its bid to become general contractor for expansion of a waste treatment facility in the city of Austin, Clearwater Constructors relied on Westech's bid to supply water treatment equipment. Westech's subsequent inability to perform caused Clearwater to purchase the equipment elsewhere at greater cost. Would the doctrine of promissory estoppel apply? *Westech Eng.* v. *Clearwater Constructors*, 835 S.W. 2d 190 (Tx. App.–Austin 1990).

7. Frederick Weisman promised to take care of Miss Bower's living expenses and salary until she got married or moved away from the United States. Weisman claims that love and affection are not legally cognizable considerations. Bower responds that her agreement not to exercise her right to end the unilateral contract is adequate consideration. What result? *Bower* v. *Weisman*, 650 F. Supp. 1415 (S.D.N.Y. 1986).

8. Elvis Presley, the king of rock 'n' roll, promised to pay off the mortgage on a house owned by Laverne Alden, the mother of his girlfriend, Ginger Alden. Elvis died unexpectedly on August 16, 1977. His promise had not been fulfilled. Alden sued Elvis's estate for $40,000, the balance of the mortgage. What result? *Alden* v. *Presley*, 637 S.W. 2d 862 (Tenn. 1982).

9. Joel Hill bought a franchise from Mobile Auto Trim for $42,000 plus 5 percent of the franchise's gross revenues. For two and a half years, Hill contacted car dealerships and made car trim repairs. After he failed to pay his franchise fees

for months, Mobile terminated the franchise agreement. When Hill contacted a prior customer about hiring him, Mobile sought to prevent Hill from competing with them under the terms of its noncompetition covenant, which he had signed when he bought the franchise. Mobile contended that its trim services were trade secrets. Hill argued that he had obtained his skills as an auto trim repairman prior to his franchise agreement with Mobile. Did Mobile give valuable consideration to Hill in return for his promise not to compete? *Hill* v. *Mobile Auto Trim, Inc.,* 725 S.W. 2d 168 (Tex. 1987).

10. The city of Lake Forest published a document entitled "Career Opportunities." It showed that the position of firefighter was open to people between the ages of twenty-one and thirty-five. Clifford Ekkert completed the required tests and was notified that his name appeared on the eligibility list. At this point Ekkert who was thirty-five, was informed that he was ineligible because state law prohibited those thirty-five or older from being accepted into the state pension fund. Ekkert sued on the basis of promissory estoppel. What result? *Ekkert* v. *City of Lake Forest,* 588 N.E. 2d 482 (Ill. App. 2 Dist. 1992).

12

Legal Capacity

Introduction
Special Rights of an Infant
Restitution
Necessities
Exceptions to the Defense of Infancy

Misrepresentation of Age
Ratification
Special Rights of the Insane
Review Questions

INTRODUCTION

Legal capacity refers to the ability of a party to enter into a valid contract. It is one of the elements of a contract. The ability to enter into a contract refers to the mental state of the party. When people enter into contracts, legal obligations arise, and the parties must have the requisite legal capacity to be bound by these obligations. To be competent to contract, the parties must intend to enter into a contract fully aware that their promise will create certain rights and duties. They must be responsible for their promises and the resulting actions. This will ensure that performance of their promises will be completed in accordance with the terms of the contract. All parties are presumed to be competent. The fulfillment of the requirements of legal age and sanity give added strength to the presumption that the parties are capable of entering into a contractual relationship. This presumption is rebuttable: One may disprove it by raising the appropriate contractual defenses.

If a person enters into a contract without the requisite capacity, the contract will be voidable. A voidable contract is legally enforceable unless one party has a special right to rescind the contract and decides to exercise that right. Rescission has the effect of canceling the contract and returning the parties to status quo—the position they were in before the contract was made. The special right to rescind is held by a party who has a viable contractual defense. We are specifically concerned with contractual defenses pertaining to lack of capacity. Parties who lack the legal capacity to make a valid contract, such as infants and insane individuals, can invoke their special right to rescind—infants by their own discretion, and the insane by their guardians.

136

SPECIAL RIGHTS OF AN INFANT

In most states any individual under age eighteen is legally termed an *infant*, or a minor. Minors do not have the legal capacity to contract because they lack the experience to understand the ramifications of contracts and to make sound judgments about them. Actually, they do not have the necessary business sense to deal with adults. This does not apply to minors who are in business for themselves. The defense of infancy gives an individual the right to rescind a contract at any time during minority or within a reasonable time after reaching majority. The real purpose of the defense is to discourage adults from entering into contracts with minors except for necessities such as food, clothing, and shelter. The minor may set forth his or her infant status by exercising the special right to rescind, or by raising it as a defense in a lawsuit for damages resulting from breach of contract. This is to protect minors against adults who might take advantage of them. The special right to rescind assures the minor of a fair deal. The minor is given the opportunity to decide if the contract is really for his or her betterment; if not, it can be abrogated. Only a minor can abrogate a contract; the minor's parents or guardian may not raise the defense on behalf of the minor, nor can people who employ minors to act for them. However, a personal representative of a minor's estate may exercise the special right to rescind or raise the defense of infancy in any situation where the minor would have had that right.

When a minor decides to rescind a contract, the whole contract must be rescinded, not part of it. The decision may be made at any point, whether the contract is fully or partially completed. Upon rescinding the contract, the minor is entitled to a return of the consideration given.

EXAMPLE | Little Boy Blue is auditioning for the lead role in a high-school musical entitled *Come Blow Your Horn*. He purchases a horn at the Pied Piper's musical instrument store, figuring that he will get the part. When the director realizes that Little Boy Blue cannot play a note, he gives the part to someone else. Little Boy Blue returns the horn, but the Pied Piper refuses to give him his money back. Can Little Boy Blue blow the whistle on the Pied Piper? Yes! He may rescind the contract because of his special status of infancy, and he is entitled to a return of his consideration.

RESTITUTION

In most states an adult is entitled to a return of the consideration belonging to him or her only when it is still in the minor's possession. When it is not, the adult does not get the item back and has no recourse against the minor for its loss. The rationale is that the importance of protecting a minor overrides the potential financial loss to an adult. Adults contract with minors at their own risk. They must run this risk, or there would be nothing to discourage them because they would be assured of getting their consideration back. This prevails even though minors may take advantage of their special status. As a matter of public policy, an adult's rights are subordinate to a minor's rights.

An adult may protect himself or herself by requiring proof of legal age or, when deciding to contract with a minor, by requiring the minor's parents to act as sureties guaranteeing payment of the debt. The minor may still abrogate the contract, but his or her parents will be responsible.

Increasingly, though, courts have been looking to the circumstances surrounding a contract to see if the minor actually received a benefit and was treated fairly. If this is the case, the minor is required to forgo part of his or her consideration. This is to pay for the reasonable benefit to the minor or the loss the adult sustains.

EXAMPLE | Jack and Jill were sweethearts. They were both sixteen. As a surprise for Easter, Jack bought Jill a large ceramic Easter egg from a gift shop. Jill's apartment had a beautiful terrace overlooking Cameron Lake. Jill sat the egg on the terrace wall. A blustery wind developed and blew the egg off the wall. It crashed into a thousand pieces. Jack and Jill fetched a pail and picked up all the pieces. They tried to put the egg back together again, but their attempt was unsuccessful. Jack returned the pieces to the gift shop, but the shop refused to reimburse him. Has Jack any recourse? Yes! In most states, Jack would be entitled to a return of his consideration because he is an minor. The fact that the gift shop's consideration is returned in pieces is part of the risk the shop must accept in dealing with minors. In states that follow the modern trend and take into account the depreciation of the consideration while it was in the minor's possession, Jack would not receive much in return because the egg was cracked.

NECESSITIES

Necessities are the things that are needed for an infant's sustenance. The definition of a necessity varies according to the infant's lifestyle, particularly financial and social status. Minors are liable for the reasonable value of the necessities furnished to them by merchants. The reasonable value of the necessities may be no higher than the contract price. Clothing, food, shelter, education, and medical expenses are categories generally included under the heading of necessities. However, not everything that falls into these categories is a necessity. A raincoat would be considered a necessity, but not a mink coat. A hamburger and a coke would be necessities, too, but not caviar and champagne. Most states do not view cars as necessities where minors are concerned; however, some states make exceptions for cars used in work or as transportation to and from work. The reason a minor may not assert the defense of infancy against a request for payment for necessities is to encourage adults to provide minors with the things they need.

EXAMPLE | Goldilocks, while hiking through the backwoods of Vermont, decides to stop at the Three Bears Inn. She enjoys a nice dish of cereal and a warm bed. The next morning she refuses to pay for the room and board, asserting infancy as a defense. Is the defense applicable? No! Food and shelter are necessities, and a minor is liable for the reasonable value of necessities.

138

...self or herself by requiring proof of legal age or, when deciding a minor, by requiring the minor's parents to act as sureties guaranteeing of the debt. The minor may still abrogate the contract, but his or her ... responsible.

Increasingly, though, courts have been looking to the circumstances surrounding ... to see if the minor actually received a benefit and was treated fairly. If this is ... case, the minor is required to forgo part of his or her consideration. This is to pay ... for the reasonable benefit to the minor or the loss the adult sustains.

EXAMPLE | Jack and Jill were sweethearts. They were both sixteen. As a surprise for Easter, Jack bought Jill a large ceramic Easter egg from a gift shop. Jill's apartment had a beautiful terrace overlooking Cameron Lake. Jill sat the egg on the terrace wall. A blustery wind developed and blew the egg off the wall. It crashed into a thousand pieces. Jack and Jill fetched a pail and picked up all the pieces. They tried to put the egg back together again, but their attempt was unsuccessful. Jack returned the pieces to the gift shop, but the shop refused to reimburse him. Has Jack any recourse? Yes! In most states, Jack would be entitled to a return of his consideration because he is an minor. The fact that the gift shop's consideration is returned in pieces is part of the risk the shop must accept in dealing with minors. In states that follow the modern trend and take into account the depreciation of the consideration while it was in the minor's possession, Jack would not receive much in return because the egg was cracked.

NECESSITIES

Necessities are the things that are needed for an infant's sustenance. The definition of a necessity varies according to the infant's lifestyle, particularly financial and social status. Minors are liable for the reasonable value of the necessities furnished to them by merchants. The reasonable value of the necessities may be no higher than the contract price. Clothing, food, shelter, education, and medical expenses are categories generally included under the heading of necessities. However, not everything that falls into these categories is a necessity. A raincoat would be considered a necessity, but not a mink coat. A hamburger and a coke would be necessities, too, but not caviar and champagne. Most states do not view cars as necessities where minors are concerned; however, some states make exceptions for cars used in work or as transportation to and from work. The reason a minor may not assert the defense of infancy against a request for payment for necessities is to encourage adults to provide minors with the things they need.

EXAMPLE | Goldilocks, while hiking through the backwoods of Vermont, decides to stop at the Three Bears Inn. She enjoys a nice dish of cereal and a warm bed. The next morning she refuses to pay for the room and board, asserting infancy as a defense. Is the defense applicable? No! Food and shelter are necessities, and a minor is liable for the reasonable value of necessities.

Parents have a duty to support an infant until the infant reaches majority. Adults supplying necessities to a minor have a legal right (a cause of action) to demand payment from the parent of the minor. Parents in turn do not have the right to raise the defense of infancy on the minor's behalf or to exercise the minor's special right to rescind. This is especially true when the parent guarantees payment for the minor's contract.

EXAMPLE | Hansel and Gretel were both seventeen when they married. They purchased a split-level house from an Englishman, who required that their parents sign a guarantee of payment on the minor's contract. When Hansel and Gretel defaulted, their parents refused to pay, raising the defense of infancy. Are the parents still liable? Yes! They are liable for payment because the defense of infancy is not available to them.

EXCEPTIONS TO THE DEFENSE OF INFANCY

Certain special contracts are designated by some states as exempt from the special rights of minor. There are two rationales for the denial of the defense of infancy. The first applies to contracts that benefit minors. Where the benefit to a minor outweighs the protection afforded by the defense, the defense will not be granted. This is to encourage adults to make such contracts readily available to minors. The contracts to which this rationale applies include life and health insurance contracts; loans; employment agency contracts; contracts with common carriers, such as airlines and railway and bus companies; and court-approved athletic and entertainment contracts. Court-approved contracts for child entertainers and athletes are enforceable and can be rescinded by the minor only with the court's permission. The court is a party to the contract.

The second rationale for the denial of the defense of infancy concerns institutions and business arrangements and the maintenance of certain standards through the enforcement of commitments. This group of exceptions encompasses the institutions of marriage and the armed forces. It also applies to business contracts involving partnerships and good-faith purchasers and to the buying and selling of corporate stock.

Marriage is the commitment of two individuals to a lifetime of mutual devotion. The commitment must be honored for the institution to be sound. A minor who enters into a marriage cannot annul that marriage on the basis of age alone. In a case where the parents did not consent, the marriage may be annulled by either the minor or the parents. The need to protect the institution of marriage outweighs the need to protect the minor. The same rationale applies to minors who enlist in the armed services.

A minor who enters into a partnership will not be able to rescind contracts made by the partnership with third parties. Although a minor may rescind a partnership agreement, the minor is personally liable for all claims made while he or she is still a partner, up to the amount of his or her investment in the partnership.

EXAMPLE | Jack and his friend, the Giant, enter into a partnership to sell beans to restaurants. Jack is a minor. One night someone cuts down all the beanstalks. When the partnership is sued by the restaurants for nondelivery of the beans, Jack immediately terminates the partnership and refuses to be liable for any debts on grounds of infancy. Do all the debts fall on the Giant's shoulders? No! A minor who enters into a partnership is presumed to have sufficient business sense to be treated as an adult. Jack may terminate the partnership, but he will not be relieved of his responsibility for debts incurred by the partnership before his termination. To place the total burden on the Giant's shoulders would be unjust.

The UCC provides that a good-faith purchaser who buys goods from a third party and is unaware that they came from a minor may retain them. The purchase must be made in good faith in order for the minor's right of rescission to be nullified. This encourages people to buy without worrying that their contracts could be voided by third-party infants. This UCC rule applies only to the sale of goods by minors, not to the sale of real estate.

EXAMPLE | Little Bo Peep lost her sheep and did not know where to find them. She later discovered that the sheep had wandered to an animal nursery run by a man known as Big Bad Wolfe. Wolfe offered to buy the sheep from Little Bo Peep. She accepted but later had a change of heart. She recovered all her sheep except a little lamb that Mary had bought from Big Bad Wolfe as a good-faith purchaser. Does Little Bo Peep regain her sheep, or does Mary have a little lamb? The UCC gives a good-faith purchaser precedence over an infant seeking to reclaim goods. So Mary has a little lamb.

A contract for the purchase or sale of corporate stock cannot be abrogated by a minor on the basis of infancy. Minors have the right to own stock and to buy and sell it. In return for this right, a minor must be bound; otherwise the minor may be unjustly enriched by rescinding the contract. This could happen in cases where stock has decreased in value.

EXAMPLE | Snow White, who is seventeen, gets a hot tip from her boyfriend about the stock of the Seven Dwarfs' Corporation, which manufactures apparel for little people. Snow White calls a brokerage company and asks them to purchase 1,000 shares of the stock at $7 a share. The brokerage company purchases the stock, and Snow White sends them the money. Two weeks later the stock drops to $2 per share. Snow White decides to get rid of her boyfriend and sues the brokerage company for return of her consideration. Will she be able to recover the money? No! The purchase of stock by a minor is an exception to the general rule permitting a minor to rescind a contract. It would be unfair to make the brokerage company bear the loss.

MISREPRESENTATION OF AGE

In most states the defense of infancy is still available to a minor who has misrepresentated his or her age to an adult. This occurs when a minor claims to be an adult and the adult is justified in believing this claim. However, some states have enacted statutes to prevent this situation because intentional misrepresentation of age on the minor's part constitutes fraud. The purpose behind the defense is to discourage contracts between minors and adults. But in these states, if a minor fraudulently induces the adult to enter a contract, the courts will deny the minor protection: A minor will not be allowed to defraud an adult and reap the benefits. In fact, a few states hold the minor liable in tort for the fraud committed. Generally, though, the court's determination will depend on whether the adult has suffered any loss, including the loss of profits. The minor's fraud gives the adult a special right to rescind the contract. This right is discretionary, and the adult may exercise it if the contract is not beneficial. Proving fraud, however, is an arduous task, particularly if there is no writing to evidence the fraudulent intent on the minor's part.

EXAMPLE | Sleeping Beauty was hired as a model to do television commercials for a well-known mattress company. She signed a contract stating that she was eighteen. The company later discovered that she was only sixteen and canceled the contract. Has Sleeping Beauty any recourse? No! An adult or company who is fraudulently induced into entering a contract by a minor who has misrepresented his or her age has the special right to rescind the contract.

RATIFICATION

Ratification is the intention to be bound by the contract; it is manifested through the objective actions of the infant. Upon reaching majority or within a reasonable time thereafter, individuals may ratify all contracts made during their minority. Ratification may be made through words; through action, such as making payments; or through inaction, such as receiving benefits. Some courts hold that receiving benefits alone is not sufficient to establish ratification without some positive action or statement on the minor's part; it depends on whether the contract was completed during the minor's minority. If the contract was completed and the minor retained benefits, ratification will be implied. If the contract was not completed, then some overt act or statement on the minor's part is usually necessary. The rule applies to cases involving payments that a minor makes on an installment contract after reaching majority. If the minor wishes to preserve the right to rescind, his or her actions should support the intent to rescind and not be inconsistent with that intent. Otherwise ratification may result. Ratification is absolutely binding on a minor once it is made, and it is retroactive to the date when the contract was made. A special rule applies to real property contracts; it requires that a minor wait until majority either to ratify or to rescind the contract.

EXAMPLE | Jack, a seventeen-year-old boy, spotted a tall candlestick while browsing through a gift shop at Christmastime. The shop owner asked Jack why he wanted such a tall candlestick. Jack replied that he was going to try out for the college track team as a hurdler and needed something to practice with. The candlestick cost $100, and Jack paid for it in full. Jack turned eighteen in January, but it was not until spring that he first used the candlestick.

Jack was nimble and Jack was quick, but Jack could not clear the candlestick. In fact he fell on it and broke it in half. Jack brought the candlestick back, but the owner refused to refund Jack's money. Has Jack any recourse? No! The contract was completed during Jack's minority and impliedly ratified in January when he reached eighteen. Suppose Jack had agreed to pay off the candlestick in ten monthly installments and made payments until April. Would the result be different? No! The installments paid after January, when Jack reached eighteen, would be a positive act on his part constituting ratification.

SPECIAL RIGHTS OF THE INSANE

Insane persons are given a special right to rescind so others cannot take advantage of them during their incapacity. There are two types of insane persons. The first, a judicially declared incompetent, is pronounced insane by the court. All contracts made by a judicially declared incompetent are void, and a void contract is unenforceable in a court of law.

EXAMPLE | The Mad Hatter, a judicially declared incompetent, entered Wonderland Fashion Store and asked Alice, the owner, to pick out a half dozen of the most expensive hats in the store. The Mad Hatter paid by check. His court-appointed guardian stopped payment on the check and returned the hats. Does Alice in Wonderland have any recourse? No! All contracts entered into by a judicially declared incompetent are unenforceable.

The second type of insane person—a nonjudicially declared incompetent—has not been reviewed by a court; however, the person's incompetent nature is evident to a reasonable observer. Temporary insanity is an example of nonjudicially declared incompetence. A person may be temporarily insane while intoxicated or under the influence of narcotics or hallucinogenic drugs. Contracts made by nonjudicially declared incompetents, including the temporarily insane, are voidable and may be rescinded by the person lacking capacity.

EXAMPLE | Cinderella, a poor unfortunate housemaid, has a few too many one night. She races out to a department store and buys a whole new outfit, including a pair of glass slippers, spending most of her savings in the process. Her condition is quite apparent. She gets into a taxi and tells the driver she is in a hurry to meet Prince Charming at the Debutante Ball. She thinks the taxi is actually a pumpkin carriage driven by mice. After having a great time at the ball, she realizes it is almost midnight. She hurries home and, in her excitement, loses one of the glass slippers. The next day she receives the bill from the department store, which sobers her up very quickly. Is she accountable for the merchandise? Cinderella was temporarily insane due to her consumption of alcohol. She may rescind the contract as long as she is able to return all the merchandise. Cinderella had better hope that her Prince Charming comes back on the scene soon with the other glass slipper.

The nonjudicially declared incompetent may make a binding contract during a lucid interval, and the defense of insanity would not apply. There are some people suffering from psychological disorders who do understand the nature of a transaction. Their contracts are binding. Thus, not all contracts made by insane persons are voidable.

EXAMPLE | Mother Hubbard was a senile old woman known to be tight with a buck. One day she went to Shoetown and purchased five pairs of rather expensive shoes for $250. When she received the bill, she refused to pay. She appeared quite normal when she bought the shoes. Is Mother Hubbard responsible for payment because she entered into the contract during a lucid interval, when she was capable of understanding the contract? Whether the contract is binding depends on her objective actions at the time the contract was made, including her appearance, demeanor, and emotional behavior together with what she said when making the purchase.

When exercising the right to rescind, an incompetent person must make restitution. If the incompetent person is unable to return the consideration, the defense of insanity may be disallowed. This situation occurs where the other party made the contract in good faith, without knowledge of the incompetent person's state of mind. Knowledge of incompetency is measured by objective actions, not the state of mind of the alleged incompetent. The incompetent person, like a minor, is liable for the reasonable value of necessities furnished.

The person alleging incompetency has the burden of proving it. To establish incompetency, a person must show either that he or she lacked sufficient mental capacity to understand the nature of the transaction or that he or she entered into the contract because of an uncontrollable reaction brought on by some mental illness and that this was known to the other party. A person who succeeds in proving his or her incompetency still may not be able to disaffirm the contract because the incompetency may not have been reasonably evident to the other party. This is an objective test. The decision will turn on whether the person dealing with the alleged incompetent is reasonable in his or her belief that the latter had sufficient capacity to appreciate the nature of the transaction and whether the contract was fair and reasonable. Contracts of the insane may be ratified or disaffirmed by the insane person when he or she regains sanity or by a legally appointed guardian or a personal representative.

Norfolk Southern Corp. v. Smith
414 S.E. 2d 485 (Ga. 1992)

Kenneth Smith was injured on the job in August 1985. Subsequently he became depressed and began seeing a psychologist. In November 1985 he went to the office of his employer, Norfolk Southern

Corporation, and fired gunshots. He was hospitalized for three weeks for his mental condition. At Smith's request, the following month he signed two releases, one for resigning and one as a settlement for his on-the-job injuries. He received $25,000 for each. Now Smith claims that he is not bound by the releases because of his mental state at the time he signed them.

The issue is whether Smith ratified the settlements after he regained his capacity. The court held,

> [I]t is well established that a contract executed by a person without the requisite mental capacity may be ratified expressly or by implication after that person is restored to mental capacity.
>
> However, there is evidence in the record other than the spending of the proceeds that indicates appellee at least implicitly ratified the releases. This evidence includes certain statements appellee made to various persons indicating his approval of the settlement, and also includes the passage of more than fifteen months between executing the releases and filing the present action.

Judgment for Norfolk Southern.

EXAMPLE   Little Red Riding Hood was mildly retarded. She lived with her grandmother, who was her legally appointed guardian. July 11 was Grandma's birthday, so Little Red Riding Hood went to a flea market to find a present for her. She purchased a set of glasses from Mr. Wolfe by writing a check in the amount of $150. The check bounced. Grandma was about to advise Little Red Riding Hood to disaffirm the contract when she discovered that the glasses were Waterford crystal. Grandma anxiously paid the $150. Does this constitute ratification? Yes! This act by Grandma, Red Riding Hood's legal guardian, amounted to ratification.

In Re Ellis
822 S.W. 2d 602 (Tenn. App. 1991)

Nellie Ellis, the eighty-five-year old owner of Ellis Funeral Home, suffered from Alzheimer's disease. Her estate was worth $1,670,000, with annual income of $160,000. Nellie requested Clyde Green, an employee, and his wife to move into an apartment above the funeral home and take care of her. This they did. Nellie executed a power of attorney in favor of Imogene Green, and in it she specified that Imogene should serve as her conservator if ever required. Walter Clark, Nellie's attorney, drafted the document.

In the following year Nellie's condition worsened. Her sister objected to Imogene Green's being appointed conservator because of the potential for self-dealing. Mr. Clark, without being asked, filed a counterpetition on behalf of Mrs. Green and Mrs. Ellis, claiming to be representing Mrs. Ellis at her request. Mrs. Ellis's sister objected to Mr. Clark's appearance, citing a conflict of interest.

Did Nellie Ellis have the capacity to contract for Mr. Clark's services?

The court held, "The ability to act 'with judgement and discretion' is not required in order to be able to contract. All that is required is that the party understand in a reasonable manner the nature and consequences of his or her transactions."

The court continued, "The uncontradicted medical evidence shows that Mrs. Ellis' mental condition had 'declined' and in June, 1990 was 'chronic' and 'poor.' Mrs. Ellis' attending physicians stated that she required a guardian to handle her financial affairs. The only reasonable conclusion to be drawn is that Mr. Clark cannot undertake to represent Mrs. Ellis at this stage of the proceedings because he failed to show that she is capable of retaining counsel and that she has retained him." Judgment for the estate of Ellis.

REVIEW QUESTIONS

1. Define legal capacity, infancy, necessities, and insanity.

2. What are the different types of necessities?

3. Wesley, owner of a funeral home, had Marilyn, age thirteen, sign a promissory note for the payment of funeral services for her father. A judgment was obtained against Marilyn for nonpayment of the note. A year after reaching majority, Marilyn discovered that her credit rating had been tarnished by the judgment against her. She brought an action immediately to disaffirm the promissory note because of her infancy. What result? If Marilyn is allowed to rescind, must she return the casket? *Terrace Company* v. *Calhoun*, 37 Ill. App. 3d 757, 347 N.E. 2d 315 (1976).

4. Lee, an infant, purchased a car from Haydocy Pontiac for $2,500 with a $100 down payment. She signed a statement certifying that she was twenty-one years of age. The car was stolen a few months later. Lee refuses to pay the balance of the contract. What result? *Haydocy Pontiac, Inc.* v. *Lee*, 19 Ohio App. 2d 217 (1969).

5. In 1954, Robertson, an infant, bought a pickup truck from Julian Pontiac. At that time he was three weeks away from reaching majority. Over a month later

electrical difficulties caused a fire that destroyed the truck. Robertson wishes to rescind the contract and recover his down payment. Pontiac asserts that Robertson is bound by the contract because the truck is a necessity. Robertson did not use the truck for work. What result? *Robertson* v. *King,* 225 Ark. 276, 280 S.W. 2d 402 (1955).

6. In 1965, Sheehan Buick sold a Riviera to Rose for $5,000. Rose was a minor at the time. At the time of the sale, Rose handled all negotiations. His parents advanced part of the cash. He used the car for school, business, and social purposes. Buick claimed that the car was a necessity and that the contract could not be rescinded. What result? If disaffirmation was allowed, should Buick be entitled to the value of depreciation while the car was in Rose's possession? *Rose* v. *Sheehan Buick, Inc.,* 204 So. 2d 903 (Fla. D. Ct. App. 1967).

7. Hanks owned farmland in Nebraska, a portion of which he used for a coal business. Hanks sold one-fourth of the coal lands to McNeil Coal Corporation in 1937. In 1940 Hanks was judicially declared insane and his son was appointed conservator of the estate. The son contended that his father had been insane at the time the contract was made. He sought to have the sale of the coal lands rescinded. The father had been involved with religious cults at the time, and his behavior often had been erratic. However, those who had business dealings with him testified that Hanks had acted rationally. What result? *Hanks* v. *McNeil Coal Corporation,* 114 Colo. 578, 168 P. 2d (1946).

8. Paolino, an infant, agreed to guarantee payment of a debt owed by Branda to Mechanics Finance. Paolino represented that he was twenty-one. Branda defaulted on the debt after making two payments. Mechanics Finance commenced an action against Paolino three months after he attained majority. They asserted that he had misrepresented his age and that he had impliedly ratified the contract by remaining silent after reaching majority. What result? *Mechanics Finance Co.* v. *Paolino,* 29 N.J. Super. 449, 102 A. 2d 784 (1954).

9. Strandberg, a minor, agreed to purchase several lots, owned by the Rubins, for $6,000. The payment was to be in monthly installments. After reaching majority Strandberg made payments in November and December, then disaffirmed the contract in February. He refused to pay the balance owed, claiming infancy as a defense. The contract had been recorded by the Rubins in January. What result? *Rubin et al.* v. *Strandberg,* 288 Ill. 64, 122 N.E. 808 (1919).

10. On a number of occasions, Stuhl, age seventeen, traveled on Eastern Airlines and paid them with checks that subsequently bounced. Stuhl took trips for business purposes. When Eastern sued Stuhl for nonpayment, he raised the defense of infancy. What result? *Eastern Airlines* v. *Stuhl,* 65 Misc. 2d 901, 318 N.Y.S. 2d 966 (Civ. Ct. N.Y. 1970).

13

Lawful Purpose

Introduction   Contracts against Public Policy
Contracts in Violation of a Statute   Review Questions

INTRODUCTION

The purpose for which a contract is made, and the acts being undertaken to accomplish this purpose, must be lawful. *Lawful* means that there must not be any contravention of any federal statute or of any state statute having jurisdiction over the subject matter of the contract. When both the means employed and the end result are consistent with the law, the contract will be valid. There is a presumption that the parties intended to form a legal contract unless the opposite is shown. If the contract contemplates the performance of an illegal act or the achievement of an illegal purpose, the contract is void. A void contract is unenforceable in a court of law. When the contract is void because of illegality, generally no remedies will be granted. A valid contract that subsequently becomes illegal through the enactment of a new law or a change in public policy will be unenforceable because the public welfare takes precedence over the contractual freedom of individuals. In a contract where one party has reason to believe that the other party will use the subject matter of a legal contract which is legal, for an illegal purpose, the contract may be valid and the innocent party may enforce it. The illegal activity must not be criminal, and the innocent party must not participate in the activity.

EXAMPLE | Billy the Kid, a card shark, purchases a deck of marked cards from a novelty shop. The shop owner knows that the Kid is going to use the cards in a showdown with Pat Garrett at the Crystal Palace Saloon in Virginia City, but the owner does not participate in that event. Is the contract to purchase the cards valid? Yes! This contract is valid because the Kid is making a legal purchase and because the shop owner's affiliation with the Kid is restricted to the sale of the deck of cards. By the way, Pat Garrett, with an ace up his sleeve, shoots the Kid down.

147

There are two types of illegal contracts: contracts in violation of either a federal or a state statute and contracts against public policy.

CONTRACTS IN VIOLATION OF A STATUTE

Laws are promulgated by federal and state legislatures through statutes. All citizens of the United States must obey federal statutes, and citizens are also bound by the statutes of the states in which they live. Agreements that contravene state statutes predominantly fall into the following categories: **CLUES**.

Contracts to commit crimes and torts
Licensing requirement violations
Usury
Engaging in gambling
Sunday laws

Contracts to Commit Crimes and Torts

Contracts to commit crimes and torts are illegal and definitely not legally enforceable. It is an accepted fact that such contracts are made and carried out. It might be said that these contracts are illegally enforceable. Criminal laws are designed to punish individuals for wrongs they have committed. Tort laws are enacted so that aggrieved parties may be reimbursed for damages sustained as a result of wrongs committed against them. Contract law discourages the making of agreements to commit crimes and torts by providing no forum for their enforcement. The courts will leave the parties where they lie, so to speak.

EXAMPLE | Al Capone puts out a $10,000 contract on the Bugsy Moran Gang, to be executed by Machine Gun Kelly on St. Valentine's Day. The massacre is carried out, but Capone refuses to pay Kelly the $10,000. Kelly sues Capone, but Capone hires the Great Mouthpiece, a defense counsel who has never lost a case. The Mouthpiece argues that contracts to commit crimes are not enforceable in a court of law. Has the Mouthpiece won another case? Yes! The Mouthpiece is correct, and the courts leave the parties where they lie.

Licensing Requirement Violations

Licenses are required of persons who intend to practice in certain professions, trades, and recreational activities. Licensure is a prerequisite for admission into professional fields including law, accounting, medicine, nursing, and teaching. Trades and businesses requiring licensure include carpentry, plumbing, masonry, contracting, meat and food processing, hair styling, and bar and restaurant operation. Hunting, fishing, and boating are recreational activities for which licenses are generally needed. There are two types of licensing: regulatory and revenue-raising.

Regulatory statutes protect the public from unscrupulous and incompetent individuals by requiring, in the first case, proof of integrity and in the second, proof of skill. Integrity is judged through personal interviews with the regulatory association, references, and examinations assessing knowledge of professional ethics. Skill is measured either through examination of knowledge or demonstration of workmanship; it can also be ascertained from years of apprenticeship. A contract made by a party who is in violation of a regulatory statute is void. That party will not be able to enforce the contract to receive the agreed-upon compensation even if the work is of the highest quality. Generally the quality of the work makes no difference because there is a strong public interest in protecting people against those not licensed. However, some courts will allow recovery where the person in violation is honest and competent and has made no claim to having a license. The reason for the recovery in that instance is to prevent unjust enrichment of the person receiving the services or goods. The court may also allow an innocent party to enforce the contract if that party lacked knowledge of the violation.

EXAMPLE | The Great Mouthpiece is at it again. This time he is defending Pretty Boy Floyd on a robbery charge in Detroit. The Mouthpiece is not licensed to practice in Michigan and does not get the court's permission to appear for this isolated case. His defense is unsuccessful, but Pretty Boy refuses to pay the fee. Has the Great Mouthpiece been foiled at last? Yes! An attorney without a license to practice will be refused compensation for his services in most states.

Revenue-raising statutes are those that allow anyone to obtain a license or permit upon payment of a fee. The purpose is to raise funds both to support the licensed activity and to maintain other government programs. Examples of revenue-raising statutes include tennis and campground permits, automobile registration, incorporation fees, transfer taxes, and other general registration fees. Courts are more lenient in enforcing contracts that involve violation of statutes intended for revenue raising. The justification of protecting the public interest from unskilled or dishonest individuals is lacking. Infringement of statutes of this type generally result in fines meant to encourage future compliance.

EXAMPLE | Clarence Darrow is licensed to practice law and has registered with the State Board of Law Examiners. Five years later he forgets to pay his yearly $50 registration fee due January 1. On January 3, Darrow agrees to represent Charles Darwin and his monkey. The trial is completed on January 30. On February 1, Darrow is notified by the state board that he is delinquent in his payment of dues, and he promptly rectifies the situation. Upon learning of this, Darwin refuses to pay Darrow for his services, alleging that Darrow was in violation of a licensing requirement at the time he rendered the services. Is Darwin's assumption correct? Darwin is correct in theory but not in practice. Darrow will be able to collect his fee because the statute he violated was designed not to protect the public from the unqualified but only to raise revenue. A person who has passed the bar exam is licensed to practice law. Failure to register can be remedied by payment of the annual fee. It has no effect on the lawyer's qualifications for practicing law.

Usury

State statutes limit rates of interest charged on borrowed money. *Usury* contracts involve the charging of interest in excess of the maximum rate allowed by statute. When money is loaned, certain additional charges are permitted for the recording of the loan and for the investigation into the borrower's financial background. These are considered separate service charges and are not included as part of the interest rate. However, "points" may be tacked on to the interest charged if they are prorated over the life of a loan. Points are an assessment charged by a lending institution for making the loan. The reason for prorating points over the life of the loan is to avoid usury in the first year when the points are charged. Courts differ on the status of late-payment penalties. Some stipulate that the penalty becomes part of the total interest charged; others do not.

The effect of usury on a contract for the loan of money depends upon the state where the contract is made. Among the states there are three prevalent attitudes toward usury, ranging from the most lenient to the most severe. First, a lender convicted of usury may recover the principal loaned together with the maximum interest allowed, thus forfeiting only the excessive interest charged. Second, the lender must suffer the loss of all interest charged. Third, the lender must relinquish both principal and interest.

EXAMPLE | Bonny and her husband Clyde are looking to buy a house in Bay Ridge, Brooklyn. They need $2,000 more for the down payment. They have been turned down by all the banks because of their bad credit rating. They get a tip to see a man named Dutch Schultz, who agrees to lend them the money at a rate of 2 percent per week. They purchase their dream house, only to find that they are having great difficulty repaying the interest on the loan. Schultz insists that they must pay the interest. Is Schultz correct? No! The loan is illegal because the interest charged is usurious.

There are three instances where the usual limitations of usury do not apply:

    Corporations
    Small loan companies
    Sales of goods on credit

Corporations cannot call on the defense of usury because it is designed to protect individuals from unscrupulous lenders.

Small loan companies were introduced for the purpose of providing loans in small amounts to deter debtors from bargaining with loan sharks. Some states limit the amount of money that can be borrowed and restrict the interest that can be charged on a monthly basis. Many states allow small loan companies to charge a higher rate of interest because of the greater risk they incur in extending credit to high-risk individuals. Typically these loans are the ones that larger institutions would not grant because of the imbalance between profit and risk.

Sale of goods on credit requires payments to be made on an installment basis. An installment sale is a contract that requires a promise to pay a certain amount at stated intervals for the consideration received until full payment is made. An interest charge is assessed each month on the unpaid balance. There is a sharp difference between sale of goods for cash and for credit. Credit sales are not subject to usury statutes because they are not loans. A maximum monthly interest rate is permitted under the truth-in-lending laws of each state. These laws generally impose a duty upon the lender to provide the borrower with a statement listing the cash price, the original payment made, the unpaid balance, and the monthly finance charge. If the borrower is obligated to make the installment payments to a bank, then the installment contract is actually a loan and will be regulated by the usury laws.

EXAMPLE | Ma Barker runs the Bullet Hole Donut Shop in Hell's Kitchen. She buys donuts from a supplier. Terms of the sale are thirty days for payment. An interest rate of 1 percent per week is charged on the unpaid balance after the thirty days. Is Ma getting a fair shake on the interest charged? Yes! The rate is within the standard set by the truth-in-lending laws for contracts involving the sale of goods on credit.

Gambling

Individuals who gamble are making wagering agreements. Most states except Nevada and New Jersey's Atlantic City prohibit gambling. People who gamble forfeit their right to the other party's consideration or to a return of their own consideration. Courts will not enforce a bettor's right to winnings, nor will they enforce a bettor's duty to pay up for money owed. Loan sharks, bookies, and other illegal betting establishments do not rely on the courts to enforce bets.

Many states allow exceptions to gambling laws for charitable and religious organizations to sponsor bingo, bazaars, nights at the races, Las Vegas nights, and the selling of chance books. Most states sanction lotteries for revenue-raising purposes. Sweepstakes are generally permissible as long as there is no request for money and no purchase necessary.

Speculative agreements involving the buying and selling of securities and commodities are legitimate because the securities and commodities represent ownership in corporations. This is true even though most investors are betting on price fluctuations to make profits. Option contracts on securities and commodities (puts and calls), which give holders the right to buy or sell specific securities or commodities at fixed prices before the expiration of specific periods, are tolerated. The prevailing theory is that the right to exercise the option implies a possibility of ownership. However, most option contracts expire unexercised. This indicates that in many cases, the reason behind investing in options is pure speculation, if not outright gambling.

Individuals are allowed to relieve themselves of possible financial burdens resulting from property damage, medical expenses, or loss of life by allocating the risk to insurance companies. A person contracting for insurance must have a substantial interest in the property or person to be insured.

EXAMPLE | Louie owns a sweet shop on the Lower East Side. He contracts with an insurance company to provide him with fire and liability coverage. Once a month, Louie rents out his main hall to the local chapter of the Knights of Columbus for bingo games and Las Vegas Nights. The other nights, Louie lets out the basement to Mugs MacGinnis, who runs his own Las Vegas Nights and employs Satch and the East Side Kids to supervise the games. Are any of these contracts legal? The insurance contract is legal because risks involving insurable interests can be allocated. Mugs MacGinnis's contract with Louie is illegal, but the contract with the K of C is valid because they, as a religious organization, are allowed to operate games of chance to raise money for their cause. Mugs's employment contract with Satch and the East Side Kids is illegal and unenforceable.

Sunday Laws

Sunday-law statutes prohibit the performance of certain work, especially work that involves manual labor and the operation of establishments selling or serving liquor, on Sundays. Sunday laws are formulated by individual states and vary greatly. There are exceptions to this rule dictated by necessity, convenience, recreation, and charity. Service stations, restaurants, hotels, and common carriers such as airlines and private bus and train companies must be allowed to operate on Sundays. Technicians and repair people needed to operate city services must be authorized to work on Sunday. Places of recreation that may be open on Sundays comprise amusement parks, theaters, sports arenas, beaches, golf courses, campgrounds, and county or state fairs. In many states supermarkets are permitted to open on Sundays because they are considered necessary to the public good. To find out the various activities that are prohibited, one should consult state statutes and local ordinances.

CONTRACTS AGAINST PUBLIC POLICY

Contracts that have detrimental effect on the general public are considered to be against public policy. The meaning of the term has changed with time and according to society's norms and values. Examples of contracts against public policy are: **PRUDE**.

Public welfare endangered
Restrict competition
Unconscionable contracts
Discriminatory contracts
Exculpatory clauses

Rinvelt v. Rinvelt
475 N.W. 2d 478 (Mich. App. 1991).

Three days before the Rinvelts were married, they entered at Mr. Rinvelt's insistence into a prenuptial agreement with the following provisions:

3. Property rights subsequent to marriage: After the solemnization of marriage between the parties, and except as hereinafter provided, each of the parties shall separately retain all rights in his or her own property, whether now owned or hereafter acquired, and, except as otherwise herein provided, each of them shall have the absolute and unrestricted right to dispose of such property free from any claims that may be made by the other by reason of their marriage, and with the same effect as if no marriage had been consummated between them . . .

11. Divorce: In the event that the marriage of the parties shall end in divorce, annulment, or separate maintenance, it is hereby agreed that their respective rights in and to the property of the other spouse shall be limited as follows:

A. The Prospective Husband shall be entitled to ten percent (10%) of the net estate of the Prospective Wife, net estate meaning gross estate less all expenses. b. The Prospective Wife shall be entitled to ten percent (10%) of the net estate of the Prospective Husband, net estate meaning gross estate less all expenses.

The parties understand that contractual provisions which attempt to deal with the event of divorce prior to the contemplation of divorce are often deemed to be in contravention of public policy. In recognition of this fact, the parties desire that the provisions of this Agreement shall be severable, and intend that, in the event that the provisions dealing with the divorce shall be found to be repugnant to public policy, then said provisions shall be severed from the remainder of this Agreement, and shall be rendered of no further force or effect.

After four years of marriage, Mrs Rinvelt filed for divorce. In compliance with the prenuptial agreement, Mrs. Rinvelt's share exceeded Rinvelt's by $228,584.

The issue is whether prenuptial agreements violate the sanctity of marriage by making provisions in the event of a divorce.

The court held,

[W]e see no logical or compelling reason why public policy should not allow two mature adults to handle their own financial affairs. Therefore, we join those courts that have recognized that prenuptial agreements legally procured and ostensibly fair in result are valid and can be enforced. The reasoning that once found them contrary to public policy has no place in today's matrimonial law.

Judgement for Mrs. Rinvelt.

Public Welfare Endangered

Contracts that endanger the public health, safety, morals, and general welfare are against public policy. Parties who attempt to impede justice by refusing to testify, suppressing evidence, or intentionally hindering court procedure, in return for some form of compensation, are engaging in contracts that have harmful effects on the general public.

EXAMPLE | Jesse James and his brother Frank are under contract to do a demolition job in downtown Manhattan on St. Patrick's Day. They are transporting nitroglycerin in a truck down the Avenue of the Americas when they are caught. A block away, over two million people are gathered to watch the St. Patrick's Day Parade. Could this blow up? Definitely! This contract endangers the welfare of over two million people, many of whom are already bombed. Because it is against public policy, the James brothers will not be allowed to continue on their preplanned route.

Individuals who exert undue influence over public officials and fiduciaries through contracts involving bribery are acting against public policy. Contracts that create conflicts between the personal interests and the duties of public officials or fiduciaries must be avoided unless complete disclosure is made. Lobbying is legal if information is presented to advance the position of one side. However, if the contract for lobbying entails the use of undue influence or is based on a contingency fee, it is void because it is against public policy.

EXAMPLE | The Quantrill Raiders, in an effort to convince Hanging Judge Parker to acquit one of their gang, offer Boss Tweed, an influential politician, $50,000 if he is successful in lobbying for their case. Tweed succeeds by informing Parker that it will be the last case that he will ever try if he convicts the raider. Are the Boss's tactics legal? No! The use of undue influence in lobbying is not lawful, and neither is the contingency fee arrangement. The Boss will forfeit the $50,000 fee.

Restriction of Competition

Contracts that individuals or corporations use to restrict free trade via monopolies, price fixing, or other forms of unfair competition are illegal because they violate the Sherman Antitrust Act. Attempts to discriminate in favor of certain purchasers by charging them preferred rates, or granting them exclusive dealing contracts are *in restraint of trade*, and thus violate the Clayton Act. It is the purpose of the antitrust laws to maintain free, open, and continuing competition.

EXAMPLE | At the intersection of Clove Road and Ridge Boulevard, Meyer Lansky operates a gas station and Bugsy Siegal operates an automobile repair shop. Their businesses are on opposite corners. On one of the other corners, Frank Nitti opens a gas and service station.

Lansky and Siegal have been doing quite well over the years by referring business to each other, but now Nitti is cutting into their profits. They enter into a contract to reduce prices to whatever extent is necessary to drive Nitti out of business. Is this a valid contract? No! It restricts free competition and is replete with violations of the Sherman Antitrust Act.

Contracts to refrain from competition are generally found to be not in the best interest of the public. However, a contract containing a covenant not to compete may be lawful where the contract is for the sale of a business or where it involves employment. A provision restricting the seller of a business from competing in the area where the business is located for a period of up to five years is generally granted for the protection of the purchaser. These are general guidelines. The court will examine whether the area and time restrictions are reasonable and sufficient to protect the purchaser against unfair competition from the seller. In most cases the contract will not fail if the area or duration is excessive, but the clause will be stricken. Some states will determine reasonable limitations and apply them. The courts watch closely to preserve free competition.

EXAMPLE Wyatt Earp sells his gun and rifle shop in Dodge City to Bat Masterson. The contract contains a clause restricting Wyatt Earp from opening another gun and rifle shop within the city limits for a period of five years. Will this clause be enforced? Yes! The clause is designed to protect Bat Masterson against unfair competition from Wyatt Earp because the town is not big enough for both of them. The time limitation is reasonable in that it gives Bat sufficient time to establish himself in the community.

A clause in an employment contract may prevent an employee leaving a position from working in the same field for a certain length of time. The courts do not look with favor upon such clauses and enforce them only where the employee's knowledge of trade secrets or the future of the business is at issue. The enforcement of employment restrictions usually applies to management.

Decker, Berta and Co., Ltd. v. Berta
587 N.E. 2d 72 (Ill. App. V. Dist. 1992)

Raymond Berta was a partner in the Decker, Berta accounting firm. When the business was sold he remained as an employee and signed the following document:

RESTRICTIVE COVENANT. For a period of three (3) years from the date of the termination of his employment, the Employee will not, within a thirty-five (35) mile radius of any present places of business of Employer, directly or indirectly own, manage, operate, or control, or be connected in any manner with any business of the type and character of business engaged in by the Employer at the time of such termination.

The contract also contained the following covenant:

DISCLOSURE OF INFORMATION. The Employees recognize and acknowledge that the list of the Employer's customers, as it may exist
from time to time, is a valuable, special, and unique asset of the
Employer's business. The Employees will not, during or after the term of
their employment, disclose the list to the Employer's customers or any
part thereof to any person, firm, corporation, association, or other entity
for any reason or purpose whatsoever. In the event of a breach or threatened breach by an Employee of the provisions of this paragraph, the
Employer shall be entitled to an injunction restraining said Employee
from disclosing, in whole or in part, the list of the Employer's customers.
Nothing herein shall be construed as prohibiting the Employer from pur-
suing any other remedies available to him for such breach.

When the contract expired, Berta joined another accounting firm.
He brought his father-in-law's account with him. Berta also phoned
several other former clients, asking them to switch firms. Decker,
Berta and Company sought a preliminary injunction, alleging that Berta
had violated the restrictive covenant.

There are two types of restrictive covenants: employment and
sale of business. Employment contracts face a much stricter test with
regard to restraints. The issue is whether this restrictive covenant is
part of the employment contract or the sale of the business.

The court concluded that the seller

purchased Decker, Berta and Co., Ltd. upon the premise that the firm
would continue to be operated by Charles R. Decker and Raymond
Berta. If either one or both of them left to do accounting work on their
own or for another accounting firm, it was conceivable that the firm's
clientele would be lost to the departing employee or employees. The
purchaser would be left with an office lease, some computers, and
whatever personal property is needed by an accounting firm. His assumption and payment of $237,200.00 in firm debts and contract to pur-
chase the firm would have been rendered totally illusory. Therefore, the
court concluded that the plaintiff had proved the employee's services
were indispensable and part of the agreement to purchase the business.

Judgment for Decker.

The limitations set forth in the contract must be reasonable. The courts will not
enforce restrictions upon employees that are unduly harsh and permit employers to de-
rive more protection than that necessary to guard their secrets or to protect their business interests.

EXAMPLE | Lucky Luciano bought a liquor store on the south side of Chicago. He hired Albert Anastasia, a kid fresh out of the school of hard knocks, to manage it for him. A provision in the contract prohibited Al from opening a liquor store within the city limits for the rest of his natural life. After learning the trade Al quit and opened his own place in the down town section of Chicago known as the Loop. Can Lucky enforce the provision? No! The provision is too broad in its geographical area and much too unreasonable in its time restraints.

Unconscionable Contracts

Unconscionable contracts are unduly harsh and one-sided, usually involving parties of unequal bargaining power. The harshness of the contract must be so severe as to shock the moral conscience of the community. These contracts are against public policy because freedom to contract is impaired by one party's taking unfair advantage through greater bargaining strength. Unconscionability especially pervades contracts that are entered into by employees and by consumers. Minimum wage and minimum hour laws, worker's compensation, and occupational safety and health standards guard against unconscionability in employment contracts. Consumer contracts are aided by the Uniform Consumer Credit Code and truth-in-lending laws, which defend against oppressive and harsh contracts imposed upon consumers. Standardized contracts containing terms and conditions to which consumers must adhere if they wish to contract are strictly construed by the courts against the drafters of the contracts.

EXAMPLE | The Dalton brothers are in the demolition business. They employ Baby Face Nelson to handle their explosive devices for a period of one year. Nelson has to work under conditions that are continually unsafe. The devices could blow up at any time. The Dalton brothers do not provide Nelson with any protective equipment or take any safety precautions on his behalf. Nelson decides that he wants out of the contract. Is Nelson bound? No! The contract is unconscionable in that it exposes Nelson to danger by making him work without proper safety equipment.

Art's Flower Shop v. C & P Telephone Co.
413 S.E. 2d 670 (W.VA.1991)

Art's Flower Shop had advertised in the Yellow Pages since 1963. In 1981 C & P promised to include Art's advertisement in the annual issue. When the Yellow Pages were published, Art's ad was omitted. The contract stipulated, "In the event of an error in or omission of the advertising for which application is hereby made, the Telephone Company will not be held liable for an amount exceeding the amount of the charge for the advertising in error or omitted." Art's Flower Shop argued that the stipulated damage clause was unconscionable.

> The issue is whether the clause was unconscionable because it involved parties of unequal bargaining power.
>
> The court decided that the clause was void. "The positions of C&P and Art's Flower Shop were grossly unequal: C&P had the only Yellow Pages directory in the area. Since Art's Flower Shop had no meaningful alternative to purchasing from C&P, it obviously was in no position to bargain for the contract." Judgment for Art's Flower Shop.

Discriminatory Contracts

Contracts discriminating against people because of religion, race, national origin, or gender are illegal because they violate both public policy and the Constitution of the United States. Their main purpose is to discriminate against people and exclude them on the basis of the classifications mentioned.

The Civil Rights Act of 1964 was enacted to ensure that all individuals would be guaranteed equal employment opportunity. The act prohibits the use of discriminatory tactics in hiring, firing, and determining compensation or other terms or conditions of employment. This prohibition not only encompasses overt discriminatory acts but also extends to acts that are subtle. The Equal Employment Opportunity Commission (EEOC) is entrusted with policing employment tactics that may be discriminatory.

EXAMPLE | The Black Hand is a national organization of funeral directors. Its membership is restricted. A pair of funeral directors named Idi Amin and Saddam Hussein applied for membership. Idi was refused because of his race and Saddam because of his religion. Idi and Saddam claimed discrimination. Are they correct? Yes! When a national organization of a particular occupation limits membership to people of a certain religion or national origin, the practice is discriminatory and unconstitutional.

Exculpatory Clauses

A party attempting to disclaim liability through use of an *exculpatory clause* in a contract may not do so when the liability is caused by his or her own negligence. This is especially true in contracts affecting the public where parties attempting to escape responsibility have superior bargaining power due to the nature of their positions, as is the case with utilities. This is to ensure that the party with greater negotiating strength does not downgrade its service or produce an inferior product by becoming lax in its workmanship; otherwise the party would be allowed to act in a manner harmful to the public, with little fear of accountability.

S.C. Electric and Gas v. Combustion Engineering
322 S.E. 2d 453 (S.C. App.1984)

A steam-generating boiler at a South Carolina Electric and Gas (SCE & G) company plant was damaged when a flexible metal hose ruptured and sprayed heated fuel oil over its surface.

> Combustion Engineering, which had manufactured and sold the hose to SCE & G argued that the claim should be barred because the one-year warranty had expired. The warranty contained an exculpatory clause that read: LIMITATIONS OF LIABILITY—The liability of Combustion to SCE & G arising out of the manufacture, sale, delivery, use, or resale of the equipment whether based on warranty, contract, negligence, strict liability or otherwise, shall not exceed the cost of correcting defects in the equipment as herein provided. Upon the expiration of the warranty period, all such liability shall terminate.

The issue is whether the exculpatory clause shields Combustion Engineering from liability that arose becasue of its own negligence.

The court decided, "Contracts that seek to exculpate a party from liability for the party's own negligence are not favored by the law. We hold, then, that the exculpatory clause does not shield Combustion from liability for negligent design." Judgment for SCE & G.

In bailment contracts, parties attempt to exonerate themselves from all blame through inconspicuous notification—for instance, on a sign or on the back of a ticket. A bailment is a contract whereby one party agrees to be responsible for the property of another in return for a fee. The party making the promise must exercise reasonable care in respect to the property. Tickets given as an indication of ownership do not effectively excuse parties from liability growing out of their own negligence. Some common carriers, parking lots, restaurant coat-check concessions, tailors, and ski lifts, for example, give tickets in an attempt to shift the risk of liability to the customer. In their dealings with the public, these businesses have a nontransferable duty to exercise due care regarding the property in their possession. Although liability cannot be disclaimed, it may be limited in certain instances. A discussion of these limitations appears in Chapter 28, "Bailments."

In private contracts one party may assign risks to another if the contract is entered into freely. The court will examine the relative bargaining strength of the parties to determine whether the assignments of risk are made freely.

Let us refer to the example of Baby Face Nelson and the Dalton brothers. Suppose Nelson continues to handle explosive devices for the brothers. Nelson is usually competent, but on one occasion a device blows up in his face because of a faulty detonator installed by the brothers. Nelson sues the Daltons, but the contract provides that Baby Face assumes all risk of injury. Has he any recourse? Yes! The Daltons cannot exculpate themselves from liability for injury caused to Nelson through their own negligence.

REVIEW QUESTIONS

1. Define lawful purpose, usury, Sunday laws, unconscionability, exculpatory clauses, and contracts in restraint of trade.

2. David Duwell left Bobcat enterprises for Portman Equipment Company, a competitor. This was in violation of the restrictive covenant that Duwell signed while employed with Bobcat. Bobcat sought an injunction. Duwell's current position involves renting industrial forklifts, a business Bobcat does not engage in. What result? *Bobcat Enterprises, Inc.* v. *Duwell*, 587 N.E. 2d 905 (Ohio App. 12 Dist. 1990).

3. Gregory Harthcock was hired as a chemist by Zep Manufacturing. He signed a nondisclosure covenant that restricted him from work in the same field for two years and did not specify geographic location. Subsequently he left Zep's employ for a job with its competitor, Panther Industries. Zep sought to enforce the restrictive covenant; Harthcock claimed that it was indefinite in its terms. What result? *Zep Mfg. Co.* v. *Harthcock*, 824 S.W. 2d 654 (Tex. App.–Dallas 1992).

4. Colonial Sales sold a motor home to Pratt pursuant to an "as is" bill of sale. Pratt claims this is unconscionable. What result? *Pratt* v. *Colonial-Sales-Lease-Rental, Inc.*, 799 F. Supp. 1132 (N.D. Ala. 1992).

5. Bud Johnson, newly elected mayor of Plano, Illinois, promised Dennis Harris, the current police chief, that he would reappoint him if Harris would forgo other employment opportunities. Harris complied, but Johnson terminated him. What result? *Harris* v. *Johnson*, 578 N.E. 2d 1326 (Ill. App. 2 Dist. 1991).

6. P.M. Palumbo Jr., M.A., Inc. is a professional corporation providing medical services. Dean Bennett was hired as an independent contractor according to the employment contract. The contract contained a restrictive covenant prohibiting Bennett from competing. Subsequently Bennett terminated the employment and violated the restrictive covenant. When sued, Bennett argued that the contract was void because the law does not permit a professional corporation to provide services through an independent contractor; the court agreed. Palumbo argued that this technicality should not prevent the court from enforcing the restrictive covenant. What result? *P.M. Palumbo, Jr., Inc.* v. *Bennett*, 409 S.E.2d 152 (Va. 1991).

7. Rozeboem, a contractor, agreed to pay $200 to Northwestern Bell Telephone for an ad in its 1980 Yellow Pages. The ad was omitted. A provision in the contract limited liability to the cost of the ad. Is the provision an exculpatory clause? *Rozeboem* v. *Northwestern Bell Telephone Co.*, 358 N.W. 2d 241 (S.D. 1984).

8. Barlow entered into an eight-year lease of dairy equipment from Agristor Leasing for a total amount of $494,127. Barlow argued that the amount charged was usurious. What result? *Agristor Leasing* v. *Barlow*, 579 N.Y.S. 2d 476 (A.d. 4th Dept 1992).

9. Owens, a bottle cap manufacturer, sold bottle-caps to Joyce Beverages, a bottler. The order form limits Owens's liability for defective bottle caps to the contract price only. Nancy Kathenes was injured when a soda bottle cap flew off and struck her in the eye. She successfully sued Joyce for her injuries, and now the bottler seeks contribution and indemnification from Owens. Joyce argues that limiting liability in an order form as Owens did is unconscionable. Owens claims that this practice is the normal way in which merchants deal with each other. What result? *Kathenes* v. *Quick Chek Food Stores*, 596 F. Supp. 713 (1984).

10. Hardin entered into an employment contract with Lance Roof Inspection on January 1, 1981. The agreement contained a restrictive covenant that prevented Hardin from competing with Lance for a period of twenty-four months from the date of the agreement. The original contract terminated on December 31, 1982, but the parties extended the term until the end of 1985. Shortly after the extension expired, Hardin started his own business in competition with Lance. Lance argued that the restrictive covenant had gone into effect only after Hardin left in 1985. What result? *Lance Roof Inspection Service, Inc.* v. *Hardin*, 653 F. Supp. 1097 (S.D. Tex 1986).

14

Form and Interpretation

FORMATION

Contracts may be formed in number of ways. They may be expressed either orally or in writing, or they may be implied from the actions of the parties. Contracts formed by any of these methods are equally valid. Generally there is no problem with the validity of an oral contract; the difficulty arises when one tries to prove its existence. Many valid contracts are dismissed by the courts because their terms cannot be proved. If, in an oral contract, one party does not fulfill his or her obligation, the other party without witnesses will have an arduous task trying to prove the existence of the contract. The old saying "It's my word against yours" is very true and applicable to oral contracts. Even with witnesses there are still problems. Over time witnesses tend to forget; their testimony is often conflicting and may even be perjured. However, for the sake of convenience, simple contracts—particularly those of nominal value—tend to be oral.

Every valuable and important contract should be in writing so there is evidence of its existence. All states have recognized this principle by adopting a *statute of frauds* that requires certain contracts to be in writing. The main purpose of the statute is to prevent fraud by requiring evidence of the contract's existence. This requirement prevents misunderstandings that lead to misrepresentations. Additionally, in the absence of the statute of frauds, oral contracts that would otherwise not be enforceable could be enforced. This would dramatically increase the legal caseload, with verdicts based on guesswork because of the conflicting oral evidence.

The idea for a statute of frauds originated in England in the latter part of the seventeenth century. Before that time all oral contracts were enforceable on the principle that a contract was as good as a person's word. However, the parties themselves were not allowed to testify because many were willing to commit perjury in order to win their cases. Only witnesses could testify on a party's behalf, but many witnesses were bribed to give false testimony. Innocent parties who lacked witnesses of their own could not rebuke the false testimony of the other parties' witnesses because of the rule forbidding parties to testify. As a result fraud became commonplace. In an attempt to protect the innocent, the British Parliament enacted the statute of frauds, which required certain contracts to be in writing.

In the United States, each state has its own statute requiring certain contracts to be in writing. If the statute's requirements are not met, enforcement of the contract is denied. This practice bars honest individuals from being able to enforce contracts that are not in writing, but the need to prevent fraud outweighs the hardship imposed upon those honest people. If, however, the denial of enforcement perpetrates a fraud upon an innocent party, the statute will be abandoned. The courts will not allow the statute to cause the fraud it is seeking to prevent.

The contracts that are generally required to be in writing are: L & M'S 500S

Land

&

Mortgages
Sale of securities

$500 or more sale of goods
One year of performance (in excess of)
Other than goods, personal property, exceeding $5,000
Suretyship contracts

LAND

Contracts for the sale of real estate must be in writing. Real estate or real property is defined as land and everything that is permanently attached to it. This includes buildings, vegetation, crops, timber, and minerals. However, a contract for the sale of crops or lumber is a contract for the sale of goods regardless of whether the buyer or seller severs the crops or timber from the land. Timber refers to trees; lumber refers to trees after cutting.

EXAMPLE | Cyrus McCormick orally contracts to sell 500 bushels of wheat and corn and to sell and deliver an acre's worth of lumber to International Harvester for a total price of $400. He uses his newly manufactured reaper to harvest the crops. When he delivers the lumber and crops, International Harvester refuses to accept, claiming that the sale of timber and crops is a contract for real estate that must be in writing. Are they correct? No! Once crops and timber are severed from the land, they become goods. A contract for the sale of goods priced under $500 does not have to be in writing.

The Uniform Commercial Code has a special rule for contracts involving the sale of minerals. If the minerals are to be removed by the seller, the contract is for the sale of goods; but if the removal is made by the buyer, it is a contract for an interest in the land and must be in writing.

MORTGAGES

Mortgages and easements that convey an interest in real estate must be in writing. An easement is the legal right to use the land of another for a specific purpose. An assignment of a mortgage does not have to be in writing because the assignment itself is not an interest in land but rather a transfer of a debt. An assignment is a transfer of rights and duties from one person to another. A further discussion of mortgages, easements, and leases is presented in Chapter 33, "Real Estate Transactions," and Chapter 35, "Landlord and Tenant."

Ancillary agreements such as those for title searches, repairs, improvements, or additions to real property are not required to be in writing. They do not qualify as interests in real property because they are personal service contracts. However, some states provide that brokerage contracts must be in writing. To satisfy the requirement many states require that the full legal description of the land be set forth in the contract. This includes lot and block numbers, and metes and bounds, in addition to the normal address.

EXAMPLE | The Wright Brothers are is looking to purchase a large tract of property to test their new flying machines. The Wright Brothers enter into a contract to purchase land in a town called Kitty Hawk. The contract and mortgage are in writing, but the only legal description of the property is in metes and bounds. The Wright Brothers inquire about whether the contract and mortgage must be in writing and about the legal sufficiency of the property description. All contracts for the sale of land must be in writing, as must mortgages because they are interests in land. The metes and bounds description is sufficient because it adequately describes the boundaries of the property. Many rural areas do not have addresses or lot and block numbers.

SALE OF SECURITIES

For the purchase or sale of securities, the UCC, under Article 8, Investment Securities, requires a writing signed by either the client or the broker who is acting as agent. The agency contract between broker and client must also be in writing. An agency contract allows the broker to act on the client's behalf, usually upon verbal instruction. The signed writing must state the quantity and price of the securities to be bought or sold. There must be delivery of the securities bought. Delivery may be made to the client's account if this is previously agreed to in writing, and it usually is. The agent must, within a reasonable time, send a writing to confirm the sale of securities. The person receiving it has ten days to send written objection to the sale.

EXAMPLE Henry Ford opens an account with his local broker. He signs a statement giving the broker authority to buy and sell for him. Ford telephones his broker, telling him to purchase 5,000 shares of Ford Motor Company stock at $30 per share. The stock drops to $20 per share and Ford refuses to pay, alleging that there was no written contract. Is he correct? No! The broker need only send a written confirmation slip to evidence the transaction within a reasonable time. Although his signature does not appear on the confirmation slip, Ford is bound by the agreement he signed when he opened the account.

$500 OR MORE FOR THE SALE OF GOODS

Under Article 2, Sales, the UCC provides that contracts for the sale of goods for $500 or more must be in writing. The $500 minimum requirement applies to a sale of a single item in excess of $500, as well as a sale of a number of items totaling more than $500. The latter applies when the parties intend the sale of a number of items to constitute a single contract. If they intended the sale of each item to be a separate contract, the writing requirement of the statute of frauds would not apply.

The required writing need only be a note or memorandum to evidence the existence of a contract. There may be an omission or mistake in one or more of the material terms as long as the parties and the goods can be identified. The quantity term must be specified, but if it is misstated, the contract will be enforceable only up to the misstated amount. The other terms— price and time and place of delivery—will be supplemented by the gap-filler provisions of the UCC if they are not mentioned in the writing (as outlined in Chapter 10, "Agreement"). The court will assume that the parties intended a reasonable price, a reasonable time for delivery, and delivery at the seller's place of business. The court will look to the parties' intentions in making the contract. This is a progressive step in liberalizing the writing requirement.

EXAMPLE Alexander Graham Bell III, in working on his new telecommunications invention, uses a tremendous amount of number eighteen wire. He calls his local supplier and asks him to deliver twenty rolls of the thin wire. The supplier agrees but never delivers. His defense to a suit for nondelivery is that the contract is not in writing. Is the supplier correct? It depends on whether the value of the contract is over $500. In accordance with the UCC gap-filler provisions, the court will assume that the parties intended a reasonable price. If the court decides that a reasonable price for the wire exceeds $500, then the contract will fail because it is not in writing. If a reasonable price is less than $500, the oral contract will be enforceable.

The UCC provides certain exceptions to the requirement of a writing for contracts involving the sale of goods priced at $500 or more. This liberalization is furthered through the **MAPS** exceptions made by the UCC to the requirement itself.

Merchants contracting with each other

Admission that the writing was a mere formality

Payment made or performance rendered

Specially manufactured goods

Merchants   Merchants contracting with each other can satisfy the statute of frauds requirement under the UCC by sending a written confirmation within a reasonable time. This is sufficient to bind the merchant who sends it. The confirmation is also binding upon the merchant receiving it—even though that party's signature does not appear on it—unless written notification of objection is sent in return within ten days.

EXAMPLE | Thomas Edison telephoned a light bulb distributor to request delivery of 5,000 bulbs, which he wanted to use to illuminate the town of Menlo Park. The contract was valued at $1,000. Edison received written confirmation of the contract a week later. The terms provide for 10,000 bulbs at a cost of $2,000. Can Edison object? Yes! His objection must be in writing and must be sent within ten days from his receipt of the distributor's confirmation.

Admission   An admission in court by one of the parties that a contract for the sale of goods was made is sufficient to require enforcement of the contract.

EXAMPLE | Singer verbally agrees to deliver ten sewing machines to its local sewing center by November 17. The company forgets to make the delivery and is sued for breach of contract. In court Singer admits that there was a verbal agreement but states that it was not in writing as required by the statute of frauds. Has Singer sewn up the case for its opponent? Yes! The contract is enforceable because of Singer's admission. The purpose behind the statute of frauds is to evidence the existence of a contract and to prevent fraud. Here Singer's admission is evidence of the contract's existence. To refuse enforcement would perpetrate a fraud on the sewing center.

Payment or Performance   An oral contract for the sale of goods will be enforceable where the goods have been received and accepted or where payment has been made and accepted. A party's receipt and acceptance of goods or acceptance of payment, in effect, stops that party from denying the existence of a contract. The contract will be enforceable against that party on the basis of the doctrine of promissory estoppel, up to the quantity of the goods received or the payment made, even though there is no writing.

EXAMPLE | Isaac Newton made a telephone call to Gravity Fruits, Inc. to place an order for 100 bushels of apples. The purchase price was $3,000. Newton received and accepted 50 bushels of apples but refused to pay, asserting that the contract was not in writing. Is Newton required to pay? Yes! Isaac must pay because his receipt and acceptance of goods constituted an admission of a valid contract under the UCC. The contract is valid, but only up to the amount Newton received and accepted, 50 bushels.

Specially Manufactured Goods   An oral contract to manufacture special goods may be enforceable against the buyer. The seller must incur a substantial loss in acquiring or manufacturing the goods, and the goods must not be readily salable in the seller's business.

EXAMPLE | Robert Fulton, president of a shipbuilding company, verbally agrees to build a steamboat for the State of Mississippi, which plans to sell tickets for excursions along the river that bears its name. After the steamboat is completed, the State of Mississippi repudiates the contract because of a lack of funds. Because there is no longer a market for steamboats, can Fulton enforce the contract even though it is not in writing? Yes! The steamboats are specially manufactured goods not suitable for sale elsewhere. The UCC permits an oral contract in this situation in order to prevent an unjust loss from falling upon the manufacturer.

ONE YEAR OF PERFORMANCE (IN EXCESS OF)

Contracts with duration of performance in excess of one year are required to be in writing. This requirement includes contracts where the duration is either fixed or indefinite. The majority of states also require contracts requiring forbearance for more than one year to be in writing. However, if there is a possibility, no matter how remote, that a contract may be completed within one year, no writing is required.

Most states require that the duration of performance for both parties exceed one year in order for a writing to be required. In many of these states, loans need not be in writing because the lender's performance, the actual loaning of the money, takes place within one year. Some states require stricter compliance by stipulating that only one party's performance in excess of one year is needed to invoke the writing requirement. This prevents future problems in long-term contracts that are difficult to resolve because of witnesses who relocate, lose their memory, or die.

The measurement of time generally commences on the day after the contract is entered into—not the day on which performance begins—and runs until performance is completed. This assures the parties that the time limitation will expire on the anniversary of the day the contract is made.

EXAMPLE | AT&T, by an oral agreement made on January 1, hires Alexander Bell and Robert Morse to perfect its telephone and telegraph systems. Bell is to begin work on April 1 and to complete the work on January 31, ten months later. Morse, who is eighty-seven years old, has a lifetime contract. Neither contract is in writing. Are the contracts enforceable? Bell's contract is not enforceable. To be enforceable it must be in writing because its duration is thirteen months, commencing at the time the contract is made—January 1. This is true even though Bell does not begin work until April 1. Morse's contract is enforceable. A lifetime contract does not have to be in writing because it is possible that the party may die within one year of making the contract.

Respect Inc. v. Committee on the Status of Women
781 F.Supp. 1358 (N.D. Ill.1992)

Ms. Must developed a sex education program called "Sex Respect." She negotiated with the Committee on the Status of Women to write three books related to the program that would be published by United Communications of America. Must claimed that she entered into a contract with the committee to develop both the books and the program and that she would be compensated for this work as well as retain rights in the publication. The committee maintained that she would be paid a fixed fee for the publications in return for relinquishing her rights to future compensation from the publications. There is nothing in writing to this effect. It is an oral agreement.

The issue is whether an oral agreement for services is enforceable.

The court held, "[A]n oral contract is unenforceable unless by its terms it is capable of full performance within one year, as measured from the date of its making . . . By Must's admission, the pilot program was to run for more than one year . . . hence the contract is unenforceable." Judgement for the Committee.

PERSONAL PROPERTY CONTRACTS OTHER THAN GOODS IN EXCESS OF $5,000

The UCC provides that contracts for the sale of personal property other than goods, such as royalty and patent rights, where the price exceeds $5,000 must be in writing.

EXAMPLE | Johann Gutenberg patents his new invention, the printing press. He orally contracts to sell the patent rights to a local manufacturer for $10,000. He subsequently realizes that the printing press has unimaginable worth because it can mass-produce books such as this one for all the world to read. Gutenberg repudiates the contract. Who gets the patent? Gutenberg retains the patent because a contract involving the sale of a patent where the price exceeds $5,000 must be in writing.

SURETYSHIP CONTRACTS

A promise to be liable for the debt of another must be in writing in order to evidence the existence of the promise. The reasoning behind this requirement is that it is unusual for people to pay the debts of others. A surety is a person who guarantees payment to a creditor for the debt of another person, who is known as a debtor. The surety's liability must be secondary. Primary responsibility for payment of the debt must rest with the debtor. Only in the event that the debtor does not pay does the surety become liable. The surety's promise must be made to the creditor.

A person's statement that he or she will be responsible for payment or that the debt should be charged to his or her account is one of primary accountability. This does not have to be in writing. Written evidence is required only where the surety's responsibility is secondary.

THE WRITING

To satisfy the statute of frauds, the writing must be sufficiently clear and understandable that it is capable of being enforced on its face without an oral explanation. This is not to say that certain oral modifications or explanations are not admissible, but to evidence the existence of a contract, the writing must stand alone. The writing must include the following material terms: subject matter, time, identification of the parties, price, number (quantity), and delivery place. The UCC is much more lenient in its writing requirement for sales contracts because of its gap-filler provisions for time, price, and place of delivery.

The writing itself may be a formal written contract, or it may be a note or a memorandum. The writing may refer to other writings or letters as long as there is some continuity between them. The party against whom enforcement is sought, or an agent of that party, must sign the writing. It need not, however, be written and signed at the time the parties exchange promises as long as this requirement is fulfilled prior to a lawsuit by one of the parties. Until the promises are put in writing and signed, they are not legally enforceable. Some states require that a party's contract with his or her agent be in writing where the contracts the agent will be entering into are required to be in writing under the statute of frauds. A signature written in pencil, stamped, or typewritten will usually be as valid as one written in ink. An oral contract may be substantiated when the material terms are set forth by a writing such as a check, invoice, sales slip, or receipt.

Courts try to determine the parties' principal objectives and look at everything else in light of those objectives. Words are given their usual meanings unless they have special significance when used in a trade or business. In such a case the special meaning will be given precedence. The court will assume that the common practices and procedures of the trade or business will be followed unless the parties specifically state otherwise. A contract is strictly construed against the party who drafted it and in favor of the other party as long as the latter's interpretation is reasonable. Written additions to standard form contracts take precedence over the printed matter in these types of contracts.

EXAMPLE

Packard purchases a Cadillac from DeSoto, a used car dealer. The contract is a printed form that provides Packard with one day for inspection; at the end of the contract, however, there is a written clause that provides three days for inspection. Packard and DeSoto quarrel about the inspection time and about whether the term *inspection* includes a test drive. Will Packard get three days for inspection and a test drive? Packard will get the three days for inspection because a written clause takes precedence over a printed form. The term *inspection* is ambiguous. The courts will look to its usual meaning in the trade to see if it includes a test drive. If the term has no definitive meaning in the trade, the court will probably decide in favor of Packard because DeSoto, in drafting the contract, had the opportunity to resolve the matter by defining the term.

Ducheneaux v. Miller
488 N.W. 2d 902 (S.D. 1992)

Ducheneaux entered into a contract in South Dakota with Miller to purchase 551 cattle for $395,965. A clean bill of health was required. The cattle in question had brucellosis (Bang's disease), which can infect humans and cause pain and weakness. Miller asserted that the term *clean bill of health* meant that the cattle would be free from quarantine, which subsequently happened in Nebraska, where the cattle were located. South Dakota would still not allow these cattle to be brought into the state. Ducheneaux argued that a clean bill of health guaranteed that the cattle had met the state and federal tests required for interstate shipment.

The issue is whether this ambiguity means that the parties did not have a meeting of the minds.

In resolving the issue of ambiguities, the court quoted from a legal treatise, 17A Am. Jur. 2d Contracts Section 338 (1991) "A contract is not rendered ambiguous simply because the parties do not agree on its proper construction or their intent upon executing the contract." Rather, a contract is ambiguous only when "it is capable of more than one meaning when viewed objectively by a reasonably in-

telligent person who has examined the context of the entire inte-
grated agreement and who is cognizant of the customs, practices, us-
ages and terminology as generally understood in the particular trade
or business.

Even if an ambiguity were found in the present contract, it must
be construed against Miller because he drafted it and by doing so had
the opportunity to prevent such mistakes. Judgment for Ducheneaux.

VIOLATION OF THE STATUTE OF FRAUDS

If a person is sued for breach of an oral contract that is required to be in writing, this
person must raise the violation of the statute of frauds as a defense in his or her answer
to the plaintiff's complaint in order to nullify the lawsuit. A contract that falls into
more than one category of the statute of frauds must satisfy each of those categories in
order to be valid. Most states hold that a contract that does not satisfy the writing requirement is void, but some states declare it to be voidable. *Voidable* means that who-
ever did not sign the writing can raise the statute of frauds as a defense and can void
the contract at any time before completion. If performance is completed by both parties, the statute of frauds defense is no longer available because performance by both
parties evidences the existence of the contract.

In situations where enforcement will not be granted, the contract will be rescinded, and the consideration given by each party must be returned. In a case where
services have been rendered, the courts will require the receiving party to pay for the
reasonable value of those services to prevent unjust enrichment of the party receiving
the benefit. Some states prevent real estate brokers from recovering the reasonable
value of their services under oral contracts. This protects the public from claims of dishonest brokers.

The writing requirement will be abandoned only where its enforcement would
perpetrate a fraud upon an innocent party. The statute of frauds must not defeat its own
purpose. Such situations arise where part performance has been rendered, where restitution is not adequate, and where an unconscionable result will follow if the contract is
not enforced. The part performance must establish the existence of the alleged oral
contract. This means that all doubt as to the contract's existence must be eliminated.
The part performance rendered must be substantial and made in reliance on an oral
contract for the court to enforce it without a writing.

EXAMPLE | Chrysler rented a warehouse in Pontiac, Michigan, from Buick for three years under an
oral lease. He made a down payment and took possession. After Chrysler converted the
warehouse into a factory for assembly of Model T replicas, Buick canceled the lease,
claiming that it was not in writing. What result? Chrysler may enforce the contract. To require compliance with the statute of frauds in this situation would be to perpetrate a fraud
that the statute is seeking to prevent.

An agreement executed in proper form, in compliance with the statute of frauds, is one element of a valid contract. This does not mean that the contract will be enforced. The party seeking to enforce the contract must prove his or her case. Evidence of a writing will be important proof, but the decision as to whether a valid contract exists and should be enforced rests with the judge or the jury and is based on their interpretation of the evidence.

PAROL EVIDENCE RULE

Parol evidence means oral evidence. The parol evidence rule forbids the introduction of all prior oral or written agreements and simultaneous oral agreements to contradict a written contract.

When the court determines from the face of a writing that it is intended to be the final expression of the parties' agreement, then the parol evidence rule applies. The rule reflects the parties' intentions to be bound by a written contract incorporating the important terms of all prior oral or written agreements. The parties protect themselves from exposure to the uncertainties connected with oral testimony, including perjury, fraud, or the death of witnesses or their loss of memory. The parol evidence rule applies to all contracts, not only to those required to be in writing. But it has special significance to the latter in that it ensures the effectiveness of the statute of frauds requirement. That is why parties should make sure that all important promises, terms, and conditions agreed upon orally or in writing, prior to the writing of the contract, are incorporated in the final written contract. This practice guarantees enforcement of terms that otherwise might be barred by the parol evidence rule.

The main drawback of the parol evidence rule is the fact that there are many situations where the court will allow an exception to the rule. These exceptions minimize the effectiveness of the rule. Some states have even allowed parol evidence to show the parties' intentions in making the contract.

EXAMPLE | Benjamin Franklin enters into a written contract on July 11 to supply Thomas Edison with keys and kites to be used in his experiments on electricity. The contract provides that fifty keys and 100 kites will be shipped to Edison's headquarters in Menlo Park for a total price of $1,000. Franklin sends sixty-five keys (fifteen more than were ordered), and seventy-five kites (twenty-five fewer than were ordered), and bills Edison for $1,500. Franklin attempts to introduce a prior written agreement made on July 4 stating that the contract was for sixty-five keys. He asserts that, at the time the July 4 writing was made, the number of kites was changed by verbal agreement to seventy-five. Finally, Franklin argues that when the July 11 contract was signed, he asked Edison for $1,500 upon delivery and Edison agreed. Can these statements be introduced into evidence? No! The July 4 oral and written statements are precluded by the parol evidence rule because they were made prior to the written contract. The parol evidence rule also bars the July 11 simultaneous oral statement. The July 11 contract is the final expression of the parties' agreement. The changes would be valid only if they had been incorporated into the July 11 contract.

The courts have allowed many exceptions to the parol evidence rule because they feel that unfair judgments will result if the rule is strictly enforced. These exceptions allow oral evidence to be admitted on its **FACE.**

Fraud
Ancillary agreements
Condition precedent fails
Explanation of ambiguities

Fraud   Parol evidence in contradiction of a written contract may be admissible where it shows evidence of fraud, duress, illegality, or mistake. The circumstances surrounding the contract and the conduct of the person making the promise are important items that the court must ascertain.

EXAMPLE | Gutenberg has successfully developed a printing business with the help of a loan from Furst, a distributor of playbills. Gutenberg contracts to print 500,000 copies of a playbill, which Furst will distribute to the various Broadway theaters in return for $70,000. In a plot to take over Gutenberg's business, Furst asks Gutenberg, at the signing of the contract, to print 50,000 additional copies. Gutenberg agrees. Furst later refuses to deliver the additional copies, claiming that there was no contract for their distribution. Knowing that Gutenberg will not be able to pay off the loan unless those additional 50,000 playbills are distributed and paid for, Furst calls for repayment. May Gutenberg introduce the oral statement made simultaneously with the making of the contract? Yes! The simultaneous oral statement may be introduced as evidence of the fraud that Furst was attempting to perpetrate.

Ancillary Agreements   Parol evidence may also be introduced to show ancillary agreements that are not contradictory to the written contract and that are of a type not ordinarily expected to be part of the writing.

EXAMPLE | Cyrus McCormick agreed to buy 1,000 bushels of cotton from Eli Whitney. At the time of the writing, Cyrus McCormick asked Whitney to throw in a case of gin. Eli agreed. When the cotton was delivered, there was no gin. May McCormick introduce into evidence the oral statement regarding the gin? Yes! The oral statement may be introduced— not to contradict the writing but to show an ancillary agreement had been made.

Condition Precedent   The failure of a condition precedent or the failure by the other party to provide consideration may be shown in court by parol evidence in an attempt to rescind a written contract. A condition precedent is a contingency that must be satisfied before the parties are bound to perform the contract.

EXAMPLE | A large engineering firm asked Albert Einstein to conduct experiments for them on his theory of relativity. The terms of the contract included a payment of $75,000 plus a $25,000 bonus. The firm told Einstein that the bonus would be given only if he proved his theory by February 2 of the following year. Later the two parties signed a written contract that did not mention the February 2 deadline for the bonus. Because of an unexpected setback, Einstein did not prove his theory until March 29. The firm paid him $75,000, and Einstein sued for the bonus. May the engineering firm introduce the oral statement made concerning the bonus? Yes! Prior oral statements are admissible to show failure of a condition. Einstein is not entitled to the bonus.

Explanation of Ambiguities   Finally, parol evidence is permissible to explain ambiguities in the language of a written contract. This exception poses the strongest threat to the viability of the parol evidence rule because of the possibility of a large number of claims based on ambiguous terms. Under this exception the UCC permits the introduction into evidence of the usual course of performance in the trade or business, as well as the meaning attributed to any ambiguous term in the particular trade or business.

EXAMPLE | Charles Atlas is opening a new health spa in Columbia, South Carolina. He telephones Hercules Barbell Company, ordering 5,000 pounds of free metal weights for the exercise and weight room. Atlas then sends Hercules a letter confirming the telephone order for 5,000 pounds of free weights. The letter omits his oral request for metal weights. Hercules sends a return letter confirming Atlas's written request. When the weights are delivered, to Altas's amazement they are plastic weights filled with sand. The cost for these weights is $3,200. Atlas expected all-metal weights, which would have cost $2,000. Atlas telephones Hercules and informs them of the mistake. Hercules replies that these weights are the latest thing and are more widely used than the metal weights. Can Atlas introduce the telephone conversation into evidence? Yes! Prior oral testimony, as well as the meaning attributed to the term *free weights* in the trade, may be admitted into evidence to explain the ambiguity confronting the parties as to whether the term means metal or plastic weights.

Subsequent oral or written agreements are always admissible to prove that a material term has been changed or that the contract has been rescinded. However, if the original written contract was required to be in writing and the change made to that contract also falls within one of the statute of frauds categories, then that change must be in writing. This requirement does not apply to modifications that remove the original contract from the purview of the statute of frauds.

EXAMPLE | Kodak hires George Eastman to develop its camera business east of the Mississippi. The employment contract is made in writing for a term of three years. A subsequent, written modification puts Eastman in charge of all operations west of the Mississippi, as well. The duration of the contract is orally modified to a period of ten months because of Eastman's ill health. Are these modifications permissible? Yes! A written modification is always admissible. The oral modification is admissible under the parol evidence rule because it takes a three-year contract out of the grips of the statute of frauds by making it into a contract for less than one year, which does not have to be in writing. On the other hand, if a contract for ten months is modified to a period of three years, the modification must be in writing to satisfy the statute of frauds.

Fecteau v. Southeast Bank, N.A.
585 So. 2d 1005 (Fla. App. 4 Dist. 1991)

Robert and Barbara Grier signed a separation agreement that provided,

> Husband hereby agrees to furnish to Wife a house to be mutually selected by the Husband and Wife, the exclusive use and occupancy of said house to be in the Wife so long as the terms and conditions of this Agreement are fully complied with. Wife agrees to execute any and all documents necessary for the purchase of said house, provided, however, Husband agrees to save and hold harmless the Wife from any obligations incurred by said signing. Husband further agrees to make all payments for the purchase of said house, as well as payments for taxes, fire insurance and other coverage as may be required by a lending institution regarding the purchase of said house. Wife agrees to maintain said house in as good condition, ordinary wear and tear excepted, as said house shall be in at the time of purchase.

A house was selected, and Robert abided by all at the terms of the agreement until his death. At that time his executor, Southeast Bank, argued that his obligation to support Barbara, who had already remarried Edward Fecteau, terminated. Barbara contended that the house was not support, but a property settlement given in lieu of Barbara's interest in Robert's business and the marital home. Robert had custody of their children.

The issue is whether parol evidence is admissible to clear up the ambiguity of whether the parties intended payment on the house, and the house itself, to be support or a property settlement.

The court ruled, "A separation agreement is a contract subject to interpretation like any other contract. Where the terms are unambiguous the parties' intent must be discerned from the four corners of the document." The court continued, "On the other hand, when a contract is ambiguous and the parties suggest different interpretations, the issue of the proper interpretation is an issue of fact requiring the submission of evidence extrinsic to the contract bearing upon the intent of the parties. There was more than one reasonable interpretation of the agreement here." Judgment for Fecteau.

REVIEW QUESTIONS

1. Define formation of a contract, statute of frauds, and parol evidence rule.

2. List the contracts that must be evidenced by some form of a writing, and explain them.

3. Barlow entered into a lease agreement with Agristor Leasing for eight years. After making payments for five years, Barlow defaulted but refused to return the machinery because the rent he paid equaled the cost of the machinery. What result? *Agristor Leasing* v. *Barlow,* 579 N.Y.S. 2d 476 (N.D. 3 Dept. 1992).

4. Keithley's Auction Service entered into a contract with Linda Hall to auction two parcels of real estate belonging to her mother, Jesse Wright. The contract was prepared by Keithley's, and one provision read, "I agree to pay unto Charles J. Keithley $200.00 **MINIMUM OR** 10% of gross sale on personal property. On real estate $50.00 **MINIMUM OR** 5% of gross sale."

   The highest bid was $70,000. The purchasers paid $7,000 down. Hall paid Keithley's $3,500. The purchasers were unable to obtain financing for the balance, and the sale was canceled, with the purchasers forfeiting their downpayment. Is Keithley's entitled to keep the commission? What result? *Keithley's Auction Service* v. *Children of Jesse Wright,* 579 N.E. 2d 657 (Ind. App. 4 Dist. 1991).

5. Art Buckalew signed a contract with the C & P Telephone Company in 1978 for a Yellow Pages advertisement, which contained a stipulated damage clause. In 1981, he signed the following:

   TO THE C & P TELEPHONE COMPANY OF W.VA.: THIS IS YOUR AUTHORITY TO INSERT IN THE NEXT DIRECTORY (INDICATED ABOVE) THE SAME ITEMS OF ADVERTISING NOW APPEARING IN THE CURRENT ISSUE OF THAT DIRECTORY.
   ALL OTHER TERMS AND CONDITIONS WILL REMAIN AS PREVIOUSLY SIGNED. DISPLAY ITEMS WILL BE ASSIGNED THE SAME POSITION NUMBER OR BETTER IN ANY DIRECTORY WHERE SPACE PRECEDENCE IS APPLICABLE.

   Do the terms of the prior agreement become part of the 1981 contract? *Art's Flower Shop* v. *C & P Telephone Co.,* 413 S.E. 2d 670 (W. Va. 1991).

6. Mark Bonk and Milton Bradley were involved in negotiation concerning the licensing of Bonk's game, "Play It Again, Juke Box." Milton Bradley sent a copy of its licensing agreement to Bonk for review. The licensing agreement stated that it would be the entire agreement of the parties and that no other representations, oral or written, would be binding. This agreement was never executed. Bonk contended that an oral contract existed. Milton Bradley retorted that the minds of the parties had never met. What result? *M.T. Bonk Co.* v. *Milton Bradley Co.,* 945 F. 2d 1404 (7th Cir. 1991).

7. Daniel Iseman signed a promissory note in which he agreed to pay David Hobbs $20,000 and 10 percent interest. The note stated that this promise was "for value received." When the note became due, Iseman refused to pay, asserting lack of consideration. Is Iseman's testimony regarding consideration admissible under the parol evidence rule? *Iseman* v. *Hobbs,* 351 S.E. 2d 351 (S.C. App. 1986).

8. The Arizona Board of Regents entered into a contract with Mardian Construction Company for the construction of the Ensphere. The dome facility was to be located on the Northern Arizona University campus in Flagstaff. Mardian entered into a subcontract agreement with Pioneer Roofing Company. Pioneer agreed to provide all labor and materials for the construction of the dome's entire roofing application. Because of severity of the cold weather during December 1976, emergency measures were taken—with the architect's verbal approval, given at a December 15 meeting—to prevent the destruction of the roof's wood and insulation. Pioneer did not submit its claims for the extra work until its final billing in June 1978. In November 1979 Mardian submitted this billing to the architectural firm, which declined to grant the change order for additional compensation. Did the architect's verbal approval amount to a waiver of the written requirement for all changes in work? *Pioneer Roofing Co.* v. *Mardian Construction Co.,* 733 P. 2d 652 (Ariz. App. 1986).

9. Schnucks, a developer, entered into an oral agreement with Glen Park, a general partnership, to share equally the cost of extending a sewer line to Schnucks' property. Glen Park then breached the agreement, damaging Schnucks in that costs increased and Schnucks had to assume Glen Park's share. Glen Park claims that David Cassilly, a general partner, did not have the authority to contract for the partnership. Is the contract valid? *Schnucks Markets, Inc.* v. *Cassilly,* 724 S.W. 2d 664 (Mo. App. 1987).

10. Banque Paribas acquired United Refining, Inc. (URI) on a public foreclosure sale. On November 15, 1985, United Acquisition Corporation (UAC) sent a letter of intent to Banque Paribas to purchase the common stock of URI for $2.5 million. The letter stated that a formal written contract would follow. In the interim there were many oral conversations between the parties. On December 5, 1985, after instructing his attorney to draft a written agreement, John Catsinatidis of UAC was waiting in Banque Paribas' office to transfer $4 million cash. After being sent away while Banque Paribas finished deliberating, he was told that his delay in the transfer of funds had caused the deal to fall through. The Creditors' Committee of United Refining made a larger offer. Then on December 9, 1985, Catsinatidis offered a certified check, which was refused.The issue is whether UAC can get an injunction based on the oral agreement to prevent Banque Paribas from selling United Refining to the Creditors Committee. Has part performance been rendered with presentation of the check? *United Acquisition Corp.* v. *Banque Paribas,* 631 F. Supp. 797 (S.D.N.Y. 1985).

15

Rights of Third Parties

Introduction
Third-Party Beneficiaries
Assignment
Contract Rights Not
   Assignable

Delegation of Duties
Rights and Duties of an Assignee
Duties of an Assignor
Review Questions

INTRODUCTION

Parties enter into a third-party contract with the intention of benefiting a third party, or of assigning rights and duties to a third party. The former situation is called a third-party beneficiary contract, and the latter is known as an assignment. In a third-party beneficiary contract, rights of the third party are created by the original contract. In an assignment, third-party rights are created after the contract is made through a transfer of rights to a third party.

THIRD-PARTY BENEFICIARIES

A *third-party beneficiary contract* is a contract entered into by two persons for the purpose of benefiting a third person. The purpose or intention to benefit a third party can be established through oral testimony in accordance with the parol evidence rule. The third person has a legal right to enforce the contract once he or she is notified of the benefit and either accepts or relies upon it. The contract cannot be canceled nor can subsequent alterations be made without the third-party beneficiary's consent unless the right to cancel or alter has been reserved through a stipulation in the contract.

There are three types of third-party beneficiaries, here referred to as **CID.**

Creditor beneficiary
Incidental beneficiary
Donee beneficiary

Creditor Beneficiary

Where consideration has been furnished to one of the two contracting parties by a third person, that third person is known as a *creditor beneficiary.* A third-party beneficiary contract occurs where a debtor furnishes another person with consideration in return for that party's promise to repay a debt owed to a creditor. The creditor beneficiary may recover the debt from either party upon nonperformance.

EXAMPLE | Cancer agrees to sell his seafood restaurant, The Crab House, to Pisces. The contract provides that Pisces will assume the mortgage on The Crab House, which is held by Scorpion Enterprises. After taking possession Pisces fails to make the monthly mortgage payments. Can Scorpion sue Cancer for nonpayment? Yes! Scorpion is a creditor beneficiary to the contract between Cancer and Pisces.

Incidental Beneficiary

A third person who will receive an incidental benefit from a contract that two other people made without that purpose in mind is an *incidental beneficiary.* If the benefit is not realized, the incidental beneficiary cannot enforce the contract because he or she is not legally entitled to it. People who are not parties to a contract and who are not intended beneficiaries of the contract have no right to enforce the contract. Enforcement is predicated upon the third person's being able to show an interest in the benefit that is substantial enough to qualify him or her as a donee beneficiary.

One can distinguish between an incidental beneficiary and an intended beneficiary by determining whether performance of the benefit is made directly to the third person, whether the third person has any right to oversee the performance, or whether the third person's right to the benefit is set forth in the contract.

EXAMPLE | The City of San Francisco employs the Gemini Twins Construction Company to reconstruct part of the roadway on the Golden Gate Bridge by November 9. The work is not completed until January 8. Libra, a justice on the California Supreme Court, must drive fifty extra miles because of the bridge construction. Can he sue Gemini Twins Construction for lost time and expenses? No! The contract was not made directly for Libra's benefit. He is an incidental beneficiary to the contract between San Francisco and the Gemini Twins Construction Company.

Donee Beneficiary

A *donee beneficiary* is a third person who has not given any consideration in return for a benefit. The party designating the third person donee beneficiary has supplied the necessary consideration to the other contracting party. That other contracting party, in turn, must promise to confer a benefit upon the third person. Either the donee beneficiary or the party making the designation has the right to sue the other party for breach of contract if the benefit is not performed.

If the party making the contract for the benefit of the third party does not perform his or her obligation, the third-party beneficiary, whether creditor or donee, will not be able to enforce the contract.

EXAMPLE | Virgo's Uncle Leo names her as beneficiary to his life insurance policy. After a falling-out Leo wants to know if he can change the beneficiary without Virgo's consent. The policy does not speak to this issue. Because Uncle Leo did not reserve the right to change beneficiaries, Virgo's consent is required. If the insurance company refuses to pay Virgo after Leo dies because she has given no consideraton, what will her argument be? Virgo will assert that the consideration paid by Leo in the form of premiums supports the insurance company's promise to pay her as beneficiary. However, if Leo had allowed the policy to lapse by failing to make timely premiun payments, Virgo would have no recourse.

Simpson v. JOC Coal, Inc.
677 S.W. 2d 305 (Ky. 1984)

James Simpson was the president of Skyuka Mining and a minority shareholder. On September 12, 1975, JOC Companies entered into a buyout agreement with the majority shareholders. Simpson was not a party to this agreement however, his interest was recognized in the contract.

> The parties to this agreement; acknowledge that . . . James W. Simpson is not a party to this agreement. It is, however, understood and agreed that the JOC Companies will undertake to conclude a similar arrangement with James W. Simpson under which said James W. Simpson will also consent to a similar amending of the Agreement.

The issue is whether Simpson was the intended or incidental beneficiary to the September 12 agreement.

The court stated that the general rule is

> that a third party for whose benefit a contract is made may maintain an action thereon; however, he must have been a party to the consideration or the contract must have been made for his benefit and the mere fact

that he will be incidentally benefited by the performance of the contract is not sufficient to entitle him to enforce it.

The court continued,

The majority shareholders and the JOC Companies, in striking their bargain, obviously recognized his interest not only by providing in the contract for JOC Companies to make Simpson a suitable offer, but also by providing in the contract that JOC Companies would "indemnify" and "hold .. harmless" the majority shareholders from all claim, causes of action and liabilities the shareholders could incur from entering into this agreement separate and apart from James W. Simpson. It is hard to imagine a situation where an individual could be more of an intended beneficiary of the contract than Simpson was in these circumstances. It was necessary for the majority shareholders to provide for his interest or risk the legal consequences. . . .

Judgment for Simpson.

ASSIGNMENT

An *assignment* is the transfer of a party's rights in a contract to a third person. A party transfers contractual rights to a third person (1) as payment of a debt, (2) in exchange for payment or performance, or (3) as a gift. The party making the assignment is known as an *assignor.* An assignor is one of the original contracting parties, who is seeking to transfer his or her contractual rights—and possibly his or her contractual duties—to a third person. The third person, to whom the assignment is made, is called an *assignee.* The other original contracting party is referred to as an *obligor.* An obligor is one who owes a duty to perform for an assignee because of an assignment. It is also possible that an assignor or an assignee owes a duty to perform for the obligor.

An assignment must be differentiated from a novation. A *novation* is an agreement made by three persons wherein one of the two original contracting parties is released from all contractual liability through the substitution of a third person. A novation is actually a new contract with the third person assuming all the rights and duties of the party who has been relieved. In an assignment an assignor is still accountable under the contract even though the assignor's rights and duties have been transferred to a third person. An assignment is not a new contract because there is no agreement to release the assignor from liability.

EXAMPLE | Taurus owns a cattle ranch in Texas. He needs an irrigation system to maintain fertile grazing areas. Aquarius is hired to construct an irrigation system. A short time later Taurus sells the ranch to Libra, a retired justice, who wants to raise cattle for investment purposes. Aquarius agrees to release Taurus and render performance for Libra, who has assumed the duty to pay. Subsequently Aquarius is offered a much larger irrigation project in the prairie lands. He assigns his rights and duties under the contract to Sagittarius, who is equally competent. What is the relationship of the parties in the two situations? The first is a novation. Taurus, an original contracting party, is released from all responsibility while Libra steps into his shoes. The second is an assignment. Aquarius, the assignor, assigns his rights and duties under the contract to Sagittarius, the assignee. Sagittarius thereby becomes primarily liable for performance; however, Aquarius can also be held accountable if Sagittarius does not perform.

Consideration is not prerequisite to the making of an assignment; therefore, gifts created through assignments are permissible. However, an assignor may revoke these gratuitous assignments by death, by bankruptcy, by a subsequent assignment of the same rights in return for consideration; or through notice, unless the assignment has become irrevocable. In many states, an assignment becomes irrevocable (1) if it is made in writing and signed by the assignor; (2) if the assignee has received payment or performance from the obligor; or (3) if the assignor has delivered to the assignee a document, which is necessary to evidence the existence of a contract, such as a deed, mortgage, stock certificate, or bankbook.

EXAMPLE | Aries assigns his interest in the Los Angeles Rams to his nephew Capricorn by transferring all the stock certificates he owns. After a falling-out Aries revokes his gift, but Capricorn refuses to return the stock. Is this assignment revocable? No! The stock certificates have been transferred to Capricorn, the assignment is thus complete. Ownership of the stock now resides with Capricorn.

Adolphus v. National Super Markets
775 F. Supp. 1243 (E.D. Mo. 1991)

In June 1979 Chippewa Watson Corporation leased a building to National Super Markets for twenty years. In December 1981 National subleased the building to Kroger for $308,000. At that point Chippewa Watson was receiving $259,000 from National. Chippewa Watson then transferred ownership to Adolphus in August 1985. In January 1987 Kroger assigned its sublease to Schnucks. In March 1987 National assigned the original lease to Kroger.

The lease provided in paragraph 8,

> [I]n no event shall the annual total rent be less than the greater of (a) the average total rent paid by Lessee to Lessor for the three (3) years immediately proceeding [sic] such assignment or subletting, or (b) an amount equal to (a) plus one-half of the amount by which the annual total rent (after deducting any third party leasing commissions) received by Lessee from such sublessee or assignee exceeds (a).

The issue is whether the assignment of the original lease from National to Kroger in March 1987 triggered an increase in rent owed to the landlord, Adolphus.

> The court held,
>
> [P]laintiffs have come to the conclusion that they are entitled to a rent increase from $259,000.00 to $283,500.00 per year. Lessee National paid to lessor plaintiffs $259,000.00 per year for each of the three years preceding the assignment. Therefore, (a) equals $259,000.00. Sublessee Schnucks paid to lessee National $308,000.00 per year. Therefore, (b) equals $259,000.00 + ½ ($308,000.00 − 259,000.00) = $283,500.00.
>
> Under the Court's interpretation of Paragraph 8, the rent received by the lessee from the sublessee is simply not taken into account when the transaction at issue is an assignment of the Lease. Instead, the formula considers the amount that the lessee received from the assignee for the assignment. Lessee National paid to lessor plaintiffs $259,000.00 per year for each of the three years preceding the assignment.
>
> Judgment for National Super Markets and Kroger.

The UCC, under Article 9, Secured Transactions, requires that all assignments of contract rights be made in writing. For this discussion contract rights include the assignor's right to payment or to return performance by the obligor either before or after performance. (The UCC defines these rights as "accounts.") The right to sue for damages based on a cause of action for breach of contract may also be assigned from a party to a third person. Under a general provision of Article 1, the UCC requires assignments of causes of action to be in writing where the assigned right is over $5,000.

CONTRACT RIGHTS NOT ASSIGNABLE

Assignments of contract rights may be made with the following exceptions: **CARS.**

> **C**lause in contract forbids assignments
> **A**lteration of obligor's duties
> **R**isk to obligor is increased
> **S**tatutes that prohibit assignments

Clause in Contract Forbids Assignments

A contract containing a clause stating that assignments cannot be made without the consent of the obligor is generally not favored. However, a person may be restricted from assigning a contract where his or her duties involve special skill, knowledge, expertise, judgment, character, trust, or confidence. In these instances, clauses prohibiting assignments will be enforced as long as consent is not withheld unreasonably. Assignments of certain rights may not be curtailed. These include ownership rights in real estate, commercial paper, checks, and securities—except for closely held corporations. Also included are accounts receivable that arise through the completion of performance by one party and contract rights that require no return performance by the assignee.

EXAMPLE | The circus has come to town! The world-renowned trapeze artists, the Gemini Twins, are the main attraction. There is a covenant in the contract restricting the Gemini Twins from assigning their rights and duties under the contract. Is this covenant enforceable? Partially! The Gemini Twins' duty to perform is properly restricted because it involves special skills and experience. Their right to payment may not be limited. Would the restrictive clause be valid if applied to the sellers of popcorn and peanuts? No! That task is routine and can be performed by almost anyone.

Obligor's Duties Are Altered

An assignment may not be made that will materially alter the obligor's duties either by placing a greater burden on the obligor to perform or by changing the performance altogether.

EXAMPLE | Virgo makes weekly deliveries of beef to Taurus, who operates a Steak and Bake Restaurant in Tulsa. This week Taurus is full of bull, so he assigns his contract with Virgo to a Steak and Bake Restaurant in Oklahoma City. Must Virgo perform according to the assignment? No! The assignment has substantially altered his duties under the contract by requesting him to perform in another city a great distance away.

Risk to Obligor Is Increased

Assignments that increase the risk an obligor must endure under a contract will not be allowed.

EXAMPLE | Leo was a clown in the Sells Floto Circus. The circus was sold, and the performers' contracts were assigned to the new owner, who requested Leo to perform in the lion's den. Must Leo accede? No! Leo's contract may not be assigned in this case because it increases the risk of physical harm.

Statutes Prohibit Assignments

Statutes may expressly forbid assignments involving benefits derived from alimony and worker's compensation, causes of action for personal injury; and right to wages. Wage assignments are generally not prohibited, but some states restrict them to a limited amount.

EXAMPLE | Pisces, who works in the Fulton Fish Market, was injured after slipping on a mackerel. Pisces received worker's compensation but attempted to assign the entire award to a gentleman who made her an offer she could not refuse. The gentleman told Pisces that she would be sleeping with the fish unless the assignment was made. Can a worker's compensation award be assigned? No! It is a personal right that can be received only by the injured party.

DELEGATION OF DUTIES

Delegation of duties occurs when the assignor transfers his or her obligations under a contract to a third person (assignee). A contractual obligation cannot be excused by delegation of one's duties to a third party unless a novation is made. An assignor remains liable to an obligor for completion of the performance agreed upon, although the actual performance may be rendered by an assignee. This is because the obligor contracted with the assignor, not the assignee. The contract between the parties is still binding on both of them even though the assignee may perform the assignor's duties. If the assignee fails to perform the delegated duties in accordance with the contract, the assignor must perform them or be liable for breach of contract.

EXAMPLE | Capricorn was a famous baseball pitcher until he lost three games in the World Series and was nicknamed "The Goat." He retired from baseball and became involved in sports field maintenance. The volume of business was so great that he ended up with two contracts for April 10. Capricorn assigned the contract with the Minnesota Twins to Aries. He handled the Masters Golf Tournament at Augusta himself. There was a rainstorm before the Twins' home opener, and Aries did a poor job of maintaining the field. As a result the Twins were forced to cancel their opener. Who is liable for the damages? Gemini, owner of the Twins, may sue both Capricorn and Aries. If Capricorn is required to pay damages to the Twins, he can sue Aries for indemnification because Aries breached the duties delegated to him under the assigned contract.

RIGHTS AND DUTIES OF AN ASSIGNEE

An assignee's rights and duties are no greater than the rights and duties of the assignor. If the obligor has any defense against the assignor, this defense will be effective against the assignee. This is true even when an assignee gives valuable consideration to the assignor. If a defense is raised by the obligor, the assignee has a cause of action for breach of contract against the assignor but not against the obligor.

An assignment is effective immediately, without notice to the obligor, unless the contract provides that notice must be given. However, an assignee should notify the obligor of the assignment in an expeditious manner once the assignment is made. This is for the assignee's protection as well as for the obligor's information. If the obligor does not receive notice of the assignment before he or she renders performance for the assignor, the obligor will not be liable to the assignee. This is based on the reasoning that, as between innocent parties, the party with the opportunity to prevent the mistake of injustice (the assignee) is the one who must bear the loss.

The assignee has the power to prevent the problem through prompt notification; otherwise the assignee will be relegated to recovering the loss from the assignor. If the obligor has notice of the assignment but performs for the assignor anyway, the obligor will be liable to the assignee for not fulfilling his or her duty under the assigned contract. If the assignor does not turn over the consideration received from the obligor, the assignee has a cause of action against the assignor as well as the obligor.

EXAMPLE | Leo, a hunter, captures an African lion and agrees to sell it to the Bronx Zoo. The Bronx Zoo assigns its right to possession of the lion to the San Diego Zoo on July 4. On July 11 the lion is delivered to the Bronx Zoo. On July 17 Leo receives notice of the assignment. Has the San Diego Zoo, as the assignee, any rights against Leo? No! Prompt notice of the assignment was not given. The San Diego Zoo must look to the Bronx Zoo to claim the lion.

A more serious difficulty arises when the assignor assigns the same contract rights to two or more assignees. The obligor will only be liable once for payment or performance. This is why immediate notice should be given to the obligor. Most states require performance to be rendered to the first assignee to whom the assignor assigns the contract rights even though this assignee may not have been the first to give notice to the obligor. This is based on the theory that once the assignment is made to the first assignee, the assignor has no more "rights" to assign, and that subsequent assignments are thus void. However, there are exceptions to this theory if a subsequent assignee gives valuable consideration and acts without notice of the first assignment.

A subsequent assignee who receives from the obligor either payment or a document essential to the enforcement of the contract, such a deed, mortgage, or bankbook, will prevail. This is similarly true of one who enters into a novation with the obligor and the assignor or who obtains a judgment against an obligor. Some states allow a subsequent assignee to recover if he or she is the first to notify the obligor and has given valuable consideration while acting without notice of the first assignment. The burden of proving this will be on that assignee. To avoid this predicament a prudent assignee will inform the obligor of the prospective assignment and inquire if the assignor has made any previous assignments.

EXAMPLE | Aquarius arrives back in a New England port with 1,000 pounds of shad roe caviar. He agrees to sell the entire catch to a new restaurant called the Scorpion's Delight. The Scorpion's Delight assigns the same contract to both the Crab Palace and Pisces Emporium. The Crab Palace is the first to receive the assignment, but the Emporium is the first to give notice to Aquarius. Who gets the caviar? Most states would give it to the Crab Palace, even though it was not the first to give notice, because it was the first to receive the assignment.

The assignee also has a duty to perform any delegated duties he or she has agreed to assume. If the assignee fails to perform the obligation, the obligor has a cause of action for breach of contract against both the assignor and the assignee for failure to perform in cases where consideration is given.

EXAMPLE | Universal Pictures wants to make a movie about Capricorn. Sagittarius agrees to deliver certain props but thereafter assigns the contract to Tops in Props, who is three days late in delivery. Who is accountable for the damages caused by the delay? Both Sagittarius and Tops in Props, although Tops in Props is primarily liable. If Sagittarius pays the damages, Tops in Props must indemnify it because Tops in Props has breached its delegated duty to deliver the props under the assigned contract.

DUTIES OF AN ASSIGNOR

An assignor has a duty to the obligor to guarantee that performance is completed by the assignee. This is why the assignor remains liable on the contract after the assignment has been made. In making an assignment an assignor impliedly warrants to an assignee that the assigned claim is valid, that any signed writing evidencing the assignment is authentic, and that no interference will be made to impair the value of the assignment. However, no warranty is made guaranteeing the obligor's solvency and performance. The assignee has a cause of action against the assignor if any of the warranties made by the assignor are breached. An assignor who receives payment or performance from the obligor is accountable to the assignee and must hold that payment or performance in trust. An assignor who assigns his or her rights under a contract to more than one assignee will be liable to those assignees who do not receive performance from the obligor.

EXAMPLE | Virgo financed her Uncle Leo in a moving picture venture. In return Leo assigns his royalty rights for writing the screenplay to the movie *The Cowardly Lion Returns to Oz.* The production folds after the producer declares bankruptcy. Has Virgo any recourse? No! As long as Uncle Leo acted without knowledge of the bankruptcy, he is not accountable for it. Virgo had a choice in accepting the assignment. The risk of the producer's bankruptcy falls upon her.

REVIEW QUESTIONS

1. Define third-party beneficiary contracts; creditor, incidental and donee beneficiaries; assignment; assignor; assignee; obligor; and novation.
2. Which contract rights are not assignable?
3. On July 14, 1987, Ducheneaux entered into a contract with Miller to buy a herd of 551 cattle for $395,968. The contract required a clean bill of health. Miller could not comply with this requirement because some of the cattle had Bang's disease, which caused them to abort. On November 9, 1987,

Ducheneaux and Miller amended the July 14 contract, reducing the number Ducheneaux purchased. Miller claims that this was a novation and that, because the bill-of-health requirement was not stated in the November 9 contract, he is not liable for the cattle's poor health. What result? *Ducheneaux* v. *Miller,* 488 N.W. 2d 902 (S. D. 1992).

4. D&B Computing Services sold Nomad, a software product, to Must Software. The contract for sale assigned to Must the right to enforce any violation of the employment agreement related to the sale of Nomad. Larry Parcler, a former D&B employee, started Diversified Business Systems to provide consulting services to users of Nomad. Two former D&B employees, who were at Must, left to join Diversified. The issue is whether the restrictive covenant in an employment contract that is assigned when the business is sold still has validity. What result? *U.S. Corp. of America* v. *Parker,* 414 S.E. 2d 513 (Ga. App. 1991).

5. When sued by Branch for dumping oil waste in Cottonwood creek, which flowed through Branch's property, Mobil Oil sought to enforce easements and releases given to it by Collier, the prior owner of Branch's property. Branch argued that the easements and releases, although lawful when given, were now against public policy. What result? *Branch* v. *Mobil Oil Corp.,* 772 F. Supp. 570 (S.D. Okl. 1991).

6. Agristor Leasing entered into a lease with Barlow for dairy equipment. Subsequently Agristor Leasing assigned the rents due to Teachers Insurance and Annuity Association as collateral for a loan. Barlow argued that once an assignment was made, Agristor forfeited its right to repossess the equipment. What result? *Agristor Leasing* v. *Barlow,* 579 N.Y.S. 2d 476 (A.D. 3 Dept. 1992).

7. Holly owed Fox $300. Lawrence asked Holly if he could borrow $300. Holly loaned Lawrence the money and told him to repay the money to Fox. Lawrence never paid Fox. Fox sued Lawrence for nonpayment. What result? *Lawrence* v. *Fox,* 20 N.Y. 268 (1859).

8. Carl Allison executed two promissory notes worth $12,000 and signed his name to both. When he failed to repay the notes, Raymond Smith sued him. Allison contends that he never received any money or anything of value himself in exchange for signing the notes. He claims that the money was for his employer, Daniel's Steakhouse. What result? *Smith* v. *Allison,* 349 S.E. 2d (N.C. App. 1986).

9. Spiklevitz loaned money to the Herons, who executed a promissory note for $4,800. Subsequently the Herons, who still owed money on the note, sold their business to Markmil Corporation, which executed an "Assumption of Obligations." Markmil failed to pay the amount due on the promissory note, claiming that Spiklevitz was not a third-party beneficiary of the contract formed by the assumption of obligations made in connection with their purchase of the Herons' business. What result? *Spiklevitz* v. *Markmil Corporation,* 357 N.W. 2d 721 (Mich. App. 1984).

16

Remedies for Breach of Contract

Breach of Contract	Reformation
Remedies	UCC Remedies
Injunction	Money Damages
Quasi Contract	Duty to Mitigate Damages
Specific Performance	Review Questions
Rescission and Restitution	

BREACH OF CONTRACT

Most contracts are completed without significant problems. Parties generally fulfill their promises under the contract. *Breach of contract* occurs when a party does not fulfill his or her promise to perform. The breach is a failure to perform a material contractual obligation. It may take the form of renunciation of the contract or restraining of the other party's performance as well as failure to perform. A breach may be either partial or total. It may be material or incidental.

A material breach is substantial and goes to the heart of the contract. The other party may treat the contract as canceled and terminate performance.

EXAMPLE | Christopher Columbus contracts to discover India for Queen Isabella by the way of the west. On October 12 Columbus sights land. He thinks it is India, but in fact he has discovered America. He decides to stay on because the natives are so friendly. Has Columbus breached the contract? Definitely! His contract with Queen Isabella obligated him to find the Third World, not the New World.

Incidental breaches involving minor defects occur where substantial performance has been rendered. The party for whom performance was rendered still has a duty to perform. However, he or she has a cause of action for damages to remedy the incidental defects.

EXAMPLE | A Portuguese trading company wanted to be the first to open a trade route to India by way of the Atlantic. Upon learning of Columbus's failure, they sent Vasco da Gama and gave him six months to complete the voyage. Vasco arrived five days late because of a brief stop at the Cape of Good Hope. Has Vasco da Gama breached the contract? Vasco has substantially complied with the contract. His delay in arriving is only an incidental breach.

McDonald's Corp. v. Robert A. Makin, Inc.
653 F. Supp. 401 (W.D. N.Y. 1986)

On November 22, 1971, McDonald's entered into a franchise agreement with Robert A. Makin permitting Makin to open a McDonald's restaurant in Clarence, New York. The franchise agreement provided for monthly payments to McDonald's consisting of license and lease fees plus a percentage of the restaurant's gross sales. It also permitted McDonald's to revoke the franchisee's license if there were a default in payment. In October 1985 Makin defaulted. As of January 1986 the accrued debt had exceeded $40,000.

McDonald's advised Makin that the franchise would be terminated on February 10, 1986, Makin refused to cease operations and to surrender the premises. He also refused to pay the franchise fees, claiming illegal conduct on the part of McDonald's.

The issue is whether Makin breached the franchise agreement.

The court stated,

> It is hornbook law that when a breach of contract occurs, the party may either retain the benefits and obligations of the contract and sue for damages or declare the contract terminated and perform no further. The defendants in this action did neither. It is clear under basic contract principles that, absent an affirmative defense excusing the defendants' failure to pay, Makin cannot refuse to meet his obligations under the contract while enjoying all of the benefits. Upon Makin's refusal to pay the amount owed, McDonald's had a clear contractual right to terminate the franchise agreement.

The court declared, "ORDERED, that defendant shall cease business operations of the McDonald's restaurant which is the subject of this proceeding and surrender possession of such restaurant to plaintiff. . . ." Judgment for McDonald's Corporation.

REMEDIES

Contractual *remedies* are the means by which a legal right is enforced where there has been a breach of contract. The purpose of a remedy is to restore the party harmed by the breach to a position as favorable as he or she would have held had the contract been carried out as promised, or to the position he or she had been in before the contract came about. This may be accomplished either through compensation or through prevention of the breach. There are two categories of remedies: legal and equitable. Legal remedies are enacted by federal and state legislatures and are found in statutes. Courts can also grant equitable remedies for reasons of fairness and justice.

An equitable remedy is granted when the usual legal remedy would be harsh to the innocent party. In requesting an equitable remedy, the party must have acted in good faith and commenced the lawsuit without unnecessary delay. Equitable remedies are preferable, especially where the breaching party has little or no money to pay for the loss. These remedies also prevent a party who is breaching the contract from becoming unjustly enriched at the expense of the party who is suffering the loss. In many cases parties may elect the remedies that they prefer. However, where remedies are conflicting, a party may choose only one. For example, in a breach of contract involving refusal to sell a house, the aggrieved party is not entitled to specific performance as well as money damages.

The equitable and legal remedies can be memorized by those who still have high **IQs** after drinking a triple **RRRUM.**

Injunction
Quasi contract
Specific performance

Rescission
Restitution
Reformation
UCC remedies
Money damages

INJUNCTION

An *injunction* is an equitable remedy that prevents a party breaching a contract from rendering the same performance elsewhere. An injunction is personal in nature and negative in effect in that it precludes a person from performing certain acts. In cases involving personal service contracts, this remedy is used instead of the remedy of specific performance because specific performance cannot be granted to compel a party to perform services against his or her will. Because the breaching party cannot be compelled to perform a certain act, an injunction can prohibit the party from performing the same act elsewhere. An injunction acts as a restraint against the party breaching a personal service contract.

EXAMPLE | Henry Hudson is under contract with an English company to explore only for them. Henry receives a better deal from a Dutch outfit and repudiates his contract with the English. Can the English prevent Henry from working for the Dutch? Yes! An injunction can be granted, but the English cannot legally force him to explore for them through specific performance.

QUASI CONTRACT

The word *quasi* means seemingly. A *quasi contract* seems to be a contract. Quasi contracts are not actually contracts but rather obligations implied in law for reasons of fairness and justice and to prevent unjust enrichment of a party at the expense of another.

Although a quasi contract lacks the elements of a contract, it has the binding effect of a contract. In a quasi contract an obligation arises in the party receiving performance to pay for the reasonable value of the services rendered or the goods delivered. It would be unjust to deny compensation to a person who performs a benefit for another in good faith because there is no formal contract.

EXAMPLE | Jacques Cartier, while journeying through the St. Lawrence River, comes upon Samuel de Champlain and his crew, who are badly in need of food. Cartier supplies them with what they need and then continues on his journey to Montreal. On the way back Cartier discovers that Champlain is doing quite well. He owns a resort and even has a lake named after him. Cartier asks Champlain to reimburse him but is refused. What result? Cartier may recover the reasonable value of the supplies given under the theory of quasi contract. Although no actual contract exists between the two, the law will imply a contract for the reasons of fairness and justice to prevent Champlain from becoming unjustly enriched at Cartier's expense.

SPECIFIC PERFORMANCE

Specific performance is granted where the only way to fulfill the party's reasonable expectations is to force the breaching party to perform the contract and where the remedies of money damages and rescission are inadequate. Specific performance can be obtained only in a contract involving something unique. Subject matters that are unique include real estate, art, antiques, other rare items, and stock of a closely held corporation. The latter is considered unique because the number of shares is restricted, the stock cannot be obtained through a public exchange, and the power to exercise control over the corporation's affairs is inherent in the stock.

EXAMPLE | Cortez, an antique dealer, agrees to purchase genuine Aztec treasures from Montezuma, who inherited them from his ancestors. Before delivery Montezuma gets a better offer from Velasquez, a fierce competitor of Cortez. Can Cortez still lay claim to the treasures? Yes! Aztec treasures are unique. Therefore specific performance will be granted because money damages are inadequate.

The remedy of specific performance does not apply to personal service contracts, including employment and construction contracts. Although these contracts are unique, one cannot force parties in breach personally to perform them. To do so would relegate a breaching party to involuntary servitude, which is in violation of the United States Constitution. Meaningful performance could not be assured because the courts do not have the capabilities to monitor mandatory personal performance or to judge whether or not it is adequate. The equitable remedy of specific performance will also not be granted where the result would be unconscionable.

EXAMPLE | Suppose that Cortez, the expert in antique treasures from in the previous example, misrepresents the value of the Aztec treasures to Montezuma and persuades him to sell the treasures for a low price. After signing the contract Montezuma learns of the fraud and refuses to perform. Will specific performance be granted for Cortez? No! The result would be unconscionable. The use of fraud precludes Cortez from taking advantage of an equitable remedy.

RESCISSION AND RESTITUTION

Rescission and *restitution* can be both legal and equitable remedies, depending upon whether they are provided by statute or invoked equitably by the court's discretion. Rescission is the cancellation of the contract; restitution is the returning of the parties to the positions they were in before the contract came about. Restitution requires each party to give back the consideration he or she received and return to the status quo. The right to rescind will expire if the party continues to perform under the contract. This right will also expire if not exercised within a reasonable time. The party wishing to rescind must evidence his or her intent by giving prompt notice.

EXAMPLE | Kubla Khan hires Marco Polo to build the Great Wall of China, which is intended to keep out unfriendly neighbors. The Khan pays Marco $100,000. Marco agrees to use a strong bonding cement. Upon inspection the Khan discovers that Marco is using the cheapest cement available. This cement will crack and can easily be demolished by the neighboring Mongolians. What recourse does the Khan have against Marco? The Khan can rescind the contract because of the material breach caused by Marco's fraud. Marco must make restitution by returning the $100,000, and he may also be liable for money damages caused by the delay in construction that will result because of his breach.

REFORMATION

Reformation is the rewriting of a contract to reflect the true intentions of the parties where the terms have been stated incorrectly. It is usually applied in cases where the parties have made a mutual mistake concerning a material fact. The remedy is available only for an error in writing, not for an error in meaning. Even if the contract falls under the statute of frauds, reformation is available to correct the written mistake. If one party has made a material mistake that the other party is aware of, or should be aware of, the contract can be reformed to evidence the mistaken party's true intent. A contract can also be reformed without resort to a lawsuit if the parties mutually agree to the reformation.

EXAMPLE | Robert E. Peary agrees to lead an expedition to the North Pole for a fee of $100 per mile. When the government secretary typed the contract, it read $10 per mile. What remedy is available to Peary? Reformation! The contract may be reformed to evidence the intent of the parties.

UCC REMEDIES

The UCC remedies will be discussed in Chapter 21, "Sales: Buyer's and Seller's Remedies."

MONEY DAMAGES

Money damages are awarded to compensate a party for a loss sustained. The innocent party has the burden of proving that he or she suffered damages as a result of the other party's breach. Money will usually be a satisfactory substitute for performance if a breach occurs, but when it is not, an equitable remedy may be granted for reasons of fairness and justice. For example, when an individual refuses to perform a personal service contract, an injunction may be granted; when a party refuses to perform a contract involving something unique, specific performance will be granted. Money damages may be awarded by one or more of the following methods, as appropriate for redressing the loss: **CRISP.**

> **C**ompensatory damages
> **R**esulting damages
> **I**ncidental damages
> **S**tipulated damages
> **P**unitive damages

Compensatory Damages

Contracting parties have the right to have their reasonable expectations fulfilled in accordance with the contract. Compensatory damages have the effect of awarding the injured party the same benefits that he or she would have received had the contract been carried out as promised.

The benefit of the bargain is the difference between the value of the performance received as a result of the breach and the actual value of the performance promised in the contract. The actual value of the promised performance is the value the innocent party would have received had the breach not been committed. The performance received, plus the difference between that value and the actual value of what was promised in the contract, will give the aggrieved party the benefit of the bargain. This is often measured as the difference between the contract price and the market price at the time of the breach.

EXAMPLE | Balboa enters into a contract to buy a clipper ship from King Ferdinand for $30,000. King Ferdinand refuses to sell the ship when he discovers that Balboa is going to search for the Pacific. Balboa finds a similiar ship, but the cost to him is $40,000. What measure of damages will compensate Balboa for Ferdinand's breach? Balboa is entitled to buy the ship for $30,000, the benefit of his contract with Ferdinand. Because he must pay $40,000 in the market, he may recover the diference between the contract price and the market price, $10,000.

Out-of-pocket damages are the reimbursement for the difference between the contract price and the value of what was received. The value received must be lower; otherwise the party would not be asking for damages.

EXAMPLE | Charles V finances Coronado's journey to America on the condition that he finds the Seven Cities of the North and returns with gold. Coronado fails in his attempt. Charles V sues Coronado for breach of contract. What will his damages be? The out-of-pocket expenses incurred in the financing of the trip.

Where the innocent party has suffered no loss, nominal damages will be awarded not for compensation, but as a sign of the breaching party's wrongdoing.

EXAMPLE | Ponce de Leon departs in early April on an expedition for a resort development company to discover new areas to build community settlements. Ponce is to return by August 31 however, he delays his return to pursue his quest for the Fountain of Youth, which he discovers one month later. Many elderly people settle in Florida because of his discovery. Because Ponce's breach actually enhanced the position of the resort development company, are they entitled to any damages? Yes! But their recovery will be limited to nominal damages, which are awarded only to evidence the wrongdoing committed by the party in breach.

Resulting Damages

Resulting or consequential damages are awarded where a direct financial loss can be attributed to the breach. This remedy is granted in addition to compensatory damages. Loss of profits is a consequence of many breached contracts. The party suffering the detriment must establish that the loss of profits stemmed directly from the breach. The party in breach must know, or should have known, that a breach would result in additional losses to the other party. In other words, the damages arising from the breach must be reasonably foreseeable. Under this theory a party in breach will be liable to an innocent party for any damages the innocent party must pay to a third person who sues the innocent party because of an unintentional breach. The innocent party's unintentional breach must directly result from the first party's breach of contract. A party may also recover interest lost on his or her money as a result of the breach.

EXAMPLE   Columbus has a contract with three different shipbuilders. Each shipbuilder is to construct a ship for Columbus's voyage. Subsequently Columbus receives a better deal elsewhere and cancels all three contracts. What will the shipbuilders' measure of damages be? The builders of the *Nina* have not yet commenced construction. Their measure of damages will be loss of profits on the contract. The company constructing the *Pinta* has commenced performance. Its measure of damages will be loss of profits plus the cost of performance to the date of the breach. The third firm has completed the construction of the *Santa Maria*. It will be entitled to recover the full contract price.

EXAMPLE   In the previous example, if each of the three shipbuilders breached its contract with Columbus, what would his measure of damages be? For the *Nina* Columbus will recover the difference between the contract price and the market price because performance has not yet begun. For the *Pinta* he will have to hire another contract to complete the ship; he need only pay the original contractor the contract price less the cost of completion. For the *Santa Maria,* which has been substantially completed, Columbus will have to pay the contract price less the cost for repairing any incidental defects.

Incidental Damages

The court awards incidental damages to reimburse an innocent party for expenses caused by a breach of contract in connection with inspection, storage, and transportation. The expenses that the innocent party incurs in attempting to locate substituted performance may also be recovered from the party in breach.

EXAMPLE   The Klondike Mining Company in Alaska agrees to sell and deliver fifty pounds of gold to the Forty-Niners in San Francisco. The Forty-Niners refuse delivery after the goods have been shipped to San Francisco. Five days later Klondike finds a buyer in Sacramento who is willing to pay the same price. May Klondike recover the costs for transportation to Sacramento and the storage cost for the five days? Yes! Damages incidental to the breach may be recovered.

Stipulated Damages

Stipulated or liquidated damages are an estimate by the parties at the time the contract is made of what the damages might be should a breach take place. Damages are stipulated in a contract for the sake of convenience. This practice spares parties the expense of a lawsuit to determine damages where damages might otherwise be difficult to prove. Parties can agree to limit damages as long as the amount stipulated is reasonable—when it approaches what the actual loss might be should a breach occur. Reasonableness takes into consideration the date of the contract, not the date of the breach. The court must determine whether the stipulated damages were reasonable on the date the contract was made. A fair estimate of loss of profits may also be stipulated. The parties need not adhere to a figure that is so excessive as to constitute a penalty. Neither does a figure that is too low restrict a party from commencing a lawsuit for the recovery of reasonable damages. Where the stipulated damage clause is nullified because of unfairness, the aggrieved party may recover damages that are fair under the circumstances. Parties may modify or limit remedies through a liquidated damage clause. However, any attempt by a party to use this clause as an exculpatory clause to disclaim liability is void because of unconscionability. This is especially true in consumer contracts.

EXAMPLE | Johnny Appleseed had a contract with a man named MacIntosh to plant apple seeds along the east coast of the United States, which is 2,000 miles long. His fee was ten dollars per mile, but for every mile not covered before the end of the year he had to repay one dollar. An early winter caused Johnny to abandon his journey in New York, 500 miles short of his destination. It was here that he dumped all of the remaining seed. That is how New York became known as the Big Apple. What are the damages recoverable by MacIntosh? Five hundred dollars. The damages stipulated in the contract may be recovered because the parties agreed to these damages, and they are reasonable.

Corral v. Rollins Protective Services
732 P. 2d 1260 (Kan. 1987)

Rollins Protective Services installed a fire and burglary system in the home of James Corral. When a fire occurred the system failed to operate, and substantial damage resulted.

The contract contained a liquidated damage clause that provided,

The parties agree that if loss or damage should result from the failure of performance or operation or from defective performance or operation or from improper installation or servicing of the system, that Rollins' liability, if any, for the loss or damage thus sustained shall be limited to a sum equal to ten per cent (10%) of one year's service charge or $250.00, whichever sum is greater, and that the provisions of this paragraph shall apply if loss or damage, irrespective of cause or origin, results, directly or indirectly, to persons or property from performance or nonperformance of obligations imposed by this agreement or from negligence, active or otherwise, of Rollins, its agents or employees.

> The damage from the fire was estimated at $185,000. Corral argued that this amount would have been less if the alarm had sounded. The issue is whether the liquidated damage clause is reasonable. The court held,
>
> There is no contention here that Corral was at any business disadvantage or that he did not or could not understand the clear terms of the contract. Also, there does not appear to be any contention that the agreement was obtained by Rollins through fraud, mistake, or duress. . . . The limitation of liability clause is not contrary to public policy.
>
> Judgment for Rollins.

Punitive Damages

A court awards punitive damages to penalize a party who commits a wrong that injures the general public. These damages are assessed in addition to the compensatory damages awarded to the injured party, usually in cases involving fraud. Punitive damages are not actually a contract remedy because the law does not exact punishment for breach of contract alone. When the breach of contract also constitutes a tort, then the court may award punitive damages for the tort in addition to the compensatory damages for the breach of contract. The purpose of punitive damages is to deter against future offenses of a similar nature and to compensate the victim for mental anguish suffered.

EXAMPLE | Daniel Boone is hired to blaze the Kentucky Trail. After Daniel advises the local used car dealer of the rugged terrain he must cross, the car dealer sells him a four-wheel-drive jeep with a busted axle, bad shocks, and worn springs. The car dealer also warrants that the engine is new, but it is actually rebuilt. The jeeps breaks down, leaving Daniel stranded in the Kentucky wilderness. Daniel sues the dealer and asks the court to award punitive damages. Will they be granted? Yes! Puntitive damages are intended to protect the public by punishing the party and discouraging him or her from committing fraud in the future.

DUTY TO MITIGATE DAMAGES

Upon learning of a breach, an innocent party has a duty to mitigate damages. This means that the innocent party must, in good faith, attempt to keep the damages as low as possible without incurring any undue risk or expense. A party who does not make a reasonable attempt to mitigate damages will be barred from recovery. A seller may fulfill his or her duty by stopping production and by attempting to resell the goods at a fair and reasonable price. A seller who continues production despite having been notified of the breach will be limited to recovery of damages suffered at the time of the breach because of the failure to mitigate damages. In certain instances mitigation of damages may require the seller to complete manufacture of the goods if they have no value unless completed. A seller who does not attempt to resell the goods for a reasonable price after notification of the breach will be barred from recovery.

In a case where the breach concerns nonconforming goods, a buyer may not continue to use these goods once he or she discovers that the goods are nonconforming. The buyer may satisfy the duty to mitigate damages by attempting to obtain substitute performance at a reasonable price. A buyer who continues to use the goods may be limited in recovery of damages or may be barred completely. A situation may arise where mitigation of damages would require the buyer to use the nonconforming goods until a suitable replacement could be furnished.

An employee under contract who has been terminated without cause has a duty to mitigate damages by making a good-faith effort to seek similar employment elsewhere. The employee need not, however, accept a lower position or look for employment outside the general vicinity.

EXAMPLE | Admiral Byrd and Floyd Bennett had a contract with the Navy to fly over the North Pole. One hour after takeoff the Navy canceled the contract and recalled Byrd and Bennett. The fliers decided to continue the flight and sued for the entire contract price. Are they entitled to it? No! Byrd and Bennett had a duty to mitigate damages at the time when they learned of the breach. They could have accomplished this by returning to the base when they learned of the breach. Their compensation will be limited to the reasonable value of their services up to the time when they received notice of the breach.

REVIEW QUESTIONS

1. Define remedies, breach of contract, injunction, quasi contract, rescission, restitution, reformation, specific performance, and money damages.

2. Art's Flower Shop sued C&P Telephone Company for loss of profits for omitting to place its ad in the Yellow Pages. The jury awarded $50,245. Is Art's Flower Shop entitled to the award? *Art's Flower Shop* v. *C&P Telephone Co.,* 314 S.E. 2d 670 (W. Va. 1991).

3. Art's Flower shop sued C&P Telephone Company for punitive damages for an intentional omission of a Yellow Page ad. The C&P salesman had stated that he was "going to take care of Art's Flowers" for notifying his wife about his delinquent account with the flower shop. Are punitive damages appropriate? *Art's Flower Shop* v. *C&P Telephone Co.,* 413 S.E 2d 670 (W. Va. 1991).

4. Art's Flower Shop contracted with C&P Yellow Pages for an advertisement. C&P omitted the ad in its annual issue. Must Art mitigate damages by using radio and television ads, letters, and flyers? *Art's Flower Shop* v. *C&P Telephone Co.,* 413 S.E. 2d 670 (W. Va. 1991).

5. On July 3, 1989, Rothner agreed to lease a nursing home facility from Louise Mermelstein for fifteen years. He paid the annual rent of $93,151 along with a security deposit of $500,000. On July 15, 1989, Rothner and Mermelstein

entered into a purchase agreement for the sale of one-half of the nursing home stock for $22,000. Rothner argued that the $22,000 was incorporated in the annual rent and that the parties agreed that the documents were silent as to this matter. No other monies would change hands. Mermelstein refused to transfer the stock because the $22,000 was not forthcoming. Is Rothner correct, and if so, what is the appropriate remedy? *Rothner* v. *Mermelstein,* 579 N.E. 2d 1022 (Ill. App. 1 Dist. 1991).

6. Gary and Debra Wells entered into a contract with Robert Minor for the building of a house. The contract price was $64,500. After paying $32,000, the Wellses noticed material defects in the workmanship. They notified Minor, but he refused to make the corrections. The Wellses had the house completed at a cost of $15,000. A local real estate appraiser valued the house at $44,500 because of the defects in workmanship that were not corrected. What is the proper measure of damages for the Wellses, and what is the appropriate remedy? *Wells* v. *Minor,* 578 N.E. 2d 1337 (Ill. App. 4 Dist. 1991).

7. Bobby and Lydia Tingle bought a house from J. Michael Leach for $66,000. They paid $3,300 in cash and borrowed the rest from a bank. The contract drafted by Leach's agent contained a guaranteed buy-back provision for $3,300 any time after the first year. Twenty-one months later the Tingles attempted to sell the house, but the best offer was $62,000. They informed Leach that they wanted to exercise the buy-back provision. He refused, claiming that it was not definite. Is Leach liable, and if so, what would be the appropriate remedy? *Leach* v. *Tingle,* 586 So. 2d 799 (Miss. 1991).

8. In 1981 Ed Vander Pas and Dean Loney terminated their partnership, with Loney assuming the assets and liabilities in return for $800,000. Loney paid Vander Pas $200,000 in cash and signed a promissory note for the remainder. In 1985 Loney defaulted. Subsequently, in 1987, Loney assigned his interest in the partnership termination agreement to First Security Bank of Anaconda. The bank in turn sued Vander Pas for breach of contract. Vander Pas claimed that he did not have to convey the deed because he was never paid. Is Vander Pas liable, and if so, what is the appropriate remedy? *First Security Bank* v. *Vander Pas,* 818 P. 2d 384 (Mont. 1991).

9. Aetna foreclosed on a farm owned by Satterlee in December 1988. Prior to this Satterlee had entered into a contract for the sale of the farm to Kirby. Both Satterlee and Kirby agreed not to contest the foreclosure sale. They also gave Aetna the right to plant the fall crop in 1988. In the summer of 1989, Kirby began to harvest the crop. Aetna got a preliminary injunction against Kirby. Kirby wanted to be paid for harvesting the crop. He claimed that Aetna has been unjustly enriched by his efforts. What remedy did Kirby pursue, and what is the result? *Aetna* v. *Satterlee,* 475 N.W. 2d 569 (S.D. 1991).

10. G&M was in dire financial straits. They needed a working capital loan and applied to Glen Fed for it. Glen Fed required a good-faith deposit of $10,000 to cover its examination expenses. Glen Fed promised either to approve the loan

within thirty days or to return the unused portion of the deposit. Glen Fed did not approve the loan and did not return the remainder of the deposit. G&M sued for breach of contract. Glen Fed claimed that its inaction was due to the disarray of G&M's financial records. What result? *G&M Oil Co.* v. *Glen Fed.,* 782 F. Supp. 1078 (D. Md. 1989).

11. Beer Mart fraudulently repackaged outdated beer in an attempt to resell the mismarked product as fresh. The Stroh Brewery Company terminated its wholesale agreement because Beer Mart intentionally sold over-age beer in violation of Stroh's marketing policies. Beer Mart sought an injunction to prevent Stroh from terminating the agreement on the ground that Beer Mart and Stroh had been transacting business for thirty-three years and that this misconduct was Beer Mart's first violation of Stroh's policy. The district court granted Beer Mart's motion for an injunction. Is the district court's decision correct? *Beer Mart, Inc.* v. *Stroh Brewery Co.,* 804 F. 2d 409 (7th Cir. 1986).

12. The City of Aliquippa agreed to sell water to the Township of Raccoon. The contract provided "that the Seller . . . must apply rate modifications equally to all like consumers purchasing water from the Seller." Thereafter Aliquippa set a different rate for Raccoon than for the customers inside its service area. Raccoon sought to have the rate increase declared invalid. What result? *Raccoon Tp.* v. *Municipal Water Auth.,* 597 A. 2d 757 (Pa. Cmwlth. 1991).

17

Contractual Defenses

INTRODUCTION

People enter into contracts to receive valuable consideration in the form of performance, forbearance, or payment from other people. A party who has not received valuable consideration from the other has a cause of action against that party for breach of contract. The nonperforming party will be liable for the breach unless he or she has a justifiable reason to excuse the failure to perform.

Justifiable reasons for nonperformance are known as contractual defenses and may be either real or personal. Real defenses are absolute defenses provided by statute for the protection of a certain class of people. They include bankruptcy discharge, duress, illegality, statute of limitations, statute of frauds, infancy, and lack of sanity. Real defenses cannot be waived. Personal defenses arise during the performance of a contract and may be asserted only by the aggrieved party. They include agreement in jest, misrepresentation and fraudulent inducement, stop in performance, insufficient consideration, failure of a condition, nonpayment, impossibility, release, unconscionability, and mistake. A party raises real and personal defenses in response to a cause of action brought by the other party. The burden of proving the validity of the defense is on the party affirming it. If the contractual defense is successfully proved, the cause of action will be dismissed. Most contractual defenses may be used in the affirmative by a party rescinding the contract. There are many contractual defenses including **BAD MISSISSIPPI RUM.**

Bankruptcy discharge
Agreement in jest
Duress and undue influence

Misrepresentation and fraudulent inducement
Illegality
Statute of limitations
Statute of frauds
Infancy
Stop in performance
Sanity is lacking
Insufficient consideration
Performance of a condition fails
Payment is not made
Impossibility

Release
Unconscionability
Mistake

BANKRUPTCY DISCHARGE

Bankruptcy occurs when a person is unable to pay his or her debts. The bankruptcy law, which is invoked by the filing of either a voluntary or an involuntary petition, provides for a fair distribution of the debtor's assets among the creditors. The bankrupt's debts are discharged in bankruptcy, which protects the debtor from all future claims made by creditors for past debts. This protection operates as a defense to a cause of action for breach of contract brought by a creditor.

EXAMPLE | The Sheriff of Nottingham filed for bankruptcy because he had no money left. A hood named Robin had taken the money from him and given it to the poor. The sheriff owed money to King Richard the Lionhearted. King Richard came to collect the debt owed to him. The sheriff had sent a notice to all his creditors, but evidently the king had not received word. In a suit for payment of a debt, is bankruptcy a good defense? Yes! The sheriff's debts, including the one owed to King Richard, have all been discharged by the bankruptcy.

AGREEMENT IN JEST

Parties contracting with each other must have the requisite legal capacity to make a contract. An agreement made in jest lacks the necessary legal capacity because there is no intent to perform. Intent to perform is manifested through the outward expressions of the parties. The requirement of intent is satisfied if the offeree is reasonable in believing the offeror is serious. A contract that lacks a party's intention to agree is voidable. The party setting forth the defense of jest has the right to disaffirm the contract if the defense can be proved. In any event, people would be wise not to make offers in jest.

EXAMPLE | The Sheriff of Nottingham was having a few beers with Robin Hood. Robin asked the sheriff if he would sell Sherwood Forest for $100,000. The sheriff replied, "Sure!" Then he laughingly continued, "But where would a peasant like you get the money?" Robin replied, "You'd be surprised," whereupon he produced the $100,000. The awestruck sheriff protested that the agreement had been made in jest. Is this a good defense? Yes! In terms of the objective actions of the parties, the sheriff's laughter while he assented to Robin's offer, coupled with the fact that they had had a few beers, would tend to prove that the sheriff was not serious and that Robin was not reasonable in believing him to be serious. Furthermore there was nothing in writing to evidence the sheriff's intention to be bound.

DURESS AND UNDUE INFLUENCE

Duress is the wrongful or illegal use of coercion by one party to force another party into entering a contract, or making a payment greater than that stipulated in the contract, out of fear of harm. The fear may arise from the threat of physical, social, or economic harm, but it must be genuine, not illusory. The threat of physical harm, which is often closely associated with extortion, may be directed at the person; a family member; or the person's property, where the damage threatened is severe. Social duress is accomplished through blackmail: threatened exposure of personal secrets that will result in public humiliation, disgrace, embarrassment, or possible loss of membership in societies, clubs, and associations. Economic duress arises where one party threatens to withhold performance unless a greater sum is paid and the aggrieved party cannot locate a satisfactory substitute within the time limits set forth in the contract. The aggrieved party may need performance immediately. The other party, knowing of that immediate need, seizes the opportunity to exploit the victim in the moment of weakness.

EXAMPLE | Sir Gawain threatens to tell King Arthur that Sir Galahad is actually Sir Lancelot's son unless Sir Lancelot and Sir Galahad each sign a promissory note for $25,000. Lancelot and Galahad know that if the king finds out, the king will have Lancelot's head, and Galahad will be dismissed from the exclusive club, Knights of the Round Table. They each sign the note but later refuse to pay, asserting duress. Is duress a good defense? Yes! Lancelot felt an immediate and justifiable fear of physical harm for himself, brought on by Gawain's statement. Galahad felt a realistic fear of social and economic harm in the form of a threat of expulsion from the prestigious club.

Undue influence is one person's use of a confidential or fiduciary relationship, based on trust and confidence, to obtain a benefit by inducing another person to enter into a contract. The key to undue influence, as well as to duress, is the victim's lack of freedom to make a decision.

People susceptible to undue influence are those who place their faith in another because of the other party's status or because of a close relationship with the other party. These relationships include attorney-client, doctor-patient, executor-beneficiary, and the like. But the most vulnerable groups, those who run the greatest risk of being exploited, are minors and elderly persons who rely on family members or guardians to act on their behalf. There is a presumption of undue influence where fiduciaries enter into contracts with their beneficiaries. An individual in a fiduciary capacity can rebut the presumption of undue influence by proving that full disclosure was made, that consideration was adequate, and that the aggrieved party had independent counseling before entering into the contract.

EXAMPLE Lady Guinevere, knowing that Excalibur is Arthur's key to power, uses her influence upon him to make him change his will, leaving the sword to Lancelot instead of to Galahad. Arthur, who had been suffering from a head wound inflicted by his archenemy King Pellinore, acquiesces to Guinevere's request. Upon King Arthur's death Galahad takes possession of the sword, but Lancelot sues to reclaim it under the provision in the will. If Galahad can prove that Lady Guinevere unduly influenced Arthur to make the change in his will, would this be a good defense to Lancelot's suit? Yes!

B.A.L. v. Edna Gladney Home
677 S.W. 2d 826 (Tex. App. 2 Dist. 1984)

B.A.L., a nineteen-year-old girl from New York, was pregnant and unmarried. She was referred to the Edna Gladney Home in Fort Worth, Texas, after she decided against having an abortion. On February 10, 1984, a baby girl was born. On February 14, B.A.L. executed an affidavit of relinquishment of parental rights before two witnesses. Her signature was notarized. The affidavit contained the following language in bold type:

> I REALIZE THAT I SHOULD NOT SIGN THE AFFIDAVIT UNTIL I HAVE READ AND UNDERSTOOD EACH WORD, SENTENCE, AND PARAGRAPH IN IT. I REALIZE THAT I SHOULD NOT SIGN THIS AFFIDAVIT OF RELINQUISHMENT IF THERE IS ANY THOUGHT IN MY MIND THAT

I MIGHT SOMEDAY SEEK TO ESTABLISH OR REESTABLISH ANY RE-
LATIONSHIP WITH THE CHILD.

B.A.L. subsequently claimed that the Edna Gladney Home unduly
influenced her to sign the affidavit by taking advantage of her youth
and emotional distress and by requesting her to sign the affidavit only
four days after giving birth.

The issue is whether B.A.L. signed the affidavit under undue influence.

The court held,

> The appellant (B.A.L.) signed the relinquishment affidavit voluntarily, in-
> telligently, and knowingly, she was aware that she could keep her baby
> if she so desired with the full support, financial and otherwise of her own
> family, and she made her own choice to place the baby for adoption
> without any undue influence, pressure or overreaching on the part of the
> Edna Gladney Home. The evidence shows plainly that this young girl
> changed her mind.

Judgment for Edna Gladney Home.

MISREPRESENTATION AND FRAUDULENT INDUCEMENT

Misrepresentation is a false statement of a material fact on which a person justifiably
relies to his or her detriment. If the misrepresentation is intentional, then it is fraudulent. The elements of fraud are **I FDR**, whereas misrepresentation consists of **FDR**
without the Intent.

Intent to deceive

False representation of a material fact
Detriment
Reliance justifiable

Intent to Deceive

Intent to deceive is the characteristic that separates a fraudulent misrepresentation
from an innocent one. One establishes intent to deceive by proving that the representation was false at the time it was made. Knowledge will be imputed to the party
making the statement where that party should have known that the statement was
false or that the statement was made in reckless disregard of whether it was false
or not.

False Representation of a Material Fact

People may make false representations innocently (misrepresentation) or intentionally (fraud), through actions as well as speech. Concealment of material alterations or defects that would not generally be noticed is an example of fraud. Material facts are facts that influence parties in their decisions to enter into contracts. Although silence usually does not constitute fraud, a duty to speak will arise in a situation where a person knows the other party believes a falsehood to be true. Individuals who have a duty to speak include a fiduciary, a person with knowledge of an alteration or a hidden defect, and a person who discovers a previous misstatement. These individuals must apprise the potential victim of the truth; otherwise their silence will constitute fraud. Parties may not disclaim their fraudulent or innocent misrepresentations at the expense of others.

Justifiable Reliance

Statements regarding predictions of future happenings or opinions about value are generally not categorized as fraudulent because a party is not justified in relying upon these types of statements. However, when the false opinion is given by an expert in the field such as a lawyer or physician, a fiduciary in a relationship of trust and confidence, or a person with superior knowledge of a product or service, then the false opinion will constitute fraud. People are justified in relying upon the opinions of these three types of individuals unless the facts of a case arouse suspicion. A person has a duty to investigate suspicious facts before entering into a contract. An individual who discovers fraud before entering into the contract may not enter into the contract and thereafter seek to abrogate it on the basis of fraud.

Detriment

The defrauded or misrepresented party must have suffered some financial loss, and be able to prove it, in order to have a cause of action.

The remedy for misrepresentation is rescission. Rescission has the effect of canceling the contract and returning the parties to status quo. Inherent in this remedy is the return of consideration by both parties. Rescission is also available as a remedy for fraud, but the defrauded party may, on the other hand, sue for money damages. The remedy of money damages has two basic forms: benefit of the bargain and out-of-pocket damages.

Benefit of the bargain is the difference between the value of the performance received as a result of the fraud and the actual value represented. The actual value represented is the value the defrauded party would have received had the fraud not been committed. The performance received plus the difference between that value and the actual value represented will give the aggrieved party the benefit of the bargain. The defrauded party is entitled to receive that difference in value as damages. It is often measured as the difference between the contract price and the market price at the time of the breach.

Out-of-pocket damages are the reimbursement for the difference between what was paid under the fraudulent contract and the actual value of what was received. The actual value would be lower; otherwise the party would not be asking for damages. Courts at their discretion may also award punitive damages. Punitive damages are penalties to punish those who commit fraud and to discourage them from doing so again.

EXAMPLE | The Artful Dodger is a con artist who devises a scheme and employs his innocent young friend, Oliver Twist, to carry it out for him. The Dodger knows that Mr. Bumble, a wealthy gentleman, is interested in purchasing a thoroughbred horse. He tells Oliver to inform Mr. Bumble that for $10,000 they will deliver a fine one. Mr. Bumble sees a good deal and gives Oliver the $10,000. Bumble trusts Oliver's judgment because he has known him since he was a small boy. Oliver believes that his representations are true. The next day an old mare is delivered to Mr. Bumble, and he refuses to pay for it. In a suit brought by Oliver and the Artful Dodger for nonpayment, what defenses could Mr. Bumble raise? Bumble could raise the defense of fraud against the Artful Dodger because the Dodger intentionally deceived Bumble through the false representations he had Oliver make concerning the horse. Bumble's reliance was justified because of his trust in Oliver. Bumble could raise the defense of misrepresentation against Oliver even though Oliver acted innocently. Bumble's remedy against both parties would be rescission and out-of-pocket damages—$10,000 less the value of the horse received. Bumble would probably not be entitled to punitive damages because the fraud was personal and not perpetrated against the general public. If the particular thoroughbred described in this contract existed, Mr. Bumble would be entitled to the benefit of the bargain—the difference between the value of the horse received and the value of the horse he would have received had the representation been true.

Hayes v. Equine Equities, Inc.
480 N.W. 2d 178 (Neb. 1992)

David Hayes bought an office condo from John Chudy. At the time Hayes expressed an interest in horses. Chudy suggested to Hayes that together they buy a horse called Chocolate Marquis from Equine Equities for $50,000. Chudy told Hayes that he had someone lined up to purchase the horse for $75,000. Hayes put up 60 percent of the money and was promised the same share of the profits. After several reassurances and other delay tactics, there turned out to be no buyer. Unbeknownst to Hayes, Chudy held a 50 percent interest in Equine Equities and had purchased Chocolate Marquis for $1,300. Hayes sued Chudy and Equine Equities for fraud. He asked for rescission and a return of the purchase price. The defendants claimed that the representations were mere sales talk.

> The issues are whether the statements were fraudulent or mere puffing and whether Hayes did not promptly seek rescission.
>
> The court held, "Chudy's statements were positive representations of fact upon which Hayes could rely, and the statements did not constitute sales talk or puffing in the sense which the law implies." The court concluded, "Hayes' delay in bringing the action was excused by 1) the continued reassurances by Chudy (not disputed)[;] 2) the later discovery of the horse's true cost to Equine Equities." Judgment for Hayes.

ILLEGALITY

The purpose of a contract must be lawful. This is one of the elements of a contract. Where either the action to be performed or the purpose to be achieved is illegal, the contract will be unenforceable. Illegal contracts are prohibited by federal, state, and local statutes and by public policy. Either party may invoke the defense of illegality without resort to a court of law because all illegal contracts are void. Courts generally do not decide matters of illegality except where an innocent party is asking for restitution. A more detailed discussion of the defense of illegality is presented in Chapter 13, "Lawful Purpose."

STATUTE OF LIMITATIONS

A statute of limitations is the period within which a person must exercise his or her cause of action—that is, the time within which the injured party must serve the summons on the other party. The time limitation begins to run from the time the harm is committed or, in some cases, discovered. Its duration varies according to the type of action brought. Contracts for the sale of goods have a four-year statute of limitations. All other contract actions are governed by the particular statute of limitations of the state having jurisdiction. Some states have a special statute of limitations for fraud: six years from the time the fraud was committed, or two years from its discovery, whichever is longer. The statute of limitations may be raised as a defense to a contract action that has been brought after the appropriate time limit has lapsed.

EXAMPLE | Robinson Crusoe sells a bunch of coconuts to his friend, Friday. Friday is to make payment after Crusoe returns from a trip to the Bahamas. However, Crusoe gets caught in a storm and ends up on Galapagos Island with a bunch of overgrown turtles. Twenty-seven years later Crusoe returns and seeks to enforce Friday's promise to pay for the coconuts. Friday raises the defense of the statute of limitations. Is this a good defense? Yes! Because this was a contract for the sale of goods, the statute of limitations expires four years after the date that payment was due.

STATUTE OF FRAUDS

The defense of the statute of frauds may be raised against an action based on an oral contract that the statute requires to be in writing. It may also be used affirmatively in an action for rescission where one party is seeking to cancel the contract. The statute of frauds is discussed more fully in Chapter 14, "Form and Interpretation."

EXAMPLE | King Arthur and King Pellinore are having a joust. Pellinore begins to get the upper hand and tells Arthur that he will spare his life if Arthur sells him Camelot and the Round Table, a valuable antique. Arthur agrees, but after retrieving his sword Excalibur refuses to perform, raising the statute of frauds as a defense. Will Arthur triumph? Yes! Both contracts are required to be in writing. The sale of Camelot is a contract for the sale of real estate, and the sale of the Round Table is a contract for the sale of goods in excess of $500.

INFANCY

The defense of infancy—explained more fully in Chapter 12, "Legal Capacity"—can be raised only by a minor. A minor may use the defense affirmatively in his or her own actions for rescission or defensively in an action brought by an adult for enforcement of the contract or for damages. The basis for the defense is to protect minors because of their lack of experience in dealing with adults. The age of majority is set by statute. Minors are individuals who have not yet attained majority; they are still in their minority.

EXAMPLE | Mark Twain sold Huckleberry Finn and Tom Sawyer a bundle of logs on credit. Huck and Tom built a raft with the logs and began sailing along the Mississippi River. After a while the raft ran aground, and the boys could not dislodge it. When Huck and Tom refused to pay, Mark Twain sued them for breach of contract. The boys raised the defense of infancy. Is this a good defense? Yes! Huck and Tom, both minors, are protected. Mark Twain assumed the risk of their nonperformance when he contracted with them.

STOP IN PERFORMANCE

A stop in performance by one party for no justifiable reason is sufficient cause for the other party to halt payment or performance. The defense can be raised by the aggrieved party in an action for payment brought by the party who stopped performance. The aggrieved party may rescind or cancel the contract by asserting a stop in performance.

EXAMPLE | Maid Marian hired two of the sheriff's yeomen to ride as bodyguards for her during a journey through Sherwood Forest to Nottinghamshire. She paid them by check. After riding a few miles through the forest, the yeomen saw Little John and Will Scarlet, two of Robin Hood's men, each with bow and arrow in hand. The yeomen quickly abandoned

Maid Marian and returned home. They deposited the checks, but Marian had immediately stopped payment. They sued her for the reasonable value of their services. Marian contended that they had abandoned her for the very reason they were hired, fear of Robin Hood's men. Is her argument valid? Yes! The yeomen's stop in performance was not justified. Marian may stop payment on the two checks.

A party who substantially performs will be entitled to the reasonable value for the work completed if the breach was unintentional. The same may be said for a partially performed contract that was breached unintentionally if the contract can be divided into more than one contract or can be made into a separate contract.

EXAMPLE | Cyrano de Bergerac, the famous poet, was hired by Christian to write twenty-five poems for Christian's beloved, Roxanne. With the help of these poems, Christian hoped to win Roxanne's hand in marriage. Each week she would stand on her balcony while he recited a different poem with Cyrano's prompting. In the twenty-fifth week, Christian planned to propose to Roxanne in poetry. Cyrano failed to show up that night because he had let his nose get in the way in a fight and was badly injured. Christian blew the proposal and Roxanne, realizing that he was a phony, refused to marry him. Cyrano sued Christian, alleging that he had substantially performed. Christian claimed that Cyrano had rendered only partial performance because the night when Cyrano failed to show was crucial. The outcome depends upon whether Cyrano knew that Christian had planned to propose that night. If the court agrees with Cyrano's argument, he will recover the reasonable value of his services because the breach was unintentional. If the court agrees with Christian, they may divide Cyrano's performance into twenty-five contracts and award him the value of each contract that he fulfilled.

SANITY IS LACKING

Sanity is a requisite for legal capacity, which is one of the elements of a contract. The defense of insanity is available only to the insane for their protection. The insane individual may raise it personally in a lucid interval, or his or her guardian may raise it. Chapter 12, "Legal Capacity," provides a more definitive explanation.

EXAMPLE | The Cathedral of Notre Dame hired Quasimodo, a well-known mental defective, to ring the church bells at wedding receptions. On the day of Esmerelda's celebrated marriage to Captain Phoebus of the king's guard, the bells were not rung. This caused the couple great embarrassment. Quasimodo had run off to a lonely place to mourn, for he had a secret love for Esmerelda. Notre Dame sued Quasimodo for breach of contract. Quasimodo raised the defense of insanity. Is this a good defense? Yes! Quasimodo is a nonjudicially declared incompetent. His contract with Notre Dame is voidable at his option.

INSUFFICIENT CONSIDERATION

A party whose performance does not fulfill his or her promise under the contract is said to have given insufficient consideration. The other party may withhold consideration until payment is made or performance is completed. If an action is brought against the party withholding consideration, the defense of insufficient consideration may be raised. If it is reasonable to assume that performance will not be completed, the contract may be rescinded, or an action for money damages may be brought.

EXAMPLE Dr. Watson kept his narcotic drugs in a locked safe in his medical office. Each Friday morning, on opening the safe, he found one bottle missing. Watson hired Sherlock Holmes, a private investigator, to solve the mystery. Holmes was to be paid only if the case was solved. Upon arriving on the scene, Holmes said, "Dr. Watson, I presume." After being briefed about the drug thefts, Holmes went to work. He discovered that Watson's nurse had left the medical office door open a crack. By using a miniature telescope, she had observed the combination of the safe when Watson turned the dial. Late in the day she would slip in and remove one bottle. Watson was astounded by Holmes's brilliance, but he was even more astounded when he received the bill for $10,000. Watson refused to pay, and Holmes sued for breach of contract. Then an amazing event took place. Another bottle was removed from the safe a week later, and another the following week. Holmes had not solved the mystery after all. Watson raised this as a defense to the suit for nonpayment. Is this a good defense? Yes! Holmes was entitled to the fee only if he solved the case. Because he did not he gave insufficient consideration in return for Watson's promise to pay.

PERFORMANCE OF A CONDITION FAILS

A condition occurs where the parties' contractual duties are contingent upon the occurrence of a future event. When making the contract, parties must expressly agree if they are conditioning their obligations on the occurrence of a particular event. Depending on whether the condition is worded positively or negatively, the occurrence of the future event may or may not require the parties to perform their contractual obligations. The condition may state that if the event occurs, contractual obligations exist. Failure of that condition would discharge the parties from their obligations. The party who must satisfy the condition has a duty to make a good-faith effort in that direction by taking positive steps.

There are two types of conditions: conditions precedent and conditions subsequent.

A *condition precedent* requires that a future event occur before parties are obligated to perform their contractual duties. The condition must be satisfied before the contract can be performed. If the condition is not satisfied, the contract is unenforceable.

EXAMPLE The Three Musketeers agreed to serve as bodyguards for Cardinal Richelieu while he traveled through the kingdom, on the condition that he could locate D'Artagnan, the fourth Musketeer. The cardinal was not able to find D'Artagnan. The Three Musketeers refused to honor their contract. The cardinal sued them for breach of contract, and the Musketeers raised the defense of failure of a condition precedent. Is this a good defense? Yes! It is a good defense because the condition had to be satisfied before the Three Musketeers would be bound by the contract.

A *condition subsequent* involves an existing contract where parties must continue to perform their contractual obligations until the condition is not satisfied. Once the condition is not satisfied, the contract can no longer be enforced, and the parties are excused from performing their duties under the contract. The distinguishing feature of a condition subsequent is that there is an existing contract and, as long as the condition is satisfied, the contract will be enforceable.

EXAMPLE | Robin Hood and his Merry Band are asked to perform every Saturday evening at Friar Tuck's Inn until King Richard returns from his crusade. The Merry Band has a contract that will continue until such time as the condition of King Richard's return is fulfilled. When this occurs the Merry Band's performance contract will terminate.

A condition may be implied where the circumstances indicate that the parties assumed that the contract would be conditioned on some stipulated event. A condition may also be implied where the type of contract entered into necessitates implying certain conditions. Courts may likewise imply conditions for reasons of fairness and justice. Where one party has substantially performed, the fact that every detail was not completed may not be raised as a failure of condition.

EXAMPLE | The Bounty was to set sail for Tahiti. Before departure Captain Cook contracted with Fletcher Christian, the first mate, to procure fifty barrels of coconut oil. He also contracted with Captain Bligh to obtain a large supply of conch shells, which Captain Cook would use to hear the ocean roar. On board the ship were breadfruit trees, which the natives had contracted to buy. When the Bounty was halfway to Tahiti, a mutiny broke out. The mutineers sent Captain Bligh adrift in a rowboat while they continued to Tahiti. The hot sun and the occasional stormy weather withered the breadfruit trees. Upon arriving in Tahiti Christian and his crew decided to remain there, knowing their lives would be worthless back home. Meanwhile Captain Bligh arrived back in England. Are any of the contracts viable? No! The contract for the conch shells was canceled because Captain Bligh never reached Tahiti. This condition was implied because the parties assumed that the contract would be carried out only if Bligh reached Tahiti. The contract for the coconut oil was canceled because Christian never returned to England. Many seamen remained on islands after voyages. Enforcement of this contract necessitated implying that Christian would return home. Because he did not the condition failed, and he is excused from performing. Finally, the contract for the breadfruit trees was canceled because they withered and died from the long journey. Neither party was aware that the journey would kill the breadfruit trees, so the court will imply a condition (that if the trees withered and died, the contract would be canceled) for reasons of fairness and justice.

PAYMENT IS NOT MADE

When one party to a contract was to receive payment in advance and did not receive it, this party may use the defense of nonpayment if the other party brings a lawsuit against him or her.

EXAMPLE | Marguerite telephones Sir Percy Blakeney and asks him to send several bouquets of scarlet pimpernel, a wayside flower that grows in the countryside, for Saturday night. She is holding a dinner party for all the French aristocrats saved from the guillotine by the Scarlet Pimpernel. Marguerite wants to place a bouquet of scarlet pimpernels on each dinner table. Sir Percy notifies her that he must have payment in advance. Sir Percy refrains from sending the bouquets because the payment does not arrive. Marguerite sues Sir Percy for breach of contract, alleging that payment would have been made when the flowers arrived. Sir Percy raises the defense of nonpayment. Is this a good defense? Yes! Because Sir Percy was to receive payment before being required to send the bouquets, nonpayment will excuse him from performing.

IMPOSSIBILITY

Impossibility of performance refers to a situation in which it is impossible for the contract to be performed either by the party under contract or by anyone else. Impossibility may be permanent or temporary. Permanent impossibility will discharge the parties from their contractual obligations. Temporary impossibility will generally suspend the duty to perform until the impossibility diminishes, at which point the duty to perform is revived. Personal inability to perform, alone, will not release the parties from their contractual obligations.

EXAMPLE | The people of Camelot hired Sir Kay and Sir Hector, specialists in metallurgy, to remove the sword Excalibur from the stone. Sir Kay and Sir Hector used various heating procedures and other methods but were unsuccessful in their attempts. The people sued them for breach of contract. Sir Kay and Sir Hector claimed the defense of impossibility. In the meantime the people of Camelot hired Arthur, at a greater cost, to remove the sword. Arthur was successful in his first attempt, and the people rejoiced. Is the defense used by Sir Kay and Sir Hector viable? No! Personal inability to perform is not equivalent to impossibility.

The event causing impossibility must be brought about by an independent intervening cause. Examples of independent intervening causes are a change in a law that makes performance illegal; the destruction of subject matter that is unique or is specially designated for a particular contract; or the illness, incapacity, or death of one party whose special skills were required in a personal service contract. Under these circumstances impossibility does not exist at the time the contract is made but arises sometime thereafter. However, in certain instances of commercial impracticability, the impossibility may exist but is not reasonably evident to the parties. The parties must not have foreseen the event nor have assumed the risk of its occurrence. Foreseeability refers to the fact that the event was anticipated or should have been anticipated and that because nothing was done to prevent the risk of loss, it was assumed. A party may assume the risk impliedly, as stated above, or expressly if that is provided for in the contract.

There is a trend to equate impossibility with impracticability. The requirements of impracticability are as follows: a contingency, which is unforeseen, must have occurred; the risk of the unforeseen occurrence must not have been allocated to either party by agreement or custom; and the occurrence of the contingency must have rendered performance commercially impracticable. Commercial impracticability means that performance can be completed only at a truly excessive and unreasonable cost.

RELEASE

Parties may release each other from their duties to perform by mutual agreement. One party may release the other party from his or her obligation to continue performance after it has been partially or substantially completed. A party's right to release another is part of the freedom to contract. The release must be supported by consideration, be in writing, and be signed by the releasing party. The UCC requires delivery of a signed writing, but it need not be supported by consideration. The form of a release may be as simple as writing "paid in full" on a check.

EXAMPLE | Robin Hood engaged in a marksmanship contest with the king's guard. Gilbert, the finest marksman of the guards, shot an arrow into the bull's-eye. Robin Hood also hit the bull's-eye and split Gilbert's arrow in two. King Richard the Lionhearted was amazed at Robin Hood's proficiency and offered to release him from all the debts he owed the kingdom if he would serve in the palace guard for one year. Robin Hood accepted, and King Richard signed a written release form. Later, Richard's brother, John, overtook the throne and called Robin to account for his debts. Robin argued that he was released from all his debts and produced the release form. Is this a good defense? Yes! A written release signed by King Richard in return for Robin's consideration—agreeing to work in the palace guard for one year—is valid.

Brown v. Simoneaux
593 So. 2d 939 (La. App. 4 Cir. 1992)

Mr. Brown and Mr. Simoneaux were involved in an auto accident. In return for $790, Mr. Brown signed a release that stated,

> For the Sole Consideration of Seven Hundred Ninety and 25/100 Dollars . . . , the undersigned hereby releases and forever discharges

Eugene Simoneaux and State Farm Mutual Auto Insurance . . . from any and all claims . . . and particularly on account of all injuries, known and unknown, both personal and property, which have resulted or may in the future develop from an accident which occurred on or about the 20th day of November, 1989. . . .

Undersigned hereby declares that the terms of this settlement have been completely read and are fully understood and voluntarily accepted for the purpose of making full and final compromise . . . of any and all claims, disputed or otherwise, on account of injuries and damages above mentioned, and for the express purpose of precluding forever any further or additional claims arising out of the aforesaid accident.

Mr. Brown argued that he did not intend to release his claim for personal injury.

The issues are whether Mr. Brown's intent governs the signed release and whether the language of the release was ambiguous.

The court held,

An individual who signs a written instrument is charged with the responsibility of having read it and is presumed to know and understand its contents. Here the language of the release is so broad and unambiguous it leaves little to be misunderstood. And where the words of an agreement are explicit and lead to no absurd consequences, no further interpretation may be made in search of the parties' intentions.

Judgment for Simoneaux.

UNCONSCIONABILITY

Unconscionability is involved in contracts that are so unduly harsh or one-sided as to constitute a violation of conscience. Unconscionable contracts usually involve parties of unequal bargaining strength, where the stronger parties use the inequality to their advantage. This is evident in many consumer contracts between individuals and large corporations where the corporations are providing goods or services to individuals. Unconscionable contracts are voidable contracts. They are against public policy and are specifically in violation of the UCC in respect to contracts involving the sale of goods. The victimized party has the special right to rescind the contract.

EXAMPLE | Injun Jo employs Tom Sawyer, Huckleberry Finn, and Becky Thatcher to work as his assistants in a cemetery. The contract provides that Injun Jo shall have the authority to determine how long they work each day, what work they do, and how long the contract lasts. Another clause in the contract provides that if Tom, Huck, and Becky abrogate the contract, they must return to Injun Jo all monies paid to that point. After two months of digging graves twelve hours a day, Tom, Huck, and Becky are at the point of exhaustion. They decide to cancel the contract, and they decide to raise the defense of unconscionability if Injun Jo sues them for a return of the money already paid. Will this be a successful defense? Yes! This contract is definitely unconscionable. It is truly harsh and one-sided.

MISTAKE

Mistake is a belief that is not in accordance with the actual facts. Mistakes must be material, not incidental. This means that the contract would have been entered into if not for the mistake. A party may have a mistaken belief as to the facts or may make a mistake in judgment as to the value of the contract. There is generally no relief afforded to a party who makes a mistake in judgment as to value: Contracts would not be binding if, every time a person made a bad deal, he or she could rescind the contract, claiming mistake. However, where a factual mistake is made, rescission may be allowed, depending on whether there is a mutual mistake or a mistake made by only one party.

A mutual mistake occurs when both parties erroneously believe that the contract can be performed as agreed or where the actual identity of the subject matter is mistaken by both parties. The contract will be canceled if a mutual mistake occurs. Because both parties did not actually agree on what they were contracting for, the court will not bind them to the contract. They will be returned to the positions they were in before the contract came about. Reformation is available as an alternative to rescission in cases of typographical mistakes in a written contract where the error is reasonably clear to both parties.

When one party enters into a contract with a mistaken belief about certain material facts, that party will not be allowed to rescind or reform the contract unless the other party has committed fraud or unless the other party knew, or should have known, of the mistake. A party should have known of the mistake when there is a noticeable discrepancy between what the mistaken party promises and what is promised by others who have knowledge of the actual facts. The question is who should suffer for the mistake. If the mistaken party is forced to perform, he or she will suffer. If the mistaken party is excused, the other party will suffer. Because one party is going to suffer, the burden of loss falls upon the party who made the mistake. This principle reinforces the precept of exercising due care when entering into a contract. A person can exercise due care by examining all the facts and by making sure they are what they seem to be. This practice will help avoid mistakes of negligence.

EXAMPLE | The French Republic hired a spy named Chauvelin to apprehend Armand Saint-Just, who the republic thought was the Scarlet Pimpernel. Chauvelin apprehended Armand, but later the republic discovered that he was not the Scarlet Pimpernel. They refused to pay Chauvelin for his services and raised the defense of mistake. Is this a good defense? No! Chauvelin was hired to apprehend Armand Saint-Just, which he did. The fact that Armand was not the Scarlet Pimpernel is a unilateral mistake on the republic's part for which it has no recourse. Chauvelin is entitled to payment. If the contract had called for the apprehension of the Scarlet Pimpernel and both Chauvelin and the republic had been under the mistaken belief that Armand Saint-Just was the Scarlet Pimpernel, then both parties would have made a mutual mistake of fact. The contract could have been re-scinded by the republic, and Chauvelin would not have been entitled to compensation for the apprehension of Armand.

Jennings v. Jennings
409 S.E. 2d 8 (Va. App. 1991)

Gary Jennings was an alcoholic and an adulterer. After the parties sep-arated, the wife's attorney drafted a separation agreement with the fol-lowing provisions:

> [T]he Wife agrees she will obtain the divorce upon the grounds of six months separation, to-wit: a no fault divorce.
>
> Husband agrees that he will make periodic support payments for the remainder of Wife's life, or until she remarries, in an amount to sup-port Wife in the style to which she was accustomed during the marriage of the parties.
>
> All of the property . . . that was obtained during the marriage . . . will be appraised. [T]here shall be a 50/50 division of all said real and per-sonal assets. . . .
>
> It is agreed that Wife's 50% of equitable distribution shall include . . . all monies received or to be received in the future, from [all rights] on . . . *Aztec, The Journeyed, Spangle,* and a book to be written . . . which has a working title of *Raptor.*

Gary refused to obtain legal counsel, but afterward he sought rescission because he did not know what he was signing. The issue is whether Gary's mistake in signing the agreement renders it void.

The court ruled, "[I]gnorance of law . . . is never ground for rescis-sion of a contract unless perhaps where the other party knowingly has taken advantage of such ignorance for fraud." Judgment for Mrs. Jennings.

REVIEW QUESTIONS

1. Define duress, undue influence, misrepresentation, fraud, condition precedent, condition subsequent, condition concurrent, impossibility, and mistake.
2. List and explain each of the contractual defenses.
3. Mr. and Mrs. Pommer executed a marital agreement two weeks after their mar-riage in 1983. The agreement provided that each party would waive his or her legal right to share in the other's property upon death. Six years later Mr. Pommer died. Mrs. Pommer claimed that this was her first discovery of the waiver. She sued Trustco Bank, the executor of the estate, for her rightful

share. The statute of limitations for fraud is six years from the contract or two years from the date of discovery. What result? *Pommer* v. *Trustco Bank,* 583 N.Y.S 2d 553 (A.D. 3 Dept. 1992).

4. The Atkinses bought land from Mrs Kirkpatrick, a realtor, the land turned out to be an unbuildable lot. Neither the buyer nor the realtor knew this. The property was sold with the following disclaimer. "Unless otherwise specified herein . . . this property is purchased 'as is' and Seller nor Agent nor Broker(s) makes or implies any warranties as to the condition of the premises." The Atkinses claim that there was a mutual mistake of fact. What result? *Atkins* v. *Kirkpatrick,* 823 S.W. 2d 547 (Tenn. App. 1991).

5. Johnny Mack Brown paid a renewal premium with a check that was later dishonored. In the meantime Progressive Insurance Company mailed a renewal acceptance to Brown. Three weeks later Shirley Brown was involved in an accident. Is the honoring of the check by the bank a condition precedent to the renewal of the policy? *Progressive Preferred Ins. Co.* v. *Brown,* 413 S.E. 2d 430 (Ga. 1992).

6. With reference to the *Jennings* v. *Jennings* case discussed in the chapter, was the phrase *all monies received* ambiguous because it did not state whether it meant net or gross? If there was an ambiguity, should the agreement be rescinded because of a mutual mistake? *Jennings* v. *Jennings,* 409 S.E. 2d 8 (Va. App. 1991).

7. ICI issued the University of Illinois an insurance policy that contained a $5,000,000 limit. This was clear and unambiguous, but it was not the true intent of both parties. The University asked the court to modify the policy. ICI argued that the University had had ample time before signing the policy to realize the mistake. Is the $5,000,000 limit enforceable? *Board of Trustees of U. of Illinois* v. *ICI,* 969 F. 2d 329 (7th Cir. 1992).

8. Clearwater Constructions was awarded the bid as general contractor to expand the Walnut Creek Wastewater Treatment Facility. Clearwater subcontracted the supply of water treatment equipment to Westech Engineering. When Westech could not satisfy the specifications required, it claimed impossibility of performance. Clearwater was forced to purchase the equipment elsewhere at a greater cost. What result? *Westech* v. *Clearwater Constructions,* 835 S.W. 2d 190 (Tex. App.—Austin 1992).

9. Frank Galli entered into a contract with James Metz for the sale of the Betuna Corporation. The contract contained the following clause: "CONDITIONS PRECEDENT TO BUYER'S OBLIGATIONS. All obligations of Buyers hereunder are subject to the fulfillment of each of the following conditions at or prior to the closing. . . . (a) All representations of . . . Sellers contained herein . . . shall be true and correct when made and as of the closing."

After closing Metz discovered that the financial position of Betuna was much weaker than what could be gleaned from the financial information he received at the time he entered into the contract. He stopped payment on the promissory note, claiming breach of the warranty clause stated previously. Galli countered that the clause cited was effective up to the date of closing and that there were other clauses to handle breaches after that. What result? *Galli v. Metz*, 973 F. 2d 145 (2nd Cir. 1992).

10. Jay Kranitz entered into a mortgage contract with the Strober Organization. A year later Kranitz was threatened with criminal prosecution if he did agree to the contract. Is this duress? *Kranitz v. Strober Organization, Inc.*, 580 N.Y.S. 2d (A.D. 1 Dept. 1992).

11. Plaintiffs purchased property that they intended to subdivide. Defendants estimated that it would cost about $32,000 to develop the subdivision. Before the final sale plaintiffs spoke with the city planning department, two paving contractors, and an experienced engineer who gave them an estimate of $90,000 in costs. Even the defendants' attorney doubted the $32,000 figure, but plaintiffs proceeded with the purchase. Over a year after they had purchased the property, plaintiffs sought rescission of their purchase of the property on the basis of fraud. What result? *Davenport v. Vlach*, 726 P. 2d. 941 (Or. App. 1986).

Special Topic: Business Ethics

WHO'S TIPPING WHOM?

Scenario A

Tom Matthews takes his girlfriend to an upscale restaurant called the Swordfish Palace for dinner and drinks. After their sumptuous meal he receives the check. The amount is $74. He hands the waitress four $20 bills. She returns in a moment with $16 change. Which is the most ethical solution?

1. Tom returns the money because he feels he has no right to keep it.
2. Tom realizes the waitress's error immediately but pockets the money.
3. Tom returns the money because he feels the waitress may have to account for it.
4. Tom returns the money because the waitress was friendly and gave good service.
5. Tom keeps the money because the service was poor.
6. Tom keeps the money. Although the service was good, the meal was lousy and/or overpriced.
7. Tom keeps the money because, when he ate there last month, they overcharged him for dinner, and either he did not realize it until later or he was too embarrassed to draw notice to it in front of his girlfriend.
8. Tom does not realize the waitress's error until he is outside, and he figures it is too late to go back.
9. Tom realizes the waitress's error the next morning and decides not to return to the restaurant.

Scenario B

The error in making change is made by the cashier, who is the owner of this expensive restaurant.

1. Tom returns the money because it is not his to keep.
2. Tom keeps the money because he feels that the owner is rich and it was the owner's mistake.
3. Tom returns the money because he is a regular customer and has a rapport with the owner.

Scenario C

Tom orders two rounds of drinks but is only charged for one. It is not this restaurant's policy to buy customers a second round for free, so it is clearly a mistake.

1. Tom notifies the waitress that she forgot to charge him for the second round.
2. Tom differentiates between this scenario and the first one because the second round of drinks was not written on the check. The likelihood that someone else will know of the waitress's mistake and make her account for it is slim, so Tom keeps the money.
3. Tom keeps the money because he feels the restaurant is losing only a few ounces of liquor.
4. Tom keeps the money but rewards the waitress with a bigger tip to show his appreciation for her mistake.

Solution

In scenario A, solution 1 is the most ethical because the reasoning behind it is unconditional. For Tom to do otherwise would be to take something that was not rightfully his. In solution 3 Tom is doing the right thing, but there should be no qualification. If he is doing it because of the waitress's accountability, then what would he do in scenarios B and C, where the owner, not the waitress, would suffer the loss?

In solution 4, Tom is also doing the right thing, but again it is conditioned on the service. This leads us to believe that Tom would keep the money if the service were poor.

In solutions 5 through 9, Tom does not perform ethically because he is able to rationalize his judgment on the basis of the service, the quality of the food, the price of the meal, or the inconvenience to him.

Solution 2 is unconditional, but the result is unethical. Here, Tom does not need any reason. Money has come his way, and he will keep it. This is the most unethical of all the responses.

In scenario B, solution 1 is the most ethical response because it is not qualified.

In solution 2, Tom reasoned that the owner could well afford this small loss. How can he make that assumption? Has he seen the owner's profit and loss statement? People commonly use this justification because they feel little guilt from a Robin Hood (take-from-the-rich) approach.

In solution 3, the result is ethical, but it is conditional. What if this happened at another restaurant? Tom seems to be saying that he would keep the money if he were not a regular customer. The reasoning must hold up under all scenarios. Otherwise an ethical result in Scenario A may be an unethical one is Scenario B.

In scenario C solution 1 is the most ethical response because it is unconditional.

Responses to 2 and 3 are common. Individuals who normally do the right thing in scenario A often change their minds in scenario C. Again, they do so because the response is conditional. If the response were unconditional, it would be the same in all three scenarios.

Solution 4 is just a common rationalization used either to ease any traces of guilt or to implement the Robin Hood approach by taking from the rich (restaurant) and giving to the poor (waitress).

In all three scenarios Tom's response should have been without qualification. Once Tom begins to rationalize the situation, the results will change: He may perform ethically in one instance and unethically in another. He is substituting his own personal inclinations for the standard ethical principle. That is, he had no right to keep the money or to drink the liquor without paying for it. And that should be the question: Does Tom have a right to an extra $10 in change? Does Tom have a right to a second round of drinks without paying for it? When the question is posed in this way, the answer is clearly no. Ethically, this is the way the question should be asked and answered: unconditionally.

WHAT A BAD BRAKE

Stellar Industries, located in Oklahoma City, is a manufacturer of brake pads for commercial aircraft. Times have been tough for Stellar. The last recession had caused Stellar to trim its work force by 40 percent. Recently United Airlines awarded Stellar a contract to design a lightweight brake pad. This contract, which will triple Stellar's revenues over a five-year period, has enabled the company to rehire half of the people it laid off and to hire some new people as well.

One of the people rehired is Megan Thomas. Her assignment is to run the brake pad testing. She works directly under Russ Hetlin, who is the chief engineer and the person directly responsible for the design of the lightweight brake pads. The purpose of the test is to assure United that the plane will stop seventy times before the pads have to be replaced. In first round of tests, the pads disintegrate after the fifty-sixth landing. Megan Thomas informs Russ, who instructs her to test that again. This time the pads last through the fifty-fourth landing. Both Megan and Russ realize that a mistake has been made. Megan asks Russ if he will inform United that Stellar can guarantee only fifty landings and that the pads will have to be replaced more frequently. Russ explains that the failure to guarantee seventy landings is a breach of contract. United will go elsewhere to have the brakes manufactured and will sue for the difference between the contract price and the market price, the price paid elsewhere. Stellar will not only have to pay damages but will lose the revenue guaranteed for the next five years. Moreover Stellar's reputation for quality will be harmed, and its financial stability will be undermined.

Russ orders Megan to do whatever is necessary to ensure that the pads work seventy times—for example, allowing the plane to coast after landing rather than applying full pressure to the brake pads. Russ's behavior is clearly unethical. What should Megan do?

A likely response is to speak to Russ's boss. Russ's superior, Fred Worthingham, is vice-president for manufacturing. Fred is also the one who negotiated the contract with United and who signed his name thereto. He is the person ultimately responsible for the deal. Upon learning this, should Megan still seek Fred out?

Megan decides to talk it over with Fred. Fred informs Megan that her duty is to follow the orders given by her direct superior. He says, "The responsibility for these decisions lies with us." Megan tells Fred that she can not live with this decision and would rather resign.

Fred tells Megan that he will assign her to a different job. Does that relieve Megan from ethical responsibility, or must she whistle-blow by informing United, the FAA, and/or the Attorney General's office? Whistle-blowing would be the most ethical decision, but the consequences can often be severe: loss of job; blackballing from the industry; threats of physical harm or even murder, as dramatized in the movie about Karen Silkwood.

The possibility of loss of life from faulty brake pads is a major consideration for whistle-blowing, as compared with defective tray tables or food carts on an airplane. Although ethical responses should be unconditional, is it realistic to expect a person to whistle-blow or lose a job over defective tray tables or food carts? Ethically no one should produce defective equipment regardless of the consequences of the defect because to do so would be to breach the duty to act in good faith.

When the rehirings took place, Russ Heflin specifically asked for Megan because she is a diligent worker. Megan was thrilled because her husband, Phil, was recently placed on disability leave from his job because of a back injury. She is now the primary support for her husband and four children. Knowing Megan's gratitude for being rehired and her personal financial dilemma, Russ emphasizes that his favor to her must be repaid; otherwise the consequences of job loss would leave Megan and her family in dire financial straits. Now Megan must balance her desire to do the right thing against her family's livelihood. Megan decides to discuss the matter with her husband. Phil says, "As long as the vice-president accepted full responsibility and relieved you from any, then do as they say." Now lacking support from her husband, Megan gives in. She is practical, but is she unethical? Must she sacrifice everything to do the right thing? What if a plane crashes because she has followed orders by doctoring the tests or has failed to prevent the disaster by remaining silent and accepting the transfer? What if she whistle-blows—losing her job and ruining her family life—and no one believes her accusations and, furthermore, no plane ever crashes?

SAVE THE LAST DANCE FOR ME

The following case illustrates a scenario wherein a gullible individual is duped into making a purchase that is not in her best interests. Keep these questions in mind as you read the case: Was the case decided in an ethical manner? Should the dance school have told Mrs. Vokes that she had no talent for dancing? Is taking a person's feelings into account when giving an opinion ethical?

Vokes v. Arthur Murray, Inc.
212 So. 2d 906 (D. Ct. App. Fla. (1968))

Vokes sued the Arthur Murray School of Dancing for rescission of a contract for dance lessons. The plaintiff contended that she had entered into the contract because of fraudulent representations about her dancing ability.

Audrey Vokes, a widow for over fifty years, had no family. She yearned to become "an accomplished dancer" and to develop a new interest in life. She was invited to a dance at Davenport's Dance School, a local franchise of the Arthur Murray School of Dancing. She took free lessons, dancing with the instructors while constantly being barraged with flattery and compliments about her dancing potential. She was baited with a trial offer of eight half-hour lessons for $14.50. The come-on worked over a period of time, for the dance school was able to induce her to buy fourteen dance courses, totaling over 2,300 hours of lessons. The cost was over $31,000. The fourteen course enrollments were evidenced by the Arthur Murray School of Dancing Enrollment Agreement.

The inducement used by the dance school included compliments concerning Mrs. Vokes's grace and poise as well as her rapidly improving and developing dancing skill. She was informed that the lessons would "make her a beautiful dancer, capable of dancing with the most accomplished dancers." The plaintiff was even given dance aptitude tests to determine how many additional hours she needed.

At one stage, Mrs. Vokes was sold 545 additional hours, which qualified her for the "Bronze Medal." Thereafter, 926 hours were added for the "Silver Medal," 347 hours for the "Gold Medal," and finally 481 hours for the classification "as a Gold Bar Member, the ultimate achievement of the dancing studio." The defendant also cajoled the widow into buying a life membership, which allowed her to take a trip at her own expense to Miami, where she was "given the opportunity to dance with members of the Miami Studio." She was also talked into buying still more hours to be eligible for trips to Trinidad and Mexico, again both at her own expense.

In reality Mrs. Vokes had no "dance aptitude" and actually had difficulty "hearing the musical beat." She was told that she was entering into the "spring of her life," but actually there was no spring in her life or in her feet.

The defendants contend that their misrepresentations relate to opinions, not facts.

The issue is whether a contract can be rescinded where it was entered into through reliance on fraudulent opinions.

The court held that the parties were not of equal bargaining strength and that the dance studio used its greater strength to its advantage. The studio's opinion of the plaintiff's dancing ability is considered to be one of superior knowledge, equivalent to a statement of fact, because of the studio's expertise. The hours of instruction were unjustified because Mrs. Vokes lacked ability for improvement. If the studio had told her the truth, she would have realized this. The widow justifiably relied on their opinion to her detriment. Judgment for Vokes.

18

Sales: Title and Warranties

INTRODUCTION

Article 2 of the Uniform Commercial Code applies to sales. *Sales* is the codification of contract law with respect to the sale of goods. It is one of the four types of contracts: **R.S.V.P.**

Real property contracts

Sales contracts

Variety of special contracts

Personal service contracts

Because the sale of goods is a contract, the elements of a contract must be present for the sale to be valid. Remember **PALACE.**

Purpose (lawful)

Agreement

Legal capacity

   Act (promise to perform)
   Consideration
   Executed in proper form

  The law of contracts is applicable to sales except for areas that have been changed by the UCC. The previous section of this book deals with contract law. In the individual chapters of that section, references are made to the changes brought about by the UCC with respect to contracts for the sale of goods. Those chapters, in conjunction with these, give an overall picture of the law of sales.

  A sale consists of the passing of title to goods from a seller to a buyer, for consideration. *Goods* are all existing movable things that have been identified to the contract of sale. An obligation to act in good faith is imposed on every party to a commercial transaction. *Commercial transaction* is a broad term encompassing contracts for the sale of goods as well as the special contracts covered by the other articles of the UCC.

  Good faith means honesty in fact; it requires a person to act in an honest manner when entering, performing, or enforcing a commercial transaction. With regard to merchants, the obligation of good faith requires honesty in fact plus the adherence to the reasonable commercial standards of fair dealing prevalent in the marketplace. A *merchant* is a person who regularly deals in a certain kind of goods or one who proclaims that he or she possesses a skill or knowledge peculiar to a certain kind of goods. This does not refer to a person making an isolated sale of goods. Goods are *merchantable* when they can pass without objection in the trade under the description of the contract.

  The sale of computer hardware is a contract for the sale of goods governed by the UCC. The sale of computer software is generally held to be sale of goods if the software is mass-produced and marketed. Computer software programs designed for individual businesses are more regularly held to be service contracts.

DOCTRINE OF CAVEAT EMPTOR

The doctrine of caveat emptor, "Let the buyer beware," has had less of an impact over the past twenty years with the development of consumer rights. This chapter on warranties illustrates the rights consumers have when they purchase products. Consumer rights have even been extended to give people the right to sue for property damages or personal injuries caused by defective products. Chapter 19, "Sales: Products Liability," is devoted to this topic. It is important for consumers to be aware of the warranties imposed by law and the way the law has changed from strict adherence to the doctrine of caveat emptor. Now it is the obligation of the sellers to market products to which they have good title and that will be fit for the uses for which they are intended.

TITLE

Title is the right to ownership of property. In sales it is evidence of a buyer's or a seller's right to the possession of goods. Title passes from the seller to the buyer at the time and place the seller physically delivers the goods to the buyer in accordance with the contract. Physical delivery may occur when the buyer picks up the goods at the seller's place of business or when the seller delivers the goods to a particular destination. If the seller is required to ship the goods, title passes to the buyer at the time and place shipment is made. The goods must be identified to the contract before title may pass.

Identification is the setting aside of goods for the purchaser. Identification occurs in a contract for existing goods when the contract is made, in a contract for future goods when the goods are shipped, and in a contract for crops when the crops are planted. When goods are identified to the contract, the buyer obtains an insurable interest in the goods. An *insurable interest* is the right a person has to insure the goods because of his or her real and substantial interest in those goods. Even though the buyer has an insurable interest in the goods after signing the contract, buyers usually request that the insurance become effective when the goods are in their possession.

An insurable interest remains with the seller as long as the seller has title to the goods or has a security interest in the goods. Therefore it is possible for both the buyer and the seller to have an insurable interest in the same goods between the time when the goods are identified to the contract and the time when title to the goods passes or the security interest in the goods is satisfied. A security interest is the interest the seller (creditor) has in goods that are transferred to the buyer (debtor) in a credit sale. This security interest secures the buyer's obligation to pay for the goods; that is, the goods act as collateral for the credit extended.

EXAMPLE | On May 28, Paul Gangin walked into an art gallery and informed the proprietor, Vincent Van Gogh, that he would like to buy a Renoir. Van Gogh showed him his collection of Renoir paintings. Gangin selected a portrait of a girl, priced at $400,000. He made a down payment of $200,000 and promised to pay the remainder in monthly installments. He told Van Gogh that he was flying to Paris for the month of June and would pick up the painting when he returned. Before he departed for Paris, Gangin insured the painting, with the policy to commence on July 1, the day of his return.

Did both parties have an insurable interest in the goods on May 28? Yes! This is true even though Gangin chose not to insure the painting until he took possession of it. When will Van Gogh's insurable interest expire? Because this is a credit sale involving installment payments, Van Gogh has a security interest in the painting until the last payment is made. Van Gogh's insurable interest will expire when the security interest is satisfied.

DOCTRINE OF ENTRUSTING

According to the doctrine of entrusting, a merchant who deals in goods of a particular kind is endowed with the power to transfer title to goods received from the original owner for storage, repair, or safekeeping. The transfer must be made to a good-faith purchaser for value. The doctrine of entrusting applies even where the merchant obtained the goods by larceny or sold them with that intent.

The reason for the doctrine is to ensure that good-faith purchasers will not be inhibited from buying from merchants out of fear that the goods may have been stolen. This preserves the smooth flow of business. A good-faith purchaser is a person who buys for value in the ordinary course of business without knowledge that the goods are stolen or that any contractual defenses exist.

EXAMPLE | Edouard Manet brought one of his paintings to Toulouse-Lautree, an art dealer, to have a new frame constructed for it. He was told to come back in three weeks. In the meantime Toulouse-Lautree sold the painting to Paul Cézanne for $50,000, a reasonable price. Manet returned to find the painting gone. Can Manet recover his painting? No! Because Toulouse-Lautree is a merchant who regularly deals in the sale of art, he may pass title to goods entrusted to him to Paul Cézanne as long as Cézanne is a good-faith purchaser who buys for value in the ordinary course of business. Manet's only recourse would be to sue Toulouse-Lautree for the value of the painting.

WARRANTIES: DEFINED

A *warranty* is a guarantee, an assurance that the facts as stated are true. The purpose of a warranty is to establish the seller's liability for the marketability, quality, and suitability of the goods sold. This liability may be assumed by the seller through the making of an express warranty, or it may be imposed on the seller by law through one of the implied warranties set forth in the UCC. The following warranties exist in all contracts for the sale of goods unless properly disclaimed: **My FEET.**

Merchantability
y

Fitness for a particular purpose
Express warranties
Encumbrances
Title

WARRANTY OF MERCHANTABILITY

The warranty of merchantability is an implied warranty given only by merchants in contracts for the sale of goods. The warranty extends to food and drink served by merchants to be consumed on their premises or elsewhere. A merchant impliedly warrants that the goods are merchantable—that is, they are fit for the ordinary use for which they are intended. They must be able to pass without objection in the trade. This means that they must be of average quality in comparison to that which is generally accepted in the trade under the description of the contract. If the goods are sold in units, each unit must be of the same kind, quality, and quantity as the rest. If the goods require packaging and labeling, then the packaging must be done in a manner adequate to prevent tampering (as in the famous Tylenol case), spoilage, or infestation, and the labeling must conform to the factual statements and promises made by the seller.

Webster v. Blue Ship Tea Room
347 Mass. 421, 198 N.E. 2d 309 (1964)

Webster brought an action based on breach of implied warranty of merchantability for injuries she sustained while eating a bowl of fish chowder.

On Saturday, April 25, 1959, Webster entered a quaint restaurant called the Blue Ship Tea Room with her sister and her aunt. The women were seated at a table and supplied with menus. Webster ordered a cup of fish chowder to accompany her crabmeat salad. After eating a few spoonfuls of chowder, she felt something lodge in her throat that prevented her from swallowing. She was rushed to Massachusetts General Hospital, where a fish bone was discovered in her throat and removed.

The court stated that the issue was whether "a fish bone lurking in a fish chowder . . . constitutes a breach of implied warranty" of merchantability.

The judge charged the jury, "But the bone of contention here—I don't mean that for a pun—but was this fish bone a foreign substance that made the fish chowder unwholesome or not fit to be eaten?"

The court held,

It is not too much to say that a person sitting down in New England to consume a good New England fish chowder embarks on a gustatory adventure which may entail the removal of some fish bones from his bowl as he proceeds. We are not inclined to tamper with age-old recipes . . . . Certain Massachusetts cooks might cavil at the ingredients contained in the chowder in this case in that it lacked the heartening lift of salt pork. In any event, we consider that the joys of life in New England include the ready availability of fresh fish chowder. We should be prepared to cope with the hazards of fish bones, the occasional presence of which in chowders is, it seems to us, to be anticipated, and which, in the light of a hallowed tradition, do not impair their fitness or merchantability.

Webster was not entitled to recover any damages for the injuries sustained to her throat. Judgment for the Blue Ship Tea Room.

A person who makes an isolated sale of goods does not impliedly warrant that the goods are merchantable because such a person is not considered a merchant. However, the person selling the goods may make an express warranty of merchantability if he or she states that the goods are guaranteed.

EXAMPLE | After the death of Peter Paul Rubens, his widow sold his paints and other art supplies to his pupil, Anthony Van Dyck, assuring him that they were of the very finest quality. Van Dyck used the paints and then complained that the pigment had gone off color. He sued Madame Rubens for breach of warranty in that she had foisted unsalable goods on him. Madame Rubens protested that she was not a merchant. What result? In an isolated sale, a nonmerchant makes no warranty of merchantability unless one is expressly stated. Madame Rubens's statement that the goods were of first quality constitutes an express warranty of merchantability, which she violated.

A merchant may exclude the implied warranty of merchantability only by using the word *merchantability* in the disclaimer or by stating the sale of the goods to be "as is."

Mercedes-Benz of North America v. Dickenson
720 S.W. 2d 844 (Tex. App.—Fort Worth 1986)

David Dickenson bought a 1982 Mercedes from Ryan Oldsmobile, an authorized Mercedes dealer. Dickenson signed a contract containing a disclaimer that excluded all warranties except those authorized by Mercedes, the manufacturer. Mercedes's warranty limited the purchaser's remedy to repairs or replacements necessary to correct defects in material or workmanship for thirty-six months or 36,000 miles.

Dickenson returned the car seven times for repairs including replacement of the transmission twice. The faulty transmission, along with numerous other defects, was never corrected. After attempting unsuccessfully to return the car for a full refund, Dickenson solicited four offers and sold the car to the highest bidder.

Statement of a New Car Warranty

There are NO WARRANTIES, express or implied, made by the Selling Dealer or the manufacturer on the new vehicle or chassis described in the order, except the most recent printed Mercedes Benz warranty or warranties applicable to such new vehicle or chassis which are made a part of this order as of here set forth in full. A copy of such Mercedes-Benz warranty or warranties will be furnished to the purchaser upon delivery of the vehicle or chassis, and they shall be expressly IN LIEU OF any other express or implied warranty, condition or guarantee on the new vehicle, chassis or any part thereof, including any implied WARRANTY OF MERCHANTABILITY or FITNESS and of any other obligation on the part of Mercedes-Benz, or the Selling Dealer. Purchaser acknowledges that this vehicle is not suitable for Trailer Towing unless specified in this order.

The issue is whether both Mercedes and Ryan breached the warranty by being unable to repair the car in compliance with the terms of the warranty.

The court found "that the limited warranty failed of its essential purpose since the warrantor was unable to correct the car's defects within a reasonable time." The court decided, "We find that the language found in the Mercedes-Benz warranty booklet cannot be construed consistently with the express warranties made. The disclaimer language is, therefore, inoperative." Judgment for Dickenson.

WARRANTY OF FITNESS FOR A PARTICULAR PURPOSE

The warranty of fitness for a particular use arises when the seller has reason to know that the buyer is relying upon his or her expertise or judgment in selecting or furnishing goods suitable to the buyer's particular purpose. This warranty is implied from the facts and applies to both merchants and nonmerchants. The buyer must prove the seller's expertise and the buyer's own reliance on it. If the buyer insists on a particular brand name, no reliance is placed on the seller's expertise or judgment. However, the warranty does apply to a brand name purchased by the buyer on the seller's recommendation.

EXAMPLE | Michelangelo sold the Vatican a fountain that he assured could be used as a baptismal font for the Sistine Chapel. When the first baptismal ceremony was held, it was discovered that the font leaked badly. The Vatican sued Michelangelo for breach of warranty. What result? The Vatican relied on Michelangelo's expertise and artistic ability to recommend a sound font. He breached the implied warranty of fitness for a particular purpose, for which he is liable to the Vatican for damages.

The warranty of fitness for a particular purpose may be modified or excluded only by conspicuous language in writing—for example, "There are no warranties which extend beyond the description of the face hereof" or "All goods are sold 'as is'." The disclaimer may be printed on a sales slip or in a formal contract.

EXPRESS WARRANTIES

An *express warranty* is created through (1) any factual statements or promises made by the seller about the goods, (2) any description of the goods made by the seller, or (3) any samples or models exhibited by the seller during the contract negotiations that become part of the basis of the contract. There is no need to prove reliance on the factual statements and promises made by the seller during the contract negotiations because these are considered a description of the goods. A description of the goods encompasses more than just words. It includes blueprints and other technical diagrams, specifications, and plans. A sample is a selection of goods indiscriminately drawn from the bulk of goods identified to the contract, whereas a model is an imitation or copy offered for inspection when the actual goods are not available.

The seller may not have intended to make any warranties, but an express warranty will be created by any of the previously mentioned statements, promises, descriptions, samples, or models introduced by the seller during the contract negotiations unless a good reason is shown to the contrary. No formal language involving the word *warranty* or *guarantee* is required, but statements by the seller concerning his or her opinion of the quality of the goods or their value are looked upon as mere puffing and do not create an express warranty. Once an express warranty is created, it may not be limited or negated.

EXAMPLE | On seeing the portrait of Whistler's mother, Lady Astor approached the artist and asked if he would do a portrait of her. After considerable dickering over the price, Whistler agreed to do the painting for $250,000 and guaranteed Lady Astor's approval. Five sittings were completed, and Lady Astor cried, "What is this? You have made me look older than your mother." She refused to continue the sittings. Whistler, steaming mad, sued Lady Astor for the full price of the portrait. What result? Whistler has not a leg to stand on because he expressly guaranteed her approval and could not earn it.

WARRANTY AGAINST ENCUMBRANCES

The warranty against encumbrances implies that the goods shall be delivered to the buyer free of any security interest or other lien of which the buyer has no knowledge at the time the contract is made. This warranty may be modified or excluded only by specific language or if the circumstances give the buyer reason to know that a security interest or other encumbrance or lien against the property exists.

EXAMPLE | Henri Matisse purchased a copy of the enormous sculpture, *The Thinker,* for $750,000 from Auguste Rodin. Matisse made a $250,000 down payment with Rodin, who retained a security interest in the sculpture for the balance. Matisse sells the statue to Picasso for $800,000, guaranteeing it to be free of encumbrances. To his astonishment Picasso learns that Rodin has a security interest in *The Thinker* and sues Matisse for breach of warranty. What result? Matisse has breached the implied warranty against encumbrances by not acknowledging the existence of Rodin's security interest in the sculpture.

WARRANTY OF TITLE

This warranty guarantees that the seller has clear title to the goods that he or she has contracted to transfer to the buyer. The warranty of good title is implied in all contracts for the sale of goods and cannot be excluded by the phrase "as is." This is to ensure that the buyer's expectations are fulfilled and to protect the buyer against lawsuits questioning the validity of the title. A buyer acquires no better title than that which he or she receives from the seller. Title does not pass through a thief, with the exception of circumstances covered by the doctrine of entrusting. Warranty of title may be modified or excluded only by specific language or circumstances apprising the buyer of the fact that the seller does not have clear title to the goods.

EXAMPLE | Raphael sold the Mona Lisa to the Louvre in Paris for $1.5 million. He guaranteed that he had clear title to the painting. Subsequently it was proved that Raphael had stolen the painting from Leonardo da Vinci, its true owner. The Louvre sued Raphael for breach of warranty of title. What result? The Louvre returned the painting to da Vinci and recovered $1.5 million from Raphael for breach of warranty of title.

BREACH OF WARRANTY

A buyer of goods may bring an action for breach of warranty on the basis of either an express warranty made by the seller or one of the implied warranties the UCC imposes on the seller. A breach may occur because the seller did not have proper title to the goods sold, because there was a lien or other encumbrance against the goods, because the goods were not merchantable, or because the goods were not fit for the particular purpose intended. A breach will give the buyer the right to sue for a remedy. Buyers' remedies will be discussed in Chapter 21. A buyer who has not sustained any damages will be permitted to cancel the contract by returning the goods and recovering the purchase price. If property damage has resulted from the use of the goods, then the buyer may sue for consequential damages. A buyer who has been forced to cover by purchasing the goods elsewhere will be entitled to the difference between the contract price and the cover price. If personal injury has resulted from the use of the product, the person injured—who may even be someone other than the buyer—has a right to sue based on breach of warranty, negligence, or strict products liability. Although we have discussed personal injury caused by breach of warranty in this chapter, Chapter 19, "Sales: Products Liability," will zero in on all the remedies available to a person who is injured by a product, including the remedy of breach of warranty.

REVIEW QUESTIONS

1. Define sales, goods, commercial transaction, good faith, merchant, merchantable, title, identification, insurable interest, and warranty.

2. What is the difference between an express warranty and an implied warranty?

3. List and explain the various types of warranties.

4. Louisiana Industries supplied concrete and Fibermesh at the request of Alfred Craft, who was building an alligator barn. The concrete cracked because of the weakness of the Fibermesh reinforcement, and Craft refused to pay for it. Louisiana Industries claimed that a preferred reinforcement was steel rods or wire mesh but that it sold Craft Fibermesh because that is what he asked for. What result? *Louisiana Industries v. Bogator, Inc.,* 605 So. 2d 231 (LA. App. 2 Cir. 1992).

5. Pratt purchased a motor home from Colonial-Sales-Lease Rental, Inc. on an "as is" bill of sale. Subsequently Pratt experienced problems with the motor home. Pratt sued for breach of warranty of merchantability. What result? *Pratt v. Colonial-Sales-Lease Rental, Inc.,* 799 F. Supp. 1132 (N.D. Ala. 1992).

6. Guaranteed Construction Company entered into a contract to refurbish the Carriage Lane Apartments. Gold Bond manufactured the drywall compound, and Dale manufactured the steel corner bead, which is a light-gauge piece of metal used to protect the outer corner of a wall. These products were used in the reconstructing of the walls in the Carriage Lane Apartments. After the corner bead was installed, the joint compound was applied. After the drywall was painted, the joint compound crumbled and the corner bead corroded. This deterioration was caused by extreme humidity in the air. Guaranteed argued that the manufacturers had breached the warranty of merchantability by selling products that were not fit for the purpose for which they were intended to be used. What result? *Guaranteed Construction Co. v. Gold Bond Products,* 395 N.W. 2d 332 (Mich. App. 1986).

7. A Pacesetter pacemaker was installed in David Larsen. Unbeknownst to Larsen's physician at the time of the operation, three other Pacesetter pacemakers had been found to have been defective. Larsen was advised to have his pacemaker removed. He agreed after being informed of the risks of two major surgeries one month apart. Complications set in, and his medical expenses and pain and suffering mounted. The pacemaker, which was removed, was not defective. Larsen sued for breach of the implied warranty of merchantability. What result? *Larsen v. Pacesetter Systems, Inc.,* 837 P. 2d 1273 (Hawaii 1992).

8. Collegiate Enterprises, the general contractor, hired Otis Elevator Company to install three elevators in Broadmoor Realty, Inc.'s condominium development. The elevators were defective. Broadmoor sued Otis for breach of implied warranties of merchantability and fitness for a particular purpose because of its inability to sell the condo units. Otis contends that Broadmoor cannot sue because Broadmoor was not a party to the contract with Otis. What result? *Collegiate Enterprises, Inc. v. Otis Elevator Co.,* 650 F. Supp. 116 (E.D. Mo. 1986).

9. Thomaston suffered serious injuries when he dove into the shallow end of his aunt and uncle's pool. He sued the pool manufacturer on the basis of breach

of implied warranty, alleging that the pool's design and construction were defective. The defendant pool manufacturer contends that the plaintiff cannot sue because no contract exists between the parties. What result? *Thomaston* v. *Fort Wayne Pools, Inc., 352* S.E. 2d 79 (Ga. App. 1987).

10. Daniel Motors sold a GM truck to the city of Colorado Springs. The city's equipment company installed the dump bed and hoist on the truck in order to use it as a pothole repair truck. Ike Shaw was injured when a city employee backed the truck over him. Shaw is suing GM because it failed to install an alarm that would sound when the truck was in reverse. The issue is whether the condition of the truck at the time of delivery was unreasonably dangerous without the alarm. Shaw argues that the truck was not fit for the particular purposes for which it was to be used. GM argues that the truck was not manufactured for use as a pothole repair truck and that the use of the truck for such purpose was not foreseeable. What result? *Shaw* v. *General Motors Corp., 727* P. 2d 387 (Colo. App. 1986).

19

Sales: Products Liability

Introduction	Strict Products Liability
Breach of Warranty	Statute of Limitations
Negligence	Review Questions

INTRODUCTION

Products liability is a separate area of the law. It incorporates principles of contracts; sales, specifically warranties; and the torts of negligence and strict liability. Products liability was developed to ensure that a consumer who sustains personal injury caused by a defective product will be compensated for the injury. Businesses are extremely concerned over products liability, evidenced by the huge amounts of insurance written to protect businesses against losses resulting from liability suits.

A person injured by a defective product may bring a lawsuit under any or all three of the following causes of action: breach of warranty, negligence, and strict products liability. *Breach of warranty* is a contract action that encompasses the express and implied warranties discussed in Chapter 18. Negligence and strict products liability are tort actions. Injured parties who may proceed under these causes of action include the purchaser, a user other than the purchaser, and an innocent bystander. The parties against whom they may seek redress are the manufacturer, including manufacturers of component parts; distributors and other intermediaries; and retailer—merchants who sell the goods.

In Chapter 18 we considered warranties covering defective products where the product was merely defective and, to an extent, cases where products caused personal injury. In this chapter we are going to examine more thoroughly warranties covering defective products that bring about personal injuries.

238

BREACH OF WARRANTY

Breach of warranty is a contract action that a purchaser of goods brings for personal injury and/or property damage on the basis of either the express warranties made by the seller or the implied warranties imposed on the seller by the UCC. (See the Webster v. Blue Ship Tea Room case discussed in Chapter 18.)

A breach of warranty action may also be brought by any member of the buyer's family or any guest in the buyer's home if that person could reasonably be expected to use the goods or to be affected by the goods. Some states have extended the warranty to include personal injury and property damage suffered by any person who would reasonably be expected to use the goods or be affected by them. In states restricting recovery to family members and guests, outsiders would be relegated to suing on the basis of negligence or strict products liability.

EXAMPLE | Rembrandt engaged an architect to design and build a little summer house for his garden. After its construction a family gathering was held. Grandma Moses was sitting having tea when the railing behind her gave way. She landed in the flower bed and broke her hip. Has Grandma Moses any recourse? Yes! Because she is a member of the family, she may sue the architect for breach of warranty.

A breach of warranty action may be brought against the seller and/or the manufacturer even though the person bringing the suit has not dealt with either of them. To establish breach of warranty, the injured person must prove that the warranty existed, that it was breached by the seller, and that the seller's breach was the proximate cause of the injury. The seller or manufacturer will attempt to rebut the buyer's allegations by establishing that he or she exercised due care in the manufacturing, processing, or selection of the goods.

NEGLIGENCE

A manufacturer will be liable to any person for reasonably foreseeable injuries and property damage (see the Palsgraf test in Chapter 5) that are proximately caused by products reasonably certain to place life and limb in danger when negligently made. This may include almost any product. The term *manufacturer* applies to both the manufacturer of the finished product and the manufacturers of component parts. The injured person must prove that the defect in the product was caused by the manufacturer's negligence in failing to exercise reasonable care in designing the product and in failing to make a reasonable inspection that would have revealed the defect.

The manufacturer also has a duty to adequately warn the prospective user of the potential danger of the product and to recall the product upon discovery that it is defective. The manufacturer's failure to warn or to recall amounts to negligence. There must be knowledge that danger is probable. A manufacturer is not compelled to put on the market a reliable product, just one that is free of negligence. If the injury is caused to someone other than the purchaser, that person must also establish that the item was used for the purpose for which it was intended and that the manufacturer knew that a person other than the purchaser would use the item without examining it to see if it was defective. Often injured persons are unable to recover from manufacturers in negligence case because of intervening inspectors; the inspectors are liable instead.

STRICT PRODUCTS LIABILITY

Strict products liability developed out of the theory of strict liability in tort. Even without proof of negligence, a manufacturer, a distributor, and a seller are strictly liable for injuries that occur when they place an article on the market knowing that it is to be used without the kind of inspection likely to uncover the defect. The term *manufacturer* includes manufacturers of component parts.

These merchants are strictly liable even though they have exercised due care in the preparation, inspection, and sale of the product and regardless of whether the person who used it is the purchaser. This is the case provided that the seller is engaged in the business of selling the product that caused the injury, the product was used in the way it was intended to be used, the injury arose from a defect in either the design or manufacture of the product, and the person who was injured was unaware of the defect. A defect in design occurs when the product as produced is inadequate to serve the purpose for which it was intended. A defect in manufacture occurs when the product is not properly made.

The injured party has the burden of proving that the defect in design or manufacture existed when the product left the seller's hands. The injured party may rely on circumstantial evidence to prove this. The party must also submit evidence that tends to prove the relationship between the defect and the injury. The court will decide whether or not the accident caused the injury on the basis of expert testimony coupled with other evidence that indicates the circumstances surrounding the accident. Some courts also require the injured party to prove that the defective condition made the product unreasonably dangerous. This concept limits the doctrine of products liability in situations involving the extent of a manufacturer's duty with regard to safe design. Similarly, it limits the doctrine of products liability where the type of injury sustained is not commonly caused by the defect and the possibility that the injured party misused the product is in issue.

Several tests are applied to determine whether the defect is unreasonably dangerous. One of the most widely used tests considers whether a reasonable manufacturer would continue to produce and sell the product in the same condition and do so with the knowledge he or she now has of the potentially dangerous consequences. Other tests consider such factors as the usefulness of the product, the availability of safer products, the potential risk of injury, and the knowledge and acceptance of this risk by the public.

EXAMPLE | The merchant of Venice, a manufacturer of gondolas, borrowed a large sum of money from Shylock. The merchant of Venice had financial difficulties because of a decline in the tourist trade and could not meet his payments. He offered to substitute one of the gondolas he had manufactured as payment for the loan. Shylock was paddling around the canals in the gondola when he suddenly realized it was sinking because of a defect in the design. Unfortunately he could not swim, so, like a captain, he went down with the ship. Does his estate have any recourse against the merchant of Venice? Yes! The estate may sue the merchant for Shylock's wrongful death under the theory of strict products liability. The gondola manufactured by the merchant had a defect in its design. The defect in construction was unreasonably dangerous because it caused the boat to sink, and Shylock's death resulted.

Some states have extended the strict liability rule to an innocent bystander for damages sustained as a consequence of a defect that is reasonably foreseeable, provided that the item was properly used, the defect could not have been discovered with reasonable care, and the injury to the bystander could not have been averted with reasonable care. A bystander deserves better protection than a user because the bystander does not have the opportunity to inspect.

A lessor is also liable for injuries that result from property that is leased to a consumer in a defective condition. However, if the person had knowledge of the defect before use or used it in an abnormal way, the consumer would be barred from recovery.

When a person or company is engaged in the business of selling food or other products for intimate bodily use and sells such a product in a defective condition that is unreasonably dangerous to the consumer, the seller is liable for bodily harm that results. A merchant selling food has an affirmative duty to check the food, thus assuring the consumer that it is safe to eat.

EXAMPLE | Alexihente operates a restaurant called The Demanding One just south of the border. Alexihente personally inspects all the meat that he purchases. During summer festival his meat distributor's supply is exhausted. Alexihente is forced to purchase the meat elsewhere. He contacts the Butcher of Barcelona, who makes prompt delivery. In his haste Alexihente forgets to inspect the beef. The meat is tainted, and his patrons suffer severe intestinal complications. Is Alexihente liable? Yes! He is liable under the theory of strict products liablity. Alexihente may sue the Butcher of Barcelona for indemnification because it was the butcher who actually caused the harm.

Shoshine Coca-Cola Bottling Co. v. Dolinski
420 P. 2d 855 (Nev. 1967)

Leo Dolinski purchased a bottle of soda from a Coca-Cola vending machine. He drank a portion of it and suddenly became ill. The bottle was examined and was found to contain a decomposed mouse and mouse feces. Apparently the mouse entered the bottle before it was filled

with soda. Dolinski claimed that he suffered physical and mental distress and that he could never drink soda again.

The issue is whether a defect in the manufacture of the bottle
caused Dolinski's injuries.

The court ruled, "[P]ublic policy demands that one who places
upon the market a bottled beverage in a condition dangerous for use
must be held strictly liable to the ultimate user for injuries resulting
from such use, although the seller has exercised all reasonable care."
Judgment for Dolinski.

Smith v. Paslode Corp.
799 F. Supp. 960 (E.D. Mo. 1992)

Kevin Luke Smith was injured when a defect in the design of a pneumatic nail gun manufactured by Paslode Corporation caused it to fire a
nail through his left hand. Smith underwent surgery and blood transfusions in December 1983 and September 1984. The blood had been collected by the American Red Cross (ARC). In September 1987 Smith
was diagnosed HIV positive. Smith sued Paslode and ARC for strict
products liability. Paslode was found guilty.

ARC contended that there was no AIDS test in 1984 and that its
blood testing satisfied FDA regulations. ARC also contended that its
distribution of blood amounted to a service, not a sale of a product, as
required by the theory of strict products liability.

The issues are whether ARC failed to test the blood properly and
whether its distribution is a sale or a service. The court held, "The collection, processing and distribution of blood by ARC is a service, not a
sale of goods. Therefore, ARC in performing these functions did not
engage in the sale of a product. Consequently, an action for strict products liability is not available against ARC under the facts of this case."

The court continued,

> [T]he reasonableness of ARC's actions must be determined in light of
> facts existing and known at the time in question, in this case 1983 and
> 1984, rather than on the basis of facts revealed by subsequent develop-
> ments. It is undisputed that HIV was not isolated until the spring of 1984.
> It is further undisputed that no test existed in 1983 and 1984 which could
> detect or remove HIV. The test to detect AIDS was developed in March
> 1985. There is still no procedure to remove AIDS from blood or blood
> components.

Judgment for Smith against Paslode, but not against ARC.

STATUTE OF LIMITATIONS

A statute of limitations is the length of time an aggrieved party has in which to begin a lawsuit. Statutes of limitations vary depending upon the cause of action. Breach of express and implied warranties pertains to contracts for the sale of goods; therefore a four-year statute of limitations applies. The four-year period begins on the date the goods are sold. In a suit based on the torts of strict products liability or negligence, a three-year statute of limitations applies, but the three-year period does not begin until the date of injury. If the injury occurs five years after the date the defective product was purchased, a suit based on breach of warranty would fail because the four-year statute of limitations would have run, but a suit based on negligence or strict products liability would prevail because the three-year statute of limitations would not have begun to run until the date of injury. This may allow an aggrieved person to recover money damages where he or she would otherwise be barred from recovery.

REVIEW QUESTIONS

1. Define strict products liability, breach of warranty, negligence, and manufacturer.

2. Pious Affolter's personal property was stolen from his boat while it was stored at the Virginia Key Marina. The storage contract contains a clause that relieves the marina from all liability even if a loss is due to their negligence. What result? *Affolter v. Marina,* 601 So. 2d 1296 (Fla. App. 3 Dist. 1992).

3. Mrs. Hauter bought the Golfing Gizmo for her thirteen-year-old son Fred. The Golfing Gizmo was designed to help improve the games of unskilled golfers. It consisted of two pegs driven into the ground about two feet apart; an elastic cord extending between them; and another cord with a golf ball on its end, tied to the middle of the elastic cord. The Golfing Gizmo resembled a large letter T with a golf ball at its base. The Golfing Gizmo was set up so that the ball would spring back after being hit. The instruction booklet stated that players should "drive the ball with full power" and furthermore asserted that the Golfing Gizmo was "COMPLETELY SAFE. BALL WILL NOT HIT PLAYER." Fred used the Golfing Gizmo several times after reading the instruction booklet. On one swing Fred hit underneath the ball and caught the cord with his golf club. This looped the ball over the top of the club, and the ball struck Fred on the left temple. He suffered brain damage. Fred's parents sued the manufacturer for breach of warranty. What result? *Hauter v. Zogarts,* 14 Cal. 3d 104, 120 Cal. Rptr. 681, 534 P. 2d 377 (1975).

4. Mrs. Amoroso was injured by a defect in the crossbar of a sailboat that her husband had rented. She sued Sunrise Water Sports, the sailboat owner, under the theory of strict liability. Sunrise contended that Mrs. Amoroso had not rented the boat and that, in any event, strict liability does not apply to lessors. What

result? *Amoroso* v. *Samuel Friedland Family Ent.*, 604 So. 2d 827 (Fla. App. 4 Dist. 1992).

5. Peggy Penland was severely burned when her BIC lighter exploded. When she sued the BIC Corporation she could not produce the fragments of the defective lighter. BIC claims that without the lighter, there is no way for Penland to prove that it was defective. What result? *Penland* v. *BIC Corp.*, 796 F. Supp. 877 (W.D. NC. 1992).

6. Billy Toney purchased a Kawasaki 750 motorcycle. The next day he was struck from the side by a truck. His left leg was amputated. He brought suit against Kawasaki, alleging that they did not provide leg guards to shield riders from this type of injury. Kawasaki claimed that the risk of injury to the legs is open and obvious. What result? *Toney* v. *Kawasaki Heavy Industries Ltd.*, 975 F. 2d 162 (5th Cir. 1992).

7. Kevin Smith contracted the HIV virus as a result of a blood transfusion that he needed when he injured his left hand. The injury was caused by a defect in the design of a pneumatic nail gun manufactured by Paslode Corporation. As a result of the HIV virus, Kevin Smith's wife Constance sued for loss of consortium. The injury occurred in November 1983. The blood transfusions were given in December 1983 and September 1984. Kevin and Constance were married in March 1987, and the HIV diagnosis was made in September 1987. Paslode contended that loss of consortium based on injuries received prior to a marriage is precluded. What result? *Smith* v. *Paslode Corp.*, 799 F. Supp. 960 (E.D. Mo. 1992).

8. Thomas Searls works at an Anheuser-Busch brewery, where he monitors a conveyor system that ejects improperly filled cans. On the date of his accident, Searls injured his back when he stepped on a beer can that had been ejected automatically at high speed. The employee sued the manufacturer of the conveyor line and the manufacturer of the machine that ejected cans from the conveyor, alleging negligence, strict liability, and breach of implied warranty. The defendants contend that a manufacturer of a component part is not under any duty to warn of potential dangers when a manufacturer assembles those components into a larger system. What result? *Searls* v. *Doe,* 505 N.E. 2d 287 (Ohio App. 1986).

20

Sales: Performance and Risk of Loss

INTRODUCTION

Both parties have a general obligation to act in accordance with the contract. The seller has a duty to transfer title to the goods and to deliver them to the buyer; the buyer has a duty to accept the goods delivered and to pay for them.

A *document of title* is a document that evidences ownership of goods. It is used in the regular course of business to prove that the person presenting it is entitled to possession and ownership of the goods it covers. Documents of title include bills of lading, warehouse receipts, and orders for delivery of goods. These documents may also be transferred by sale, exchange, or gift.

A *bill of lading* is a document of title evidencing the receipt of goods for shipment. It is issued by a common carrier. A *common carrier* is a company engaged in the business of transporting goods. A negotiable bill of lading specifies that delivery must be made either to the person named in the bill of lading or to the person in possession of the bill of lading, who is commonly known as the bearer. A negotiable bill of lading can be transferred by sale, gift, or exchange. A bill of lading in any other form is nonnegotiable. A nonnegotiable, or straight, bill of lading may not be transferred.

A warehouse receipt is a document of title issued by a warehouse upon receipt of goods. A warehouse is a company that is engaged in the business of storing goods.

A bailment is a contract to deliver goods or to hold them for safekeeping in return for a fee. A bailee is the person to whom the goods have been entrusted. The bailee will deliver the goods to the buyer upon the buyer's presentation of a document of title.

Documents of title are required only where (1) the seller and the purchaser expressly provide for them in the contract of sale or (2) the circumstances of the case or usage of trade dictates that the documents of title are necessary. A further discussion of bailees, common carriers, and warehouses may be found in Chapter 28, "Bailments."

TENDER OF DELIVERY

Tender of delivery is the seller's notice to the buyer of willingness and ability to perform. This must be followed by the actual performance, which consists of delivery of the goods. The buyer need not pay if tender of delivery is not made. When tender is made the buyer must accept the goods, if they conform to the contract, and pay for them; otherwise the buyer will have breached the contract.

Tender of delivery may be made when the seller holds conforming goods for the buyer and gives the buyer notice that he or she may take delivery. The tender of delivery must be made at a reasonable hour, and the buyer must be given adequate time to take possession of the goods. It is the buyer's obligation to furnish sufficient facilities to store the goods upon receipt; this does not affect the seller's tender.

EXAMPLE | The Texas gentleman is a rancher living in Dallas. He owns several cattle farms throughout the state. All deliveries are made through the Dallas ranch. On March 30 he enters into a contract to sell 1,500 head of cattle to Big Bad John. On April 3 the Texas Gentleman notifies Big Bad John that the cattle are at his Dallas ranch waiting to be picked up. Big Bad John arrives and picks up the cattle the very next day. Has proper tender of delivery been made? Yes!

In a *destination contract* the seller must tender the appropriate document of title in correct form to the buyer. A negotiable document of title is one in bearer form. The bailee must transfer the goods covered by the document of title to any person who presents it. A negotiable document of title may also be assigned. A nonnegotiable document of title is payable only to the person named on the document; it may not be assigned. A nonnegotiable document of title or a written direction to the bailee to make delivery will suffice as tender unless the buyer objects. If the bailee refuses to honor either the document or the direction, tender has not been made.

EXAMPLE | Diamond-Tooth Gertie is working as a stripper in the Silver Spoon Saloon on the Barbary Coast in San Francisco. She contracts with Le Boudoir, Gentleman Jim's lingerie shop in Crystal City, Colorado, to furnish her with twelve stunning costumes with "lots of lace and space." Gentleman Jim ships the goods via Union Pacific Railroad, with written instructions directing the carrier to deliver the goods to Diamond-Tooth Gertie on the Barbary Coast. When the goods arrive the carrier refuses to deliver them to Gertie. Has tender of delivery been made? No! The carrier refused to honor the written instructions given by Gentleman Jim.

The buyer has a right to reject a tender of delivery that fails to conform to the contract. The seller may cure an improper tender of delivery that is rejected because the goods are nonconforming. The seller must notify the buyer of his or her intention to deliver conforming goods and must make delivery before the expiration of the time for performance.

EXAMPLE | In the previous example suppose that the contract calls for delivery on or before July 17. Diamond-Tooth Gertie receives the shipment on July 11 but rejects the costumes because there is too much space and not enough lace. Gentleman Jim informs Gertie that he will send her another shipment of costumes with more lace and less space. The shipment arrives on July 15, and this shipment conforms to the contract. Is Gertie bound to accept this shipment? Yes! Because the expiration date has not passed, Gentleman Jim must be afforded the chance to cure the nonconformity. He accomplishes this by notifying Gertie of his intention to cure and by delivering conforming goods before July 17.

The *risk of loss* remains on the seller until a cure of either the goods or the document of title is made. The seller may not shift the risk of loss until his or her performance conforms to the contract. If the seller had reasonable grounds to believe that the original tender would be accepted, the seller may be afforded a reasonable time beyond the expiration date for performance to cure the nonconformity. Whether the seller had reasonable grounds to believe that the tender would be accepted can be determined from the prior course of dealing or from the circumstances surrounding the contract.

EXAMPLE | In the ongoing tale of Diamond-Tooth Gertie and Gentleman Jim, suppose that Gentleman Jim has made annual deliveries of costumes to Gertie for the last five years. Gertie accepted the delivery each time, relying on Gentleman Jim's taste in selection. This time Gentleman Jim cannot cure the nonconformity by July 17. What result? Because Gentleman Jim had reasonable grounds to believe that his tendered delivery would be accepted, he will be allowed a reasonable time beyond the expiration date to cure the nonconformity.

TENDER OF PAYMENT

Tender of payment must be made before the seller is required to deliver the goods unless the contract provides that delivery is to be made first, as in the majority of credit sales. Tender of payment may be made in any ordinary business manner. If the payment is made by check and, when the check is presented to a bank, it is dishonored, then tender of payment has not been made.

A buyer who wishes to purchase goods on credit is often required to secure a letter of credit from a bank that is willing to act as a surety and assume the risk of nonpayment by the buyer. The buyer must then deliver the letter of credit to the seller.

EXAMPLE | Diamond Jim Brady, a big spender, wants to purchase a diamond necklace from Tiffany's for his new girlfriend, Darlin' Lil. The necklace costs $30,000, and Diamond Jim promises to pay for it in thirty equal installments. Tiffany's asks Diamond Jim to obtain from his bank a letter of credit guaranteeing the extension of credit. Diamond Jim secures the letter of credit from the Franklin Savings Bank. Will Darlin' Lil now become Diamond Lil? Yes! By all means! The bank's issuance of a letter of credit means that it will honor all checks drafted by Diamond Jim in regard to the installment payments.

INSPECTION OF GOODS

The buyer has a right, before payment or acceptance, to inspect the goods at a reasonable place and time and in a reasonable manner to discover any defects that do not appear on the surface. When the seller is sending the goods to the buyer, the buyer may inspect them after they arrive. If the contract requires payment before inspection, the buyer must pay but later may revoke acceptance if the goods are nonconforming. The buyer has the responsibility of paying for the inspection. If the goods are found to be nonconforming, the buyer may be reimbursed for the inspection expenses.

EXAMPLE | Little Joe from Kokomo agrees to purchase 100 pounds of Boston Baked Beans for $200 from Boston Blackie, who is the proprietor of the Boston Beanery. Little Joe sends the money to Blackie, who in turn ships the beans to Kokomo. After the beans arrive Little Joe tastes them and discovers they are actually jumping beans and not the baked beans he ordered. Now he is known as Jumpin' Joe from Kokomo. Has Jumpin' Joe any recourse? Yes! Even though Jumpin' Joe paid for and accepted the beans, his acceptance was conditioned on his right to inspect them after arrival. He may revoke his acceptance and revoke his payment together with any incidental expenses incurred for the inspection.

When there is a dispute concerning the quality of the goods after the buyer has paid for, inspected, and rejected them, each party has the right to inspect, test, and sample the goods to establish evidence for his or her case. The parties may agree to have an arbitrator inspect the goods to determine their condition and conformity, and the parties may also agree to be bound by the arbitrator's decision.

RISK OF LOSS

Risk of loss is the placement of the financial responsibility for lost, damaged, or destroyed goods. Actually, anyone who has an interest in the goods suffers by their destruction. A person having a security interest loses the right to exercise that interest as well as the right to resell or reclaim the goods on the buyer's default if the goods are destroyed. When the risk of loss falls on the seller, he or she loses the right to the goods even though no payment is received.

SHIPMENT CONTRACTS

In a *shipment contract* the risk of loss is transferred to the buyer when the seller delivers the goods to the carrier at the place of shipment. The seller also bears the expense of transferring the goods to the carrier. Shipment contracts are denoted by the terms *F.O.B., F.A.S., C.I.F,* and *C.&F.*

F.O.B.

The term *F.O.B.* means free on board. It requires the seller to deliver the goods to the F.O.B. point, the place of shipment or destination. It is usually written as "F.O.B. Charlotte" (place of shipment) or "F.O.B. Milwaukee" (place of destination). The seller must bear the expense and risk of transferring the goods into the possession of a carrier. The seller also is responsible for contracting with the carrier who will deliver the goods to the place of destination. In a shipment contract the risk of loss is placed on the seller until the time the goods are transferred to the carrier at the place of shipment. After the goods are in the carrier's possession, the risk of loss transfers to the buyer.

F.A.S.

The term *F.A.S.* means free alongside ship. F.A.S. is a delivery term in a shipment contract that obligates the seller to transport goods to the place of shipment at the seller's expense and risk. The seller must make delivery on the dock alongside the ship. The name of the ship and the port must be specified.

EXAMPLE | Dapper Dan runs the Masquerade House in St. Louis. He contracts with the city of New Orleans to supply all the costumes for the annual Mardi Gras on Bourbon Street. The terms of the contract state, "F.A.S. Kansas City on the Riverboat Queen." Dapper Dan delivers the costumes to the dock in Kansas City, alongside the steamboat. The costumes are loaded on board, and the Riverboat Queen sets sail for New Orleans. During the journey a masked villain makes off with the costumes. Who must bear the risk of loss? Although the carrier will ultimately be responsible for the stolen costumes because it failed to exercise reasonable care for their protection, the risk of loss initially falls on the city of New Orleans as the buyer. An F.A.S. contract is a shipment contract. Dapper Dan, as seller, must bear the risk of loss only until the time he delivers the goods to the dock alongside the Riverboat Queen. After that the city of New Orleans assumes the risk of loss.

C.I.F. and C.&F.

The terms *C.I.F.* and *C.&F.* mean cost, insurance, and freight and cost and freight, respectively. Both terms indicate shipment contracts where the seller is obligated to pay all costs for transportation, insurance, and freight to the place of destination. These costs are reflected in the price charged.

EXAMPLE | Tucker's Inn in Skagway, Alaska, ordered 300 pounds of sourdough from Yukon Joe in Dawson City. Sourdough was used as a substitute for yeast in baking. The terms of the contract were: C.I.F. Skagway. While the shipment was crossing the Chilkoot Pass en route to Skagway, it was destroyed by an avalanche of snow. Is Tucker covered for the loss? Yes! A C.I.F. contract is a shipment contract with the risk of loss falling on Tucker; however, as a part of the C.I.F. contract, Yukon Joe had procured insurance for the goods being shipped. This protects Tucker.

In a shipment contract the seller must (1) assume the risk and expense of transporting goods to a common carrier, (2) transfer the goods to the carrier, (3) make a reasonable contract for their transportation, (4) forward to the buyer any document of title that will be necessary for him or her to get possession, and (5) promptly notify the buyer of shipment. The seller may satisfy the notification requirement by sending the documents of title. In a case where there are no required documents, an invoice may be sent.

DESTINATION CONTRACTS

In a *destination contract* the seller must be responsible for the expense and risk of loss until the goods are delivered to the place of destination. The seller must notify the buyer when the goods arrive at the place of destination so that the buyer may take delivery of the goods. It is only when the buyer takes delivery at the place of destination that the risk of loss passes from the seller to the buyer.

> ### Ninth Street East, Ltd. v. Harrison
> ### 5 Conn. Cir. 597, 259 A. 2d 772 (1968)
>
> Ninth Street East brought an action to recover the purchase price of goods that were delivered to Harrison, were not accepted, and were later lost.

Ninth Street East, a Los Angeles manufacturer of men's clothing, agreed to supply The Rage, a Connecticut men's clothing store owned by Harrison, with the clothing that Harrison ordered for $2,210. The goods were delivered to the Denver-Chicago Trucking Company, which issued a bill of lading for the goods. Ninth Street East mailed the bill of lading, together with four invoices covering the total sale, to Harrison. In Massachusetts, Denver-Chicago Trucking transferred the shipment to Old Colony Transportation Company, which delivered the clothing to Harrison's store. Harrison's wife refused delivery because Old Colony would not make delivery inside the store. Old Colony drove off with the clothing, which, after that, was never seen again.

The issues are whether the buyer made a rightful rejection of the goods and on whom the risk of loss will fall.

The court held that the buyer, Harrison, wrongfully rejected the goods because delivery was made to the store and that the risk of loss remains on him. Ninth Street East may recover the entire purchase price of the clothing. The contract was satisfied when the goods were delivered to the store. The goods need not be brought inside the store unless that was specifically agreed to. Judgment for Ninth Street East.

In either a shipment or a destination contract, if the goods are destroyed while in transit, the buyer and/or the seller having an insurable interest in the goods will have a cause of action against the common carrier transporting the goods. The party upon whom the risk of loss falls may collect from his or her insurance company for the damaged or destroyed goods. The insurance company will then have a right of subrogation against the common carrier. A right of subrogation accrues when the insurance company pays the proceeds of the policy to the insured. The insured then assigns his or her cause of action to the insurance company pursuant to the subrogation agreement contained in the insurance policy.

EXAMPLE | John Sutter enters into a contract to purchase fifty gold nuggets from Klondike Bill. The terms of the contract are: F.O.B. Sutter's Mill, California. Klondike Bill arranges to transport the nuggets by a team of huskies to Whitehorse, then by stagecoach to California. While Klondike Bill is en route to California, Dangerous Dan McGrew attacks the stagecoach up at Donner Pass and steals the gold. Who must bear the risk of loss? This is a destination contract, so Klondike Bill as seller must bear the risk of loss. If Klondike Bill is insured he will be compensated on proof of loss. The insurance company will then have a right of subrogation and may exercise that right by suing the operators of the stagecoach, which is a common carrier, for failing to exercise reasonable care against the likes of Dangerous Dan McGrew in the delivery of the gold.

A contract that specifies neither a shipment term nor a destination term is presumed to be a shipment contract.

Eberhard Manufacturing Company v. Brown
61 Mich. App. 268, 232 N.W. 2d 378 (1975)

Eberhard Manufacturing Company sued Brown to recover the price of goods sold that were lost in transit.

The parties did not expressly agree as to who would bear the risk of loss because the contract contained no written evidence of an F.O.B. term. Eberhard Manufacturing claimed that delivery was F.O.B. their factory. This claim may be considered usage of trade.

The issue is who must bear the risk of loss when the contract contains no F.O.B. term.

The court held,

> Under Article 2 of the Uniform Commercial Code, the "shipment" contract is regarded as the normal one and the "destination" contract as the variant type. The seller is not obligated to deliver at a named destination and bear the concurrent risk of loss until arrival, unless he has specifically agreed so to deliver, or the commercial understanding of the terms used by the parties contemplates such delivery. Thus, a contract which contains neither an F.O.B. term nor any other term explicitly allocating loss is a shipment contract.

Furthermore, the court stated that

> Brown's argument that the words "ship to" are equivalent to "F.O.B. place of destination" is without merit because "a 'ship to' term has no significance in determining whether a contract is a shipment or destination contract for risk of loss purposes. . . . Since the presumption of a shipment contract controls in this case, the seller, Eberhard, may recover the price from Brown for the goods lost in transit.

Judgment for Eberhard Manufacturing Company.

STATIONARY CONTRACTS

When stationary goods are to be picked up by the buyer at the seller's place of business or at the place where the goods are located, the risk of loss remains on the seller until the buyer actually receives the goods. This is true even though the buyer has made full payment for the goods and has been notified that he or she may take possession of them. The reason for this is that the merchant is still in physical control of the goods and is in the best position to have the goods insured. It is unusual for a buyer to insure goods before taking possession of them.

EXAMPLE | The Crystal Palace Saloon, located on the Barbary Coast in San Francisco, was a distributor and retailer of distilled spirits. On April 14 a group of descendants of the original Forty-Niners contracted to purchase 100 cases of distilled spirits from the Crystal Palace for $5,000. They paid the contract price and informed the Crystal Palace that they would take possession of the liquor on April 21, the night of their annual reunion. On April 18 and April 19, an earthquake erupted in San Francisco that devastated the Barbary Coast region, including the Crystal Palace Saloon. Who must bear the risk of loss? The risk of loss remains on the Crystal Palace because they were in the best position to have the liquor insured until the Forty-Niners took possession of it.

When the goods are held by a bailee without physically being moved, pending receipt by the buyer, performance is complete. Risk of loss passes to the buyer when he or she receives the document of title or when the bailee acknowledges that the buyer has the right to possession of the goods.

EXAMPLE The Kentucky Colonel owned a tobacco plantation in Virginia. He entered into a contract to sell Beauregard Clayton five tons of tobacco leaves. The Colonel told Clayton to pick up the tobacco at a warehouse on the outskirts of Roanoke, where it was stored. He gave Clayton the warehouse receipt. That evening a forest fire swept across the Blue Ridge Mountains and consumed the warehouse. Who had to bear the risk of loss? The risk of loss passed to Beauregard Clayton when he received the warehouse receipt for the tobacco.

The risk of loss is placed on the person who is in the best position to guard against the loss and is most likely to have the goods insured. The risk of loss may be altered by the agreement of the parties. In the contract the risk of loss may be directly allocated, or the parties may use any of the delivery terms that fix the risk of loss, such as F.O.B.

CONDITIONAL SALES CONTRACTS

Sale on Approval

In a contract providing for *sale on approval,* goods are transferred to the buyer for a certain period during which the buyer may use the goods to determine whether he or she wishes to purchase them. The buyer must be the ultimate consumer—the person who is going to use the product—rather than a merchant who is purchasing the product for resale.

The reason behind sale-on-approval contracts is that sellers want to entice buyers to try their products by providing money-back guarantees if the purchasers are not satisfied. Satisfaction is a personal test to be applied by the consumer; the product may be returned even if it conforms to the contract. During the approval period title and risk of loss remain with the seller because the sale is not complete. Title and risk of loss pass to the buyer when he or she accepts the goods by making payment.

EXAMPLE | The Mississippi Gambler was watching Benny Hill on television one night. During a commercial break he saw an advertisement for a wok and related implements. He thought this would be great for frying up grits. (The wok, which originated in China, is a round-bottomed pan used for frying.) The total package cost was $19.95 with a money-back guarantee. The Gambler called right away and placed an order. When he received the products, he discovered that the wok was nothing more than an ordinary large frying pan. The Gambler returned the "wok" and requested his money back. Is he entitled to it? Yes! This is a sale-on-approval contract. The consumer may return the goods even though they conform to the contract because the consumer was not satisfied. Is this true even when the returned goods are lost in the mail? Yes! The risk of loss remains on the seller until the goods have been accepted and paid for by the consumer.

Sale or Return

In a sale-or-return contract, goods are transferred to the buyer on consignment. If the buyer is unable to resell them, he or she may return them to the seller. A sale-or-return contract usually occurs between merchants where the buyer is purchasing the goods expressly for resale. During the period of consignment, the title and risk remain with the buyer because the sale is considered complete even though the buyer may return the goods. If the goods are returned, it must be at the buyer's risk and expense.

EXAMPLE | Old Zeke from Cabin Creek was the manufacturer of Louisiana Lightning, a distilled spirit made from potatoes. Zeke agreed to sell 100 cases of the potato whiskey on consignment to Johnny Walker Red, a city slicker from Memphis. The Louisiana Lightning proved so potent that when a customer at the Red Garter, owned by Johnny Walker Red, lit a cigarette near an open bottle, that bottle exploded and ignited fifty of the 100 cases delivered. The fifty cases burst into flames. Who must bear the risk of loss? Johnny Walker Red, as buyer, must bear the loss on a consignment contract because the goods were accepted, and the risk of loss remains with the buyer until the goods are returned, if ever. If Johnny Walker Red returns the other fifty cases because he cannot sell them, is he entitled to reimbursement? Yes! This is a sale-or-return contract. Even though risk of loss falls on the buyer while the goods are in his or her possession, the remaining goods may be returned even though they are conforming.

THE RISK OF LOSS AFTER BREACH

The previous discussion assumed that there was no breach of contract. If the buyer breaches the contract by repudiating it after the goods have been identified to the contract but before the risk of loss normally passes to him or her, then the risk of loss will rest with the buyer for a reasonable time. The buyer will assume this risk of loss only to the extent of any deficiency in the seller's insurance coverage. If the seller breaches the contract and the buyer revokes his or her acceptance, then the risk of loss will rest on the seller for a reasonable time, but only to the extent that the buyer's insurance is not sufficient to cover the loss.

EXAMPLE | The Hatfields and the McCoys are at peace. The McCoys, who are in the coal mining business in the hills of Kentucky, are planning to build a new mine shaft. The Hatfields, who are in the construction business, agree to supply them with two tons of dynamite for $4,000. The terms of the contract are F.O.B. Hills of Kentucky. After shipping the goods the Hatfields receive a call from the McCoys repudiating the contract. An hour later the dynamite blows up en route to the hills of Kentucky. The Hatfields have insurance coverage of $1,000. Who must bear the loss? The feud between the Hatfields and the McCoys is on again. The contract is a destination contract. The risk of loss is usually on the seller, but because of the McCoys' breach, they are liable for $3,000—the extent to which the Hatfields' insurance does not cover the loss.

REVIEW QUESTIONS

1. Define document of title, bill of lading, common carrier, tender of delivery, risk of loss, shipment contract, destination contract, F.O.B., F.A.S., C.I.F., C.&F., sale on approval, and sale or return.

2. John Kottis entered into a contract to sell his shares of stock in Hammersmith Farms to Benedetto Cerilli. Kottis appeared on the date of closing with the required documents. Cerilli refused to buy the property, contending that he did not have the ability to perform because Kottis did not have marketable title to the farm. Kottis claimed that his actions constituted a satisfactory tender of performance. What result ? *Kottis* v. *Cerilli*, 612 A. 2d 661 (R.I. 1992).

3. Multiplastics contracted to manufacture and deliver 40,000 pounds of brown styrene pellets to Arch Industries for $.19 per pound. Arch Industries agreed to accept delivery of 1,000 pounds per day after production had been completed. Arch Industries refused to accept delivery in accordance with the terms of the contract. Multiplastics advised Arch Industries to pick up the brown styrene pellets because they had stored them for more than forty days. One month later the Multiplastics plant was destroyed by fire. Their insurance did not cover the pellets. Multiplastics sued for the contract price plus interest. Did Multiplastics make a valid tender of delivery, and on whom should the risk of loss fall? *Multiplastics* v. *Arch Industries, Inc.,* 166 Conn. 152, 348 A. 2d 618 (1974).

4. On June 11, 1974, Martin, a farmer, agreed to purchase a truck and haystack mover for over $35,000 from Melland's dealership. Martin was to receive over $17,000 as a trade-in allowance on his old unit. Because the new unit would not be ready for two to three months, Martin was allowed to retain the old unit. In August a fire destroyed the truck and haystack mover unit. The parties had no risk of loss provision in their contract. Did Martin tender delivery of his old unit, and on whom does the risk of loss fall? *Martin* v. *Melland's, Inc.,* 283 N.W. 2d 76 (N.D.) 1979.

5. Scampoli purchased a television set from Wilson. The set was warranted for ninety days of free service. After the set was delivered, there was a reddish tint to the picture. A service representative arrived to adjust the color, but after

encountering some difficulty, he maintained that he would have to remove the television chassis and take it to the shop. Scampoli's adult daughter, who was home at the time, refused to allow Wilson's representatives to remove the chassis, insisting that she wanted a brand-new set, not a repaired one. Scampoli later demanded a return of her purchase price, but Wilson refused and again offered to cure the defect. What result? *Wilson v. Scampoli,* 228 A. 2d. 848 (D.C.) 1967.

6. Sterling agreed to ship goods to Electric Regulator F.O.B. Norwalk, Connecticut, which was the seller's place of business. The goods were damaged during shipment. Electric Regulator asserted that the contract was a destination contract rather than a shipment contract because the "ship to" addresses took precedence over the F.O.B. term. Sterling argued that the contract must state the destination and the carrier must be supplied with the destination in order for the goods to be delivered. This is the only purpose fulfilled by the "ship to" addresses. Who must bear the risk of loss for the damages to the shipment? *Electric Regulator Corp. v. Sterling Extruder Corp.,* 280 F. Supp. 550 (D. Conn.) 1968.

7. Ramos contracted to buy a motorcycle from Wheel Sports Center and tendered payment of $893. Delivery was to be made June 30. Ramos was given the papers necessary to register the motorcycle and to obtain insurance for it. On July 11 a power blackout occurred, and the motorcycle was stolen by looters. Who must bear the risk of loss? *Ramos v. Wheel Sports Center,* 96 Misc. 2d 646, 409 N.Y.S. 2d 505 (1978).

8. Ray Schock delivered $3,900 as the purchase price of a mobile home to the sellers, Pablo and Colette Ronderos, on April 15, 1985. He received a bill of sale along with the promise that title would be delivered soon. Schock was going to remove the mobile home on April 22, 1985. During the interim the house was to remain on the property with their permission. On April 19 the mobile home was destroyed by high winds. Schock received title in the mail on April 23rd. He sought rescission of the contract, claiming that risk of loss remained with the Ronderoses until title passed. The Ronderoses claimed that risk of loss passed on April 15. What result? *Schock v. Ronderos,* 394 N.W. 2d 697 (N.D. 1986).

21

Sales: Buyer's and Seller's Remedies

INTRODUCTION

Both the buyer and the seller are entitled to have their reasonable expectations with regard to performance fulfilled. When a breach occurs it gives the aggrieved party the right to sue for a remedy. This chapter addresses first the buyer's, then the seller's remedies.

BUYER'S RIGHTS

The buyer is entitled to a remedy when the seller breaches the contract. A breach of contract by the seller occurs when the seller

repudiates the contract,
fails to make delivery, or
delivers nonconforming goods.

The seller's repudiation or failure to make a delivery is an automatic breach of contract, and the buyer may immediately exercise his or her right to a remedy. With respect to nonconforming goods, the buyer has the right to reject the goods upon inspection,

accept the goods and later revoke, or

accept the goods and recover damages.

Any action taken by the buyer is not effective until the seller receives notification.

BUYER'S REJECTION

The buyer's rejection of nonconforming goods must be in relation to commercial units. A buyer may reject an unlimited number of units but may not reject part of any one unit. The whole unit must be rejected; otherwise it is considered accepted.

To make an effective rejection, the buyer must

reject the goods within a reasonable time after they have been tendered or delivered,

notify the seller of particular defects to give the seller the opportunity to cure them,

refrain from exercising any ownership over the goods that would be inconsistent with his or her rejection, and

exercise reasonable care with regard to the rejected goods and hold them for a reasonable time to allow the seller to reclaim them.

If the buyer is a merchant, he or she has a further duty to follow the seller's reasonable instructions with respect to the rejected goods. The merchant must make a good-faith effort to salvage the value of perishable goods, or other goods rapidly declining in value, by selling them and applying the proceeds to the seller's account. The buyer may deduct the expenses incurred in selling the goods.

EXAMPLE | The Cheyennes order 1,000 pounds of buffalo meat from the Apaches. Both tribes are merchants dealing in the sale of meat. After delivery is made the Cheyennes inspect the meat and discover that the so-called buffalo is horse meat. They promptly notify the Apaches of the defect. The Apaches instruct the Cheyennes to sell the horse meat at a nearby market. Do the Cheyennes have to follow the instructions? Yes! The Cheyennes, as merchants, have a duty to follow the instructions if they are reasonable. If the Cheyennes sell the goods as instructed and apply the proceeds to the Apaches' account, have they made a valid rejection? Yes! They promptly notified the Apaches of the defect, followed their instructions with respect to the goods, and did not exercise any ownership over the goods inconsistent with the Apaches' wishes.

A buyer who receives no instructions may reship the rejected goods to the seller, resell them and apply the proceeds to the seller's account, or store the rejected goods for the seller.

BUYER'S REMEDIES PRIOR TO ACCEPTANCE

In a case where the seller has breached the contract by repudiating it, by failing to make delivery, or by delivering nonconforming goods that are properly rejected, the buyer's remedies prior to acceptance are **CC RIDERS.**

Cancellation
Covering

Recovering goods from an insolvent seller
Interest, security
Damages for nondelivery
Expenses incidental to the breach
Resulting damages
Specific performance and replevin

Cancellation

The buyer may cancel the breached contract and recover any consideration given. This is equivalent to rescission and reimbursement for out-of-pocket expenses. In addition to seeking this remedy, the buyer may also cover or recover damages for nondelivery.

Garfinkel v. Lehman Floor Covering Company
60 Misc. 2d 72, 302 N.Y.S. 2d 167 (1969)

Garfinkel sued Lehman Floor Covering Company for reimbursement of the purchase price paid for the installation of carpeting. Garfinkel alleged that the carpeting was installed in a defective condition and sought to cancel the contract.

On March 8, 1967, Lehman installed the carpet in Garfinkel's home. Immediately after the installation Garfinkel informed Lehman that he noticed an unsightly condition about the carpet. Lehman's representatives attempted to cure the defect on two occasions without success. Garfinkel alleged that he was entitled to a return of his purchase price because his rejection and immediate notification were timely made. Lehman contended that Garfinkel's retention and use of the carpet interfered with the company's ownership rights.

The issue is whether the buyer, after notifying the seller of his or her rejection, has any further duty with respect to the rejected goods other than to hold them with reasonable care until the seller removes them.

> The court held that the buyer has no further obligation concerning the goods. After notifying Lehman that the goods were defective and nonconforming, Garfinkel was allowed to retain the carpet and to use it until Lehman removed it. Lehman delivered the carpet, and it is fair that he should bear the burden of removing it. Judgment for Garfinkel.

Covering

The buyer may cover by purchasing substitute goods elsewhere in good faith, and in a reasonable manner, without delay. The buyer is entitled to the difference between the contract price and the cost of cover together with the incidental damages. Consequential damages may be awarded only if the buyer is unable to cover or for damages occurring between the time of the breach and the time when adequate cover is made.

EXAMPLE | In the example involving buffalo meat, let us assume that the Apaches do not cure the defect by the delivery date specified in the contract. The Cheyennes thereupon purchase the 1,000 pounds of buffalo elsewhere for $2,500. The original contract price was $2,000. What will the Cheyenne's measure of damage be? Five hundred dollars—the difference between the contract price, $2,000, and the cost of cover, $2,500, which must be reasonable under the circumstances.

Recovering Goods from an Insolvent Seller

The buyer has the right to recover goods identified to the contract if the seller becomes insolvent within ten days after receiving the first installment of payment from the buyer. The buyer must tender the balance of the payment owed to the seller. This remedy is designed to prevent the seller from fraudulently inducing the buyer to enter into a contract shortly after the seller becomes insolvent.

EXAMPLE | Custer is an ice cream manufacturer located in Montana. He has a statewide franchise of ice cream stands bearing his name. His chief competition comes from the Sioux, headed by Chief Sitting Bull. The Sioux, through price wars, are slowly putting Custer out of business. He is down to his last stand. The operator of the last stand, located in Little Big Horn, orders 500 gallons of ice cream from Custer at $1 per gallon and sends $300 as a down payment. One week later, after the goods have been identified to the contract, Custer files for bankruptcy. Will Custer's last stand be able to recover the 500 gallons of ice cream from him? Yes! By tendering the balance owed, it may recover the ice cream because Custer became insolvent within ten days after the down payment was made.

Security Interest

The buyer has a security interest in the rejected goods for any payments made on them and for any incidental expenses incurred. Pursuant to that security interest, the buyer may resell the goods and recover the payments together with the incidental expenses. The amount that remains must be applied to the seller's account. The buyer may not determine what his or her measure of damages should be in addition to the payments made and retain the proceeds of the sale for that purpose.

EXAMPLE | The Arapaho order ten dozen peace pipes from the Choctaws for $3,900. The Arapaho send a check for $3,000 with the order. When the peace pipes are delivered, they are found to be of inferior quality and worth much less than the contract price. The Arapaho want their money back. What recourse do they have against the Choctaws? First, the Arapaho must make a valid rejection of the peace pipes by notifying the Choctaws. Then they may retain the peace pipes until others conforming to the contract are sent. The Arapaho also have a security interest in the peace pipes for the amount they paid, $3,000. If the defect is not cured, they may exercise their security interest in the peace pipes by selling them and applying the proceeds to satisfy the $3,000 debt owed to them. If anything remains the Arapaho must apply it to the Choctaws' account.

Damages for Nondelivery

As an alternative to the remedy of cover, the buyer may cancel the contract and sue for damages for nondelivery. The buyer is entitled to the benefit of the bargain when he or she makes a contract. Granting that benefit means awarding the buyer the difference between the contract price and the market price, along with any incidental or consequential damages resulting from the breach. The market price is the prevailing price of goods at the time when the breach occurs and at the place where performance was to be made.

EXAMPLE | On May 28 the Blackfoot contract to purchase fifteen tons of tobacco from the Pawnees at $2,000 per ton—the current market price. Delivery is to be made on June 13. The Pawnees breach the contract by refusing to deliver on the date specified. The Blackfoot opt for recovering damages caused by the Pawnees' nondelivery. On June 13, the date of the breach, the market price of tobacco is $2,200 per ton. What will the Blackfoot's measure of damages be? $200 per ton. The Blackfoot will be entitled to the difference between the contract price ($2,000 per ton) and the market price ($2,200 per ton).

Expenses Incidental to the Breach

Incidental damages are awarded to compensate the buyer for expenses incurred because of the seller's breach of contract. Incidental damages include disbursements made for inspection, receipt, storage, transportation, care, custody, and resale of the rejected goods. The incidental expenditures made by a buyer in attempting to cover may also be recovered.

EXAMPLE | The Navajos operate a souvenir shop on their reservation. They order and pay for 100 bow and arrow sets from the Pueblos. The Pueblos mistakenly send 100 tomahawks. Both items are priced at $20 apiece. The Navajos exercise their remedy to cover by purchasing the bow and arrow sets from the Iroquois. The Navajos make a valid rejection of the tomahawks, but the Pueblos refuse to refund their money. The Navajos sell the tomahawks for $15 each to the Cherokees in the Smoky Mountains. They are the only tribe that could handle such a quantity. What damages are recoverable by the Navajos out of the proceeds of the sale in addition to the cost of cover? The Navajos may recover any incidental expenses incurred in the inspection and resale of the nonconforming goods, the storage of the goods, the transportation of the goods to the Smoky Mountains, and the procurement of substitute goods through the remedy of cover.

Resulting Damages

Resulting damages, also known as consequential damages, are awarded to compensate the buyer for any direct financial loss he or she suffers as a result of the seller's breach. Consequential damages include any loss stemming from the buyer's needs or requirements that was reasonably foreseeable by the seller and any injury proximately caused to a person or property by the seller's breach. If the buyer could have prevented the loss by utilizing the remedy of cover and obtaining substitute goods, he or she will not be allowed consequential damages.

EXAMPLE | In the previous example assume the following: (1) The Navajos ordered all of their supplies from the Pueblos, (2) the Pueblos refused to deliver, and (3) the Navajos could not cover until the following week. Would the Navajos be entitled to the loss of profits for the week they were forced to shut down their souvenir shop? Yes! Their loss of profits would result from the Pueblo's breach. The burden of proving the actual loss of profits would be on the Navajos.

Specific Performance and Replevin

The buyer may be awarded the equitable remedy of specific performance where the goods involved are unique and money damages are not a satisfactory substitute. The remedy of replevin makes the party in possession of the goods turn them over to the rightful owner. Replevin is also an equitable remedy granted when the goods have been identified to the contract and the buyer is unable to cover because substitute goods cannot be found. Identification of goods to the contract occurs when the goods have been set aside specifically for the buyer. Both specific performance and replevin allow the purchaser to enforce the contract and recover the goods under the circumstances previously set forth.

EXAMPLE | The Mohicans are the only tribe that continues to manufacture wigwams. The Algonguins contract to purchase five wigwams from the last of the Mohicans for use in the re-creation of an Indian village, which they hope will prove to be an attraction for their entertainment park. After completing manufacture of the wigwams, the Mohicans get a better offer from the Walla Wallas. Do the Algonguins have any recourse against the Mohicans? Yes! The Algonguins can regain possession of the wigwams through the remedy of replevin because the goods have been identified to the contract and substitute goods cannot be found elsewhere.

BUYER'S ACCEPTANCE

Acceptance of goods by the buyer occurs in one of the following ways: (1) The buyer signifies that the goods are conforming after inspection or decides to take the goods even though they are nonconforming, (2) the buyer fails to reject the goods after having a reasonable opportunity to inspect them, or (3) the buyer acts in a manner inconsistent with the seller's ownership of the goods.

If the buyer accepts the goods, he or she must pay the contract price. Although the buyer must keep the goods, acceptance does not deprive the buyer of the right to a remedy for accepted goods if they are nonconforming.

BUYER'S REMEDIES AFTER ACCEPTANCE

The remedies available to a buyer after acceptance of nonconforming goods include Maryla**D CRAB.**

> **M**iscellaneous expenses incidental to the breach
> **D**eduction from the price
>
> **C**onsequential damages
> **R**ecoupment
> **A**cceptance revoked
> **B**reach of warranty

Miscellaneous Damages Incidental to the Breach

Miscellaneous damages incidental to the breach have just been discussed under the heading "Expenses Incidental to the Breach."

Deduction from the Price

The buyer may deduct all or part of the damages caused by the seller's breach if payment has not already been made. The buyer must notify the seller of his or her intention before any deduction may be made.

EXAMPLE | Geronimo, a catering establishment in Niagara Falls, New York, orders 100 cases of white wine. By mistake the Catawbas, distributors of fine wine, send fifty cases of white wine and fifty cases of rosé wine. The rosé wine is $2 per case less expensive than the white wine, but in the billing, the Catawbas charge the same price for both rosé and white wine. Geronimo accepts the delivery but notifies the Catawbas that it is deducting $100 from the price because of the inclusion of the less expensive rosé wine. Is this valid? Yes! After giving notification to the seller, the buyer may deduct from the price the damages caused by the seller's breach.

Consequential Damages

Consequential damages, which were discussed previously in the section on resulting damages, entitle the buyer to recover for any injury or damage caused by nonconforming goods that have been accepted.

Recoupment

The buyer who has accepted and paid for nonconforming goods, and who no longer has the option of revoking acceptance, may still recoup damages for the nonconformity. The measure of damages is the difference in value between conforming goods and the nonconforming goods that have been accepted. If payment has not already been made, the damages may be deducted from the price, as previously discussed.

EXAMPLE | In the previous example suppose that Geronimo had already paid for the wine. Would he still be able to recover the $100 per case? Yes! Its remedy would be recoupment. It would be entitled to $2 per case, the difference in price between the fifty cases of the nonconforming rosé wine and the fifty cases of the conforming white wine for which they were charged.

Revocation of Acceptance

Acceptance of the goods prevents the buyer from later rejecting them unless he or she can revoke the acceptance. Acceptance may be revoked when the nonconformity could have been cured by the seller and no attempt to cure it has been made. Acceptance may also be revoked when the defect was not discovered until after acceptance, whether because of the buyer's reliance on reasonable assurances from the seller or because of the buyer's difficulty in discovering the defect.

In order for the revocation of acceptance to be valid, the buyer must notify the seller within a reasonable time after the buyer discovered the defect or should have discovered the defect. A buyer who effectively revokes has the same remedies available as a person who has rejected the goods before acceptance.

EXAMPLE | The Dakotas ordered 500 beaver pelts from the Pawnees. After the distributor made delivery, the Dakotas inspected the shipment. Each case was marked "Beaver Pelts." The distributor had assured the Dakotas that the pelts were the finest available. The Dakotas made payment on the pelts and began to sell them to general stores in the Black Hills of South Dakota. They soon discovered that almost half of the cases were filled with opossum pelts, a less expensive pelt. Do the Dakotas have any recourse against the Pawnees? Yes! The defect was not discovered within a reasonable time because of the distributor's fraudulent assurances and labeling. The Dakotas may revoke their acceptance and proceed as though they had rejected the goods initially, thereby taking advantage of the remedies available to a buyer who makes a valid rejection.

Lanners v. Whitney
247 Ore. 223, 428 P. 2d 398 (1967)

This is an action brought by the purchaser of an airplane for revocation of acceptance due to the nonconformity of the goods (airplane) delivered.

Whitney sold his airplane to Lanners. An inspection by a mechanic from the Federal Aviation Agency (FAA) indicated that the airplane was suitable for flying. After Lanners received delivery he found that the airplane burned an excessive amount of oil, overheated regularly, and had unusually high cylinder pressure. He sought to revoke his acceptance because the airplane did not conform to the assurances given by the seller. Whitney claimed that Lanners did not reject the nonconforming goods within a reasonable time.

The issue is whether Lanners could revoke his acceptance even though an unreasonable amount of time had passed.

The court held that Lanners could revoke his acceptance because his failure to inspect the airplane before accepting it was due to his reliance on the assurances of Whitney and the FAA mechanic. This reliance was reasonable. Lanner may cancel the contract and recover the payments he made. Judgment for Lanners.

Breach of Warranty

The damages awarded for breach of warranty are explained in detail in Chapter 18, "Sales: Title and Warranties."

SELLER'S RIGHTS

The seller in a contract for the sale of goods has a right to expect the buyer to accept and pay for the delivery of goods if they conform to the contract. The buyer may breach the contract by

Repudiating the contract

Failing to make timely payment

Wrongfully rejecting the goods

Inappropriately revoking acceptance

SELLER'S REMEDIES UPON BUYER'S REJECTION

The seller must act in good faith in choosing and carrying out the available remedies: **DRIP DROP.**

Delivery withholding

Recalling delivery in transit

Identifying conforming goods to the contract

Prompt cancellation

Damages for nonacceptance

Reselling and recovering damages

Occurrence of damages incidental to the breach

Price recovery

Delivery Withholding

The seller may withhold delivery when the buyer repudiates the contract or fails to make a timely payment on or before delivery. The seller may then cancel the contract, resell the goods, and recover damages or just recover damages for nonacceptance. The seller may also withhold delivery when he or she discovers the buyer to be insolvent, except if the buyer pays in cash.

Recalling Delivery in Transit

The seller may stop and reclaim goods in transit when the buyer breaches the contract or becomes insolvent. The seller must notify the carrier or bailee of his or her intention to halt the delivery of the goods, and the carrier or bailee must follow the seller's instructions. The seller's right to stop the goods in transit lapses when the buyer is in receipt of the goods, when the buyer is in receipt of a negotiable document of title, or when the carrier or bailee acknowledges that the goods are being held for the buyer.

EXAMPLE | The Kansas City Chiefs contract to purchase forty-five pairs of Jim Thorpe track sneakers from the Carlisle Shoe Palace for their contest with the Washington Redskins. After the goods are delivered to the railroad carrier for shipment, the Chiefs notify the Carlisle Shoe Palace of their intention to cancel the contract. What recourse does

Carlisle have? They may recall delivery of the sneakers while the goods are in transit by notifying the railroad carrier. They must act promptly before their right to stop delivery in transit lapses.

Identifying Conforming Goods to the Contract

The seller may identify conforming goods to the contract to make them available for resale. This means that the seller has set aside certain goods for the purchaser. With respect to unfinished goods, the seller must use reasonable judgment to mitigate his or her losses by either completing them or stopping their manufacture, depending on how far the seller has progressed in manufacturing the goods. When unfinished goods are completed, they may be identified to the contract for the purpose of making them available for resale.

EXAMPLE | The Comanches agree to purchase eighty-five woolen blankets for $5,000 from the Florida Seminoles, a group of senior citizens who weave them for profit. After the Seminoles procure the necessary materials and the pattern is measured and cut, they begin work on the blankets. The Comanches then inform them of their intent to cancel the contract. What recourse is available to the Seminoles? They may finish manufacturing the blankets, identify them to the contract, and resell them. They may recover the difference between the contract price and the resale price.

Prompt Cancellation

A material breach by the buyer permits the seller to cancel the contract. The seller must promptly notify the buyer of the cancellation; from that point on the obligations of the parties are discharged. The seller may identify conforming goods to the contract, withhold delivery of the goods to be transferred, or stop delivery in transit. The seller may then proceed to recover damages for nonacceptance, resell the goods and recover damages, or sue for the price if the goods cannot be resold.

Damages for Nonacceptance

The seller may choose not to resell the goods when the buyer repudiates the contract or refuses to accept the tendered goods. Instead the seller may opt to retain the goods and sue the buyer for damages for his or her nonacceptance. The court will determine these damages by measuring the difference between (1) the market price at the time and place of tender and (2) the unpaid contract price together with incidental damages but less any expenses saved by the seller because of the breach. The seller is entitled to be placed in a position as favorable as the one he or she would have held had the contract been carried out. If this measure of damages is not adequate, the seller will be reimbursed for the loss of profit resulting from the buyer's nonperformance.

EXAMPLE | A group of Eskimos contracted to supply the Mohawks with 150 tons of whale blubber at $800 per ton. Before delivery was made the Mohawks refused the whale blubber because their needs had suddenly diminished. The market price for whale blubber had dropped to $750 per ton. The Eskimos chose to retain the whale blubber for their own use. Do they have any recourse against the Mohawks? Yes! The Eskimos may recover $50 per ton as damages for the Mohawk's nonacceptance. This amount is determined from the difference between the contract price of $800 and the market price at the time of tender, $750.

Neri v. Retail Marine Corporation
30 N.Y. 2d 393, 334 N.Y.S. 2d 165, 285 N.E. 2d 311 (1972)

Retail Marine Corporation sued Neri for lost profits resulting from Neri's nonacceptance of conforming goods.

Neri contracted to buy a boat from Retail Marine Corporation for $12,500. Less than a week later, Neri repudiated the contract and sued Retail Marine for the return of his $4,250 down payment. Retail Marine sold the boat for the same price to someone else. Retail Marine argues that they have lost the profit on the repudiated sale to Neri because they would have made the other sale anyway. Retail Marine also requests reimbursement for incidental damages of $675 incurred for storage, finance charges, and insurance until the resale.

The issue is whether a seller who has an unlimited supply of merchandise may recover loss of profit when the item is sold to another person for the same price.

The court held that where the difference between the market price and the unpaid contract price puts the seller in a worse position than he would have been in had the sale been completed, the seller may recover the profits lost because of the breach plus any incidental damages. Neri was entitled to a return of his down payment less Retail Marine's loss of profit and incidental damages. Judgment for Retail Marine Corporation.

Reselling and Recovering Damages

Goods that are finished and conform to specifications may be identified to the contract. The seller may resell these goods, along with goods already identified to the contract that have been withheld or recalled from transit. The resale may be made at a public or private auction upon notification to the buyer. The seller may then recover the difference between the resale price and the contract price together with incidental damages but less the expenses saved because of the buyer's breach. If the seller makes a profit on the sale, he or she need not apply it to the buyer's account.

A buyer cannot reclaim goods resold to a good-faith purchaser for value even though the seller failed to notify the buyer of the resale or otherwise failed to comply with the resale requirements.

EXAMPLE | The Shawnees agree to supply Crazy Horse with seventy-five cases of firewater for $7,500 on November 17, with payment due on or before that date. On November 17 the Shawnees have not yet received payment. They sell the firewater to Hiawatha, a good-faith purchaser, for $6,600. Does Crazy Horse have any right to sue for the firewater or for other damages? No! Crazy Horse's right to the firewater was conditioned upon his making payment on or before November 17. Because his payment was not timely, he has breached the contract. May the Shawnees recover damages? Yes! The Shawnees may recover the difference between the contract price of $7,500 and the resale price of $6,600, which amounts to $900. The resale to Hiawatha was made without notice to Crazy Horse. Would this affect the outcome? No!

Occurrence of Damages Incidental to the Breach

The seller may recover damages incidental to the breach, including charges assessed by the carrier for stopping delivery; expenses for transportation, custody, and care of the goods halted in transit; and any disbursements resulting from the resale of the goods.

Price Recovery

If the seller cannot resell the goods after making a reasonable attempt, the seller may sue the buyer for the contract price. The goods must be in the seller's possession and must have been identified to the contract for the buyer. The seller must transfer the goods to the buyer upon recovery of the contract price from the buyer.

EXAMPLE | Sitting Bull, a forty-two portly, orders a custom-made tribal gown for $800 from his tailor, Osceola. Osceola procures the necessary material and starts to work. After the material is cut on Sitting Bull's measurements and is partially sewn, Sitting Bull notifies Osceola of his intention to repudiate the contract. What recourse is available to Osceola? Osceola may sue Sitting Bull for $800, the full cost, because custom-made clothing cannot be resold. When Osceola recovers the purchase price, he must finish the tribal gown, if Sitting Bull requests it, and transfer it to him.

SELLER'S REMEDIES AFTER BUYER'S ACCEPTANCE

A buyer who accepts conforming goods for which he or she does not pay is in breach of contract. A seller's rights against a buyer who has breached the contract after acceptance can be found in the following remedies: **RIP.**

Reclaim goods
Insist on cash or reclaim goods from insolvent buyer
Price may be recovered

Reclaim the Goods

The seller has the right to reclaim goods delivered to and accepted by the buyer if the buyer does not pay for them. This rule applies to situations where payment is made by a check that is later dishonored. Payment by check is conditioned on the bank's honoring the check when it is presented.

Insist on Cash or Reclaim Goods from Insolvent Buyer

Upon learning of the buyer's insolvency, the seller may refuse to deliver the goods except for cash. If delivery has been made and accepted, the seller may reclaim the goods by giving prompt notice of demand within ten days after the buyer's receipt of the goods. The seller must discover the buyer's insolvency within the ten-day period or be precluded from reclaiming the goods.

Either party has the right to demand adequate assurance in writing that performance will be forthcoming where reasonable grounds for insecurity exist. If a response is not made within thirty days of receipt of the demand, the party making the request may consider the contract breached. This is to ensure that the contracting parties' reasonable expectations will be fulfilled. If the buyer gives the seller adequate assurance in writing of his or her solvency within three months before delivery is tendered, the ten-day limitation does not apply.

A seller who elects to reclaim goods from an insolvent buyer will be barred from all other remedies because of the preferential treatment afforded the seller over the buyer's other creditors. The seller cannot reclaim goods delivered to an insolvent buyer if the goods are sold to a good-faith purchaser who buys them for value in the ordinary course of business.

EXAMPLE | The Creeks enter into a contract to purchase twenty pairs of moccasins, on credit, from the Leather Factory. A week after making delivery, the Leather Factory learns of the Creeks' insolvency. Can it reclaim the moccasins? Yes! The Leather Factory can recover the moccasins by giving prompt notice of demand before the ten-day limit expires. If the Creeks had given the Leather Factory an adequate assurance of their ability to pay, would the ten-day limit apply? No! Not as long as delivery was made within three months from the written assurance.

Price Recovered

The seller has the right to sue for the price where the buyer has accepted conforming goods but has not paid for them. This is the seller's main remedy after the buyer has accepted the goods.

REVIEW QUESTIONS

1. Explain each of the buyer's remedies both prior to and after acceptance.

2. Explain each of the remedies available to the seller both upon the buyer's improper rejection of the goods and after the buyer accepts the goods.

3. Cohn placed an ad in the newspaper to sell his boat. Fisher saw the ad and purchased the boat from Cohn for $4,650. Fisher gave Cohn a check for $2,535 as a down payment. On the check Fisher noted that the purchase price was $4,650. Fisher decided not to go through with the contract and stopped payment on the check. Cohn placed another ad in the paper and resold the boat for $3,000, which was the best offer he received. Then Cohn sued Fisher for breach of contract. What will Cohn's measure of damages be? *Cohn* v. *Fisher*, 118 N.J. Super. 286, 287 A. 2d 222 (1972).

4. Star Grain assigned its right to purchase grain from Meyer and other farmers to Duffe Grain because Star Grain was in bankruptcy. Duffe Grain notified Meyer of the assignment but not of the new delivery place. Must Meyer make inquiries concerning delivery, or may he sell the grain elsewhere? If the price of the grain rises above the contract price, does this change things? *S&S* v. *Meyer*, 478 N.W. 2d 857 (Iowa App. 1991).

5. C.T. Chemicals entered into a contract with Vinmar Impex to deliver two lots of goods. The first lot was delivered in January. Because Vinmar Impex did not pay for this lot, C.T. Chemicals sued it for breach of contract. Vinmar Impex's defense was that although it had requested separate deliveries, payment was not due until the second lot was delivered because there was only one contract. What result? *C.T. Chemicals* v. *Vinmar Impex*, 588 N.Y.S. 2d 1 (A.D.I Dept. 1992).

6. In 1982 Commonwealth Edison agreed to purchase coal leases from Decker Coal Company. Each interest gave Commonwealth the right to mine certain quantities of coal at specific prices. Subsequently the development of alternative energy sources became more economical. Commonwealth no longer had an interest in mining the coal and did not want to pay for the mining rights. Commonwealth was liable, but for how much? The contract price was approximately $5,500,000. There was no market for coal resources because the cost of mining exceeded the sale price. Decker argued that it should receive loss of profit, which would allow it to retain the coal reserves as well as recover the contract price. Commonwealth contended that Decker's remedy should be the contract price, with Commonwealth retaining the mining rights until the contract expired in 1990. What result? *Commonwealth Edison Co.* v. *Decker Coal Co.*, 653 F. Supp. 841 (N.D. Ill. 1987).

7. Oloffson, a grain dealer, contracted to purchase 40,000 bushels of corn from a farmer named Coomer for $1.1225 per bushel. The contract was signed in April, with delivery to be made in October. On June 3 Coomer notified Oloffson that he had decided not to plant corn because of the wet season. The

market price of corn on June 3 was $1.16 per bushel. Oloffson waited until October to cover by purchasing substitute corn at $1.35 and $1.49 per bushel. Oloffson then sued Coomer for the difference between the contract price and the respective cover prices. What result? *Oloffson* v. *Coomer,* 11 Ill. App. 3rd 918, 296 N.E. 2d 871 (1973).

8. The city of Austin awarded Clearwater Constructors a contract to expand Walnut Creek Wastewater Treatment facility. Clearwater subcontracted with Westech Engineering to provide water treatment equipment. The equipment did not meet the required specifications. Clearwater obtained the equipment from another supplier at a greater cost. What is the appropriate remedy? *Westech Eng.* v. *Clearwater Constructors,* 835 S.W. 2d 190 (Tex. App.—Austin 1992).

9. Traynor contracted to buy Christmas trees from Walters, who grew them. The contract specified that the trees were to be top quality. Traynor inspected the Christmas trees after receipt and discovered that they were not top quality. Traynor immediately notified Walters of his rejection and resold the trees because he considered them to be perishable, with Christmas but a short time away. Walters had not given Traynor any instructions as to the disposition of the trees. Did Traynor act correctly by reselling them, and what must he do with the proceeds of the resale? *Traynor* v. *Walters,* 342 F. Supp. 455 (M.D. Pa. 1972).

10. Charles Dutten purchased a Model 800 planter from Hoefling, a franchise dealer for International Harvester, on April 1, 1981. The contract provided that Hoefling was not Harvester's agent. The planter malfunctioned; Hoefling made the repair and extended the warranty to two planting seasons. Problems continued. Dutten rescinded the contract and sued for damages for rental replacement and loss of profit. Dutten also sued for incidental and consequential damages under the theory of breach of warranty. What result? *Dutten* v. *International Harvester Co.,* 504 N.E. 2d 313 (Ind. App. 4 Dist. 1987).

22

Consumer Law

INTRODUCTION

A consumer is a person who buys goods or services for personal, family, or household use. The main pupose of consumer law is to safeguard consumers in their transactions with businesses by requiring businesses to provide complete information about products and services. This will enable consumers to make educated decisions.

WARRANTIES

The expansion of implied warranties mandating that goods be merchantable—fit for the purpose for which they were intended to be used—is an important part of consumer law that helps to minimize the doctrine of caveat emptor, "Let the buyer beware." A consumer's contract with a business is not voidable at his or her option. Although a consumer has the capacity to contract, he or she may lack one or more of the following:

the information to make an educated decision,

the right to inspect to discover whether any defect in the product exists,

the bargaining power to realize a fair deal.

A consumer cannot enter a Sears department store, open a box containing a power tool, and operate it to see that it functions. To do so would be neither convenient nor appropriate. That is why the implied warranty of merchantability exists—to allow the consumer to take the product home and test it. If it does not function properly, the warranty of merchantability has been breached, and the consumer can return the item. The retailer has the opportunity either to remedy the defect by repairing or replacing the item or to rescind the contract by refunding the purchase price. Refer to Chapter 18, "Sales: Title and Warranties," for a more in-depth analysis of warranties.

PRODUCTS LIABILITY

Consumers must also be protected against injury from products. Products must be properly packaged and labeled and accompanied by detailed instructions regarding their use and operation. Certain safety devices are also mandated by law for the protection of consumers. If a customer who uses a product in the way it was intended to be used and for the purposes for which it was intended suffers an injury, he or she may recover damages for that injury under strict products liability, negligence, or breach of warranty. This protection applies to the purchaser of the product as well as to other users and bystanders. Consult Chapter 19, "Sales: Products Liability," for more detailed information as well as illustrative cases.

CONSUMER CREDIT TRANSACTIONS

Many consumers purchase goods through the use of credit cards or on installment plans. The sale of goods on credit is known as a consumer credit transaction. It may be defined as a contract between a consumer and a business where payment is deferred to a later date, with interest charged periodically on the unpaid balance.

The business to which the payments are owed is known as the creditor. The term *creditor* may also include a business that extends credit on a regular basis to a consumer, with repayment being made in more than four installments and a finance charge being assessed on the unpaid balance.

CREDIT CARDS

The credit card is the most frequently used device for consumer credit transactions. Equal credit opportunity must be given to all who apply. Discrimination because of religion, race, sex, national origin, marital status, or age is prohibited. The creditor must notify the consumer of its decision within thirty days. No credit card may be issued in a person's name unless he or she has requested it; there is an exception for renewals and replacements. If a credit card is lost or stolen or otherwise used by someone who lacks authorization, the consumer's liability is limited to $50. This liability is contingent upon the consumer's receiving both notice of the $50 liability and instructions for notifying the card issuer if the card is lost or stolen. The issuer (the company that issued the card) will be responsible beyond the $50 limit unless it can prove that the use of the card was authorized.

CONSUMER CREDIT PROTECTION ACT

The Consumer Credit Protection Act of 1968 requires creditors to show clearly and conspicuously, on the application and the statement the total finance charge, which must include interest and fees. This finance charge also must be reported as an annual percentage rate. The Federal Trade Commission (FTC) is entrusted with the responsibility for enforcing this act. If a consumer is overcharged, the creditor must within sixty days of discovery make an adjustment, including reimbursement for any finance charge mistakenly imposed. If the creditor fails to make the adjustment, the FTC will determine whether there was gross negligence, a pattern of mistakes, or an intentional desire to mislead. The FTC will then require the creditor to make an adjustment in the consumer's account. Willful failure to obey is a crime punishable by a fine of up to $5,000, one year's imprisonment, or both.

A consumer has the right to cancel a consumer credit transaction by midnight of the third business day following the consummation of the consumer credit contract. Upon receiving notification within the time limit, the creditor must refund all monies received from the consumer without deducting any finance charges.

FEDERAL TRADE COMMISSION

The Federal Trade Commission (FTC) is an administrative agency created in 1914, along with the Clayton Act, as part of an antitrust program. The FTC is composed of five individuals appointed by the president with the advice and consent of the Senate. The purpose of the FTC is to prevent deceptive or otherwise unfair methods of competition in commerce. This includes administering the Sherman, Clayton, and Robinson-Patman antitrust laws. To carry out its duties, the FTC is entrusted with investigative powers. Upon discovering alleged unfair competition, the FTC will hold a hearing to determine the truth of the allegations and will render a decision. If the corporation is found guilty of unfair competition, the FTC will issue a cease-and-desist order, the equivalent of an injunction. If the order is not complied with, the FTC may have its order affirmed by the District of Columbia (D.C.) Circuit Court of Appeals to give the order judicial effect. A corporation wishing to contest a decision of the FTC board may bring an appeal in the D.C. Circuit Court of Appeals. The court of appeals will usually affirm the FTC's decision unless it is arbitrary and capricious and bears no relation to the facts presented.

The majority of cease-and-desist orders declared by the FTC relate to false advertising, mislabeling, deceptive packaging, violation of trademarks through passing off of an imitation as the original product, and commercial bribery through illegal kickbacks, discounts, and rebates.

EXAMPLE | Francis Clark and Albert Gifford manufacture jeans of inferior quality and pass them off as products of the top designers by attaching various brand labels to them. They sell the jeans at a competitive price and make huge profits. When several of the top designers find out, they notify the FTC, which holds a hearing to determine the validity of their allegations. What remedies are available against Clark and Gifford? The FTC may issue a cease-and-desist order preventing them from engaging in the further practice of unfair competition. The top designers may sue Clark and Gifford in tort for violation of their trademarks and recoup profits they lost when consumers bought the imitations, thinking they were originals. The designers may also recover damages caused by Clark and Gifford's selling of inferior merchandise under their brand names.

OPEN-END CONSUMER CREDIT

An open-end consumer credit plan is one in which there will be numerous consumer credit transactions. Open-end plans usually involve credit cards such as VISA, American Express, MasterCard, Diners Club, Sears, J. C. Penney's, Macy's, Exxon, and Mobil. The creditor must make the following disclosures in accordance with the Consumer Credit Protection Act:

- The conditions that will result in the imposition of a finance charge.
- The grace period after which a finance charge will be imposed (If there is no grace period, then this fact must be disclosed.)
- The method that will be used to determine the finance charge, including the minimum fee, if any
- The method that will be used to calculate the unpaid balance against which the finance charge will be assessed
- Any other charges
- The fact that the creditor has retained a security interest in the property purchased on credit

The Consumer Credit Protection Act also requires the creditor to provide the consumer with a statement for each billing period itemizing the following:

- The outstanding balance at the beginning of the term
- The consumer's credit limit, if any
- Any payments credited to the consumer's account
- The finance charge assessed
- The unpaid balance on which the finance charge was based
- The outstanding balance remaining

CLOSED-END CONSUMER CREDIT

A closed-end consumer credit plan is one involving an extension of credit for a single purchase. The creditor must set forth the loan principal, less any down payment, trade-in or both. Examples of closed-end plans include purchases of automobiles, furniture, appliances, and electronic equipment.

CONSUMER CREDIT REPORTING AGENCIES

A consumer credit reporting agency checks the consumer's credit and issues a report on his or her creditworthiness, character, general reputation, and mode of living. Consumer credit reports are usually requested by creditors in connection with applications to purchase goods on credit or credit card applications. The consumer must sign a form acknowledging that the creditor is going to undertake a credit investigation.

The Consumer Credit Protection Act mandates that the consumer credit reporting agency must disclose the following to the consumer at his or her request:

• All personal and financial information compiled by the agency except medical information.
• The sources of such information, except if these sources were used solely for the preparation of the report
• The companies to which the agency has sent the report

If the consumer disagrees with any information contained in the report, the reporting agency must either reinvestigate the issue and delete any information that is unsubstantiated or permit the consumer to write a rebuttal, which will be attached to the report.

The following actions by a creditor or collection agency are prohibited:

• Threats of violence
• Use of obscene language
• Publication of a consumer's name
• Harassment by telephone

Johnson v. Chrysler Corp.
598 N.E. 2d 941 (Ohio Com. Pl. 1992)

Timothy Johnson leased a 1987 Chrysler Conquest from Mike Alber Leasing, Inc. The car was defective and nonconforming as defined by Ohio's lemon law, which stated: (A) "Consumer" means the purchaser other than for purposes of resale of a motor vehicle, any person to whom the motor vehicle is transferred during the term of the express warranty that is applicable to the motor vehicle, and any other person who is entitled by the terms of the warranty to enforce the warranty. . . .

(B) If the manufacturer, its agent or its authorized dealer is unable to conform the motor vehicle to any applicable express warranty by repairing or correcting any defect or condition that substantially impairs the use, safety, or value of the motor vehicle to the consumer after a reasonable number of repair attempts, the manufacturer shall, at the consumer's option, replace the motor vehicle with a new motor vehicle acceptable to the consumer or accept return of the vehicle from the consumer and refund.

The issue is whether a lessee of a motor vehicle is entitled under the Lemon Law to the same protection as a purchaser. The court ruled, "First, a cause of action is provided to 'any purchaser of a new motor vehicle.' A lessee merely acquires the right to use the vehicle during the term of the lease and is not a 'purchaser of a new motor vehicle.' Therefore, Ohio's 'Lemon Law' does not explicitly provide a cause of action for a lessee of a nonconforming new motor vehicle. The court continued, "It is clear that 'consumer' applies to a purchaser and not a lessee of a motor vehicle." Judgment for Chrysler Corporation.

REVIEW QUESTIONS

1. What is an open-end consumer credit plan?
2. What is a closed-end consumer credit plan?
3. What information must be set forth in each billing statement?
4. What disclosures must be made by credit reporting agencies?
5. What is a lemon law?

23

Commercial Paper: Form and Negotiation

INTRODUCTION

Commercial paper is a negotiable instrument that is readily transferable between parties as a substitute for money. It is a contract creating an obligation on one party's part to pay another party a certain amount of money. There are four types of commercial paper: drafts, checks, notes, and certificates of deposit.

FORMS OF COMMERCIAL PAPER

Draft

A draft is an order to pay a certain amount of money. It involves three parties: the drawer, the drawee-payor, and the payee. The drawer is the person making the order, the drawee-payor is the person to whom it is made and who must pay the amount of money stated in the draft, and the payee is the person to whom the money is paid.

Check

A check is a special form of draft drawn on a bank and payable on demand. The drawer is the person making the check. The drawee-payor is the bank at which the drawer has a checking account and which must pay the amount of money stated on the check upon presentment. The payee is the person to whom the bank must pay the money, usually the person who receives the check. If that person maintains an account at a different bank, the payee may be the bank in which the check is deposited or cashed.

EXAMPLE | Achilles was a sprinter training for the Olympics. He developed a severe pain in his right tendon, so he made an appointment with a podiatrist. The podiatrist advised Achilles to stay off his feet for two weeks and to train on a surface softer than cement. Achilles was billed eighty dollars for the examination. He paid the podiatrist with a check drawn on the Olympia Savings Bank in Washington State. The podiatrist also maintained his account there. Who are the respective parties to this check? Achilles is the drawer, the person who is making out the check. Olympia Savings Bank is the drawee/payor, the bank against which the check was drawn and which must pay the amount stated on the check upon presentment, and the payee is the podiatrist. If the podiatrist had his account at the Bank of Athens, who would be the payee? The Bank of Athens. After the podiatrist deposited or cashed the check, it would be the Bank of Athens that would present the check to the Olympia Savings Bank for payment.

Drafts and checks are three-party instruments, whereas notes and certificates of deposit involve two parties. A person could, however, make two of the three parties, the drawer and the payee, the same.

Note

A note is a promise to pay a certain amount of money. A promissory note involves two parties. The maker of the note is the person promising to pay the amount stated, and the payee is the person to whom the promise to pay is made. Promissory notes range from IOUs to notes securing loans for automobiles, businesses, and houses; the latter is called a mortgage note.

EXAMPLE | Andromeda decided to purchase a Buick Apollo. The purchase price was $12,000. Andromeda made a down payment of $2,000 and financed the remainder through General Motors Acceptance Corporation. Andromeda signed a statement saying, "I agree to pay GMAC $10,000 plus 12% interest in equal installments over a period of forty-eight months." What is the effect of this statement? This is a promissory note in which Andromeda, as the maker of the note, agreed to pay the amount stated to GMAC, the payee, in return for the $10,000 loan.

Certificate of Deposit

A certificate of deposit (CD) is a special form of promissory note evidencing receipt of money by a bank with its promise to repay the sum at a future date—for example, in six months or two and one-half years—with a guaranteed rate of interest. The bank is the maker of the certificate of deposit, and the payee is the person who deposits the money with the bank.

REQUIREMENTS FOR NEGOTIABILITY

Commercial paper must meet certain requirements to be negotiable, which means that it may be transferred to another by indorsement or by delivery. The requirements for negotiability are that the commercial paper be signed by the drawer or maker, that it contain an unconditional order or promise to pay a certain sum in money, and that it be payable on demand or at a definite time to order or to the bearer.

Signature

The drawer or the maker must sign the commercial paper. The signature may be in the usual written form, or it may be printed, typewritten, stamped, initialed, or finger-printed. In case of doubt the court must determine whether the drawer or maker actually used or intended to use the symbol as his or her authentication of the commercial paper.

Unconditional Order or Promise

The order or promise to pay must be made without reservation, not subject to any other agreement. The holder of the commercial paper must be able to ascertain his or her right to payment from the instrument itself. Payment also must not be restricted to a particular fund. The holder must be confident that the drawer or maker will be personally liable if the commercial paper is dishonored, without worrying whether a particular fund exists or is sufficient to make payment.

Certain Sum in Money

The holder of the commercial paper must be able to determine the amount payable from the face of the instrument. The face of the instrument includes any computation necessary to arrive at the correct figure. The amount must be payable in money. Money is currency, the agreed-upon medium of exchange. Money means the dollar or any foreign currency that can be converted into dollars. It does not encompass precious metals, jewels, or other forms of personal property.

EXAMPLE | Pandora, who is engaged to be married, is searching for a box (trousseau or hope chest) in which to keep all of her treasures until she is married. Pandora finds the perfect one for $260. She makes a down payment of $20 and signs a promissory note for the remainder. The note reads, "I agree to pay $240 in twelve monthly installments with 13% interest; if, however, the principal is repaid within four months or less, the interest rate shall be discounted to 10%." Is this promissory note negotiable? Yes! Although the interest on the amount owed may differ depending on when full repayment is made, it can be computed from the terms stated on the promissory note. So Pandora may keep her box, but she would be wise not to open it.

Smith v. Rushing Construction Co.
353 S.E. 2d 692 (N.C. App. 1987)

Richard Smith entered into a contract to purchase a mobile home and a lot for $14,000 from Rushing Construction Company. Smith signed a promissory note that stated his promise to pay "the principal sum of FOURTEEN THOUSAND AND NO/100 DOLLARS ($14,000.00), with interest from (date), at the the rate of twelve percent (12%) per annum on the unpaid balance until paid or until default. . . ." This provision was typed in the blank spaces provided. Payment was due as follows: "Payable in eighty-four equal monthly installments of $306.67 each, beginning the 27th day of March 1980, and continuing on the 27th day of each month thereafter until paid in full." This provision was typed onto the form.

The issue is which typewritten provision controls. There is a discrepancy concerning the number of payments required. To satisfy the 12 percent interest requirement, sixty-two payments would be needed; that is what Smith made. If he had made eighty-four payments, the interest rate would have been 15 percent.

The court held,

> [T]he typewritten provisions control over printed provisions in a document. In this note, there is ambiguity within the typewritten material itself . . . words control figures unless the words themselves are ambiguous. There is not ambiguity in the phrase 'until paid in full,' therefore, those words control over the number '84'.

Judgment for Smith.

Time for Payment

The commercial paper may state that payment is either on demand or at a definite time. Payable on demand means that the payee must be paid when he or she presents the commercial paper for payment. Payable at a definite date means that the time for payment is fixed and that payment may not be demanded before that date. Notes and certificates of deposit are payable at a definite time in the future, whereas checks are usually payable on demand unless they are postdated.

Payee: Order or Bearer

A drawer or maker may make the commercial paper payable to the order of himself or herself, to the order of the drawee, or to some other specific person or persons. To receive payment the person to whom the commercial paper is payable must indorse the instrument by signing his or her name. Commercial paper may be made payable to two or more persons. If the payees are designated in the alternative, then any one of them may indorse the instrument; if not, all of the payees must sign it. Commercial paper may also be made payable to bearer, to the order of bearer, to a specific person or bearer, or to cash. In any of those cases, to receive payment, the holder—who may be anyone in possession of the instrument—need only indorse the instrument with his or her name and present it for payment. There is greater risk that an instrument payable to bearer will be indorsed and presented for payment by someone other than the person whom the drawer or maker intended because that person's name was not designated on the instrument.

PURPOSE

The purpose of commercial paper is to act as a substitute for money and, in certain cases, as a credit device. Checks are the most popular and convenient substitute for money. A promissory note serves as a credit device through which money is loaned to a borrower in return for his or her promise to repay the loan in a lump sum or in certain installments at an agreed-upon rate of interest.

EXAMPLE | Hercules was an Olympic wrestler and weight lifter well known to people who followed those sports. However, when Hercules traveled he was not immediately recognized. For that reason he filled out an application for an American Express Card. On the application it was stated that the applicant agreed to pay all debts incurred through the use of the card within thirty days free of interest, or otherwise at the rate of $1\frac{1}{2}$ percent per month thereafter. Hercules signed the application and was later accepted. What is the significance of the application he signed? It is a promissory note that remains open for as long as the credit card is authorized in his name. This promissory note is a credit device permitting Hercules to purchase things on credit through use of the American Express Card.

NEGOTIATION

Negotiation occurs when commercial paper is properly transferred to a person (*transferee*), who then becomes a holder of the instrument. If the commercial paper is payable to the order of a specific person, an indorsement of that person's signature and delivery of the instrument to the transferee are required for the transferee to become a holder. If the commercial paper is payable in bearer form to the person possessing it, delivery of the instrument to the transferee suffices for him or her to become a holder.

A *holder* is a transferee who has possession of commercial paper payable to his or her order or to bearer. A holder acquires all of the rights of the *transferor*, the person who transferred the commercial paper to him or her. A holder may negotiate the commercial paper by transferring it in the required manner or by presenting it for payment.

INDORSEMENTS

An *indorsement* is the signature of the person to whom the commercial paper is payable; it is required for negotiation (transfer) of the instrument. The person to whom the commercial paper is payable may be any of the following: the payee, the drawee, or the holder or accommodation indorser. An accommodation indorser is a person who extends his or her credit to the commercial paper to enable the holder to negotiate it to a person who is not satisfied with the holder's credibility.

EXAMPLE | Poseiden was a world-class swimmer who missed the Olympic trials. He came to Atlanta to watch his fellow countryman, Zeus, compete in the discus throw. When Poseiden attempted to purchase tickets, he discovered that he had lost his traveler's checks; they were not from American Express. All he had in his possession was a check from his parents made out to his name. He attempted to negotiate the check to the Olympic Ticket Committee by indorsing the back, but they would not accept the check. He could not cash the check and wait for it to clear, so he contacted his friend Zeus, who offered to indorse the check himself, thus vouching for Poseiden's credibility. What is Zeus's status? Zeus is an accommodation indorser. He indorsed the check for Poseiden's benefit to enable the latter to transfer it to the Olympic Ticket Committee. Zeus is liable as a surety if the check should bounce.

Dillard v. NCNB Texas National Bank
815 S.W. 2d 356 (Tex. App.—Austin 1991)

The NCNB Texas National Bank received from the FDIC several promissory notes with the following indorsements: "Pay to the Order of Federal Reserve Bank–Dallas" and "Pay to the Order of NCNB Texas National Bank." The first indorsement was by the First Republic Bank of Austin, the original owner of the notes and now bankrupt; the second indorsement was by the FDIC, which was the receiver (trustee) in bankruptcy. NCNB attempted to collect on the notes from Dillard, who had guaranteed payment on the notes, but he claimed that NCNB did not have ownership.

The issue is whether the notes were properly indorsed to NCNB.

The court ruled, "[T]he note was sold, negotiated, or in some manner 'conveyed' to the Federal Reserve Bank–Dallas, thus augmenting the evidence of an assignment to the Federal Reserve

Bank–Dallas as this is reflected on the reverse of the note." The court continued,

> And if there was an assignment to the Federal Reserve Bank–Dallas, title to the note and underlying debt could be shown in the First Republic Bank Austin, N.A. only if the record *also* had shown that title had somehow left the Federal Reserve Bank–Dallas so that First Republic Bank Austin, N.A. might acquire it for subsequent assignment by the Federal Deposit Insurance Corporation to the plaintiff. *In this respect the record is silent.*

Judgment for Dillard.

Special Indorsement

A special indorsement consists of the indorser's signature and specifies the person to whose order the instrument is payable. The person specified is the only one who can negotiate the instrument again. This may be done through his or her indorsement coupled with delivery to another.

Blank Indorsement

A blank indorsement is signed by the indorser but does not mention to whom the instrument is payable. Therefore it is payable to bearer—the person in possession of the instrument indorsed in blank.

EXAMPLE | Adonis and Medusa were married but were living separately because of incompatibility. They sold their home in Olympia, Washington. The net amount they were to receive from the sale of the house was $140,000. Adonis and Medusa agreed to divide the proceeds equally pursuant to a separation agreement. They informed the purchaser of this. At the closing of title, the deed was signed and delivered to the purchaser. Medusa was present at the closing, but Adonis, not wishing to see Medusa, did not attend. The purchaser brought two certified checks of equal amounts made out to himself. The reason the purchaser made the checks out to himself was that if the deal should fall through, he could indorse the checks and cash them. If the certified checks had been made out to Adonis and Medusa, he would have had to obtain their indorsements before he could negotiate the checks. The purchaser indorsed his name on the first check and handed it to Medusa. He indorsed his name on the second and then wrote, "Pay to the order of Adonis." The purchaser gave this check to Medusa also. What types of indorsements were made? The first was a blank indorsement, which could be negotiated or presented for payment by the bearer, the person possessing it. The second was a special indorsement, which could be negotiated or presented for payment only by Adonis even though Medusa was in possession of it.

Restrictive Indorsement

An indorsement for deposit or collection restricts the commercial paper from being negotiated by anyone other than the bank to which it is presented. If the bank negotiates the instrument without crediting the depositor's account, it is guilty of conversion.

Qualified Indorsement

A qualified indorsement is made by a person who transfers a negotiable instrument to another without guaranteeing that payment will be made. The qualified indorser may disclaim any contractual liability by signing the negotiable instrument "without recourse."

REVIEW QUESTIONS

1. Define commercial paper, negotiation, indorsements, holder, transferor, and transferee.
2. What are the four types of commercial paper?
3. Which types of commercial paper are two-party instruments and which are three-party instruments?
4. Explain the requirements for negotiability.
5. List and explain the various types of indorsements.
6. What is the purpose of commercial paper?
7. A promissory note was transferred from the First Republic Bank of Austin to the Federal Reserve Bank of Dallas by the endorsement, "Pay to the Order of Federal Reserve Bank–Dallas." Because the note was nonnegotiable, meaning that First Republic could not be paid for it, what theory of law would give the Dallas Fed the right to collect from the maker of the note? *Dillard* v. *NCNB Texas Nat. Bank,* 815 S.W. 2d 356 (Tex. App.—Austin 1991).
8. Michael Norton signed a promissory note payable to Lynda Nugent. Subsequently Kendrick Hollis produced a copy of the promissory note and claimed payment from Norton. Hollis asserted that the original note was lost. There was no endorsement on the copy held by Hollis. What result? *Hollis* v. *Norton,* 586 So. 2d 656 (La. App. 5 Cir. 1991).
9. A promissory note required payment as follows: "Lender's Prime Rate Plus 2.00%." Is this note negotiable? *Dillard* v. *NCNB Texas Nat. Bank,* 815 S.W. 2d 356 (Tex. App.—Austin 1991).
10. During the fall of 1982, Mary Giles received four Veterans Administration disability checks made out to her husband James, who was in prison. She cashed the checks by indorsing her husband's name and then her own. When James learned of this, he wrote to the VA, asserting that Mary was claiming his benefits without his authorization. The VA demanded reimbursement from the bank. The bank in turn sued Mary, claiming forgery. What result? *First National Bank in Eureka* v. *Giles,* 733 P. 2d 357 (Mont. 1987).

24

Commercial Paper:
Holder in Due Course

Introduction   Shelter Doctrine
Requirements   Review Questions
Rights of a Holder in Due Course

INTRODUCTION

A *holder* is a person who has possession of commercial paper and has the power to negotiate it either by delivery or by indorsement and delivery.

A *holder in due course* (HDC) is a holder who acquires commercial paper for value; in good faith; and without notice that it is overdue, has been dishonored, or has any other defenses against it. The payee, as well as any person who subsequently receives the commercial paper, may qualify as a holder in due course by satisfying the following requirements.

REQUIREMENTS

Value

To qualify as a holder in due course, a holder must give valuable consideration in return for receiving the commercial paper. If the holder receives the instrument as a gift, he or she does not qualify as a holder in due course.

EXAMPLE | Thor sold his interest in a privately owned corporation that manufactured hammers for use in the Olympic hammer-throwing competition. Thor indorsed the check he received over to his father, Odin, for Odin's 100th birthday. Does Odin qualify as a holder in due course? No! Odin is the recipient of a gift. This qualifies him as a mere holder because he gave no valuable consideration. If Thor negotiated the check to his father in return for his promise to repay the amount by doing work for Thor, would he be a holder in due course? No! The valuable consideration must be given at the time the commercial paper is negotiated. Odin would still be a mere holder.

Good Faith

Good faith means honesty in fact. The purchaser must acquire the instrument in an honest manner. This requirement does not preclude the transferor, the person from whom the holder receives the commercial paper, from being an unscrupulous person or a thief. The good-faith requirement applies only to the transferee (purchaser).

EXAMPLE | Medusa stole Venus de Milo's pocketbook in a supermarket while Venus was reaching for some beauty aid cream. Inside the pocketbook were a check made payable to Venus, which had already been indorsed, and a passbook from Olympic Savings Bank. As Medusa searched through the wallet, she came across Venus's driver's license and registration. Medusa proceeded to Olympic Savings Bank and cashed the checks against Venus's account by providing the bank with the passbook and proper identification. Does the bank qualify as a holder in due course? Yes! The bank acted in good faith when it paid valuable consideration to Medusa whom it believed to be Venus de Milo.

If Medusa found no identification belonging to Venus and offered to negotiate the checks at a neighborhood drugstore for $90 in cosmetic supplies, would the proprietor qualify as a holder in due course? No! The proprietor has not paid valuable consideration for the checks and has not acquired them in good faith. Good faith is lacking on the part of the proprietor because the suspicious circumstances through which he acquired the commercial paper, coupled with the inadequate consideration requested, should have alerted him to refuse the instrument.

No Notice of Defenses

The purchaser must acquire commercial paper without notice that it is overdue or has been dishonored and without notice that a valid defense or claim exists against it. A purchaser has notice of a defense if the instrument is irregular. An instrument is irregular if it is visibly incomplete, forged, or altered.

EXAMPLE | Andromeda received a check for $250 from Hercules in return for some body-building equipment. Andromeda altered the check to read $2,250. He negotiated the check to the Athenian Savings Bank and received payment when the check cleared. Assuming that the alteration is perfect, does the bank qualify as a holder in due course? Yes! The bank was not on notice that the check had been altered because the alteration was not visibly irregular. Is the bank liable in a suit brought by Hercules to have his account recredited? Yes! The bank is still liable because the real defense of alteration is valid against the claim of a holder in due course.

RIGHTS OF A HOLDER IN DUE COURSE

Personal Defenses

The rights of a holder in due course are greater than those of a mere holder because a holder in due course is not subject to personal defenses, whereas a mere holder is subject to personal defenses. These personal defenses are: **MUFFLERS.**

Mistake
Unconscionability
Failure of a condition precedent
Fraudulent inducement
Lack of consideration
Expected delivery not being made
Release or discharge of debt
Stolen by a thief

If the drawer or maker or a prior transferor who indorsed the commercial paper raises any of the listed defenses in a suit brought by a holder in due course, it will have no effect because of the special status of the holder in due course. If any of these defenses is raised against a mere holder, it will have the effect of nullifying his or her suit. Most of these defenses are discussed more fully in Chapter 17, "Contractual Defenses."

Perry v. Welch
725 S.W. 2d 347 (Tex App.—Corpus Christi 1987)

R. J. Welch was a partner in an accounting firm in the Rio Grande Valley. On July 1, 1980, Lester Perry and Noble Allen became partners in the accounting firm by buying into it. Perry and Allen executed nonnegotiable promissory notes to evidence this. The notes provided in part:

> This note, principal and interest, is payable in installments, with each installment being applied first to interest accrued to the date of such installment, and then to principal, and with the amount and payment date of each such installment being determined by the date and amount of each cash withdrawal of net profits made by the partners of Welch, White and Co. pursuant to their written Partnership Agreement.

Perry and Allen made payments until Welch retired on July 31, 1981. They claimed that his remaining in the partnership was a condition precedent to their duty to pay.

The issue is whether Welch's active participation in the firm was a condition precedent to Perry and Allen's payment of the note.

The court held,

Here, appellants Lester Perry and Noble Allen each received a one-seventh interest in the partnership, including the right to receive profits and a share of the taxable and intangible assets of the firm. Contending now that they had not foreseen the mandatory retirement of appellee during the term of the note and that appellee took some of the firm's clients with him is not sufficient to defeat appellants' obligation to pay. It merely shows now that they may not have obtained all they were hoping for when they made the deal. Again, if appellants had foreseen such event as a condition for the payment of the notes, they could have so provided.

Judgment for Welch.

Fraudulent Inducement   A drawer or maker who is induced to sign commercial paper on the basis of false representations of another has no defense if the instrument is negotiated to a holder in due course who requests payment. If the person requesting payment does not qualify as a holder in due course, the personal defense of fraudulent inducement will nullify the request.

EXAMPLE | Hades participated in a Health Fair Exhibition. At his booth he advertised his Hot Springs Health Spa. He induced Adonis to join, claiming that all the beautiful women at the spa would be at his feet. Adonis negotiated a check to Hades for $600, the cost of initiation and one year's membership. Hades indorsed the check over to Perseus, a good-faith purchaser, for value. Adonis soon discovers that there is no health spa, that the whole episode is a scam. Meanwhile Hades has gone to _____. The check has cleared, so Adonis sues Perseus, claiming that he issued the check because of Hades's fraudulent inducement. Is Adonis's argument viable? No! Perseus qualifies as a holder in due course and is not affected by the personal defense of fraudulent inducement. The reason for this is that, as between the drawer victimized by the fraudulent inducement and the holder in due course, the drawer was in a better position to detect the fraud perpetrated. Adonis's only recourse is to go to _____ to sue Hades.

Stolen by a Thief   A thief may negotiate commercial paper to another person; that person may even become a holder in due course. If that person becomes a holder in due course, then in a suit for payment against the drawer or maker, the fact that the instrument was acquired from a thief will have no effect. Refer to the earlier example concerning Medusa and Olympic Savings. In that example Medusa was a thief who presented checks signed by Venus de Milo for payment. Olympic Savings made payment to Medusa because she possessed Venus's identification. In that case Olympic Savings would be a holder in due course.

Real Defenses

Both a holder and a holder in due course acquire commercial paper subject to real defenses. Real defenses include: **FADS 'N FIB.**

Forgery
Alterations
Duress
Statute of limitations has run

No capacity to contract because of either infancy or insanity

Fraud in the execution of the instrument
Illegality
Bankruptcy discharge

Forgery and Alteration Forgery is the unauthorized signing of another person's signature. An alteration is something that materially changes the terms of the commercial paper, usually the amount. A holder has no right to payment when this defense is raised. A holder in due course has only the right to payment up to the original amount authorized before the instrument was altered.

Fraud in the Execution Fraud in the execution occurs when the drawer or maker does not know that he or she is signing commercial paper. (In fradulent inducement, by contrast, the drawer or maker knowingly and voluntarily signs a negotiable instrument.) The fraud occurs when the consideration promised is not received or is not valuable.

EXAMPLE | Zeus, president of the International Olympic Committee, is signing invitations to the 1998 Winter Olympics in Nagano, Japan. His assistant, Apollo, tapes a check payable to himself underneath one of the letters written on carbonized paper. Zeus's signature appears on the check as a result of the carbon paper trick. Apollo fills in the amount and then cashes the check at the Five Rings Savings Bank. Zeus later discovers the missing check. Will Zeus be successful if he brings a lawsuit to recover payment from the bank? Yes! Zeus may assert the real defense of fraud in the execution! This is effective against the bank even if it is a holder in due course.

Gross v. Ohio Savings & Trust Co.
116 Ohio 230, 156 N.E. 205 (1927)

Ohio Savings & Trust Company sued Gross for nonpayment on a note that Gross claimed to have executed because of fraud.

Hill and Pittinger offered to sell Gross preferred stock in a drugstore corporation that they represented. After a quick glance at the paper, Gross agreed and signed what he thought was a contract for delivery of the shares of stock. The paper that Gross signed was actually a promissory note that was conveyed to the Bank of Athens and then to the Ohio Savings & Trust Company. The latter qualified as a holder in due course. Gross argued that he did not know he was signing a promissory note.

The issue is whether Gross's defense amounts to fraudulent inducement or fraud in the execution.

The court ruled,

> The distinction must be kept in mind between cases in which a party, through fraudulent representations, signs an instrument which he intends to be a negotiable promissory note, usually referred to as fraud in the inducement, and those where through fraud and misrepresentations or deceit and trickery his signature is procured to a negotiable promissory note, when he had no intention or purpose to sign any such instrument, termed fraud in the inception of the instrument. It is quite well settled that fraud in the transaction out of which the instrument arose, or in respect to the consideration for which it was given, is no defense against a holder in due course. A different rule prevails where the signature of the maker of a negotiable instrument was obtained by fraudulent trick or device and the maker did not know that the paper he was signing was a negotiable instrument and had no intention of making or delivering such instrument.

In this case the court held that Gross had been fraudulently induced to sign the note. This defense is valid against a holder but not against a holder in due course. The bank qualified as a holder in due course. If the signing of the note had been ruled to be fraud in the execution rather than fraudulent inducement, this defense would have been valid against both holders in due course, including the bank.

The court decided,

> It is better that defendant, and others who so carelessly affix their names to paper, the contents of which are unknown to them, should suffer from the fraud which their recklessness invites, than that the character of commercial paper should be impaired, and the business of the country thus interfered with and unsettled.

Judgment for Ohio Savings & Trust Company.

SHELTER DOCTRINE

A transferee who acquires commercial paper from a holder in due course, but who does not qualify as one, is still entitled to the rights of a holder in due course under the shelter doctrine. The reason for this is that a transferee acquires all of the rights of his or her transferor.

EXAMPLE | In the first example in this chapter concerning Thor's gift, a check made payable by him to his father, Odin, what are Odin's rights if the drawer asserts a personal defense? Odin is a holder, but as long as Thor qualifies as a holder in due course, Odin will be entitled to the rights of a holder in due course under the shelter doctrine. Because a holder in due course is not subject to any personal defenses, Odin will be entitled to payment.

REVIEW QUESTIONS

1. Define holder in due course, holder, value, good faith, and without notice of defenses.

2. What personal defenses are not valid against a holder in due course who is seeking to enforce the commercial paper for payment?

3. What real defenses are valid against a holder in due course?

4. Explain the difference between fraudulent inducement and fraud in the execution.

5. Can a person who acquires commercial paper from a thief qualify as a holder in due course?

6. What is the shelter doctrine?

7. Ray Orrill defaulted on promissory notes held by American Bank and Trust Company. When American went into receivership in 1990, the FDIC took possession of the promissory notes executed by Ray Orrill and attempted to collect on them. Orrill raised certain personal defenses against American. He contended that the FDIC was not a holder in due course because it had taken possession of the notes with knowledge of these defenses. In other cases, the FDIC has been substituted as a party and given holder-in-due-course status. What result? *FDIC v. Orrill*, 771 F. Supp. 777 (E.D. La. 1991).

8. Frank L. Fancher signed a note for $75, which Lester also indorsed as an accommodation indorser. The check was subsequently altered to $375 and negotiated to the National Exchange Bank of Albany. The bank argued that Lester was liable if he had carelessly placed his name on the commercial paper without observing the spaces that Fancher had left open, which would permit an alteration to the check. Lester contended that a drawer is not under a legal duty to prepare a check so carefully as to avoid any chance of alteration. Is the defense of alteration raised by Lester valid against the bank, who is a holder in due course? *National Exchange Bank of Albany* v. *Lester*, 194 N.Y. 461, 87 N.E. 779 (1909).

25

Commercial Paper: Liability of the Parties and Bank Deposits and Collections

CONTRACTUAL LIABILITY OF PARTIES

Drawer and Maker

In a two-party instrument, it is the maker who is primarily liable for payment when the promissory note or certificate of deposit matures. In a three-party instrument, the drawer has only secondary liability. He or she becomes liable to the holder of the check or draft if the drawee dishonors it.

Power Equipment v. First Alabama Bank
585 So. 2d 1291 (Ala. 1991)

Power Equipment negotiated a $900,000 line of credit with First Alabama Bank. The promissory note gave First Alabama a security interest in all of Power Equipment's equipment. It also contained a provision allowing the bank to demand the entire payment at any time. Robert Ferguson, who was on another bank's board of directors and loan committee, signed the note without reading it. Subsequently Power Equipment defaulted on the note.

The issue is whether the note is enforceable.

The court held, "The law is equally clear that ordinarily when a competent adult, having the ability to read and understand an instrument, signs a contract, he will be held to be on notice of all the provisions contained in that contract and will be bound thereby." Judgment for First Alabama Bank.

Drawee

The bank or the drawee becomes primarily liable when it accepts a check or draft for payment. The reason the bank must accept the check before it incurs primary liability is that the bank needs the opportunity to examine the drawer's account to verify that it contains sufficient funds to cover the check. If the drawer's account is maintained at a different bank, the depositor may cash the check against his or her own bank account. In that case the depositor must have sufficient funds to cover the check if it bounces. A check bounces when the drawer's account lacks sufficient funds to cover outstanding checks.

A bank has a contract with the drawer to pay all checks signed by the drawer when he or she maintains sufficient funds in an account to cover the checks issued. If a bank wrongfully dishonors a check by refusing to accept it when adequate funds have been maintained, the drawer will be liable to the holder for payment, but the bank will be liable to the drawer for breach of contract. If the bank accepts a forged or altered instrument, it cannot charge the drawer's account, because the drawer is not liable for forgery or a subsequent alteration unless his or her negligence substantially contributed to the forgery or alteration.

Check Reporting Service v. Michigan National Bank
478 N.W. 2d 893 (Mich. App. 1991)

Check Reporting Service (CRS) purchased checks received by merchants from their customers for a discount. CRS would then attempt to collect the unpaid amounts to earn a profit. CRS entered into an agreement with Michigan National Bank (MNB) in Lansing whereby CRS would deposit the merchant-endorsed checks into the bank and, in return, the bank would pay the drafts given to the merchants up to the amount of funds CRS collected. MNB was providing a service. CRS assumed the risk of collection. The collection period lagged, but because the drafts had to be paid, MNB gave CRS overdraft protection. CRS signed a promissory note to repay any overdrafts. The amount of this protection gradually grew from $50,000 in June 1984 to $300,000 by February 1985. In February 1986 MNB refused to pay the drafts, citing an overdraft of $352,000, which was in excess of the limit. MNB demanded payment of CRS's promissory note. CRS said that it was impossible to pay at that time. So, as collected funds came into CRS's account, MNB set them off against the $352,000 outstanding debt and did not pay the drafts issued to the merchants, citing insufficient funds. CRS sued MNB for failing to pay the drafts.

The issue is whether MNB wrongfully dishonored the drafts.

The court stated that MNB might exercise "its right to use the funds in that account to set off the amounts outstanding on the line of credit and term loans." The court held, "[T]he dismissal of plaintiff's (CRS) wrongful dishonor claim . . . was proper." Judgment for MNB.

Indorser

An indorser who signs an instrument agrees to pay its face value when it becomes due or upon presentment. This agreement is a surety contract. A surety is a person who agrees to be liable for the debt of another. An indorser agrees to be liable for the debt of the maker or drawer of a negotiable instrument.

If commercial paper is dishonored when presented for payment, the indorser is liable to the holder of the instrument or to any subsequent indorser who receives it from the holder. The holder must give notice of dishonor to the indorser. If there is more than one indorser, the indorsers are liable to one another in the order in which their signatures appear on the commercial paper. An indorser's liability is limited to the amount stated on the instrument when the indorsement is made. An indorser can disclaim his or her contractual liability by signing the check "without recourse." This protects the indorser from liability for any subsequent indorsement.

Accommodation Indorser

An accommodation indorser is a person who lends his or her signature to an instrument to help the holder negotiate it. As an indorser of the holder's instrument, the person making the accommodation is liable as a surety. Presentation and notice of dishonor are required. An accommodation indorser is considered to be a surety because he or she is guaranteeing the payment of another. An accommodation indorser is not liable to the person being accommodated; instead, the accommodation indorser has the right to reimbursement for any payments made on behalf of the person accommodated.

PRESENTMENT

Presentment is a demand by a holder either for payment from the maker or for acceptance by the drawee. Commercial paper must be presented before a drawer or an indorser can be liable. The time of presentment must be reasonable. If an instrument matures on a specified date, presentment must occur on or before that date. With regard to checks, presentment must occur within thirty days from the date of issue, or else the check will be considered stale. This puts the holder on notice that the check is overdue. The drawer's liability coincides with this rule, extending thirty days from the date of issue. An indorser's liability is limited to seven days following the date of his or her indorsement. Unexcused or unreasonable delay in presentment or notice of dishonor will result in discharge of the drawer or the indorser.

PROOF OF SIGNATURE

The signature of the drawer or maker, or of an indorser, on an instrument is deemed admitted by that party unless it is specifically denied. The burden of proof is on the holder, but the holder is aided by the presumption of the authenticity of a signature in all cases except where the signer has died or has become incompetent. The signer must establish a real or personal defense to the holder's claim. If the holder can prove that he or she has fulfilled all the requirements of a holder in due course, or is entitled to the rights of a holder in due course under the shelter doctrine, then the holder will not be subject to any personal defense raised by the signer.

No person is liable unless his or her signature appears on the instrument. If the signature is forged or otherwise unauthorized, it is ineffective against the person whose name was unlawfully signed. This includes an agent exceeding his or her authority.

SIGNATURE OF AN AUTHORIZED AGENT

An authorized agent must sign in his or her authorized capacity. The agent must also sign the name of the person he or she represents or else risk personal liability. Authorized capacity may be either express or implied.

LIABILITY UNDER SPECIAL CIRCUMSTANCES

Impostors

An indorsement by an impostor is effective if the impostor, through use of the mails or in person, induces a drawer or maker to sign an instrument payable to the person whom the impostor is impersonating and to mail the instrument to the impostor. The person receiving the instrument (usually a check) from the impostor is entitled to payment from the maker or drawer if the receiver acted in good faith and exercised ordinary care in accepting the instrument. In other words, the person receiving it must be a holder in due course.

EXAMPLE | Murf the Surf sent Darlin' Lil the following letter:

> Dear Preferred Customer,
>
> I am writing to advise you of our liquidation of diamond inventory at greatly reduced prices. One-carat heart-shaped blue-white diamond regularly $3,500 now only $2,000. This offer is good for only ten days. Make checks payable to the signer as agent for Diamonds Are Forever, Inc.
>
> Signed,
>
> Diamond Jim Brady

Darlin' Lil ordered a diamond and mailed a check to the imposter Murf the Surf under the impression that she was mailing it to Diamond Jim, agent for Diamonds Are Forever. Murf signed the name of the payee, Diamond Jim, then indorsed the check to the First National Bank of Miami, which paid him cash for it. After discovering the scam Darlin' Lil sued the bank for wrongful payment. Is she entitled to recover the amount of the check from the bank? No! The imposter's indorsement is effective as long as the bank acted in good faith and exercised ordinary care in accepting the check. The bank is the more innocent party and should be entitled to payment because the drawer, Darlin' Lil, had the opportunity to prevent the fraud by not dealing with the impostor.

Padded Payroll

A padded payroll is one to which a dishonest employee has added names that are unauthorized and commonly fictitious. Checks are issued to these fictitious payees and indorsed by the dishonest employee. An indorsement by an agent or employee who supplies the drawer or maker with the name of a payee, usually fictitious, and who induces the drawer or maker to issue a negotiable instrument to that person is effective even though the impostor intends the named payee to have no interest in the commercial paper. The person or bank receiving the indorsed instrument is not liable if that party acted in good faith and exercised ordinary care.

EXAMPLE | Richelieu works as treasurer for the Candy Man Company, which manufactures candy bars. There are 142 employees, but Richelieu issues 145 checks. The three additional checks are made out to the order of the Three Musketeers. Richelieu indorses their names and cashes the checks at a nearby bank. When Candy Man discovers the scheme, it sues Richelieu, but he is bankrupt after spending all of the money. Does Candy Man have any recourse against the bank? No! The indorsements of the imposter Richelieu are effective against Candy Man as long as the bank acted in good faith. Candy Man was in a better position than the bank to prevent the scam.

Conversion

Conversion is the theft of another's property. Conversion of commercial paper occurs when it is delivered to a person or bank and that party misappropriates it. A person or a bank also becomes guilty of conversion by accepting a forged instrument and crediting the account of the person whose name was forged. The reason this amounts to conversion is that funds are transferred from the account of the rightful owner to the forger even though the party may be acting in good faith. Conversion does not require intent to steal; otherwise, it would be a crime. See Chapter 5, "Torts," for a more detailed discussion of conversion.

Negligence

Any negligence on the part of the drawer that substantially contributes to a forgery or alteration will prevent the drawer from asserting either of these defenses against a holder in due course, including a bank that makes payment in good faith. If the bank was also negligent in accepting the commercial paper for payment, this rule would not apply, and the defenses of forgery and alteration could still be raised.

Certification

A bank is not under any obligation to certify a check, but when it does so, certification operates as an acceptance of the check. This means that the drawer and all prior indorsers are discharged from liability. The bank has agreed to honor the check as presented for payment.

Lost, Stolen, or Destroyed Instruments

A person who claims to be the owner of a lost, stolen, or destroyed instrument may recover from any person liable on the instrument (the maker, the drawer, the indorser, or the bank that accepted the instrument for cash) if the claimant can prove the following:

    Ownership of the instrument
    Facts lending to the instrument's loss
    Terms of the instrument

The court may require the purported owner to provide security indemnifying the person or bank from any future superior claims. When a check is stolen through the mails, the person who was to have received it must file a sworn affidavit testifying that the check was never received.

EXAMPLE | Mickey is vacationing at Disneyland in Florida with his wife Minnie. He accidently drops his wallet while moving through the pavilion "It's a Small World." Donald finds the wallet with some blank checks inside. He forges Mickey's name and cashes the checks at a nearby bank. Later that day Mickey discovers that he has lost the checks. He and Minnie run to a nearby security guard, who asks them if the checks were American Express. They answered no, with the words "Don't leave home without them" running through their minds. Do Mickey and Minnie have any recourse? Yes! They may sue the bank to have their account recredited because the bank paid out on a forged check. Forgery is a real defense that Mickey and Minnie can raise successfully in a suit against the bank.

BANK DEPOSITS AND COLLECTIONS

Classification of Banks

The depository bank is the first bank to which commercial paper is transferred for collection.

An intermediary bank is the bank through which commercial paper is transferred during the course of collection. Intermediary banks are usually large banks that maintain accounts with the Federal Reserve Banks in their districts. Intermediary banks provide access for smaller banks to the Federal Reserve Bank check-clearing process by allowing smaller banks to maintain accounts with them for this purpose.

Collection banks include the thirteen Federal Reserve Banks, which handle commercial paper for collection.

The payor bank is the bank on which payment is drawn. It may be the same as the depository bank.

EXAMPLE | In Disney World, Florida, Donald draws a check on the Bank of Orlando and mails it to his good friend Goofy in Disneyland, California. Goofy deposits the check in his account at the First National Bank of Anaheim. The check-clearing process begins. The First National Bank of Anaheim transfers the check to the Bank of America, with which it maintains an account for collection purposes. The Bank of America transfers the check to the San Francisco Federal Reserve Bank, with which it in turn maintains an account for collection. The San Francisco Federal Reserve Bank transfers the check to the Atlanta Federal Reserve Bank, which covers the state of Florida. The Atlanta Federal Reserve Bank transfers the check to the Bank of Orlando, which maintains an account with the Atlanta Federal Reserve Bank for collection purposes. The Bank of Orlando finally returns the check to Donald along with his other checks and monthly bank statement. What are the classifications of the respective banks? The Bank of Orlando is the depository bank. The Bank of America is an intermediary bank. The San Francisco and Atlanta Federal Reserve Banks are collection banks. The First National Bank of Anaheim is the payor bank.

Process of Posting

The process of posting is the usual procedure that a payor bank follows in determining whether to make payment and in recording payment. The bank will

> verify the signature,
> check the drawer's account to determine whether sufficient funds are available,
> stamp the check "paid," and
> make an entry to the drawer's account.

Bank's Right to Revoke

A depository bank has the right to revoke, charge back, or obtain a refund of any amount credited to the customer's account until the time when payment becomes final.

Final Payment

Payment becomes final when

> the process of posting is completed,
> the payor bank has paid cash, and
> the payor bank has settled the instrument without reserving the right to revoke it or has provisionally settled the instrument and failed to revoke within the statutory period.

Stop Payment Order

The payor bank must receive a stop payment order within a reasonable time in order to act on it. This means that the order must be received before the bank has

> accepted or certified the check,
> paid cash for the check,
> settled the check without reserving its right to revoke, and
> completed the process of posting the check to the drawer's account.

The effect of a stop payment order is to suspend the bank's duty to pay on a check or to charge the drawer's account for it. Oral stop payment orders are effective for fourteen days; written ones are effective for six months. If the bank pays on a check after receiving a stop payment order within a reasonable time, the bank will be liable only for the loss actually suffered by the drawer. If the check was negotiated to a holder in due course and then negligently paid by the bank in spite of a stop payment order, the holder in due course and the payor bank (which would be subrogated to the rights of a holder in due course) would prevail—that is, unless the drawer could set up a real defense to justify the stop payment order.

Payor Bank's Rights and Duties

The payor bank has the following rights:

- The right to charge a customer's account for any check that is properly payable
- The right to subrogation of the rights of a holder in due course or a payee against the drawer, or the right to subrogation of a drawer's rights against the payee or other holder
- The right to dishonor stale checks
- The right to dishonor checks for ten days after the date a person becomes incompetent or dies unless notified to stop payment

The payor bank has a duty to act by midnight of the banking day on which it receives the check by paying the check, returning it, or sending a notice of dishonor.

Drawer's Rights and Duties

A drawer has the following rights:

- The right to damages for the bank's wrongful dishonor. This is a breach of contract action. The drawer's recourse includes consequential damages for arrest or prosecution for passing a bad check.
- The right to stop payment.

The drawer has the duty to examine his or her bank statement and canceled checks to discover and report unauthorized signatures and alterations. After receiving the bank statement, the drawer must use reasonable care and promptness in discovering forgery or alteration and must notify the bank promptly if any is found. If the bank establishes that the drawer failed to comply with this requirement, then the drawer cannot assert forgery or alteration if the bank has suffered a loss or if the drawer has had the bank statement and canceled checks for fourteen days before notifying the bank. The drawer can assert forgery or alteration regardless of the time requirement if the bank was negligent in paying the check. Even if the bank is negligent, the drawer must report forgery of his or her signature or an alteration within one year, or unauthorized indorsement of another within three years, for the defense to be valid. If the bank waives its defense against the drawer, it forfeits its claim against any collecting bank or prior transferor.

ELECTRONIC FUND TRANSFERS

Electronic fund transfers (EFT) are governed by the Electronic Fund Transfer Act of 1979 (EFTA). An EFT is a transfer of funds through an electronic terminal, telephone, or computer. The financial institution is instructed to debit or credit a savings, money market, or checking account. EFTs include depositing checks, switching funds from one account to another, and receiving cash. To make an EFT through an automated teller machine (ATM), the consumer introduces a card, similar to a standard credit card, into the ATM and inputs an individual secret access code.

When a consumer applies to a financial institution for the ATM access card, the EFTA requires that the contract specify the following:

- The consumer's liability for unauthorized use
- The time limit for reporting unauthorized use
- The method of notification (telephone or mail) concerning unauthorized use
- The type of EFT that may be used, including the frequency of use and the maximum dollar amount that may be withdrawn each day
- The charges for use
- The consumer's right to stop payment on the EFT
- The consumer's right to a receipt of the transfer

Automated Teller Machines

The EFTA requires that the ATM provide documentation of the transfer, including the following:

- The amount of the transfer
- The date and time of the transfer
- The type of transfer
- Identification of the accounts involved in the transfer
- The location of the ATM where the transfer was made

The financial institution must send the consumer a monthly statement setting forth the following:

- Each EFT
- Fees charged
- Beginning and ending balance
- Address and/or telephone number for consumer inquiries

A consumer must notify the financial institution, orally or in writing, of any errors in his or her account within sixty days. The notice must contain the following:

- The consumer's name and account number
- A description of the error
- The reason for the error

The financial institution must investigate and issue a report to the consumer within ten business days. If the consumer initially gives oral notice, the bank may require a written follow-up statement.

Consumer Liability

The consumer's liability for an unauthorized electronic fund transfer is limited to the lesser of $50 or the amount of the EFT. If the consumer fails to report the error within sixty days of receipt of the periodic statement, he or she is not entitled to reimbursement. If the consumer fails to report loss or theft of the access card within two days of learning of it, his or her liability will be the lesser of $500 or the amount of the EFT. To refute the consumer's claim, the financial institution must prove that the use was authorized or, if it was unauthorized, that the consumer did not file timely notice. The financial institution will not be liable for technical malfunctions, acts of God, lack of sufficient funds in the consumer's account, or lack of cash in the ATM.

REVIEW QUESTIONS

1. Explain the banking deposit and collection process.
2. What are the payor bank's rights and duties?
3. What are the drawer's rights and duties?
4. How does an agent properly sign for a principal in order to absolve himself or herself from all liability?
5. What is the contractual liability of the drawer, maker, drawee, indorser, surety, and accommodation indorser?
6. Who is liable when an impostor defrauds a person by inducing that person to send the impostor a check payable to an individual being impersonated?
7. List and explain the warranties made on transfer and on presentment.
8. On March 10, 1987, Service Typesetting and Printing, Inc. signed a promissory note with a bank for $124,000. Robert Dillard guaranteed the note in writing. He was obliged to pay if Service Typesetting failed to do so. Under what theory of law would Dillard be held liable? *Dillard* v. *NCNB Texas Nat. Bank,* 815 S.W. 2d 356 (Tex. App.—Austin 1991).

26

Secured Transactions

INTRODUCTION

Transactions involving consumers and businesses may be made on a cash or a credit basis. No debt is incurred in a cash transaction because payment is made when performance is rendered. In a credit transaction part or full payment is deferred until a later date. This creates a debt owed by the purchaser to the seller. The purchaser becomes known as a *debtor,* and the seller becomes known as a *creditor.* Credit transactions may be secured or unsecured. A *secured credit transaction* is one in which the creditor has a security interest in personal property belonging to the debtor. The personal property acts as collateral for the debt owed. The security interest, once attached and perfected, gives the creditor the right to sell the collateral if the debtor defaults, with the proceeds applied to the debt. A security agreement is generally signed by the debtor, thus evidencing the existence of a security interest in the collateral. An unsecured credit transaction is one in which no security interest exists; no collateral is offered to secure the debt owed. A consumer or a business enters into an unsecured credit transaction on the strength of the name, goodwill, and reliability of the debtor for prompt payment. Secured transactions are covered by Article 9 of the Uniform Commercial Code.

COLLATERAL

There are two general classifications of personal property that may serve as *collateral:* tangible (goods) and intangible (commercial paper, accounts, chattel mortgage, documents of title, and other general intangibles).

CREATION OF A SECURITY INTEREST

A *security interest* is created and attaches to the specified collateral when the following criteria are satisfied: First, either the collateral must be in the creditor's possession, or the debtor must have signed a security agreement in which the collateral is described. If the collateral consists of crops or timber, then the agreement must include a legal description of the real estate on which the timber or crops are located. Second, the creditor must have given valuable consideration for the security interest. Third, the debtor must have rights in the collateral. The creation of a security interest gives a creditor the right to sell the property upon the debtor's default in payment and to apply the proceeds to the debt.

PERFECTION OF A SECURITY INTEREST

When a security interest is created, it protects the creditor against the debtor alone. The creation of a security interest in and of itself does not protect a creditor against other secured creditors, general creditors represented by a trustee in bankruptcy, and good-faith purchasers. The security interest must be perfected.

There are three methods of perfecting a security interest: transferring collateral, creating a purchase-money security interest, and filing a financing statement.

Transfer of Collateral

A security interest is perfected when the debtor transfers possession of the collateral to the creditor.

EXAMPLE | Royalty Cruise Lines has a fleet of five extravagant but outdated cruise ships named after English queens. Recently they have decided to construct a brand-new fleet. They borrow three and one-half million dollars from Bermuda Triangle Associates, which finances the construction of the new ships. In return Royalty Cruise Lines transfers one of its older ships, the *Queen Mary,* to Bermuda Triangle Associates as collateral for the loan. Will Bermuda Triangle Associates have a perfected security interest? Yes! Bermuda Triangle Associates' security interest was perfected when possession of the collateral was transferred to them.

Purchase-Money Security Interest

A security interest is automatically perfected when a purchase-money security interest is created. This rule applies only to the sale of consumer goods on credit, pursuant to a security agreement signed by the debtor. The purchase money is advanced in return for a security interest in the goods sold.

EXAMPLE | Christopher Columbus bought three ships called *Nina, Pinta,* and *Santa Maria* from Queen Isabella for $75,000. Before he set sail for the new world, Columbus made a down payment of $15,000 and signed a security agreement pledging the ships as collateral for the $60,000 debt. Does Queen Isabella have a security interest in the three ships, and is it perfected? Yes! This is a purchase money security interest. The security interest was created and perfected pursuant to a signed security agreement in which possession of the ships was transferred to Columbus in return for his promise to repay the debt owed, with the ships serving as collateral.

Filing of a Financing Statement

A security interest is perfected when a financing statement is filed. The financing statement must include the names and addresses of the debtor and creditor and a statement describing the collateral. If the collateral is timber or crops, a description of the real estate on which it is located must be set forth as well. A copy of the security agreement may be used if it conveys the pertinent information. The financing statement must be filed with the appropriate government official designated by state law. In most states the designated official is the secretary of state or—when the collateral involves consumer goods, farm products, or farm equipment—the county clerk. Designation of the secretary of state means that a statewide, centrally located filing system has been adopted. This system affords businesses operating nationally or throughout the state easy access to information concerning prospective customers who wish to borrow on credit. It would be a burdensome task for such businesses to contact each county clerk throughout one or more states. However, where consumers, farmers, and other local businesses are concerned, information filed with the county clerk is more convenient. This is why some states require filing with the secretary of state except for local matters, in which case the financing statement is filed with the county clerk

A financing statement, giving rise to a perfected security interest, is effective for five years. At the end of that period, a continuation statement may be filed; otherwise the security interest will lapse. The creditor's filing of the financing statement puts all prospective purchasers of the secured property on constructive notice of the existence of a perfected security interest in that property. This perfected security interest is a lien, and others may purchase the secured property subject only to this lien. Thus a person who buys subject to a perfected security interest cannot qualify as a good-faith purchaser.

GOOD-FAITH PURCHASERS

A purchaser who buys goods in the regular course of business in good faith, for value, and without notice of a perfected security interest is given preference to the goods over a creditor with a perfected security interest.

EXAMPLE | DiMaggio buys a sailboat called the *Yankee Clipper* from Boats and Floats, Inc. for $20,000 cash. The inventory carried by Boats and Floats is financed by Waterlogged Shipbuilders, Inc. They have a purchase-money security interest that has been automatically perfected. Shortly thereafter Boats and Floats defaults on the debts it owes to Waterlogged Shipbuilders. Can Waterlogged reclaim the *Yankee Clipper* from DiMaggio? No! DiMaggio is a good-faith purchaser who paid valuable consideration for the sailboat and who bought it without knowledge of the perfected security interest. He is entitled to the sailboat against the claims of Waterlogged shipbuilders. Waterlogged must look to Boats and Floats for the proceeds from the sale of the *Yankee Clipper*.

If a good-faith purchaser buys goods from a consumer who in turn bought the goods pursuant to a credit transaction in which the retailer had a purchase-money security interest in the goods, the purchaser is also given preference over the retailer regardless of the latter's perfected security interest unless the retailer has filed a financing statement.

EXAMPLE | Mr. Rourke purchased a ticket on the *S.S. Titanic* for $1,400 on his MasterCard. Two weeks later he learned of a new cruise ship called the *Love Boat,* which sailed to Fantasy Island. Rourke had always wanted to visit Fantasy Island, so he sold his ticket on the *S.S. Titanic* to a good friend, Tattoo, for $1,100. After the sale to Tattoo, Rourke stopped payment on his MasterCard. MasterCard tried to enforce its perfected security interest by suing Tattoo for return of the tickets. MasterCard never filed a financing statement because its security interest was automatically perfected on the creation of the purchase-money security interest. Who has the paramount right to the tickets? Tattoo! He is a good-faith purchaser of the tickets for valuable consideration without knowledge of MasterCard's perfected security interest. MasterCard was protected against Rourke's other creditors but not against Tattoo, a good-faith purchaser for value. Bon voyage!

PRIORITIES

A perfected purchase-money security interest in collateral other than inventory has priority over conflicting security interests where the perfection of the purchase-money security interest occurs at the time when, or within ten days after, the debtor takes possession of the collateral. Perfection of a purchase-money security interest occurs when the debtor signs a security agreement.

A perfected purchase-money security interest in inventory has priority over conflicting security interests in the inventory, and any cash proceeds received by the debtor on or before delivery to a buyer, provided that the following criteria are satisfied: First, the security interest must be perfected when the debtor receives the inventory; second, the holders must be notified of the conflicting security interests.

Priority among conflicting security interest in the same collateral is given to the person who first filed the financing statement or, otherwise, to the person who first perfected the security interest. One may accomplish the latter by receiving possession of the collateral pursuant to a signed security agreement. Among conflicting security interests that remain unperfected, the first security interest created and attached to the specified collateral has priority.

The creditor having priority may use the collateral to satisfy the debt owed to him or her either by retaining the collateral or by selling it and keeping the proceeds. If the value of the collateral exceeds the amount owed, the creditor must return the proceeds to the debtor.

REVIEW QUESTIONS

1. Define secured credit transaction, collateral, security interest, debtor, and creditor.
2. How can a security interest be perfected?
3. In what order will priorities be accorded among conflicting security interests?
4. What are the rights of a good-faith purchaser as against those of a person holding a perfected security interest?
5. How is a security interest created?
6. List and explain the various types of collateral.
7. Alfred Klass and his company entered into a security agreement giving Klass a security interest in funds contributed to the company when he knew that the company would likely file for bankruptcy. The company argued that the security agreement was invalid, contending that Klass sought preferential treatment over other creditors because of his inside knowledge. What result? *Klass v. Winstein, Kavensky, et al.,* 579 N.E. 2d 365 (Ill. App. 3 Dist. 1991).
8. Stumbo delivered logs to Keystone Lumber Company under a contract of sale. Thereafter a fire destroyed Keystone's lumber mill. Keystone could not continue to operate, and the insurance proceeds were not sufficient to pay Stumbo the value of the logs. Stumbo removed his remaining logs from Keystone and sold them to Hult, who made them into lumber. M.D.M. Corporation held a security interest in the logs and contested Stumbo's right to them. The seller made no demand to reclaim the goods within ten days after the buyer had received them. Is the claim of Stumbo as seller superior to the claim of M.D.M. as a holder of a security interest? *Stumbo v. Paul B. Hult Lumber Co.,* 251 Ore. 20, 444 P. 2d 564 (1968).

Special Topic: Business Ethics

Advertising may be defined as an impersonal method of communicating information to consumers. Ethical advertising may be defined as an impersonal method of communicating truthful, unbiased, objective information to consumers. But must an advertisement be truthful, unbiased, and objective to be legal? Which of these characteristics, if any, are necessary?

Advertising slogans such as "A new generation of Olds," "The Pepsi Generation," "Jordache Jeans," and "Coke Is It" are biased and unobjective. Ads also stretch the truth in some cases by their zealous advocation of products. An example is the BIC shaver commercial in which the little guy in the locker room full athletes is the one who gets all the girls. Whereas legal standards are designed primarily to protect the public, ethical standards advocate what is right.

FALSE STATEMENTS IN ADVERTISING

The Lanham Trademark of 1946 Act prohibited advertisers from making false statements about their own products. An amendment to this act in 1988 extended the prohibition to false statements about competitors' products. Before the amendment was passed, a competitor had no recourse in federal court but was relegated to suing in a state court. The difficulty with that proceeding was the difficulty in proving actual damages. For example, if Digital Equipment, without mentioning its own computers, falsely alleged that IBM computers broke down after one year of use on average, IBM would have to present the testimony of consumers who had not bought their computers specifically because of the advertisement. Those consumers might not be easy to locate. However, if the ad had falsely mentioned that DEC computers lasted five years longer than IBM computers on average, then IBM would be entitled in most federal courts to bring an action under the original Lanham Act for false comparative advertising. The key would be the use of the Digital Equipment name in the false advertising.

The 1988 amendment to the Lanham Act permits a competitor to bring an action in Federal court if an ad makes a false statement with regard to the competitor's goods or services. Upon proving the statement false, the competitor will be entitled to general damages. Editorials, political ads, and reviews of goods and services are exempt from the terms of the amendment. Opinions are also not actionable because they are protected under the First Amendment's Freedom of Speech clause. To date, protection afforded competitors against false statements in advertisements extends to print media only. The protection will be extended to television and radio broadcasters under the new amendment. Finally, under the new amendment, only competitors, not consumers, may sue.

Lefkowitz v. Great Minneapolis Surplus Store, Inc.
251 Minn. 188, 86 N.W. 2d 689 (1957)

Lefkowitz responded to two newspaper advertisements. The first one read:

> Saturday 9 A.M. Sharp
> 3 Brand New Fur Coats Worth to $100
> First Come First Served
> $1 Each

The second ad, published the following week, read:

> Saturday 9 A.M.
> 2 Brand New Pastel Mink 3-Skin Scarfs Selling for $89.50
> Out They Go Saturday, Each . . . $1.00
> 1 Black Lapin Stole, Beautiful, Worth $139.50 . . . $1.00
> First Come First Served

On both occasions Leftowitz was first in line, but the store refused to sell him the merchandise, claiming that only women could respond to the advertisement. Furthermore, the store claimed that the general rule with regard to newspaper advertising was that the ad is an invitation to the consumer, who in turn may make an offer that can be accepted only by the store.

The issue is whether an exception to the general rule should be made when the advertisement is so clear and definite that no terms are left open for negotiation.

The court ruled in the affirmative for the exception, and Lefkowitz won. The court held,

> Circulars, catalogs, advertisements, and price quotes are all forms of invitations intended to acquaint the prospective purchaser with certain items, property, or services the seller provides. In doing so, the seller hopes that prospective customers will discuss terms that will eventually lead to enforceable offers. These forms of invitations are not enforceable unless they are so clear and definite, as in the Lefkowitz case, that no terms are left open for negotiation.
>
> When the recipient of the invitation or advertisement offers to buy something, then the seller may accept or reject the offer requested depending on whether it is available. As you know, all sellers do not carry every color, size, and style of every product that is made. They are free to carry what they feel are the most popular items. It would restrict their freedom if they were requested to act otherwise.

Was the Great Minneapolis Surplus Store's ad deceptive?

State of New York v. Terry Buick, Inc.
137 Misc. 2d 290, 205 N.Y.S. 2d 497 (1987)

Terry Buick had advertised by displaying in its showroom window large signs: "NO MONEY DOWN" "$99 MO." The purpose of the signs was to capture people's attention as they drove by. The actual terms were printed on small stickers legible only from a short distance.

The issue is whether Terry Buick disclosed terms of payment and financing for its automobile sales in an adequately clear and conspicuous manner.

The Federal Truth-in-Lending Act provides,

> If any advertisement . . . states the amount of the downpayment, if any, the amount of any installment payment, the dollar amount of any finance charge, or the number of installments or the period of repayment, then the advertisement shall state all of the following items . . .

> 1. the downpayment, if any,
> 2. the terms of repayment;
> 3. the rate of the finance charge expressed as an annual percentage rate.

Regulation Z, which has amplified the truth-in-lending laws, stipulates that "[t]he creditor shall make the disclosures required by this subpart clearly and conspicuously."

The court held that "defendant's place of business and its advertising material showed beyond question that the announcement signs were a come-on designed to lure the eager seeker of a good deal." The court went on to say, "[W]hat you see is not what you get." The advertisement constituted a material misprepresentation of fact, which is exactly what the truth-in-lending laws were designed to protect against. The court found Terry Buick in violation and granted the preliminary injunction. Was Terry Buick ethical?

Geismar v. Abraham & Strauss.
109 Misc. 2d 495, 439 N.Y.S. 2d 1005 (1981)

A & S published a full page ad in Long Island's *Newsday* that showed four sets of china for sale. The first set was regularly priced at $100 but was on sale for $59.95. The second, normally at $140, was on sale for $59.95. The third, at $120 was on sale for $69.95. The fourth set, the one in question, was listed as $280, on sale for $39.95. A & S refused to sell the china, claiming that there had been a mistake in the advertised price. Geismar sued A & S, claiming that it was guilty of false advertising.

The issue the court addressed in this case was whether the aggrieved party must prove that the advertising was "misleading in a material respect" and that she sustained a loss or that she must go beyond that requirement and prove that the store intended to deceive the public.

Section 350-a of Article 22-A of the General Business Law addresses false advertising. It states,

> The term "false advertising" means advertising, including labeling, which is misleading. There shall be taken into account (among other things) not only representations made by statement, word, design, device, sound or any combination thereof, but also the extent to which the advertising fails to reveal facts material in the light of such representations with respect to the commodity to which the advertising relates under the conditions prescribed in said advertisement, or under such conditions as are customary or usual.

The court decided, "that judicial interpretation of article 22-A and the clear language of the statute dictate the conclusion that the plaintiff need not establish an intent to deceive."

The argument that the price was too low and should have been viewed as a mistake has no merit. With regard to this matter, the advertisement showed sale prices 40 percent to 50 percent off regular prices. The second and fourth sets of china were reduced beyond 50 percent. Where would one draw the line as to what is reasonable? After all, A & S drafted the ad and should have taken care in doing so. A & S's error, whether intentional or not, was misleading in a material way. Was A & S's conduct unethical?

Golstein v. Garlick
65 Misc. 2d 538, 318 N.Y.S. 2d 370 (1971)

The Garlick Parkside Funeral Home had developed an excellent reputation over forty years, in part through substantial advertising. Joseph N. Garlick Funeral Home published advertisements in *The New York Times* and *The New York Post,* which Garlick Parkside, believed confused and misled the public and misappropriated the reputation and goodwill of Garlick Parkside.

In its allegations against the newspapers, Garlick Parkside raised the issue of the circumstances under which a newspaper can be held liable for publishing a false advertisement. The court held,

> [I]f a newspaper publishes false and misleading advertisements maliciously or with the intention to harm another or so recklessly and without regard to its consequences that a reasonably prudent person would anticipate the damage, that newspaper should be held accountable for its conduct in the same manner as is any other person who commits such a tortious act.

Garlick Parkside's argument was that once a competitor of an advertiser notified a newspaper that the advertisement was false or misleading, the newspaper should cease publishing the advertisement or be potentially liable in a court action. The court felt that this would place the burden of determining which side was correct on the newspaper, which was not in a position to conduct investigations and to serve as arbiter. Furthermore, the newspaper would have to turn away many advertisements for fear of the threat of lawsuits by the advertiser's competitors where no valid claim might really exist. This threat, if allowed to stand, would have a chilling effect on a newspaper's right to publish and would create a conflict with the First Amendment's Freedom of the Press clause. The court continued,

> Therefore, this court is of the opinion that a standard that is consistent with protecting the public from irresponsible conduct by newspapers and that at the same time preserves the right of newspapers to publish advertisements should be that the newspaper is only liable if it publishes a false advertisement maliciously or with intent to harm another or acts with total reckless abandon.

Were the newspapers acting ethically?

Eastern Airlines v. New York Air, Inc.
559 F. Supp. 1270 (D.C.N.Y. 1983)

Eastern claimed that New York Air's use of the term *shuttle* or *shuttle service* in its advertising was an infringement on Eastern's "Air-Shuttle" trademark. The court determined that the term *shuttle* was a generic term associated primarily with short, frequent trips made by a plane, bus, or train and not with Eastern per se. When the term *shuttle* was used, most people would not immediately associate it with Eastern. However, the court pointed out that because in air travel a particular service and style of traveling have come to be associated with Eastern's Air-Shuttle, the term *shuttle* should not be used indiscriminately to mislead the public as was the case here.

The court held,

> After viewing the advertisement, individuals were asked whether the statement "New York Air offers all that Eastern offers, plus more" was conveyed by the ad. Ninety-one percent of all respondents and 94 percent of the more frequent fliers replied in the affirmative that this was the impression NYA conveys. This impression is clearly deceptive as NYA does not guarantee a trip at departure time or within a short interval of traveler's arrival at the airport. This feature of the shuttle is clearly a significant aspect of air travel and the fact that the advertisement suggests that NYA provides all the affirmative associations that the term shuttle has come to connote on EAL's Air-Shuttle shows that the advertisement is clearly misleading.

An injunction was granted restraining New York Air from incorporating in its advertisements features of Eastern's Air-Shuttle that New York Air does not in fact provide. Was New York Air's behavior unethical?

CONCLUSION

With increasing attention drawn to ethics in advertising, consumers should be more aware of the nature of the advertisements themselves and should scrutinize them more closely for credibility. Legislative actions together with ensuing case law should provide consumers more protection against deceptive advertising.

27

Bankruptcy

INTRODUCTION

Bankruptcy is the relief afforded an honest debtor through discharge of all of the debts he or she owes. A *debtor* is an individual, association, joint venture, partnership, or corporation that owes a debt to a creditor. A *creditor* is a person or entity to whom a debt is owed. A *debt* is an obligation owed by a debtor to a creditor.

The following is a discussion of the Federal Bankruptcy Reform Act of 1978, which was the first major revision of the bankruptcy laws in forty years.

BANKRUPTCY REFORM ACT

Provisions

The following are the provisions of the Bankruptcy Reform Act:

Chapter 1: General Provisions
Chapter 3: Case Administration
Chapter 5: Creditors, the Debtor, and the Estate
Chapter 7: Liquidation
Chapter 9: Adjustment of Debts of a Municipality

Chapter 11: Reorganization

Chapter 13: Adjustment of Debts of an Individual with Regular Income

Chapters 1, 3, and 5 are general provisions that apply to all bankruptcy proceedings. Chapters 7, 9, 11, and 13 are four types of bankruptcy proceedings. Chapter 7, Liquidation, is also known as straight or ordinary bankruptcy. It provides for the termination of the debtor's business through liquidation of its assets. Chapters 9, 11, and 13 provide for reorganization plans geared to keeping the debtor's business operational. Chapter 9 will not be discussed in detail because it refers to the reorganization of a municipality.

Bankruptcy Courts

On April 1, 1984, a United States bankruptcy court was established in each of the ninety-eight judicial districts in which a district court was located. This plan originated in the Bankruptcy Reform Act of 1978. Appeals from the bankruptcy court may be heard either by a panel of three bankruptcy judges or by the district court. Judges appointed by the president preside over the bankruptcy courts for fourteen-year terms.

ADMINISTRATION OF A BANKRUPTCY PROCEEDING

Chapter 3 of the Federal Bankruptcy Reform Act deals with commencement of a bankruptcy proceeding, bankruptcy officers and their administrative powers, and creditors' meetings. A bankruptcy proceeding may be commenced by filing a voluntary or involuntary petition.

Voluntary Petition

A voluntary petition may be filed under any chapter of the Bankruptcy Reform Act by any person who has accumulated debts that he or she is unable to pay. This person, known as a debtor, is seeking relief by asking in the petition that his or her debts be discharged. In addition to individuals, any association, partnership, joint venture, or corporation may file a voluntary petition for bankruptcy in the judicial district where it is incorporated or where its principal place of business is located. The following are prohibited from filing voluntary petitions and are relegated to proceeding under Chapter 7, Liquidation, or Chapter 11, Reorganization, through involuntary petition:

Bank

Railroad

Insurance company

Municipal corporation

Savings and loan association

A voluntary petition must set forth the following information: **NAME.**

Names and addresses of all secured and unsecured creditors and the amount owed to each

Assets and property owned by the debtor

Material facts leading to bankruptcy

Exempt property claimed by the debtor

If the information set forth is determined to be accurate and the debtor has not filed for bankruptcy within the last six years, then the court will transform the petition into an order for relief in bankruptcy.

Involuntary Petition

The creditor of a debtor who is not paying his or her debts may force the debtor into bankruptcy by filing an involuntary petition. If the number of creditors totals twelve or more, the petition must be signed by three or more creditors whose claims collectively amount to at least $5,000. If there are fewer than twelve creditors, the petition need only be signed by one of the creditors who has a claim of $5,000 or more. A debtor can contest the petition, but it will be upheld if he or she is not paying the debts owed. An involuntary petition may be brought against any debtor except a farmer or nonprofit corporation.

Once a petition is filed voluntarily or involuntarily, the debtor is protected against creditors, attempts to collect debts owed whether by bringing lawsuits, enforcing judgments, or attacking the debtor's property. This is because the debtor has been declared bankrupt by a court order and the bankruptcy court acquires jurisdiction over the debtor's assets.

Appointment of a Trustee

The court appoints an individual as trustee in all bankruptcy proceedings except those under Chapter 7, where the trustee is selected by a vote of the creditors at their first meeting. However, in a Chapter 7 proceeding, the court may appoint a receiver to act as a temporary trustee until one can be elected at the first meeting.

Duties of Trustees

A trustee has a duty to file a fidelity bond ensuring the faithful performance of his or her duties. In a Chapter 7 proceeding, a trustee has a duty to take title to and to sell and apportion the debtor's property among the creditors according to the priority of their claims. The trustee takes title to property owned by the debtor on the date the petition was filed, property inherited within six months after the filing of the petition, and property transferred to an unsecured creditor within ninety days before the petition was filed. Transfer of property to a good-faith purchaser for value after the bankruptcy petition was filed will be upheld. Certain property owned by the debtor is exempt from the creditors' claims. In reorganization proceedings the trustee has a duty to keep the debtor's business operational and to invest and distribute any income earned from the continued operation of the business.

First Meeting of the Creditors

The court will notify the creditors of the time and place of their first meeting. Before the meeting each creditor must submit a claim stating the amount owed to him or her. The bankruptcy judge will not be present at this meeting; the court-appointed trustee or temporary receiver will preside. In Chapter 7 proceedings the creditors will elect a trustee who will assume the duties of the temporary receiver. The debtor is required to attend the creditors' first meeting to have his or her debts discharged in bankruptcy. The debtor must respond to questions concerning the amount and location of his or her assets. The creditors will be trying to discern whether the debtor has concealed or fraudulently transferred any assets.

RIGHTS OF CREDITORS AND DEBTORS

Creditors' Claims

After the first meeting all creditors must file proof of their claims. Claims will be allowed unless the debtor objects, at which time the court will hold a hearing to determine the validity of the debt. If a creditor was not informed of the bankruptcy proceeding because of an omission on the debtor's part and therefore did not file proof of claim, that debt will not be discharged in bankruptcy but will survive the proceeding. The debtor is responsible for providing an accurate list of all creditors so the court can give them proper notice.

Moureau v. Leaseamatic
542 F. 2d 251 (5th Cir. 1976)

Leaseamatic appealed from the court order discharging all of Moureau's debts because Moureau had purposely failed to notify the court of the debt he owed to Leaseamatic.

Moureau filed a voluntary petition of bankruptcy, and in his schedule of creditors, he failed to disclose a debt owed to Leaseamatic. The court notified all of Moureau's creditors listed in the schedule. Leaseamatic repeatedly placed demands on Moureau that went unsatisfied. Leaseamatic learned of the bankruptcy proceeding just before the time for submitting claims expired, and therefore it never filed a proof of claim. The bankruptcy judge discharged all debts owed by

Moureau. When Leaseamatic learned that Moureau's debts had been discharged in bankruptcy, it appealed the bankruptcy judge's decision. Leaseamatic's argument was predicated on the fact that Moureau might not profit from his own fraud and concealment. The company contended that its claim was not discharged because it had not received timely notice. Moureau argued that sufficient time remained during which Leaseamatic could have filed proof of claim.

The issue is whether the time limitation for filing proof of claims applies to a creditor who has not received timely notice of the bankruptcy proceeding.

The court held, "[T]he debtor must take great care in the scheduling of creditors. His failure to do so will make the unscheduled debt non-dischargeable. . . ." The court found in the present case,

> [N]otice of the discharge was provided two months after the fact. Furthermore, we cannot ignore Moureau's neglect to list the Leaseamatic debt in any of his schedules—despite its repeated demands for payment. . . . While these facts do not establish fraudulent intent, they do indicate Moureau's complete disregard for the obligations imposed by statute. . . . We therefore hold that the debt was not discharged.

Judgment for Leaseamatic.

Nondischargeable Claims

EXAMPLE | The Scarecrow left his wife and children without support and obtained a $22,000-a-year position hanging around. One day a group of crows trespass upon the farm he is guarding. Instead of scaring the crows away, he inflicts severe bodily harm on them by clipping their wings. After failing to pay taxes for four years, he decides it's time to move on. He encounters a girl named Dorothy who tells him she is trying to find her way back to Kansas. He tells her that for $350 he can arrange transportation for her and her dog Toto. She gladly pays him. He asks her to wait on the yellow brick road for him, but he never returns. Instead he is on his way to Oz. When he arrives there he enrolls in the local college run by the Wizard to improve his intelligence. He takes out a student loan to pay for his tuition. But after embezzling $13,000 from the school's bursar's office where he has worked as a student aide, he leaves the college, defaults on the loan, and heads west, only to be caught from behind by the good fairy. Having squandered most of his money, the Scarecrow immediately files for voluntary bankruptcy, claiming that all of his debts are discharged. Is he correct? No!

The following debts are not dischargeable in bankruptcy: **TAPIOCA.**

Taxes

Alimony and child support payments

Property or money obtained under false pretenses

Intentional tort claims

Obligations incurred by students with regard to their education

Claims arising because of fraud, embezzlement, or breach of a fiduciary duty

Any claims that a debtor waives his or her right to discharge

EXAMPLE | In the previous example the Scarecrow failed to pay his past-due income taxes and alimony and child support payments; he obtained money from Dorothy under false pretenses; he committed an intentional tort against some crows; he defaulted on his student loan; and he embezzled $13,000 from the College of Oz. All of these debts will not be discharged but will survive the Scarecrow's bankruptcy.

Priority Claims

There are two classes of creditors: secured and unsecured. A secured creditor is one who has a security interest in the debtor's property. The security interest acts as collateral and may be sold, with the proceeds being used to satisfy the debt owed. If the proceeds from the sale of the security interest are insufficient to cover the secured creditor's claim, he or she has an unsecured claim for the amount unsatisfied and will share with the other general unsecured creditors.

A secured creditor is assured of collecting the money owed to him or her out of a specific asset offered by the debtor as collateral. Thus a secured creditor has an advantage over unsecured creditors, whose claims are paid out of the debtor's remaining assets, which may not be sufficient to satisfy completely the claims of all the creditors. That is why unsecured creditors often collect as little as twenty, thirty, or forty cents for every dollar owed to them.

EXAMPLE | The Wicked Witch of the East sold Dorothy a pair of glass slippers for $600. Dorothy paid the Wicked Witch $200, with the Witch retaining a $400 security interest. The Wicked Witch had told Dorothy to save the slippers for Kansas, but Dorothy wore them as she eased on down the yellow brick road, and one of the glass slippers cracked. Dorothy could not repay the amount owed to the Wicked Witch. In fact, her financial difficulties became so pressing that she filed a Chapter 7 liquidation proceeding. The Wicked Witch exercised her security interest by taking possession of the glass slippers. The amount remaining on the loan was $400. What priority will be given to the Wicked Witch's claim if we assume that the present value of the slippers is only $100 because of their condition? The Wicked Witch is a secured creditor up to $100 because she possesses a security interest in the slippers. As to the other $300 owed, the Wicked Witch will become a general unsecured creditor of Dorothy.

An unsecured creditor is one to whom a debt is owed but is not secured by any specific property of the debtor. An unsecured creditor will be paid from the liquidation of the debtor's assets according to a priority schedule. Payments are made in the following order:

Bankruptcy administration expenses, including such items as court costs, attorney fees, trustee's compensation and expenses, and appraisal fees.

Unsecured claims of a creditor arising between the time when the petition was filed and the time when a trustee was appointed. Such a creditor is referred to as a gap creditor.

Wages or commissions earned by employees within ninety days before their employer's filing of a bankruptcy petition. The amount is limited to $2,000 per employee.

Unsecured claims relating to an employee benefit plan made within 180 days before the filing of a bankruptcy petition. The amount is limited to $2,000 multiplied by the number of employees covered by the plan.

Unsecured claims for money paid to the debtor for rent, goods, or personal services that were never delivered, performed, or provided. This amount is limited to $900 per claim.

Taxes owed to federal, state, and local governments that were due within three years before the bankruptcy filing.

The amount remaining will be apportioned among all the general unsecured creditors. This includes any of the aforementioned unsecured priority claims to the extent that they exceed the stated limitations. If anything remains it will be returned to the debtor.

EXAMPLE   On October 1 the Lion, a furrier, filed a voluntary petition for Chapter 7 liquidation proceeding for the Lion's Mane, Inc. because he lacked the courage to make the innovative marketing decisions necessary to keep pace with his competition. A trustee was appointed one month later. The Lion's assets totaled $140,000. The following claims were filed against the Lion's Mane: Pelts and Felts, Inc., a $56,000 claim, with ten mink stoles that had been delivered securing the entire debt; bankruptcy expenses, $6,100; $8,000 worth of rabbit jackets purchased on October 17; wages earned by eight employees for the previous twelve weeks—$3,250 per employee; unpaid claims by the employees' health insurance plan for $1,250 per employee; unpaid rent for the month of October $900; unpaid state and federal income taxes, $3,000; personal loans made to the Lion's Mane, Inc. by the Scarecrow, $30,000, and by the Tin Man, $20,000. In which priority will the claims be paid?

Total Assets	$140,000
1. Secured claims	$ 56,000
2. Bankruptcy administration expenses	$ 6,100
3. Gap creditors	$ 8,000
4. Unpaid wages	$ 16,000
5. Unpaid employee health insurance	$ 10,000
6. Unpaid rent	$ 900

7. Income taxes		$ 3,000
8. General unsecured creditors		
Scarecrow	$ 30,000	$ 20,000
Tin Man	$ 20,000	$ 13,333
Employees	$ 10,000	$ 6,667
Total debts discharged	$140,000	

Because the general unsecured creditors' claims exceeded the amount of assets remaining for distribution after the priority classes had been satisfied, each will receive two-thirds of a dollar for every dollar of his or her claim.

Exempt Property

The Bankruptcy Reform Act allows a debtor to retain certain property and assets that will be exempt from the creditors' claims. These exemptions, which may be restricted by state law, are as follows:

House or burial plot up to $7,500

Motor vehicle up to $1,200

Household furnishings, goods, appliances, clothing, and the like to $200

Jewelry up to $500

Any other property up to $400 plus the unused portion of the $7,500 house or burial plot exemption

Professional tools and books up to $750

Outstanding life insurance

Health aids prescribed

Social Security, disability, and veterans' benefits

Pension, profit-sharing, and annuity payments

Unemployment compensation

Alimony and child support

Preferential Transfers

An important objective of the Bankruptcy Reform Act is to ensure equal treatment for all creditors in the same class. To enforce this stipulation, the trustee in bankruptcy is given the power to set aside all preferential transfers of money or property made by the debtor in favor of one or more of the creditors at the expense of the others. A *preferential transfer* is one in which a creditor receives an amount greater than his or her proportionate share, thereby reducing the proportionate shares of the other members of that class. Preferential transfers occur within ninety days before the filing of a bankruptcy petition unless the recipient of the preferential transfer knew of the debtor's insolvency at the time the transfer was made. In preferential transfer cases, any property transferred may be reclaimed for a period of up to one year preceding the date when the bankruptcy petition was filed.

EXAMPLE | The Munchkins run a donut shop in Oz. The business is failing because the donuts the Munchkins make have no holes. The Munchkins realize that they have to file a petition for bankruptcy. Their total assets are $15,000. The Munchkins have three creditors: the Wicked Witch, to whom they owe $6,000 for unpaid rent; the Wizard, to whom they owe $20,000 for ovens and other equipment; and the Good Fairy, to whom they owe $12,000. The Munchkins decide to satisfy the full amount of the debt owed to their close friend, the Good Fairy, three weeks before the petition is filed. This leaves only $3,000 to be split between the Wicked Witch and the Wizard. Can this transfer be voided? Yes! This is a preferential transfer in which one creditor is favored over the others. This preferential treatment causes the victimized creditors to suffer financial loss. Preferential transfers can be set aside as long as they occur within ninety days of the time when the bankruptcy petition is filed.

If a creditor receives payment from a debtor for the sale of goods or the performance of personal services in the ordinary course of business, the trustee cannot recover the amount transferred. The fact that it occurred during the ordinary course of business is decisive because there was no preferential treatment. A trustee cannot recover the proceeds of the sale of collateral by a secured creditor because of the security interest held unless the proceeds exceed the secured creditor's claim. Unlike the trustee in bankruptcy, a good-faith purchaser who buys goods from an unsecured creditor who received them because of preferential treatment is entitled to retain the goods.

EXAMPLE | In the previous example suppose that the Munchkins had paid Dorothy $400 for dough two weeks before they filed for bankruptcy. Could these payments be set aside as preferential transfers? No! These payments occurred during the ordinary course of business. It was in the best interest of the business to keep making and selling donuts.

Fraudulent Conveyances

A *fraudulent conveyance* made by a debtor with the intent to conceal nonexempt property from the creditors and to delay or otherwise obstruct the bankruptcy proceeding is void and may be set aside by the trustee. This stipulation applies to fraudulent transfers made after the filing of the bankruptcy petition or up to one year before the filing of the petition. Some states have extended the period to as much as five years before the filing. A fraudulent conveyance differs from a preferential transfer. A preferential transfer is made by the debtor for the benefit of one or more of the creditors. It deprives the remaining creditors of any claims they may have had to the transferred property. A fraudulent conveyance is usually a transfer made to a friend or relative of the debtor with the intent to deprive all creditors from making claims against the asset conveyed.

EXAMPLE | The Tin Man has filed a voluntary petition for a Chapter 7 bankruptcy proceeding for the purpose of liquidating his personal assets and discharging his personal debts. The Tin Man's personal assets total $47,000, including a collection of golden valentine hearts worth $14,000. His debts exceed his assets by $12,000. The Tin Man does not want to part with the valentines, so he sells them to his girlfriend Dorothy for $50. The creditors demand that the trustee set aside the transfer as a fraudulent conveyance. Does the trustee have the power to do this? Yes! Fraudulent conveyances made by a debtor with the intent to deprive creditors of his assets may be set aside by a trustee.

Acts of the Debtor that Will Prevent Bankruptcy

A debtor's obligations will not be discharged if the debtor has committed any of the following acts: **FADS.**

Fraudulently conveyed property or concealed assets with intent to defraud creditors

Admitted into a bankruptcy within the previous six years

Destroyed, falsified, or otherwise concealed accounting records so as to hinder investigation into the financial condition of a business

Secured credit by falsifying documents concerning one's own financial status or the status of his or her business

There are three basic bankruptcy proceedings:

Liquidation
Business reorganization
Individual rehabilitation

LIQUIDATION PROCEEDING

Liquidation is the only bankruptcy proceeding in which the debtor's business will be terminated, with its assets liquidated and then distributed to the creditors in accordance with the priority of their claims. Liquidation proceedings are also referred to as straight or ordinary bankruptcy and are covered under Chapter 7 of the Bankruptcy Reform Act. A liquidation proceeding under Chapter 7 incorporates all of the elements previously discussed: commencement of the proceeding through filing of a voluntary or involuntary petition, appointment of a temporary receiver, election of a trustee at the first meeting of creditors, stipulation of the trustee's duties, exemption of certain property, exclusion of certain debts from discharge, priority distribution of claims, and setting aside of preferential transfers and fraudulent conveyances.

BUSINESS REORGANIZATION

Introduction

Business reorganization is governed by Chapter 11 of the Bankruptcy Reform Act. It provides an alternative to terminating and liquidating the debtor's business under a straight bankruptcy proceeding, and it may be initiated pursuant to either a voluntary or an involuntary petition. The main purpose of a Chapter 11 proceeding is to formulate an effective plan for reorganization.

After the court issues its order for relief in bankruptcy, it will appoint a committee composed of the seven unsecured creditors having the largest claims. The committee's duties include consulting with the trustee or debtor concerning the administration of the bankrupt's affairs; investigating the financial background of the debtor, especially concerning any preferential or fraudulent transfer of property; and participating in the drafting of the plan for reorganization. A trustee will be appointed only if the debtor acted in a fraudulent, dishonest, or negligent manner in conducting the business or if the court determines the appointment to be in the best interest of the creditors. A reorganization proceeding may be converted to a Chapter 7 liquidation proceeding by the court for cause or by the debtor, unless a trustee has possession of the business's assets or the proceeding was triggered by an involuntary petition.

Reorganization Plan

The plan for reorganization must be filed within four months after the order for relief in bankruptcy is granted. This filing is the debtor's exclusive right unless a trustee has been appointed. The court-appointed creditors' committee, a trustee, or a creditor may propose a reorganization plan after 120 days if the debtor has not presented one, or after 180 days if the creditors did not accept the debtor's timely presentation. A plan must be approved by the court before it is made available to the creditors. A plan is accepted if more than one-half of the creditors holding at least two-thirds of the value of all claims vote in favor of it. After the creditors have accepted the plan, the court must determine whether the plan is feasible, is made in good faith, and is fair and equitable with respect to each class of unsecured creditors. The court may assess the latter by comparing what each creditor would have received under a Chapter 7 liquidation proceeding with what he or she will purportedly receive under the reorganization plan. A creditor's compensation under a Chapter 11 reorganization must be comparable; otherwise the plan will be disapproved for impairing the creditor's claim.

The debtor's successful adherence to the reorganization plan, which entails making all payments, revives the business and allows it to continue operating free of all debts.

Matter of Landmark at Plaza Park, Ltd.
7 B.R. 653 (D. N.J. 1980)

Landmark at Plaza Park, Ltd. owned a 200-unit garden apartment. City Federal held a first mortgage on the property for $2,250,000 at an interest rate of 9.5 percent. Landmark defaulted on its payments, and City Federal took possession of the garden apartments and began to collect the rents. Landmark's debt to City Federal exceeded the value of the garden apartment complex. City Federal wanted to sell the complex and apply the proceeds to satisfy the debt owed to it.

Landmark filed for reorganization under Chapter 11 and proposed the following reorganization plan:

1. Possession of the apartment complex is to be redelivered to Landmark.
2. Landmark will pay City Federal 12.5 percent on the face value of the property from the sixteenth month after the date the plan is approved through the thirty-sixth month.
3. In lieu of the interest at 12.5 percent for the first through the fifteenth month plus interest on the unpaid interest, City Federal will receive a note for $2,705,820, payable in three years.
4. City Federal's existing mortgage will secure the $2,705,820 note.

Landmark's plan for repayment at the end of three years was contingent upon its ability to secure refinancing for the first mortgage by the end of the three-year period.

City Federal rejected the plan, contending that its rights were impaired. The plan called for redelivery of possession of the apartment complex to Landmark. This amounted to a 100 percent loan with interest deferred for the first fifteen months.

The main issue is whether the court should approve the plan. In considering the issue the court must decide whether the debtor will be able to repay the loan and whether the proposed interest rate reflects the risk undertaken by the secured creditor.

The court decided that a 12.5 percent interest rate was modest in comparison to the risk undertaken by City Federal. The interest rate stipulated in the plan should correspond to the market interest rate that would be charged on the basis of the risks involved.

The court held, "It appears clear to the Court that the forced loan proposed by the debtor includes terms less favorable to City than would typically be found in the market and that any confirmable plan

must compensate City for this deficiency. . . ." The court denied approval of the plan because it believed that fulfillment of its proposals
was highly unlikely and that the plan would result in either further reorganization attempts or liquidation.

INDIVIDUAL REHABILITATION

Individuals may avoid having all of their assets liquidated under straight bankruptcy
proceedings by rehabilitating themselves under Chapter 13. The individual rehabilitation proceeding, which must be filed voluntarily, is open to any individual who has outstanding secured debts less than $350,000 and unsecured debts less than $160,000.
The court may convert this proceeding to a Chapter 7 liquidation proceeding for cause
or upon the debtor's request.

Rehabilitation Plan

The debtor must file a plan for rehabilitation. The court will appoint a trustee to monitor administration of the plan. Under the plan the debtor must agree to furnish all or
part of his or her future income to the trustee for repayment of the creditors' claims, to
repay all creditors within three years according to the priority distribution schedule,
and to treat all members of a class equally.

Court Approval

The court will determine whether the plan is made in good faith and is feasible—that
is, capable of being carried out by the debtor; whether the unsecured creditors are assured
of receiving amounts at least equivalent to what they would have received under a Chapter
7 liquidation proceeding; and whether the secured creditors are sufficiently protected either
by having possession of the collateral or by being allowed to retain their security interests
in property with value equivalent to their claims.

Discharge of Debts

The debtor will be rehabilitated, and the debts will be discharged, when he or she has
made all payments in accordance with the court-approved plan. This discharge is of
greater scope than that granted by Chapter 7. The debtor may also be discharged after
making part of the payments if the failure of the plan was not directly attributed to the
debtor and if all of the creditors received amounts at least equivalent to what they
would have received under a Chapter 7 liquidation proceeding.

REVIEW QUESTIONS

1. Define bankruptcy, debtor, creditor, and debt.

2. When is a trustee appointed, and what are the trustee's duties?

3. Explain the terms *preferential transfer* and *fraudulent conveyance.*

4. List the priority distribution of unsecured claims.

5. What claims are nondischargeable?

6. List the property that will be classified as exempt.

7. Explain the three major types of bankruptcy proceedings.

8. Winstein, Kavensky Company executed a security agreement in favor of Alfred Klass, one of its owners, giving Klass a security interest in funds that he contributed to the company. Klass wanted to qualify as a secured creditor because he knew that the company might go bankrupt and that this would assure him of getting repaid. The company did go bankrupt, but the bankruptcy trustee set aside Klass's secured claims. What result? *Klass* v. *Winstein, Kavensky, et. al.,* 579 N.E. 2d 365 (Ill. App. 3 Dist. 1991).

9. Alfred Klass paid himself $84,500 as accrued salary before his company, Winstein, Kavensky filed bankruptcy. The company sought to have this payment set aside as a preferential transfer. What result? *Klass* v. *Winstein, Kavensky, et. al.,* 579 N.E. 2d 365 (Ill. App. 3 Dist. 1991).

10. Johnson was traveling south on Highway 55 when his car was struck from behind by Perrett. Both cars traveled more than 300 feet after the point of impact, and Johnson was thrown from his car and killed. A nearly empty bottle of vodka was found in Perrett's car. Subsequent tests proved that Perrett was drunk. A wrongful death action was brought by the widow of the deceased. She received a judgment for $23,000, which was to be enforced through garnishment of Perrett's salary. A week later Perrett filed a voluntary bankruptcy petition and raised the defense that his debts, including this judgment, were discharged in bankruptcy. What result? *Perrett* v. *Johnson,* 253 Miss. 209, 175 So. 2d 497 (1965).

28

Bailments

INTRODUCTION

A *bailment* is a temporary transfer of possession of personal property to another for a specific purpose with the understanding that it will be returned upon the fulfillment of that purpose or at the owner's request. The *bailor* is the owner of the personal property. The *bailee* is the person to whom the personal property has been transferred. The bailee must exercise a certain degree of care toward the property while it is in his or her possession. The purposes for which bailments are made include (1) loan of property; (2) delivery of property for servicing, such as cleaning, repairing, or remodeling; and (3) delivery of property for storage or safekeeping until requested.

The key to determining whether a bailment exists is knowing whether the owner has turned over possession or title of the personal property. Delivery of possession constitutes a bailment; delivery of the title constitutes a sales contract. A sales contract is covered by Article 2 of the Uniform Commercial Code; a bailment is not. A sales contract in excess of $500 must be in writing to satisfy the statute of frauds; a bailment contract need not be in writing. A bailment may be expressed orally or in writing, or it may be implied from the actions of the parties. It is wise to have a writing to evidence the transfer of possession, but it is not a legal requirement.

STANDARD OF CARE OWED BY A BAILEE

There are three types of bailments: for the benefit of the bailee, for the mutual benefit of the bailor and the bailee, and for the benefit of the bailor. Each type requires a different standard of care on the part of the bailee.

Benefit of the Bailee

When the bailor transfers possession of property to the bailee solely for the bailee's use and enjoyment, the bailee is held to a high standard of care toward the property and will be liable for the slightest negligence.

EXAMPLE | Hughes was attending his first black-tie affair but did not own a tuxedo. He borrowed one from his friend Getty, then purchased a pair of pure white sneakers to complete his outfit. While discussing the manufacture of his overgrown airplane, Hughes accidentally dribbled tomato sauce on the tuxedo. When Hughes returned the tuxedo, Getty asked him to pay for the cleaning costs. Hughes strenuously objected. Was Hughes responsible? Yes! This is a bailment contract for the sole benefit of Hughes, the bailee.

Mutual Benefit of the Bailor and the Bailee

The most prevalent type of bailment is for the mutual benefit of both parties. If a bailor transfers possession of property for the purpose of renting the property to the bailee or having the bailee store the property or perform a service on it in return for compensation, then the bailee must take reasonable care of the property. Should damage occur the bailee would be liable if he or she could reasonably have been expected to prevent the damage in question.

EXAMPLE | Hilton brings his Rolls-Royce to DeLorean's service station for repairs. He leaves the car overnight. DeLorean has taken steps to guard against vandalism by installing a sophisticated security system with an alarm that rings at a central station. Despite the protective device vandals attack DeLorean's station during the night and strip Hilton's car. Hilton sues DeLorean for damages. Is he entitled to collect? No! This is a bailment for the mutual benefit of both the bailor and the bailee. Hilton is deriving valuable consideration in the form of repairs to his car, while DeLorean is receiving payment for the work performed. DeLorean is a bailee, not an insurer. He owes Hilton a duty to exercise reasonable care over the car, and he will be liable for only ordinary negligence. By taking the precaution of installing a security system, DeLorean has satisfied his duty of reasonable care; he is not responsible for the damages to Hilton's car.

Thomas v. Supermarkets General Corp.
586 N.Y.S. 2d 454 (Sup. 1992)

The Reverend Alan Thomas rented the video *Who Framed Roger Rabbit* from Pathmark for his children aged four and seven. At the end of the film, a pornographic passage had been added on. Thomas claimed that both he and his children suffered extreme emotional distress. The issue is whether Pathmark violated the standard of care required in a bailment contract by failing to examine the contents of their videotapes.

The court ruled,

> The standard of care to which defendant must conform is that of a reasonably prudent merchant or supermarket under these circumstances. There is nothing in the record to indicate the defendant reasonably knew or should have known of the existence of this passage on the tape. Contrary to plaintiff's suggestion, this duty does not extend to an examination of each videotape, in its entirety, in their inventory.

The court concluded, "Although plainly an unfortunate and unpleasant experience, simply stated, the law does not provide a remedy for every wrong." Judgment for Pathmark.

Benefit of the Bailor

If the bailee receives possession of the bailor's property and agrees to hold or store it without compensation, then the bailment is solely for the benefit of the bailor. The bailee owes a lower standard of care to the property and will be liable only if grossly negligent.

EXAMPLE Two old friends, Rockefeller and Morgan, are vacationing on the Riviera. Rockefeller, deciding to go for a swim, gives his watch to Morgan and asks him to keep an eye on it. Morgan tells Rockefeller he will wrap the watch in a beach towel. When Rockefeller returns he dries himself off, and the two of them head back to the hotel. They suddenly realize the watch is gone. They search frantically but to no avail. Rockefeller insists that Morgan pay for the watch. Morgan says, "To hell with you!" Is Morgan responsible? No! Because this contract is for the sole benefit of Rockefeller, the bailor, Morgan, the bailee, has only a slight duty of care. Because both he and Rockefeller forgot about the watch, he is not liable. His actions were not grossly negligent.

A bailment for the mutual benefit of both the bailor and the bailee is a contract. A bailment solely for the benefit of the bailor or bailee is a gratuitous bailment because no consideration is received in return. Bailees will be liable for loss or destruction of property resulting from accident, fire, or theft only if it occurs through their negligence in failing to meet the appropriate standard of care. They are not insurers of property unless the contract so stipulates.

LIABILITY OF A BAILEE

A bailee is liable for failing to exercise the proper standard of care with regard to the safety of the bailed property. This liability may be limited by contract to a certain value. The bailor must be informed of the limitation by conspicuous notice. A ticket given as an indication of ownership that attempts to limit or disclaim liability is not conspicuous; something more is required. The privilege of limiting liability does not extend to damages resulting from unauthorized use of the bailed property by the bailee or an agent of the bailee. In such a case the bailee is liable for any loss regardless of the care exercised over the property.

SPECIAL TYPES OF BAILMENTS

Finders

A bailment is implied when a person finds lost property. The finder is a bailee for the true owner. Because the bailment is created solely for the benefit of the true owner–bailor, the finder owes a lower standard of care to the found property.

EXAMPLE | J. P. Morgan had agreed to deliver 5,000 gold bars to the Rothschilds in London. He placed the gold aboard a brand-new ocean liner called the *Titanic*. The *Titanic* embarked for London, but while crossing the icy Atlantic it rammed the top of an iceberg and sank. A number of years later, deep-sea divers discovered the wreck and claimed its treasure. The Rothschilds sued the divers for return of the gold and produced the bill of lading for it. Are they entitled to recover the gold? Yes! A finder of lost property is entitled to it against all save the true owner. The divers actually became constructive bailees for the true owners, the Rothschilds, once they had taken possession of the gold.

Safe-Deposit Boxes

A bank that maintains safe-deposit boxes is liable for the contents of a box if it has been damaged, destroyed, or stolen through the negligence of the bank. This is true even though the contents of the box have not been declared because the bank realizes that people keep valuable property in safe-deposit boxes. Because rental of a safe-deposit box is a bailment for the mutual benefit of both the depositor (bailor) and the bank (bailee), the standard of care owed by the bank is a reasonable one—reasonable in light of the high caliber of security maintained over the safe-deposit vault.

EXAMPLE | The ever-popular Mrs. McLean placed her Hope diamond in a safe-deposit box at Mellon Bank. Later that year the notorious bank robber, Willie Sutton, robbed the bank's safe-deposit vault. Mrs. McLean sued Mellon for $2,000,000, the value of the diamond. Is she entitled to the full value? Yes, if she can prove ownership of the diamond, its value, its presence in her safe-deposit box at the time of the theft, and the bank's negligence in maintaining its security system.

Coat Checks

An establishment providing coat checks creates a bailment when the customer relinquishes possession of a coat to the cloakroom attendant. The degree of care required of the establishment depends on whether a fee is charged. If a fee is charged, the bailment is for the mutual benefit of both the establishment and the customer, and reasonable care must be exercised. When a fee is not charged, a bailment is created for the sole benefit of the customer, and the establishment owes a lower standard of care. Generally, if a person hangs a coat in an unattended cloakroom, no bailment is created. But courts have ruled to the contrary where a coat is hung in a closet provided by a physician or a dentist in his or her reception room.

EXAMPLE | Lady Astor was having dinner at the Copa with her husband. When she entered the nightclub, she checked her sable coat for a two dollar fee. In return she received a ticket disclaiming all liability. After a gala evening of wining and dining, she sought to reclaim her coat. The fur coat had slipped off the hanger because it was too heavy. The coat had lain on the dusty floor, where it was trampled on and a large hole was burned in it by a cigarette stub. Lady Astor sued the Copa for the damages stemming from their negligence in handling her fur coat. The Copa asserted that they had effectively disclaimed all liability. Will Lady Astor triumph? Yes! The coat-check attendant acted negligently in placing such an expensive coat on a hanger that would not support it. Furthermore, a ticket given as an indication of ownership cannot be used to disclaim liability for negligence.

Parking Lots

A parking lot that requires car owners to leave their car keys with an attendant has created a bailment for the mutual benefit of the lot operator and the car owner. Once possession of the keys has been transferred, the parking lot, through its attendant, has the right to exercise dominion and control over the car. This gives rise to a bailment contract. In addition to being responsible for property left in a car's passenger compartment, a parking lot is generally responsible only for property ordinarily expected to be in the trunk of a car unless the contents of the trunk have been made known to parking lot personnel.

A park-and-lock, where car owners park in a lot without transferring possession of the keys, does not create a bailment contract because the parking lot is not exercising any control over the car. The car owner is merely being given permission to park in the lot. This relationship is something less than a bailment. The permission guarantees the car owner that the operator of the lot will refrain from removing the car from the lot or otherwise causing it damage. If the damage is caused by someone other than the parking lot operator or an attendant, then the lot has no liability.

A parking lot that requires the car owner to present a ticket to a guard for access to the lot is considered to have created a bailment contract even though the lot operator does not have the keys to the car and therefore does not have control over it. The relationship is a bailment because of the guard's power to exclude from the lot all but car owners who pay.

EXAMPLE | Vanderbilt and Dupont were attending a Broadway musical called *If I Were a Rich Man*. Vanderbilt parked his car in a lot across the street from the theater and gave the attendant the ignition key. Dupont parked a few blocks down in a park-and-lock on Tenth Avenue to save a few bucks. After they left the theater, both men found that their cars had been vandalized. Both men sued the parking lot owners. Will either Vanderbilt or Dupont recover? Vanderbilt may recover for breach of the bailment contract because the lot owner failed to exercise reasonable care in denying vandals access to cars parked in the lot. Dupont will not recover because he received a mere license to park. No bailment contract was created between him and the park-and-lock owner.

Car Rentals

In car rental situations, the bailment is for the mutual benefit of both parties. The person renting the car is the bailee, and the owner of the car rental business is the bailor. The bailee has a duty to pay for all ordinary repair and maintenance expenses. This duty may be altered by a stipulation in the contract. The bailor's duty is limited only to extraordinary repairs that are not normally needed by a car of similar condition, age, and mileage. If a third person is injured by the person renting the car (bailee), the bailee is responsible for those injuries as though he or she were the original owner; the owner of the rented car is not liable.

EXAMPLE | The Kennedys are inviting a few New York associates for an afternoon of sipping tea, trimming sails, and playing touch-tackle on Cape Cod. They hire a Volkswagen minibus from Budget Rent A Car to transport their guests to Massachusetts. On Interstate 95 they experience a sudden stop in motion when a piece of glass punctures a tire. Because neither Kennedy nor his associates wish to soil their hands with a laborer's task, they have the car towed off the expressway to the nearest service station, where the tire is repaired. The tow-and-repair bill comes to $54. Kennedy pays the sum and sues Budget for reimbursement. Is Kennedy entitled to reimbursement? No! A flat tire caused by glass is an ordinary expenditure that must be anticipated by the individual renting the car.

Amoroso v. Samuel Frieland Family Int.
604 So. 2d 827 (Fla. App. 4 Dist. 1992)

While Mr. and Mrs. Amoroso were staying at the Diplomat Hotel in Hollywood, Florida, they rented a sailboat through a rental stand on the hotel grounds. The boats were owned by Sunrise Water Sports. The stand was operated by Atlantic Sailing Center. The fee was charged to the hotel bill. While they were sailing, the crossbar on the sailboat cracked, injuring Mrs. Amoroso. A welder had repaired the crossbar a few days before, but it cracked in the same place. An expert testified that the crossbar should have been replaced, not repaired. Mrs. Amoroso sued the Diplomat, Sunrise, Atlantic, and the welder on the basis of breach of the implied warranty of merchantability.

The issue is whether implied warranties extend to lessors of rental property.

The court held,

> [T]he renter must rely on the lessor to provide a chattel fit for its ordinary use. The renter of a car expects that it will function as an automobile, and its wheels won't fall off during the rental period. Likewise, the renter of a sailboat should expect that its mast will not break and fall down during the period of the rental. We hold that there is an implied warranty of fitness for ordinary use in a lease transaction.

The court found against the Diplomat and Sunrise. Atlantic was not liable because it was the agent of Sunrise, and a third party cannot recover against both principal and agent. The welder was not liable because the weld was not defective, and the welder had no duty to inform Sunrise that the crossbar should be replaced. Judgment for Amoroso against the Diplomat and Sunrise.

Hotels

Hotels are liable to their guests for the full value of property that is stolen or destroyed because of the negligence of the hotel for its employees. A guest is a person who is staying at the hotel for a limited time while traveling. By providing a safe and posting conspicuous notices of its availability, a hotel may limit its liability when a guest's property is stolen or damaged without negligence on the hotel's part. For items not placed in a hotel safe, each state restricts recovery to a maximum amount, which is usually not very high. A hotel providing parking facilities becomes a bailee only if it takes possession of the keys to the guest's automobile.

EXAMPLE | Lady Diana Windmere and her husband, while vacationing in Las Vegas, are staying at the Lucky "7." When they check in the desk clerk informs them that all valuables should be placed in the hotel safe; otherwise the hotel's liability will be limited to $500 for personal effects, as set forth by the state statute. A sign conveying the same message hangs in the lobby. Lady Diana places her tiara in the safe but retains her diamond necklace and bracelet. While Lady Diana is taking a dip in the pool, the hotel maid steals her necklace. Later that evening her bracelet is stolen by the occupant of a suite down the hall. Lady Diana had carelessly left her door open when she went to dine in the hotel restaurant. Lady Diana sues the hotel for the full value of her stolen jewelry. Will she recover it? She will recover the value of the necklace because it was stolen by a hotel employee. Her award for the stolen bracelet will be limited to $500 because it was not placed in the safe according to the notification.

Warehouses

Warehouses are businesses engaged in the storing of goods in return for compensation. When a warehouse receives goods he issues a warehouse receipt, which is a document of title. It entitles the holder to title and possession of the goods, it evidences the existence of a contract for storage, and it sets forth the terms of that contract. Warehouse receipts along with negotiation and transfer are governed by the Uniform Commercial Code under Article 7.

Warehouses may limit their liability by conspicuous notice. The limitation must be set forth in terms of units or by weight. The person storing the goods must also be given the choice of paying a higher rate for unlimited liability. Although warehouses are bailees, they are subject to extensive state and federal regulation in addition to Article 7 of the UCC.

EXAMPLE | On Saturday Willy Hearst stored 1.5 million copies of the Sunday edition of his newspaper, the *Journal American,* in a warehouse on Park Row. The contract provided for unlimited liability on the warehouse's part. That evening a fire broke out, burning the contents of five warehouses on Park Row, including the one where Hearst's newspapers were stored. Hearst sued the warehouse for the value of his newspapers. Will the warehouse have to pay even if he did not cause the fire? Yes! The unlimited liability provision is designated to cover instances where the warehouse is not at fault. If Hearst had not paid the additional cost for unlimited liability, would the result be different? Yes! Hearst would be entitled to recover only the amount per pound stipulated in the limited liability provision. If Hearst could prove that—even though the fire was not caused by the warehouse—the installation of a sprinkler system would have minimized damages, would this change the result? Yes! This evidence would go to prove that the warehouse failed to exercise reasonable care in regard to the safety of the newspapers.

Common Carriers

Common carriers are transporters of goods and passengers who offer their services to the general public in return for compensation. A common carrier is a special type of bailee. On receipt of goods it is held to an extraordinary standard of care, almost that of an insurer. Common carriers are responsible for all damages or injuries that occur, without regard to fault or negligence. Common carriers occupy a position of privilege and in consequence hold a public trust. Furthermore they must serve all who apply, and they have an affirmative duty to provide reasonable services.

A common carrier issues a bill of lading for land or sea transportation, or an air bill for transportation by air, when it accepts goods from a shipper. The shipper may negotiate this bill to his or her purchaser. Bills of lading and air bills are documents of title evidencing the receipt of goods for shipment. The person holding the bill of lading (the purchaser of the goods) is entitled to title and possession of the goods on the presentation of the bill. Bills of lading and their negotiation and transfer are treated in Article 7 of the UCC.

The common carrier has a duty to deliver the goods listed in the bailment contract on time. A carrier's failure to fulfill this duty gives the shipper a cause of action for damages. Common carriers are extensively regulated by federal and state statutes as well as by Article 7 of the UCC. They may limit their liability by contract in accordance with the governing statutes. Common carriers generally limit their liability for goods to a certain value per package. An additional higher rate must be offered for individuals who want unlimited liability for their packages.

EXAMPLE | The Shah of Iran sent 10,000 barrels of oil to Hunt by ship. When the ship passed through the Sargasso Sea in the Bermuda Triangle, it sank. The Shah's bailment contract with the shipping line provides that liability for each barrel shall be limited to $750. Each barrel is worth $1,000. What will the Shah recover? He will recover $750 per barrel. This is true as long as the limitation placed in the contract is in accordance with the appropriate federal statute governing common carriers and interstate shipments.

Although common carriers have a duty to serve the general public, they need not accept goods that are not within their capacity, are not of the kind normally carried, are improperly prepared, or are dangerous to the health and safety of the carrier's passengers and crew.

Although a common carrier is generally not responsible for loss of, destruction of, or damage to goods occasioned by an act of God, the public enemy, the negligence of the shipper, or the inherent nature of the goods, it can be held responsible if it is negligent in dealing with the conditions that result. The burden of proof remains on the carrier, which must prove that it was not negligent.

An act of God is a force of nature that cannot be anticipated and provided against. Examples are extreme weather conditions in places with no past records of such conditions, earthquakes, and volcanic eruptions. If the force of nature unexpectedly destroys goods in the carrier's possession, the carrier will be absolved from liability.

The term *public enemy* refers not to hijackers, looters, or the FBI's ten most wanted, but rather to enemy nations at war with the United States, pirates of the seven seas, and revolutionists seeking to overthrow the government.

A common carrier is not liable for any destruction or damage to goods if they are packaged, labeled, or loaded in a negligent manner by the shipper. The carrier has a duty to follow reasonable instructions from the shipper. If the goods are damaged as a result of the shipper's instructions, the carrier is not responsible.

A common carrier is held to a higher standard of care for perishable goods. However, a carrier will not be liable for natural spoilage of perishable goods if they are shipped without delay. Concerning fruits and vegetables it is not the carrier's responsibility to examine each piece to see how ripe it is and whether it may spoil during shipping; this is the shipper's obligation.

Connecting Carriers

Where two or more carriers are required to make delivery, the initial carrier is liable for a loss even though it may be occasioned by a connecting carrier. The shipper may sue either carrier or both for damages. If the initial carrier is relegated to paying the damages, it has a right to be indemnified by the connecting carrier where the connecting carrier is at fault for the loss.

Passengers

A common carrier has a contractual obligation to take reasonable care of passengers while the passengers are on the carrier and when they enter or leave the carrier. This reasonable care extends to protection of passengers from negligence of the carrier's employees and from other passengers. What is reasonable will vary with a passenger's age and health. Because a cause of action against a common carrier is predicated on negligence, the three-year statute of limitations for negligence applies.

REVIEW QUESTIONS

1. Define bailment, bailor, bailee, warehouseman, and common carrier.
2. List and explain the various kinds of bailments.
3. What is the standard of care owed by a bailee in each of the three types of bailments?
4. Capezzaro was the victim of a robbery. The police arrested a suspect named Winfrey and found the money that had been stolen from Capezzaro in Winfrey's girdle. Subsequently the indictments against Winfrey were dismissed, and the police returned the allegedly stolen money to her without

notifying Capezzaro. Capezzaro sued the police for returning the money to Winfrey. He argued that his claim for the money did not lose its validity solely because the indictments against Winfrey were dismissed. What result? *Capezzaro* v. *Winfrey,* 153 N.J. Super. 267, 379 A. 2d 493 (1977).

5. Noreen Wolf had arthroscopic surgery performed on her left knee by Dr. Chapman. A piece of metal was left inside. Subsequently the piece of metal was removed in another operation at Cleveland Metro Hospital. In Wolf's malpractice suit against Dr. Chapman, the piece of metal was key. When she requested it from the hospital, the hospital said that the piece of metal had been discarded. The request was made two weeks after the operation; the hospital had a thirty-day retention period. What result? *Wolf* v. *Lakewood Hospital,* 598 N.E. 2d 160 (Ohio App. 8 Dist. 1991).

6. Barlow leased dairy equipment from Agristor Leasing in 1981. In 1986 Barlow defaulted on the payment. Agristor sought to repossess the equipment for nonpayment. Is this a bailment? What result? *Agristor Leasing* v. *Barlow,* 579 NYS. 2d 476 (A.D. 3 Dept. 1992).

7. Pius Affolter stored his boat at the Virginia Key Marina. Personal property was stolen from his boat. The bailment contract provided, "Owners to have their own insurance coverage." The marina argued that this clause shifts the risk of loss to the bailor even if the bailee is negligent. What result? *Affolter* v. *Marina,* 601 So. 2d 1296 (Fla. App. 3 Dist. 1992).

8. Advian Ruiz fell off a scaffold when it was struck by a bobcat machine. The scaffold equipment had been leased to Ruiz's employer by Scaffolding & Shoring Systems, Inc. The scaffold had not been erected by Scaffolding & Shoring, and there was no defect in its design. Ruiz argued that Scaffolding & Shoring had a duty to inspect the scaffold after it had been erected. What result? *Ruiz* v. *Pardue,* 420 S.E. 2d 1 (Ga. App. 1992).

9. Timothy Passamano claimed that a car rental agreement signed with North-West was a contract of insurance between North-West and him. North-West argued that the renting of a car is a bailment. What result? *Passamano* v. *Travelers Indemnity Co.,* 835 P. 201 514 (Colo. App. 1991).

10. Mr. and Mrs. Moore were granted a divorce. Mrs. Moore was awarded the horses and sheep, and Mr. Moore was awarded the ranch, although she was given access to the livestock. Mrs. Moore claimed that the fact that the livestock remained on the ranch created an implied bailment and that Mr. Moore did not care for them properly. What result? *Moore* v. *Moore,* 835 P. 2d 1148 (Wyo. 1992).

29

Insurance

INTRODUCTION

Insurance is a contract in which the insurer agrees to indemnify the insured, or the designated beneficiary, if loss to property or injury or death of a person ensues. Insurance protects people against risk of loss. An insurance policy is a contract between the insurer and the insured that sets forth the rights and responsibilities of each, including the limit of the insurer's liability and the premiums to be paid by the insured in consideration for the insurance. The *insurer* is an insurance company that agrees to be liable for any loss sustained by the insured up to the face value of the policy. The face value of an insurance policy is the insurer's limit of liability. The *insured* is any individual, family, partnership, or corporation that pays premiums in return for insurance coverage. An insurance company designates premiums at a certain rate depending on the amount of insurance purchased by the insured.

An insurance company operates through its agents, specifically individuals who convince people to buy insurance. These insurance agents are employees of the insurance company and are usually paid salaries plus commissions based on a percentage of the face value of insurance policies they sell. An insurance broker is an independent contractor who is the agent of the insured rather than an agent of the insurance company. An insurance broker services clients by attempting to place their insurance needs with any of a number of insurance companies. Brokers receive compensation by charging their clients fees for the services they render. Brokers may become agents for an insurance company if the company authorizes them to accept premiums on its behalf.

341

The law of contracts is applicable to insurance policies because they are special contracts. The following contractual elements must be present for an insurance policy to be valid: **PALACE.**

Purpose (lawful)
Agreement
Legal capacity
Act
Consideration
Executed in proper form

When a person expresses a wish to take out an insurance policy, this is considered to be an offer. The insurance agent who suggested taking out a policy is merely inviting the person to make an offer. An agent does not usually have the authority to accept an offer to contract for insurance. With the possible exception of fire and casualty insurance, an insurance policy must be approved by the insurance company's home office. A question of fact may arise concerning the agent's apparent authority when a premium is paid and the agent has given the insured a binding receipt with the assurance that a policy is in effect.

A person buying insurance must have sufficient capacity to contract. A minor who purchases insurance can not abrogate the contract solely because of his or her age. Otherwise a minor could purchase fire, automobile, health, or term life insurance and then request a return of the premiums upon reaching legal age. The result would be that no insurance company would insure the property, automobile, health, or life of a minor. This is an exception to the general rule concerning legal capacity because the benefit of a minor's being able to purchase insurance outweighs the underlying risks of incapacity.

Progressive Preferred Ins. Co. v. Brown
413 S.E. 2d 430 (Ga. 1992)

On January, 18, 1988, Progressive Insurance mailed a notice to Johnny Mack Brown stating that it would renew his auto insurance. "Your policy will expire on 02/23/88. Payment must reach Progressive before 02/23/88 to keep your coverage in continuous effect through 08/23/88." The policy stated, "If you pay your premium, we, the Progressive Insurance Companies, agree to insure you. . . . Your failure to pay the required continuation or renewal premium means that you have declined our offer."

Upon receipt of Brown's check on February 25, Progressive issued a renewal statement. On March 2 Brown's bank dishonored the check for insufficient funds and did so again on March 11, when the check was redeposited. On March 17 Shirley Brown had an auto accident. Progressive denied coverage because of the Browns' failure to pay the premium.

The issue is whether Progressive's issuance of a renewal notice obligates it to pay.

The court held, "[W]here a check is taken for an insurance premium, it will ordinarily be assumed that the acceptance was conditioned upon proper presentation, so that if payment is refused, and in the meantime the period in which payment could be made has elapsed, the insurer may declare the policy forfeited for nonpayment." Judgment for Progressive.

LIFE INSURANCE

Life insurance is a third-party beneficiary contract in which the insurer agrees to pay the face value of the policy to a designated beneficiary on the death of the insured.

Insurable Interest

A party must have an *insurable interest* to insure the life of a person. A person can insure his or her own life, a spouse can insure the life of the other spouse, and a parent can insure the life of a child.

A person may also establish an insurable interest in the life of another based on blood ties, love and affection, or employment   or on the fact that a debt is owed, if it can be shown that the person requesting the insurance will suffer a financial loss if the person he or she wishes to insure should die. In addition to establishing an insurable interest, the prospective purchaser must secure the insured's consent. Before an insurance company will issue a policy, it will usually require the insured's signature consenting to the creation of a policy on his or her life. This requirement applies to all relationships except one involving a young child who is not able to sign. In this case the policy will be issued to the parent on the basis of his or her signature alone.

A partnership may insure the life of each partner up to the value of each partner's interest. The partnership will pay the proceeds of the policy to the heirs of the deceased partner in lieu of permanently dissolving the partnership and accounting for the deceased partner's share. A corporation may insure the lives of its executives for the expected financial loss it will suffer if an executive dies. A creditor can insure a debtor up to the amount of the debt owed. An insurable interest need exist only at the time when the insurance is taken out.

EXAMPLE | Elvis married Priscilla when he was thirty-two. Each had taken out a life insurance policy on the other. Six years later they were divorced. When Elvis was forty-two years old, he died. Priscilla, as beneficiary, attempted to collect the proceeds of the policy on Elvis's life, but the insurance company refused to pay her because she no longer had any insurable interest in her husband after the divorce. Has Priscilla any recourse? Yes! The insurer's contention is true but insignificant. Priscilla is entitled to the proceeds as the named beneficiary because she had an insurable interest in her husband when the policy was taken out.

Types of Life Insurance

Ordinary Straight Life On the death of the insured, a fixed sum is payable to the designated beneficiary; premiums must be paid for the entire life of the insured.

Limited Payment Life Limited payment life is the same as ordinary straight life except that premiums need be paid only for a specified period, such as fifteen, twenty, or twenty-five years.

Endowment The insured pays premiums until he or she reaches a designated age, at which time the insurer will pay a lump sum to the insured. If the insured dies prematurely, the lump sum will be paid to the named beneficiary on the date of the insured's death.

Annuity The insured pays either one premium in a lump sum at the time the policy is taken out or makes period payments until retirement. In return the insurance company promises to make periodic payments to the insured either for a fixed amount of time or until the insured dies. The amount of the periodic payments is usually fixed at the time the policy is taken out, but the insured may elect for payments to fluctuate with prevailing interest rates by choosing a variable annuity.

Term Insurance A fixed sum is payable to a covered beneficiary if the insured dies within the term covered by the insurance. Premiums must be paid for the duration of the term.

EXAMPLE

1. At age nineteen Elvis takes out an $800,000 policy on his own life, with quarterly premiums payable until the date of his death. Elvis dies at the age of forty-two. His beneficiary will be entitled to the face value of the policy as long as his premiums have been paid up to date. What type of life insurance policy is this? Ordinary straight life insurance!

2. Assume the facts as given above, but assume that Elvis is only required to pay premiums for fifteen years, until he is thirty-four. What type of policy would this be? Fifteen-year limited payment life!

3. Elvis is thiry years old when he takes out a $200,000 insurance policy that requires him to pay premiums until he reaches the age of sixty-five, at which time a lump sum will be paid to him. If Elvis dies at forty-two, his beneficiary will be entitled to the $200,000. What type of coverage is this? Endowment!

4. For each of the next ten years Elvis, at age thirty, invests $50,000 with a life insurance company. The insurance company agrees to pay Elvis or his named beneficiary $30,000 a month when Elvis reaches or would have reached sixty. What type of insurance has Elvis purchased? An annuity!

5. Elvis is thirty-two years old when he marries. Nine months later he and his wife have a child. Elvis decides to take out a $50,000 term policy on his life for ten years with his daughter as beneficiary. Because Elvis dies within the term, his daughter will be entitled to the $50,000. If Elvis had lived beyond the term, the policy would have been worthless. What type of insurance is this called? Term insurance!

The policy issued by the company constitutes the entire agreement between the parties. Although the statute of frauds does not require a life insurance policy to be in writing because it is possible for the insured to die within one year, many states now require a life insurance policy to be in writing.

Standard Provisions

An incontestable clause provides that the validity of the policy may not be disputed because of material misrepresentations after two years from the issuance of the policy. The two-year period gives the insurer sufficient time to investigate the statements made by the insured.

Misstatement of age is not a material misrepresentation; the beneficiary may recover the amount of insurance the premiums would buy on the basis of the policyholder's correct age.

A change of beneficiary clause allows the policyholder to change the name of the beneficiary, usually upon written notice, at any time before the death of the insured. Although this provision is usually standard, if it were not included in the policy, the policyholder would have no right to change the beneficiary without the consent of the beneficiary.

A grace period of twenty to thirty days past the due date is allowed, during which the policyholder may pay the premium. In most states the insurer must send a written notice to this effect.

A nonforfeiture clause provides that if the premium is not paid by the end of the grace period, the owner of the policy has a choice to

terminate the policy and accept the cash surrender value,

apply the premiums to purchase paid-up life insurance in a reduced amount,

apply the premiums to purchase term insurance, or

apply for a loan against the cash value of the policy in an amount sufficient to pay the required premium.

The cash surrender value is the amount of reserves built up in addition to the portion of the premium used to pay claims. Not all of the premium is used to pay life insurance claims; the extra amount is placed in a reserve fund. The amount in the reserve fund is known as the cash surrender value. This is the amount that will be paid to a policyholder who decides to terminate insurance coverage.

EXAMPLE | The Colonel purchases a one-million-dollar straight life insurance policy on his client, Elvis, who is twenty years old at the time. After paying premiums for twelve years, he defaults. Assume that the annual premium is $10,000, the cash value of the policy is $130,000, ten years of term insurance with a face value of one million dollars could be purchased with the cash value, and the premiums paid would also buy $350,000 worth of paid-up life insurance. What options are available to the Colonel? (1) Terminate the policy and accept the cash surrender value of $130,000, (2) apply the cash value to purchase one million dollars' worth of term insurance, (3) use the $100,000 premiums paid to purchase $350,000 of paid-up life insurance, or (4) apply for a $10,000 loan against the cash value of the policy to pay the annual premium and retain the present insurance coverage.

FIRE INSURANCE

Fire insurance is a contract created for the purpose of indemnifying the insured for property loss caused by fire.

Substantial Economic Interest

The insured must have a substantial economic interest in the property to satisfy the insurable interest requirement. Of course one can insure one's own property. In addition the following relationships give rise to an insurable interest in property:

>   Bailee
>   Tenant
>   Contractor
>   Buyer of goods
>   Shareholder of corporate property
>   Mortgagee

A bailee can insure goods incident to a bailment contract when they are in his or her possession. A tenant can insure the property rented for the duration of the lease. Usually a landlord will maintain adequate insurance, but a tenant will be required to insure his or her own personal property. A contractor who is building a house on land owned by another may purchase insurance because he or she has a substantial economic interest in the house until it is completed. A buyer may insure goods once they have become identified to the contract of sale. A shareholder has an insurable interest in corporate property because the assets of the corporation are directly related to the value of the shareholder's stock. A lending institution or an individual mortgagee has a substantial economic interest in the mortgaged property and may acquire insurance coverage up to the balance remaining on the mortgage. The insured's substantial economic interest must exist at the time the insurance is purchased and at the time the loss occurs.

Coinsurance Provisions

Insurance coverage of 80 percent of the fair market value of the property must be maintained; otherwise the insured becomes a coinsurer. A coinsurer is liable for the proportion of the loss to the property for which he or she is underinsured.

EXAMPLE | Elvis purchased Graceland for $100,000 and took out an insurance policy for the required 80 percent of its value. Six years later the house had doubled in value, but Elvis never increased the insurance. That same year a fire partially destroyed the study. The insurance adjuster estimated the loss to be $20,000. What percentage of the loss will Elvis recover from the insurance company? Fifty percent of $10,000! Because Elvis did not have Graceland insured for 80 percent of its fair market value of $200,000, he will be entitled to $80,000 divided by $160,000, or 50 percent. This is the amount of insurance Elvis had divided by the amount he was required to carry. Elvis became a coinsurer for the other 50 percent, or $10,000.

A person who intentionally ignites a fire on property that he or she has insured will be barred from recovering the proceeds of the policy.

EXAMPLE | King Creole purchased the Elvis Wax Museum in New Orleans. For many years the museum attracted thousands to see the King of Rock 'n' Roll. King Creole wanted to move the museum to a larger area where he could build a bigger facility and have enough parking spaces to accommodate all of the Elvis fans. He had difficulty selling the museum because of its unusual construction. Late one night King Creole entered the building with a can of kerosene and ignited a fire. The building was consumed in flames, and the museum literally melted. King Creole notified the insurance company immediately and submitted a claim to collect the proceeds. The insurer paid out the claim and then discovered King Creole's fraud. Will the insurance company be able to recoup its payment of the proceeds? Yes! Arson is a crime. King Creole may not profit from his own criminal conduct.

LIABILITY INSURANCE

Businesses acquire liability insurance to protect themselves from lawsuits by people who are injured on their premises or through the negligence of employees acting within the scope of their employment. Businesses also need liability coverage in a variety of areas. Employers have workers' compensation coverage for injuries sustained by employees on the job. Manufacturers carry product liability insurance to protect them from lawsuits arising from injuries caused by the use of their product. Common carriers use insurance to indemnify shippers whose goods are damaged or destroyed through the fault of the carrier. Insurance protects contractors by covering employees and subcontractors who are injured due to unsafe working conditions or other workers' negligence. Landlords need liability coverage for injuries caused to their tenants through neglect in maintenance of the tenants' apartments or areas of common use such as hallways, sidewalks, and courtyards.

Homeowners also need liability insurance to protect them from lawsuits brought by individuals injured on their premises—for example, guests, repair people, delivery people, and gas and electric meter readers. This protection is usually afforded in a homeowner's policy.

HOMEOWNER'S INSURANCE

A homeowner's policy provides comprehensive coverage incorporating standard fire insurance, liability insurance, and casualty insurance plus an assortment of riders to suit the needs of the individual homeowner.

CASUALTY INSURANCE

In most states casualty insurance applies to accidental damage to property. It may cover property of the insured that is damaged or stolen during a burglary or other civil commotion. It also covers the insured's real or personal property damaged by vandalism or malicious mischief. Personal property of the insured may also be covered while the insured is away from his or her principal place of residence—that is, while visiting, vacationing, or traveling on business.

Casualty insurance also covers the property of others that is accidentally damaged by the insured. Casualty insurance is usually included in a homeowner's policy, but it may be acquired separately. In some states casualty insurance applies to personal injury caused to the insured or others, but for convenience these areas are dealt with under health insurance, liability insurance, and automobile insurance.

HEALTH INSURANCE

Health insurance protects individuals who need medical treatment. There are two types of coverage: hospital service and surgical-medical service. These services may be administered jointly, as when a patient is admitted to a hospital for surgery, or separately, as when a patient visits a physician at an office or clinic for medical care. Coverage may be extended to home care services. Health insurance may be provided for an individual, family, or group. Group coverage is a plan purchased by an association, partnership, or corporation for its members or employees.

AUTOMOBILE INSURANCE

An automobile policy may cover personal injury, property damage, or both. Insurance for property damage may encompass collision insurance, fire and theft insurance, or both. Collision insurance protects the value of the insured's car against resulting damage even if the damage was caused by the insured's negligence. A person who does not have collision insurance and was not at fault may still collect from the insurance company of the negligent driver by making a claim, or the person may collect from the negligent driver by suing the driver in court.

NO-FAULT AUTO INSURANCE

The significance of no-fault insurance is that insurance companies may issue medical payments to their insured individuals without first determining which party is at fault. The insurance companies resolve that matter among themselves by apportioning the fault among the parties. Meanwhile the insured's medical expenses are being paid. No-fault insurance was also designed to relieve court calendar congestion by prohibiting an individual who is a "covered person" from suing in court for basic economic loss up to $50,000 (this amount may vary from state to state) unless a serious injury was sustained. Some form of no-fault insurance has been adopted in most states.

Passamano v. Travelers Indemnity Co.
835 p. 2d 574 (Colo. App. 1991)

Antonio Passamano rented a car from North-West. The next day he was in an accident with an uninsured motorist. Passamano's passenger was badly injured. The law "[p]rovides that uninsured motorist coverage must be offered in any automobile or motor vehicle liability policy, except that the named insured may reject each coverage in writing." North-West, as the named insured of the policy issued by Travelers, had rejected the uninsured motorist coverage. Passamano argued that the lessee of the motor vehicle is in reality the named insured and that he was given no opportunity to accept or reject the uninsured motorist coverage. He argued further that the rental agreement did not disclose that uninsured motorist coverage was unavailable because of North-West's rejection.

The issues are (1) whether a lessee of a rented vehicle should be considered the named insured and given the option to accept or reject uninsured motorist coverage and (2) whether the rental agreement is a contract of insurance.

The court ruled,

We conclude that neither this Rental Agreement, nor any portion thereof, constituted an automobile liability policy between North-West and plaintiff. Consequently North-West was not required to offer uninsured motorist coverage to him in its Rental Agreement, and the trial court was correct in so holding. Furthermore, since no contract of insurance existed, it follows that there was no "named insured." Therefore, plaintiff's assertion that he was the named insured of this nonexistent insurance policy between himself and North-West and that, as such, he was empowered to accept or to reject uninsured motorist coverage, is without merit.

Judgment for Travelers Indemnity Company.

INSURER'S RIGHT OF SUBROGATION

Once an insurance company makes a payment to an insured for a loss suffered, it has the right of subrogation. This means that the insurer takes the place of the insured and is entitled to whatever rights and remedies the insured has against the person who had caused the loss.

EXAMPLE Elvis was entertaining at the *Heartbreak Hotel,* singing "*If I Can Dream,*" when the woman of his dreams sat in the front row. Her name was Marie, and she was soon to be *His Latest Flame. After* his performance Elvis told her, "*My Wish Came True,*" and *I Need Your Love Tonight.* She said, "*My Baby Left Me,* and *I'm All Shook Up.*" Elvis responded, "*Are You Lonesome Tonight?*" She answered yes and then said, "*Love Me Tender.*" He took her out to an out-of-the-way place he had *In The Ghetto* because he knew the people in his neighborhood would have *Suspicious Minds.* Marie told him, "*I Can't Help Falling in Love With You.*" Elvis replied, "*It's Now or Never, and we'll do it My Way.*" But she said, "*Don't,*" and he did, so she yelled, "*What'd I Say,*" and with that she stepped on his *Blue Suede Shoes,* kicked his *Hound Dog,* and pulled the stuffing out of his *Teddy Bear.* Elvis cried "I was only *Loving You*" and pleaded, "*Don't Be Cruel,* but *Treat Me Nice.*" With that his daughter arrived and sobbed, "*Don't Cry, Daddy,*" but Elvis retorted, "*It Hurts Me, Too Much.*" The next day Marie found herself in prison sitting on the *Jailhouse Rock* with a *Mess of Blues.* Elvis had his *Blue Suede Shoes* and *Teddy Bear* insured. The insurance company paid Elvis for their value. Do they have the right to proceed against Marie for the amount they paid in fulfillment of Elvis's claim? Yes! After paying the claim the insurance company may exercise its right of subrogation—that is, they step into Elvis's *Blue Suede Shoes* and assume all the rights he has against Marie. Elvis's daughter asked who Marie was, to which Elvis replied, "*A Hard-Headed Woman* who has left me with *One Broken Heart for Sale* and lots of *Memories.*"

REVIEW QUESTIONS

1. Define insurance, insurer, insured, and insurable interest.
2. What does the term *coinsurance* mean?
3. What are the various types of life insurance?
4. Describe the other major kinds of insurance.

5. What is no-fault insurance?

6. Who is a "covered person" under no-fault insurance?

7. Passamano was involved in an accident with an uninsured motorist. The car that Passamano was driving was a rental from North-West. The rental agreement provided, "[North-West] will not provide 'Uninsured Motorist' coverage, 'Underinsured Motorist' coverage, or supplementary 'No Fault' coverage unless such coverages are required to be provided by applicable law and cannot be rejected." Passamano argued that this clause was confusing and that not providing uninsured motorist coverage was unconscionable. What result? *Passamano* v. *Travelers Indemnity Co., 835 P. 2d 514 (Colo. App. 1991).*

8. The University of Illinois negotiated a professional liability insurance policy with the Insurance Corporation of Ireland (ICI) on March 1, 1984. The policy was to run from July 1, 1984, to June 30, 1985, in accordance with the university's fiscal year. The policy was amended to cover the gap from March 1, 1984, to June 30, 1984. For the four-month gap, the university paid $165,000—exactly one-third of the annual premium. The policy clearly provided for a single $5,000,000 limit. The actual parties to the contract testified that it was the parties' intent to have a separate $5,000,000 limit for the gap period. A large claim was made against the policy during the gap period. ICI claimed that the university had no recourse because it had not carefully read the policy. What result? *Board of Trustees of the U. of Illinois* v. *Insurance Corp. of Ireland, 969 F. 2d 329 (7th Cir. 1992).*

9. Earl Dwayne Hunter sustained an eye injury on the job as a result of the negligent manufacture of a metal punch by Mayhew Steel Products. Dr. Max Hirschfelder committed malpractice in treating the injury. Hunter settled out of court with Mayhew for $162,500, with Hunter's employer paying an additional $67,500. Hunter continued his lawsuit against Hirschfelder and was awarded $335,436 less the amount paid by the other joint tortfeasors. Mayhew sued Hirschfelder, claiming a right of contribution, because it had paid more than its proportionate share. What result? *Mayhew Steel Products, Inc.* v. *Hirschfelder, 501 N.E. 2d 904 (Ill. App. 5 Dist. 1986).*

10. Paul Stallo purchased a pizza parlor, which he insured with the Insurance Placement Facility of Pennsylvania. He explained to Fran McManamon, an employee of the insurance broker, Ferrario Insurance Agency, that he wanted his daughter's name to appear on the policy. The policy was issued as Stallo requested. Subsequently a fire destroyed the building. When Stallo attempted to collect the insurance proceeds, the insurer refused to pay, claiming that they had contracted with Stallo's daughter, not Stallo, and that she had no insurable interest in the building. Stallo claims that because the Ferrario Agency knew he was the real owner and issued the policy on that basis, the insurer is bound by the knowledge of the insurance broker, who is acting as the insurer's agent. What result? *Stallo* v. *Insurance Placement Facility of Pennsylvania, 518 A. 2d 827 (Pa. Super. 1986).*

30

Real Estate Transactions

INTRODUCTION

A real estate transaction is a special type of contract involving the sale of land. All of the rules of contract law are applicable and should be consulted in the drafting of the contract. This refers especially to the statute of frauds, which requires a contract for the sale of real estate to be executed in proper form—that is, in writing.

A real estate transaction involves the buying and selling of land for use or speculation, a house for habitation and/or investment through rental or price appreciation, or a building for commercial use. The seller and purchaser may be individuals, partnerships, corporations, or any combination of these.

Buying and selling real estate involves three major stages:

Contacting a broker
Signing a contract
Closing the title

CONTACTING A BROKER

The first step in selling or buying real estate is to find a buyer or a seller. Although the individual parties themselves can accomplish this—through word of mouth or by posting signs or advertising in local newspapers—the most utilized and accepted method is through the services of a *broker.*

Real estate brokers help create a market for real estate transactions by listing a variety of land parcels, houses, and commercial properties for sale or rent. Brokers have the resources to market these products through advertising and telephone contact, and they have continually updated files of prospective buyers. They attempt to screen prospective purchasers to ensure that they have the ability to finance the transactions.

A broker is licensed with the state to list real estate for sale. The broker employs salespeople, who must be licensed to sell real estate and to act as the broker's agents. Where the parties cannot agree on a price, the broker acts as a mediator in negotiations between seller and purchaser and attempts to bring the parties together on an agreeable price.

For the rendering of these services, the broker is entitled to a commission based on a percentage of the sale. The broker actually earns the commission when he or she produces a purchaser who is ready, willing, and able to pay a price agreeable to the seller on the seller's terms. For the seller's protection the brokerage agreement should be amended to state that the broker's commission is due and payable only after the closing of title, when the purchase price is paid and the deed is delivered to the buyer. This protects the seller from having to pay a commission in all cases where title does not close except where the seller willfully breaches the contract.

The seller pays the broker's commission unless the parties provide otherwise in the contract. The broker's commission can be as high as 8 percent for the sale of a house. The more expensive the land, house, or business property, the smaller the commission because the broker's task of locating a purchaser remains the same.

| **EXAMPLE** | Morgan the Pirate operates a brokerage office in New Orleans. He hires Redbeard as a sales representative. Redbeard and Morgan successfully negotiate the sale of Key West. For this they earn an 8 percent commission. The sale of the land was $400,000. How much will the brokerage be entitled to? $32,000. |

The commission earned will be split between the broker and his or her agent if the latter brought about the sale. A 50-50 split is the usual arrangement. However, the more successful a salesperson is, the more likely this arrangement will be altered to 55-45 or 60-40 in favor of the salesperson. The reason for this is that the broker's costs for each salesperson are basically fixed. These fixed costs include desk space, telephone use, mailings, advertisements, and overhead expenses. The broker will spend this fixed amount regardless of the number of homes sold by a particular salesperson. A successful salesperson can use this fact as leverage in demanding a greater percentage of the commissions.

| **EXAMPLE** | In the previous example assume that it was Redbeard who actually brought about the sale. He receives a 50-50 split. How much of a commission will he be entitled to? $16,000— one-half of the amount earned by the brokerage company. |

Sellers can enter into a variety of *brokerage agreements.* These include open listing, exclusive agency, exclusive right to sell, and multiple listing.

Open Listing

The seller reserves the right to sell the property himself or herself or to contract to sell with other brokers. A broker who accepts an open listing will be entitled to a commission only if he or she brings about the sale.

Exclusive Agency

The seller reserves the right to sell the property himself or herself but agrees not to contract with other brokers. A broker who accepts an exclusive agency will be entitled to a commission in all cases except where the seller brings about the sale.

Exclusive Right to Sell

The seller reserves no rights, and the broker is entitled to a commission no matter who brings about the sale.

It is important to read a brokerage agreement before signing it regardless of the broker's oral representations. A person who has difficulty understanding the language of an agreement should consult an attorney, preferably one who will represent him or her at the signing of the contract and at the closing of the title.

EXAMPLE | Captain Hook signed an exclusive agency brokerage agreement with Peter Pan Realty to sell his Kohala Ranch on the Big Island of Hawaii. Captain Blood signed an exclusive right to sell brokerage agreement with Blackbeard Real Estate to sell his condo in St. Petersburg, Florida. Both Captain Hook and Captain Blood succeeded in selling the property themselves. Will either of them be responsible for paying the broker a commission? Yes! Captain Blood gave the exclusive right to sell his condo to Blackbeard. This means that Blackbeard was entitled to the commission even though he did not bring about the sale. Captain Hook reserved the right to sell the property himself by signing an exclusive agency agreement; therefore Peter Pan Realty is not entitled to a brokerage fee.

Multiple Listing

Multiple listing is a subscription service for brokers in which all members pool their exclusive listings and agree to split the commissions earned with the brokers who bring about the sales. A broker will usually place the property with a multiple listing service after first trying to earn the full commission by selling the property himself or herself.

EXAMPLE | The sultan, a broker, got an exclusive listing on a palace in Dariabar through his agent Sinbad. Unable to sell the property, the sultan places it in a multiple listing service.

> Dariabar is sold by Ali Baba, a salesman for The Sheik of Arabique. The commission is 6 percent, divided 60-40 in favor of the selling broker. The sale price is $500,000. Both sales representatives are operating on the usual 50-50 commission split. How much will each party get? The sultan's brokerage will earn $12,000 (40 percent of the total commission of $30,000). This $12,000 will be split between Sinbad and the sultan evenly. The Sheik of Arabique will earn $18,000 (60 percent of the total commission). This $18,000 will be split evenly between the Sheik of Arabique and Ali Baba.

A broker will usually ask an interested purchaser to sign a binder, which is a statement setting forth the amount the prospective purchaser wishes to offer. It is often accompanied by a check for $100 or more. A binder amounts to a good-faith demonstration of interest on the prospective purchaser's part. However, an interested purchaser should be wary of signing a binder because, if it includes all the contractual elements, it may constitute a contract.

SIGNING A CONTRACT

After a ready, willing, and able purchaser is found, the next step is the signing of a contract that sets forth the rights and liabilities of each party. Before a contract is signed, both parties should hire lawyers to represent them at the signing of the contract and through the closing of title. An attorney's fee generally ranges from .5 percent to 1 percent of the sale price. The reason a purchaser or a seller hires an attorney is for advice on the contract and protection against fraud and other unfair consequences.

The contract must be in writing. Its signing will give effect to the oral agreement of the parties. The contract must set forth the consideration given by each party. Each party must have the legal capacity to enter into the contract. A contract entered into by a minor is valid only during the period of minority; the party may void the contract within a reasonable time after reaching majority. A real estate contract made by a nonjudicially declared incompetent is voidable; this means that the contract is valid unless the incompetent person chooses to void it. A judicially declared incompetent's contract is absolutely void. A sale of real estate by a partnership must be made in the partnership's name; the signature of any general partner will be valid. A contract entered into by a corporation must have stockholder approval to be valid. A nonprofit corporation's real estate contract may have to be court approved before the contract is signed.

The sale of real estate by a fiduciary possessing power of attorney, such as an executor, trustee, or agent, is valid only if the document conferring the authority to act for another is in writing, signed by the person delegating the authority, and acknowledged by a notary public. A fiduciary is a person who has been given the authority to act for another in a relationship of trust and confidence.

The contract for sale is generally prepared by the seller's attorney, then forwarded to the purchaser's attorney for approval. The contract incorporates the provisions described in the following sections.

Preliminary Provisions

The first provision sets forth the date of the contract together with the names and addresses of the seller and purchaser.

> DATE: THIS AGREEMENT, MADE THE 17th DAY OF NOVEMBER, NINETEEN HUNDRED AND NINETY-NINE.

> PARTIES: BETWEEN JOHN JUDE MORAN residing at One Cameron Lake, Staten Island, New York HEREINAFTER DESCRIBED AS THE SELLER, AND RITA HOLOCHWOST residing at 271 Bay Ridge Boulevard, Brooklyn, New York, HEREINAFTER DESCRIBED AS THE PURCHASER.

Legal Description

The legal description of the property must be set forth to satisfy the writing requirement of the statute of frauds. The legal description includes the street address; the section, lot, and block numbers; and the metes and bounds.

> LEGAL DESCRIPTION: WITNESSETH, THAT THE SELLER AGREES TO SELL AND CONVEY, AND THE PURCHASER AGREES TO PURCHASE, ALL THAT CERTAIN PLOT, PIECE OR PARCEL OF LAND, WITH THE BUILDINGS AND IMPROVEMENTS THEREON ERECTED, SITUATED, LYING AND BEING IN THE [Here denote the county, city, and state of location together with the address and the lot and block number or the metes and bounds of said property].

> LOT AND BLOCK NUMBER OF EACH PARCEL OF LAND IS FILED ON A MAP IDENTIFYING SUCH PROPERTY WITH THE COUNTY CLERK'S OFFICE.

> METES AND BOUNDS: RELATIONSHIP OF SAID PROPERTY TO THE CORNER OF AN INTERSECTION OF TWO STREETS.

Personal Property and Fixtures

Certain personal property and fixtures become part of the structure of the house once they have been installed. These objects are generally conveyed with the house, but a description of each must be set forth in the contract.

The sale of real estate includes all of the following articles of personal property and fixtures unless specifically excluded: lighting, heating, plumbing, bathroom and kitchen fixtures and cabinets, stoves and refrigerators, dishwashers, washers and dryers, storm doors and windows, awnings, shades, screens, mantels, mailboxes, toolsheds, and wall-to-wall carpeting. The sale of real estate does not include household furnishings.

Purchase Price

The contract must denote the purchase price together with the method of payment. On the signing of the contract, the buyer will make a down payment, which the seller's attorney will hold in an escrow account. An escrow account is a special account that an attorney sets aside from his or her personal account for the purpose of safeguarding a client's funds until the proper disposition of those funds has been determined either by the parties themselves or by a court of law.

If the purchaser is to assume the mortgage, the amount remaining on any existing mortgages will be deducted from the purchase price. Otherwise, the seller must be paid in full, and the mortgage will be satisfied out of the proceeds from the sale. The amount of a purchase money mortgage to be held by the seller will also be deducted from the purchase price.

The balance remaining must be paid at closing either by an official check from a bank located within the state or by a personal check that has been certified by a bank located within the state. Provision is made for a personal check or a small amount of cash to be used as payment generally not exceeding $1,000. This limitation is because of the problems that will arise if a personal check bounces and also because of the inconvenience of carrying a great deal of cash—especially if the closing is after banking hours.

Purchase Price

The purchase price is:	$120,000
It is payable as follows:	
Down payment on the signing of the contract	12,000
The unpaid principal remaining on any existing mortgages	None
Purchase money note and mortgage executed by the purchaser and given to the seller	28,000
Balance at closing	80,000

"Subject to" Provisions

The premises are sold subject to the following:

Zoning laws and other governmental regulations that affect the use and maintenance of the property.

Encroachments by stoops, fences, and cellar steps on any street or highway.

Any facts that an accurate survey may show provided they do not render the title unmarketable.

Utility easements such as telephone, gas, electric, fuel, water, and sewer lines. An easement is a right of way, the right to use the property of another for a limited purpose. A utility easement is a right to install and maintain utility lines on the property of another.

Title

The seller's *title* to the premises must be verified for the purpose of determining whether he or she has proper ownership in the land to convey to the purchaser. This is known as marketable title. A marketable title is required unless the contract includes a clause requiring the seller to transfer an insurable title, one that must be approved and insured by a reputable title company. An insurable title may be something less than marketable title. This means that a title search must examine whether there is a proper chain of title leading up to the seller from the time the house was built. The records are kept in the clerk's office in the county in which the property is located.

The title search may be done by a lawyer, but more often than not it is handled by either an abstract company or a title insurance company, which specializes in these matters. An abstract company will issue a title report from which the purchaser's attorney can judge whether the seller has proper title. A title insurance company, upon satisfying itself that the seller has good title, will grant a title insurance policy in return for a fee. This policy insures the purchaser against claims others might make questioning the validity of the purchaser's title. If the purchaser's title were successfully contested, the purchaser would be entitled to reimbursement for the value of the property at the time the sale was made.

A title insurance company will not insure property if the validity of the seller's title is in question. Only in a rare case based on a major mistake in the title search would the company have to pay out. A purchaser of property that had greatly appreciated would lose heavily if the title proved to be invalid because title insurance is limited to the value of the property at the time of purchase. In some states the owner can increase the value of title insurance to reflect appreciation in return for payment of an additional premium.

The title conveyed by the seller to the purchaser must satisfy the requirements of a reputable title company in the state where the property is located. The title company must be willing to approve and insure the title conveyed. A reputable title company is usually insured by the state's board of title underwriters.

Deed

The deed delivered may be a general warranty deed, a specific warranty deed, or a quitclaim deed.

In a general warranty deed, the seller guarantees that neither the seller nor any preceding owner of the property has committed any act that would make the title unmarketable.

In a specific warranty deed, more popularly known as a bargain and sale deed, the seller guarantees that from the date of purchase, he or she has not committed any act that would make the title unmarketable.

In a quitclaim deed, the seller only relinquishes whatever interest he or she had in the real estate by transferring that interest to the purchaser. No guarantees are made as to whether the seller had any interest. If three people hold title to property and one of them wishes to buy out the other two, the other two may issue quitclaim deeds transferring their portions of ownership in the property.

Time and Place of Closing

The contract must state the time and place for the closing of title. These terms may be altered thereafter by mutual agreement in writing or at the request of one party as long as a request for a time extension is not unreasonable.

The closing of title usually takes place either in the office of the seller's attorney or, when a mortgage is involved, at the lending institution.

Gordon v. Schumacher
733 P. 2d 35 (Or. App. 1987)

Willamette Savings & Loan held a mortgage on John Gordon's house with monthly payments of $619 required.

In December 1983 John Gordon entered into a contract to sell his house to the Schumachers for $83,500, payable as $13,500 in cash with monthly installments of $619 to cover the balance. The contract required the payments to be made on the first of each month; the following provision was annexed: "Time is of the essence in this contract. A default shall occur if: (a) Purchaser fails to make any payment at the time required, or within ten (10) days thereof. . . ."

During the four consecutive months following the signing, the Schumachers' payments were late; however, Gordon accepted these payments. Subsequently Gordon's attorney sent two letters reinstating the aforementioned "time is of the essence" clause. Following is an excerpt from the first letter:

> Notice is hereby given that the "time is of the essence" clause is reinstated, and any delinquent payments not received by the escrow company on or before the due dates will not be accepted, a default will be declared, the full balance of the contract will be accelerated, and such action as appropriate will be taken to foreclose the contract.

On May 10 the Schumachers mailed the check. Gordon received it on May 14, but he returned it and instituted a foreclosure action.

The issue is whether payment mailed within the grace period but received after the grace period expires is timely.

The court concluded, "The land sale contract contains a provision that 'time is of the essence' in performing the conditions of the contract. Although plaintiff waived the time-essence clause by accepting several late payments, he reinstated it by sending the two letters. . . ." The court continued, "In fact, the letters from plaintiff's counsel reinstating the time-essence clause specifically state that any payment not received within the grace period would constitute a default under the contract." Judgment for Gordon.

Broker

The contract states the name of the broker and includes an indemnification clause protecting the seller against claims made by other brokerages that allegedly found and dealt with the purchaser. The following is such an indemnification clause:

> Purchaser states that he or she has not had dealings with any broker other than the broker who brought about the sale and agrees to indemnify seller against any claims made by other brokers with whom he or she has had dealings in connection with the property. Seller agrees to pay the named broker the commission agreed on in the separate brokerage agreement.

Compliance with State and Municipal Orders

The seller must cure all outstanding violations associated with the premises including those cited by the health department, building department, fire department, department of housing, and department of labor conditions.

Adjustments

The following items must be apportioned between the seller and the purchaser: real estate taxes, water and sewer taxes, fuel remaining on premises, and rents.

EXAMPLE Long John Silver sold his bungalow on Treasure Island to Squire Trelaway. The closing of title took place on July 15. At the time of closing a tenant was occupying the bungalow pursuant to a two-year written lease and paying a monthly rent of $600. There were 200 gallons of fuel left in the oil tank. The water and sewer bill was $120 for the fiscal year beginning July 1 and ending the following June 30. The real estate taxes, $2,400 per year, were assessed on a quarterly basis for the same fiscal year as the water and sewer taxes. The seller had paid the annual water and sewer bill and the first quarterly real estate tax bill. What adjustments must the seller and purchaser make at closing?

Adjustments	Credit to Purchaser	Credit to Seller
Fuel 200 gal. @ $1.25/gal		$250
Real estate taxes		$500
Water and sewer taxes		$115
Rent	$300	

Adjustments	Credit to Purchaser	Credit to Seller
Total	$300	$865
		$565 Adjustment added to the purchase price

Personal Judgments or Violations

The title report will usually disclose any personal judgments or violations against the seller's name. Any judgment that actually pertains to the seller is a lien against the property, and the seller must pay it to ensure that his or her title is marketable. An unpaid judgment creates a defect in the title that renders it unmarketable; the title insurance company, if any, will not insure the transfer of title. If a violation or judgment found is against a person with the same name as the seller's but does not pertain to the seller, then the seller must sign an affidavit to this effect before a notary. The affidavit must detail the violation or judgment found in the title report against the seller's name and must state that the violation and judgment does not apply to the seller.

Transfer and Recording Taxes

The seller must pay a real estate transfer tax at the closing of title. The transfer tax is usually a percentage of the sale price—for example, 1 percent. A recording tax may also be charged as a dollar amount—for example, $4 for every $1,000 of the purchase price. Thus on the sale of a $120,000 house, the transfer tax would be $1,200 (1 percent of the purchase price), and the recording tax would be $480 ($4 for every $1,000 of the actual purchase price). The seller agrees to deliver a certified check payable to the appropriate state, city, or county offices for the transfer and recording taxes in connection with the property to be transferred.

Limitation of Liability

If unable to convey a marketable or insurable title, the seller usually will limit his or her liability to a refund of the purchaser's down payment together with the expenses incurred by the purchaser for the title search and survey charges.

The purchaser's liability is usually limited to the down payment made. The purchaser is wise to include a provision conditioning the contract on his or her obtaining a mortgage for a certain amount, within a certain time. This condition implies that the purchaser must make a good-faith effort to secure a financing commitment.

Condition of Property

The purchaser inspects the property and agrees to accept it "as is" subject to reasonable use and wear and tear between the time of inspection and the closing of title. The purchaser would be wise to make a brief reinspection the day before closing and to stipulate in the contract that on the day of the closing, the roof should be free of leaks and the plumbing, heating, and lighting should be in good working order. This warranty made by the seller does not continue after the closing of title.

The purchaser should also insist on a provision allowing for an inspection for termites and carpenter ants within ten days to two weeks after the signing of the contract. If termites or ants are present, they may be exterminated and the damage repaired at the option of the seller. If the seller does not choose to exterminate and to repair the resulting defects, the purchaser can cancel the contract.

Incorporation of Prior Agreements

When a single writing is intended to be the final expression of the parties' intentions, then the writing must incorporate all prior oral and written agreements in order to have effect. This provision is in accord with the parol evidence rule, which prohibits the introduction into evidence of prior oral or written agreements to contradict the written contract.

Subsequent Changes

Any changes made subsequent to the signing of the contract must be in writing and signed by both parties.

Signatures

In the presence of the following witnesses   s/John Jude Moran, seller
    s/Harry Mullins, witness
    s/Nellie Regan, witness   s/Rita Holochwost, buyer

The signatures must be acknowledged by a notary public.
    STATE of _____, County of _____ ss:
    On the _____ day of _____ 19 _____, _____ personally
came before me. This person I know as the individual described as the seller or purchaser, who executed this contract in proper form, and acknowledged that fact before me _____ Signature of Notary
                    Stamp of Authority

A promise regarding the allocation of risk of loss is not included in the standard contract of sale form; this matter is governed by the Uniform Vendor and Purchaser Risk Act, which has been adopted by most state legislatures and then incorporated in the states' own statutes. The Uniform Vendor and Purchaser Risk Act places the risk of loss, if the premises are destroyed by fire or other means, on the seller until either title or possession of the premises is transferred to the purchaser. At the time of the closing of title, or at the time when possession is transferred if that is before the closing of title, the risk of loss passes to the purchaser. The purchaser should make provisions to have the real estate insured from the time when he or she assumes the risk of loss.

CLOSING OF TITLE

The *closing of title* is the final step in a real estate transaction. In the interim between the signing of the contract and the closing of title, the purchaser will run a title search and try to secure financing by obtaining a mortgage from a bank or other lending institution. Upon the satisfactory completion of both of these tasks, the closing of title will take place.

The basic scenario at the closing is the delivery of the deed, in which the seller transfers his or her title to the purchaser in return for payment of the balance owed on the purchase price. The seller must pay his or her attorney's fee; the broker's commission; the real estate transfer and recording taxes; any outstanding real estate taxes and water and sewer taxes; and parking violations or other judgments that remain unpaid. The contract will usually contain a provision that these encumbrances can be paid out of the proceeds of the sale. The purchaser must pay his or her attorney's fee, the title company fee, charges assessed in connection with the mortgage, and any adjustments to the purchase price in favor of the seller.

The deed must state the date of the closing of title, the names of the parties, and the legal description of the premises including the metes and bounds. It must be signed by the seller, whose signature must be acknowledged by a notary public. Then either a representative of the title insurance company or the purchaser's attorney will take the deed to the clerk's office in the county in which the property is located to have the deed recorded. This step gives notice to all other prospective purchasers that title to the property now belongs to the purchaser. Recording makes it official; the transfer of title is now on the records of the county clerk's office. The county clerk will then mail the deed back to the purchaser for safekeeping.

If a deed or any other interest in real estate is not recorded, it is practically worthless because a subsequent good-faith purchaser who records a deed with no knowledge of a prior unrecorded deed has paramount title to the land.

REVIEW QUESTIONS

1. Explain the steps in a real estate transaction.
2. Define broker, title, real estate contract, brokerage agreement, and closing of title.
3. Identify the three types of brokerage agreements, and explain how they differ.

4. Why are all real estate transactions required to be in writing?

5. Explain how a commission is split between a broker and his or her salesperson.

6. Explain the types of deeds that can be conveyed.

7. How does a multiple listing service operate?

8. Stern, a broker, procured a purchaser named Pierce for property owned by Gepo Realty. On the day Gepo Realty entered into the contract of sale, Pierce, Stern, and Gepo Realty signed a written brokerage agreement stipulating that the commission was payable on the closing of title. Title was never closed because Gepo Realty as owner and seller refused to satisfy certain taxes and assessments that constituted liens against the property. Pierce, the purchaser, was able to recover his down payment because the seller had breached the contract by impeding the conveyance of marketable title. But is Stern entitled to the brokerage commission regardless of the clause in the contract conditioning payment on the closing of the title? *Stern* v. *Gepo Realty Corporation,* 289 N.Y. 274, 45 N.E. 2d 440 (1942).

31

Forms of Ownership and Mortgages

Forms of Ownership Mortgages	Review Questions

FORMS OF OWNERSHIP

Individuals can own property in various forms:

Tenancy in common
Joint tenancy
Tenancy by the entirety
Community property
Condominiums
Cooperatives

Tenancy in Common

Tenancy in common is the concurrent ownership of real estate by two or more individuals with no right of survivorship and with each individual owning an undivided interest in the entire parcel of real estate. The phrase "no right of survivorship" means that when one of the tenants in common dies, that tenant's interest passes to his or her heirs by will or intestate succession; the heirs may not necessarily be the other tenants in common.

EXAMPLE | Alexander the Great died, leaving a will devising his house in Carthage to the Spartans, the Athenians, and the Persians in equal shares. What form of ownership has been created, and what are the rights of the Spartans? A tenancy in common has been created, with each group owning a one-third individual interest in the house. This means that although the Spartans own one-third of the real estate, the house or property cannot be divided to reflect their interest unless it is sold.

Joint Tenancy

Joint tenants have undivided concurrent ownership in the entire parcel of real estate with a right of survivorship. This means that when one joint tenant dies, his or her share passes to the other joint tenant.

EXAMPLE | Wellington and Napoleon held Waterloo as joint tenants with the right of survivorship. Napoleon died, leaving all of his property, both real and personal, to the people of France. Who is entitled to Waterloo? Wellington, as the survivor of a joint tenancy, has exclusive ownership of Waterloo regardless of the contents of Napoleon's will.

Overheiser v. Lackey
207 N.Y 229, 100 N.E. 738 (1913)

Hester Marsh died, leaving a will that devised the real estate she owned in the following manner: "I give and devise to my daughters Elaine Jane Marsh and Hester Marsh, jointly, the lot of ground with the dwelling house and improvements thereon situated in the City of New York and known as No. 15 Christopher Street."

The younger Hester Marsh died some time thereafter. Overheiser, one of her heirs, has brought an action to partition the real estate so that he may get his fair share. His suit rests upon the claim that Hester Marsh and Elaine Jane Marsh, both daughters of Hester Marsh, were tenants in common. If this is the case, Overheiser will be successful because a tenant in common's share passes to his or her heirs. However, if the two daughters were joint tenants, Overheiser's suit will fail because Hester Marsh predeceased Elaine Jane Marsh. A joint tenant's share passes to the surviving tenant rather than to the deceased's heirs.

The issue is whether a joint tenancy or a tenancy in common was created by the elder Hester's will.

The court held, "The rule of common law that a grant or devise to two or more persons without other words that created a joint tenancy was abolished early in the history of this state. . . ." This rule was replaced by the revised statutes, which declared, "Every estate granted or devised to two or more persons, in their own right, shall be a tenancy in common, unless expressly declared to be a joint tenancy." The court decided,

> In view of the indications that the devise in question here was formulated by a layman who did not use the word "jointly" in its distinctive technical sense, we conclude that it is not a sufficiently express declaration of an intent to create a joint tenancy to negate the presumption established by our statute that a tenancy in common was intended.

> Because the bequest to the two daughters was a tenancy in common, Overheiser inherited a portion of Hester Marsh's half share in the real estate, and his request for a partition was granted. Judgment for Overheiser.

Tenancy by the Entirety

Tenants by the entirety is a special form of joint tenancy reserved to married couples. This tenancy may be terminated only by divorce or by mutual agreement of the husband and wife, whereas a joint tenancy can be terminated by one joint tenant.

EXAMPLE Henry VIII and his wife own Nottingham Castle as tenants by the entirety. The purchase price was paid exclusively with Henry's funds. Three years after the purchase, Henry dies of a social disease. His will leaves his entire estate to his mistress, Anne Boleyn. Is she entitled to the castle? No! Henry's eighth wife is the surviving member of the tenancy by the entirety. On Henry's death she becomes exclusive owner of Nottingham Castle.

Community Property

Community property may be defined as property acquired by a husband and wife during their marriage. It does not include property acquired through gift or inheritance. Each spouse owns an undivided half interest in the community property regardless of who earned or acquired it. Community property laws have been adopted in a number of states. Most of these laws provide that the surviving spouse will receive half of the community property, with the remainder passing according to the deceased spouse's will or the laws of intestacy. If the husband and wife divorce, each will receive half of the community property. Most other states provide for equitable distribution when divorce occurs, with property divided between the spouses according to need.

Condominiums and Cooperatives

There are two other special forms of ownership: condominium and cooperative. A condominium or cooperative may be purchased by an individual, a corporation, or a partnership or by two or more individuals in any of the tenancies previously described.

The purchaser of a *condominium* acquires individual ownership in an apartment unit and becomes a tenant in common, along with the other apartment owners, of the common property. The common property includes the land on which the apartments are built, roofs, corridors, lobbies, stairways, elevators, fire escapes, basements, gardens, recreational facilities, parking and storage areas, and the like.

A *cooperative* is formed by the establishment of a corporation that owns title to the real estate on which the cooperative apartments are built. The corporation owns the common property. Each purchaser becomes a shareholder in the corporation and thus owns not real property but rather personal property in the form of stock certificates. A shareholder in the cooperative corporation is entitled to lease an apartment owned by the corporation as long as he or she owns the shares. Each purchaser-shareholder is actually a tenant of the corporation. The number of shares allocated to each tenant must bear a reasonable relationship to the rental value of the apartment occupied.

A condominium owner can usually sell, lease, assign, or sublet the apartment without any restrictions, whereas a shareholder in a cooperative must obtain the written consent of the corporation. Both condominium and cooperative purchasers must pay their proportionate shares of the maintenance costs attributed to the common property.

MORTGAGES

A *mortgage* is a lien securing payment of a debt, called a loan, through the creation of an interest for the lender in the property purchased. A mortgage creates a debtor-creditor relationship. The *mortgagor* is the one who is mortgaging his or her property by giving an interest in the property to the lender in consideration of a loan. The *mortgagee* is the one who is holding the mortgage by giving the loan in consideration for an interest in the borrower's property. The mortgagee's interest in the property is a qualified or dormant one that develops into a viable right of ownership only upon foreclosure. Foreclosure is the satisfaction of the mortgage debt through the judicial sale of the real estate pledged as collateral. A judicial sale, the sale of property to achieve a fair and reasonable price with judicial supervision, arises upon the mortgagor's default in payment. A *mortgage note* accompanies the mortgage and serves as a promissory note evidencing the debt. A parcel of real estate may be subjected to several mortgages; however, the entire first mortgage has preference over the second mortgage, with the second mortgage having preference over the third, and so on. The preference is created by the order in which the mortgages are recorded against the particular property.

EXAMPLE William of Orange and Mary, Queen of Scots, own a large fiefdom in England. Because of the uprising of rebellious serfs, William and Mary must spend an enormous amount of money to finance an army to squash the rebellion. They obtain a series of mortgages against their fiefdom. The Bank of England owns the first mortgage of $700,000. Cromwell, the previous owner, holds a second mortgage of $500,000, and three English barons hold a third mortgage of $200,000. William and Mary have invested a large sum of money in a college in Virginia that bears their name, and because of this they default on all three mortgages. All three mortgages are foreclosed, and the fiefdom is sold at a judicial sale for one million dollars. How will the proceeds from the judicial sale be distributed? The Bank of England will be entitled to the face value of its mortgage, $700,000, because it had just priority. Cromwell, the previous owner, will be entitled to collect the remaining $300,000 as holder of the second mortgage. Because he is not paid in full, he becomes a general creditor in regard to the other assets owned by William and Mary. The mortgage held by the three barons will go unsatisfied because the proceeds of the sale were insufficient to satisfy the third mortgage. They will become general creditors for $200,000.

Recording the Mortgage

A mortgage must be recorded to insure that the mortgagee's lien against the real estate is given priority against all subsequent mortgagees. Recording puts these subsequent mortgagees on notice of the existence of a prior mortgage to which their claims must be subordinated. If a mortgage is not recorded, it is practically worthless.

EXAMPLE In the previous example assume that the bank's mortgage was granted subsequent to the mortgages given by Cromwell and the barons. Assume further that the bank's mortgage was recorded, but the other two mortgages were not. Would the bank have a preferential claim to the proceeds of the foreclosure sale? Yes! The bank would have preference because it was the first and only party to have its mortgage recorded. This presupposes that the bank acted without knowledge of the other two unrecorded mortgages.

Types of Mortgages

There are various kinds of mortgages. A blanket mortgage covers all of the debtor's property. A special mortgage covers a particular parcel of real estate. There may be more than one mortgage. A purchase-money mortgage arises when the former owner takes back a mortgage as security for the unpaid balance of the purchase price. A balloon mortgage requires periodic payments, with a substantial final payment becoming due (ballooning) at a stated time.

EXAMPLE Napoleon Bonaparte buys a house in Waterloo. He takes out a mortgage of $140,000 that provides for $8,000 yearly payments, with a final payment of $60,000 after ten years. What type of mortgage is this? A balloon mortgage.

Federal Land Bank of Omaha v. Woods
480 N.W. 2d 61 (Iowa 1992)

The Woodses entered into a contract to buy the Schmitt farm from the trustee after foreclosure. Federal Land Bank of Omaha (FLB) loaned the Woodses funds. In return the Woodses signed a promissory note for $76,500. After occupying the farm they were dispossessed by the Mosers, who had superior title because they had signed an earlier contract. When they bought the farm, the Woodses had notice of the Mosers' claim. The Woodses defaulted on the note, and FSB sued.

The Mortgage

Donald J. Woods and Lola Jean Woods, husband and wife . . . in consideration of the advance of the principal sum recited in the note hereinafter described, receipt of which is acknowledged, hereby mortgage and convey to [FLB] mortgagee, . . . the following described real estate [the farm]. . . . This mortgage is given to secure a promissory note . . . executed by mortgagors to mortgagee, in the principal sum of seventy-six thousand five hundred and no/100——dollars. . . .

The Note

For value received, I/we jointly and severally, as principals, promise to pay to [FLB] . . . the principal sum of seventy-six thousand five hundred and no/100——dollars.

The issue is who is responsible for determining whether any prior liens against the property exist.

The court held that the mortgage language required the Woodses to warrant good title to FSB: "The mortgagors, and each of them, hereby warrant that they are fee owners of the mortgaged real property. . . ." Judgment for FSB.

REVIEW QUESTIONS

1. List and explain the various forms of ownership.
2. Define condominium and cooperative.
3. What is the difference between the two?
4. Define mortgage, mortgage note, mortgagor, and mortgagee.
5. List and explain the different kinds of mortgages.
6. How is priority determined if there is more than one mortgage?
7. David Ebersohn purchased two Treasury bills, one in the name of "David Ebersohn or Ruth Lowenberg," his niece, and the other in the name of "David Ebersohn or Nathan Lowenberg," his niece's husband. When Ebersohn died he had not changed his will to leave the Treasury bills to his niece and her husband. The executor of Ebersohn's estate refused to give Ruth and Nathan the

Treasury bills, claiming that Ebersohn could not have intended a joint tenancy because it would contradict the provisions of his will. What result? *Estate of Ebersohn,* 512 N.Y.S. 2d 768 (Sur. 1987).

8. The Andersons executed a promissory note to FLB for $125,000. A mortgage covering 720 acres of farmland secured the note. When the Andersons failed to make a payment, FLB served a notice of intention to foreclose the mortgage. Anderson contends that there was a failure of consideration and a lack of free consent when the loan agreement was entered into. What result? *Federal Land Bank of St. Paul v. Anderson,* 401 N.W. 2d 709 (N.D. 1987).

9. Herman Schroeder, a real estate broker, negotiated a deal on behalf of Granite City Realty to buy Alfred Mateyka's farm for $115,000. When the realty company defaulted on the mortgage, Mateyka sued. The defendants urge that Mateyka's only remedy is to foreclose on the property because, in the absence of a note, they are not personally liable. What result? *Mateyka v. Schroeder,* 504 N.E. 2d 1289 (Ill. App. 5 Dist. 1987).

10. Morgan and Halliburton owned property as joint tenants. Halliburton borrowed $100,000 from Texas American Bank by securing a note and mortgage covering that jointly owned property. Morgan was not a party to the loan or the mortgage. When Halliburton defaulted the bank sued for foreclosure. Morgan contended that another joint tenant could not execute a mortgage that would encumber her interest in the property without her consent. What result? *Texas American Bank/Levelland v. Morgan,* 733 P. 2d 864 (N.M. 1987).

32

Landlord and Tenant

Introduction	Assignment and Subletting
Types of Tenancy	Termination of Tenancy
Landlord's Duties	Review Questions
Tenant's Duties	

INTRODUCTION

A landlord and tenant relationship is a contractual one in which both parties are bound by a lease. A *lease* is a contract that sets forth the rights and duties of both parties as well as the terms on which the parties agree. An oral lease is enforceable unless its duration exceeds one year, in which case a written lease signed by both parties is required by the statute of frauds. The *landlord* is the owner of the premises who is granting the lease. The *tenant* is the person to whom possession of the premises is given in return for payment of rent.

TYPES OF TENANCY

The following are the basic types of tenancies:

  Tenancy for years
  Periodic tenancy
  Tenancy at sufferance

Tenancy for Years

A tenancy for years is one created for a definite time, usually by a written lease. No notice of termination need be given because the lease automatically expires at the end of the term. The lease may then be renewed if the landlord and tenant so desire. The landlord has the option of increasing the rent as much as he or she wishes unless the apartment is rent controlled or rent stabilized. This means that the local municipality regulates the amount by which the rent for an apartment may be increased.

EXAMPLE | On April 1 Mary, Queen of Scots rented an English tudor in Edinburgh for a term of three years, with the monthly rental fixed at 200 silver pieces. What type of tenancy has been created? A tenancy for years!

Periodic Tenancy

If the tenant pays rent for a certain time period, such as one month, and the landlord accepts it, then a periodic tenancy has been created. This tenancy will continue for the duration of the period. Either party must give adequate notice of termination, which is usually construed to be the length of a period.

EXAMPLE | Prince Rupert has been renting a castle in Hastings-on-the-Hudson for eighteen years. The rental period began with a one-year lease. After the lease expired Rupert paid rent on a monthly basis. What type of tenancy has been in effect for the last seventeen years? A periodic tenancy with a duration of one month, which is renewable each time the rent check is offered by Rupert and accepted by the landlord.

Tenancy at Sufferance

A tenant at sufferance is one who wrongfully stays on beyond the duration of the tenancy without the landlord's permission. He or she may be treated as a trespasser and evicted. A tenant at sufferance may also be sued for the rent due during the period he or she wrongfully stayed over.

EXAMPLE | The Duke of Marlborough rented a villa from Louis XIV in Oudenaarde for a term of one year. After the lease expired Marlborough remained in possession of the premises and offered to continue to pay rent, but Louis XIV refused. If Marlborough will not vacate the villa, what type of tenancy does this become? A tenancy at sufferance! Louis XIV may treat Marlborough as a trespasser and commence eviction proceedings.

LANDLORD'S DUTIES

A landlord has the following duties:

> Duty to deliver possession
> Duty to fulfill warranty of habitability
> Duty to ensure tenant's right to use and quiet enjoyment of the premises
> Duty to make repairs

Duty to Deliver Possession

A landlord has a duty to deliver possession of the premises on the date on which the tenancy is to begin. This means that the landlord must oust any holdover tenants. A landlord may disclaim liability for failure to deliver possession because of a holdover tenant by incorporating a provision to this effect in the lease. This disclaimer will be conclusive as long as the landlord has taken every step necessary to oust the holdover. The new tenant may take possession when the holdover tenant is removed or may cancel the lease for the landlord's failure to deliver timely possession. In either event, if both parties agreed to the disclaimer provision, the new tenant may not look to the landlord for damages caused by the breach.

EXAMPLE A man who lived in England has rented a house in southeastern New Hampshire. The man made all the necessary sea transportation arrangements for himself and his belongings. While en route to the United States, he was advised, the day before the tenancy was to commence, that the former tenants refused to move out and that the landlord did not have prior knowledge of this. The man without a country is forced to keep his furniture in storage aboard ship and remain aboard ship until the holdover tenants are ousted. Their eviction occurs four weeks later. When the man moves in, he sues the landlord for the expenses he incurred because of the landlord's failure to deliver the house for occupancy on time. Will he recover? No, if there was a disclaimer provision in the lease. The man has the option to occupy the house when the tenants are ousted, which must be done expeditiously, or the lease will be considered void. If the man moves in after four weeks, is he responsible for the full month's rent? No! The landlord is precluded from collecting for the full month because he failed in his duty to deliver timely possession. Will the lease now run from the date of occupancy? No! It will run from the original date agreed on as stated in the lease.

Duty to Fulfill Warranty of Habitability

A landlord has a duty to guarantee that the premises are habitable. This means that the premises must be in a condition fit for human occupancy—clean, safe, and sanitary. Local housing codes have set forth minimum standards by which habitability is judged. Separate standards apply to conditions within an apartment and to areas of common use where the landlord has retained control.

Minimum standards requiring the landlord's compliance within an apartment include adequate kitchen and bathroom facilities, lighting and ventilation, and temperature controls for hot water and heat. The landlord must also comply with the criteria for the maintenance of areas of common use. The minimum criteria include maintaining sidewalks free from ice, snow, and deep cracks; roofs free from leaks; lighting in hallways and lobbies; elevators in working order; and the like.

EXAMPLE In August Sir Thomas More rents a furnished room from Henry VIII in the Tower of London pursuant to a one-year lease. During November Thomas More discovers that there is no heat or hot water in the premises. Is there any way for Thomas to escape from the legally binding lease? Yes! Thomas may vacate the premises, claiming that Henry VIII has breached the implied warranty that the premises were habitable. Thomas More will be responsible for paying rent only for the period during which he occupied the premises.

A landlord has a further duty to disclose any condition dangerous to the tenant of which the landlord has actual knowledge or even a belief that such a condition exists unknown to the tenant. Many states also require the landlord to take additional precautions to protect tenants from criminal conduct by properly securing the house or building with adequate locks, burglar alarms, or security patrols and by providing adequate lighting on the outside of the building for tenants walking to and from the entrance.

EXAMPLE | Thomas à Becket resided at the Canterbury Apartments owned by Geoffrey Chaucer. Becket, along with other tenants, complained of inadequate lighting and security. One evening Becket entered the foyer and proceeded up the stairs to his second-floor apartment. He was attacked by thieves, whom he could not see because of the lack of adequate lighting. The thieves entered the building through the front door, which they could open thanks to a broken lock. Does Becket have any recourse against Chaucer for his injuries? Yes! Chaucer, as landlord, is responsible for the injuries because of his failure to maintain the areas of common use, in this case the hallways and entrance, by providing proper lighting and locking devices.

P.H. Inv. v. Oliver
818 P. 2d 1018 (Utah 1991)

Cathy Oliver lived with her seven children in a building with forty-two housing code violations against it. The violations included electrical hazards, a stairway without handrails, holes in the walls of every room, a collapsed bathroom ceiling, broken windows, and rotting floors. Cathy stopped paying rent because of the deteriorated condition of the building, but she continued to live there. The landlord, P.H. Investment, argued that the warranty of habitability did not apply because Cathy had waived her rights by renting the premises with knowledge of the dilapidated condition.

The issue is whether the tenant must vacate the premises to invoke breach of the warranty of habitability.

The court held,

In the present case, the tenant is typical of the individuals we sought to protect by adopting the warranty of habitability. Ms. Oliver is a woman with little or no resources or income, with seven children, and pregnant with an eight at the time of this action. Because of a lack of bargaining power, low income tenants often have no meaningful choice but to accept and continue to live in substandard housing. To protect persons similarly situated, our approach will invalidate boiler plate language, eliminate any duty of inspection, and protect against uninformed waivers of any latent defects.

Judgment for Oliver. To hold otherwise would support the landlord's violation of the housing code.

Landlord's Duty to Ensure Tenant's Right to Use and Quiet Enjoyment of the Premises

This is an important provision in which the landlord makes the following guarantees: He or she has title to the premises; the tenant has the right to absolute possession for the duration of the tenancy; the use and quiet possession of the premises will not be disturbed by either the landlord or other objectionable tenants; the tenant will not be evicted without just cause—that is, without violation of a major provision of the lease.

EXAMPLE   Wolsey lives in the Tower Hill Apartments. He has a job at the palace that requires him to be at work early in the morning. Henry VIII lives in the apartment next to Wolsey and on many occasions carries on with his mistresses until early dawn. Wolsey has confronted Henry VIII only to be threatened. Wolsey wonders, is the owner of Tower Hill responsible for setting Henry straight? Yes! Each tenant has a duty to respect the other tenants use and quiet enjoyment of the premises. Because Henry VIII does not respect this duty, the landlord has an obligation to enforce Wolsey's rights by informing Henry VIII of his duty not to disturb other tenants. If Henry does not abide by this warning, then the landlord has a further obligation to evict Henry from the premises.

Duty to Make Repairs

A landlord generally has no duty to make repairs and will not be liable for injuries due to a defective condition unless

the repairs are of the kind required to maintain the habitability of individual apartments and areas of common use,

a major repair involving a structural defect is needed,

an injury-causing defect resulted from intentional concealment on the part of the landlord,

the landlord has agreed to make the repairs,

the landlord voluntarily undertakes to make the repairs even though he or she has not expressly agreed to do so, or

an injury is caused by the inherently dangerous work of an independent contractor.

EXAMPLE | Eleanor of Aquitaine was an elderly widow living in the east wing of Pontifact castle, which had recently been purchased by Henry II. Eleanor's wing was rent controlled; her rent was only $150 per month. Henry was desirous of removing Eleanor and renting the wing at a much higher fee. He offered to find Eleanor lodging elsewhere, but she refused to move. On the brink of winter, the heating system failed, and Henry refused to repair it. Within a short time Eleanor contracted pneumonia and was hospitalized. Is Henry liable for her medical expenses? Yes! A landlord is responsible for making repairs of the kind required to maintain the habitability of the rented apartment. Since lack of heat would cause the wing to become uninhabitable and since Eleanor could not vacate the apartment due to her advanced age, Henry would be liable for Eleanor's medical expenses.

TENANT'S DUTIES

A tenant must fulfill the following duties:

Duty to make ordinary repairs
Duty to refrain from disturbing other tenants and making material alterations
Duty to pay rent and to give a security deposit

Duty to Make Ordinary Repairs

A tenant has a duty to make all repairs necessary for the general upkeep of the apartment. The tenant will be liable for injuries caused by a neglect of this duty, as was seen in the previous example, unless the injury occurs in one of those instances where the landlord is responsible.

Duty to Refrain from Disturbing Other Tenants and Making Material Alterations

A tenant has a duty to refrain from disturbing others and to refrain from altering the premises or otherwise causing any material or substantial change that results in permanent damage.

EXAMPLE | The Duke of Lancaster rented the west wing of a castle owned by the Duke of York in Towton. The Duke of York had the perimeter of the castle lined with white roses. Unfriendly conditions developed between the two dukes. The Duke of Lancaster dug up all the white roses and replanted the perimeter with red roses. Thus began the War of the Roses. Has the Duke of York any recourse against the Duke of Lancaster? Yes! The Duke of York may commence an eviction proceeding against the Duke of Lancaster for materially altering the nature of the premises without the landlord's permission. The Duke of Lancaster will be responsible for the damage caused by the alteration. The War of the Roses was won by the Duke of York.

Duty to Pay Rent and to Give a Security Deposit

The tenant has a duty to pay rent and to give a security deposit in accordance with the provisions of the lease. The duty to pay rent is conditioned upon the premises' being habitable and upon the tenant's being able to enjoy quietly the use of the premises.

EXAMPLE | Harold Wessex rented a fiefdom in Hastings from William the Conqueror for 300 hundred gold sovereigns a month. Subsequently a battle in Hastings forced Harold to abandon the fiefdom for two weeks because it was unsafe. Harold seeks reimbursement for half the month's rent for the period when he was not in possession. Will Harold win? No! William the Conqueror is not responsible for extraneous circumstances that render the premises uninhabitable unless he causes them or they are of the kind he can remedy. This responsibility does not include maintaining the quality of the air or safety in the neighborhood or fiefdom. If the manor had been destroyed or rendered uninhabitable by the battle, then Harold could vacate the premises because of constructive eviction.

In most states the landlord is obliged to keep the security deposit in a separate interest-bearing account. If there are no damages to the premises, the landlord must return the security deposit in full together with the interest earned. The tenant's duty to leave a security deposit with the landlord is designed to protect the landlord from tenants who abandon the premises, refuse to pay rent, or materially alter the condition of the premises. The security deposit will be applied to such losses. If the losses exceed the security deposit, the landlord will have a cause of action, a right to sue for the remaining damages.

A tenant who breaks the lease becomes liable for the rent payments throughout the remaining portion of the tenancy. In most states the landlord has a duty to mitigate damages by trying to rerent the vacant apartment.

EXAMPLE | Alfred the Great rented Wedmore Manor for 500 silver pieces pursuant to a two-year lease to a group of Danish students participating in a foreign exchange program. After eight months the Danes became homesick and decided to leave for home. Alfred the Great was able to rerent the apartment in two months for 400 silver pieces. How much will Alfred be able to recover from the Danes? Two thousand four hundred silver pieces! When the Danes broke the lease, the remaining payments became due. Alfred had a duty to mitigate damages, to keep them low by rerenting Wedmore Manor. Alfred the Great is entitled to recover for the two months the apartment was vacant (1,000 silver pieces) plus the difference (1,400 silver pieces) between the original rental price of 500 silver pieces and the rerental price of 400 silver pieces for the fourteen remaining months. If the Danes had left a security deposit, it would have been applicable to the amount owed.

ASSIGNMENT AND SUBLETTING

A lease is a contract. Like any contract, a lease is assignable unless (1) a clause in the lease forbids assignment, (2) the assignment will materially alter the provisions of the lease, or (3) the risk to the landlord will be greatly increased should the assignment be made. Most leases incorporate a clause prohibiting assignment without the landlord's consent. In leases involving commercial buildings and owner-occupied rental properties, the landlord can arbitrarily withhold consent as long as doing so does not involve discrimination that violates the Fourteenth Amendment. In leases involving multiple dwellings—that is, generally four or more apartment units—the landlord cannot arbitrarily withhold consent. In an assignment of a lease, the assignee pays the rent directly to the landlord.

EXAMPLE | Oliver Cromwell rented an apartment in Huntingdon Manor on St. James Place pursuant to a two-year lease. After six months he was forced to relocate to Marston Moor. Cromwell entered into a contract assigning to Charles I his right to occupy Huntingdon Manor and his duty to pay the agreed-upon rent. Three months later Charles was forced to leave the manor for the gallows in Whitehall. At the very least Charles was reluctant to leave. All of Charles's wealth had been confiscated. Has the landlord of the Huntingdon Manor any recourse against Cromwell? Yes! An assignor remains liable to the landlord if the assignee fails to perform the assignment.

Subletting occurs when the tenant rents either part or all of the premises to a third party in return for payment of rent. The third party makes rental payments directly to the original tenant. In subletting, a new landlord and tenant relationship is actually created, with the original tenant being the landlord and the third party the subtenant. In both assignment of a lease and subletting of the premises, the original tenant remains liable for the rent. Refer to Chapter 15, "Rights of Third Parties," for more information.

EXAMPLE | King Duncan rented a very large shop in Aberdeenshire with the intent to open a donut shop. However, he soon realized that the shop was much too big for his needs. With the permission of the landlord, he rented a portion of the shop to Macbeth. What would this arrangement be called? Subletting! King Duncan has sublet a portion of the premises to Macbeth, a third party, who is a subtenant and has a duty to pay King Duncan a monthly rental.

Northside Station Assoc. v. Maddry
413 S.E 2d 319 (N.C. App. 1992)

Northside leased space in a shopping center in Cary, North Carolina, to the Video Shoppe. In turn the tenant, with Northside's consent, rented half of the space for the remainder of the lease to the Floral Emporium, owned by Carolyn Maddry. The lease provided that upon its expiration, failure to negotiate a new lease would result in a month-to-month tenancy with a 50 percent increase in rent. Northside offered Maddry a new lease. She refused both to sign a lease and to pay the stipulated rental increase. She claimed that in the sublease her only duty was owed to the Video Shoppe. Northside claimed that the lease had been assigned to Maddry by the Video Shoppe.

The issue is whether an assignment or a sublease has been made. The court decided,

[A] conveyance is an assignment if the tenant conveys his entire interest in the premises, without retaining any reversionary interest in the term itself.

A sublease, on the other hand, is a conveyance in which the tenant retains a reversion in some portion of the original lease term, however short.

For the forgoing reasons, we hold that the Agreement is a partial assignment . . . . allowing Northside to assert a direct claim against Maddry on the original lease.

Judgment for Northside.

TERMINATION OF TENANCY

A tenancy most often terminates when the duration of the tenancy comes to an end. A tenancy may also end before its normal expiration by mutual agreement, abandonment, constructive eviction, or eviction.

Abandonment

A tenant who abandons property immediately becomes liable for all of the remaining rental payments. The landlord has a duty to mitigate damages by attempting to rerent the premises. Refer to the example concerning Alfred the Great.

Constructive Eviction

The tenant may abandon the premises, and be justified in so doing, if the premises become uninhabitable through no fault or negligence of the tenant. Constructive eviction is an alternative when there is loss of heat or hot water; uninhabitability of the premises, perhaps caused by fire; deterioration of structural supports; rat infestation; presence of other tenants who disrupt the quiet enjoyment of the premises and against whom the landlord has not commenced eviction proceedings; and the like. In the previous examples concerning tenants Sir Thomas More, Thomas à Becket, and Wolsey, if the conditions affecting the quiet enjoyment and habitability of the premises were not promptly remedied by the landlord, the named tenants could permanently abandon the premises, refuse to pay the rent, and claim that the conditions of the premises caused them to leave. This is constructive eviction.

Eviction

A landlord may bring an eviction proceeding against a tenant for the tenant's failure to pay rent or to abide by the provisions of the lease. Common lease provisions prohibit the tenant from making any structural changes; installing a clothes washer, dryer, or dishwasher; harboring pets; inviting third parties to live in the apartment; and assigning or subletting the apartment without the consent of the landlord. It is important for a tenant to read a lease thoroughly before assenting to it. If a tenant wants to do something that the lease prohibits, such as keep a pet, then either the lease provision should be changed or the landlord's consent should be obtained in writing.

REVIEW QUESTIONS

1. Define landlord, tenant, and lease.
2. What are the various types of tenancies?
3. List and explain the duties of a landlord.
4. List and explain the duties of a tenant.
5. Cuntrell was a tenant at Hidden Lakes Apartments. A perpetrator was able to force Cuntrell's door open because the screws anchoring the deadbolt system were only one-half inch long. Two months before the robbery, the police had advised the apartment manager and the tenants that three and one-half inch screws were necessary to anchor a deadbolt system. Tenants were forbidden to add supplemental locks. What result? *Cuntrell v. State,* 410 S.E. 2d 193 (Ga. App. 1991).
6. Landlord wants to evict tenant, Martin Lubarsky, without giving him the required thirty-day notice. Because the housing accommodations are not the tenant's primary residence, the landlord claims that Martin is not a periodic tenant and therefore is not entitled to notice. Tenant argues that he falls within an exception to the primary-residence requirement and therefore is a month-to-month tenant who requires thirty-day notice before the landlord can terminate the tenancy. What result? *Charlotte Realty Co.* v. *Lubarsky,* 509 N.Y.S. 2d 691 (Sup. 1986).
7. A&P, the tenant, operates a supermarket in a shopping center owned by Berkeley, the landlord. After the initial lease term ended, A&P informed Berkeley that it intended to lease the premises to Drug Fair, a drugstore. A&P and Drug Fair entered into an agreement of sublease, whereby A&P

transferred all of its interest in the store for the entire unexpired term of the lease. Is the agreement between A&P and Drug Fair an assignment or a sublease? Why? *Berkeley Development Co. v. Great Atlantic & Pacific Tea Co.,* 518 A. 2d 790 (N.J. Super. L. 1986).

8. Joseph Waters owned four parcels of land. He leased two of them to Rose Metal Industries. The lease gave Rose Metal the first right of refusal on the leased premises. Thereafter James Kassouf offered to purchase the four parcels from Waters. Waters agreed to sell subject to Rose Metal's right of first refusal on the leased premises. Rose Metal agreed to purchase the four parcels. Waters refused to sell all four parcels to Rose Metal. What result? *Rose Metal Industries, Inc. v. Waters,* 579 N.E. 2d 767 (Ohio App. 8 Dist. 1990).

9. Vogel rented an apartment from Haynes pursuant to a written contract signed on January 6, 1983, that stipulated that the tenancy would commence on January 15 and could be terminated on a thirty-day written notice. On June 26 Vogel gave Haynes written notice that she intended to vacate the premises on or before July 31. Haynes refused to return Vogel's security deposit, claiming liquidated damages. The contract required a $110 security deposit, which would be returned to the tenant if the apartment were not damaged and the tenant had remained in possession for one year. What result? *Vogel v. Haynes,* 730 P. 2d 1096 (Kan. App. 1986).

10. The Klucznicks and the Yonicks leased a restaurant in a building owned by Tom Nikitopoulos for five years. The air conditioning was not functioning. A repairman advised the tenants that the heating and air conditioning were a single unit and that the cost of repair would be $1,600. The landlord refused to make the repairs. During the summer the lack of air conditioning caused the tenants to lose customers and finally forced them to close for two months. At the end of the summer, they reopened, but their business continued to suffer during the winter because of lack of heat. Are the tenants entitled to reimbursement for the months they were forced to close the restaurant and for loss of profits? *Klucznick v. Nikitopoulos,* 503 N.E. 2d 1147 (Ill. App. 2 Dist. 1987).

33

Wills and Trusts

WILLS

A *will* is a declaration that states the intention of the testator or testatrix concerning **DAD.**

Distribution of his or her property

Administration of his or her estate

Disposition of his or her remains

The testator or testatrix is the person who is making the will. That person will decide what relatives, friends, or charities will be the beneficiaries of the estate. An *estate* consists of all the property owned by a person at the time of death. The decedent's estate must be administered by a person designated by the testator or testatrix in the will. That person is known as the executor or executrix. If a person should die intestate (without a will), the court will appoint a public administrator to handle the decedent's estate. There is a fee set by statute that must be paid to the executor or public administrator for services rendered.

REASONS FOR MAKING A WILL

In the United States we have certain guaranteed freedoms. One is the right to distribute our property on our death as we choose and to designate who will carry out our wishes. To take advantage of this freedom, one must draft a legal document known as a will.

Where there's a will there's a way to leave the property to the people one wishes to have it. Where there's no will the decedent's property will be distributed according to the laws of intestacy, which require that the property be given to the spouse or the closest blood relatives. Without a will there's no way for property to be given to a good friend or a charitable institution.

EXAMPLE | Scarlett O'Hara was the owner of Tara, a Georgia plantation. She was very fond of Mammy, a servant, who had taken care of Scarlett when she was a child. Scarlett had desired to leave Mammy a portion of Tara to live on for the rest of her natural life. Scarlett died of a fever that bears her name. She left no will. Her only blood relation was her father, who had become shellshocked in the Civil War when Sherman marched through Atlanta. Mr. O'Hara seeks to dispossess Mammy. Has Mammy any recourse? No! This example dramatizes the importance of making a will. If Scarlett had made a will devising a portion of Tara to Mammy, then Mammy would have been protected.

FORMAL REQUIREMENTS

The will must comply with the laws of the state in which it is drafted, and it must be drafted in the state where the person making the will is domiciled. A person may have many residences but only one domicile. A person's domicile is the state in which the permanent home is located and from which the person votes.

The will must be in writing and signed at the end, either by the testator or by his or her agent in the presence and at the discretion of the testator. If an agent signs for the testator, the agent must sign his or her own name as well (Rita Connolly by John Burns). In drawing the will the testator must declare and sign or acknowledge his or her signature in the presence of at least two witnesses (some states require three). The witnesses also must sign the will at the direction of and in the presence of the testator, attesting to the testator's signature and competency. If the witness is an interested party—one who is to receive property through the will—the will remains valid, but the witness is apt to lose his or her share of the estate unless there is another witness who signs. This is to prevent fraud. Otherwise nothing would keep two individuals from conspiring to influence a weak-minded person to draft a will leaving them the bulk of his or her estate, with the two individuals signing as witnesses. However, if the witness is a spouse, child, or other close relative who would be entitled to receive an intestate share if the will were declared invalid, then that witness will be entitled to the lesser of either the share provided in the will or the intestate share.

EXAMPLE | In his later years Charles Dickens was befriended by a small boy named Oliver Twist. Dickens was desirous of making a will and leaving half of his estate to Oliver, with the remaining half bequeathed to his first cousin and only blood relative, David Copperfield. Dickens, being a writer, drafted his own will, to which he signed his name, but the will was not attested to by any witnesses. Is the will valid, and will Oliver be entitled to his one-half share of the estate? No! The will did not comply with the formal requirements mandating the attestation of at least two witnesses; therefore it is invalid. Dickens's estate will pass intestate. This means that David Copperfield, his only blood relative, will inherit the entire estate. If there were two witnesses to the will and Oliver were one of them, would this affect the will's validity? No! The will would be valid, but Oliver would forfeit his share. If David Copperfield signed as a witness, would the will be valid? Yes! The will would be valid, but Copperfield would get the lesser of the share under the will or his intestate share. In this case the lesser would be the one-half share under the will, but if there were four other cousins, Copperfield would be entitled only to his intestate share of 20 percent.

TESTAMENTARY CAPACITY

The testator must have the capacity to understand and appreciate the nature and extent of his or her property, the persons who are the natural objects of his or her bounty, and the disposition that he or she is making in regard to such persons and property. The testator must be eighteen years of age or older in most states and must be of sound mind. However, an insane person may make a will during a lucid interval.

If a person making a will lacks testamentary capacity or does not make the will freely of his or her own initiative, the will may be challenged and rendered invalid.

EXAMPLE | Rip Van Winkle fell asleep for a very long time. When he awoke he found himself to be up in years, so he decided to make out a will leaving his entire fortune to Ichabod Crane and the headless horseman, who had awakened him. He totally forgot his cousin Washington Irving, who had given Rip his start in the literary world. When Rip Van Winkle died, Irving contested the will on the grounds of senility. Will he be successful? Yes! Rip lacked the testamentary capacity to make a valid will because he did not remember his blood relatives, who were the natural objects of his bounty. Rip's estate will pass intestate to his cousin according to the laws of intestacy. If Rip had recognized the existence of his cousin and then chosen to disinherit him (which should have been written in the will), then the will would have been valid.

In Re Estate of Hutchins
829 S.W. 2d 295 (Tex. App.—Corpus Christi 1992)

Nancy Kilgore, the decedent's only child, sought to have the probate of her father's will set aside on the grounds that there was no evidence of her mother's testamentary capacity.

The attestation clause, which appears immediately below the signature of the decedent (testator), reads:

> The above and foregoing instrument was now here published as his last will and signed and subscribed by William Merritt Hutchins, the testator, in our presence, and we, J. B. Trimble and Charlotte Johnson, being both over the age of twenty-one years, at his request, in his presence, and in the presence of each other, sign and subscribe our names thereto as attesting witnesses this day of August, 1954.
>
> s/J. B. Trimble
> s/Charlotte Johnson

The two witnesses to the will are deceased.

The issue is whether testamentary capacity can be inferred from the attestation clause.

The court ruled that the witnesses must attest to the testator's sound mind either at the time of the making of the will by a statement to that effect in the attestation clause or at the time of the testator's death by a sworn statement. Because the will did not contain such a provision and the witnesses did not survive the testator, there was no evidence of testamentary capacity. Judgment for Kilgore.

CLASSIFICATIONS OF INDIVIDUALS AND PROPERTY

A *testator* is a person disposing of his or her property by will. A woman who makes a will is referred to as a testatrix.

An *executor* is a representative of the decedent who handles the administration and disposition of the estate. A woman who is appointed as a representative is known as an executrix.

An *administrator* is a representative appointed by the court for a person who dies intestate (without a will.)

A *guardian* is a representative appointed to look after the decedent's children. A guardian is appointed by the testator through a will or by the court if the decedent has died intestate or the will failed to appoint a guardian for minor children.

A *conservator* is a representative of a judicially declared incompetent, appointed by the court to administer the estate of the incompetent while he or she is still alive.

Issue means the legitimate children of a decedent, including those conceived before but born alive after the decedent's death.

Adopted children are treated as natural children for the purpose of inheriting. One-half blood relations—stepbrothers and stepsisters—are treated as full-blood relations for the purpose of inheriting. Illegitimate children inherit from the mother and from the maternal grandparents and great-grandparents. They inherit from the father only if he is acknowledged through an order of paternity or if he makes a specific bequest in his will. A father may inherit from an illegitimate child only by an order of affiliation.

A *devise* is a disposition of real property through a will.

A *devisee* is the recipient of the disposition of real property through a will.

A *bequest* is the disposition of personal property (such as money, jewelry, or silver) through a will.

A *legatee* is the recipient of the disposition of personal property through a will.

A *distributee* is an heir who is entitled to share in the estate of a decedent who died with or without a will.

A *residuary clause* in a will determines to whom the remainder of the decedent's real and personal property shall be given after specific devises and bequests have been made. In the absence of a residuary clause, the property remaining would pass according to the laws of intestacy. An example of a residuary clause is set forth in the sample will.

Intestate refers to a person who dies with no will and whose property will be distributed in accordance with the laws of the state in which he or she has died.

SAMPLE WILL

THE LAST WILL AND TESTAMENT
OF
JAMES BOND

I, JAMES BOND, residing at the headquarters of Her Majesty's Secret Service, being of sound and disposing mind and memory, do make, publish, and declare the following as for and to be my Last Will and Testament.

FIRST: I hereby revoke any and all Wills and Codicils by me at any time heretofore made.

SECOND: I direct the payment of all my just debts and funeral and testamentary expenses as soon after my decease as may be practicable.

THIRD: I give and bequeath my Astor Martin to GOLDFINGER with my best wishes for his being able to fit inside the car.

FOURTH: I give and bequeath my top hat to ODD JOB to replace the one he lost in Fort Knox.

FIFTH: I give and bequeath a golden wedding band to MISS MONEYPENNY because she had always wanted to be Mrs. James Bond.

SIXTH: I give and bequeath to ERNST BLOFELD my white kitten, Pussy Galore, to replace his cat that died.

SEVENTH: I give and bequeath $2,000 to JAWS for the purpose of buying a new set of dentures.

EIGHTH: I give and devise and bequeath all the rest, residue, and remainder of my estate, both real and personal, of whatsoever kind or nature and wheresoever the same may be situated, of which I may die seized and possessed, or be entitled to at the time of my death, in equal shares to my two sons of my late wife, 008 and 009.

NINTH: I hereby nominate, constitute, and appoint my good friend, FELIX LICHTER, to be executor of my Last Will and Testament, and I direct that no bond or other security shall be required of him in any jurisdiction in which he may seek to qualify.

TENTH: I direct that any and all estate, inheritance, legacy, succession, or other death taxes payable in respect of my estate, or any devise, legacy, or distribution under this, my Will, or levied by reason of my death, including but not limited to those levied on proceeds of policies of insurance on my life, whether or not the property, transfer, or proceeds with respect to which said taxes are levied pass by virtue of my Will or outside my Will, shall be paid out of my residuary estate as administration expenses, and said taxes shall not be apportioned.

IN WITNESS WHEREOF, I have hereunto subscribed my name and affixed my seal this 17th day of November in the year of our Lord, One Thousand Nine Hundred and Eighty-Eight.

James Bond (L.S.)

WITNESSES:

_____"M"_____

_____"Q"_____

The foregoing instrument was on this 17th day of November, 1988, subscribed by JAMES BOND, the Testator therein. In the presence of each of us, said Testator did, in advance of signing said instrument, declare to us that he had read the same; that he understood it and that it expressed his wishes and purposes; and said Testator did, immediately subsequent to making said subscription, declare and publish the instrument so subscribed by him to be his Last Will and Testament, whereupon we, at his bequest, in his presence and in the presence of each other, did on the same day hereunto subscribe our names as witnesses thereto.

REVOCATION OF A WILL

A will may be revoked by the drafting of a new will that contains a provision that all prior wills are thereby revoked. A will may also be revoked by physical destruction or by a writing manifesting the testator's intention of revocation. Divorce or annulment revokes any distribution of property to a spouse; the spouse is treated as though he or she had predeceased the testator. Marriage entitles the surviving spouse to exercise the right to elect against the will and take the statutory share. In most states the statutory share is one-half if there are no children and one-third if there are children. A child who is born or adopted after the parent made his or her last will is entitled to the intestate share if there are no other children. If there are other children, then the after-born or after-adopted child shall be entitled to a proportionate share of what the other children receive. If the other children receive nothing, then the after-born child will receive nothing.

PROBATE

Before a decedent's property can be distributed in accordance with the will, the will must be probated. *Probate* is the procedure for proving that the will is valid and genuine and that it manifests the testator's true intent. The probate or surrogate court in the state where the decedent died has jurisdiction over the will and estate. The disposition of real estate located in a state other than the one where the decedent died will be governed by the laws of the state where the real estate is located. No state has the power to make a decision regarding ownership of real estate in another state.

The original will must be filed with the court along with an affidavit of subscribing witnesses and a probate petition that sets forth the testator's heirs and any person named in the will as either an executor or a beneficiary who is not an heir. Notice of probate must be sent to the parties named in the probate petition to advise them that the decedent has died and that the will has been admitted to probate. An heir who is not named in the will, or a person named in the will who is not satisfied with the bequest or devise he or she received, may contest the validity of the will at a hearing.

Once the will has been approved by the surrogate or probate judge, letters will be issued to the executor or executrix giving that person authority to administer the estate and to dispose of the property according to the directions in the will.

INTESTATE DISTRIBUTION

The estate of a person who has died with no will is governed by the intestacy laws of the state where the decedent has died. The laws of intestacy are based on spousal and blood relationships. The following outline describes the distribution priorities under a typical state's laws of intestacy.

Surviving spouse and child
a. Spouse gets one-half
b. Child gets one-half
Surviving spouse and children
a. Spouse gets one-third
b. Children split two-thirds
Surviving spouse and parents, no children
a. Spouse gets one-half
b. Parents get one-half
Surviving spouse, no children or parents
a. Spouse gets whole
One or more children, no surviving spouse
a. Child or children get whole

Parent(s), no surviving spouse or children

a. Parent(s) get whole

Brothers and sisters or their children

a. Brothers and sisters or their children (cousins) split whole

EXAMPLE | Mark Twain lives in St. Louis. He has two sons named Tom Sawyer and Huckleberry Finn. Both boys have floated on down the Mississippi to the city of crawfish and creole. Mark Twain rarely hears from them. He spends most of his time alone, except for frequent visits from his niece Becky Thatcher. Mark Twain enjoys telling Becky stories of the good old days. He promises her all of his possessions when he dies. Eventually Mark Twain dies, but without a will. Will Becky share in his estate? No! Mark Twain's estate will pass according to the laws of intestacy, to his closest blood relations, who are his two sons, Tom and Huck.

Meador v. Williams Ky. App.
827 S.W. 2d 706 (Ky. 1992)

In the will of W. G. Meador, his property was left to his three children. Ervin and Mildred received their shares outright, while a spendthrift trust was created for Sterling. The will provided:

ITEM IV. Spendthrift Trust: I give and bequeath to the Citizens National Bank of Bowling Green, Kentucky, the other *one-third share in trust,* however, for the following uses and purposes, to wit: to hold, manage, control, invest, and reinvest the same in its absolute and unqualified discretion *during the life of my son, Sterling Meador,* from time to time, to pay him all or any part of the income thereof, or portions of the principal *for the support and maintenance of said Sterling Meador,* and to make such payments in such amounts and at such times and in such manner as my said trustee, in its absolute and unqualified discretion, may from time to time deem proper and *at his death, the remainder of said trust shall pass to and vest in his next of kin.*

If Sterling had died first, his share would have passed to Ervin and Mildred. However, Ervin died first. Mildred argued that she was the next of kin and should receive Sterling's share. Ervin's children argued that they should receive their father's distribution and share equally with Aunt Mildred.

The issue is whether *next of kin* means closest blood relatives or whether it allows the children of deceased siblings to inherit by their representation of their parents.

The court ruled that it was presumed that the testator meant for his children or their heirs to share equally. Therefore, Ervin's children are entitled to his one-half share of the trust. Judgment for Williams.

RIGHT OF ELECTION

A surviving spouse cannot be disinherited. The statutory right of election provides against this by allowing the surviving spouse to elect against the will for a one-third share of the estate if there are children or a one-half share if there are no children. For the purpose of determining the spouse's right of election, all testamentary substitutes are included in the estate: Testamentary substitutes include real or personal property held jointly by the decedent and someone other than the surviving spouse, including joint bank accounts, gifts made to others with knowledge of impending death, and trusts established with others named as beneficiaries.

EXAMPLE | Scarlett O'Hara is married to Rhett Butler but has always had fond desires for Ashley Wilkes. In her will she leaves one-half of her estate to her daughter Bonnie Blue and the other half to Ashley. In one of her frequent arguments with Rhett, Scarlett tells him the contents of her will. Rhett responds by saying, "Frankly, my dear, I don't give a damn." Will Scarlett's attempt to disinherit Rhett be successful? No! Rhett may exercise his statutory right of election against the will and receive a one-third share of Scarlett's estate. What remains will be divided equally between Bonnie Blue and Ashley Wilkes.

Although a testator cannot totally disinherit a spouse, the testator can create a trust in an amount equal to or greater than the surviving spouse's right of election, with the income from this trust payable to the surviving spouse for life and with the principal paid on the surviving spouse's death to a beneficiary designated by the testator. Under this arrangement the surviving spouse does not have free use of the entire trust principal but has only the income from it for his or her lifetime. This trust cannot be terminated before the surviving spouse's death nor be invaded by or for anyone else. The trust must pay out all income to the surviving spouse. If any of these contingencies is violated, the surviving spouse is entitled to the principal of the trust outright.

CONTESTING A WILL

A will may be contested by an heir or by any other person named in either the last will or a prior will on the following grounds:

Lack of capacity
Improper execution
Undue influence
Fraud

Lack of Capacity

The burden of proving capacity is on the proponents of the will. They must prove that the testator was of legal age and sane at the time of the signing of the will. The sanity requirement is usually sworn to by the subscribing witnesses, who must attest truthfully with no motive to lie.

Improper Execution

A contest because of improper execution arises when it is alleged that one of the formal requirements has not been met. The person contesting the validity of the will has the burden of proving this.

Undue Influence

The question of undue influence hinges upon whether the testator's mind was dominated to the extent that no testamentary intent existed. Evidence may be presented concerning the susceptibility of the testator, the opportunity of the accused to unduly influence the testator, and the accused's motive for doing so. The burden of proving undue influence rests with the person contesting the estate.

Rose v. Dunn
679 S.W. 2d 180 (Ark. 1984)

Mills O. Pierce, aged eighty-nine, lived on the family farm with his brother Vernon Pierce. After the brother's death Delma Dunn, a neighbor, moved in with Mills Pierce. Delma Dunn accompanied Mills to speak with Dunn's lawyer about Vernon's estate. After several visits to the lawyer, Mills decided to execute a will. Dunn's lawyer drafted the will as Mills requested, leaving all of Mills's personal property to Dunn and his wife. In addition Mills devised his 160-acre farm to Dunn and his wife for $1.00.

The heirs of Mills O. Pierce asserted that Delma Dunn had unduly influenced Mills O. Pierce to execute a will and a deed in Dunn's favor.

The issue is whether Dunn procured a will in his own favor by unduly influencing Pierce.

The court stated,

> Undue influence which voids a will is not the influence which springs from natural affection or kind offices, but is such as results from fear, coercion, or any other cause that deprives the testator of his free agency in the disposition of his property, and it must be specially directed toward the object of procuring a will in favor of particular parties.

> There was no presence of fear or coercion dinned into the mind of Mills O. Pierce. The court added, "The mere fact that a beneficiary is present while a will is made does not give rise to a presumption of an undue influence." Judgment for Dunn.

Fraud

A will is not valid if the testator was the victim of a deception that led him or her to disinherit an heir. That heir is entitled to his or her intestate share.

TRUSTS

A trust is the legal title to real or personal property held by one party for the benefit of another. The person creating the trust is called the creator; the person for whom it is created is known as the beneficiary; and the person who has been entrusted by the creator with the legal title to the trust funds until the designated time for payment to the beneficiary is referred to as the trustee. A trust involves a fiduciary relationship in which the trustee must administer the trust property in good faith, as a reasonably prudent person would.

TYPES OF TRUSTS

A trust may be created during the life of the creator through an *inter vivos* or living trust, or it may be created on the death of the creator through a will. The latter is known as a testamentary trust. A living trust may incorporate a provision giving the creator the right to revoke the trust and reclaim the principal. If the creator does not reserve this right, the trust is irrevocable unless it is a Totten trust.

A Totten trust is a special trust consisting of a bank account opened in one's own name for the benefit of another, with the creator retaining possession and control of the passbook. Any funds on deposit on the date of the decedent's death will automatically pass to the named beneficiary. The creator who is also the trustee, may revoke the trust at any time by withdrawing the funds from the bank account.

PURPOSES OF TRUSTS

Trusts may be created for varied purposes. Some trusts are set up to provide for the support and education of children. In such a case, money or other property may be held in trust for a child until he or she reaches an age of financial responsibility that is predetermined by the creator. One may also create a trust for the purpose of providing for a relative or friend who is not capable of managing his or her financial affairs. The beneficiary is thus assured of a fixed income without the need to manage or otherwise be accountable for the money, and the creator is assured that the principal of the trust will not be squandered.

EXAMPLE | Robert Louis Stevenson died, leaving all of his property in trust for his good friend Mr. Hyde. He appointed Dr. Jekyll as trustee because he knew that Mr. Hyde was two-faced and irresponsible. Was Stevenson wise to set up a trust fund for Mr. Hyde? Yes! He knew that Mr. Hyde lacked the mental capacity to invest the trust funds prudently. Instead Dr. Jekyll will manage the trust and provide Mr. Hyde with a consistent source of monthly income.

A person may create a scholarship trust fund, where the income from the principal will be used to pay the tuition of promising students. Many universities, societies, and clubs have funds designated for this purpose. Trusts may also be created for other educational, religious, or charitable purposes. If for some reason circumstances change and make it impracticable to carry out the purpose of the trust concerning religious, education, or charitable dispositions, the court may invoke the cy-pres doctrine. This allows the court to alter the purpose or beneficiary of the trust to prevent the trust from failing and to fulfill the creator's intention in a feasible manner.

EXAMPLE | Louisa May Alcott died with no blood relations, leaving her entire estate in trust for the little women of the world. The executor of her estate was perplexed as to who should receive the money. The executor petitioned the court for guidance. What should the court do? The court should invoke the cy-pres doctrine and alter the specific purpose of the trust to best serve Louisa May's intentions. The money may be paid to a group for the advancement of womens' rights.

REVIEW QUESTIONS

1. Define will, estate, testator, executor, administrator, guardian, conservator, issue, devise, devisee, bequest, legatee, intestate, distributee, residuary clause, and probate.
2. What are the rights of adopted children, one-half blood relations, illegitimate children, and after-born children?
3. Why should a person make a will?
4. Define trusts and state the purposes for which they may be used.
5. The executor of the estate of William Kalenak sought to introduce an exact copy of the decedent's will into probate because the original will was lost. The copy was held by the decedent's attorney, and the attorney's secretary attested to the fact that it was an exact copy. What result? *Matter of the Last Will and Testament of Francis Kalenak, Deceased,* 583 N.Y.S. 2d 332 (A.D. 4 Dept. 1992).

6. Robert Daley left all his property equally to his two children Marguerite Boroughs and Franklin Daley in his will of November 1989. In August 1990 Daley was admitted to the hospital for fever and disorientation. On August 21, 1990, he executed a new will witnessed by four individuals and leaving everything to Marguerite. The attorney who drafted the will did so after being advised by Marguerite that her father wished to leave her his house and that the rest of the property would be shared equally. The testator disagreed with this assertion and expressed his desire to leave everything to her. The hospital chart described Daley as being more alert and feeling better on August 21, 1990. What result? *Daley* v. *Boroughs,* 835 S.W. 2d 858 (Ark. 1992).

7. Clifford Pommer and his wife were married in 1983. It was her third marriage. Two weeks later they signed a marital agreement in which both waived their respective rights of election to each other's wills. Mr. Pommer then executed a will leaving all his property to his daughter. He died six years later. It was at his death that Mrs. Pommer alleged that she first discovered she had waived her right of election. She claimed that her husband had fraudulently induced her to sign the marital agreement. Mrs. Pommer sued Trustco Bank, the executor of the estate. What result? *Pommer* v. *Trustco Bank,* 583 N.Y.S. 2d 553 (A.D. 3 Dept. 1992).

8. Marie Gonzales lived in California with her sister Cecil Pope, to whom she left one-third of her estate. Subsequently Marie deeded her house to Cecil before moving to live in South Dakota with her other sister, Mildred Brown, and Mabel Martin. Marie decided to draft a new will in South Dakota, substituting her niece Stephanie for her sister Cecil because she claimed that Cecil would be getting her house, which constituted over half of her estate. Cecil brought action, claiming undue influence on the part of her sister Mildred. It was determined that Mildred was in a confidential relationship with Marie and actively participated in the formulation of the will. Mildred claims that she did not exert undue influence because she had nothing to gain by the change. What result? *Pope* v. *Brown,* 357 N.W. 2d 510 (S.D. 1984).

9. In Virgil Williams's will he left his wife a life estate in all the Florida real estate he owned. The remainder of his property passed to his children. When he died he owned no property in Florida. His wife Patsy had severe mental and physical problems. She filed a notice of intention to exercise her right of election. The estate contended that this was not tantamount to electing against the will. What result? *Harmon* v. *Williams,* 596 So. 2d 1139 (Fla. App. 2 Dist. 1992).

10. Jessie Olsen died at the age of ninety in 1982. Her relationship with her granddaughter had deteriorated after her son's death in 1979. In 1980 Jessie executed a new will, leaving her estate to her niece Audrey, who had cared for her in her waning years. Audrey's husband, a lawyer, drafted the will. Jessie's granddaughter claimed that Audrey had procured the will by exercising undue influence and that she was otherwise precluded from benefiting under a will

that was drafted by her husband, a lawyer. The three witnesses to the will testified that Jessie was of sound mind and that she claimed that the will clearly expressed her wishes. What result? *Matter of Estate of Olsen,* 357 N.W. 2d 407 (Minn. App. 1984).

Special Topic: Business Ethics

ETHICAL DILEMMAS

The following are scenarios illustrating a variety of ethical dilemmas:

1. You are a supervisor of telephone operators. Two operators, Bertha and Myrtle, approach you regarding Bruce, a fellow employee who they believe has AIDS. They want him transferred, or else they will inform the other operators and initiate a strike. Bruce has never spoken to you about this matter. How do you handle this? Discuss the ethical and legal implications.

2. Businesses suffer because of poorly educated employees. Do businesses have an ethical obligation to resolve this dilemma? If so, develop a strategy for resolving it?

3. Do you think commercials are deceptive? Name three that are and three that are not, and explain whether or not they are ethical.

4. In the United States Tennis Open, the men players were always paid more than the women players. One year the women refused to play unless they got equal pay. The USTA relented and paid them equally. The men argued that the women played the best of three sets, whereas the men played the best of five sets, and that the men drew more spectators. Ethically how should this be resolved?

5. Doris's uncle Stuart is vice-president of Code Blue, Inc. Doris asks her uncle how the company is doing. He says that they are going to be acquired by Genetics Company. Doris purchases 1,000 shares for $20,000. Three weeks later Stuart announces the acquisition of Code Blue by Genetics. Over the next five weeks, the Code Blue stock triples. Doris sells and realizes a $40,000 profit in two months. Has Doris acted ethically? What about her uncle?

6. New York creates more garbage than London, Paris, and Tokyo combined. Staten Islanders don't want a garbage dump on the island, yet New York—including Staten Island—must be responsible for disposing of its garbage. Is it ethical for the dump to be on Staten Island? What about the practical problem of where to put the garbage?

7. Research, Inc. is using monkeys and rabbits in its testing to discover a cure for AIDS. This testing is very painful for the animals. There is an alternative method, which does not involve animals, but it is twice as expensive. Research,

Inc. has limited funding. Is Research, Inc. acting ethically? What would you recommend that it do?

8. XYZ Department Store has been experiencing every imaginable kind of employee theft. The store executives hire you, a human resource consultant, to advise them on ways to decrease theft. Ever mindful of XYZ's cherished ethical image, discuss the solution that you would suggest while balancing the employees' rights. Also state what rights the employees have.

9. Fred asks his fiancée Wilma if her father Barney would find Fred a job at the Flintstone Quarry. Barney, who is a senior manager there, agrees. After working at the quarry for two months, Fred learns that Barney is embezzling funds and stealing supplies. Fred confides in Wilma. Wilma threatens to break off their engagement and tell her father to fire Fred if Fred turns Barney in. Fred was fired from his last two jobs, so his job prospects are poor. Fred also is up to his ears in wedding expenses. Should Fred turn Barney in? Would your answer be different if Fred were laid off by Barney two weeks later?

10. In 1987 Mary, age twenty-one, obtained a secretarial position with Amco, Inc. Her boss Tom, forty-four, was very fond of Mary. He was also executive vice-president. Mary and Tom lunched often. She accompanied him on business trips, and they had a continuous affair, about which Mary was very candid. As a result Mary moved up the ranks until she reached the rank of assistant vice-president. She was not qualified, but Tom covered for her. At this point Mary felt secure and wanted her independence. At the annual summer picnic, she ignored Tom in a very obvious manner. Tom continued to make advances such as sending flowers to Mary's office, using computer mail to leave love notes, and leaving sexual messages on her answering machine. Without notice to Tom, Mary filed a sexual harassment suit against the company in October. Tom, hurt but angered as well, fired Mary for incompetence. What are the issues? Ethically, what would be the desired result? Discuss the arguments of both sides.

34

Agency: Creation and Duties

Introduction
Types of Authority
Agent's Duties

Principal's Duties
Review Questions

INTRODUCTION

Agency is a contractual relationship, involving an agent and a principal, in which the agent is given the authority to represent the principal in dealings with third parties. The most common example is an employer-employee relationship wherein an agent (employee) is given the power by a principal (employer) to act on the latter's behalf. An *agent* may be an employee, an independent contractor, or a professional agent. A *principal* is a person who employs an agent to act on his or her behalf.

A principal (employer) has full control over his or her employee, who must complete the assigned work by following the principal's instructions. An independent contractor and a professional agent are individuals hired by a principal to perform specific tasks. The principal has no control over the methods used by an independent contractor or a professional agent. The following are among those who act independent of a principal: independent contractors such as electricians, carpenters, plumbers, television repair technicians, and automobile mechanics and professional agents such as lawyers, physicians, accountants, securities brokers, insurance brokers, real estate brokers, and investment advisors. These special agents may also employ others in their fields who will be bound to them as employees.

A principal may be disclosed or undisclosed. An agent acting for a disclosed principal will make that relationship known to the third parties with whom he or she is dealing. When an agent represents an undisclosed principal, the agent will pretend to act for himself or herself, thus ensuring anonymity for the principal.

EXAMPLE | Her Majesty's Secret Service has reason to believe that Sotheby's is offering to sell a diamond Easter egg at its next auction. The secret service does not want to make it known that they are bidding for the egg. Instead they send their secret agent, James Bond. If Bond is successful in his bidding to buy the egg, he will transfer it to the secret service. What type of relationship has been created? An agency has been created, with Bond acting as an agent for the secret service, an undisclosed principal. If Bond represented to Sotheby's that he was purchasing the egg for the secret service, the secret service would be a disclosed principal.

All of the requirements of contract law apply to the creation of an agency. Both a principal and an agent must have the capacity to contract.

A minor may act through an agent but will not be liable for the reasonable value of the agent's services or any contracts the agent enters into unless they involve necessities or come under one of the other exceptions to the defense of infancy, such as hiring an employment agency. This is because contracts entered into by a minor are voidable at his or her discretion.

An agency contract of an insane person is voidable by that person unless he or she has been adjudicated incompetent, in which case the agency contract would automatically be void.

A partnership enters into contracts through its individual partners, who are both agents and principals of the partnership. A corporation also acts through officers and other designated employees, who are agents of the corporation.

An agency contract may be created expressly, through a writing or a verbal conversation, or impliedly, through the actions of the parties. However, if an agent's duties on behalf of the principal involve entering into a contract that is required to be in writing under the statute of frauds, then the agency contract must likewise be in writing.

EXAMPLE | In the previous example the secret service's agency relationship with James Bond was required to be evidenced by a signed writing because it involved the purchase of real estate.

TYPES OF AUTHORITY

Actual Authority

The scope of an agent's authority is usually determined by the principal. Actual authority is the express authority conveyed by the principal to the agent; it includes the implied authority to do whatever is reasonably necessary to complete the task. This implied authority also gives the agent power to act in an emergency.

EXAMPLE | James Bond is a secret agent for Her Majesty's Secret Service. Along with his license to kill, his actual authority includes investigating security problems throughout the world. He has no authority to decide which security problems he will investigate. One day while he is investigating a case in Monte Carlo, a sudden breakthrough requires him to fly to Rio de Janeiro. Does he have the authority to make the travel arrangements? Yes! Inherent in the authority delegated to Bond is the implied authority to perform those tasks necessary to ensure the successful performance of his work.

Apparent Authority

Apparent authority is the authority the agent professes to have that induces a reasonable person to believe in the agent. The reliance on apparent authority must be justifiable.

EXAMPLE | "Q," a specialist in manufacturing the equipment used by Her Majesty's Secret Service, has the actual authority to manage the construction of the equipment. He does not have the authority to order the materials that he needs for manufacturing. One day "Q" contacts the Astor Martin Corporation, provides them with his identification as head of secret service manufacturing, and orders one of their subcompact cars, which he intends to modify with an ejector seat. Astor Martin delivers the car, but the secret service refuses to pay for it. Can the secret service raise the defense that "Q" did not possess the actual authority to purchase the Astor Martin? No! Although "Q" did not possess the actual authority to bind the secret service to a contract, he appeared to have the authority to enter into the contract. Astor Martin was justified because a reasonable person would believe that the head of equipment and manufacturing would possess the authority to order the car for the secret service.

Lundberg v. Church Farm, Inc.
502 N.E. 2d 806 (Ill. App. 2 Dist. 1986)

Church Farm, Inc. purchased a well-bred stallion named Imperial Guard for $700,000 in 1982. Thereafter Gil Church, owner of Church Farm, Inc., advertised the breeding rights to Imperial Guard. The fee was $50,000, and all inquiries were to be directed to Herb Bagley, manager.

Vern Lundberg signed a contract with Herb Bagley entitling Lundberg to three breeding rights to Imperial Guard in the 1982 and 1983 breeding seasons. In 1984 the breeding rights were to be converted into one share of ownership in Imperial Guard. This part of the contract was signed "Herb Bagley" and "Gilbert G. Church by H. Bagley." The contract also provided that the horse would remain at Church Farm in Illinois unless 50 percent of the shareholders voted to move him. This portion of the contract was signed "Church Farm Inc. H. Bagley, Manager." The contracts were on printed forms.

Between the 1982 and 1983 breeding seasons, Gil Church moved Imperial Guard to Oklahoma without giving notice to the shareholders. Unable to exercise his 1983 breeding rights, Lundberg brought an action for damages.

Gil Church argued that Bagley had not been authorized to sign the contracts, nor had he been given the authority to add or amend its terms. Lundberg retorted that he had dealt exclusively with Bagley.

The issue is whether Bagley had the apparent authority to bind Church Farms, Inc. to the contract with Lundberg.

The court declared an agent's apparent authority to be the authority that the principal holds his agent out as possessing. In view of the principal's actions, it is the authority that a reasonable person would naturally presume the agent to have.

The court stated,

> Plaintiffs produced evidence at trial that Gil Church approved the Imperial Guard advertisement listing Herb Bagley as Church Farm's manager and directing all inquiries to him. Church also permitted Bagley to live on the farm and to handle its daily operations. Bagley was the only person available to visitors to the farm. Bagley answered Church Farm's phone calls, and there was a preprinted signature line for him on the breeding rights package.

The court concluded,

> The conclusion is inescapable that Gil Church affirmatively placed Bagley in a managerial position giving him complete control of Church Farm and its dealings with the public. We believe that this is just the sort of "holding out" of an agent by a principal that justifies a third party's reliance on the agent's authority.

Judgment for Lundberg.

AGENT'S DUTIES

Duty of Loyalty

The relationship between principal and agent is a fiduciary one, based on trust and confidence. Inherent in this relationship is the agent's duty of loyalty. An agent has a duty to disclose all pertinent information he or she learns of that will affect the principal, the principal's business, or the task at hand. An agent must not take advantage of the principal's prospective business opportunities or enter into contracts on behalf of the principal for personal aggrandizement without the principal's knowledge. An agent may not work for two principals who have competing interests.

EXAMPLE | Solitaire works as a sales clerk in Mr. Big's Tarot Card Shop in Harlem. One day James Bond enters the shop and informs Solitaire that he would be interested in financing a Mr. Big shop in London. Solitaire takes Mr. Bond's card, and instead of passing the information along to Mr. Big, she visits James Bond that evening. By the following morning they have agreed that Solitaire will manage the London tarot card shop. After learning what has transpired, Mr. Big wishes to know what recourse he has against Solitaire. Mr. Big may sue Solitaire for breach of contract because Solitaire violated her duty of loyalty in failing to disclose Bond's offer and in taking advantage of Mr. Big's opportunity.

Duty to Act in Good Faith

An agent is obligated to perform all duties in good faith. He or she must carry out the task assigned by using reasonable skill and care. The agent has a further duty to follow the principal's instructions and not to exceed the authority delegated to him or her.

EXAMPLE | Goldfinger is in charge of security at Fort Knox. He hires Odd Job, a karate expert, to maintain night watch. However, Odd Job falls asleep one night, and James Bond is able to steal the gold. What recourse does Goldfinger have against Odd Job? Goldfinger may sue Odd Job for breach of his agency contract because Odd Job failed to act in good faith in carrying out his assigned task with reasonable skill and care.

Duty to Account

An agent has a duty to account for all compensations received, including kickbacks. Upon the principal's request the agent must make a full disclosure, known as an accounting, of all receipts and expenditures. The agent must not comingle funds but rather must keep the principal's funds in an account separate from his or her own. Furthermore the agent must not use the principal's funds for his or her own purposes.

EXAMPLE | Miss Moneypenny is the executive secretary for "M," head of Her Majesty's Secret Service. One day she elopes with a James Bond lookalike while stealing all the money in the petty cash. What recourse does "M" have against her? "M" may sue Miss Moneypenny for breach of contract in failing to account for the funds in the petty cash account. She is also liable in tort for conversion of funds.

PRINCIPAL'S DUTIES

Duty to Compensate

A principal has the duty to compensate an agent for the work performed. The agent will be entitled to the amount agreed upon in the contract; otherwise he or she will be entitled to the reasonable value of the services rendered. A principal must also reimburse an agent for expenses the agent incurs while conducting the principal's business. For tax purposes a principal has a duty to keep records of the compensation earned by an agent and the reimbursements made for expenditures.

Duty to Maintain Safe Working Conditions

The maintenance of safe working conditions is another obligation placed on the principal. Any tools or equipment furnished to the agent must be in proper working order; otherwise the principal may be liable for harm resulting to an agent.

Plouffe v. Burlington Northern, Inc.
730 P. 2d 1148 (Mont. 1986)

Douglas Plouffe sued Burlington Northern for injuries he received while on the job. Plouffe asserted that the injuries resulted from Burlington Northern's failure to abide by the Federal Safety Appliance Act. This statute was enacted to protect railroad employees and the public against defective equipment on railroad cars and locomotives that might cause injury.

The accident occurred when Plouffe was attempting to free a hand brake on a railroad car that was stuck. After bleeding the brakes and attempting to turn the hand brake wheel, Plouffe bent down to rattle the chain connected to the brakes under the car. When he did so, the hand brake slipped, knocking him on the head.

The issue is whether Burlington Northern is absolutely liable for the injury sustained where Plouffe may have been contributorily negligent.

Contributory negligence is not a factor in determining whether the Safety Appliance Act (Title 45 U.S.C. 53) has been violated. The act states that "no such employee who may be injured or killed shall be held to have been guilty of contributory negligence in any case where the violation by such common carrier of any statute enacted for the safety of employees contributed to the injury or death of such employee."

EXAMPLE | Spectre hires Dr. No to work in its nuclear reactor plant. Spectre provides Dr. No with a pair of treated black plastic gloves for safety. While Dr. No is climbing a ladder, his hands slip and he falls into a radioactive tub, where he sustains severe chemical burns. Does he have any recourse against Spectre? Yes! Spectre breached its agency contract with Dr. No by violating its duty to provide employees with safe equipment.

REVIEW QUESTIONS

1. Define agency, principal, and agent.

2. What is the difference between express and implied actual authority? Give an example of each.

3. What is apparent authority? Give an example.

4. Define the agent's duty of loyalty, and give an example of a breach of the duty.

5. Define the agent's duty to act in good faith, and give an example of a breach of that duty.

6. Debi Eyerman worked her way up through the ranks of Mary Kay Cosmetics until she was appointed a national sales director. At that time she signed a National Sales Director Agreement. It provided that Eyerman would be an independent contractor, not an employee, and that she would earn a commission based on the performance of her sales group. Eyerman was required to maintain an office, provide advice to salespersons, and attend meetings when necessary. She was given no power to bind Mary Kay Cosmetics, and the company would exercise no control over her as well. Either party could cancel the agreement upon sixty days' notice. Is Eyerman an employee or an independent contractor? *Eyerman* v. *Mary Kay Cosmetics, Inc.,* 967 F. 2d 213 (6th Cir. 1992).

7. Lorentz was hired by Coblentz, who had an appliance repair business. Lorentz had to provide his own truck and stock his own parts. At 8:00 every morning Lorentz had to call in to receive his assignments for the day. He was paid a 50 percent commission. Coblentz withheld federal payroll taxes. The issue is whether Lorentz is an employee or an independent contractor. What result? *Lorentz* v. *Coblentz,* 600 S. 2d 1376 (La. App. 1 Cir. 1992).

8. Mrs. Amoroso was injured by a defective crossbar on a sailboat, which she and her husband had rented at the Diplomat Hotel. The sailboats were owned and operated by Sunrise Water Sports. The rental stand was on the hotel's grounds, the fee was billed to the hotel room, and the rental was advertised in the hotel room. Mr. Amoroso sued the Diplomat on the theory of apparent authority. What result? *Amoroso* v. *Samuel Friedland Family Ent.,* 604 So. 2d 827 (Fla. App. 4 Dist. 1992).

35

Agency: Liability and Termination

Liability of Agents	Termination of an Agency
Liability of Principals	Review Questions
Liability of Third Parties	

LIABILITY OF AGENTS

Agents will be liable for breach of contract if they fail to uphold their duties, including duty of loyalty, duty to act in good faith, and duty to account for all receipts and expenses. An agent will be liable for all unauthorized acts or misrepresentations made to third parties in the principal's name.

An agent's liability extends to a situation where the agent contracts with a third party on behalf of a nonexistent principal or contracts in his or her own name on behalf of a principal who does exist. For protection against personal liability, an agent should always sign the principal's name and then his or her own name as agent. Of course, when an agent represents an undisclosed principal, the agent will have to contract in his or her own name to protect the identity of the principal; in this case the agent would be personally liable.

Except in an emergency, an agent will be personally liable to a third party when he or she acts without actual or apparent authority. A principal will be liable to a third party for an agent's acts during an emergency if the agent's acts were reasonable, even though the agent may have acted without authority.

EXAMPLE | Rosa Klebb, an agent of Spectre, represented to James Bond that Spectre would sell its Star Wars space weapons to Her Majesty's Secret Service and signed a contract to this effect as an agent for Spectre. Spectre disaffirmed the contract, claiming that Klebb had acted without authority. What recourse do James Bond and the secret service have? They may sue Spectre for breach of contract. Spectre will be bound because of Rosa Klebb's apparent authority. Spectre's recourse lies against Rosa Klebb for breach of her duty of loyalty and her duty to act in good faith.

Jessee v. Amoco Oil Co.,
594 N.E. 2d 1210 (Ill. App. 1 Dist. 1992)

Amoco leased a service station to Tommy Baker. The lease provided that Amoco would be responsible for major repairs including replacement of the furnace. Baker had full discretion in hiring. He hired Anna Jessee to work as cashier. Subsequently the heating system stopped functioning. Baker advised Amoco, which then hired Standard Heating to replace the system. After installation of the new heating system, Jessee became ill and was rushed to the hospital to be treated for carbon monoxide poisoning. She suffered brain damage. The fresh air return duct had not been reconnected to the new furnace; therefore the cashier's booth became filled with carbon monoxide. Standard Heating had been hired to install the furnace but not to reconnect the ducts.

The issue is whether Amoco is liable for the work of Standard Heating, an independent contractor.

The court ruled, "Generally, an employer of an independent contractor is not liable for the acts or omissions of the independent contractor; however, an exception to the rule provides that an employer who retains control of any part of the work will be liable for injuries resulting from his failure to exercise his right of control with reasonable care." Judgment for Jessee.

LIABILITY OF PRINCIPALS

Contractual Liability

A disclosed principal is bound by his or her agent's contract with a third party where the agent acted with actual authority, either express or implied, or with apparent authority. A disclosed principal is not liable for the unauthorized acts of an agent unless he or she ratifies them.

When a contract is made on behalf of an undisclosed principal, the third party may elect to hold either the principal or the agent responsible. The agent is responsible because he or she is contracting in his or her own name for an undisclosed principal. The undisclosed principal will become liable only when his or her identity is disclosed.

EXAMPLE | Felix Lichter and James Bond each contracted with Scaramanga to purchase one of his golden guns for $5,000. Felix Lichter represented the CIA and signed the contract as an agent of the CIA, while James Bond represented Her Majesty's Sercet Service but failed to disclose this. Both men were authorized to pay only up to $3,000. Each of their principals refuses to pay Scaramanga when the golden guns are delivered. Scaramanga, the man with the golden guns, sues the CIA and Her Majesty's Secret Service. Who will be liable? The CIA is a disclosed principal and is liable for the acts of its agent, Felix Lichter, even though Felix exceeded his authority because he acted with apparent authority. Her Majesty's Secret Service will not be liable for James Bond's actions because its identity was not disclosed. James Bond is personally liable because he signed his own name to the contract. If Bond sued the secret service for reimbursement, would he be successful? No, because Bond breached his duties of loyalty and good faith by exceeding his authority.

A principal is not liable for the unauthorized acts of an agent in a case where the third party has a duty to inquire about the agent's actual authority when that authority is not apparent. A third party who unjustifiably assumes that the agent possesses the authority to contract will have no recourse against the principal but will be restricted to recovering from the agent alone.

Tort Liability

A principal is liable for the torts committed by his or her agent if a tort is committed within the scope of employment—that is, if it is related to the business at hand. Principals may contract for liability insurance to minimize their risk and to avoid paying for damages out of the business profits.

EXAMPLE | Jaws is an attendant in the shark tank in Octopussy's Aquarium and Water World. On a day when the facilities are closed, some of the show performers' guests are swimming in a pool adjacent to the shark tank. Jaws lifts open the steel door that separates the pools, and the sharks nip the swimmers. Do the guests have any recourse against Octopussy? Yes! Octopussy is responsible for the tort of assault and battery committed by her agent because it occurred within the scope of Jaws' employment. If Jaws had bitten one of the guests himself after leaving the Aquarium and Water World, would Octopussy still be liable? No! Jaws' actions did not occur within the scope of employment.

Collum v. Argo
599 So. 2d 1210 (Ala. Civ. App. 1992)

Kenny Collum sold a mobile home to the Dawsons. He arranged with Stanley Wilson to have a septic tank installed. During the installation Wilson knocked over fifteen fruit trees on adjacent property owned by the Argos. The Argos brought suit against Collum, alleging that Wilson was in his employ when he committed the trespass.

The issues are whether Collum is Wilson's employer and whether an employer is liable for the torts of his or her employee.

The court ruled,

> An employer's liability for general trespass is based on the doctrine of respondent superior; that is, an employer may be liable for consequential damages when his employee, acting within the course of the employer's business, wrongfully trespasses on the property of another. The employer need not have even been aware of the employee's actions, because liability arises from the employment relationship itself.

The court continued,

> The test for determining whether one is an agent or employee, as opposed to an independent contractor, is whether the alleged employer has reserved the right of control over the means and method by which the work is done. We must conclude that there was no employer-employee relationship between Collum and Wilson. Instead, the record indicates that Collum merely acted as an agent of the Dawsons and engaged Wilson to install the septic tank at their behest. He did not have any right of control over the work to be performed and certainly did not direct Wilson to trespass onto the Argo property. Accordingly, Collum cannot be subjected to liability for the damage Wilson caused to the Argos, nor can he be held liable under a theory of trespass.

Judgment for Collum.

A principal is also liable for fraud or misrepresentation committed by an agent where the principal has placed the agent in a position that leads people to believe that the agent has the apparent authority to make certain actual representations.

EXAMPLE | "M" asked Miss Moneypenny if she would work overtime every night for the next three weeks. She inquired concerning the rate of pay. "M" advised her that she could not be paid because of budget restrictions but assured her that he would arrange a date for her with James Bond. She assented, but after she performed the work, the date never materialized. Has she any recourse against Her Majesty's Secret Service? Yes! The secret service as a principal is responsible for the false representations made by its agent within the scope of his or her employment. Given "M"'s position as head of the secret service, Miss Moneypenny would reasonably believe that he has the authority to make such a statement.

Ratification of an Agent's Unauthorized Acts

Ratification is approval or sanction given by the principal to an agent's unauthorized acts. The principal may ratify unauthorized contracts made by the agent as well as torts committed by the agent. Following are the requirements for ratification:

The agent acts in excess of or without authority.

The principal is made aware of all important facts.

The principal ratifies the entire act, not part of it.

Ratification must be made in the same manner as the authority given to the agent.

Ratification may be implied when a principal fails to condemn an agent's acts within a reasonable time after learning of all of the important facts. Once the principal ratifies the agent's contractual acts and the third party is notified, a contract exists between the principal and the third party that the principal is now legally obligated to perform. When a third party is notified that the principal assumes all responsibility for an agent's torts, the principal will be liable for the injuries sustained by that third party.

EXAMPLE | Ernst Blofeld, Spectre's Number One, hires Mr. Good and Mr. Will to procure fifty diamonds from Tiffany Case, president of Diamonds Are Forever. Mr. Good and Mr. Will give Tiffany Case a bad check for the diamonds and then transfer them to Ernst Blofeld. Blofeld is advised of the theft but makes no attempt to rectify the matter. Is he liable in a suit brought by Tiffany Case for payment? Yes! Blofeld ratified his agent's unauthorized acts by accepting the diamonds and refusing to pay for them.

LIABILITY OF THIRD PARTIES

A third party is liable only to the principal, whether the principal is disclosed, partially disclosed, or undisclosed. A third party is not liable to an agent unless the agent signs the contract in his or her own name.

EXAMPLE | In the earlier example concerning Scaramanga and the sale of his golden guns, if he refused to sell the gun to James Bond after Bond's bid had been accepted, could Bond and Her Majesty's Secret Service both enforce the contract? Yes! Bond has the right to enforce the contract against Scaramanga because he signed the contract in his own name. The secret service, an undisclosed principal, may enforce the contract by disclosing its identity and ratifying Bond's unauthorized act of exceeding his authority.

TERMINATION OF AN AGENCY

An agency relationship may terminate in the following ways: **RAP UP,** as "wrap up."

Revocation of authority
Agreement
Purpose fulfilled

Unfulfilled condition
Prohibition by operation of law

Revocation of Authority

An agent's authority may be revoked if the duration of the contract is indefinite or if no time limit has been specified. The principal may also revoke an agent's authority for cause where the agent has breached one of the duties owed. The agent must be notified that his or her authority is revoked. If the agency contract was in writing, then the revocation must also be in writing. Under other circumstances it may be oral. Notice of revocation is effective when the agent receives it.

Notice of termination by revocation or mutual agreement must also be communicated to third persons who have dealt with the principal through the agent. Otherwise the principal will be liable to third persons who contract with the agent. The principal's liability is based on the agent's apparent authority to act, which is based on prior dealings and which the third party is justified in believing. Third parties who have dealt with the agent on prior occasions must be sent actual notice of termination. Notice becomes effective when the third party receives it. For all other third parties, the principal may satisfy the duty to notify by publishing a statement regarding termination of the agent's authority in a newspaper.

EXAMPLE | Spectre's Number Two was assigned the task of eliminating James Bond. Number Two proved to be a double agent and double-crossed Spectre. What recourse does Spectre have against Number Two? Ernst Blofeld, director of Spectre, may permanently revoke Number Two's authority because of Number Two's violation of his duty of loyalty. Blofeld may have Jaws put the bite on Number Two.

Agreement

Like any other contract, an agency contract can be terminated by mutual agreement of the parties. This termination is valid even if the contract had called for a longer term of employment.

Purpose Complete

The authority of an agent hired for a specific term of employment, as in an employee-employer relationship, will terminate upon the expiration of that term. An agency relationship created for the fulfillment of a specific purpose will terminate when that purpose is fulfilled.

EXAMPLE | Spectre contracts with Emilio Largo to have Largo manufacture the arcade game "Battle of the World" where the participants receive electric shocks in increasing magnitude for each country they lose in battle. Domino is hired by Spectre for a three-year period, mainly to act as a liaison between Spectre and Largo. What is the status of the agency relationships created, and when will they terminate? Emilio Largo is an independent contractor who is free to use his own methods in manufacturing the game. His agency relationship with Spectre will terminate when the game is manufactured. Domino is an employee of Spectre, who must follow Spectre's instructions in dealing with Largo. Domino's agency relationship terminates at the end of the three-year employment period.

Unfulfilled Condition

The creation of an agency relationship may be conditioned on the occurrence of an event. If the condition precedent fails, the agency will not be created. An agency may also be created with its continued existence dependent on the fulfillment of a condition subsequent. If this condition should fail, the agency will be terminated.

EXAMPLE | Spectre hired Pussy Galore to be 007's personal bodyguard for the rest of his natural life. When will the agency relationship terminate? On Bond's death! James Bond, unlike a cat, only lives twice. Pussy Galore may be unemployed if Bond is bumped off.

Prohibition by Operation of Law

An agency may terminate by operation of law in the following ways: **BID**.

Bankruptcy of the principal or the agent (which will terminate the agent's authority in financial transactions)

Insanity or death of either the principal or the agent

Destruction or loss of the subject matter, if the agency was created for a purpose related to that subject matter

REVIEW QUESTIONS

1. When is an agent personally liable?
2. Under what circumstances will a principal be liable for an agent's torts?
3. When will an undisclosed principal be liable for his or her agent's acts?
4. In what ways can an agency relationship be terminated?

5. The Hudginses entered into a contract with Bacon to build a house for them. Bacon hired an independent contractor who poured the footings and laid the foundation. Within a few months after the Hudginses moved into the house, it began to fall apart. The Hudginses brought action against Bacon for negligence and for breach of contract for failure to build the house in a workmanlike manner. Bacon contends that he cannot be held liable for any negligence caused by the independent contractor. What result? *Hudgins* v. *Bacon,* 321 S.E. 2d 359 (Ga. App. 1984).

6. Equitable Life Assurance instructed Dr. Arora to administer a stress test to Sidney Rosenberg, a fifty-one-year-old with a history of heart problems. Rosenberg died a month after taking the stress test, and the test was determined to be the proximate cause of his death. His estate sued Equitable for wrongful death. What result? *Rosenberg* v. *Equitable Life Assurance Society,* 584 N.Y.S. 2d 765 (Ct. App. 1992).

7. Sparks sued the Northeast Alabama Regional Medical Center, her employer, claiming to be sexually harassed by Dr. Garland. Sparks alleged that Dr. Garland joked about her breast size and sex life and cursed her in front of her co-workers for being late. The hospital claimed that this behavior was outside the scope of Dr. Garland's employment. What result? *Sparks* v. *Regional Medical Center Bd.,* 792 F. Supp. 735 (N.D. Ala. 1992).

8. Power Equipment's president Robert Ferguson signed a promissory note without reading it. The note contained a provision that the bank could demand payment at any time. Power Equipment alleged that the bank had breached its fiduciary duty to inform Ferguson of the demand provision before he signed the note. What result? *Power Equipment* v. *First Alabama Bank,* 585 So. 2d 1291 (Ala. 1991).

9. Kimberly Bunce entered the Parkside Lodge for rehabilitation from cocaine addiction. Bryan Brown, a senior counselor, comforted Bunce on a few occasions. This led to a sexual relationship. After several encounters Bunce revealed her relationship with Brown to Parkside, then left the facility. Brown resigned. Bunce sued Parkside for sexual assault, malpractice, and intentional infliction of emotional distress. Parkside claimed that it was not responsible for the intentional torts of its employee. What result? *Bunce* v. *Parkside Lodge of Columbus,* 596 N.E. 2d 1106 (Ohio App. 10 Dist. 1991).

10. Sixteen-year-old Cory Grote was a high school rodeo champion. After receiving permission from Bruce Bushnell, foreman, he was allowed to visit his brother Brad at Joy Ranch, a division of Meyers. During his visit Cory helped Brad release twelve colts into a corral. One of the colts, known to the ranchers to be uncontrollable, kicked Cory, causing him to have a skull fracture. Cory sued the ranch, claiming that the ranch was negligent in not informing him of the colt's dangerous propensities. Is the ranch liable for its employees' failure to warn Cory? *Grote* v. *Meyers Land and Cattle Co.,* 485 N.W. 2d 748 (Neb. 1992).

36

Partnerships:
Formation and Duties

Introduction
Partnership Compared to Other
   Legal Entities

Organization of a Partnership
Rights and Duties of Partners
Review Questions

INTRODUCTION

A *partnership* is a voluntary association of two or more persons who

act for each other as agents;

are involved in a fiduciary relationship (one of trust and confidence);

operate a business, trade, or profession for profit; and

share in the profits and the losses of the partnership as well as the partnership
property by express or implied agreement.

Simply stated, a partnership is a voluntary association of two or more persons established for profit. Partnerships are governed by the Uniform Partnership Act, which
has been adopted in almost every state. A partner is an individual who voluntarily enters
into an agreement with one or more individuals to operate a business and to share the
resulting profits or losses. A partner is an agent of the partnership. This means that he
or she has the right to act on behalf of the partnership. The relationship between the
partners is based on principles of agency involving a fiduciary relationship—one of
trust and confidence.

Because a partnership is created by contract and in fact is a special kind of a contract, all the rules of contract law apply, and all the requirements of a contract must be

met, including the requirement of capacity. A minor may be a partner. Because a partnership is a form of business contract, he or she will be liable as a partner but only up to the amount of his or her capital contribution. In the legal sense the term *person* also includes corporations and other partnerships. A corporation may become a partner in states where permission has been granted by statutory authority; otherwise corporations lack the requisite capacity. Partnerships may become partners with other partnerships if all of the partners of both partnerships agree. Sharing of profits is evidence of a partnership.

PARTNERSHIP COMPARED TO OTHER LEGAL ENTITIES

A partnership must be distinguished from other legal entities formed for profit, such as corporations, associations, and joint ventures. A partnership may be created without legal formalities, whereas formation of a corporation requires state approval and the filing of a certificate of incorporation. A partnership is not a legal entity for tax purposes. Therefore it may have favorable tax consequences for a person who would prefer his or her share of the profits to be taxed as individual income. In certain instances partnerships may act with greater expediency because they do not require stockholder approval for action. Partners are personally liable for all the debts of a partnership, whereas stockholders' liability is limited to their investment in the corporation. Partners' unlimited liability may lead to greater borrowing power because they can pledge their individual assets, in addition to those of the partnership, as collateral in consideration for a loan. A partnership lasts only as long as the partners are alive or as long as they desire to remain associated. A corporation's existence, in contrast, is perpetual.

A joint venture is organized for a specific purpose and continues in existence until the purpose is achieved, at which time it terminates. A joint venture may be considered a special form of partnership because it is subject to all the rules of partnership law. Religious, fraternal, charitable, and labor associations are not partnerships because they are not created for the purpose of profit. Examples of such organizations are the Knights of Columbus, the Masons, the Elks, the Moose, the Kiwanis, Covenant House, the Teamsters, the AFL-CIO, the United Federation of Teachers, and the United Auto Workers.

ORGANIZATION OF A PARTNERSHIP

A partnership is a special contract that is not required to be in writing under the statute of frauds unless it is organized for the purpose of selling real estate or otherwise comes under one of the provisions of the statute of frauds. A partnership may be created orally or by implication through the actions of the parties, but most often it is created in writing. A writing is important for the protection of the individual partners because it evidences the existence of the partnership and sets forth the partners' rights and duties.

This writing is the partnership agreement, which is often referred to as the articles of partnership.

The partnership may choose any name as long as it does not deceive or otherwise mislead the general public. The partnership may use the name of one of the partners, as well. Usually one of the following is added to the partnership name to distinguish it from a corporation or sole proprietorship: Company, Co., Associates, or Firm.

A partnership must file a certificate of partnership with the county clerk in the county where it intends to have its principal place of business.

RIGHTS AND DUTIES OF PARTNERS

A partner has the following basic rights and duties in a partnership:

Make capital contributions
Share in the partnership property
Participate in management
Share in the profits
Fulfill the duty of loyalty

Capital Contributions

Each partner's share in the profits is determined by the value of his or her contribution. This contribution may be in the form of money, real estate, fixtures, goods, or services.

EXAMPLE | Duke, Pee Wee, and Campy form a partnership that buys the Brooklyn Bums, a baseball team that is continuously in the cellar. The purchase price for the Bums is one million dollars. The partnership agreement calls for the three partners to share profits and losses in proportion to the percentage of capital they contribute. Duke contributes $500,000, Pee Wee $300,000, and Campy $200,000.

Partnership Property

All property, both real and personal, that is held in the partnership name, bought with partnership funds, or used in the partnership business is presumed to be an asset of the partnership. This presumption can be rebutted because property held by a partner individually can be loaned or otherwise used in the business. The assets of the partnership are held by the partners as tenants in partnership. Each partner has an equal right to use the partnership assets, but only in connection with the partnership business. If one partner dies the remaining partners have the right of survivorship to all property held by the partnership. The heirs of the deceased partner have no right to the assets of the partnership, but they must be paid the proportionate value of the assets representing the decedent's interest therein. The heirs are third-party beneficiaries of the partnership agreement.

EXAMPLE | If Campy dies his heirs have no right to any of the assets of the Brooklyn Bums. However, Duke and Pee Wee must pay the heirs the value of Campy's interest in the partnership on the date of his death. If the net assets of the Bums on the date of Campy's death were determined to be two million dollars because of a pennant-winning season, Campy's heirs would be entitled to $400,000. If Duke and Pee Wee do not have the $400,000 in cash to pay the heirs, they may be forced to (1) take out a loan, (2) form a new partnership with the heirs as partners, or (3) liquidate the partnership assets by selling the Bums. As an alternative the surviving partners might be able to work out an agreement with the heirs to reimburse them for the deceased partner's proportionate share over a period of time, with interest. The prudent thing for the partners to do when setting up the partnership would have been to take out a life insurance policy on each partner in an amount equivalent to each partner's interest in the partnership and to pay the premiums from the partnership's assests. The face value of the policy could have been increased as the value of the partners' interests grew.

Management

The partnership agreement designates the officers and specifies the responsibilities of each. The voting power of each partner is also stipulated. In the absence of such stipulation, voting power is considered equal. The articles also specify whether matters must be decided by a simple majority, by a two-thirds majority, or by unanimous vote. Routine matters might be decided by a majority vote, whereas special or important matters might require a unanimous vote. Also, the articles must state the number of partners who must be present to constitute a quorum.

EXAMPLE | In the partnership agreement of the Brooklyn Bums, decisions concerning the players' salaries or changes in the profit-sharing structure require unanimity of all three partners. What are each partner's responsibilities? Duke is in charge of all legal and accounting matters. Pee Wee is in charge of recruitment and dismissal of coaches and players. Campy is in charge of advertising and equipment purchasing.

Because each partner is an agent of the partnership, he or she has the power to act on behalf of the partnership in such matters as making contracts for employment, for the sale of goods, for the purchase or sale of real estate, and for the rendering of personal services. A partner need not have written authority to bind the partnership because a partner is both a principal and an agent of the partnership.

EXAMPLE | Tinker, Evans, and Chance form a partnership to sell and distribute baseball equipment. Tinker enters into a contract with Campy to supply the Brooklyn Bums with 120 gloves, 280 bats, and 600 baseballs for $4,500. Because this contract must be in writing as it involves the sale of goods in excess of $500, must Tinker's authority to bind the partner-ship to this contract be in writing? No! Because Tinker is both an agent and a principal of the partnership, his authority is not required to be evidenced by a writing, but the articles of partnership must be in writing to satisfy the statute of frauds requirement.

Profit Sharing

The partnership agreement dictates the percentage of the profits that each partner will receive. The percentage is based on the capital contributions made and the services rendered by each partner. Partners are liable for the partnership's losses to the extent to which they share in the profits. If there is no agreement as to profit sharing, then the profits and—impliedly—the losses will be divided equally among the partners regardless of capital contributions made or time devoted to the partnership business.

EXAMPLE The Brooklyn Bums' partnership agreement provides that Duke gets 50 percent of the profits, Pee Wee 30 percent, and Campy 20 percent. The first year the Bums are in the red for $30,000. The second year they turn a profit of $60,000. After the second year the partners vote unanimously that Duke will receive 45 percent of the profits, Pee Wee will earn 33 percent, and Campy 22 percent. In the third year the Bums win the World Series and earn a profit of $200,000. How much will each of the partners receive in the respective years? In the first year Duke will be responsible for $15,000 of the $30,000 loss, Pee Wee will be responsible for $9,000 of the loss, and Campy will be liable for the remaining $6,000. In the second year Duke will earn a $30,000 profit, Pee Wee will receive $18,000, and Campy will earn $12,000. In the the third year Duke will be entitled to $90,000 in profits, Pee Wee will earn $66,000 in profits, and Campy will get $44,000.

The partnership agreement may also provide for salaries to compensate the partners for their individual services, although normally each partner's compensation is determined through profit sharing.

A partner has the contractual right to assign his or her share in the profits to a third person. For more information on assignments consult Chapter 15, "Rights of Third Parties."

All partners have the right to inspect the bookkeeping and accounting records of the partnership to assure themselves that they are receiving fair distribution of the profits in accordance with the percentages set forth in the partnership agreement.

Duty of Loyalty

A partner as an agent of the partnership must fulfill an agent's duty of loyalty and duty to act in good faith. Inherent in these duties are the following: duty to avoid self-dealing, duty not to compete, duty to exercise reasonable business judgment, and duty not to exceed authority.

Duty to Avoid Self-Dealing Each partner has a duty of loyalty to the partnership, which means that he or she must act in good faith with regard to all transactions entered into on behalf of the partnership. A partner may buy from or sell to the partnership but must avoid self-dealing—entering into contracts with the partnership solely for personal benefit. To avoid self-dealing, the partner should disclose to the other partners all pertinent information relating to the purchase or sale.

EXAMPLE The recent success of the Brooklyn Bums has caused Prentice-Hall to offer the Bums a contract to write their success story, *From the Bowery to Broadway.* Prentice-Hall approaches Duke with the idea. Duke accepts and signs a contract to write the book in his own name without informing his partners. When Pee Wee and Campy learn of Duke's actions, they bring a lawsuit against him. Will they win? Yes! Duke is guilty of self-dealing. He has violated his duty of loyalty to the partnership.

Duty Not to Compete It is inherent in a partner's duty of loyalty to refrain from engaging in any business that will compete with or otherwise affect the partnership in a detrimental manner. This includes taking advantage of the partnership's business opportunities for one's own use or profit. A partner has a duty to inform the other partners of all material relating to new business or the operation of the partnership. If a partner is guilty of self-dealing, competing with the partnership, or usurping the partnership's business opportunities, the partner must account for all profits earned at the partnership's expense.

EXAMPLE Gehrig, Ruth, and Aaron form a partnership to manufacture candy bars that will bear Ruth's name. Aaron becomes jealous because Ruth is receiving all the publicity and a greater share of the profits. While still remaining a partner, Aaron opens his own candy manufacturing company and markets a candy bar called Oh Henry. The sales of Oh Henry cut into the market share of Baby Ruth. When Gehrig and Ruth discover that Aaron is behind Oh Henry, do they have any recourse against him? Yes! Aaron has breached his duty of loyalty to the partnership by taking advantage of the partnership's business opportunity. Aaron must account for the profits that the partnership lost because of the competing sale of Oh Henry candy bars.

Meinhard v. Salmon
249 N.Y. 458, 164 N.E. 545 (1928)

Meinhard sued Salmon for breach of his duty of loyalty in taking advantage of the partnership's opportunity for his own benefit.

Salmon was in the process of negotiating a twenty-year lease with Louisa M. Gerry for the rental of the Hotel Bristol on Forty-second Street and Fifth Avenue in New York when he used Meinhard's financial backing to complete the deal. A partnership was formed, with Meinhard contributing half of the funds required to reconstruct, manage, and operate the hotel. Meinhard was to share in 40 percent of the profits for the first five years and 50 percent for the remaining fifteen years, at the end of which time the lease would expire.

Before the lease expired Louisa passed away. Her heir, Elbridge T. Gerry, became the owner of the Hotel Bristol. He entered into a long-term lease with a corporation called Midpoint Realty, which was owned by Salmon. Salmon did not advise Meinhard of the new leasing arrangement until after the lease had been signed. Meinhard sued Salmon to make the latter hold half of the lease in trust for him.

The issue is whether Salmon breached his duty of loyalty to Meinhard by taking advantage of the partnership's opportunity for his own benefit.

The court held, "[O]ne partner may not appropriate to his own use a renewal of a lease, though its term is to begin at the expiration of the partnership." The problem with Salmon's conduct is that he excluded Meinhard

> from any chance to enjoy the opportunity for benefit that had come to him alone by virtue of his agency. This chance, if nothing more, he was under a duty to concede. The price of its denial is an extension of the trust at the option and for the benefit of one whom he excluded.

Judgment for Meinhard.

Duty to Exercise Reasonable Business Judgment A partner's duty to act in good faith means that the partner must exercise reasonable care in representing the partnership and in making business judgments on its behalf. However, a partner will not be liable for honest mistakes resulting from his or her judgments if they were reasonable in light of the surrounding circumstances.

EXAMPLE | The Brooklyn Bums take in four new partners, O'Malley, Alston, Hodges, and Robinson. The partnership agreement provides that each partner is entitled to one vote. These four partners, who have business and personal interests on the West Coast, vote to move the Bums from Brooklyn to Los Angeles without evidence that the Bums will be accepted. Duke, Pee Wee, and Campy object, but to no avail.

When the Bums arrive in L.A., they find that people are more interested in sun, surfing, and Hollywood. The Bums suffer severe financial losses. The three original partners sue the other four for failing to exercise reasonable business judgment in moving the team. Will they win? Yes! The new partners failed to exercise reasonable care in making their decision, which adversely affected the team as well as the three original partners. This is more than an honest business mistake because the new partners acted out of self-interest.

Duty Not to Exceed Authority The partnership agreement spells out the managerial responsibilities of each partner. A partner has an obligation not to exceed the authority granted to him or her by the partnership agreement. If a partner exceeds that authority or fails to exercise reasonable judgment in transacting partnership business, the partner is negligent and will be liable for the consequential damages.

EXAMPLE | Pee Wee hires a wild throwing pitcher named Koufax for $100,000 a year. In the opinion of Pee Wee's partners, Koufax is not worth the money. They breach the contract with Koufax, who sues for damages. After paying Koufax the damages, the Bums sue Pee Wee for exceeding his authority. Will they succeed? Yes! Although Pee Wee was right concerning Koufax's ability, he only had the authority to recruit Koufax, not to sign a contract with him for a set salary. The player's salary required the unanimous vote of all the partners.

REVIEW QUESTIONS

1. Define partnership.
2. What is the difference between a partnership and the following: corporation, joint venture, and association or club?
3. What are the rights of the individual partners?
4. Dr. Witlin was one of forty-five physicians who formed a partnership for the purpose of opening a medical center that they would operate together. After Dr. Witlin died the surviving partners offered his widow $65,000, which they claimed represented the book value of Dr. Witlin's interest in the partnership. The partnership agreement stated that the determination of the deceased partner's interest should represent its corresponding fair market value. Dr. Witlin's widow claimed that the partnership was in the process of negotiating a sale of the medical center that would place the value of her deceased husband's interest at almost triple the amount offered to her. The widow sued the partnership for the fair market value of her husband's interest, alleging a breach of the partnership duty to act in good faith. The partnership claimed that she was precluded from maintaining the lawsuit because she had already accepted the partnership's offer. What result? *Estate of Witlin,* 83 Cal. App. 3d 167, 147 Cal. Rptr. 723 (1978).
5. Lindsey and Stranahan were copartners in a business called J. K. Lindsey & Company. Lindsey managed the business and did more than his share of the work. Lindsey claimed that he should be awarded a salary for the reasonable value of the services he rendered. No provision about a salary was made in the partnership agreement. Is Lindsey entitled to a salary in addition to his right to share in the profits earned from the partnership business? *Lindsey* v. *Stranahan,* 129 Pa. 635, 18 A. 524 (1889).

6. Okura & Company loaned money to the Carean group, owners of an egg ranch named Egg City, pursuant to a loan agreement. Okura hoped that the loan would enable Carean to generate sufficient revenues to service debt. Instead Carean defaulted. Carean alleged that the relationship was a joint venture and that Okura had breached its fiduciary duties toward Carean by exercising control over Carean's decision making. What result? *Okura & Co.* v. *Carean Group,* 783 F. Supp. 482 (C.D. Cal 1991).

7. Williams and Pedersen were copartners in a logging business. The partnership agreement did not specify the division of profits between them. Pedersen claimed that Williams was away from the logging camp much of the time and that because of these absences, the burden of operating the logging business fell upon him. Pedersen further claimed that he should receive a greater share of the profits because of the added responsibility forced on him. Williams claimed that because the partnership agreement was silent, both he and Pedersen must divide the profits equally. What result? *Williams* v. *Pedersen,* 47 Wash. 472, 92 P. 287 (1907).

8. Latta, Kilbourn, and Osborn were partners in a real estate brokerage. Their partnership agreement stated that the purpose of their partnership was to negotiate the sale and purchase of real estate for other individuals. There was no mention in the partnership agreement of giving the partners authority to buy or sell real estate in the partnership's name. On several occasions the partners purchased property in their individual names. On one occasion Latta speculated by purchasing real estate with a third party named Stearns. The joint venture was very successful, and huge profits were realized. Kilbourn and Osborn sued Latta, claiming that Latta had acted without informing them of the speculation and that in doing so he had directly competed with the partnership and should account to it for the profits he had realized at the partnership's expense. What result? *Latta* v. *Kilbourn,* 150 U.S. 524, 14 S. Ct. 201 (1893).

9. J. David Cassilly and Joseph L. Masan were general partners in Glen Park Properties. Cassilly entered into a contract with Schnucks Markets, Inc. to share the cost of extending a sewer line to the Schnucks's property. Subsequently Cassilly and Schnucks orally agreed to split the cost equally. Glen Parks breached the contract, claiming that Cassilly had no authority to bind the partnership. Is the partnership liable? *Schnucks Markets, Inc.* v. *Cassilly,* 724 S.W. 2d 664 (Mo. App. 1987).

37

Partnerships: Dissolution and Liabilities

Liability of Partners	Distribution of Assets
Dissolution	According to Priority
Winding Up	Review Questions

LIABILITY OF PARTNERS

Generally

A partnership is liable for the actions of its partners, and it will be primarily responsible for the contracts that they enter into. This is because a partner is both a principal and an agent of the partnership. The partners are also jointly and individually liable for debts incurred by the partnership.

A partnership and the individual partners will be liable for any crime or tort committed by any of the partners while he or she is engaging in partnership business. However, the partnership and the individual partners are not liable for any debts incurred or crimes or torts committed by a partner outside the scope of the partnership business.

Partners take a risk that one of the other partners may bind the partnership to a contract that may place unlimited liability on the partnership and on themselves as individuals. There is a definite risk when one enters into a partnership—that one's personal assets may be sold to cover the debts of the partnership. For this very reason individuals should be very careful with whom they enter into partnerships. Many individuals take the risk because of their trust and confidence in their partners.

EXAMPLE | Johnny Reb and Billy Yankee form a partnership to construct two iron-clad ships, the *Monitor* and the *Merrimac,* for the Union. After the construction Johnny Reb secretly delivers the *Merrimac* to the Confederates. The Union sues the partnership for breach of contract. Is the partnership liable? Yes! The partnership is liable for Johnny Reb's unauthorized actions. If the partnership is unable to pay the Union's damages, would Billy Yankee be personally liable? Yes! Billy Yankee is personally responsible for the acts of his partner. If Johnny Reb entered into a contract in his own name with the Confederates to sell and deliver the other ship, the *Monitor,* could this contract be enforced against the partnership? No! By signing his own name, Johnny Reb did not bind the partnership.

A partnership may be sued in its own name. The summons must contain the name of the partnership, and service may be made personally to any one of the partners. In order for the partners to be personally liable, they must be named in the summons, and each one of them must be personally served.

EXAMPLE | Caesar Brothers Company operated a health spa that employed "specialists" to give massages. This service helped to entice members of established health spas to join Caesar's Health Spa. Eventually the competing health spas offered the same attraction. As a result the Caesar Brothers' business dwindled, and they were forced to close down. They did not return the current membership fees paid. The remaining members of Caesar's Health Spa sued collectively for return of their membership fees.

The summons named Caesar Brothers Company and individually named Tiberius and Augustus but not Julius. Only Augustus was personally served. The partnership's debts greatly outweigh the partnership's assets. After the assets are sold and the proceeds are paid to the members, only Augustus will be personally liable because he was the only partner named on the summons and personally served. Tiberius was named but not served; Julius was neither named nor served. It would be a violation of their constitutional rights to hold them personally liable if they were not given proper notice.

If only one of the partners is personally accountable and must pay, his or her recourse lies in the right to contribution from the other partners for their proportionate shares of the profits as dictated by the partnership agreement. If the partnership agreement is silent on this matter, the partners' shares in the profits and losses will be equal. If this were the case in the previous example, Augustus might look to Tiberius and Julius for one-third each of what he had paid out.

A judgment against a partnership must be enforced first against the assets of the partnership; only when they are depleted are the partners' individual assets subject to the claims of the partnership's creditors.

EXAMPLE | In the previous example concerning Caesar's Health Spa, assume that the debts of the partnership were $350,000 and that its assets totaled $200,000. The $200,000 would be applied to the debt, leaving the partners jointly liable for the remaining $150,000. Each partner would be liable for $50,000, but the entire $150,000 might be collected from one partner, Augustus. Augustus would then have the right to sue Tiberius and Julius for $50,000 each.

U.S. v. Broude
593 F. Supp. 1402 (N.D. Cal. 1984)

The Pacific Far East Liner (PFEL) decided to file for bankruptcy. PFEL paid $125,000 to Richard Broude, a partner in the law firm of Irell and Manella, to retain the firm's services. This left PFEL with insufficient funds to meet its payroll tax.

The U.S. government sued to recover the monies the law firm received. The government claimed that a constructive trust was imposed on the law firm because it knew that the funds it received had been set aside to pay the unpaid payroll tax.

Broude argued that he was not liable because the retainer had been paid to the law firm, Irell and Manella, not to him personally. Furthermore, he had since left the firm.

The issue is whether Broude is personally liable.

The court held, "Partners are jointly and severally liable for partnership obligations and such liability is not discharged simply because one leaves the partnership." Judgment for the United States.

Incoming Partners

An incoming partner is not personally responsible for the past debts of the partnership. However, the capital contribution of an incoming partner will be subject to the claims of past debts because once the contribution is made, it becomes an asset of the partnership.

Moseley v. Commercial State Bank
457 So. 2d 967 (Ala. 1984)

On September 17, 1980, five individuals founded the Southern Distilleries partnership. The partnership agreement provided that authorization to borrow money and to execute promissory notes on behalf of the partnership required the signatures of any three or more partners having a combined interest of at least 60 percent. The agreement also stated that any action taken by any three partners would bind the partnership as well as the individual partners.

On December 19, 1980, three of the partners entered into two promissory notes totaling $758,784. On July 21, 1981, Southern Distilleries satisfied the existing notes after a new note for $140,000 was executed by the same three partners. Prior to this, three new partners had joined Southern Distilleries, and the partnership agreement had been duly amended. Julius Moseley, one of the incoming partners, contributed $100,000 to the partnership's capital.

Southern Distilleries defaulted on the July 21 promissory note when it matured. Commercial State Bank sued the partnership and the partners individually. Moseley claims that as an incoming partner he is not liable for the past debts of the partnership. He claims that the July 21 note was merely a renewal of a preexisting obligation, which preceded the date of his entry into the partnership.

The issue is whether Moseley is personally liable or whether his liability is limited to his capital contribution. The key is whether the debt in question arose before or after his acceptance into the partnership.

The court held,

> Although the defendant chooses to categorize the debt created by the note sued on as the renewal of a preexisting debt, it is clear that the obligation created by the old note terminated when the bank accepted the new note. . . . After it accepted the new note and satisfied the old one, there was no obligation which was due and payable to the bank until the new note matured. The court continued, "[T]he bank relied on the representations of the partnership agreement that the partners, including Moseley, would be bound by the new note."

Judgment for Commercial Bank.

EXAMPLE The Alamo is a condominium complex. The owners employ Sam Houston and Davy Crockett, partners in a security firm, to protect its residents. After a territorial conflict with a gang from the South, many of the apartments have been looted and damaged. Two months later Teddy Roosevelt joins the security firm. Shortly thereafter the partnership is sued by the owners of the complex and of individual apartments for breach of contract in failing to protect the facility adequately. The partnership's assets are insufficient to cover the damages awarded by the court. Is Teddy Roosevelt personally liable? No! Unlike Houston and Crockett, Teddy Roosevelt became a partner after the breach of contract occurred. However, he will lose his capital contribution because that has become an asset of the partnership subject to the claims of the condominium owners.

Retiring Partners

A retiring partner is liable for present debts as a surety, but not for future debts, as long as notice of his or her retirement has been conveyed and actually received by the partnership's customers. New customers are not entitled to notice because they would not be relying from past experience on the retiring partner's presence in the partnership.

EXAMPLE | Robert E. Lee, Ulysses S. Grant, and William Sherman enter into a partnership to refurbish historic landmarks. Their first assignment is the Appomattox Court House in Virginia. Before completion Lee resigns at Appomattox. This notice is conveyed to the city. After completion the partnership is sued by the city for breach of contract due to the inferior quality of workmanship. Is Lee personally liable? Yes! A retiring partner is liable as a surety for all contracts entered into while he or she was a partner. The fact that notice was conveyed will protect Lee only from being personally responsible for future contracts.

DISSOLUTION

A partnership's existence is not perpetual like that of a corporation. Rather it may be dissolved because of a number of factors: **BAD WIL.**

> **B**ankruptcy
> **A**greement
> **D**eath
>
> **W**ithdrawal
> **I**llegality
> **L**ack of capacity

Bankruptcy

Personal insolvency of a partner will not dissolve a partnership. But if the insolvent partner files for bankruptcy, that may dissolve the partnership because inherent in transactions extending credit to a partnership is the guarantee that each of the partners will be individually liable. If one partner is bankrupt, then this guarantee no longer exists.

EXAMPLE | Paul Mason, Stan Dixon, and Clarence Line form a partnership called Mason-Dixon Line. Line is heavily invested in Confederate dollars. After the war these dollars are practically worthless. Line files for bankruptcy. What effect does this have on the partnership? The partnership will be dissolved by operation of law. Mason and Dixon may form a new partnership and may continue the business without interruption if they are able to pay Line his share of the partnership's assets.

Agreement

A partnership may be voluntarily dissolved at any point by the mutual agreement of all partners. Even at the outset the partners can stipulate in the partnership agreement that the partnership will continue for a definite duration or until the occurrence of a contingency, at which time the partnership will end. The partners can override the partnership agreement by mutually agreeing to extend the partnership beyond the stipulated duration or to end it earlier.

Death

Death of a partner terminates the partnership; however, the remaining partners can carry on the business by forming a new partnership or a corporation. If there is only one partner left, he or she can continue the business as a sole proprietorship.

EXAMPLE | Abe Lincoln, John Wilkes Booth, and a man named Ford form a partnership for producing plays called Ford's Theatre Company. Shortly thereafter Lincoln dies in Ford's Theatre. Lincoln's heirs sue the partnership for Lincoln's share of the partnership's assets. Must Booth and Ford liquidate the assets of the partnership to pay Lincoln's heirs? Yes! Lincoln's heirs are entitled to the deceased partner's interest. The partnership could have avoided the problem of liquidation by taking out an insurance policy on each partner's life tantamount to the partner's interest in the partnership's assets. Then the partnership would be dissolved in name only, and the surviving partners could continue business operations without interruption.

Withdrawal

Any partner may withdraw from the partnership upon giving the other partners sufficient notice of that intent. Every partner must be apprised of the partner's withdrawal; otherwise the withdrawing partner will be liable, along with the rest of the partners, for any contract entered into or other action engaged in by a partner who acted without notice.

EXAMPLE | Andrew Johnson, U.S. Grant, and Abe Lincoln form a partnership called the Presidential Review. The purpose of the partnership is to monitor the activities of the executive branch and report its findings to local political organizations. After two years Johnson resigns from the partnership. After notifying the other two partners, is Johnson liable for any future debts of the partnership? No! Johnson would remain liable only for past debts, not for future debts.

The partnership agreement may include a buyout provision allowing the remaining partners to buy out a withdrawing or retiring partner without dissolving the partnership. A partner may also be forced to withdraw from the partnership because of a breach of the duty of loyalty. A breach of that duty may occur where a partner is guilty of self-dealing, has taken advantage of a partnership business opportunity, has failed to exercise reasonable care in making business judgments, or has exceeded the authority given to him or her by the partnership agreement.

Illegality

If a partnership is formed illegally or with an unlawful purpose in mind, or if it is operating legally but a change in the law renders the business of the partnership unlawful, then the partnership must comply with the legal requirements of formation, change its type of business, or dissolve the partnership.

EXAMPLE | Jefferson Davis and Stonewall Jackson formed a partnership to engage in slavery. Their business continued for a number of years until the Thirteenth Amendment, prohibiting slavery, was enacted. Must their partnership be dissolved? Yes! The purpose of the partnership is now illegal.

Lack of Capacity

A partnership may be dissolved where it is shown that one of the partners no longer possesses the mental capabilities to perform his or her managerial responsibilities adequately.

EXAMPLE | John Brown was a partner in the Harpers Ferry Company. Because of his uncontrollable passion for civil rights, John Brown became unable to manage his duties at the ferry. The other partners decided to dissolve the partnership because of Brown's incapacity. Can they do this? No! The other partners may dissolve the partnership by agreement, or they may attempt to dismiss Brown because of his failure to perform his duties, but his political views do not affect his mental capacity.

WINDING UP

A partnership that is being dissolved may immediately be recreated in the form of a new partnership, and business may be continued without need for liquidating the partnership's assets. However, if the remaining partners have no plans to form a new partnership, or if they cannot afford to buy out a partner who has withdrawn or to pay off a deceased partner's heirs, then the partnership must be dissolved. During the period of winding up, the partnership may continue to operate as such only for the following purposes: completing unfinished business, liquidating the assets of the partnership, and accounting for all claims made against it.

DISTRIBUTION OF ASSETS ACCORDING TO PRIORITY

The following priorities exist in the distribution of the partnership's assets: First, the creditors of the partnership are entitled to payment, then the creditors of the individual partners. With regard to the assets of individual partners, the individual's creditors have preference over the partnership's creditors. Next, the partners' claims will be satisfied if there are assets left. Loans made by a partner to the partnership will be refunded first. Second, the capital contributed by each partner will be returned. If the partnership's assets are insufficient, then each partner will be entitled to a proportionate share of his or her capital contribution. Finally, whatever remains will be distributed to the partners in accordance with their right to share in the profits of the partnership.

EXAMPLE | Robert E. Lee, Stonewall Jackson, and Jefferson Davis form the Confederate Company to sell Civil War artifacts below the Mason-Dixon Line. A few years later, after facing severe competition from the North, the Confederates decide to dissolve and liquidate their business. The total assets of the partnership are $325,000. The debts owed the general creditors of the partnership amount to $90,000. Robert E. Lee loaned the partnership $15,000 and contributed $50,000. Stonewall Jackson contributed $30,000, and Jefferson Davis contributed $20,000. The partnership agreement provided that the partners would share in all the profits and losses in the same proportion as their respective capital contributions. How will the partnership's assets be distributed?

		Total assets	$325,000
		Total creditors' claims	−$ 90,000
			$235,000
Partners' claims			
Loans			
Robert E. Lee	$15,000		
		Total loans	−$15,000
			$220,000
Capital contributions			
Robert E. Lee	$50,000		
Stonewall Jackson	$30,000		
Jefferson Davis	$20,000		
		Total capital contributions	−$100,000
			$120,000
Profit sharing			
Robert E. Lee: one-half share	$60,000		
Stonewall Jackson: three-tenths share	$36,000		
Jefferson Davis: two-tenths share	$24,000		
			−$120,000
		Total profit sharing	-0-

EXAMPLE | Assume that the monetary value of the Confederate Company's assests after liquidation totaled $165,000. In what priority would the assets be distributed?

		Total assest	$165,000
			−$ 90,000
			$ 75,000

Partners' claims

Loans
Robert E Lee. $15,000

		Total loans	$15,000
			$60,000

Capital contributions

Robert E. Lee	$50,000	$25,000	
Stonewall Jackson	$30,000	$15,000	
Jefferson Davis	$20,000	$10,000	

		Total capital contributions	−$60,000
			-0-

Each partner receives one-half of the amount he contributed to capital. The other half becomes a partnership debt for which each of the partners is personally liable. However, their proportionate liabilities are the same as the amounts owed to them. So they will each get back one-half of their capital contributions and have to suffer the loss of the other half.

EXAMPLE | Assume the following; The total assets of the Confederate Company are $210,000, the total debts are $310,000, and no loans were made by any of the partners. Robert E. Lee has $150,000 in personal assets, and Stonewall Jackson has $10,000 in personal assets, and Jefferson Davis has $10,000 in personal assets. What is the priority of distribution?

	Total assets	$210,000
	Total creditors claims	$310,000
		−$100,000

Partner's shares of the losses

Robert E. Lee: one-half share	$50,000	
Stonewall Jackson	$30,000	
Jefferson Davis: two-tenths share	$20,000	

	Total liabilities of partners	$100,000
		-0-

Partners' Individual Assets
Robert E. Lee
   Assets $150,000
   Proportionate share of the partnership liability   −$ 50,000
                    $100,000

Stonewall Jackson
   Assets $10,000
   Proportionate share of the partnership liability   −$30,000
                    −$20,000

Jefferson Davis
   Assets $10,000
   Proportionate share of the partnership liability   −$20,000
                    -$10,000

Because all of the partners are jointly and severally liable for the partnership's debts and because $30,00 of partnership debts remain unpaid, the creditors may sue Robert E. Lee for the amount because he is the only partner who is still solvent. Lee must pay the $30,000 and then look to the other two partners for his right of contribution: $20,000 from Jackson and $10,000 from Davis.

REVIEW QUESTIONS

1. What are the liabilities of an incoming and a retiring partner?

2. In what ways can a partnership be dissolved?

3. Explain unlimited liability.

4. The *M/V Solena* physically damaged a dock facility owned by Star Enterprise. SRI was a 50 percent partner in Star Enterprises. SRI sought consequential damages from *M/V Solena* because it lost the use of the dock facilities. *M/V Solena* argued that the dock was deeded to Star Enterprise and that only Star Enterprise could bring a suit for damages. What result? *Star Enterprise* v. *M/V Solena,* 791 F.Supp. 655 (E.D. Tex. 1992).

5. Pursuant to a written contract Horn's Crane Service supplied materials and services to a partnership comprising of Prior, Cook, and Piper. The partnership failed to pay for the materials and services when billed. Horn's Crane Service sued Prior and Cook individually for breach of contract. They claim that a creditor cannot sue a partner individually until all of the partnership's assets are depleted. Here the partnership is not dissolved or insolvent. What result? *Horn's Crane Service* v. *Prior,* 182 Neb. 94, 152 N.W.2d 421 (1967).

6. Respass and Sharp were partners in crime. They were bookies who accepted wagers on horse races. On Sharp's death his personal bank account contained almost $5,000 that was attributed to the partnership. Respass sued Sharp's estate for his half share of the profits. The estate refused to account to Respass for half of the money in the bank account. Has Respass any recourse? *Central Trust & Safe Co.* v. *Respass,* 112 Ky. 606, 66 S.W. 421 (1902).

7. Fred Henefeld and Eileen Henefeld were partners in H & K Garage Doors. The partnership had on a number of occasions bought supplies from Taylor Building Products. After Fred withdrew from the partnership, Taylor Building Products extended credit to H & K Garage Doors, but this time without knowledge of Fred's departure. Is Fred still liable for the partnership's debts? *Taylor Building Products* v. *Henefeld,* 500 So. 2d 722 (Fla. App. 2 Dist. 1987).

8. Zev Parnes, Nash Kestenbaum, Alex Edelman, and Lori Friedman were partners, with Parnes and Kestenbaum each owning a one-third interest and Edelman and Friedman sharing equally a one-third interest. The partnership agreement provided that upon a partner's death, his or her share would be transferred to his or her spouse and children. Parnes's widow, upon acquiring her late husbands interest, brought suit against Edelman, claiming that as managing partner he had misappropriated and mismanaged partnership assets. Edelman claimed that Mrs. Parnes had no standing to sue because the partnership had been dissolved by Parnes's death. What result? *Parnes* v. *Edelman,* 512 N.Y.S. 2d 856 (A.D. 2 Dept. 1987).

38

Limited Partnerships

INTRODUCTION

Until this point we have been speaking about a partnership formed by general partners; this is called a general partnership. A general partner is an individual who actively participates in the management and operation of the partnership and who has unlimited liability for the debts of the partnership. A general partner may also be required to make a capital contribution.

The other form of partnership is called *limited partnership.* A limited partnership consists of one or more general partners and one or more limited partners. The general partners, as just explained, actively manage the partnership and have unlimited liability for its debts. The limited partners make capital contributions, are liable for partnership debts but only up to the amounts of their capital contributions, and do not participate in any way in the managment of the partnership. Individuals, corporations, and other partnerships become limited partners for investment purposes. If such a party surmises that a business has potential for expansion and success but lacks adequate funds, it may form a limited partnership to provide the business with funding. In return the limited partner will receive a fixed rate of return on the contributed capital.

A limited partnership must be formed in accordance with state statutes. Every state except Delaware, Lousiana, and the District of Columbia has adopted the Uniform Limited Partnership Act of 1916. The Revised Uniform Limited Partnership Act of 1976, which has modified the original act, was undertaken for the purpose of replacing the original act. What follows is a discussion of the 1976 Revised Act.

LIMITED PARTNERSHIP CERTIFICATE

A certificate attesting to the formation of a limited partnership must be signed and sworn to in writing. The certificate should set forth the following:

1. The name of the limited partnership
2. The type of business the partnership plans to engage in
3. The duration of the partnership
4. The name and address of each partner, with his or her title of general or limited partner specifically designated
5. The capital contribution of each limited or general partner
6. The percentage of the profits that each general partner will receive
7. The rate of return that each limited partner will receive on his or her capital contribution and the method by which the return will be distributed
8. The right of a limited partner to assign his or her rights, duties, or both to a third person

The name of the limited partnership must not include the name of a limited partner, otherwise that limited partner may be liable as a general partner.

RIGHTS OF A LIMITED PARTNER

Limited partners have the right to limitation of liability up to the amounts of their capital contributions as long as they do not take an active part in the partnership's managment or operations.

A limited partner has the same rights as a general partner in regard to the following:

1. Inspecting the books and accounting records of the partnership
2. Being informed of all pertinent information affecting the partnership
3. Seeking a court order dissolving the partnership and winding up its assets

A limited partner also has the right to a return of his or her original investment (capital contribution) at one of the following points:

1. When the partnership is dissolved
2. On the date specified in the limited partnership certificate
3. On six months' written notice if no provision exists for (1) or (2). The notice must be given to all partners.

DISSOLUTION

On dissolution of a limited partnership, the following priority of claims will govern the distribution of the partnership's assets:

1. Creditors' claims
2. Limited partners' claims
   a. Return on capital contributed
   b. Capital contribution
3. General partners' claims
   a. Loans
   b. Capital contribution
   c. Profit sharing

The limited partners' claims are subordinate to the claims of other creditors but are given preference over all of the claims of the general partners.

EXAMPLE | The Three Stooges form a limited partnership for the sale of used cars. Moe and Larry each contribute $45,000 and agree to be responsible for the management and operations of the business. Curly contributes $150,000 as a limited partner. A certificate of limited partnership is signed and sworn in writing to this effect. The certificate sets forth the annual rate of return guaranteed Curly at 15 percent of his capital contribution. Moe and Larry will split the remaining profits equally. At the time specified in the certificate for payment to Curly of $22,500, his guaranteed return on his investment, Moe and Larry inform him that the partnership is operating at a loss and that they can not afford to pay him at this time. Curly brings a lawsuit seeking a dissolution of the partnership by court order and an accounting of the financial operations of the partnership. The accounting produces the following results: Partnership assests $372,500, partnership liabilities $70,000. How will the distribution of assets be made?

		Total assets	$372,500
Creditors' claims			
General Creditors	$ 90,000		
		Total creditor claims	−$ 90,000
			$282,500
Limited partners' claims			
Curly			
Return on capital contributed	$ 22,500		
Capital contribution	$150,000		
Claim of limited partner			−$172,500
			$110,000
General partner claims			
Moe			
Loans	$ 0		
Capital contribution	$45,000		

(one-half of amount contributed)	
(Profit sharing)	$10,000
Larry	
Loans	$ 0
Capital contribution	$45,000
(one-half of amount contributed)	
(Profit sharing)	$10,000

Total claims of
general partners   −$110,000

-0-

Deporter-Butterworth Tours, Inc. v. Tyrrell
503 N.E. 2d 378 (III. App. 3 Dist. 1987)

The Quad City Blackhawks and the American Professional Football Tour of Europe were both operating under assumed names as limited partnerships without having filed certificates disclosing the names of the owners. Deporter-Butterworth Tours, Inc. supplied the Blackhawks and the American Professional Football Tour with goods and services for which they were never paid. The owners of the Blackhawks and the Tour argue that they are limited partners and that their liability is thus limited to the capital contributions of the partnership.

The issue is whether the owners of the Blackhawks and the Tour are personally liable as general partners.

The court held,

> The rule, as established by the Act, is that the certificate required by the Uniform Limited Partnership Act is a statutory prerequisite to the creation of a limited partnership. Until it is filed, the partnership is not formed as a Limited Partnership and all partners will be treated as general partners. Therefore, any contract entered into prior to June 22, 1979, the date on which the Limited Partnership certificate was filed and made of record, would be a contract entered into by a general partner and all partners individually would be liable as general partners.

Judgment for Deporter-Butterworth Tours, Inc.

REVIEW QUESTIONS

1. What is a limited partnership?
2. What information must be included in the limited partnership certificate?
3. What are the rights and liabilities of a limited partner?
4. What is the priority in the distribution of assets upon the dissolution of a limited partnership?

39

Corporate Formation

INTRODUCTION

A *corporation* is legal entity, organized for profit, with limited liability in accordance with state law. *Capital stock* is issued by a corporation to raise money and to determine ownership of corporate assets. *Shareholders* are individuals who purchase the capital stock of a corporation and who own the corporation. Shareholders are not principals or agents; they do not have the power to bind the corporation in any way. Their liability is limited to their investment in the capital stock corporation. The *board of directors* is elected by the shareholders. The board is responsible for managing the corporation for the shareholders. The board of directors appoints officers to manage the corporation's day-to-day activities. The officers of the corporation include the president, vice-president, secretary, and treasurer.

FORMATION

A corporation is formed when individuals agree to invest in the proposed corporation by purchasing stock subscriptions from promoters. *Promoters* issue a prospectus to persuade investors to become owners in the proposed corporation. A *prospectus* is a statement, made by the promoters of a corporation, that invites the public to purchase stock subscriptions. A *stock subscription* is a contract, entered into by the promoters and the subscribers, wherein subscribers agree to pay a certain amount of money per share in return for a designated number of shares in the corporation when the proposed corporation has become legally incorporated. At that point the stock subscriptions become shares of capital stock, and the subscribers become shareholders.

CERTIFICATE OF INCORPORATION

The formation of a corporation requires legal formalities. A certificate of incorporation must be filed with the secretary of state in the state of incorporation. Filing of that document, along with payment of a filing fee, gives rise to corporate status. (In addition the corporation must pay the state a yearly fee for the privilege of doing business.) The certificate of incorporation, when filed and approved, is conclusive evidence that all conditions precedent have been met and a corporation is formed. The person filing the certificate of incorporation is an *incorporator*.

The following are the provisions included in the certificate of incorporation.

Corporate Name

The corporate name must be cleared with the secretary of state for the purpose of ensuring that it is distinct enough not to defraud or confuse anyone. The name must include one of the following: Inc., Incorporated, Corp., Corporation, Ltd., Limited, Co., or Company (as long as the latter is not written _____ and Company," which would tend to indicate a partnership).

Purpose of Formation

The corporation must be formed for lawful purposes. Because the corporation will be restricted to the purposes set forth, this provision should be sufficiently broad and flexible to include all the areas in which the corporation may wish to become involved.

Location of Corporate Offices

The corporation must have an office where it may be contacted by the secretary of state in the state of incorporation. In most states the corporate headquarters may be located outside the state. The promoters may choose to incorporate in a particular state, even though they do not intend to do business there, because of certain tax advantages or a lack of restrictions.

Capital Stock

The certificate must specify the aggregate number of shares that the corporation shall have the authority to issue, as well as the class of stock (common or preferred) and its par value, if applicable. The capital stock of the corporation may be fixed at a certain value (par value) below which it may never fall, or it may have no designated minimum amount (no par value).

Share Transfer Restrictions

Shareholders may be restricted from freely transferring shares, especially in a closely held corporation. Restrictions of shareholders' freedom to transfer shares must be specified on the stock certificate. Article 8 of the UCC provides that a good-faith purchaser who acquires a stock certificate is not bound by transfer restrictions that do not appear on the face of the certificate.

Designation of the Secretary of State as Agent

The secretary of state in the state where the incorporation takes place must be designated as the corporation's agent upon whom service of process may be made. Service of process refers to the serving of a summons and complaint on the corporation.

Directors

The number of directors must be set forth, along with the quorum and voting requirements for approval of transactions confronting the board of directors at their meetings.

Shareholders

The quorum and voting requirements for shareholders must be delineated so that the shareholders can conduct proper meetings.

Dividends

An accounting of earned surplus, with possible distribution to shareholders, shall be made at regular intervals.

Establishment of an Accounting Period

The corporation must select either a fiscal or a calendar tax year for the purpose of accounting for income received.

Requirements for an Incorporator

An incorporator must be a human being eighteen years of age or older.
The following is a sample certificate of incorporation.

CERTIFICATE OF INCORPORATION
OF PRACTICAL BUSINESS LAW, INC.

Under the Business Corporation Law of the State, the undersigned for the purpose of forming a corporation pursuant to the Business Corporation Law of the State, certifies:

Section 1. The name of the corporation shall be Practical Business Law, Inc.

Section 2. The purpose for which it is to be formed is: to publish a college textbook for students and to do everything necessary, suitable, or proper for the accomplishment of this purpose or of any objective incidental to or connected with this purpose.

Section 3. The offices of the corporation shall be located at 271 Tennis Court, in Fun City, County of Kings, in the State.

Section 4. The aggregate number of shares which shall be authorized and which the corporation shall have the authority to issue is TWO THOUSAND (2,000) shares at no par value, all of one class which shall be designated as common stock.

Section 5. The shareholders shall not transfer, sell, assign, pledge, or otherwise dispose of their shares of the stock of the corporation without first obtaining the written consent of the other shareholders to the sale or disposition, or without first offering to sell shares to the corporation at a value to be determined by an arbitrator to be selected by the American Arbitration Association. The offer shall be in writing and shall be open for a period of 30 days. If the corporation fails to accept the offer within that period, a second offer, also in writing, shall then be made to sell the shares on similar terms, to the other shareholders, first on a pro rata basis, then individually. This offer shall also remain open for a period of 30 days following the expiration of the offer to the corporation. If the offer is not accepted by either the corporation or the other shareholders, the shares shall thereafter be freely transferable.

Section 6. Upon the death or retirement of any shareholder, the remaining shareholders shall purchase and the estate of the decedent shall sell all the decedent's shares in the corporation now owned or hereafter acquired, and in the case of a shareholder's retirement, the remaining shareholders shall purchase and the retiring shareholder shall sell all his or her shares in the corporation now owned or hereafter acquired. The value of the shares purchased shall be determined according to the terms of Section 5, stated above.

Section 7. The Secretary of State of the State is designated as the agent of the corporation upon whom process in any action or proceeding against it may be served. The address to which the Secretary of State shall mail a copy of process in any action or proceeding against the corporation which may be served upon him or her is 271 Tennis Court, Fun City.

Section 8. There shall be nine directors of the corporation. A two-thirds vote by the quorum of the board of directors shall be necessary to approve a transaction being considered. A quorum shall consist of the chairman of the board plus five other directors. The position of the chairman of the board shall be held by the same person occupying the position of the president of the corporation.

Section 9. The presence in person or by proxy of a majority of the holders of common stock of this corporation shall be necessary in order to constitute a quorum for the transaction of any business at any meeting of the shareholders of the corporation. The affirmative vote of a majority of the shareholders of the common stock of the corporation shall be necessary for the transaction of the following items of business:

The removal of any director and the filling of any vacancy on the board, however created.

The fixing of any of the compensation and the duties, and any changes therein, of any director.

Any merger or consolidation of the corporation with any other corporation, domestic or foreign, and any contract which in effect constitutes a merger or consolidation.

Any guaranty not in the furtherance of the corporate purposes.

Any amendment of the bylaws of the corporation.

Section 10. The earned surplus of the corporation shall be determined quarterly by the corporation's regular accountant, in accordance with generally accepted accounting principles on a basis consistent with that normally used in determining a corporation's earned surplus, and the board of directors shall determine, by a two-thirds vote of the quorum, the amount of said earned surplus that shall be distributed, provided that the corporation is not then insolvent or would not thereby be made insolvent.

Section 11. The accounting period which the corporation intends to establish as its first fiscal year for reporting of the franchise tax is July 1 to the following June 30.

Section 12. The incorporator is a natural person over the age of 18.

In witness whereof, the undersigned have signed this Certificate of Incorporation on May 1,

_____

Clifford Gardener

Dixie Pipe Sales, Inc. v. Perry
834 S.W. 2d 491 (Tex. App.—Houston 14th Dist. 1992)

Irma Beeley owned 2,000 shares of Dixie Pipe Sales, a closely held corporation. In her will Irma left the 2,000 shares to her niece Rebecca Perry and her nephew Edward Thompson. When Irma died the executor, Charles Johnson, transferred her stock to Rebecca and Edward. They in turn requested that Dixie issue new shares in their names. Dixie refused and paid them the book value of $798,000 instead. Dixie cited a provision of its bylaws giving the corporation the right of first refusal on any stock transfer. It read in part as follows:

> *Section 2.* Each stockholder prior to the disposition of any Stock shall give written notice by post-paid registered mail, which shall be effective on the day it is received by the corporation at its principal office.

[I]n said notice [each stockholder] shall offer to sell and transfer such shares to the corporation and, subject only to the prior right of the corporation to acquire any of such shares, to its stockholders or such of them as may elect to purchase, severally or collectively, any of such shares

(i) at a price per share equal to the cash price or consideration per share specified in such notice, or

(ii) in the event that no consideration is to be received by the stockholder for such share, the value per share of such shares as determined by Section 4 hereof.

The issue is whether Dixie is entitled to the right of first refusal when the transfer is made through a will.

The court ruled,

The Texas Business Corporation Act provides that a reasonable restriction noted conspicuously on the stock certificate shall be enforceable against the successor or transferee of the holder. An executor under a will is a successor or transferee of the holder. Therefore, Dixie's right of first refusal is triggered by Johnson's delivery of the stock to Perry and Thompson.

Judgment for Dixie.

BYLAWS

Bylaws are the rules by which the corporation agrees to govern itself. The bylaws may be adopted either by the board of directors or by the shareholders, as determined by the law of the state in which the business is incorporated. The following is a sample set of bylaws, including the important articles and provisions necessary to organize and operate the corporation.

BYLAWS OF PRACTICAL BUSINESS LAW, INC., ORGANIZED UNDER THE BUSINESS CORPORATION LAW

ARTICLE I
SHAREHOLDER'S MEETING

Annual Meeting
Special Meeting
Location of Meetings
Voting Allotment
Proxy Entitlement

ARTICLE VIII
DIVIDENDS

Authorization and Distribution

ARTICLE IX
NEGOTIABLE INSTRUMENTS

Signature Requirements

ARTICLE X
CORPORATE OFFICES

Location

ARTICLE XI
AMENDMENTS

Bylaw Amendments by Shareholder Vote

ARTICLE XII
AUTHORITY

Authoritative Effect of Bylaws

FIRST MEETING OF THE BOARD OF DIRECTORS

The first meeting of the board of directors will be called after the certificate of incorporation has been filed and approved by the secretary of state in the state where the incorporation takes place. The purpose of the board of directors' first meeting is to get the business under way. Officers will be elected; bank accounts will be established; and corporate documents, such as the certificate of incorporation, bylaws, and specimen shares of stock, will be ratified. The following is a sample of the minutes of a board of directors' first meeting.

MINUTES OF THE FIRST MEETING OF THE BOARD OF DIRECTORS
OF PRACTICAL BUSINESS LAW, INC.,
HELD ON MAY 1

The first meeting of the board of directors of Practical Business Law, Inc. was held at 10:00 A.M. at the offices of the corporation. The following directors, constituting a quorum, were present:

Donald Vanderveer
Julia Michelson
Scott Meyers

Clifford Gardener
Joann Werner
Priscilla Peterson
Dennis O'Brien
Anthony Morano
Nancy Hamilton

Waiver of notice of the meeting of directors: We, the undersigned, being all of the directors of Practical Business Law, Inc., hereby severally waive notice of the time and place of the first meeting of the board of directors of said corporation and hereby consent that it be held at 271 Tennis Court, Fun City, at 10:00 A.M. on May 1, for the purpose of electing officers and for such other business as may come before said meeting.

Dated May 1   All Sign _____

RESOLUTIONS

Election of Officers

Resolved: Donald Vanderveer has been elected president of the corporation at an annual salary of $125,000. He will assume his duties immediately and is to take over for the temporary chairman of this meeting. Clifford Gardener has been elected secretary of the corporation at an annual salary of $75,000 and is to assume his duties immediately and to take over for the temporary secretary of this meeting. Julia Michelson has been elected treasurer of the corporation at an annual salary of $75,000 and is to assume her duties immediately.

Ratification of Documents

Resolved: The following have been ratified and agreed to by the board:

1. Certificate of incorporation, attached hereto.
2. Bylaws of the corporation, attached hereto
3. Specimen shares of stock, attached hereto
4. Corporate seal, affixed hereto

Establishment of Bank Accounts

Resolved: Bank accounts are to be started at the Chase Manhattan Bank, 1 Chase Plaza, New York, New York. The president and/or treasurer shall sign all corporate obligations with said Bank.

Proposal for Distribution of Stock

Resolved: A written proposal is to be prepared by the newly elected secretary for the distribution of the stock certificates. The secretary is to have this proposal prepared and ready for review at the first regular meeting of the board so that the shares can be issued.

Designation of Tax-Filing Status

Resolved: The corporation agrees to be treated as a Subchapter S corporation for the purposes of filing its tax returns. The secretary shall prepare the necessary papers for this election and have them ready for the first regular meeting of the board.

Motion to Adjourn

Resolved: A motion to adjourn the meeting until the next scheduled meeting was approved, and the board adjourned.

Dated: May 1

Clifford Gardener, Secretary

CORPORATE CHARACTERISTICS

A corporation has the following characteristics: **LOLLIPOP.**

Legally capable of suing and being sued in its corporate name and contracting in its corporate name

Organized for profit

Legal entity that possesses the rights of a person under many federal and state laws

Limited liability up to the value of the investment made in capital stock. This is often the main reason for incorporating because partners and sole proprietors are personally liable.

Inherent tax advantages

Perpetual duration, unlike a partnership, which may be dissolved for a variety of reasons.

Ownership evidenced by stock that is freely transferable unless properly restricted

Powers of management invested in a board of directors

PIERCING THE CORPORATE VEIL

The law encourages individuals to limit their liability through incorporation. A shareholder will be liable only up to the amount of his or her investment. The corporate veil will be pierced only where the corporate form is used to perpetrate fraudulent, illegal activities. In such an instance the shareholders will be personally liable for all debts incurred or injuries caused by the corporation. The corporate veil will not be pierced solely because the corporation is 100 percent owned by one shareholder or by a parent corporation with the same board of directors.

U.S. v. BCCI Holding (Luxembourg), S.A.
795 F. Supp. 477 (D.D.C. 1992)

In January 1992 the four corporate defendants in the BCCI banking scandal entered a plea of guilty. An Order of Forfeiture was entered; the order provided that all property located in the United States must be forfeited. ICIC Investments Ltd. is an overseas corporation located in Luxembourg. The United States claimed that assets held by ICIC in the United States were transferred to it by BCCI after the United States sought to recover the assets. The United States also claimed that ICIC was an alter ego of one of the BCCI defendants.

The issue is whether the corporate veil at ICIC should be pierced and its assets held in the United States be forfeited just as though they were held in the name of the defendant.

The court held as follows: "The court disregards the corporate form of investments and considers the assets of investments forfeitable 'interest' of the named corporate defendants. To do otherwise would seriously undermine the legislative purpose of RICO." Judgment for the United States.

TYPES OF CORPORATIONS

Public Corporations

Public corporations include municipalities formed by cities, towns, or villages and government corporations such as the U.S. Postal Service and the Federal Deposit Insurance Corporation (FDIC).

Private Corporations

Private corporations encompass all other corporations that are organized for profit and owned by members of the public, such as IBM, GM, and AT&T.

Nonprofit Corporations

Nonprofit corporations usually are religious, social, athletic, or educational societies or clubs organized for the benefit of the community. Any monies earned by a nonprofit corporation must be used exclusively for community purposes; they may not be distributed to the members. Examples of nonprofit corporations include churches and synagogues, libraries, YMCAs, fraternal organizations, private schools, colleges, and universities.

Closely Held Corporations

A closely held corporation is owned by a finite number of shareholders, often family members or relatives. There are usually share transfer limitations, specified in the certificate of incorporation as well as on the face of each stock certificate, which restrict the shareholders from transferring their stock to anyone outside the corporation. This is how a corporation remains closely held.

Professional Corporations

Professional corporations allow individual practitioners in professions such as law, medicine, and accounting to incorporate their professional practices to reap tax advantages unavailable to partnerships or individual proprietorships.

Subchapter S Corporations

Subchapter S corporations are small business corporations that, for income tax purposes, are treated as partnerships while still retaining the other characteristics of a corporation, especially that of limited liability. In a Subchapter S corporation, all income earned will be allocated among the various shareholders by agreement. The shareholders in turn will be taxed on that income as individuals. This avoids the double taxation that most corporations face: first, the corporation must pay corporate income tax; second, individual shareholders must pay personal income tax on their portions of that same corporate income, which they receive in the form of dividends.

Domestic Corporations

Domestic corporations are those incorporated in the state.

Foreign Corporations

Foreign corporations are those incorporated in a state other than in the one where they are doing business. For example, Practical Business Law, Inc. was incorporated in New York, but it also does business in New Jersey and Connecticut. Practical Business Law is a domestic corporation in New York and a foreign corporation in New Jersey and

Connecticut. Corporations incorporated in other countries, such as British Petroleum and Mitsubishi, are referred to as international corporations.

FRANCHISES

A *franchise* is a license given by the owner of a trade name (the franchisor) to another (the franchisee) in return for a fee that allows the recipient to operate a business under the trade name. Inherent in this arrangement is the stipulation that the products used in the business by the franchisee must be purchased from the franchisor. Other restrictions may be set forth in the franchise agreement.

The benefit to the franchisee, the person purchasing the franchise, is the opportunity to operate an independent business while being affiliated with a much larger organization that will guarantee the supply of products and the advertising. Examples of businesses in which franchises flourish are car dealerships, gas stations, car rentals, ice cream shops, fast food establishments, and distributorships for soft drinks.

Franchise operations have grown remarkably over the last few decades, but laws regarding franchises have not kept pace. Currently fifteen states have laws designed to deal specifically with franchises, while the other states rely on principles of contract law and on agency, employment, independent contractor, and antitrust laws. Problems encountered by franchises are often novel and call for the adoption of specific laws designed to deal with the difficulties.

Many franchisees have been defrauded because pertinent information was not disclosed to them at the start. The Federal Trade Commission requires a franchisor to disclose to prospective franchisees certain information such as the franchisor's name and address; the franchisor's financial statements for the last five years; a detailed description of the franchise offered, along with a copy of the franchise agreement setting forth the restrictions and stipulations the franchisee must abide by; and the amount of the royalties that must be paid to the franchisor and how they are calculated.

A typical franchise agreement will set forth the name of the franchisor and the franchisee; the duration for which the franchise will be granted; the type of business authorized by the granting of the franchise; the royalty payments required for the use of the trade name; a restrictive covenant stating that the franchisee may use only the products marketed by the franchisor or may distribute them only in a certain area (the latter may have antitrust considerations); the requirement that the franchisee comply with the franchisor's standards of service, which must be detailed either as part of the franchise agreement or in a separate manual; a clause requiring the franchisee to maintain liability insurance and a provision allowing the franchisor to inspect the franchisee's books and records to determine their accuracy with regard to the royalty payments made.

The franchisor may in no way dictate the prices to be charged for the products sold by the franchisee; to do so would be to engage in price fixing in violation of the federal Sherman Antitrust Act as well as state antitrust laws. The franchisor may, however, suggest an appropriate price, often referred to as the manufacturer's suggested retail price.

REVIEW QUESTIONS

1. Define corporation, capital stock, shareholder, board of directors, prospectus, promoter, stock subscriptions, incorporator, and franchise

2. How is a corporation formed?

3. State the function of a certificate of incorporation, and list what must be included in it.

4. State the purpose of bylaws, and explain their main provisions.

5. What happens at the first meeting of the board of directors?

6. List the various types of corporations.

7. What are the various characteristics of a corporation?

8. While in the employ of Tall Ships Sales, Inc., a wholesale distributor of frozen fish, Stanley Kroen loaned the corporation $50,000. After six months' employment he was terminated when he attempted to stop delivery of fish to another cooperation owned by Tall Ships' president and vice-president, Rocco and Joseph Fuda. Subsequently Tall Ships filed bankruptcy. Kroen sued the Fudas personally for repayment of the loan. He contended that corporate funds had been used for the Fudas personal expenses: travel, dry cleaning, housing, and the like. What result? *Fuda* v. *Kroen,* 420 S.E. 2d 767 (Ga. App. 1992).

9. Four Davis brothers formed D&D Manufacturing Company. A share transfer restriction in the bylaws provided that if one brother wished to sell his stock, he had to sell it in equal shares to the others. In this way no brother could have an advantage over the others. James Davis served as president from the company's inception until he resigned after conflicts with Walter Davis. Then Walter took over, and sales plummeted from $800,000 to $250,00 in five years. At that juncture the business was put up for sale. When no offers were forthcoming, the brothers decided to stop operating the business. James bought out Ralph's and Wilson's shares, fired Walter, and took control. Walter brought suit to obtain one-quarter of the stock from James, this would give each of them one-half ownership. What result? *Davis* v. *Davis,* 419 S.E. 2d 913 (Ga. 1992).

10. Howard Davidson performed services for Beco Corporation with regard to a construction contract for which he was never paid. Davidson asserts that the court should pierce the corporate veil and render Doyle Beck, the sole shareholder of Beco, personally liable. Davidson's reasoning is based on the fact that the corporation maintains no individuality from Beck; that it keeps no records; that it holds no meetings; and that it perpetrates a fraud by being a mere shell providing Beck with limited liability. Beck is able to show that the book value of Beco Corporation is $150,000, many times the amount of Davidson's claim. Beck argues that Davidson's claim should be satisfied out of Beco's corporate assets. What result? *Davidson* v. *Beco Corp.,* 733 P.2d 781 (Idaho App. 1986).

40

Corporate Management

Corporate Powers

Ultra Vires Doctrine

Powers of Directors

Powers of Officers

Duties of Directors and Officers

Business Judgment Rule

Shareholders' Rights

Shareholders' Derivative Action

Review Questions

CORPORATE POWERS

A corporation is a legal person. It has the powers that a natural person has to accomplish the purpose for which it was formed—usually, to earn a profit in a particular business. These powers include: **CLAMS.**

Contract in its own name, establish employee benefit plans, and make and alter bylaws

Lend or borrow money and make political or charitable contributions in its own name

Act as a partner in a joint venture or a partnership

Mortgage and/or hold title to real estate in its own name

Sue and be sued in its own name

The actions of a corporation must not exceed these powers or any other powers set forth in the certificate of incorporation, or they will be *ultra vires* acts, acts that exceed corporate powers.

ULTRA VIRES DOCTRINE

If the *ultra vires* act has not begun, or has begun but has not yet been completed, a shareholder of the corporation or the attorney general of the state of incorporation may prevent the act from being performed through a request for an injunction. The court will grant the injunction if it feels that the result would be fair and equitable. By the court's discretion a party suffering financial loss because of the injunction may recover damages from the corporation, or vice versa, but loss of profits is not recoverable. Rather the shareholder's remedy lies against the officers or directors responsible for the prescribed act. This remedy may be sought through a derivative suit, to be discussed later in this chapter. If the corporation illegally exceeded its powers, the attorney general may commence a proceeding to have the corporation dissolved.

The doctrine of *ultra vires* has been restricted to a great extent because most certificates of incorporation provide for very broad corporate purposes and extensive corporate powers.

POWERS OF DIRECTORS

The board of directors has certain powers through which it administers corporate affairs. A few of the more important powers include: **LEADER.**

Lease, sell, or otherwise exchange corporate assets
Elect and remove officers
Amend, create, alter, or repeal bylaws
Determine the price to be paid for newly issued shares
Empowered to declare dividends
Responsible for approving mergers and acquisitions

POWERS OF OFFICERS

The board of directors elects individuals to fill the officer positions of the corporation as dictated by the bylaws. These positions usually include president, vice-president(s), secretary, and treasurer. The powers of the respective officers of the corporation are contained in the bylaws. The officers manage the day-to-day business of the corporation and are agents of the corporation. Their terms of office are often regulated by contract. The board of directors has the power to remove officers with or without cause. If an officer who is under contract is removed without cause, he or she may sue the corporation for breach of contract.

President

The president shall be the chief executive officer of the corporation and, subject to the control of the board of directors, shall exercise general supervision over the property, affairs, and business of the corporation. the president shall call and preside at meetings of the shareholders and of the board of directors. He or she shall, unless otherwise provided by the board of directors, be an ex-officio member of the executive committee and call and preside at meetings thereof. He or she shall, in general, perform all duties and have all powers incident to the office of president and shall perform such other duties as from time to time may be assigned to him or her by the bylaws or by the board of directors.

Vice-President

The vice-president shall have the respective powers and duties delegated to him or her by the president.

Secretary

The secretary shall act as secretary at, and keep the minutes of, meetings of the shareholders and of the board of directors and shall cause the same to be recorded in books provided for that purpose. He or she shall, in general, perform all duties and have all powers incident to the office of secretary and shall perform such other duties and have such other powers as may from time to time be assigned to him or her by the bylaws, by the board of directors, or by the president. He or she shall have custody of the seal of the corporation and shall have authority to cause such seal to be affixed to, or impressed or otherwise reproduced upon, all documents the execution and delivery of which, on behalf of the corporation, shall have been duly authorized.

Treasurer

The treasurer shall have custody of the corporate funds and securities and shall keep full and accurate accounts of receipts and disbursements in books belonging to the corporation. He or she shall cause all monies and other valuable effects to be deposited in the name and to the credit of the corporation in such depositories as may be designated by the board of directors. He or she shall cause the funds of the corporation to be disbursed when such disbursements have been duly authorized, taking proper vouchers for such disbursements, and shall render to the president and the board of directors, whenever requested, an account of all his or her transactions as treasurer and of the financial condition of the corporation. He or she shall, in general, perform all duties and have all powers incident to the office of treasurer and shall perform such other duties and have such other powers as may from time to time be assigned to him or her by the bylaws, by the president, or by the board of directors.

DUTIES OF DIRECTORS AND OFFICERS

Fiduciary Duties

Fiduciary duties are those that grow out of a relationship of trust and confidence.

1. Duty of loyalty
2. Duty to act in good faith

   Officers and directors have an obligation to refrain from

   misappropriating corporate funds,
   oppressing minority stockholders,
   taking advantage of corporate opportunity for their own personal benefit
   trading with the use of inside information, and
   creating conflict of interest with the corporation.

Managerial Duties

Managerial duties include the following:

   Duty not to exceed authority; an officer or director who exceeds his or her authority will be absolutely liable only if negligent.
   Duty to exercise due care; an officer or director who fails to exercise due care in the management of corporate funds will be liable for any loss that occurs if he or she is negligent

---

Case v. Murdock,
   488 N.W. 2d 885 (S.D. 1992)

Hickocks, Inc. was formed by Case, Sides, Murdock, and Hamm for the purpose of operating a gambling casino in Deadwood, South Dakota. Case and Sides were elected president and secretary, respectively. Hickocks rented a building owned by Brockley. The lease gave Hickocks the right of first refusal to match any acceptable offer. Subsequently Hickocks decided to purchase the building. After Hickocks' offer of $1,500,000 and Brockley's offer of $1,750,000, negotiations stalled. Hickocks decided to back off and let Brockley think about it. During this supposedly dormant period, Case and Sides entered into a contract with Brockley for $1,650,000.

   The issue is whether Case and Sides violated their duty of good faith to Hickocks.

The court ruled, "Directors of a corporation occupy a fiduciary position in respect to the corporation and its shareholders, and are required to exercise the utmost good faith in all transactions touching a director's duty." The court continued, "The doctrine of corporate opportunity has a long history in the law. Essentially, the doctrine holds that one who occupies a fiduciary relationship to a corporation may not acquire, in opposition to the corporation, property in which the corporation has an interest or tangible expectancy." Judgment for Murdock and Hamm.

BUSINESS JUDGMENT RULE

Officers and directors are not insurers of corporate investments or transactions. The business judgment rule renders management immune from responsibility and ratifies transactions where they are within the powers of the corporation, within the authority of management, and in compliance with the managerial and fiduciary duties just set forth.

Michaud v. Morris,
603 So. 2d 886 (Ala. 1992)

Bernard Michaud, Marc Michaud, and James Morris formed Edge Corporation for the purpose of operating a Rax restaurant franchise. James Morris held 25 percent of the stock and served as manager. After a $20,000 loss in seven months operation, Morris was replaced by Bernard Michaud. Under his tenure the restaurant lost over $100,000. Morris brought a derivative action against the Michauds.

The issue is whether the Michauds violated the business judgment rule and oppressed a minority shareholder by replacing Morris.

The court ruled, "As majority shareholders in the corporation, the Michauds were confronted with the fact that the corporation was losing money at an alarming rate. . . . The majority cannot be held liable to the corporation in a derivative action for exercising a business judgment to replace management under these facts." The court continued, "Shareholders in close corporations have a right to share in corporation earnings, and a majority cannot deprive minority shareholders of that right by failing to declare dividends. . . ." Here Morris was not oppressed because the corporation earned no money. Judgment for Michaud.

Mid-Continent Aggregate, Inc. v. Brandt
499 So. 2d 1117 (La. App. 3 Cir. 1986)

Hank Brandt issued four checks to pay personal debts during his tenure as president of Mid-Continent Aggregate, Inc. (MCA). The checks totaled $10,690. The first and second checks were to the Downtown Motor Inn, at which Harry Tubbs and Robert Larios were staying. Tubbs asked Brandt to pay the bills, which Brandt did. Tubbs was neither an officer nor a director of MCA authorized to act on its behalf. The third check was a disbursement to Central Flying Service for a 100-hour inspection made on an airplane owned by Brandt. Brandt claimed that the plane was used for charter flights at the request of Harry Tubbs. The fourth check was a loan to Robert Larios, which was never repaid. Larios had aided Brandt in acquiring funds to pay for Brandt's airplane.

The issue is whether Brandt acted within his authority as president of MCA in issuing these four checks.

The court adopted the language of the trial court in holding Brandt personally liable;

> In his capacity as president the defendant was authorized to sign checks and disburse corporate funds. But he was also bound to restrict his disbursements to the satisfaction of actual corporate obligations. He was in a fiduciary capacity and was responsible for his acts. Whenever he acted irresponsibly his acts were beyond his legitimate authority as an officer of the corporation and he is answerable for such acts. The debts which the defendant paid with corporate funds were not debts of MCA. Nor has it been established that these payments were justified or authorized as being related to or in furtherance of business of the plaintiff.

Judgment for Mid-Continent.

SHAREHOLDERS' RIGHTS

Shareholders have the right to **TRAVIL MAP'D** (pronounced "travel mapped").

Transfer shares by sale, gift, or exchange

Ratify corporate acts by shareholder resolution

Amend bylaws; this right coexists in the board of directors

Vote in person or through proxies

Inspect the books and records of the corporation, including accounting records, bylaws, minutes of the shareholders' and board of directors' meetings, contracts, tax returns, and property owned

Limited liability up to the amount of their investment

Maintain their percentages of ownership when new shares are issued by exercising their preemptive right to purchase proportionate shares of the new stock; preemptive rights do not apply to the issuance of original shares

Approve amendments to the certificate of incorporation

Preserve the corporation by removing directors for cause, with court review, where they violate their managerial and/or fiduciary duties

Dividends, although the declaration and the amount is discretionary with the board of directors.

SHAREHOLDERS' DERIVATIVE ACTION

Shareholders may bring a derivative action against the officers and directors or other shareholders of the corporation, either on their own behalf or on behalf of the corporation. A suit on behalf of the corporation is brought to recover damages sustained by the corporation from a director or officer who has breached a managerial or fiduciary duty; to recover improperly paid dividends; to recover from a third party who has perpetrated a wrong on the corporation, whether in contract or in tort; or to compel payment of lawfully declared dividends that were withheld or otherwise not paid. A derivative suit on behalf of the shareholders is initiated to enforce their right of inspection; to protect their preemptive right to maintain their percentages of ownership in the corporation, to enforce their right to vote, to enjoin directors before they exceed their authority or commit an *ultra vires* act, to recover from insiders trading without proper disclosure, or to compel corporate dissolution. In small business corporations, shareholders often draft agreements to protect their rights.

Citron on Behalf of United Technologies v. Daniell
796 F. Supp. 649 (D. Conn. 1992)

In their complaint United Technologies shareholders stated, "For several years, defendants have knowingly or recklessly caused UT to unlawfully extend bribes, monies and other gratuities to government officials and industry consultants in return for classified confidential information and favorable consideration and treatment in the procurement of defense contracts.

Plaintiffs claim that a

UT official paid $218,453.29 to Melvyn R. Paisley, former Assistant Secretary of the United States Navy, for confidential information which Paisley "stole" from the government before leaving the Navy. Using this information, UT was able to procure a government contract for the manufacture of the F404 engine, for which it had been competing with General Dynamics. Paisley eventually pled guilty in United States District Court to a charge of conversion of government property in connection with this scheme.

The issue is whether a shareholder must demand action from the board of directors before litigating.

The court ruled, "Before a shareholder may seek to litigate claims that rightly belong to the corporation, a shareholder must first make a "demand" on the board to commence suit." If the board fails to act because he or she is an interested party, then an action may be commenced. Here the opportunity to act was not given to the board; therefore the shareholder's derivative action failed. Judgment for Daniell and the other U.T. directors.

REVIEW QUESTIONS

1. Name the powers that a corporation, its board of directors, and its respective officers possess.

2. What is the *ultra vires* doctrine?

3. Marie Grandon inherited stock of a closely held corporation from her husband. A restriction had been placed on the shares providing that the purchaser of the stock agreed to resell the stock to the corporation for $250 per share upon the shareholder's death. When Marie died her assets were left to a trust for the benefit of her children. The trust refused to sell the stock back. What result? *Grandon* v. *Amcore Trust Co.*, 588 N.E. 2d 311 (Ill. App. 3 Dist. 1992).

4. G&M Soybean Oil, Inc. sued Diamond Crystal Specialty Foods for bottling an inferior brand of oil under the G&M name. Marc Heiden, vice-president and a principal shareholder of G&M, also sued Diamond Crystal for fraud. Diamond Crystal argued that Heiden had no right to sue as a shareholder. What result? *G&M Soybean Oil* v. *Diamond Crystal Sp. Foods*, 796 F. Supp. 1214 (S.D. Iowa 1992).

5. Morad, Thompson, and Coupounas operated Bio-Lab, Inc. One of Bio-Lab's main purposes was to open another office. The cost for an additional office was $44,000. Bio-Lab would have had that amount if the corporation had not declared an exorbitant dividend of $20,000. This precluded Bio-Lab from opening the new office. Morad and Thompson used their dividend payments to open a competing office called Med-Lab. Coupounas brought a derivative suit on behalf of Bio-Lab against Morad and Thompson for breach of their fiduciary duties of loyalty and good faith in taking advantage of corporate opportunity for their own benefit. Coupounas requested that the profits earned by

Med-Lab be transferred to Bio-Lab. What result? *Morad* v. *Coupounas, 361 So. 2d 6 (Ala.) 1978.*

6. A criminal accusation was filed against Military Circle Pet Center No. 94, Inc. by the solicitor of Cobb County in Georgia. It was alleged that the corporation should be held criminally responsible for deceptive business practices, which included causing the animals to suffer pain and sickness through neglect and selling these sick animals, which the pet center represented to be healthy. The pet center argued that engaging in deceptive business practices does not constitute a crime. What result? *Military Circle Pet Center No. 94* v. *State, 353 S.E. 2d 555 (Ga. App. 1987).*

7. John Imperatore owned a 20-percent interest in Forest Transmissions, Inc. The remainder was owned by John Jordan and Charles Fox. Imperatore invested $10,000 in cash and $7,000 worth of tools in the corporation with the understanding that he would be employed as a mechanic at $409 per week. Subsequently Jordan and Fox discontinued paying him, claiming that the corporation had financial difficulties because of Imperatore's incompetence. Imperatore claimed that the action taken against him by the majority shareholders was oppressive and that because of it the corporation should be dissolved. What result? *Matter of Imperatore, 512 N.Y.S. 2d 904 (A.D. 2 Dept. 1987).*

8. Fred Hester was in charge of Ladsco's operations. In 1979 he decided to leave Ladsco and open his own foundry supply business called Hessco. Hester purchased equipment and a warehouse before departing from Ladsco. When he left, Alan Draper of L.A. Draper & Son, Inc., owner of Ladsco, attempted to induce the remaining employees to sign a restrictive covenant not to compete. When they refused Draper fired them. Subsequently they were hired by Hessco. Eventually Hessco was purchased by Wheelabrator-Frye, Inc. Ladsco, which could no longer compete with Hessco, filed for bankruptcy. Draper claims that Wheelabrator-Frye and Hessco are liable for the action of their agent in luring Draper's employees away. What result? *L.A. Draper & Son, Inc.* v. *WheelabratorFrye, Inc., 813 F. 2d 332(11th Cir. 1987).*

9. Mary Jean Lower, a policyholder of Lanark Mutual Fire Insurance Company, brought a shareholder's derivative action against Lanark's board of directors. Mary Jean alleged that Alma Dollinger, as secretary of Lanark, had endorsed and deposited service fee checks into Dollinger's personal account and had covered up these transfers by fraudulent bookkeeping. The directors did not seek to recover the converted funds. They responded by stating that Mary Jean had no standing to sue because she was no longer a policyholder. Mary Jean had canceled all but one of her insurance policies with Lanark. What result? *Lower* v. *Lanark Mutual Fire Insurance Co., 502 N.E. 2d 838 (Ill. App. 2 Dist. 1986).*

Special Topic: Business Ethics

IS IT WORTH BEING ETHICAL?

By being ethical you are assured of a clear conscience, but you may suffer financially and emotionally for it. Sometimes through no fault of your own, you can be placed in an ethical dilemma that results in a no-win situation. The price of doing the right thing for a guiltless conscience may be loss of reputation, employment, money, or even relationships. The hope is that leading an ethical life will give you peace of mind in the long run, but in the short run you may lose. On the other hand, if you are unaware of potential ethical problems or if you disregard them and act unethically, eventually you will get caught and have to pay for your actions. Unethical action may bring short-term success, but it often leads to long-term ruin. Some may plan to reap the short-term benefits and then mend their ways before their luck runs out, but people who start along an unethical path rarely change. The long term result must be the paramount consideration in ethical decisions. Without the peace of mind from acting ethically, you have the stress of worrying about getting caught. This can lead to irritability, ulcers, and an unhappy life.

In this world, in this country, and even in business, we have the free will to choose. Decide early on to exercise that choice consistently in an ethical manner, and in the long run your life will be better.

1. Ruth, a middle-aged widow, gives Tim, her stockbroker, discretion to buy and sell stock for her. (a) Tim can try to make solid, long-term income-producing selections, which will be in Ruth's best interest, but will generate only a one-time commission for him. (b) Tim can invest Ruth's funds in short-term ventures such as options to generate hefty continuous commissions while trying to make money for her at the same time. What should Tim do?

2. Mabel asks her brother Ralph to get a job for her son Mark, who just graduated from college. Uncle Ralph has an entry-level position open for which Mark would qualify, but there are three other more qualified applicants. Is it ethical to select a candidate who, although qualified, is not the most qualified? (a) Ralph can accede to his sister's request and select Mark; he will not be faulted because Mark is qualified. Assume Ralph also knows that the other candidates have alternative job opportunities so they will not be out pounding the pavement. (b) Ralph can lie to his sister and tell her that there are no openings. (c) Ralph can

tell his sister that there is no current opening for which Mark is the most qualified. What course of action should Ralph follow?

3. On Guido's graduation from Vo-Tech, his father buys him a silver Corvette. One night Guido is driving back from the Westbury Drive-In with his girlfriend Roxanne after seeing *Rambo V—The Ultimate Encounter.* As they drive over the Throgs Neck Bridge, a fog has rolled in. Traffic is stalled ahead because of a disabled car. Guido can't see, and he plows into the stopped vechiles. The fiberglass Corvette body shatters, leaving Guido a quadraplegic and Roxanne brain damaged. It is a matter of common knowledge that Corvettes are made from fiberglass. The parents of Guido and Roxanne sue Chevrolet. Is the making of a car from fiberglass ethical?

4. Do businesses have any responsibility for reforming the welfare system and the educational system? If so, what can they do, and what's in it for them.?

5. Dudley works as an office clerk for Fuji Bank in its New York Office. One day when Dudley delivers a memo to Mr. Fujimoto, Mr. Fujimoto tells Dudley that he had better start looking for other employment because Mitsubishi Bank is going to acquire Fuji Bank, and 60 percent of Fuji's U.S. employees will be laid off. Regretfully Dudley goes home and tells his grandfather Homer that he is about to lose his job. Homer suggests that Dudley pour his life savings into Fuji Bank stock. Dudley places a purchase order with Nomura Securities, which executes the trade on the Japanese stock exchange. Under Japanese law insider trading is legal. Discuss the ethical implications for all the parties involved in this case.

6. Twinkle Toes Dance School of Atlanta ran an advertisement:

> You don't have to participate in the Olympics to win a medal. Enroll in the Twinkle Toes Dance School for eight half-hour lessons for $25, and you will be on your way toward earning points for bronze, silver and gold medals.

Myrtle, a widow for over fifty years (she was a child bride), enrolled. She was constantly flattered and complimented on her dancing potential. Over a period of five years she earned the gold medal, the dance studio's ultimate achievement. She spent $45,000 for 2,000 hours of lessons. In reality Myrtle had no talent for dancing. She even had difficulty hearing the beat. She did not perform any better after the five years of lessons. What are the arguments for Twinkle Toes and Myrtle? Ethically, who should prevail?

Subject Index

Case Index